Michael Foot

Mervyn Jones is the author of twenty-three novels including *Holding On*, *Two Women and their Man* and *That Year in Paris*, based on the events of 1968 of which he was an eye-witness. As a journalist he was on the staff of *Tribune* under Michael Foot's editorship between 1955 and 1960, was subsequently assistant editor of the *New Statesman*, and has contributed to various other papers including the *Guardian*, the *Observer* and the *Sunday Times*. His autobiography, *Chances*, was published in 1987. His most recent book is *A Radical Life*, a biography of Megan Lloyd George. Mervyn Jones lives in London.

Michael Foot

MERVYN JONES

VICTOR GOLLANCZ

LONDON

First published in Great Britain 1994
by Victor Gollancz

First Gollancz Paperback edition published 1995
by Victor Gollancz
A Division of the Cassell group
Wellington House, 125 Strand, London WC2R 0BB

© Mervyn Jones 1994, 1995

The right of Mervyn Jones to be identified as author of
this work has been asserted by him in accordance with
the Copyright, Designs and Patents Act, 1988.

A catalogue record for this book is
available from the British Library.

ISBN 0 575 05933 8

Typeset at The Spartan Press Ltd,
Lymington, Hants
Printed and bound in Great Britain
by Cox & Wyman Ltd, Reading, Berks

The seat of knowledge is in the head; of wisdom, in the heart. We are sure to judge wrong, if we do not feel right.

William Hazlitt, quoted by Michael Foot in
The Politics of Paradise

Keep her facing it. They may say what they like, but the heaviest seas run with the wind. Facing it – always facing it – that's the way to get through.

Joseph Conrad, *Typhoon*, quoted by Michael Foot in
articles and speeches from 1940 to 1977

CONTENTS

ILLUSTRATIONS

Cartoon by Vicky: Hugh Gaitskell and Anthony Crosland react to Michael's by-election campaign, 1960.

Sketch by Vicky, 1960s: 'Dear Michael, I'm sorry I lost my temper last night.'

Michael returns to the House of Commons, 1960.

In hospital after the car accident, 1963.

With Beaverbrook at Capponcina, 1964.

On the 1964 Aldermaston march: Michael with his step-grandson, Jason Lehel, and James Cameron.

Keeping an eye on Harold Wilson. County Hotel, Durham, on the day of the Durham Miners' Gala, 1969.

Following page 430

At the party conference, 1973: James Callaghan, Michael, Ted Graham, Ian Mikardo, Tony Benn.

After a Cabinet meeting, 1975.

With Indira Gandhi, 1976.

With Callaghan on the conference platform, 1977.

Michael and Jill walk on Hampstead Heath with their dogs.

Tribune meeting, 1980: Eric Heffer, Tony Benn, Michael, Jo Richardson, Neil Kinnock.

Michael arrives at St Patrick's Cathedral, Dublin, 1980.

A speech by the Labour leader, 1981.

At the Bevan memorial on the Waun-y-Pound.

Michael and Denis Healey on their way to Moscow, 1981.

At the Wembley conference, 1981: Frank Allaun, Tony Benn, Judith Hart, Michael, Ron Hayward, David Hughes.

Michael's farewell speech as leader, 1983.

With Neil Kinnock in Tredegar, 1988.

Michael leaves the House of Commons for the last time, 1992.

FOREWORD

On walks round Hampstead Heath with Michael Foot during the years that followed his retirement from the leadership of the Labour Party, I repeatedly urged him to write his memoirs. Others, doubtless, urged him too. He firmly declined, without giving reasons for his refusal, but in a manner that showed that the matter had been considered and decided.

When word got round that there would be no Foot memoirs, several writers proposed a Foot biography as the next best thing. He resigned himself to its inevitability, and I took on the project. Michael and Jill Foot were unfailingly generous in supplying me with information, advising me on sources and giving me access to hitherto unpublished letters and other documents. I had worked on *Tribune* under his editorship between 1955 and 1960; we have met ever since at intervals never longer than a few months; and I am proud to call him a friend.

It is worth recording, therefore, that Michael Foot's first words to me after we had agreed on the project were: 'You can say what you like about me, you know.' We had engaged in enough arguments, on the Heath or elsewhere, for him to be aware that I had disagreed with a number of his opinions, decisions and actions. I have made the assumption that he did not seek invariable justification from me, but did desire understanding. The duty of a biographer, as I conceive it, is neither to defend nor to attack the conduct of the subject of the biography at this or that point, but to elucidate the motives for it.

I wish to express my gratitude to people who gave me valuable imformation through interviews: Abu Abraham, Leo Abse, Ian Aitken, Alexander Baron, Tony Benn, Michael and Cornelia Bessie, Albert Booth, Sir Geoffrey Brand, Alan Brien, James (Lord) Callaghan, Moni Cameron, Barbara (Lady) Castle, Nikhil Chakravarty, Richard and Bridget Clements, Diana Collins, Una Cooze, Constance Cummings, Lawrence Daly, Reginald Davis-Poynter, Sir Donald Derx, Maureen Duffy, Robert J. Edwards, Winifred Ewing, George Fernandes, John (Lord) Foot, Paul Foot, Sarah Foot, Martin Gilbert, Geoffrey Goodman,

I. K. Gujral, P. N. Haksar, Julie Hamilton, Ron Hayward, Denis (Lord) Healey, Louis Heren, Clive Jenkins, Jack Jones, K. S. Karol, Gerald Kaufman, Neil and Glenys Kinnock, Joan Lestor, Harold (Lord) Lever, Jenny Little, Sheila Lochhead, Sir Tom McCaffrey, Kevin Macnamara, Dr E. J. Madden, Ray Morgan, Jim Mortimer, Frederic Mullally, Len (Lord) Murray, Natwar Singh, Sheila Noble, Stan Orme, Ivor Parton, Swraj Paul, Enoch Powell, John Powell, Sir Michael Quinlan, Merlyn (Lord) Rees, Caerwyn Roderick, David Ross, Peter du Sautoy, Peter Shore, Sir Douglas Smith, Peter Tatchell, Elizabeth Thomas, George Malcolm Thomson, Mark Tully, Alan Watkins, Bill (Lord) Wedderburn, Andrew Welsh, Janet Whitaker, Shirley (Lady) Williams, Sir Geoffrey Wilson and Woodrow (Lord) Wyatt. In addition, I wish to record my gratitude to those who have died since I began work on this book: Sir John Cripps, Judith (Lady) Hart, Jon Kimche, Ian Mikardo, Robert Millar, Jo Richardson, John Smith, George (Lord) Strauss and Ted (Lord) Willis.

Cledwyn Hughes (Lord Cledwyn) generously allowed me to quote from his unpublished diary. I have quoted extensively from the published diaries of Barbara Castle, Tony Benn and the late R. H. S. Crossman. Doubts may be felt – and they are shared by Michael Foot, as readers of my Chapter 11 will see – about the value of diaries as historical evidence, but their vividness and immediacy persuade me to bring them into the narrative and leave it to readers to make such reservations as they may decide.

The first draft of this book has been considerably reduced in length after discussion with the publisher. I have no complaint to make in this regard, but some readers may be interested to know that an uncut typescript has been given to the Museum of Labour History, Manchester. I am also grateful to the Museum for permission to quote from unpublished reports relating to the 1983 election.

Michael Foot

— Chapter 1 —

ON FREEDOM FIELDS

I

Lipson Terrace was eighty years ago, and still is, one of the best addresses in Plymouth. There, at Number 1, Eva Mackintosh Foot gave birth, on 23 July 1913, to her fifth child, a boy who was named Michael.

The Foot family did not stem from any long-established elite. Michael's grandfather, Isaac Foot, was a carpenter and undertaker, trades which were linked by skill in making coffins and often combined. He also went into the building business and benefited from the demand for new houses as the town grew in the later decades of the nineteenth century. A staunch Methodist, he built a mission hall to rescue sinners from the hard drinking and sexual misconduct that were rife where sailors and dockyard workers mingled in Notte Street and the Barbican. He promised each of his grandchildren twenty-five pounds if they abstained from alcoholic liquor until reaching the age of twenty-one. All made the promise and stuck to it without evasion, but all made up for lost time in adult life.

His son, also named Isaac, was born in 1880. He left school at the age of fourteen and initially set his sights on a clerkship in the Admiralty, but then changed course and qualified as a solicitor. In 1904, with a friend named Edgar Bowden, he set up the firm of Foot and Bowden, which is still flourishing. He was already married to Eva Mackintosh, whom he had met on a Methodist outing. Her father was a Scottish doctor, while her mother came from Cornwall and had the maiden name of Dingle, an authentic West Country surname (Dingle's is still the leading clothing store in Plymouth). Eva's home until her marriage was in Callington, a Cornish town a dozen miles from Plymouth.

The second Isaac Foot, like his father, was a devout Methodist and a campaigner in the cause of temperance, but his nature was that of a passionate romantic. Characteristically, he proposed to Eva the day after he set eyes on her. In politics, he was spurred by idealism and scornful of patient calculation. He spent money as fast as he made it, or faster, and never tried to save. No worldly success could excite him so much as a Handel oratorio or a Wordsworth sonnet. A theme on which Michael Foot is insistent is that the adjective 'puritanical', as generally used, does an injustice to the English Puritan tradition. In an essay in praise of his father, Michael has written that the Foot household 'was, like so many Puritan households, suffused with music and song'. As a title for this essay, Michael found the perfect phrase to describe Isaac Foot: 'A Rupert for the Roundheads'.[1]

Greatly though Isaac loved music – even as an old man, he would travel to London for a choral concert – his dominant passion was literature. To his children, it seemed that he had read everything ever written in or translated into the English language. He was devoted, above all, to Shakespeare, Milton and Wordsworth; in prose, to Swift, Burke, Hazlitt and Macaulay. Book-buying was his adventure, his delight and his addiction. In Michael's words, he was 'a bibliophilial drunkard'. A trip to London, whatever the official purpose, always found him sneaking off to the second-hand shops or the antiquarian dealers. The addiction had the same consequence as other addictions in other men – he could not keep money in the bank. His wealth was in his library, which ultimately comprised 52,000 books and was among the finest private collections in the world. There were 240 Bibles, including several medieval illuminated manuscripts, a Tyndale 1536 New Testament and the Great Bible of 1640; 3,000 pamphlets or tracts from the period of the Civil War; and first editions of many writers across the centuries from Milton to H. G. Wells.

While he read, he memorised. He could recite, says Michael (perhaps with some pardonable exaggeration) 'whole plays of Shakespeare and whole books of *Paradise Lost*'. When he was living in a Cornish village and working in Plymouth, he selected passages that were just the right length to recite as he walked the three miles to catch the morning train at Liskeard and back in the evening. Trained in this discipline, Michael can still correct a misquotation, name the author of a little-known line, or launch into a recitation. As a dramatic performer, Isaac Foot was equally impressive whether he was acting out a scene from *Les Misérables*, speaking from a Liberal election platform or preaching from a Methodist pulpit. A ripe Devon accent, never modified, enhanced the effect. Some good judges ranked him among the great old-style orators, able to stand comparison with Joseph Chamberlain or David Lloyd George. While he extolled the beliefs and values to which he was dedicated, he was the incarnation as well as the guardian of his traditions. 'Look unto the rock whence ye are hewn and to the hole of the pit whence ye are digged' – these words from the Book of Isaiah became a motto for the Foot family. To this day, any Foot is likely to end a letter or a telephone conversation with 'Pit and rock', and every Foot knows what is meant.

As Isaac's wife, Eva devoted herself to being a loyal helpmeet and making a comfortable home for him, but she was a woman of strong character and decided opinions, and she did not submerge her personality in his. Her determination to make her mark is shown by the names given to their seven children. In order of age, they were Dingle Mackintosh Foot, Hugh Mackintosh Foot, John Mackintosh Foot, Margaret Elizabeth Foot, Michael Mackintosh Foot, Jennifer Mackintosh Foot and Christopher Isaac Foot. (In the family, Hugh was called Mac, or occasionally Tosh, and Margaret was called Sally. Since 'Mac' and 'Sally' stuck throughout adult life, the names will be used in this book. Dingle was sometimes called Bob, but this did not stick.)

Eva was a proud matriarch, and when she wrote a letter to the *Western Morning News* it was always signed 'Mother of Seven'. Everyone in Plymouth knew who that was. But her ambitions for the future, if not her affections, were concentrated on her sons. When John's American fiancée first came to stay at the Foots' home, she found to her indignation that Eva had brought up the girls to make the boys' beds and tidy their rooms, thus giving them time to read and study. There were priorities which both Isaac and Eva took for granted. The boys went to Oxford or Cambridge; the girls did not.

Eva's conception of family life is well illustrated by a piece of didactic verse which she composed when the Foots lived temporarily at Ramsland House, in the Cornish village of St Cleer:

> This is the Ramsland list of rules
> (Not quite so strict as at some schools) . . .
> First, every morning, not too early
> (And this too that shall apply to Girlie)
> Each boy shall rise and dress and wash.
> Then Bob and John and naughty Tosh
> Shall clean their teeth and come to table
> To eat what breakfast they are able.
> Before his lips and food have met
> Each boy must wear his serviette.
> He surely too must see it's right
> With everyone to be polite . . .
> And when the day draws to a close

And time has come for night's repose
Each boy must go at once upstairs
And have his bath and say his prayers.
This is the list of Ramsland laws
And if they're broken without cause . . .
On Saturday there'll be no penny
And as for sweets there won't be any.
There'll be no toast but only bread,
So please keep these rules in your head.
But if these rules you learn and keep
Then every night you'll fall asleep
Thankful for your home and food
And jolly glad that you've been good.

Except for a three-year sojourn at Ramsland House, 1 Lipson Terrace was Michael's home from his birth until the age of fourteen. The house, a handsome and roomy Victorian residence, stood at the crest of a hill and overlooked an open space called Freedom Fields. It was on Freedom Fields that Michael played his first games; it was across Freedom Fields that he walked to school. The name was rich in meaning – a meaning that Isaac Foot, an ardent Roundhead who became president of the Cromwell Association, explained to his children as soon as they could understand it. In the Civil War, Plymouth was the only Parliamentary stronghold in the West Country and withstood a three-year siege, in which a third of the population died of hunger. In 1643, the Royalists launched a surprise attack on the strategic Lipson Fort and were beaten back by the citizens' militia. For the Foot family, that battle was a link in a sequence that encompassed Marathon, the defeat of the Spanish Armada, Marston Moor, Valmy and Gettysburg – the long and still-continuing fight for freedom.

Growing up in Plymouth, Michael soon acquired the sense of history that remained a vital part of his mental equipment. As far back as 1292, the town sent members to the assembly in which Isaac Foot and his sons Dingle and Michael took their places centuries later – the House of Commons. In 1385, a popular uprising defied the power of the Prior of Plympton. A sixteenth-century MP and mayor was Francis Drake, Devon's supreme hero, who left behind him the legend that he would wake from the dead and beat his drum if England were ever endangered as it had been in 1588. Isaac Foot stoutly maintained that he believed it, and Michael was never sure whether he was serious. In the next century, Plymouth maintained its traditions by its defiant courage in the Civil War and again by being the first English town to declare for William of Orange, who showed his gratitude by bringing into existence the Royal Dockyard at Devonport.

The cause of political freedom was indissolubly linked with that of religious Dissent. Plymouth people were attracted almost by instinct to sects that repudiated the Established Church: Baptists, Unitarians, Quakers, Methodists and the rigorously nonconforming Plymouth Brethren, whose members maintained that 'official ministry is a denial of the spiritual priesthood of all believers' and that 'established churches are as foreign to the spirit of Christianity as the Papacy is'.[2] The political significance of Dissent was seldom in doubt; in 1793, Unitarians were banned from working in the dockyard because of their sympathy with revolutionary France. No one inherited the dual tradition more fully than Isaac and Eva Foot. Both were prominent Methodists and both, also, were prominent Liberals, in a region where the Liberal Party had a radical coloration and the Tories were denounced as incurable enemies of freedom.

Liberalism was nourished by the social structure of the West Country, with its population of farmers on a family scale, fishermen, craftsmen and self-made entrepreneurs like the elder Isaac Foot. Absent from this picture were the large estates and the subservience to 'great families' that made the south of England from Wiltshire to Kent a Conservative domain. Absent, equally, were the concentrations of heavy industry that, in South Wales or Yorkshire, generated a collective rather than individual concept of freedom, the growth of trade unionism and the beginnings of the Labour Party. In the hard-fought election of January 1910, Devon and Cornwall returned thirteen Liberal and seven Tory MPs. At a national level, this election resulted in deadlock and another was held in December of the same year. Isaac Foot stood for the Bodmin constituency, which included Callington and Saltash and was familiar territory for him. He lost by forty-one votes.

2

The Foots of Lipson Terrace and Ramsland House were a warm and affectionate but also a competitive family. Eva expected great things of her sons, praised their successes and was sternly critical of their faults or failures. At the age of twenty-five, Michael recalled: 'I was No. 5 in the family. There were plenty of others to keep me in my place. I often revolted against these "overlords" and this must have had something to do with my becoming a Socialist.'[3]

The 'overlords' – the three eldest children – were boys. Sally was next in seniority, one year older than Michael, his natural associate and protector. She was a highly intelligent child and, quite as much as any of her siblings, a precocious inheritor of her father's love of reading. Many years later, when Michael was asked to record his introduction to the world of books, he wrote:

> My beloved sister, Sally . . . was already captivated by my father's imaginative excursions and volunteered to take me along too. She was my white witch, mischievously good, and she would always find room for me on her broomstick. She had already started, in her early teens, as all children should, with the great novelists, while I was still stuck with the *Magnet*, the *Gem* and the *Popular*.[4]

It is reasonable to think that his close comradeship with Sally, and his respectful gratitude to her, predisposed him to regard women as the equals of men and pointed him towards the genuine friendships with women that he developed in adult life. Englishmen, especially of Michael's generation, who really like women are a minority. Moreover, he became gradually aware that Sally, as a girl, was not being encouraged to make full use of her potential. She was fond of horses, and her parents felt that this was a suitable interest. Her later unhappiness and instability may well have sprung from a sense of frustration.

Sally and Michael were drawn still closer together for another reason. Both suffered severely from eczema and in 1918, when they were six and five years old, they spent several months away from the family home with their mother. Eva had heard of a doctor, in Norwood, in the southern suburbs of London, who claimed to cure eczema by a salt-water treatment, and she went with the children to rented lodgings near his surgery. The treatment did little good, but Michael enjoyed his introduction to London – long bus rides, picnics in the parks, visits to the Zoo.

When Michael, as a young man making his way in journalism and politics, was known to suffer from both eczema and asthma, some people supposed that these afflictions were psychosomatic, or arose from his highly strung temperament. In fact, atopic eczema and asthma are hereditary ailments and derive from the same gene, which causes a defect in the body's immunity system. Six of the seven Foot children suffered to some extent from eczema in their early years, with John as the only one who escaped it. In the next generation, Mac's son Paul had an attack at the age of five. There is no real cure for eczema or asthma, but they normally disappear in childhood or at latest in the teenage years. Michael was extraordinarily unlucky. Only 2 per cent of sufferers from eczema also have asthma, as he did. Ninety per cent of youngsters with eczema are free from it before they become adults; with Michael, it persisted until he was about forty.

When Michael returned from Norwood, he was sent to a local kindergarten and then to a preparatory school, Plymouth College. His memories of this period are unhappy; he was waylaid and attacked by bigger, rough boys as he walked across Freedom Fields and down to the centre of Plymouth. However, his school reports were excellent. The history teacher noted: 'He remembers every detail of the stories,' and he was rated as 'very good' in reading, writing, arithmetic and geography. At the age of ten, he moved on to Forres, a boarding prep school at Swanage. The Foots, following middle-class custom, sent their sons away to school, and the boys took to it cheerfully. When John started at Forres, Dingle (who was at a different school) inquired in a letter home: 'How is John getting along at school, does he like it? Well, I suppose that's rather a silly question as every chap likes his school. At least he'd be a funny chap who didn't.'

John did like Forres, and so did Michael, but he resented the severe discipline. He was once caned and, while he could put up with this philosophically, he was revolted when another boy had to undergo a public caning in front of the assembled school – a humiliation piled on the standard punishment. But he continued to get good reports and earned strong approval from the headmaster, who wrote to Isaac when Michael left the school:

> We shall miss Michael sadly. He has been the leading boy in the school in every way . . . and we have had no hesitation at all in saying he must have the highest honour we can pay him, by putting his name on the Honours Board . . . What he does will not lack a spirit of grit and keenness behind it – and I think he will always have the right ideals in view.

For the years leading up to university entry, Michael was at Leighton Park School, near Reading. If the Foots were conventional enough to send their sons to fee-paying boarding schools, they nevertheless made a choice that was consistent with their liberal outlook. Military training – the Officers' Training Corps, which was an integral part of the system at most public schools – was non-existent at Leighton Park, which had been founded with endowments from wealthy Quakers. A boy who passed through this school, as Michael did, in the decade following the First World War learned that war was not glorious but tragic, that internationalism was a nobler creed than patriotism, and that human beings had an equal value regardless of race or colour.

Michael was praised for his progress in history, English literature and maths, but his French was not so highly commended and he had to drop chemistry and physics after the teachers commented regretfully that he had 'not much aptitude'. Under 'hobbies', politics was mentioned in every report. Although his eyesight had been very poor since childhood and he was virtually helpless without his spectacles, and although he was intermittently plagued by eczema and asthma, he was generally in good health and was successful both at rugger ('a good wing forward') and cricket ('a promising batsman'). But his preference was for soccer, and from boyhood to the present day he has been a warm supporter of Plymouth Argyle.

During the years of Michael's boyhood, his father became what newspapers call 'a controversial figure' – a status of which no Foot has ever been afraid. In the First World War, while Edgar Bowden went into the Army, Isaac Foot kept the law firm going and gave much of his time to defending conscientious objectors before military tribunals. Isaac was not himself a pacifist, but the objectors had a legal right to be represented and other lawyers were declining the job. When he stood for Parliament in post-war elections, he was fiercely attacked for having defended 'conchies'.

He made what he considered to be another principled decision when the Prime Minister, H. H. Asquith, was ousted in 1916 by David Lloyd George, who governed with Tory support. Isaac was among the Liberals who remained loyal to Asquith, and paid for it in the 'coupon election' of 1918, which was a triumph for the coalition of Tories and Lloyd George Liberals. Fighting Bodmin again, he was heavily defeated. This did not deter him from standing in a 1919 by-election in the Sutton division of Plymouth, caused when the Tory MP Waldorf Astor succeeded to the peerage. The Tory candidate was his wife Nancy. Women had only just been enfranchised and the citizens of Plymouth had never before been asked to vote for a woman, let alone an American woman with a strong Virginia accent. But the coalition was still popular, the Labour candidate polled surprisingly well and Isaac was pushed into third place. At a personal level he was on friendly terms with Lady Astor – they were both ardent supporters of the cause of temperance – and he was happy to congratulate her on being the first woman to take her seat in the House of Commons.

By 1922, when a by-election came up in Bodmin, the coalition was on the verge of collapse and a Liberal untainted by dealings with the Tories could claim his reward. Isaac won Bodmin at last and held it in two general elections, in November 1922 and December 1923. His maiden speech was in support of a bill moved by Nancy Astor banning the sale of alcoholic drinks to persons under the age of eighteen. It became law and is still in force.

After the brief interlude of the first Labour government in British history, the election of October 1924 resulted in a Tory landslide and Isaac lost his seat. A dejected Liberal wrote to him: 'I will not attempt to divine the cause, the Tory sweep is abnormal, but behind it is a hidden wisdom which we trust will work out for the good of the People and the Glory of God.' The writer of this letter must have been confirmed in his faith when Isaac regained Bodmin in the 1929 election, which produced the second Labour government.

In 1927, the Foots had moved from Lipson Terrace to a house named Pencrebar, set in open country three miles from Callington. Parents of seven children might be expected to move to a smaller house when the children are growing up, but Pencrebar was an imposing mansion with no fewer than twenty-eight rooms. The view over the valley of the Lynher was entrancing and the spacious grounds were useful for Liberal or Methodist garden parties, but the family were in no doubt that Isaac had acquired Pencrebar to get more room for his books. Inevitably, the extra space was filled within a few years and merely encouraged the passionate bibliophile to buy and buy. His granddaughter Sarah gave this description of Pencrebar:

> To go to the lavatory you had to climb over stacks of books; up the back stairs to the attic they were piled; in the laundry room where the old-fashioned boiler was fixed to the middle of the floor, books were stacked everywhere and for as long as I can remember, that room was no longer used for its original purpose but was yet another place to store the books . . . Often you would find people sitting down in the passage or on the stairs having found a book they had always wanted to read, starting to browse through it and soon forgetting where they were.[5]

At the time of the move to Pencrebar, Dingle had graduated from Oxford and was reading for the Bar, Mac was at Cambridge and John was about to enter Oxford. In brainpower, Dingle was generally given the highest ranking among the brothers and Mac the lowest. A *Daily Mail* profile of Sir Hugh Foot published in 1958, when he was Governor of

Cyprus, described him as 'the slightly out-of-step hearty in the intellectual menage.' He wrote to the paper: 'This is the culmination of a
whispering campaign put about, I am sure, by my brothers . . . I got
exactly the same university degree as all of them — second-class
Honours . . . I would thank them to remember that, except for our
father, who is, as we all know, head and shoulders above all of us, we are
intellectually equal — all second-class stuff.' Michael's comment, in an
Evening Standard article, was:

> Put the point crudely: Sir Hugh was never considered the brightest of
> the brood . . . He picked up bad habits that never entirely left him.
> Over the years it became increasingly evident that he had acquired
> strange tastes and was ready to indulge in pastimes which the rest of us
> wouldn't be seen dead at — such as rowing, playing polo, dressing up in
> Goering-like uniforms and enjoying it, and occasionally even — at a
> pinch — placing some trust in the word of Tory Prime Ministers.

3

History was Michael's strongest subject at school, and in the summer of
1931, when he was eighteen and in his last term at Leighton Park, he sat
the examination for a history exhibition to Oxford and won it. When the
holiday came, he and a schoolfriend joined an International Peace
Crusade. They were the only English participants, the others being
French and German. The crusade was a long march across France,
following the track of the trenches in which, only fourteen or fifteen years
before, young men had slaughtered one another with bullets and
bayonets. The marchers, united in pledges never to be dragooned or
fooled into another war, and eager to spread the word, tramped the dusty
roads all day and held meetings in the towns and villages every evening.
They slept in youth hostels, in barns or out in the open in the warm
August nights. It was an experience that Michael remembered when —
thirty years later, and with a car to take him to a comfortable home at
night — he was again a peace marcher.

In 1931, most people were worrying less about war dangers than about
the grave economic depression which, stemming from the Wall Street
crash of 1929, had plunged Britain and other industrial nations into
industrial decline and mass unemployment. The Labour Prime Minister,
Ramsay MacDonald, was a captive of the economic orthodoxy preached
by 'experts' and rejected Keynesian policies of reflation, urged by the

Labour left wing and by the Liberals. He appointed a committee consisting mainly of businessmen to find remedies for what had now become an acute crisis. Its report, published on 31 July, proposed a 20 per cent cut in the already miserable level of unemployment relief. For MacDonald, this was a sad necessity; for half his Cabinet and almost the whole of his party in the Commons and outside, it was unacceptable. On 24 August, he resigned as Labour Prime Minister and re-emerged as Prime Minister of what was called a National Government, dependent on Tory support and with the Tory leader, Stanley Baldwin, as a weighty presence in the Cabinet. In November, a general election produced a landslide victory for the National Government. Its supporters had 551 seats in the House, of which 470 were won by Conservatives. Labour was down to 52 seats.

The crisis shattered the unity of the Liberal Party. One section, headed by Sir John Simon, happily joined the National Government and was entirely committed to supporting it. These MPs were known as Liberal Nationals, or less formally as Simonites. The main body of Liberals, led by Sir Herbert Samuel and known as Samuelites, promised conditional support to the government, the condition being that it should maintain Britain's traditional policy of free trade. Lloyd George, with three followers, stood in firm opposition to the government.

Isaac was defending Bodmin, and Dingle was facing his first election as Liberal candidate for Dundee. Since they were both Samuelites, and thus members of a party represented in the government, they had no Tory opponents at the polls. With Labour failing to find a candidate for Bodmin, Isaac had an unopposed return – the only easy election in his life of battles. Dundee was a double-member constituency (that is, a voter had two votes and the two candidates at the top of the poll were elected) so that Dingle and a Tory were able to defeat the Labour candidates. Somewhat uneasily, Isaac accepted the only government post he ever held, that of Parliamentary Secretary, or number two, in the Ministry of Mines.

At Oxford, the arrival of Michael Foot was viewed with interest by dons as well as other undergraduates. Having won his exhibition before his eighteenth birthday, he was younger than most first-year men. He came from a notable family; both Dingle and John had been elected to the coveted post of President of the Union. The university authorities were trying to upgrade Wadham, then a college of little distinction, and Michael was steered towards it in pursuit of this policy. Fortunately, he fell in love with Wadham. A fine example of Jacobean architecture, the college was the creation of Dorothy Wadham, a West Country widow.

Years later, Michael called it 'wondrous, exquisitely proportioned Wadham; founded by a woman and thereby perhaps escaping the Oxford vice of misogyny'. Reviewing James Morris' book on Oxford, he wrote: 'This book recalls Oxford in all her green glory, and Wadham, the greenest, the most gracious, the peerless, the most perfect.'[6]

Michael's Oxford contemporaries and friends included John Cripps, son of Sir Stafford Cripps, who had been Solicitor-General in the Labour government and now sat on the Opposition front bench; Anthony Greenwood, son of Arthur Greenwood, who had been Minister of Health but had lost his seat in the 1931 typhoon; and Paul Reilly, son of Charles Reilly, a progressive-minded pioneer of town planning. In their second year, John Cripps and Michael Foot shared lodgings in a house near the New Theatre, but Michael's asthma was exacerbated by the dust from a nearby building site and he had to move to the healthier environment of Headington.

At first encounter, Michael did not make a strong impression. He was shy, sometimes gauche in social gatherings, and clearly conscious of his embarrassing eczema and asthma. But once he began to speak – in the Union, which he joined at once, or even in an informal discussion or argument – his self-confidence increased with every minute and the listeners were struck by his fluency, his flair for the vivid phrase, indeed his eloquence. In these youthful days, as in later life, a character sketch would have struck a note of paradox. He had a genuine modesty, he was grateful for new pieces of knowledge on which he would quietly reflect, he was considerate towards other people to the point of being self-effacing. By general agreement, he was a nice chap. Yet his basic convictions (or, some might say, prejudices) were firm and unshakeable, he could indignantly denounce an institution or a course of action which he considered to be wrong, and when he had decided that something had to be done he pressed on with determination, reinforced by impatience. Anyone who imagined that he was a nice chap and nothing more would be surprised by his capacity for aggression, in the strict sense of the word used by psychologists – the will to attack and overcome obstacles that stood in the way of achievement. It was a good bet that he would forge a career of distinction.

But what sort of career would it be? He seemed equally well equipped for politics or for literature. Like his father, he read voraciously and kept a commonplace book which furnished him with quotations when needed. He wrote so well, so fast and so easily that he could be expected to produce remarkable books, or at the very least to excel in journalism. If he went in for politics, he could certainly be envisaged as a brilliant independent *franc-tireur*, but he would not take happily to the restrictions of party discipline and it was hard to see him making a steady ascent through the system. If he ever became a party leader, he would be the most improbable as well as the most variously gifted leader since Disraeli – a predecessor with whom Michael felt a natural empathy, to whom in later years he devoted an affectionate essay, and after whom he named a much loved dog.

John Cripps, who knew Michael as well as anyone, never had any doubt that he was headed for the political life. His strongest opinions and his most ardent passions were concentrated on the aim of making a better world. He had, much to his mother's distress, discarded all religious belief to become an agnostic humanist. (Surprisingly, it was the apparently hedonistic Mac who became a pillar of the Methodist community.) But Nonconformists had often concerned themselves with social evils as much as with individual salvation; and this aspect of the tradition of Dissent contributed towards Michael's developing convictions, just as it contributed both to the radical wing of Liberalism and to the Labour movement. At this period, Michael was a Liberal sharing the ideals and loyalties of his father and a warm admirer of Lloyd George, to whom Isaac Foot had been reconciled after the death of Asquith. While John Cripps was President of the university Labour Club, Michael was President of the Liberal Club.

He was studying PPE – philosophy, politics and economics. He realised with hindsight that he might have got a first-class degree if he had stuck to history, instead of his second-class in PPE. He had difficulty in understanding most of the philosophers who were covered in the course, and responded enthusiastically only to Bertrand Russell. Russell's blend of scepticism and humanism was much to Michael's taste, and a visit to Oxford by Russell excited him almost as much as a visit by Lloyd George. He found economics tough going too, but his tutor, Russell Bretherton, was a disciple of Keynes and the tutorials strengthened Michael's belief in Keynesian remedies for the depression. Even so, politics was the only division of the degree course in which Michael was comfortably at home with all the material.

For Michael, Toryism was the enemy and the National Government was a transparent cover for Tory power. He wrote to his father in 1932:

> L.G. came to Oxford on Tuesday. It was superb. I went to breakfast with him on the following day and he let this government have it. Well, I hope you are feeling thoroughly uncomfortable in your present position. I hope the responsibility for a niggardly disarmament policy

and blustering dealing with Ireland rests heavily on your shoulders. I hope that you squirm in your seat at the pronouncement of each new tariff order. I suppose you will vote with patriotic resignation for further economy cuts.

Fortunately for family amity, these reproaches were no longer necessary after the government decided on tariffs which were unacceptable to the Samuelite Liberals. In September 1932, Isaac Foot was able to resign from the government and move to the Opposition benches.

In these depression years, only those who were either callously insensitive or totally uninterested in the political and social scene could ignore the sufferings being endured by millions of British people. One of Michael's friends came from Wales and took him on a conducted tour of the mining valleys in the university vacation. It was an unforgettable experience for a young man coming from a comfortable middle-class home. Capitalism was visibly failing to fulfil its promises, credulously accepted before 1929, of economic stability and broadening prosperity. America, the source of the proudest boasts, was also the source of the breakdown and seemed incapable of recovery until the election of Franklin D. Roosevelt in November 1932 offered grounds for hope. But Roosevelt had not yet been inaugurated when the uncouth demagogue Adolf Hitler, whose Nazi Party was subsidised by such capitalist tycoons as Krupp and Thyssen, became Chancellor of Germany. Within a few months, other parties were outlawed, Dachau opened its gates as the first of the concentration camps, and Albert Einstein and Thomas Mann were exiles. More than anything else, it was the advent of Hitler that swung wavering sections of British opinion, including Oxford opinion, to the left. Einstein was an interested spectator when, in October 1933, the Oxford Union voted that 'Toryism offers no solution of the nation's economic and social problems.' As Michael Foot recorded: 'Oxford politics in the past few years have taken a decidedly radical turn.'[7]

By contrast, Soviet Russia claimed achievements that won unstinted praise from visitors like Shaw and Sidney and Beatrice Webb. Full employment and enormous percentage increases in industrial production under the Five Year Plan seemed to show that Stalin had solved the problems that plagued wealthier nations – though, as Shaw put it, 'not on a basis of private property, and not in all cases without a gentle but persistent pressure of a pistol muzzle'.[8] John Strachey's influential book *The Coming Struggle for Power*, published in 1932, convinced many young people, not least at Oxford and Cambridge, that Marxism was the key to a true understanding of the problems that baffled both politicians and academics in the Western world. Michael noted in 1933 that the October Club, so named in tribute to the October (1917) Revolution, was 'the most lively and enthusiastic club in Oxford'.

Was it true, as Strachey argued, that the capitalist system was incapable of reform or repair and must be destroyed? Before very long, Michael would follow that logic and declare himself a socialist – but not until he left Oxford. If he was a distinctly left-wing Liberal, he was still a Liberal, not yet ready to cross the ideological divide. An obvious restraining factor was the Foot tradition; one could, like Isaac Foot, repudiate the motivations of self-interest and be an irreconcilable antagonist of the Tories, and remain a Liberal. Another factor was that he was President of the Liberal Club, and to change his allegiance would leave followers who had trusted him in the lurch. More fundamentally, he doubted whether the revolutionary change advocated by Strachey could be brought about without sacrificing the values of democracy, pluralism and tolerance. In a 1934 article on 'Why I Am a Liberal',[9] he wrote that socialist rule might rely on 'suppression of criticism' and 'measures which seem to commend themselves to Mr G. D. H. Cole and the intelligentsia of the socialist movement'. He declared: 'I am a Liberal because I believe it is Liberalism in its more radical moods which established the social and democratic institutions which this country already enjoys' – a formulation which left open the question of whether the 'radical moods' would always prevail in the Liberal Party.

This abiding concern with democratic values explains why Michael, even when he moved from Liberalism to socialism, could not make the further move that would have brought him, like some other idealistic young people in the 1930s, to Communism. If he suspected Cole of a tendency to intolerance, he was bound to suspect Stalin and Stalin's acolytes with far greater reason. No inheritor of the Foot tradition could allude smoothly and wittily to the 'persistent pressure of a pistol muzzle'. In 1933, he stated firmly: 'Force is not the proper instrument to establish the rights and wrongs of any case; reasonable and just ends can only be achieved by reasonable and just methods.'[10] In the 1990s, after the bitter experiences of half a century, that principle may be read as axiomatic or even platitudinous; it did not appear so in 1933.

Nevertheless, the clear alternative to classical Liberalism was the Labour Party. A number of left-wing Liberals of the Isaac Foot generation – Dr Christopher Addison, Sir Charles Trevelyan and William Wedgwood Benn among others – had transferred their allegiance to Labour in the past decade. These were honourable men, so the option was patently justifiable, especially for a young man with his life ahead of him.

At the time when Michael was considering whether to join the Labour Party, its leader was George Lansbury, the only member of the 1929–31 Cabinet who had not either followed MacDonald into apostasy or been swept out of the Commons in the electoral disaster. Lansbury was a devout Christian and a committed pacifist, but his record was that of a left-winger and he had even, as a borough councillor in Poplar, gone to prison rather than implement Tory financial policies. In reaction to the cautious, compromising paths followed by the first two Labour governments, the mood of the bloody but unbowed party that emerged from the wreckage of 1931 was ideologically purist. Cripps responded to that mood when he declared that the aim of the next Labour government must be 'a rapid change-over to socialism'. Hugh Dalton, a prominent representative of the right wing in the party, took a scathing view of Cripps: 'He began to go wild soon after the 1931 election. Then, stimulated by increasing publicity and attacks, especially in the Tory press, and by eager cheers from our own lunatic fringe, he went wilder and wilder.'[1] But Dalton, along with other right-wing luminaries such as Arthur Henderson and Herbert Morrison, was out of Parliament, while Cripps was in.

In 1932, the Socialist League was founded as a sort of Jesuit Order within the Labour church. Cripps and Clement Attlee, another Labour front-bencher, were on its committee; the chairman was the strongly left-wing Frank Wise; and other committee members, whose names will recur in this book, were Aneurin Bevan, H. N. Brailsford, Harold Laski, William Mellor, D. N. Pritt and Ellen Wilkinson. Its programme called for nationalisation of the banks, the land, the mines, power, transport, iron and steel and the cotton industry; abolition of the House of Lords; and an Emergency Powers Act to enable a Labour government to forestall any sabotage by financial interests.

Thanks to his friendship with John Cripps, Michael soon met Sir Stafford, who had been a wealthy barrister before entering politics and owned a beautiful house, called Goodfellows, near Lechlade. It was less than thirty miles from Oxford, so the two young men often went there at weekends. Sometimes, Lansbury and other Labour personalities were among the guests. Michael was also invited for holidays with the Cripps family in the Scilly Isles. His view of Cripps fell considerably short of whole-hearted admiration. Writing later, he credited Cripps with 'burning sincerity' and 'intellectual power' but described him as 'a political innocent'. The criticism continues:

He knew little of the Labour movement, less of its history, and among all his other preoccupations had had little time or inclination to repair the deficiency by a reading of Socialist literature. His Marxist slogans were undigested; he declared the class war without ever having studied the contours of the battlefield.[12]

For Michael, brought up to venerate books, Cripps' limited reading was a grave fault. Also, he was put off by Cripps' dictatorial and self-centred airs in the home. At Pencrebar, anyone was free to tease, contradict or argue with Isaac Foot, but at Goodfellows Stafford Cripps' word was law.

Rather embarrassingly, Cripps soon became very fond of Michael. His own son was not inclined to take on his political inheritance; although a Labour supporter, John was primarily devoted to the welfare of the countryside, became editor of the *Countryman* after leaving Oxford, and is best described as a premature Green. Michael was more likely to develop into a stalwart of the Socialist League – if only he would stop being a Liberal.

In Michael's second year, the Oxford Union was the setting for a political storm whose echoes have still not entirely died away. The motion 'That this House will in no circumstances fight for King and country' was debated and carried by a narrow majority. Michael, although by this time he had a high reputation as a Union speaker, did not take part in this debate, but voted for the motion. Since 'King and country' was the hallowed incantation of the traditional patriot, the phraseology was deliberately chosen to scandalise the older generation, and it certainly succeeded. But the language had another purpose; it secured the support of those, including Michael, who were not absolutely opposed to all war, but who considered national loyalty an inadequate ideal. Very unwisely, two recent graduates, Randolph Churchill and Frank Pakenham, came to Oxford and tried to persuade the Union to expunge the now celebrated motion from the minutes – that is, to recant. This time, the atmosphere was violent and the proceedings were disrupted by stink-bombs. Michael tried to speak, but did not get the floor. Eventually, Churchill and Pakenham withdrew and no vote was taken.

In his final year, Michael was President of the Union. Dingle and John had preceded him and Mac had been President of the Cambridge Union, so four brothers had attained this distinction – a record which is unlikely ever to be equalled. Other elective posts went to John Cripps, who became treasurer, and to an Indian student, D. F. Karaka, who became librarian. Michael was a member of the Lotus Club, which consisted of an equal number (twenty-five) of British and Indian students.

Soon afterwards, Michael joined the India League, which had been founded by V. K. Krishna Menon to press the case for Indian freedom, and was supported by Stafford Cripps and others on the political left. Michael became friendly with Menon, met Jawaharlal Nehru when he came to London in 1938, and thus began a lifelong association with India, its leaders and its people. His first meeting with Menon, however, was to discuss plans for a book, to be called *Young Oxford and War*, which Menon was planning to edit as a follow-up to the furore created by the 'King and country' episode. There were to be four contributors, each writing an essay of about fifty pages: Michael to express the Liberal viewpoint, a Conservative, a Labour supporter (Frank Hardie, who had been President of the Union at the time of the debate) and a Communist. The essays were completed by the end of 1933 and the book was published early in 1934.[13]

Michael's contribution came very close to an advocacy of pacifism. He began by quoting the declaration made by the early Quakers in 1660: 'We utterly deny all outward wars and strife, and fightings with outward weapons, for any end or under any pretence whatever.' He conceded that a war could be motivated by a just cause, such as justice or liberty, but pointed out:

> Even the victor in a just cause is susceptible to the passions which war arouses. Every inhuman feeling is at once exacerbated. Truth, decency, morality, justice are the first casualties in any war. The accumulated effect makes a just settlement impossible . . . The pacifist treasures justice, liberty; but he believes that they can only be lastingly secured by peaceable means and that the use of force will only contaminate them.

He went on to discuss the prospects of disarmament, given that 'armaments themselves provide an independent cause of war owing to the suspicion and fear which they breed'. Disarmament by agreement – 'collateral disarmament', as Michael called it – was not within reach, for the international disarmament conference at Geneva was plainly heading towards breakdown. Hence: 'Unilateral disarmament offers the only way of escape once the policy of collateral disarmament has failed.' Hardie contested this view, arguing that unilateral disarmament might create a moral impression but the example was unlikely to be followed by other nations. The arguments of 1933 were to be echoed with uncanny precision in the 1960s and the 1980s.

He also crossed swords with the Communist contributor, who took the line that capitalism was the cause of war and socialism was the only cure. Michael's reply was: 'It cannot seriously be argued that capitalists are desirous of bringing about war. The Great War almost dealt capitalism its death blow.' Indeed, he went further:

> Socialism with its ideal of the national control of consumption and production, its substitution of national barter for the processes of foreign trade, is by no means an international force . . . It looks inwards rather than outwards and sets up a national economy, which every true protectionist should envy. Russia is a powerful national state and has indulged in nationalist policies . . . Even a Socialist state cannot provide against war unless a world authority has been formed.

These were the words of a Liberal engaging in polemic against socialism. It was the last time that Michael Foot wrote from that stance.

Yet something that derived from the Liberal (or it might be truer to say liberal) heritage remained as a vital part of Michael's outlook. This was the value that he attached to the politics of free debate, persuasion and tolerance of opposing opinions. In the left of the 1930s – and to some extent in later years – there were some who believed that a socialist government which meant business should curtail parliamentary delays by means of an Emergency Powers Act, or should ban reactionary newspapers which spread lies and prejudices, or should put obstructive opponents out of circulation in one way or another. No such ideas were ever part of Michael's socialism, and we can find the reason in his upbringing as a son of Isaac Foot. Years later, Barbara Castle – herself brought up in a socialist family with no tinge of Liberalism – noted with some exasperation: 'These Foot brothers all merge into one collective Foot type: rational, radical and eminently reasonable. They even speak in the same voice and the same tones; they are natural Liberals.'[14] When she made this comment in 1975, Michael had long been a convinced and passionate socialist; but there was truth in the insight.

— *Chapter 2* —

THE MAKING OF
A SOCIALIST

I

Michael left Oxford with no definite plans for future employment or career, but eager for new experiences and particularly for travel. He had a small amount of cash in hand, due to be augmented on his twenty-first birthday – 23 July 1934 – by the twenty-five pounds promised by his grandfather as a reward for abstention from alcohol. He celebrated the birthday in Paris, staying with his brother John, who was living there for six months, and they both got joyfully drunk on Pernod.

John would be spending his working life as a partner in the family law firm of Foot and Bowden. Mac had entered the Colonial Service and was an Assistant District Commissioner in Palestine, then a British mandate. A visit to Mac was Michael's next objective; he went by train to Italy – taking a look at Venice, in later years one of his best-loved cities – and by ship from Trieste to Haifa. All the other passengers were Jews, escaping from the Nazi persecution that had clamped down on Germany and was threatening Austria. The only common language between the Oxford graduate and the graduates of the cafés of Berlin or Vienna was the language of chess. Michael lost all the games he played, emerging with enhanced respect for Jewish intellectual standards.

Mac's district was centred on Nablus, in the mountainous country that runs down the centre of Palestine between the coastal plain and the Jordan valley. In ancient times, and again in modern Israeli parlance, this region has the name of Samaria. It was in 1934 and is to this day a stronghold of Arab nationalism. The Arabs had never accepted the Jewish immigration that followed the establishment of the British mandate in 1919, nor would they accept the more rapid influx caused by the flight from Hitler.

Mac was happy among the Arabs. He wrote later: 'Their manners are superb, their endurance almost superhuman, their hospitality spectacular, their courage romantic and their dignity unequalled . . . I have never ceased to rejoice that I had the privilege of spending my early years in overseas service with the Arabs.'[1] Although he did not share the anti-Jewish prejudices of other British officials, he sympathised with Arab resentment over the increasing Jewish settlement. In the antagonism between Arabs and Jews, arising from conflicting promises made in Britain's name during the First World War, Mac leaned towards the Arab side of the argument, and of course voiced his opinions to his brother. It was Lord Caradon – the title that Mac earned – who drafted UN Resolution 242 after the war of 1967, calling for Israeli withdrawal from occupied territories, including Samaria.

Michael's attitude was more balanced, or more undecided. Two book reviews which he wrote in 1936 reveal his reactions. Commenting on a book called *Yellow Spot*, which described the Nazi system of discrimination, he wrote: 'The ordered terrorism of Hitler is as thoroughly bestial and menacing as anything devised by Nebuchadnezzar or Torquemada.'[2] He also noted: 'In Germany, the home of assimilation, such a policy has provided no escape from the pogrom and the ghetto.' Evidence that it was futile for a Jew to strive for acceptance as a true German (or, as the Dreyfus case had shown, a true Frenchman) was a cogent and emotionally powerful part of the Zionist argument. Remembering his own journey to Palestine, Michael wrote: 'When he [the Jew] boards the ship at Trieste he takes with him the aspirations not merely of a lifetime but of twenty centuries of repression. As he sits in the cafés of Jaffa Road in Jerusalem or walks along the promenade in Tel Aviv, he breathes for the first time in his life the air of freedom.'[3]

Hence, it was 'difficult to resist the appeal of the Jewish case'. But there was also an Arab–Palestinian case, as Michael well knew from Mac. By 1936 the Arab rebellion was in full swing and British troops were shooting down Arabs, as they had been shooting down Indians a few years earlier. Michael reminded his readers: 'We have another and older tradition which it would be perilous to betray' – the radical tradition of solidarity with the oppressed. He was reviewing a book by Lord Melchett, a wealthy and conservative British Jew, which advocated a partnership between British power and Zionism. This, Michael commented, was 'a dangerous game to play', and he reflected: 'One doubts whether Zionism does in fact provide a solution to the Jewish problem.' He concluded: 'If this is the meaning of Zionism, there will be little hope of peace and no secure future for the Jews in a country in which neither the British nor the Jews will in the last resort have the dominant voice.'

Leaving Palestine, Michael took ship from Beirut to Athens. His money was running out, so he travelled fourth-class; the accommodation was so revolting that he stayed on deck throughout the journey. The cheapest possible train, stopping at every station through Macedonia and Serbia, took him on to Belgrade. He spent a day in Budapest and a day in Vienna before heading for home.

In October he was off again, on a very different kind of expedition. Michael Foot and John Cripps were to represent Oxford University in a debating tour in the United States. This was a regular plum for stars of the Oxford Union in the autumn after graduating, and had been enjoyed in past years by both Dingle and John Foot. In 1934, the Oxford pair spoke in twenty-two debates at all sorts of academic institutions: Yale, which was Oxford's counterpart in prestige, four state universities, a segregated black college in Virginia, and two women's colleges (reporting on the debate at Smith in a letter to his mother, Michael wrote: 'The debaters were more notable for their beauty than their speaking'). At St Lawrence University, he spoke in favour of the nationalisation of armaments production and declared: 'We should prevent people from putting weapons into the hands of the madman Hitler.' An unexpected difficulty confronted him at New Jersey Law School, as he told Eva: 'To my horror I was informed just before the debate that I was supposed to speak for military training and not against it. I managed to get through, however, by being generally facetious and I fully believe that my championship of it was the most mortal blow that cause has ever received.'

Facetiousness was an aspect of the Oxford technique that proved somewhat baffling to American audiences. The *Atlanta Journal* explained to its readers: 'Debating in England is not the deadly serious affair it is in this country . . . English students address the audience, intersperse their arguments with humorous remarks, and debate more for the fun of it.' The *Yale News* complimented Michael: 'Winning the sympathy of the audience, he cleverly made an informal and humorous beginning . . . Every statement was void of boring detail.'

After the end of the tour, which lasted from 26 October to 4 December ~34, Michael hoped to stay on in the US for a while and pay his way by writing articles for British newspapers on the progress of Roosevelt's New Deal. He contributed one article to the *News Chronicle* and reported excitedly: 'The country is seething with new movements of a radical or pseudo-radical character.' However, it was John Cripps who stayed on in America; he was offered a job as secretary to his uncle, Major Leonard Cripps, who was in the shipping business in Liverpool, but he decided not to take it and proposed Michael in his place. The job did not sound very interesting, but it might not be very demanding and Michael would, he hoped, be able to make more forays into journalism and write his first book. He was planning a biography of Charles James Fox, a political figure whose personality was much to his taste. On 8 December, he wrote to his mother:

> We have now finished the debating tour and I expect to be returning on the Olympic which leaves here on Dec. 21 and gets to Southampton about the 25th or 27th. I would have stayed longer but I have the chance of getting a job starting on Jan. 1st. The job is one which John Cripps was offered by his uncle . . . I don't know much about what the job offers, but it includes the possibility of visits to foreign ports, and small salary. I think it will also give me time to write the Charles James Fox book.

Fox's life spanned the period of the French Revolution and the Napoleonic wars. A Tory in youth, he moved to a posture of defiant and uncompromising Radicalism. He was known, too, for the flamboyant recklessness of his personality, his entanglements with women and the heroic scale of his gambling. Everything about him was in dramatic contrast to the prudent, unemotional William Pitt, who ruled as Prime Minister while Fox was shunned by the Establishment of the time.

The characteristics that attracted Michael in Fox were akin to those of the three figures from the past who most strongly and durably captured his imagination. Over the years, he wrote a book about Swift, wrote a book about Byron and devoted three essays to Hazlitt.[4] All three men were rebels against the dominant political forces and power structures of their times. However, they did not give unconditional allegiance to the official opposition. We can describe them as independent spirits, or mavericks, or loners. (One collection of Michael's occasional pieces was entitled *Loyalists and Loners* – a significant distinction.)

All three, in their lifetimes and when they were in their graves, were mercilessly attacked or treated with contempt. Michael wrote indignantly about the calumny, first spread by Dr Johnson, that Swift declined into senility and madness. His book on Byron, *The Politics of Paradise*, is subtitled 'A Vindication of Byron'. Hazlitt, too, was in need of vindication; he had been denigrated both as a writer and as a man even by those who shared his ideas. In each case, the role that Michael assumed was that of defender, or restorer, of an injured reputation.

It is worth adding that Swift, Byron and Hazlitt all had unorthodox sexual lives, which furnished material for the attacks. Their irregular habits were readily excused by the Michael Foot who included Tom Driberg among his friends.

2

Major Cripps (it was customary for men who had been officers in the First World War to use their military titles in civilian life) was, in contrast to his brother, a firm believer in the virtues of the capitalist system. He was a director of the Blue Funnel Line, then headed by Sir Richard Holt. Its headquarters were in Liverpool, and Michael reported for duty in a city entirely strange to him – a city of wretched slums by the waterfront and gracious Georgian houses a little way inland and uphill, of bitter enmities between the Catholic Irish and the Orange Irish. In addition to his responsibilities with Blue Funnel, Cripps was closely involved with a combine which sought to establish a monopoly in trade with the Far East. One could hardly imagine a task more uncongenial to a budding socialist than work in the service of Major Cripps. In 1980, giving his first press conference as leader of the Labour Party, Michael recalled: 'I first joined the Labour Party in Liverpool because of what I saw of the poverty, the unemployment and the endless infamies committed on the inhabitants of the back-streets of that city.' Perhaps he was just as strongly impelled by what he saw of capitalism from the inside. On 27 January 1934, after only a few weeks in Liverpool, he was writing to Eva:

> I do not yet know enough about the job to be able to get really interested in it . . . All the big shipping firms in England and Europe trading with China, Japan and the Far East are organised in a ring or combine and have agreed to maintain the same charges in the cargoes they carry. There is still, however, one German firm refusing to enter into the agreement. In order to make the combine effective it is necessary to keep a close watch on all persons trading with the Far East and to refuse to carry the cargo of anyone who trades at all with the competing German firm. Major Cripps is chairman of the committee appointed to see that the affairs of the combine work smoothly and I am going to . . . keep him informed of what is happening . . . Learning up all the back stuff is as dull as ditchwater . . . Major Cripps is quite a good person, although not nearly so interesting as Sir Stafford . . . All the big men in the firms are just intolerable, with dwarfed, stunted intelligences . . . Sir Richard Holt is just the last word in malignant density . . . I have rarely met a less pleasant individual and I feel that a conspicuously dull career of sordid and unrelieved money-making has received a fitting recognition in a knighthood at the hands of the National Government . . . I am the only person in the whole firm who does not split his infinitives . . .

You will gather from all this that I am not exactly thrilled and overcome by all the good things that Liverpool has to offer.

Michael had signed on for the job for a year, with the option of a permanent career if both sides were agreeable. It was soon obvious that this was out of the question; the surprise, indeed, is that he stayed with Blue Funnel for nine months. One reason was that he had his own little office and was able to work on his life of Fox when the boss left him alone, writing on the backs of official documents which could be swiftly turned over if necessary. Those that survive make curious reading, with typescript on one side and Michael's pencilled handwriting on the other. For example:

Item 7 (b) Ref: SC 296
BONE GLUE IN BAGS FOR SHANGHAI

Dr Berg: 'I am of opinion that under the circumstances the Conference should allow the reduction to 42/6 W. Shanghai basis' . . .
Mr McGregor: 'In view of the fact that average exports have gone forward during the last five years from Holland, I see no necessity to reduce the rate.'

On the reverse:

The members of the Ministry, Lord North, Thurlow, etc, whose names according to Junius read like a satire on all government, were recruited with a few exceptions from the dregs of political society. Lord North was probably the ablest and least objectionable of the lot . . . Fox lavished upon him the finest flower of his invective; yet they were always good personal friends . . .

On the obverse:

LABOUR. At Pukow is very bad. Coolies control the entire situation, and vessels must not expect work as at Shanghai . . . They are however willing to work Sundays and holidays, without extra pay (except China New Year when no work is done). When cargo is stowed in a difficult place they have a habit of demanding extra pay to get it out.

On the reverse:

The idea of attracting power into his own hands only came to George after years of experience had impressed him with the impossibility of establishing a firm government under the existing regime of party intrigue. The Whigs were a rabble and George's antagonism is not inexplicable. The gravamen of the charge against George III is not that he refused to accept the Whig nominee of the moment, but that he attempted to force on his own chosen leader the same squalid views of government as he himself had.

The book was intended for a series called 'Brief Lives', published by Duckworth; but the series itself was not a success, so Michael's book was never published nor completed.

Soon after arriving in Liverpool, Michael crossed the Rubicon on whose brink he had stood since his last year at Oxford: he made up his mind that he was a socialist and joined the Labour Party. The news reached Pencrebar in a rather unfortunate manner. The activities of the former President of the Union were still a matter of interest in Oxford, and a report of his political move appeared in the *Isis*, to be picked up by the *Daily Herald*. According to John Foot, the news caused no real trouble in the family – 'the only trouble would have been if anyone had become a Tory'.[5] Sarah Foot recalls that when she was a child Isaac said to her with his air of mock solemnity: 'I think I could just forgive you if you voted socialist, but I could never forgive you if you voted Tory.'[6] She says, too, that Michael ingeniously ascribed his conversion to the reading of Hazlitt, and his father responded: 'Oh well, if William Hazlitt was responsible that's all right with me.' John remembers, however, that Eva Foot was 'rather upset', and she evidently sent Michael a reproachful letter. He wrote to her on 5 March 1935:

I am very sorry about the announcement in the *Herald* . . . The information was obtained from the *Isis* and must have been given to them by a friend of mine at Oxford. The announcement, however, expresses my considered views on the subject and I think it a little hard that in your letter you should (a) be sarcastic about the honesty of my motives and (b) speak as if I was to be blamed for letting you down . . . I have come to the conclusion that in the present circumstances Liberalism offers absolutely no contribution to the problem of poverty which with peace is far and away the most important problem and that Socialism is the only solution . . . I realise, of course, that the Labour Party possesses a rotten set of leaders, but as I believe in Socialism and still believe in democracy and parliamentary methods I do not think there is any other course but to support the Labour Party in the hope that it will improve. I am very sorry if the change makes you sad, but I think you will agree that I have a perfect right to come to my own political conclusions . . . Greater men than I, from Charles James Fox downwards, have disagreed with their parents.

In an account given a few years later, Michael explained:

I was brought up in the traditions of West Country Liberalism . . . At Oxford I met friends who came from South Wales. I went frequently to the valleys of Wales. I saw the same distress, misery and spoliation as I had seen in the big cities of America and the slums of Liverpool. I saw that something bigger and more revolutionary than Liberalism was wanted to deal with the problems of our social and economic system . . . I therefore decided to break with the family tradition and become a Socialist. Such a break was bound to cause some measure of distress to my family but, this must be said, my family accepted this decision with a true spirit of Liberal tolerance.[7]

Whatever her distress, Eva told a meeting of the Women's Liberal Association: 'I think he is grievously mistaken, but I believe he is entirely honest and sincere.'

Michael stayed in Liverpool until October 1935. Despite the boring job, he looked back on this period without regret. He found lodgings with a Jewish family whose roots were in Russia; although the mother spoke nothing but Yiddish, he found the household congenial and extended his knowledge of Jewish customs and traditions. The Labour Party was lively and emphatically left-wing and Michael made a new friend in Sydney Silverman, a Liverpool solicitor who became an MP in the 1935 election. When he could snatch time off from the Blue Funnel treadmill, he went to London to keep up his association with Stafford Cripps. Through Cripps, he made other new friends.

Of these, by far the most impressive and fascinating – and the most significant influence on Michael's life for the next twenty years – was Aneurin Bevan. In 1935 he was thirty-seven years old: too young to be a father-figure for Michael, but the right age to fill the role of an elder brother. A Welsh miner, he had entered the House of Commons in 1929 as MP for Ebbw Vale, which included his home town, Tredegar. The constituency was so solidly Labour that the Tories could not hope to mount a challenge even in 1931. The thinning of Labour's ranks in that disaster year, and Nye Bevan's qualities of energy and pugnacity, brought him to the forefront. In debates on a bill which set up the Unemployment Assistance Board – a relief system that preserved the hated 'means test' – he took up more space in Hansard than any other MP. Michael has recorded: 'It was one evening after a debate on this bill that I first met Aneurin Bevan. Thereafter I knew him as well as almost anybody else for the rest of his life. He was never a hero-worshipper; but I was.'[8]

If ever two men can be said to have 'clicked', and to have found an
intuitive affinity, it was these two. When Michael wrote of Nye: 'His
eyes were fixed on the horizons of politics. He was obsessed by the broad,
tumultuous movements in society and the world at large . . . Ideas were
his passion and he was interested in power as the vehicle for ideas,'9 he
might have been writing of himself. Both men had been shaped by books
and by ideas derived from books. Bored by routine tasks, they found it
essential as well as fascinating to read and to reflect on what they read.

However, their interests were never narrowly political. They responded eagerly to the arts, to music, to poetry, to the theatre. 'He
wanted a world of light and gaiety and beauty for everyone else and he
wanted it for himself' – again, Michael was describing his friend and
speaking for himself too.

Both came from Methodist families devoted to the cause of temperance. In adult life, both rejected religion and both took pleasure in their
wine and whisky, while despising anyone who surrendered to helpless
drunkenness. They were gregarious men who loved a good party,
whether at the home of a friend or a familiar venue like the Café Royal
(which was fairly cheap in the 1930s). But they also loved the ruminative
quietness of a hillside deep in the country.

With both, informality in dress and manners was a natural taste,
perhaps felt to be a guarantee of sincerity. In the thirties, when wearing a
hat was the badge of respectability, all photographs of Michael and Nye
show them bare-headed – even one of Nye handing in a petition at
10 Downing Street in pouring rain.

Each man had been forced to battle with an infuriating physical
handicap: Michael's asthma, Nye's stammer. Yet they were rated as
superb orators (though both distrusted the word) and also excelled as
debaters; they rank among the few politicians who have been equally
effective on the platform and in the House of Commons. When Nye
spoke, his aim was to enlighten, even to educate. 'He seemed', wrote
Michael, 'to wrestle with the problems of his audience, and, as the
argument mounted in intensity, the language became direct and
simple . . . His perorations might rise to a tremendous emotional
climax, but the argument always came from the intellect.'10 His guiding
rule was: 'Always address yourself to the strength of your opponent's
case, not the weakness' – a piece of advice that Michael did not forget.

Naturally, these men saw eye to eye in their likes and dislikes. They
loathed careerists. They were impatient of dull, pedantic politicians like
Clement Attlee. They could not stand intolerant, overbearing bosses
such as Ernest Bevin and Hugh Dalton. They reserved their trust and

their affection for men and women who could be called, as they themselves wished to be called, comrades.

Yet there was a difference between the two, and it was the outcome of their origins. Bevan was, indeed, fully at home with the highly educated; his political allies at this time included Professor Harold Laski, the theoretician (and Old Etonian) John Strachey and the top-ranking barrister D. N. Pritt. But he never broke his links with the working people of Tredegar, and one of his strengths was an inborn understanding of the thought-processes, the reactions, even the prejudices of those who lived their lives in the mining valleys, the steel towns, the docksides. This was a strength that Michael was not equipped by experience to acquire, and which he therefore respected.

At this time, Bevan was newly married to Jennie Lee. They had both entered Parliament in 1929, but she had lost her seat at North Lanark in 1931. She had been elected as a member of the Independent Labour Party, which was strong in Scotland, and she stayed with the ILP when it disaffiliated from the Labour Party in 1932.

Baldwin, the Tory leader, replaced the senescent Ramsay MacDonald as Prime Minister on 7 June 1935. He had to deal with the prospect of an attack by Fascist Italy on Abyssinia (now called Ethiopia). Mussolini, far from concealing his intentions, was rousing his people to a warlike frenzy with bombastic, menacing speeches. It was the duty of all members of the League of Nations to force an aggressor to desist, if possible by economic sanctions and if necessary by military action. But neither the British Tories, who were inclined to admire Mussolini – the man who had saved Italy from Bolshevism and made the trains run on time – nor the French government, headed by Pierre Laval, wished to do anything of the kind. On 10 September, the Foreign Secretary, Sir Samuel Hoare, conferred in Paris with Laval, who later recorded: 'We found ourselves instantaneously in agreement upon ruling out military sanctions, not adopting any measure of naval blockade, never contemplating closure of the Suez Canal.'[11] Of course, no such account was given at the time. Next day, Hoare addressed the League Assembly at Geneva and pledged Britain to support 'steady and collective resistance to all acts of unprovoked aggression'.

For the Labour Party, the obvious policy was to insist on the implementation of sanctions and to warn of any lukewarmness or duplicity on the part of the government. However, there were divided counsels. Lansbury, the party leader, was an absolute pacifist. Cripps declared that the government, while claiming 'to be fighting on behalf of the League system . . . will in fact have led the country into war to preserve the interests of British imperialism'.[12] Within the Labour left and the Socialist League, there were anguished debates. Michael, hearing opposing arguments from older comrades whom he respected, had difficulty in reaching a consistent position. He told his mother:

> My view is that I believe it is necessary to be willing to support economic and military sanctions against the aggressor in order to establish the collective system. But I certainly wouldn't fight in a pseudo-League of Nations war started by France and this government to impose conditions on Germany, when we have most flagrantly refused to accept the implications of the collective system ourselves.

A few months later, he was still more dubious about the 'collective system', and wrote: 'The emasculated League system acts as a mirage for diverting the Socialist movement from its true path.'[13]

When the Labour Party conference opened on 1 October, it was clear that a resolution supporting sanctions would be easily carried, mainly by the votes of the big trade unions – primarily, Ernest Bevin's Transport and General Workers' Union. Lansbury announced that he saw it as his duty to give up the leadership. The reaction of the delegates was to sing 'For he's a jolly good fellow', but Bevin's reaction was to deliver a brutal attack which reduced Lansbury to tears. Cripps, who resigned from the National Executive Committee because of his divergence from party policy, was treated just as roughly and accused of 'a cowardly stab in the back', a phrase of which Bevin grew increasingly fond. The resolution in favour of the sanctions policy, moved by Dalton, was carried by a huge majority. Within a week, Italian bombs were falling on Addis Ababa.

Labour MPs now had to choose a new leader and settled without enthusiasm for Attlee, acidly described by Beatrice Webb in her diary as 'the least disliked member of the Front Bench'. In the view of the *Manchester Guardian*, it was 'hardly more than an interim appointment'.

Despite the overwhelming conference vote, the Labour Party was seen as divided. Thanks to Hoare's speech, the government appeared to be pursuing the right policy. Besides, there had been a distinct recovery from the worst of the depression, with unemployment still high but at only half the 1931 level. Baldwin called a general election, with polling set for 14 November.

The idea of standing as a Labour candidate came immediately to Michael's mind. He had nothing to lose, since he was only twenty-two years old and his political life was ahead of him. At the least, he had the prospect of putting down a useful marker.

Being adopted as a candidate was a much simpler business then than it is now. Michael took a train to London, walked into Transport House (the party headquarters), asked to see James Middleton, the party secretary, and inquired whether there were any seats without a candidate. Middleton produced a list. Michael looked at it and said that he fancied Monmouth. Middleton told him that the management committee was to meet the next evening. Michael took another train, walked in again, introduced himself and was accepted with smiles all round.

The first job was to produce the election address. Michael named peace and poverty as the 'major problems' and declared that 'only a Socialist Government' – not just a Labour Government, one notes – could solve them. He gave priority to peace and, first of all, to disarmament. In capitals, the address urged: 'THE ARMAMENTS RACE IN EUROPE MUST BE STOPPED NOW.' Michael accused the government of betraying the League Covenant, but did not refer specifically to Abyssinia and continued: 'I am not in favour of going to war in order to defend the Foreign Investments of British financiers, or the protective tariffs of British industrialists.'

In the sphere of home policy, the address kept more closely to the standard Labour programme. It advocated nationalisation of the banks 'and the staple industries'; state aid to agriculture, minimum wages for farm workers, rural housing at low rents and the abolition of the tied cottage; the raising of the school–leaving age (which was then thirteen) and a better scholarship system; and the abolition of 'the iniquitous Means Test'.

In a final appeal, Michael told the voters:

I am a young man. I appeal to the Youth of the Monmouth Division to consider what the world offers to our generation. WAR and POVERTY are the twin dangers which threaten our chances of a decent, happy life in the World. All over Europe youth is being recruited into the ranks of Fascism. Fascism represents the last attempt of those who control economic power to maintain their supremacy . . . I WANT TO SEE A GOVERNMENT IN THIS COUNTRY WHICH WILL SERVE THE INTERESTS OF THE DESERVING MANY, AND NOT THOSE OF THE WEALTHY FEW.

He knew that he had no real hope of winning Monmouth. The Tory MP, Major Jack Herbert, was Lord Lieutenant of the county and a dominant local figure; he had secured a majority of over 9,000 in a by-election only the year before. It was (and is) a generally prosperous farming constituency, with four market towns – Monmouth, Abergavenny, Chepstow and Usk – but not a whiff of smoke from the industries a score of miles to the westward. The Labour organisation was rudimentary and the party secretary, Tom Powell, had to spend most of his time guiding Michael around and introducing him at meetings. Powell's warming-up speeches were not always wisely phrased; having set up the portable platform in Usk, he announced to the gathering crowd: 'Well, here we are in bloody Tory old Usk.' The party had no loudspeaker, and Michael was several times shouted down by Major Herbert's adherents. In those days the possession or use of cars was a crucial factor in an election, and Labour in Monmouth had only one car.

Michael increased the Labour vote by 3,000, but (in a higher turnout) the Tory vote went up too, and Herbert again scored a 9,000 majority.

At a national level, the Tories were easy winners. Labour had 154 MPs in the new House, but this only meant that seats were regained which should never have been lost in 1931, and the government still had a commanding majority. Morrison, Dalton and other senior figures returned to Westminster. The left was strengthened by the election of George Strauss (a close friend of Cripps), Sydney Silverman, D. N. Pritt and Ellen Wilkinson, who won Jarrow, a shipbuilding town hard hit by the depression and still grievously suffering. In the ensuing few years, she led a column of unemployed men in a march to London that became a Labour epic and wrote a widely read book, *The Town That Was Murdered*. Jennie Lee put up a good fight as ILP candidate for North Lanark, but the Labour Party – to Bevan's disgust and fury – ran an official candidate, thus enabling the Tories to hold the seat.

A few weeks after the election, a press leak revealed that Hoare and Laval, at their discreet meeting, had agreed to make a deal which would give Italy half of Abyssinia. The revelation caused an uproar and Hoare had to resign, though he returned to the Cabinet in another post six months later. There were indeed no effective sanctions and Italian troopships passed freely through the Suez Canal. After a savage campaign, marked by the bombing of undefended towns and the use of poison gas, the conquest of Abyssinia was completed by May 1936.

3

As soon as the votes were counted in Monmouth, Michael went to London to live and, if possible, find work. Walking out of Paddington Station with his suitcase, he found a furnished room at 33 Cambridge Terrace – his home for the next four years. The rent was thirty shillings a week. He had paid the same in Liverpool, but there it had covered all meals, and in London it only included breakfast.

What he wanted to do, above all, was to serve the cause of socialism in whatever way was open to him. Naturally, he had thoughts of a political career, but there would not be another general election for four or five years and there was no telling whether he would find a winnable seat. (As it turned out, the Parliament elected in 1935 sat for ten years through the turmoil of a world war.) Meanwhile, he had to earn money and the obvious way to do so was with his pen. He became a freelance journalist – not a very successful one, for his articles were accepted only by small-circulation weekly or monthly journals whose budgets were as frugal as his own, and he was scarcely able to make enough to live on.

To equip himself for any staff job in journalism that might appear, he learned the techniques of layout and typography. His teacher was Allen Hutt, who was a dedicated Communist and assistant editor of the *Daily Worker*, but also laid out the pages of the Sunday *Reynolds' News*. Founded in 1849 by a Chartist, George Reynolds, it was still required reading for left-wing socialists, thanks largely to the column written by H. N. Brailsford. Sixty-two years old at this time, Brailsford had earned unquestioning respect for his idealism and integrity, and won Michael's limitless trust and admiration. Another man whom Michael held in high esteem was William Mellor, who had been editor of the *Daily Herald* (succeeding George Lansbury) when it was a campaigning socialist paper, and had been dismissed because of his left-wing views when it came under the joint ownership of the press baron Lord Southwood and the Trades Union Congress. Michael already knew Mellor, who liked to play the role of a mentor and guide to young people and had often visited Oxford and other universities.

Mellor's enthusiasm for youth was not exclusively political and di-dactic, and he was (although married) the lover of a young woman named Barbara Betts. The red-haired Barbara – strikingly attractive, full of self-confidence, vehement in manner, endlessly talkative and argumentative – made a vivid impression on everyone who met her, not least on Michael. In 1984, he wrote in a tone of affectionate remin-iscence: 'It is indeed fifty years ago since we first became acquainted and spent many happy hours together, reading from the works of Beatrice Webb or Karl Marx, and engaging in a whole gamut of even more joyous pursuits.'[14] Michael would have been glad if these com-radely evenings had developed into a love affair; but, as Barbara has written, 'Michael knew of my relationship with William, whom he deeply respected.'[15] Her account is: 'We were never lovers and I do not think either of us ever seriously thought of each other in that way. For one thing I was not beautiful enough to attract him sexually. Under that shy exterior there was a lover of beautiful women waiting to burst out.'[16]

Barbara remained devoted to Mellor until he died in 1942. She then married Ted Castle, a journalist on the *Daily Mirror*. Michael Foot and Barbara Castle were two of the new Labour MPs elected in the triumph of 1945, and eventually sat round the Cabinet table together.

Three months after arriving in London, Michael found a job. In one sense it was a very good, indeed enviable job; he was to work on the *New Statesman*, which had developed under Kingsley Martin's editorship into the liveliest and most successful political weekly in London. In another sense it was less than fully satisfactory, for Martin was paying only a retainer of £250 a year, regarded Michael as a trainee and would give no guarantee that the job would last beyond the training period. On 21 May 1936 Martin wrote to another job applicant, Frank Hardie:

> I'm not sure how long Michael Foot, who has been working here for the last few months, is stopping. He is not on the staff and is not in any case going to be put on it, but he is working here doing some jobs and some writing . . . He is looking for another job and may soon get one. He's a good fellow and not a bad journalist, but not A plus . . . I tried him out on the clear understanding that we shouldn't keep him unless he was brilliantly successful.[17]

In the *New Statesman* office, Michael did routine sub-editing work and wrote some of the unsigned 'Notes' which were brief commentaries on events; it would be impossible now to identify those that were his handiwork. His only signed contributions were nine book reviews, appearing between 22 February and 3 October 1936. Those relating to Palestine and the Jewish–Arab antagonism have already been mentioned. The others illustrate, and conform to, the left-wing attitudes of the period. Reviewing the memoirs of the Communist MP William Gallacher, and praising him for his opposition to the 1914–18 war, Michael wrote: 'The acceptance today of the myth of national solidarity in the face of some menace to British Imperialism would mean the final betrayal of whatever economic and emotional appeal Socialism is able to possess.' In a review of a book which extolled the benefits conferred by Soviet rule on the peoples of Central Asia, he laid down: 'Colonial peoples in revolt must be regarded by a Socialist opposition as allies in the fight against the common enemy; they must never be looked upon as chattel-slaves to be bought and sold in the market of European diplomacy.' The writing was fluent and trenchant, but Kingsley Martin may well have felt that the didactic manner was at odds with the open-minded, sceptical style that *New Statesman* readers liked. He decided that Michael was less than 'brilliantly successful' and advised him to pursue his career elsewhere. The next trainee, also on £250 a year, was R. H. S. (Richard) Crossman.

Leaving the *New Statesman* was no disaster for Michael, for he had another prospect in view. Cripps had for some time been thinking of starting a weekly paper as a mouthpiece for the Labour left, and in June 1936 he made plans to launch it at the New Year of 1937. The initial capital would be provided by Cripps himself and by George Strauss, who was also a rich man. The name chosen was *The Tribune* (later, the definite article was dropped). Mellor would be appointed as editor and there would be a job for Michael. Barbara would also be invited to write for the paper, but as a freelance contributor.

4

If one had to point to a moment at which Europe became vulnerable to the menace of Nazi and Fascist aggression and the danger of a Second World War became clearly visible, it would certainly be in the year 1936. Hitler had denounced the disarmament clauses of the Treaty of Versailles, had introduced conscription with a view to creating an army capable of large-scale war, and was building up a Luftwaffe with a formidable array of bombers. Germany's neighbours – Austria, Czechoslovakia and Poland – were vulnerable and anxious. Indeed, the Nazis had been poised to take over Austria in 1934 and had been checked only by the disapproval of Mussolini, who rushed Italian troops to the Brenner Pass. But by 1936 the two dictators were acting in close co-operation, linked in an alliance which they called the Axis. In March 1936 Hitler sent his troops into the Rhineland, a part of western Germany which was demilitarised under the provisions of Versailles. Britain and France protested, but submitted to the *fait accompli*.

The first theatre of war was Spain. The People's Front, an alliance of Socialist, Communist and Liberal parties, had scored an electoral victory in February, but the Spanish right refused to accept its defeat. Military chiefs conspired to seize the main cities on 18 July. In Madrid and Barcelona, the uprising was crushed by hastily assembled workers' militias. The coup was successful only in Seville, where thousands of members of left-wing parties were shot. One man paid with his life for possessing a book entitled *Socialism*, written years earlier by Ramsay MacDonald.

General Francisco Franco, who had been sent to the Canary Islands by the Republican government because of his suspect loyalties, emerged as the rebel commander. A British freelancing pilot flew him to Morocco. This was to be the base for an advance towards Madrid, but the first problem was to ferry the troops across the straits, which were patrolled by a cruiser loyal to the Republic. A German businessman with interests in Spain appealed to Hitler (catching him at the Wagner festival in Bayreuth) and he despatched twenty Junker aircraft with German crews, which not only transported Franco's troops but also bombed and sank the cruiser.

From the outset, Franco received massive aid from Germany and Italy, but his sympathisers also included British Tories, the Catholic hierarchy (notably in the United States), owners of big newspapers, and professional military men. In some instances this sympathy took a practical form; thus, British officers in Gibraltar placed their phone lines at the disposal of General Kindelan, Franco's man in Algeciras, enabling him to talk to Rome and Berlin without going through Spanish exchanges.[18] One Tory MP, Commander R. T. Bower, wrote: 'The Spanish war is a conflict between Christian civilisation and the Beast. That is why so many of us hope that Franco will win.'[19]

But sympathy for the Republic took a practical form too. Within a few months, thousands of men crossed the Pyrenees to enlist in the International Brigade. The greatest numbers were French, but they also included Welsh miners and London dockers, German and Italian anti-fascists who had been living in France, Americans and Canadians, and men from Cuba, Bulgaria, Finland and virtually every country reached by political idealism. Most of them were of course young men, but Brailsford volunteered and was deeply disappointed when he was told that he was too old. He had fought for Greece with the Philhellenic Legion in 1897.

Michael Foot, like thousands on the left, shared the passionate feelings aroused by the Spanish conflict, which still evoke emotional memories. Since 1980, he has unveiled two memorials to the British volunteers, one in London and the other in Cardiff. At the time, he wrote:

Some had begged for their passage money; some had scaled the Pyrenees by night; some had dropped over the mountains with not a penny in their pockets and only a trade union card as a passport . . . Some had stood, maybe, in the prison yard at Dachau and seen their comrades bruised by Nazi lash and boot; some had crossed a wild German frontier with the hand of a woman clasped in their own and a child clinging about their necks; some had sat for ten years in the dingy home of an exile with their eyes turned to their native Italy, hearing no sound but the voice of desecration; some, indeed, came from England, believing, like the heroes of old, that shame could be expiated in battle . . . Such were the Ironsides of Democracy, the International Brigade.[20]

The shame to be expiated was that of 'non-intervention'. Although the Spanish government had a legal right to buy arms from abroad, a scheme to ban the supply of arms to either side in the civil war was proposed by Britain and France. France now had a People's Front government, headed by the Socialist Léon Blum, which had to be pressured into endorsing non-intervention,[21] and the French Air Minister, a Socialist named Pierre Cot, managed to get fifty fighter planes into Spain by arranging fake sales to Brazil. However, a Non-Intervention Committee was soon set up in London, headed by Lord Plymouth, a Tory peer, with representatives from Britain, France, Germany, Italy, the Soviet Union and Portugal.

Plymouth ruled that complaints of intervention had to be submitted in writing by a committee member – not by the Spanish government – and answered in writing before they could be discussed. Thus the committee took little cognisance of the massive aid furnished to Franco by Germany and Italy from the outset and throughout the war. Units of bombers, fighters, tanks and artillery formed part of the Condor Legion, operating under German command; the bombing of Guernica, which inspired Picasso's famous painting, was a German technical experiment. Mussolini sent entire divisions of Italian regular troops, amounting to 70,000 men. The capture of Malaga in the south and that of Santander in the north were all-Italian operations. The Soviet Union withdrew from the Non-Intervention Committee when it became clear that the system was a farce and sent tanks and planes to Republican Spain, but its aid was never on the same scale as the lavish flow that was reaching Franco.

The Labour Party conference met in October 1936 in Edinburgh. The National Executive Committee, mainly thanks to the urging of Dalton and Bevin, decided to ask the conference to support non-intervention, using the argument that Blum had agreed to it (and was alleged, wrongly, to have been the first to suggest it). It was thought prudent to take the vote before the speech made by a Spanish Socialist guest, and the NEC won a majority by the usual comfortable margin guaranteed by union block votes. The Spanish comrade was Isabel de Palencia, who had a Scottish mother and spoke fluent English with the accent of the city where the conference was meeting. She made a moving appeal, which roused some delegates to demand that the vote should be taken again – in vain, of course. Dalton recorded contemptuously: 'A large number of delegates were now wildly excited. They were wallowing in sheer emotion, in vicarious valour.'[22]

Franco's forces were now in the outskirts of Madrid. General Mola boasted that four columns were advancing on the city and there was a fifth column within it, thus coining a durable phrase. But on 8 November 3,000 International Brigaders marched through the streets and took up positions at the front. Three days later, the first Russian tanks and planes went into action. The difference in the military balance was small; the effect on morale was incalculable. For another two and a half years, Madrid was in the front line, repeatedly threatened with encirclement, incessantly bombed, weary and hungry, but defiant. For those years, Spain was the focus of the faith and pride, the hopes and fears of the left. Thousands of men and women were caught up in supporting the volunteers, helping their families, raising money for ambulances and medical aid, sheltering Spanish children who came as refugees, and campaigning against non-intervention.

One effect of the Spanish war was a change in the left's attitude to the use of armed force. It was not easy for people who had hitherto regarded war as the supreme evil to start talking in terms of courage, heroism, self-sacrifice, the values that had seemed to be the property of the patriotic right; it was never true, as subsequent mythology maintains, that all the issues were clear and all the choices simple. Yet, for most socialists, it was impossible to concede that the workers of Madrid and Barcelona, on that fatal 18 July, should have passively allowed the military conspirators to gain the upper hand. Michael Foot was typical enough of his generation. In 1933, as we have seen, he was writing that justice and liberty 'can only be lastingly secured by peaceable means and the use of force will only contaminate them'. A few years later, he was pouring out his admiration for the International Brigade.

Another effect was a rapid increase in the prestige of the Soviet Union and, by extension, of the Communist Party. While Attlee and Blum were clinging to the futility of non-intervention, Stalin was sending real aid to the Republic, although he had to maintain his own defences – the defences of the land of socialism – against the visible threat of a Nazi attack. Moreover, it was the efficient network of the Communist International that mobilised volunteers all over Europe. Although the British Communist Party had only 10,000 members while the Labour Party had about half a million, roughly two-thirds of the men who left Britain to fight in Spain were Communists. There was no need to stress the contrast.

Hence, Spain greatly strengthened the argument for alliance and joint action between socialists and Communists. It was an alliance of this kind that had won victory at the polls in France and Spain, and was now the backbone of the fighting Republican government. In Britain, the idea of the united front might have had little attraction in ordinary times. Given their minuscule voting strength, the Communists could make little contribution to winning an election (at all events under the British system) and it could indeed be argued that association with them was a handicap. But Spain drastically altered, if not the logic, certainly the mood. It did not seem reasonable that Joe of the Worktown Labour Party and Jim of the Worktown Communist Party should fight together in Spain while their Jean and Joan could not run a campaign committee together. The edicts of the Labour Party, banning co-operation with Communists and imposing penalties, including expulsion, for disobedience appeared to many simply petty and mean-minded.

There was, however, a difficulty to be confronted even for those who were, in principle, all for unity. The united front, as understood up to 1935, meant co-operation between Labour and the Communist Party: that is, between two parties both subscribing to socialism as a political philosophy and an ultimate goal. The People's Front meant an alliance of three forces: the Communists, the socialists or social democrats, and any moderate or middle-of-the-road groups which were in favour of democracy and against fascism. In France, the third partner was the historic and still formidable Radical–Socialist Party (so called, though in truth neither radical nor socialist). Its leader, Edouard Daladier, did indeed sign on the dotted line and was to be seen, not very happily, in the forefront of a march with Blum and the Communist leader, Maurice Thorez. The result was electoral victory and coalition government, but the power of the Radicals gradually increased at the expense of the Socialists (Blum was replaced as Prime Minister after a year) and Mellor commented that one should be 'wary of experiments in government that give renewed weight to the Right of the Left in order to defeat the Right of the Right.'[23] In Britain, the third partner was the Liberal Party. There certainly were Liberals who inherited the Lloyd George tradition of social progress and reform, and there were Liberals who were sincerely devoted to the League of Nations and to the cause of Republican Spain, but even these Liberals were not socialists, and some Liberals were strongly anti-socialist in their outlook. It was impossible to forget that the Labour Party had fought hard to displace the old Liberal hegemony, and had won the battle in South Wales or Yorkshire as recently as the 1920s. Still more difficult to swallow, but visible in the Communist idea of the People's Front concept, was an alliance that would include a section of Tories. Here the key figure was Winston Churchill, who was clearly against Hitler (it was less clear whether he was against Mussolini or Franco) but in other respects was an incorrigible reactionary.

Cripps, however, was unreservedly enthusiastic for the People's Front policy. A major influence on his thinking was Harry Pollitt, the Communist leader, a jovial Lancashire man with a salty sense of humour who was widely liked and trusted among the Labour left. Ben Pimlott, the best historian of the period, considers that Cripps 'had fallen under Pollitt's spell' and that 'the splits in the Labour Party from 1936 to 1939 owed much to Pollitt's adept management of Cripps'.[24] When representatives of the Communist Party, the Socialist League and the ILP met to hammer out a Unity Manifesto, the successful outcome was secured largely by Pollitt's negotiating skill. Nevertheless, the manifesto did not call for a People's Front in the broader sense, but only for 'unity of all sections of the working-class movement within the framework of the Labour Party and trade unions'. Even so, a special conference of the Socialist League, despite Cripps' personal authority, endorsed this manifesto only by a majority of 56 to 38 votes, with 23 abstentions.

On 24 January 1937, the Unity Campaign based on the manifesto was launched at an enthusiastic meeting in the Free Trade Hall, Manchester. This was followed up by a series of successful rallies up and down the country, and the campaign soon had a hundred local committees. It was, however, one of the most short-lived campaigns in political history. The NEC of the Labour Party reacted swiftly by declaring that the Socialist League was no longer an affiliated organisation, and that membership of the League was incompatible with membership of the party. Attlee, in a private letter to Harold Laski, regretted that 'Stafford & Co have played into the hands of every right-wing influence in the party . . . I fight all the time against heresy-hunting, but the heretics seem to seek martyrdom.' Pollitt advised Cripps that he could achieve nothing as an exile in the wilderness and the only realistic course was to dissolve the League. Over protests from William Mellor, Cripps agreed. On 17 May, an unhappy League conference voted for dissolution, with Barbara Betts bravely explaining that it was 'not a funeral but a conscious political tactic'. Inevitably, the Unity Campaign was wound up too. It could scarcely be carried on by the CP and the ILP without participation by any section of the Labour Party.

5

The first issue of *The Tribune* appeared on 1 January 1937. It was an attractive sixteen-page paper, well laid out (often by Allen Hutt's pupil), with bold headlines and good photographs and always with a front-page cartoon by a gifted artist, Arthur Wragg. Despite these assets, and despite the cover price of only twopence (twice that of a daily paper) sales were disappointing. As Pimlott has written: '*Tribune* would have quickly collapsed without massive contributions from Cripps.'[25] In the other sense of the word, there was no lack of contributions. Lansbury, Nye Bevan, Laski, Cole, Krishna Menon and Sidney Webb all wrote for the paper.

Michael wrote almost every week, but did not often have a by-line. He and Barbara, jointly using the name 'Judex', were responsible for the industrial news and comment. Until now, Michael's knowledge of the world of industry had been slight and mainly theoretical, but he soon developed an ability to dig for facts, including those concealed in the small print of company reports, and to grasp and interpret what he was told face to face by working-class people with grievances.

Miners in Nottinghamshire were on strike, battling not only against the coalowners but against the company union, which had been set up after the General Strike and was totally subservient to the employers. Men who belonged to a real union, affiliated to the nation-wide Miners' Federation, were victimised and sacked. In a centre-page signed report from Harworth, the village which was the centre of resistance, Michael wrote: 'Every collier knew that destitution was the price of defiance. During the past ten years thousands of miners who valued the right to speak as free men have been forced to leave the county.' Yet the atmosphere in Harworth was inspiring: 'Six months ago it was the coalowners' preserve. Today it is the spearhead in the fight against company unionism. The miners throughout the county have made clear how precious they hold the principles for which the Harworth men have fought.'[26]

In May 1937, the newspapers devoted their space to the coronation of George VI and to the retirement of Baldwin, who was succeeded by Neville Chamberlain. The organisers of the coronation invited four working men and women to attend the ceremony in Westminster Abbey, mingling with dignitaries of Church and state to create a show of national unity. Michael's headline for another signed piece was: 'FOUR HONOURED GUESTS AT A RICH MAN'S FESTIVAL'. The men were a Derbyshire miner and a Welsh tinplate worker; the women, a Birmingham assembly-line worker and a Glasgow carpet-weaver. Enquiries established that only the tinplate man was decently paid, at 69 shillings a week, and he was a highly skilled worker. The miner was earning only 45 shillings, barely enough for family needs, and the weaver a mere 30 shillings. Michael wrote:

> Follow these four back to their homes and you will see what a cheap piece of deception the whole thing was. You will realise something of the vulgarity of a ruling class which takes delight in flaunting its power in the faces of the poor . . . The majesty of monarchy and the glory of empire are founded on the economics of the sweatshop . . . When we ask for bread, they give us a circus.

At the Labour conference of 1937, the Executive made a prudent concession and decided that the constituency parties should be allowed to elect seven NEC members; hitherto, all seats had been filled by grace of the union block votes. Alongside Morrison, Dalton and other right-wingers, the left succeeded in electing Cripps, Laski and Pritt. However, the united front was now a forlorn cause and when Cripps moved a resolution in favour of it he lost by an overwhelming majority. Meanwhile, the Executive vetoed the selection of Mellor as Labour candidate for Coventry.

The united front was victorious in only one sphere: that of the youth movement. A young man named Ted Willis, known to stand firmly on the left, was elected as chairman of the Labour League of Youth, defeating George Brown – an event hailed by Cripps as 'a good augury'. In *Tribune*, Willis wrote complacently: 'Youth has always been in advance of the adult movement politically.' Cripps was greatly taken with young Willis, regularly invited him to tea, and once told him that he might well be a future Labour Prime Minister.[27] But Ted's real soul-mate was John Gollan, leader of the Young Communist League, and the two organisations were working closely together. Gollan was invited to contribute to *Tribune*; his article, on 28 May, was headed: 'We Can Bring Hope to Our Youth.' In fact, although Willis did not hold a card in the YCL for tactical reasons, his loyalties were to Communism. According to another leading light in the League of Youth, Alec Bernstein, when Cripps gave a tea-party for members of the League's committee, he was unaware that ten of the twelve were undercover Communists.

While Harry Pollitt pleaded eloquently for co-operation between Labour Party people and Communists, and many of the former were strongly in agreement, the appeal was to some extent undermined by disturbing news from Moscow. Between August 1936 and January 1938, three sensational trials resulted in the conviction of men who had been high in the Soviet power structure on charges of espionage, treason and plotting to assassinate Stalin and overthrow the Soviet government. All made abject confessions; almost all were executed. We now know that these show trials were only the tip of the iceberg. In a huge reign of terror, millions of innocent people were summarily shot or sent to perish in the Siberian prison-camps.

The full truth emerged only decades later. In 1937, Barbara Betts spent seven weeks in the Soviet Union, reporting for *Tribune* on the life of Russian women and children. Her articles were full of praise for the schools, the hospitals and 'the shops overflowing with good things to eat', and only one thing puzzled her: every school she visited had a photograph of Andrei Bubnov, the Commissar for Education, but by the time she got back to London he had lost his job. She confided to *Tribune* readers: 'Naturally I am curious to know in what way Bubnov was considered inadequate.' In fact, Bubnov – a veteran Bolshevik who had been in the party leadership on the eve of the 1917 revolution – had been summarily arrested, and he was shot in 1940. Barbara wrote many years later: 'Re-reading them [her articles] today I realise how much I had to learn journalistically. I faithfully reported what I was shown by my Intourist guide.'[28]

She was young and equipped with little background knowledge; others should have known better. Just before the first big trial, the American journalist Louis Fischer wrote: 'The reign of law is now definitely established in the USSR.'[29] After it, the *Observer*'s correspondent reported: 'It is futile to think that the trial was staged and the charges trumped up.' D. N. Pritt, a luminary of the English Bar, told the *News Chronicle*: 'I am completely satisfied that the case was properly conducted and the accused were fairly and judicially treated.' But one man of the left took a different view, and he was a man whose attitude carried much weight with Michael Foot. H. N. Brailsford was outraged by what he called 'this shocking trial' and by 'the purge of the Communist Party that recalls Hitler's slaughter of his rivals'. In his *Reynolds' News* column, he described the trial as 'a relic of the Middle Ages, worthy of the Inquisition rather than a Socialist tribunal'.[30] In reply to protesting letters, he insisted: 'I hold to the opinion which rationalist and humanitarian thinkers have maintained since the eighteenth century: civilised justice does not rely on confessions.'

Given that the Soviet Union was credited with many admirable achievements, was the target of fascist threats and was the only nation to help Republican Spain, even the sceptical were reluctant to condemn. An editorial in the *New Statesman* pleaded: 'Let us see this matter in perspective. A social revolution is accompanied both by violence and by idealism.' Readers were reminded: 'The Russian Revolution is the great achievement of this generation.' In *Tribune*, Mellor took the same line:

> Many Socialists may be horrified by the suppression of those in Soviet Russia who are critical of the regime . . . But who can believe that the transformation of the old Russia into a Socialist society could proceed without severity or without errors? . . . The defence of the Soviet Union against capitalist and Fascist enemies is a common vital interest for the working classes of all countries.[31]

More anxieties – and more cover-ups excused by loyalty to the cause – arose from a distressing event in Spain in May 1937. This was a clash between the Communists, now dominant in the Republican government, and the Anarchists, allied with a small party called the POUM (Workers' Party of Marxist Unity) which had links with the British ILP. Street-fighting in Barcelona took a toll of 400 or 500 lives. A British volunteer, George Orwell, who was an ILP member, took part in the defence of the POUM office against the Civil Guards. As he saw it, the aftermath of the struggle was a 'horrible atmosphere produced by fear, suspicion, hatred, censored newspapers, crammed jails, enormous food queues, and prowling gangs of armed men'.[32] On his return to England, Orwell wrote an article called 'Spilling the Spanish Beans' which was rejected by the *New Statesman*. He also proposed to write a book about Spain for Victor Gollancz, but Gollancz refused to consider it. *Homage to Catalonia* was eventually published by another firm.

Gollancz was a man of passionate convictions and overbearing personality. In 1936 he had launched the Left Book Club, which offered its members political books in cheap editions, selected by Harold Laski, John Strachey and Gollancz himself. The Club was a huge success, attracting 50,000 members and creating a spin-off of hundreds of local discussion groups. Indeed, this network of groups, with its incessant activities and its annual rally in the Albert Hall, was almost a political movement. Gollancz claimed: 'In the Left Book Club we are creating the mass basis without which a true Popular Front is impossible. In a sense, the Left Book Club is already a sort of Popular Front.'[33]

Gradually, however, it became clear that Gollancz, subscribing with his usual whole-heartedness to the Communist line, was exercising an intolerance of his own. He commissioned an 'educational' book by Brailsford, entitled *Why Capitalism Means War*, but then demanded changes unacceptable to the author (the book was saved by Laski and published after a delay). The main problem arose from Brailsford's criticism of the extinction of freedom in the Soviet Union. Gollancz told him: 'The Soviet Union is in a war situation; in that situation it is not only justified but impelled to take every possible measure that can prevent the faintest chance of disloyalty or disruption within.'[34] On the Soviet trials Gollancz had no doubts; he published a book by a Communist lawyer praising the Radek trial, and the *Left News*, the Club's organ, carried a vehement Strachey article headed 'The Guilty'.

One other result of Stalin's ruthlessness should be noted. His attack on his army was as devastating as any of his purges; among the victims were most of the generals and senior officers. This disaster came at just the time when the left was pressing for an alliance between Britain, France and the Soviet Union as the only possible way to deter, or if necessary defeat, a Nazi aggression. Tory politicians and British military men, reluctant in any case to welcome co-operation with the Red Army, were given a perfect excuse to decide that it would be pointless. A key adviser to the Foreign Secretary summarised the official view in these terms: 'No one thought the Russians were any good or would last more than a fortnight.'[35] Sir Samuel Hoare recalled in his memoirs: 'We had to depend for our estimate on the unanimous verdict of the British and French General Staffs that the Russian Army was completely demoralised. Their second conclusion followed that Poland was a more valuable ally than Russia.'[36] When the need for an alliance with Russia became urgent in 1939, these opinions may have swayed the balance.

Michael was watching these events with foreboding, aware of Mellor's suppressed dissent from the Communist or pro–Communist line and of Brailsford's more open disagreement. He took part in *Tribune* editorial conferences and in many informal discussions over coffee or cheap red wine, but he was not called upon to write political articles and was busy enough with industrial affairs. In 1938 he attacked the Bata shoe company, of Czechoslovak origin, which had set up factories and shops in Britain and was forbidding employees to join trade unions. There was a strike, supported by only a hundred workers. Brigadier-General Spears, who was chairman of Bata in Britain and also a Tory MP, dismissed the strike as a negligible event and was rebuked by Michael in an Open Letter: 'The hundred on strike have forfeited their livelihoods in the cause of trade unionism. The fourteen hundred still working fear the same fate. The courage of those hundred and the fear of those fourteen hundred are things you would know nothing about.'[37]

On 6 May Michael wrote a profile of Leslie Hore-Belisha, the Minister of War. Originally a Liberal, then a National Liberal from 1931, Hore-Belisha was MP for the Devonport division of Plymouth. He had written for the Beaverbrook papers – or, as Michael put it: 'Press Lord Beaverbrook took him up, paid him £3000 a year for feature floridity in the *Evening Standard* and *Daily Express*, where he kept his name bold at the top of the page.' He then joined the government as Minister of Transport and introduced pedestrian crossings marked by what were popularly known as Belisha beacons. Michael's version of this phase was: 'He became the great embellisher, exhibited his one Disraelian trait to the full. Painting his room at the Ministry peacock-blue, plastering London with inelegant orange traffic beacons, he publicised himself – ostensibly his department – to the limit.'

By 1938 Hore-Belisha was Minister of War, but was far from safe in the job. The military expert Liddell Hart was told by a friend: 'Hore-Belisha is hated in the Cabinet . . . They resent his advertising and obvious ambition, complain that his recruiting figures are deceptive, and are afraid that he will leave them in a mess.'[38]

As Prime Minister, Neville Chamberlain was bent on appeasement, a word which he uttered with pride and which acquired its pejorative meaning only with retrospect. He made his own foreign policy, often without consulting the Foreign Secretary, Anthony Eden, who had been appointed in 1936 to calm the outcry over the Hoare–Laval deal and was associated by reputation with a collective security policy. When Chamberlain decided to open discussions with Mussolini, over-ruling Eden who opposed doing so until at least some Italian troops had been withdrawn from Spain, Eden resigned, to be replaced by Lord Halifax.

This was the moment when Hitler made his first overtly aggressive move. On 13 March, Austria was occupied by German troops and ceased to exist as an independent state. For the first time, the world was presented with the reality of Nazi brutality, not behind the gates of concentration camps but in the city streets. The Jews of Vienna, a large community, were dragooned into scrubbing the pavements with brushes dipped in an acid solution. Hundreds, perhaps thousands, killed themselves, thus forestalling the journey to the gas chambers which the survivors made a few years later. Others tried to escape; a British journalist wrote:

All roads to the frontier were jammed with fleeing taxicabs and motor-cars. At the aerodrome and the stations a medley of princes, peasants and paupers, world-famous bankers, obscure proletarians, Jews from the highest rank to the lowest, army officers, police officials and the Communists and Socialists they had arrested and punished, Catholic priests, civil servants and journalists desperately tried to find places on the departing train.[39]

The British psychoanalyst Ernest Jones, who hurried to Vienna to rescue Sigmund Freud, gave this description of what he found at the psychoanalytic publishing house:

The stairs and rooms were occupied by villainous-looking youths armed with daggers and pistols, Martin Freud was sitting in a corner under arrest, and the Nazi 'authorities' were engaged in counting the petty cash in a drawer. As soon as I spoke I was also put under arrest, and the remarks made when I asked to be allowed to communicate with the British Embassy (to which I had special introductions) showed me how low my country's prestige had fallen after Hitler's successes.[40]

In Spain, meanwhile, Franco launched a powerful offensive, and in April 1938 his troops reached the Mediterranean, cutting off Catalonia from the rest of Republican territory. Barcelona was mercilessly bombed. In desperate battles that summer on the Ebro river, it was reckoned that Franco's forces had a superiority of fifteen to one in artillery, the same in bombing aircraft, and ten to one in fighters. The Republic's most ardent friends could not conceal from themselves that defeat was only a matter of time.

6

A rift was rapidly developing between those on the left who supported a broad People's Front, arguing that the immediate necessity was the defence of democracy and that the advance towards socialism must be put into temporary cold storage, and those who could not stomach the dilution of their socialist faith. Orwell wrote sardonically: 'The People's Front is only an idea, but it has already produced the nauseous spectacle of bishops, Communists, cocoa magnates, publishers, duchesses, and Labour MPs marching arm in arm to the tune of "Rule Britannia".'[41] However, the People's Front was the doctrine of the Communist Party, of the Left Book Club, and of Cripps and his closest political friends, such as Strauss, Ellen Wilkinson and Pritt. Bevan too was a supporter, although Michael remarked in his later biography: 'Bevan might have been expected to insist on the purity of his Socialist faith.' He silenced his inner doubts because of the urgency of the situation, and Michael's paraphrase of his attitude is doubtless a valid summary of Michael's own attitude too:

> No one could gauge what would be the magnetic effect of a realignment on the Left . . . Maybe the Popular Front was always a desperate, forlorn bid. But what other card in the Socialist hand was there left to play? Better this than the infuriating inertia of official Labour in the face of calamity.[42]

The obvious propaganda vehicle for the People's Front was *Tribune*, announced by street-sellers as 'Stafford Cripps' paper'. The awkward fact, however, was that *Tribune*'s editor, William Mellor, was on the other side of the argument. True, he did not advertise his dissent, and the only sign of it in *Tribune* files is a review of G. D. H. Cole's book *The People's Front*, a Left Book Club choice. Cole had argued that the People's Front was a corollary of the earlier United Front, and Mellor commented: 'If one doubts the reality of the corollary – as I do so far as Britain is concerned – one must admire the persuasiveness of the argument.'[43] But Mellor's attitude was no secret to Cripps, Strauss and the other members of the Board.

Besides, Cripps and Mellor jarred on one another at a personal level. Mellor – described by Michael as 'an endearing ogre' – was passionate in argument, quick-tempered and utterly devoid of tact. As Michael recalled: 'Working with William Mellor was like living on the foothills of Vesuvius. On slight provocation the molten lava would pour forth in protest against the imbecilities of the world in general and anyone who dared cross him in particular.'[44]

Such a man could find nothing in common with the legalistic Cripps, who was equally sure of himself and indeed arrogant, but was always controlled and precise. Cripps also laid great stress on financial probity and Mellor, according to Ted Willis, was capable of spending the huge sum of ten pounds of *Tribune*'s money – which, of course, was Cripps' money – on lunch for two.

In the summer of 1938, Cripps negotiated with Gollancz – it is uncertain which of them first approached the other – for a deal between *Tribune* and the Left Book Club. They reached agreement that two pages of the paper were to be placed at the disposal of the Club, which would extol the merits of its books and publish the sort of articles that had hitherto appeared in *Left News*. Gollancz would join the *Tribune* board. Some of the financial burden would be lifted from the shoulders of Cripps and Strauss. It was hoped that an increase in circulation, with Club members urged to read *Tribune*, would make it possible to increase the size of the paper to twenty-four pages (this was never achieved). Politically, the line would be that of the People's Front.

Cripps was having trouble with his delicate stomach – it plagued him all his life – and had been advised by his doctor to take a long rest. He was due to leave for Jamaica in July. Only one matter remained to be decided: the editorship of the revamped paper. Gollancz, in the name of the three Left Book Club selectors, advised (or demanded) that Mellor should be dismissed. Cripps agreed without reluctance.

With only a few days left before he had to board the ship, Cripps summoned Mellor to a brief interview and told him that he must give up the editorial chair. The manner of this dismissal is described by Michael as 'brusque and dictatorial'. In fact, Michael was outraged at seeing a comrade, and a man of stature in the socialist movement, treated as subordinates were treated in the capitalist press.

Cripps' next move was to offer the position of editor to Michael. This must have struck him as an excellent idea. Here was a young man, devoid of any of Mellor's irritating characteristics, to whom he stood in a quasi-paternal relationship. It can never have occurred to him that Michael would not gratefully accept the job.

Clearly, Michael realised that he was faced with a flattering offer and a considerable opportunity. He was just twenty-five years old and had barely two and a half years' experience in journalism. To become an editor – a person who wrote major policy articles, made vital decisions and commissioned contributors – was more than he had any right to expect. Moreover, he was being invited to edit a socialist paper, founded to preach the ideas in which he believed.

On the other hand, he disagreed with Cripps and Gollancz – and agreed with Mellor – on the issue of a broad People's Front. Still not far distant from his renunciation of Liberalism, Michael took his socialism very seriously and could not subscribe to a strategy that relegated it to irrelevance. Since the disagreement on the People's Front was – overtly, at least – the reason for Mellor's dismissal, it could not be logically justifiable for Michael to move into Mellor's editorial chair.

Beyond the political problem, there was a straightforward question of right conduct, or decency or integrity. Mellor, whatever his idiosyncrasies or faults, was Michael's friend. Mellor had been treated badly.

Had he resigned after a quarrel with Cripps, it might have been debatable whether Michael should also resign in solidarity; but he had not resigned – he had been brutally kicked out. For Michael to benefit from this dismissal was, he decided, morally impossible.

It was a decision that Michael could easily have evaded. Mellor himself made no demands on loyalty and advised Michael to accept the job. Brailsford, who was the soul of integrity, wrote to dissuade Michael from resignation:

> As to Mellor, I should agree that if you and he had been standing together against the proprietors on a matter of policy or principle, you would in honour have to go with him. But that I gather wasn't the fact . . . Why capitulate in advance? I assume that you would enjoy full editorial discretion . . . One may be too subjective – that's in the Liberal–Nonconformist tradition – and forget that to run a good paper matters more than to perform prodigies of conscience.[45]

In a subsequent letter, Brailsford wrote sadly: 'The Socialist Left is allowing itself to be driven from all its strategical positions by the Communist Party. With great subtlety it drove the Socialist League to suicide and now it is capturing *The Tribune*.'

However, Michael wrote to Cripps without delay declining his offer. In a letter which has not survived, he evidently took his stand on apprehensions that Gollancz was moving into the driving-seat. Cripps replied on 25 July:

> I got your long letter this morning and I am most grateful to you for giving me your reasons at length. I appreciate what a difficult position you have been put in but it is one of those unavoidable happenings that do occur in life and for which no one can be blamed! I disagree with your decision as you know but I am very glad indeed that it has not been influenced directly by William . . .
>
> Certain facts must be made clear and two of them seem important. *First*, it was not Gollancz who alone imposed the condition as to change of Editor. It came from all three of the selectors, nor was it based on or because of any policy of The Tribune in the past or future. I think you may give me credit for the fact that I don't propose to pay many thousands a year to run a paper which is not in harmony – broadly – with my views.
>
> *Second*, Gollancz and the LBC will not control the policy of the Tribune in the future. I may be foolish politically in William's

view . . . but I am not to be completely ignored as chairman of the Board and broadly the paper will carry out my policy . . . You may be quite assured that I shall not continue putting my money and energies into running a paper for a policy I don't believe in . . .

I only elaborate these points, Mike dear, to try and show you that I am not such a completely negligible political factor in the Tribune as you would seem from your letter to think . . .

I admire your sense of loyalty to William and, as you say, the Tribune won't come to an end because you leave us, but it does make me sad to think that I shan't have the joy of working with you in the future as I had hoped since we first met at Oxford some years ago. You must make your own choice and you must satisfy your conscience which is certainly the most important thing in this life. If you are straight with yourself you can hold up your head and fight through any difficulties that may come . . . I am most anxious, not to persuade you to do anything, but that you should come to your decision upon a real basis and not upon an imaginary one which seems to be the position at the moment . . .

> God bless you,
> Stafford

With these Polonius-style counsels, Stafford Cripps and Michael Foot parted company for a considerable time. Cripps and Gollancz had given little or no thought to the question of who should be the new editor in the event of Michael's refusal – it was clearly undesirable to choose an obvious Communist – so Michael agreed to be acting editor until an appointment was made.

On 16 September, with Cripps still in Jamaica, the words 'The Left Book Club and *The Tribune* – a Statement' appeared in large type on the front page. Readers were informed of Gollancz's membership of the board, the two Club pages, and the expectation of producing a twenty-four-page paper. They also learned that 'William Mellor has ceased to be editor and managing director of the company.' 'We believe', the announcement concluded, 'that readers of *Tribune* will warmly welcome this development.'

The new editor was H. J. Hartshorn, a name known to very few people. He assured readers that *Tribune* was known for 'its fearlessness of attack, its sincerity of opinion, its devotion to the cause of the Labour movement' and that 'these characteristics will be continued and developed'. Alec Bernstein, who was shortly to join the staff, was aware that Hartshorn was a 'closed member' of the CP.

It was far from being the end – merely an interruption – of Michael's association with *Tribune*. But it was the end of a chapter in his life; a new one was about to open.

— Chapter 3 —

THE FINEST HOUR

I

Pressing on after his triumph in Austria, Hitler fixed his avaricious eyes on Czechoslovakia. Ostensibly, he wanted only to liberate the frontier districts inhabited by ethnic Germans. Chamberlain accepted this claim, explaining to a group of journalists invited to meet him at Lady Astor's house: 'Hitler wants all the Germans he can lay his hands on, but positively no foreigners.'[1] Daladier, the French Prime Minister, was more perceptive and told Chamberlain that 'he was convinced in his heart that Germany was aiming at something far greater'.[2]

As the crisis developed, Chamberlain saw the solution in saving peace by granting Hitler's demands. A German diplomat reported that he had been told by Sir Horace Wilson, an influential adviser to Chamberlain:

> Britain and Germany were in fact the two countries in which the greatest order reigned and which were the best governed . . . It would be the height of folly if these two leading white races were to exterminate each other in war. Bolshevism would be the only gainer . . . A constructive solution of the Czech problem by peaceful means would pave the way for Germany to exercise large-scale policy in the South-east.[3]

In the aftermath of the crisis, Keynes wrote succinctly: 'The actual course of events has been dictated by the fact that the objectives of Herr Hitler and Mr Chamberlain were not different, but the same.'[4] The obstacle was that the Czechs were prepared to fight rather than surrender their defensive positions on the frontier. Moreover, France had a treaty commitment to come to the aid of Czechoslovakia, and Russia in turn had a commitment to France. Stalin informed Edvard Beneš, the Czech President, that 'the Soviet Union was ready to give military aid to Czechoslovakia even if France did not do so'.[5] The Nazi General Jodl confided anxiously to his diary: 'Most certainly the Western Powers will interfere and we are not yet equal to them.'[6]

Chamberlain flew to see Hitler at Berchtesgaden on 15 September, and they reached agreement on a handover of territory. The Czech government, under British pressure, agreed to submit, but mass demonstrations in Prague led to the formation of a new government which was defiant. A second meeting between Hitler and Chamberlain achieved nothing, and Europe prepared for war. Trenches were dug in the London parks; gas masks were distributed. Many on the left were torn between their horror of war and their hatred of the appeasement policy. Gollancz wrote in his *Tribune* pages: 'A European war would be so terrible that people of imagination hardly dare to think of it . . . We must strive to preserve peace on any conditions except intolerable conditions.'

On 28 September, while Chamberlain was speaking in the House of Commons, he was handed a telegram from Hitler inviting him, along with Daladier and Mussolini, to another meeting the next day in Munich. The great majority of MPs on both sides of the House burst into cheers of encouragement and relief. Attlee, for the Opposition, said: 'We agree to adjourn now, and hope that when the House reassembles the war clouds may have lifted.' The meeting resulted in a firm agreement on the transfer of territory. Czech representatives were excluded and merely told afterwards that they must accept the decision; the Russians had not been invited.

In the week of Munich, Michael was on holiday. Hartshorn had taken over at *Tribune*, so Michael and Barbara crossed to Dieppe and stayed at a small, cheap hotel at Veules-les-Roses, a few miles along the coast. The kindly *patron* gave them rooms with a connecting door. One night, Michael had a violent attack of asthma, and the sound of his wheezing alarmed Barbara so much that she rushed to be with him; we can only wonder how the *patron* interpreted the noise. Otherwise, she never stopped talking, arguing, lecturing and delivering tirades against Hitler, Chamberlain and sometimes Stafford Cripps. Far from getting a rest, Michael found that a holiday with Barbara was more exhausting than work. They returned to London on the day when Chamberlain, back from Munich, told a cheering crowd: 'It is peace for our time.' Michael's comment to Barbara was: 'I hope that goes for us.'

Cripps, too, arrived home at this eventful moment. The next issue of *Tribune* carried a front-page article which began with perhaps the most tactless sentence ever to appear in a left-wing paper: 'On Monday last I returned from ten weeks' holiday in Jamaica.' It did not occur to Cripps to tell the readers that he had gone for health reasons. He continued, however, with a forthright denunciation of Munich: 'A gallant democratic nation has been sacrificed . . . The power and prestige of Fascism has been vastly increased.'

The effect of Munich on British public opinion is a matter on which it is hard to make a definite judgement. Certainly, Chamberlain was cheered by those who gathered in Downing Street to greet his return and by cinema audiences who watched the newsreels. But the impression of a nation-wide outburst of rejoicing was somewhat exaggerated, and has been further exaggerated in retrospect. John Strachey wrote in *Tribune*: 'Chamberlain has secured for a moment the support of those simple-minded, unreflective, uneducated people whom it is so easy and so cruel to deceive.'[7] Other people, who saw Munich as a shame and a disaster, were more likely to sit sadly at home than to come out on protest demonstrations which were now futile. Aneurin Bevan, also writing in *Tribune* of 7 October, judged: 'Gone completely is the relief and elation of last Wednesday. The silly hysteria of last week has given place to grim foreboding.'

In the autumn months, the verdict of the polling booths did not show that Chamberlain had scored a political triumph. Six by-elections produced an average swing of 5.7 per cent against the Tories. Two seats that had been Tory in 1935 changed hands; Labour won Dartford, and Bridgwater was won by the *News Chronicle* journalist Vernon Bartlett, standing as an Independent Progressive with local Labour and Liberal support – a success for the People's Front policy and in particular for the Left Book Club groups in the constituency. Even so, it was hard to be confident that the political landscape could be changed before the next general election – or, as it turned out, the next war.

2

While most of the British press supported Chamberlain's policy throughout the crisis, no newspaper was more emphatic than the *Daily Express*. With considerable intuitive skill, its leading article on 17 September (the Monday after the Berchtesgaden meeting) put into words a mood shared by many of its readers: '*No more war*. We do not wish to be disturbed with the thought of it at breakfast in the morning. We want to sit down to our midday meal in the contemplation of plenty. And when night comes we desire to sleep well and soundly.'

Two days later, the *Express* used for the first time the 'strap-line' on the front page which it has never lived down: 'The *Daily Express* declares that Britain will not be involved in a European war this year or next year either.' The leader insisted: 'No more war! And no more war-talk!' On 22 September the *Express* had this to say: 'We must detach ourselves from the quarrels of Europe, which are not of our making and which should not be of our seeking . . . For the resolution which Mr Chamberlain has shown in turning aside from the ways of war, we are thankful.' And on 25 September: 'Do we want to fight for the boundaries of Czecho-slovakia? . . . How can it be? . . . Participation by us in a European war, fought in defence of foreign frontiers, is not and cannot be good business for the British people.'

Naturally, the news of the Munich agreement found the *Express* ecstatic. Above the word 'PEACE' in outsize type, the famous prediction appeared again on the front page. The leader read:

> Be glad in your hearts. Give thanks to your God . . . A war which would have been the most criminal, the most futile, the most destructive that ever insulted the purposes of the Almighty and the intelligence of man has been averted . . . Through the black days, this newspaper clung to the belief that peace would prevail, that common-sense would triumph . . . Now is the moment when our persistent faith is justified.

The proprietor of the *Daily Express*, the *Sunday Express* and the *Evening Standard* was Max Aitken, Lord Beaverbrook. He was much more than the proprietor, a word which in some cases implies passive ownership; he was an extremely active, vigilant, autocratic super-editor. Fifty-nine years old at this time, he was a Canadian who had never lost either his rasping accent or his attachment to his home town, Fredericton, New Brunswick. Brilliant at financial manipulation, he was already a rich man when he arrived in England before the First World War. He was a Conservative MP for a few years, but found his true métier as a press lord. By the 1930s – thanks to Beaverbrook's personal flair, but also to his choice of Arthur Christiansen to edit the *Express* and Frank Owen to edit the *Standard* – his papers were highly successful and profitable.

At his two mansions, Stornoway House in the West End of London and Cherkley Court near Leatherhead, Beaverbrook liked to gather round his dinner-table men and women whose talk interested him. They were often distinguished, sometimes powerful – although men who were out of power, such as Winston Churchill, got a good share of the invitations – and, as a condition of their presence, always ready with strong opinions frankly voiced. One frequent guest was Aneurin Bevan.

Beaverbrook had no objection to enjoying the eloquence of this left-wing socialist and sworn enemy of capitalism, nor did Nye have any objection to enjoying the good food and wine and exchanging knock for knock with Tory guests. It could be said, indeed, that he was the token lefty of the dinner-parties. Few others of his persuasion were asked; Beaverbrook detested both Stafford Cripps and Harold Laski.

It was Nye who, when he heard of Michael's resignation from *Tribune*, recommended him for a job with Beaverbrook. According to one account, his words on the phone were: 'I've got a young bloody knight-errant here. They sacked his boss, so he resigned. Have a look at him.'[8] Michael has related that Beaverbrook invited him to Cherkley Court for a weekend and ordered him to summarise the Sunday papers. Relying on his excellent memory, Michael did it without notes and was able to repeat the performance when the host told the other guests: 'Mr Foot will now tell you what most of you no doubt have been too damned lazy to read for yourselves.'[9] By the time lunch was served, Michael was on the payroll as an *Evening Standard* feature-writer.

It was a good job – paying, to start with, nine pounds a week, exactly double Michael's salary on *Tribune* – but it was always more than a job. The relationship between the ageing tycoon and the 'young knight-errant' was as warm and affectionate as between a father and an adopted son: all the more so because Beaverbrook's actual son, Max the younger, inherited neither his strong character, his executive ability nor his passionate interest in politics. Michael kept the job only for five years, but the relationship endured, with interruptions, until Beaverbrook's death in 1964. At various times during that long period, Michael received unsolicited gifts of money, lived rent-free in a cottage on the Cherkley estate and spent holidays at Beaverbrook's villa in the south of France. Since Michael was a rising star of the left, his acceptance of this benevolent patronage was viewed by some with raised eyebrows. Bevan, who had involved Michael in this situation, was himself more cautious. When offered the loan of the cottage, he replied: 'It would be politically indiscreet.'[10]

For people who took the austere view that the function of a newspaper was to provide information, Beaverbrook was a demonic figure. He made no secret of the fact that he ran his papers to make propaganda for his chosen causes, and thus incurred the reproach that Baldwin expressed in a famous phrase: 'power without responsibility, the prerogative of the harlot throughout the ages'. Beaverbrook and Lord Rothermere, owner of the *Daily Mail*, were notoriously guilty of twisting the news, suppressing inconvenient facts (even in reports from their own correspondents), pursuing personal vendettas, and perpetrating all the morally despicable tricks of the trade. A widespread feeling was summed up in a rhyme current in the 1930s:

> Great Britain's stream of crystal truth
> Can never flow both pure and clear
> Till we have dammed the Beaver brook
> And drained the Rother mere.

It was common knowledge, too, that Beaverbrook's management of his papers was dictatorial. His employees, including the editors, were plagued by memoranda, phone calls – they learned to dread the imperious rasping voice – or telegrams from Beaverbrook's residences overseas, instructing them to change this, highlight that or kill the other.

For the left, what mattered about Beaverbrook was that the policies he promoted were consistently reactionary. The cause he had most at heart was protection through tariffs – always designated in his papers, with an Orwellian inversion, as 'Empire free trade'. (The Empire, of course, meant the white Dominions.) In foreign policy, his theme was an anachronistic revival of the 'splendid isolation' of bygone days. The *Express* papers derided the League of Nations and urged that Britain should cease to be a member. They opposed the doctrine of collective security. In Spain, they supported the rebels (always called 'Nationalists') against the Republicans (always called 'Reds'). It was natural, therefore, that in 1938 they were in the vanguard of appeasement.

In the light of this record, the month of Munich was not exactly the best time for Michael to start work on the *Evening Standard*, but he did not hesitate over his decision and in later years he wrote of it without a shadow of regret. Indeed, a convincing case for it can easily be made out. He was a journalist by profession and he needed a job. He had resigned from *Tribune* on a point of honour, and there was a limit to the amount of knight-errantry that he could indulge in without acquiring a reputation for inflexible priggishness (the worst sort of reputation to have in Fleet Street). True, he was going to work for the capitalist press. But if he did not fit in at the *New Statesman* or *Tribune*, and if his disagreements with the Communists ruled out the *Daily Worker*, the capitalist press was virtually all that remained. Finally, it would have been extremely difficult to reject the door-opening which he owed to a comrade whom he admired and trusted as much as Nye Bevan.

It was also important that he was to work on the *Standard*, not the *Express*, and that the editor of the *Standard* was Frank Owen. Owen was a delightful and hugely entertaining person whom Michael at once found most congenial – 'we became bosom companions, night and day'. He was, in Michael's view, 'a superlative journalist and editor, being capable of enlisting an incomparable allegiance from those who worked for him'.[11] And he was, without any question, a man of the left. Eight years older than Michael (another elder brother), he had been a Liberal MP in 1929–31. While he never became a socialist or joined the Labour Party, he was vehemently anti-Tory. He was hoping that, in the course of time and with the aid of fast-moving events, Beaverbrook could be shifted from his support for appeasement, and in this enterprise Michael could well be a useful fellow-campaigner.

When all this is said, there is no doubt that Michael's move to the *Evening Standard* can be explained by one simple fact: he was captivated by the personality of Beaverbrook. Writing long afterwards, in 1980, he put his feelings on record: 'I loved him, not merely as a friend but as a second father, even though throughout I had . . . the most excellent of fathers of my own.'[12] In that long and nostalgic essay, Michael made a defence of Beaverbrook designed to rebut all the charges levelled against him by the left.

His first substantial point was that Beaverbrook listened to what was said to him:

> He *listened*. He took in everything said to him, everything overheard . . . Nothing but candour could survive his sensitive powers of cross-examination and recollection. Yet on this same level of personal exchange there was no cant, no personal pretension, no side, no snobbery, not the smallest tincture of it. I soon discovered I could say anything to him.[13]

No doubt this was true, and no doubt it makes a laudable contrast with the habits of other press lords and other rich men in general. It must nevertheless be borne in mind that the great argument of the time was about appeasement, and that its fallacies were pointed out at the Cherkley dinner-table not only by the very authoritative Sir Robert Vansittart (recently demoted from being head of the Foreign Office to the decorative post of Diplomatic Adviser) but also by Churchill, the dissident Tory MPs Robert Boothby and Brendan Bracken, H. G. Wells, Aneurin Bevan, Frank Owen and Michael Foot. Yet Beaverbrook persisted in his faith in appeasement not only until the outbreak of war in 1939 demonstrated its futility, but even for some months thereafter. One must question, therefore, whether Beaverbrook 'listened' in the sense of considering what was said or whether he was merely enjoying a spectator sport.

Beaverbrook has also been praised for the tolerance he extended to employees whose opinions differed from his own. Michael, from 1938, was a feature-writer with liberty to choose his topics and deal with them as he wished. However, there were limits to this tolerance. Winston Churchill's contract to write a fortnightly article was terminated in 1938 on the grounds that 'your views on foreign affairs . . . are entirely opposed to those held by us'. The brilliant cartoonist David Low was invited to lunch with Lord Halifax and urged to tone down his derisive portrayals of Hitler and Mussolini. Frank Owen in June 1938 received a proprietorial note which read: 'Frank, be careful of your attacks on Ribbentrop. If you get making attacks on Ribbentrop, you are going to disturb the great efforts that are now being made for an accommodation with Germany . . . We have got to give over criticism of those foreign powers for the time being.'[14]

Michael's least convincing claim was that 'Beaverbrook's radicalism was deep and abiding.' It is true that, as an outsider from Canada, he was never in sympathy with the traditional Establishment. He was informal in his manners, unprejudiced in choosing his associates (his mistress when Michael first went to Cherkley was a Jewish refugee) and certainly no snob. Some of the phrases used by Michael – 'emotional radicalism' and 'instinctive radicalism' – can be justified. But none of this can reasonably be taken to imply a consistent radical philosophy, nor a radical line of policy on any significant issue. While at the dinner-table he showed his dislike of the tedious and pompous nonentities who sat in Chamberlain's Cabinet, he applauded what that Cabinet was doing. Bevan hit the nail on the head when, in a letter to Beaverbrook, he expressed his admiration for 'those qualities of heart and mind which, unfortunately, do not appear to inspire your public policy'. In 1946 a paragraph in Tribune commented derisively on the 'legend' that Beaverbrook was 'a radical within the Tory Party', adding that in reality he was 'merely a fellow passenger divagating frequently to the far Right'.[15] Presumably this (unsigned) paragraph was not written by Michael, but it expressed accurately enough the general view on the left.

Yet in the narrative of Michael's life this critique fades into irrelevance when juxtaposed with the simple and sincere confession: 'I loved him.' Michael was happy in his relationship with Beaverbrook, happy when he took his seat at one of the fascinating Cherkley dinners, and happiest of all at his desk in the Evening Standard office.

One other event brought him cheer in the dismal year of 1938. On 10 December, by a unanimous vote, he was adopted as prospective Labour candidate for Devonport. The seat was not thought to be winnable; Hore-Belisha was a very adept politician, well ensconced for the last sixteen years, always ready with the jovial smile and the accurately remembered name, recognised whenever he walked down a street. Indeed, there can be little doubt that he would have won an election in 1939 or 1940. But Michael too was on his home ground, and at the least it was a better prospect than Monmouth.

3

In January 1939, Stafford Cripps made a last desperate attempt to revive the Unity Campaign. He submitted a paper arguing for the People's Front policy – it became known as the Cripps Memorandum – to the National Executive Committee of the Labour Party. It was rejected by 17 votes to 3 – Cripps himself, Pritt and Ellen Wilkinson (Laski was away). The party leaders were angered by this reappearance of a policy which they thought they had buried in 1937, and especially by Cripps' warning that if the memorandum were rejected he would circulate it 'with the object of gaining support within the movement'. It was indeed sent without delay to all Labour MPs, prospective candidates, constituency parties and trade unions. The response was encouraging; 134 local parties sent in resolutions backing Cripps, while exactly the same number took a stand in support of the Executive. The NEC moved swiftly to avert the threat of a party split, always a Labour nightmare. Cripps was ordered to withdraw his memorandum, refused, and on 25 January was expelled from the party.

His following was beginning to melt. Only Wilkinson voted against the expulsion, and she soon had second thoughts and resigned from the board of *Tribune*. Pritt, as he put it in his memoirs, 'decided that I ought to obey Party discipline and not follow Cripps into exile'.[16] (Ironically, he was expelled a year later for supporting Stalin's war on Finland.) But Bevan, addressing a crowded and excited meeting on the evening of the expulsion, announced his solidarity with Cripps: 'They can expel me. His crime is my crime.' He was duly expelled, along with George Strauss, Sir Charles Trevelyan and two others. The Unity Campaign did not survive these hammer-blows.

The audience at that meeting on 25 January knew that time was running out for the Spanish Republic too. The International Brigade volunteers had been withdrawn from Spain to save them from the perils of a Franco victory, and some spoke at the meeting. The next day, Franco's troops entered Barcelona. Thousands of Republican soldiers

crossed the French frontier, handing in their weapons and going into
internment. The Republic's Foreign Minister, Alvarez del Vayo, stood
by the roadside:

> It was heart-breaking to watch that procession of men who had been
> defeated merely because the means of defending the country and the
> cause which they loved so passionately had been withheld from
> them . . . men who had defied death a hundred times, men who had
> known the excitement of the advance . . . men who still saw before
> them the faces of comrades who had fallen without losing the hope of
> victory.[17]

By the end of March, Madrid ceased its resistance and the war was
over. Perhaps as many as 300,000 Spaniards with a Republican record
were hunted down, court-martialled and shot in ensuing years.

The left of Europe was in mourning, not only for Spain but for
Czechoslovakia too. On 15 March, German troops marched into Prague
to set up the 'Protectorate of Bohemia and Moravia'. To Chamberlain's
dismay, the pretence that Hitler wanted to rule only over Germans was
exploded. His reaction, in a speech two days later, was to ask: 'Is this the
last attack upon a small state or is it to be followed by others? Is this, in
fact, a step in the direction of an attempt to dominate the world by force?'

Obviously, it was. Hitler's next demand was for possession of Danzig
(now Gdansk), which had the status of a 'free city' under the Versailles
settlement. Danzig had a German population and the municipal council
was already Nazi, but it was clearly, like the Sudetenland, a pretext;
Hitler's aim was to reduce Poland to the same helpless condition as
Czechoslovakia. Hastily, Chamberlain issued a guarantee of protection
to Poland and also to Romania, which was thought (inaccurately, as a
matter of fact) to be under imminent threat. But these were indeed 'far-
away countries' and in the event of attack Britain would be able to do
nothing whatever to help them.

Very reluctantly, some of Chamberlain's colleagues began to come
round to the idea, which had been urged by the left since Hitler's
aggressive designs became plain, of an alliance between Britain, France
and the Soviet Union. A firm proposal was made on 18 April by the
Soviet Foreign Minister, Maxim Litvinov. Chamberlain's reply was:
'The time for a military alliance is not yet ripe.' On 3 May Litvinov (who
was Jewish and had an English wife) was dismissed, to be replaced by
Stalin's most senior comrade, Vyacheslav Molotov. It was a sign,
unheeded by Chamberlain, that Stalin was considering an alternative

course of action if he could not get the alliance with Britain, namely a deal with Germany.

Under pressure and without conviction, Chamberlain opened negotiations with the Russians. The stumbling-block, in addition to the intense distrust on both sides, was the attitude of Poland's bitterly anti-Russian leaders. They refused to give their approval to any plans which involved aid from Russia to check a German attack, partly because they had an unrealistic faith in their own army. They would simply send their cavalry into battle against the German tanks; and when the assault came they did, heroically and suicidally, exactly that.

The course of negotiations after Litvinov's proposal has been carefully chronicled by A. J. P. Taylor:

The British took three weeks before designing an answer on 9 May; the Soviet delay was then five days. The British then took thirteen days; the Soviet again took five. Once more the British took thirteen days; the Soviet government answered within twenty-four hours. Thereafter the pace quickened. The British tried again in five days' time; the Soviet answer came within twenty-four hours. The British next needed five days; the Soviet two. Five more days for the British; one day for the Russians. Eight days on the British side; Soviet answer on the same day. British delay of six days; Soviet answer the same day.[18]

Since discussions at the diplomatic level were getting nowhere, it was felt that a military mission might do better. Travelling by sea (the possibility of flying via Scandinavia was ignored) it reached Moscow in August. The crucial session was on 14 August, when the Soviet Marshal Voroshilov asked bluntly whether his forces would be allowed to enter Poland 'in order to make contact with the enemy'. There was no clear answer. The talks were adjourned. The Admiral and his team were still in Moscow when Hitler's Foreign Minister, Joachim von Ribbentrop, arrived there (by air, of course) to sign a non-aggression pact with the Soviet Union. Hitler's hands were now freed for an invasion of Poland.

Chamberlain and Halifax were worried, but not hopeless. They still thought it possible to arrange a deal with Hitler on Munich lines. Contacts were maintained, notably through the very appeasement-minded Foreign Office minister R. A. Butler and a rather mysterious Swedish businessman, Birger Dahlerus. On 29 August a friend of Halifax noted in her diary: 'Edward thinks if we can keep Hitler talking for two more days the corner will be turned.'[19]

But this hope was vain. On 1 September the annexation of Danzig was announced, targets in Poland were bombed, and German troops crossed the frontier at numerous points from East Prussia to Silesia.

Even now, Britain and France hesitated to declare war. On 2 September, after the fighting had been going on for thirty-six hours, Chamberlain told the House of Commons that he was hoping to get the invaders to withdraw and then 'the way would be open to discussion on the matters at issue'. Patriotic Tories writhed. When Arthur Greenwood rose from the Opposition front bench (Attlee was ill), Leopold Amery shouted the appeal: 'Speak for England!' – a phrase that acquired longevity. The reluctant, anti-climactic declaration of war came the next day.

The sad tale of the annihilation of Poland is soon told. On 6 September, German troops captured Cracow and the Polish government left Warsaw, which was directly threatened. On the western front, French units made a local advance and withdrew to their positions in the Maginot Line. By 15 September the Polish army was no more than a scattering of disintegrating fragments and the government was taking refuge in Romania. On 17 September Soviet forces, acting in accordance with a secret clause of the non-aggression pact, occupied the eastern half of the country. A brave Polish commander, on his own initiative, organised a defence of Warsaw which began to evoke memories of the defence of Madrid, but it was all over by 27 September. The word *Blitzkrieg* – lightning war– had shown its significance for the first time.

4

Michael Foot, with his friends of the British left, experienced mixed feelings in the early weeks of war. There was a certain sense of relief now that the years of anxious waiting were at an end; at least the battle-lines were drawn and the enemy officially designated. There was shame and anger at the failure to strike a single blow while Poland went down into the shadows. There was some bewilderment at the continuing normality of life. The buses and trains were running, the newspapers appeared, the often predicted bombing of London did not happen, and the only signs of war were the blackout and mild rationing. It was the beginning of what came to be called the 'phoney war', which lasted for seven months.

Indeed, it was by no means certain that the war would be kept going at all. With Poland lost and the Soviet Union more friendly to Germany than to the West, it was tempting to accept the regrettable realities.

Hitler, it was understood, was preparing to offer peace proposals. The attitude of Stafford Cripps was: 'It would in my view be the height of unjustifiable folly to turn down his proposals without putting forward in clear and precise terms our own objective.'[20] Cripps then departed on a lengthy world tour, and on his return was appointed British ambassador in Moscow. Never again was he known as a left-wing socialist and a rebel. He did not apply for readmission to the Labour Party, but Bevan and Strauss were quietly readmitted.

The Communist Party, on Stalin's orders, performed a dramatic *volte face* and declared its opposition to the 'imperialist war'. In a tense meeting of its Central Committee, Pollitt refused to follow the new line, saying: 'I don't envy the comrades who can so lightly in the space of a week, and sometimes in the space of a day, go from one political conviction to another.'[21] He warned presciently: 'The Soviet Union will yet find itself in a position where it will need . . . the friendship of the international working-class.' He was removed from the leadership and, in accordance with party discipline, apologised for his error. In private, however, he maintained his belief that the error was that of the docile majority. Pollitt was fond of beer and congenial company, especially the company of journalists. In this frustrating period, he shared many a pint with Michael Foot and Frank Owen, who warmly sympathised with him.

The People's Front was now only a memory. Gollancz put a stop to Communist influence in the Left Book Club and laid down in its journal, *Left News*, that it was 'clearly the duty of all members in their various ways to do all in their power to win the war and defeat Fascism'. Hartshorn was removed from the editorship of *Tribune* and replaced by Raymond Postgate, who had impeccable socialist credentials as a son-in-law of Lansbury and a brother-in-law of Cole (but is best remembered today as the founder of the *Good Food Guide*). But *Tribune* had lost its causes – aid to Spain, the fight against appeasement, the Unity Campaign – and circulation fell badly.

Beaverbrook, displeased by the outbreak of war despite his assurances to *Express* readers, was – as Michael put it later – 'sulking in his appeaser's tent'. He extended his approval to Joseph Kennedy, the US ambassador (and father of the future President) who thought that the war was futile and Britain could not possibly win. An instruction to editors read: 'Mr Kennedy is not to be criticised in the columns of our papers . . . he is to receive favourable comment.' The *Express* paid due heed to the proprietor's wishes, but the *Standard* – perhaps because of Beaverbrook's kindly feelings towards Frank Owen and Michael Foot – was able to take its own line. A leader written by Michael on 6 October in reaction to a speech by Hitler, offering peace over the corpse of Poland, was headed by the one word 'NO!' and continued:

> It is Hitler's hope to consolidate his flimsy gains and, more important still, grapple with the problems in the East, which he himself has raised by the pact with Russia . . . Never again will he be able to indulge in the one-sided contest which the bully always chooses. The power of democracy in Britain and France, aided by those who love freedom the world over, has taken the decision from his hands. They have decided to finish with Hitler.

Another leader next day concluded: 'He hoped to make us cowards by his cunning. He has failed and he is finished.' And on 10 November the *Standard* described Hitler as 'locked in his room' and warned: 'The only way he can escape is if someone comes along and unlocks the door for him. And the only people who can do that for him are those who would like to see peace on Hitler's terms.'

These shafts were not aimed at Hitler so much as at Beaverbrook. After a while, Frank Owen mobilised the editors of the three papers in the *Express* group to confront the boss and urge him to change his line. But the change, when it came, was not brought about by persuasion so much as by the cataclysmic events of May 1940.

At this time, Michael did not generally write the leaders. He was acting as Owen's chief assistant, working on the Diary – then, as now, the most-read page of the *Standard* – and writing signed feature articles. These, for the most part, were historical; there was, for example, a series on the life of Kemal Atatürk, the dictator who had striven to make Turkey a modern nation. The story was dramatic and dramatically presented, but it was also a safe subject since Beaverbrook had little interest in Turkey, and Kemal Atatürk had died in 1936. Having written a number of articles of this kind, Michael decided to work them up to extended length, add some new subjects, and thus produce a book which gave an outline of recent history. The fact that Europe was again at war provided him with a title: *Armistice 1918–1939*. It was accepted by George Harrap and published in April 1940 – the first book written entirely by Michael Foot.

As a book, *Armistice* was presented as the work of an independent writer, not a Beaverbrook journalist, and clearly the work of a man of the left. One chapter was a eulogy of Rosa Luxemburg, then and later a heroine for Micheal. The chapter on the Spanish Civil War contained a passionate tribute, already quoted, to the International Brigade. Hitler was assailed; appeasement was denounced. There was certainly no trace of Beaverbrookian attitudes in the comment on Britain's declaration of war:

> A people so long deluded by the prospect of immunity for themselves discovered at last that Nazi-ism challenged the frontiers of elementary freedom . . . They were ready to expiate by the only means they could the twenty years of pride and pusillanimity which their rulers had displayed . . . If tragedy is not to recur, guilt must be apportioned to those who nurtured Hitler in the first decade and magnified him in the second.

Read as history, *Armistice* is narrative writing with a strong emphasis on personalities and bears distinct traces of its journalistic origin. There is little analysis of the influence of ideas, nor of social and economic forces. Yet we are often presented with a judgement that stays in the mind for its validity as well as for its effective phrasing. This, on the statesmen who steered Britain on the path to 1939: 'Because they only respected force, they smote Germany when she was civilised but weak, and grovelled before her when she became barbarian but strong.' Or this on Stalin:

> Stalin was determined to seize his Gibraltars and his Singapores. Because he was a lesser man than Lenin, he did not understand that they would be dearly bought if they involved the forfeit of some great part of the allegiance which the Soviet Union had gained in other countries. He was ready to employ lies and deceit in pursuit of his aims. Again because he was a lesser man than Lenin, he did not recall that the Soviet Union's strength in all her diplomatic dealings resided in her open diplomacy and her unmasking of deceit.

The principal interest of *Armistice* is in the development of Michael's style. The phrase 'crimes and follies', a favourite that across the years became a hallmark, appears for the first time. Especially, Michael was mastering the art of shaping sentences that were forceful without being crudely violent, witty without being strained or ornate. On Poincaré: 'Only the most final retribution would satisfy his stunted intelligence.' On Mussolini: 'It was his sensitive nose as much as his violent jaw which was to make him the dictator of Italy.' On Baldwin: 'He was left standing in lonely eminence like a hillock in the Fen country.'

It must have been fun to write. But more serious – more desperate – needs were soon to arise.

5

For millions of people, and most surprisingly and abruptly for Lord Beaverbrook, the world was transformed on 10 May 1940, the Saturday of the Whitsun holiday weekend. On that day, Winston Churchill took over as Prime Minister from the humiliated Neville Chamberlain. On that day, German armies surged forward into Holland, Belgium, Luxembourg and France. On that day, too, the first bombs fell on Kent, the bank holiday was cancelled, and scores of weddings were postponed. The *Evening Standard*'s leader concluded: 'As illusion ends, a glittering superb confidence possesses our people.' The end of illusion was a fact; the confidence was a matter of faith.

The overture to the drama had begun on 8 April, when the Germans attacked two neutral nations, Denmark and Norway, and seized their capitals in an unexpected lightning stroke. Denmark attempted no resistance. British troops landed at small fishing ports along the Norwegian coast, tried to fight their way into Trondheim, and failed. No one had reckoned with the devastating effectiveness of German dive-bombers operating from nearby airfields. By 2 May the troops had withdrawn from Norway except for one town in the Arctic north, which was pointlessly held until the end of the month. With the retreat came stories of muddle, indecision and lack of co-ordination between Army and Navy. The government faced an inquest in the form of a two-day debate, opening in the House of Commons on 7 May and known in political history as the 'Norway debate'.

On the eve of the debate, Beaverbrook wrote a signed article in the *Express* minimising the military failure and assuring readers that there was no cause for alarm: British cities would not be bombed, nor would the Germans attack the Maginot Line. But Michael Foot, in the *Standard*, made a ruthless analysis of the mistakes that had led to defeat. The towns chosen as British bases, he wrote, were 'naked, inviting, splintered targets for the Nazi blitzkrieg'. His conclusion was: 'Britain in Norway chose to defy the Nazi air power without preparing the means for combating that air power. That was the root cause of our expulsion from southern Norway. By this blunder we presented Hitler with his victory.'

The headline was: 'REMEMBER THIS WHEN THE PREMIER SPEAKS TOMORROW'. Evidently, many MPs did. The debate opened with Michael in the press gallery. He is probably the only person still alive who heard Leopold Amery hurl his damning quotation from Cromwell – 'Depart, I say, and let us have done with you!' – and Lloyd George demand that Chamberlain should 'give an example of sacrifice' by surrendering the seals of office. When the House divided, forty-one Tories voted with the Opposition and sixty abstained. Chamberlain resigned and Churchill became the Prime Minister of a coalition government, with Attlee and Greenwood in his small inner Cabinet and Bevin as Minister of Labour. Beaverbrook became Minister of Aircraft Production, with the crucial task of providing the Royal Air Force with the planes that would be desperately needed in coming battles and in the protection of British cities. As Michael wrote later: 'He had to relinquish the detailed day-to-day supervision over his property which was his normal custom, but telepathic communication was fully maintained.'[22]

From this day, the *Evening Standard* of Frank Owen and Michael Foot entered upon its glory. The connection with Beaverbrook, telepathic or otherwise, was no longer a hampering control, for he had erased all thoughts of appeasement from his flexible memory and was fully committed to the Churchillian pledges of resistance and victory. As the news became worse and inspiration more necessary, Londoners turned hungrily to the leaders in the *Standard*. It was more than a newspaper; it was, as Michael claimed , 'the flaming herald of the embattled city'.[23]

At this distance, it is impossible to say precisely which leaders were written by Michael, which by Frank Owen, and which – the most likely – were drafted by one man and revised or added to by the other. They do, however, bear the marks of Michael's knowledge of history and his immersion in literature. On 10 May, the *Standard* declared that Britain needed not merely a new government but a Committee of Public Safety – the all-powerful executive that governed the France of the Revolution. On 15 May, when the Nazis triumphed in Holland, it recorded: 'A nation which fought the tyranny of the Spanish Hapsburgs for forty years and the exorbitant power of Louis XIV for half a century has been struck down by this modern Moloch in five days.' On 19 May, it reckoned the menace of Hitler as worse than those of Philip of Spain, Louis XIV, Napoleon or the Kaiser.

It should also be recorded with awe that within a couple of months *Standard* leaders quoted Leonidas of Sparta, Pericles, Cato, the Bible (several times), Shakespeare (also several times), Milton, Cromwell, Gibbon, Pitt, Benjamin Franklin, Saint-Just, Walt Whitman, Mazzini and Joseph Conrad. Never in the field of journalism can so much learning have been dispensed by so few to so many.

Four main themes can be traced through the 1940 files of the *Standard*. The first is the determination to resist the enemy and contemplate no alternative. On 10 May: 'Without flinching we will give our answer to the abomination which Nazism has let loose on innocent peoples. For today we understand what would be the meaning of defeat at the hands of such an enemy . . . Either we awaken every energy in our being or this soil of England will be drenched by blood and unending tears.' The insistent point was that compromise with Hitler implied not merely disadvantageous peace terms, but subjection to a force understood by men who had been anti-fascists through the 1930s. On 19 May: 'All the foul work that was done in the back alleys of Berlin, all the horror that has transformed Prague and Warsaw into cities of slaves, all the same devilish instruments of hatred and murder are prepared for us.'

It may be thought that, with Churchill at the helm, there was no need to stress that Britain would go on fighting. But Chamberlain and Halifax were two members of the inner Cabinet of five, and in an argument on 28 May they both maintained that, in Chamberlain's words, nothing would be lost 'if we were ready to consider decent terms if such were offered to us'. According to a biography of Halifax, the argument was conducted 'in a tough, heated and gladiatorial atmosphere, principally between Halifax and Churchill'.[24]

The soldier in France and the Spitfire pilot on the Kent airfield knew nothing of such discussions. But – whether through talk in the Fleet Street pubs or through telepathic communication – Michael knew, and whatever he did not know he could guess. Thus the *Standard* was consciously extending support to Churchill in a battle that he had to wage behind the scenes.

On 14 June, the Germans entered Paris. Three days later, Marshal Pétain sued for an armistice. The *Standard* printed Low's famous cartoon of a British soldier defiant on a rock amid stormy seas, with the caption: 'Very well, alone!' The leader on 30 May had quoted, from Joseph Conrad's *Typhoon*, Captain MacWhirr's advice – words that came recurrently to Michael's mind throughout his life: 'Keep her facing it. They may say what they like, but the heaviest seas run with the wind. Facing it – always facing it – that's the way to get through.' The conclusion drawn from the Captain's advice was: 'How many lives would have been saved if we had studied that maxim in the past nine months!' For the *Standard*'s second theme was that determination to win the war implied a stern judgement on those who had brought Britain to this mortal danger. On 22 May: 'Our delinquency in preparation has condemned thousands to their death and decreed a longer war.' On 31 May: 'Not in the previous few weeks but in preceding months and years, prodigious miscalculations were made by the military commands and governments in Britain and France.'

A third theme was that the war could only be fought and won by the people: a people proud of their democracy and drawing on democratic resources. 'We shall win this war because we are still a democracy, because the eye of criticism is still kept imperious over those who might sink into slothful, unoriginal methods, because at last democracy is shaking itself free from the vamping embrace of bureaucracy' (7 June). In protest against bumbling regulations churned out by civil servants, against excessive censorship of the press and against a Ministry of Information which (said the *Standard*) saw itself as a Ministry of Exhortation, the leader of 18 July declared:

Some in authority seem to suppose that they are dealing with a collection of schoolchildren who need to be exhorted, cajoled, rapped over the knuckles and sent on errands which their all-wise masters need not even explain. This is insult and imbecility . . . These people know little of the spirit of England at this supreme hour and nothing of the spirit of democracy if they do not yet realise that this throb of freedom in the breasts of common men provides exactly the impetus from which we must draw the strength for victory.

Nor did the *Standard* forget to demand: 'The same axe that cuts the rights of labour must be wielded against the rights of property. Without that, the call to sacrifice is a shabby hypocrisy . . . [The government must] break vested interests, banish privilege and exorcise luxury' (20 May). Hence another theme: the war was being waged for the freedom of all the peoples of Europe, even including those of Germany and Italy (on 10 June, Italy declared war). 'It is not a war of nations at all. It is a mammoth civil war. Goethe and Garibaldi, a great German and a great Italian, are on our side. We should recognise no boundaries except those which exist in the human mind' (15 June). The leader of 18 June, the day when General de Gaulle called on Frenchmen to reject Pétain's surrender, proclaimed: 'Every rebel is our ally. We do not only fight a war. We must conduct a Continental revolution.'

Logically, and yet courageously in the anxious atmosphere of 1940, the *Standard* protested against the wholesale internment of aliens, now recognised as one of the most shameful episodes of the war. Of the thousands of men and women of German nationality who were rounded up and taken from their homes, many were refugees, Jewish or anti-Nazi or both. Michael reacted with a signed article headed: 'WHY NOT LOCK UP GENERAL DE GAULLE?' 'There are German de Gaulles and Italian de Gaulles,' he pointed out; they had been fighting Nazism and Fascism for years. He concluded:

Let us tell the world that our aim is a European revolution, that all
who can give proof of their solid anti-Nazi and anti-Fascist resolution
will be welcomed by us as treasured allies . . . This is our finest hour,
says Mr Churchill . . . Let us not smudge this fine faith by meanness
or sheer stupidity. Let us act on the proud boast with wide vision and
humanity.

6

A letter from Michael to his mother, though undated, clearly belongs to
this 1940 summer. She had written to complain that Isaac Foot (often
called Pop in the family) could not get work connected with the war,
and to express her anger with the business-as-usual atmosphere that still
prevailed. Michael answered:

I am sorry I did not reply to your letter before. I wanted to do so
immediately as it did me a lot of good. A little of that anger mobilised
and we would get the revolution which is necessary to enable us to
win this war. Simon and his friends of course should have been put in
gaol along with the other Quislings . . .

Pop should certainly be given a job. But of course our civil service
is still so riddled with public school spirit, snobbery, old school
tieism and all the other stupidities which have brought us into this
plight that it is difficult to get through them. It will be done,
however. At last the British people are awakening to the fact that they
have been ruled by traitors. When they are fully awakened their
wrath will be terrific. Only a truly Socialist England can win this
war.

In his own anger, Michael was convinced that the politicians of the
Chamberlain era, such as Sir John Simon, were not merely blunderers
but virtually Quislings. That word was just beginning to gain currency;
Vidkun Quisling was a Norwegian Nazi who had been installed as the
head of a puppet government. If it was too much to expect that Simon
and his like would actually be thrown into prison, they should at least
suffer public denunciation. They were guilty men. As usual, a historical
memory came to Michael's mind. In 1793, when things were going
badly for revolutionary France, an angry crowd burst into the hall
where the Convention was meeting. Their leader declared: 'The people
haven't come here to be given a lot of phrases. They demand a dozen
guilty men.'

It was on the night of 31 May, when ships were still busy rescuing exhausted soldiers from the Dunkirk beaches under the fire of Nazi dive-bombers, that Michael and two friends talked over these matters on the roof of the *Standard* building. One was Frank Owen; the other was Peter Howard, a feature-writer with the *Express* group. They had all heard disturbing stories brought back from France – the same stories that had been brought back from Norway. One soldier's words summed it up: 'We never had a fair chance.' The three journalists agreed that the root causes of this terrible situation must be explored and made public. But, despite the *Standard*'s boldness, the subject was probably too hot to handle in newspaper articles. Press censorship was in force and the censors did not always confine themselves to vetoing military information; there might well be irritating arguments, causing delay. Besides, with news pouring in all the time, it would be difficult to set aside enough space. The solution was to write a book.

Decisions were quickly made. The book must be written at top speed – why not that very weekend? Each of the three men would take a share of the work. (Howard did not have the same radical convictions as the others and was accustomed to writing pretty much whatever was desired, but he was highly competent and fluent.) Michael supplied the title: *Guilty Men*. It would be presented as though from the pen of a single writer and a pseudonym would be used, because Beaverbrook disapproved of his employees doing anything (even in their own time) except writing for his papers. Michael also supplied the pseudonym: Cato. A figure in early Roman history, Cato was known for his stern, incorruptible character. From his official position, but also because of this character, he was remembered as Cato the Censor – not, as Michael remarked, Cato the Censored. The obvious publisher, thanks to his interest in politics and anti-appeasement record, was Victor Gollancz. He was a celebrated hustler and could be counted on to get the book out faster than anyone else. The clash over the control of *Tribune* was now history, so Michael felt confident in approaching him.

Fifty years later, Michael recalled:

I well remember the London of that July: how the sun blazed more brilliantly each day, how the green parks, the whole city indeed, had never looked lovelier. All of us who lived through those times had a special instruction in the meaning of patriotism. The sense of the community in which we had been born and bred suffused all else, made everything else subordinate or trivial. And one essential element in the exhilaration was the knowledge that the shameful Chamberlain era had at last been brought to an end, and that English people could look into each others' eyes with recovered pride and courage.[25]

The book, 40,000 words long, was written in four days. Over the weekend the writers worked at a house in Suffolk belonging to Peter Howard; on the two succeeding days they worked through the afternoon and at night after producing the *Evening Standard*. The sections – there were twenty-four short chapters – were shared out. When a chapter was completed, the man who had written it read it aloud to the two others. Any changes, additions or deletions were agreed on after brief discussion and written in on the spot. On 5 June, Gollancz read through the typescript and, matching the pace of the authors, accepted it and gave orders for the speediest possible publication. Exactly a month later, on 5 July, *Guilty Men* went on sale. Gollancz was paying an advance of £100 which, if not enormous, was quite large for the period.

The opening pages, written by Michael, described the grim ordeal of Dunkirk. 'The assault became hotter. More planes obscured the sky. The machine gunners came lower and more daring . . .' The reasons why the desperate evacuation had become inevitable were hammered home: 'Relays of Nazi bombers against non-existent British fighters . . . Unconquerable spirit against overpowering weapons . . . Flesh against steel. The flesh of heroes, but none the less, flesh. It is the story of an Army doomed *before* they took the field.' With this in mind, the reader was led through a history of the blunders, the miscalculations, the negligence and the complacency of which British governments had been guilty from 1929 right up to the Norway campaign.

Fifteen men (including MacDonald, who was dead, and Baldwin, who was retired) were listed on the first page as 'The Cast' and bore the brunt of the indictment. The thrusts were more deadly because they were treated fairly: Chamberlain 'was not and is not either vain or foolish'. Their record, however, was mercilessly dissected. Three men received praise: Churchill and Lloyd George for being right about Munich, and Beaverbrook because he had sponsored a 'Grow more food' campaign. Nothing was said about his support for appeasement or his rejoicing over Munich. Michael remarked after Beaverbrook's death: 'He himself emerged from the whole story better than he might have dreamed and deserved; how much more deadly the indictment could have been!'[26]

The book concentrated on British inadequacies in preparing for war rather than on the conduct of foreign policy. Despite pressure from Churchill, in the 1930s the government had neither a Minister of Defence to co-ordinate the three Services nor a Minister of Supply to look after armaments production. Baldwin eventually appointed a Minister for the Co-ordination of Defence – not a Minister of Defence with real authority – in the person of Sir Thomas Inskip, a lawyer who admitted that he had no qualifications for the job. 'Cato' quoted the comment by 'a famous statesman' (actually Churchill): 'There has been no similar appointment since the Roman Emperor Caligula made his horse a Consul.' Chamberlain refused to appoint a Minister of Supply until April 1939, when he chose the utterly undistinguished Leslie Burgin. 'Cato' wrote: 'A sound like the escape of gas from a barrage balloon arose from the packed benches of Westminster and as it penetrated to the outer lobby it took on the profounder note of a human moan. It was the sound of MPs gasping when Mr Chamberlain announced the name of the new Minister.'

Here and there, readers were treated to inside stories. For example, Chamberlain was asked at a dinner-party why Hitler should be trusted after his record of broken promises, and replied solemnly: 'Ah, but this time he promised *me*.' Complacent pronouncements were quoted to damning effect. On 3 August 1939 Inskip said: 'War today is not only not inevitable but is unlikely. The Government have good reason for saying that.' On 3 April 1940, five days before Hitler struck at Norway, Chamberlain confidently declared: 'Hitler has missed the bus.'

The names of the principal 'guilty men' recurred again and again. In April 1940, Lloyd George had asked in the Commons whether anyone could say he was satisfied with the 'speed and efficiency' of preparations for battle. As 'Cato' described the scene: 'He waited seconds for an answer. None came. The House was utterly silent. Among those who kept their seats were Mr Chamberlain, Sir John Simon and Sir Samuel Hoare.' Another passage cited the unemployment figures, contrasting them with the mobilisation of labour in Germany: 'There were still nearly a million unemployed persons in Britain in May 1940 – the month of Hitler's invasion of Belgium. They might have been blind and crippled for all the contribution they were allowed to make to the national war effort. They were not idlers . . . Not only did these citizens, disfranchised in the most heartbreaking way, contribute nothing to the nation. They were compelled to continue as a burden on it.'

Such eminently quotable passages – one imagines them being read aloud in Army barrack-rooms or factory canteens – can be found in almost every chapter. If we read *Guilty Men* in cool retrospect half a century later, we can find faults in it. Being (as we now know) the work of three writers, it sometimes moves rather jerkily from mood to mood, from anger to irony. It was probably too long for a topical pamphlet and too short for a book dealing thoroughly with its subject. A chapter analysing the campaign in France (doubtless written by Frank Owen, who was an authority on military matters) went into excessive detail. Sometimes, too, the tone may strike us as too rhetorical and strident. But we must allow for the speed of composition and for the emotional tension of the days in which it was written – and read.

The central accusation against Chamberlain and his colleagues – that of sending men into battle without 'a fair chance' – has been abundantly borne out now that confidential papers are available to historians. General Montgomery, who commanded a division in France in 1939–40, wrote later: 'It must be said to our shame that we sent our army into that most modern war with weapons and equipment which were quite inadequate.'[27] The men who had the responsibility either could not or would not envisage what Hitler had in store for them by 1940. Captain Liddell Hart, military correspondent of *The Times*, was told in 1936 by the Chief of the Air Staff: 'There cannot be war until 1942.' When he was asked why not, the reply was: 'Because our rearmament programme will not be completed until then.'[28] Liddell Hart did his best to publicise the real state of affairs, but the Chamberlainite editor of *The Times* refused to print his articles.

The supreme guilty man was undoubtedly Chamberlain. In 1934, when he was Chancellor of the Exchequer, he recorded proudly: 'I have practically taken charge now of the defence requirements of the country.'[29] Under Chamberlain and his successor as Chancellor, Simon, the Treasury set a fixed sum for defence spending and the three Services had to compete within that limit. As the historian Keith Middlemas writes: 'Strategic policy, in its widest sense, was subject to dictation from the Treasury boardroom in a way which had not occurred before 1937.'[30] When the allocation was made, priority went to the Air Force. The Army's plan to build up a field force was scrapped, with the full agreement of Hore-Belisha as Minister of War. Chamberlain told the Cabinet that 'he did not believe that we could or ought . . . to enter a continental war with the intention of fighting on the same lines as in the last war'. Thus no preparation was made to send a British expeditionary force to France. When the war began, it had to be sent nevertheless to maintain good relations with the French – but it was inadequately equipped, and therefore doomed.

Given the priority selected, the aircraft should have been sufficient. When Chamberlain spoke in 1938 of 'this enormous power, this almost terrifying power which Britain is building up', he was referring to air power. The government stood officially by the pledge given by Baldwin in 1934 that the RAF would never be inferior to 'whatever air force may be raised in Germany in the future'. But in 1938 Germany was producing 440 aircraft in a month and Britain only 250. The result was the desperate strain placed on the RAF in 1940. A soldier back from Dunkirk said: 'Fifty or more Jerries would come and drop bombs. Just as we were recovering another fifty or so came in relays. We longed to see our own fighters.' The words were duly quoted in *Guilty Men*.

When the book was being written, the war situation was not utterly desperate in spite of the nightmare of Dunkirk. The French were still fighting and fresh British troops were being landed at Cherbourg (they eventually came home without firing a shot). But while *Guilty Men* was being printed, Gollancz had to reckon with the French surrender and with rumours that Chamberlain, Halifax and others were urging consideration of German peace terms. He showed a proof copy to a few of his friends to get their views. The day after an anxious discussion, he wrote to Ralph Pinker, agent for the authors:

> Inevitably the effect of the book is highly depressing as a record of total unpreparedness . . . This being so (I am quoting what was put to me last night) won't the effect of the book be to make people say: 'If we were in that ghastly state of unpreparedness even a month ago, isn't it obvious that we must be in almost as bad a condition now? Might it not be wiser, therefore, to try and seek a way out?' The book, far from fulfilling our intention of strengthening the war effort, might, in the new situation brought about by the capitulation of France, actually strengthen capitulationist elements . . . I know that all this is exceedingly upsetting; but we dare not let any considerations whatever about lost work on the one hand or lost money on the other lead us into making what, in the rapidly changing situation, may now be a false move.

Some of those consulted by Gollancz advised that the book should not be published, 'but should be held in reserve and then published at what seemed to be the right moment, if that arrived'. Others recommended inserting either a foreword or an addendum to strike a note of optimism. Tom Wintringham favoured an addendum 'as he thought the Dunkirk note was the wrong one to end on' and he drafted a paragraph which assured the reader: 'This is a book about the *past* . . . The whole atmosphere has changed; an immensely rapid drive is taking place which every day gives us a surer hope of victory.' Gollancz sent the draft to Pinker, asked him to discuss the problem with the authors, and told him to destroy the letter – 'one doesn't want the part about fears of capitulation to lie about and be read by all sorts of people who may quickly spread a defeatist atmosphere'. However, a copy stayed in the Gollancz office files in accordance with normal practice.

The book appeared with the addendum, revised and enlarged by 'Cato' and printed, on Gollancz's suggestion, in block capitals. In part, it read:

> *At long last, the aeroplanes, the tanks, the arms of every kind are piling up. But in the meantime the French state has fallen under the control of Hitler. An immense new strain has been placed on Britain, and an immense new effort is now required of her.*
>
> *In Mr Churchill as premier, and in his three service supply chiefs, Ernest Bevin, Herbert Morrison[31] and Lord Beaverbrook (to name only four) we have an assurance that all that is within the range of human achievement will be done to make this island 'a fortress'.*
>
> *But one final and absolute guarantee is still imperatively demanded by a people determined to resist and conquer: namely, that the men who are now repairing the breaches in our walls should not carry along with them those who let the walls fall into ruin . . . Let the guilty men retire.*

From the day of publication the book was in tremendous demand, but people who wanted to buy it ran into difficulties. The two big bookshop chains, W. H. Smith's and Wyman's, refused to stock it, and the central distributors serving all bookshops, Simpkin Marshall, refused to handle it. Bookshop owners who were ready to sell it had to go direct to Gollancz for copies. Geoffrey Pyke, a friend of Gollancz, wrote to ask why it had been published at the relatively high price of two shillings and sixpence, five times the price of a Penguin at that time. Gollancz explained that he had foreseen a boycott by Smith's, so a large printing was impossible and he had fixed the lowest feasible price. A commander in the Navy, who had been a Left Book Club member in peacetime, wrote to Smith's to inquire the reason for the boycott and sent Gollancz a copy of the reply: 'We are not at liberty to disclose all the considerations that led to our decision, but you can rest assured that not the least of these was the desire to preserve national unity and see the present conflict marching on to a triumphant victory for the Allied cause.'

A shop assistant at Stoneham's bookshop wrote in with the information that she had been instructed to say that *Guilty Men* was unobtainable. 'A clear example of capitalist suppression of the truth,' she commented. A customer at Wyman's in Watford was told that the book had been banned by the government. Jon Kimche, who ran the ILP bookshop in London, was visited by the police, who warned him that he was selling a banned book.

Of course, stories of suppression stimulated the sales. The three authors (still concealing their identity) sold the book from barrows in Farringdon Road and recruited friends to take a turn. Newspapers carried reports on the queues that formed, and thus added to them. Independent bookshops reordered and reordered again. There was even a sale in Soho, thanks to a misapprehension about the meaning of the title. Gollancz, seeing that he had a runaway success on his hands, abandoned all caution; six impressions were printed in the month of July. In the end, *Guilty Men* sold over 217,000 copies.

Who was 'Cato'? There was much speculation, but the secret was well kept. The three friends amused themselves by laying false trails. Michael reviewed the book in the *Standard*, recommending it but making some criticisms. In his headline, he too asked: 'WHO IS THIS CATO?' Peter Howard wrote the review in the *Express* and referred to 'the mysterious author'. Candidates were suggested: perhaps it was Alfred Duff Cooper, who had resigned from the government over Munich and was now Minister of Information; or perhaps Randolph Churchill, the Prime Minister's son. Even Beaverbrook mischievously hinted that he was the author and once told Halifax that he was living on his royalties from *Guilty Men*. He had every reason to read it with pleasure; it attacked men whom he had always disliked, such as Baldwin and Simon, and it praised him instead of including him in the indictment. But he did not guess, so far as Michael could tell, that it had been written by three of his employees.

Several months later, he circulated an office memo warning all employees of the *Express* group that they were not allowed to write for publication in any form without his permission. Michael and the others took this as a signal that he had found out or at least guessed who 'Cato' was. But he said nothing to them on the subject, and naturally they said nothing to him.

7

The summer of 1940 marked a breathless pause in the war. One question was earnestly asked: would Hitler, with his formidable and victorious armies which had suffered few casualties in France, launch an invasion of Britain? The country was defended only by the exhausted men who had struggled home from Dunkirk, new conscripts who were still untrained, and the part-timers who joined the Home Guard, known to a later generation as Dad's Army. Britain seemed to have no assets but her spirit.

That spirit inspired Isaac Foot when, recalling the legend of Drake's drum, he made a broadcast on 16 August:

> The Drum was heard to beat when we had the miracle of the deliverance of Dunkirk. Drake's heart went out to those men who manned the little ships that saved the British Army. Those ships were very like his own . . .
>
> Hitler, threatening invasion, reckons his forces and tries to calculate ours. He will have to meet a good deal that is altogether beyond his reckoning and beyond his understanding . . . Destitute himself of any moral greatness or spiritual resource, this mean cruel man . . . seeks to crush the land of William Tyndale and John Hampden and Oliver Cromwell and John Milton – the Britain of Marlborough (another famous Devonshire man) and John Wesley, of Chatham and Burke and Tom Paine and Charles James Fox . . . For the defence of this land of dear souls, this dear, dear land, all these will rally at the sound of Drake's drum, with Wordsworth and Burns and Shelley and Scott and Cobbett and David Livingstone and Florence Nightingale and Edith Cavell and countless others.

Eva Foot was concerned for the sons whom she had brought up to strive for a life of achievement. Two of them, John and Christopher, were going into the Army. Dingle had a government post in the Ministry of Economic Warfare; Mac had been recalled from Palestine to work at the Colonial Office. Michael had volunteered for military service at the beginning of the war and been rejected because of his asthma. The application cleared his conscience and assured him that he was a true anti-fascist, but he did not feel that he would have been in his element as a soldier and knew that he was fulfilling himself through his work on the *Evening Standard*. Eva's mind was not entirely set at rest. From what she knew of the world of journalism, it was strongly marked by heavy drinking. She may have heard rumours about Michael's best friend, Frank Owen, of whom Michael wrote later: 'He could drink all night everything and anything set before him' (and whose career was indeed truncated by alcoholism). Michael had to send his mother a reassuring letter:

> You must believe me that the picture you draw of a prodigal son dependent on whisky is totally false. I have no craving for drink and can refrain from it for weeks and often do. I am quite aware of its dangers. I have seen the effects on some persons and am fully resolved that I should not follow the same path . . .

My chief, absorbing passion is to discover fresh things about the world. I long for every hour that I can spend with books that thrill me. Those hours are cut monstrously short by many occupations, but if you think that I would throw any of them needlessly away on a stupid habit you are wrong. I do drink occasionally but the chief reason is that it is the easiest way of talking to people I want to meet.

That was presumably an effective answer, but Eva had another worry. She and Isaac had seen four of their children married before the war began: Dingle to Dorothy Elliston, Mac to Sylvia Tod, John to Anne Bailey Farr and Jennifer to James Highet, a man in the oil business whom she had met in Haifa while visiting Mac in Palestine. Apart from Christopher, who was still young, only Sally and Michael were still single. Michael was now twenty-seven, and there was no sign of an engagement or even a serious attachment. In Eva's view he was in need of a woman, if only to keep his clothes in repair and feed him. Perhaps he was not drinking too much, but was he eating? His way of life was distinctly unsettled. He was living with Frank Owen in bachelor rooms in Lincoln's Inn; then, when Frank married, with the Owens in Banstead; then with Mac and Sylvia in a flat in Battersea; then with Dingle and Dorothy in another flat, this time in Westminster. Sometimes, when he was a guest of Beaverbrook's, he stayed at Cherkley. Sometimes, caught by an air raid, he slept at the *Standard* office (luckily, he wasn't there when it was hit by a bomb). Seen from the comfort of Pencrebar, this wandering could not be good.

The truth was, though Eva did not know it, that Michael was hopelessly in love with Lili Ernst. 'Hopelessly' was the *mot juste*; she was Beaverbrook's resident mistress. Once again, as with Barbara Betts, Michael had allowed himself to be attracted by a woman who was firmly attached to an older man. Lili came originally from Yugoslavia and had been a ballet dancer in Vienna. She was, in Michael's description, 'beautiful and delicate and fragile'. Beaverbrook met her when she was touring in Cannes and helped her to escape from Vienna after the Nazis marched in. Michael set eyes on her on his first weekend in Cherkley in 1938. As he remembered:

I was tongue-tied by the general company and atmosphere but also by the apparition who sat at my side, an exquisitely beautiful girl who had some trouble with her English, but who seemed otherwise at ease and whom I took to be a Hungarian countess or something of that sort. Next day also she was floating through the house; her disturbing presence seemed to be everywhere.[32]

He knew from the start that he had no chance with Lili. She was five years older, and regarded him as a brilliant boy, still immature (except intellectually) by comparison with men she had known. In any case, she was deeply grateful to Beaverbrook and faithful to him, and hoped that he would marry her (he had been a widower since 1927). This he had no intention of doing, for as Michael wrote later: 'he could be hard and demanding as well as sensitive, possessive and wayward by turns, as he was in politics'.[33] Eventually she relinquished her hopes, broke with Beaverbrook in 1946, married another man and lived into a happy old age as Lady Hornby. But in the 1940s she became, as Barbara had been, Michael's friend and comrade. They went around London together and even stayed together in a cottage on the Cherkley estate. Lili recalled later that she told him: 'You must find a young woman and go and get married' – to which he replied: 'As long as you don't mind, I want to stay with you.'[34]

However, if Eva suspected that a young single man in the big city was likely to be involved in light-hearted, transitory sexual relationships, she was right. Amid the uncertainties of wartime, the normal formalities and constraints – and loyalties – tended to melt away. Young men were in short supply, disappearing suddenly to remote Army camps. Young women were filling jobs, notably in journalism, that had hitherto been male preserves. As a leader-writer on the paper that practically everyone in London read, Michael was inevitably a focus of interest. Besides, he had discarded, along with his religious heritage, any hold that traditional morality had ever exerted on him. Of the outlook which he adopted as a young man and maintained thereafter, these words are a typical expression:

> Why is it that in so many fields sex is condemned, outlawed, banned, frowned upon, sniggered at; so rarely welcomed as a normal and steady delight? A strong case can be made for the accusation that, thanks to the cruel lies taught about sex, our language is depleted and gangrenous, our arts vapid and cold, our lives furtive and thwarted, compared with what they could be.[35]

According to Frederic Mullally, a young journalist who was then writing for *Picture Post* and joined *Tribune* in 1942, Frank Owen and Michael Foot were 'the romantic models of Fleet Street'. Mullally recalls: 'The girls simply swooned.'[36] This was certainly true of Owen, who was a remarkably handsome man and an extrovert of limitless self-confidence. Michael has paid this tribute to him: 'Women fell for him in droves, at a glance; no one else I ever saw was ever in the same competition.'[37] By comparison, Michael was shy with people he did not yet know and not inclined to make aggressive advances to women, and he was handicapped by his eczema and asthma, which sometimes prevented him from going out for two or three days at a time. But his initial reserve heightened the interest, and women who got to know him were attracted by his charm and humour, fascinated by his flow of talk, and drawn to admiration by his idealistic vision of the new Britain and the new Europe that he saw with eyes turned to the future.

In the early 1940s, he had a succession of affairs or relationships, but none of them had real importance for him, partly because he did not feel ready to settle down, partly because he was absorbed by his work, and partly because he was in love with Lili Ernst. He was particularly attracted by women with a foreign background who were spending the war years in London. In June 1942 his mother wrote anxiously: 'These rumours of ladies of various European nationalities, I presume they are entirely legendary?' They were not; the girlfriend whom Michael recalls most affectionately was Helvi Rintalla, from Finland.

Yet the one human relationship that mattered more to him than any other was still with his 'second father', Beaverbrook. As Minister of Aircraft Production, Beaverbrook was rushing and roaring round the country, demanding from employers and workers the same tireless effort that he himself made, breaking the rules and conventions both of industry and of the Civil Service, and achieving what scarcely any other man could have achieved at this critical time. However, he did not forget that he was a newspaper owner and was delighted with the progress of his protégé, Michael Foot. He noted, especially, that work on the *Standard* was well advanced at an early hour. In a letter in May 1940, he remarked: 'When a man is admired most in the early morning, he is a great fellow,' and enclosed a cheque for Michael 'in recognition of your splendid work in the early mornings'. He advised Michael to invest the money and predicted that he would soon be a capitalist. There is no record of how big the gift was, but it must have been considerable, for Michael replied: 'I now discover that I have become not merely a capitalist but a bloated capitalist. Thank you for your great kindness to me.' A few months later, he benefited by another unsolicited award and wrote to his patron: 'I have today received a note that leaves me breathless. To receive reward in such an exaggerated manner for work which I have so much enjoyed baffles all attempt at thanks.'

Over the ensuing years, a number of similar letters reached Lord Beaverbrook. This, dating from 1943, is a good example: 'I have been wanting ever since Saturday to write and thank you for the princely bonus which you have given me. But I have been wondering what I should say. This is but one example of the unbounded generosity and kindness which you have always bestowed on me in a way that I trust I will never forget.' The gifts were, of course, additional to Michael's salary, which went up repeatedly. In 1943 Kingsley Martin, no doubt regretting that he had not kept Michael on the *New Statesman* in 1936, wrote in extremely courteous – even humble – terms to ask Beaverbrook to allow Michael to write occasionally for the weekly journal. Beaverbrook replied:

> I can well understand your desire to make use of the fine talents of Michael Foot . . . But the proposition you put forward is not one that I could possibly entertain.
>
> If newspapers opened that door, it would swing very wide indeed.
>
> The newspaper pays Foot nearly £4000 a year. If he were to do similar work for another paper, the directors would ask 'Is Beaverbrook losing his punch? Is he going down into the valley where all the newspapermen before him have gone?'
>
> And they may be right.
>
> I am very sorry that this is my answer to you, but it must be so.

At the time, a member of Parliament was paid £600 a year, a county court judge £2000, the Commissioner of the Metropolitan Police £3000, the permanent head of a government department also £3000, and the Lord Chancellor £4000. Only Cabinet ministers, the most senior generals and admirals, and some bishops had the edge on Lord Beaverbrook's star journalist.

Chapter 4

VICTORIES

I

In Michael's eyes, it was the persecution of the Jews of Europe that, more glaringly than anything else, stamped Nazism as an evil and regressive force. When the collaborationist regime in Vichy France adopted the anti-Jewish laws prevailing in Germany, the *Evening Standard* of 29 November 1941 carried a scorching leader:

> One hundred and fifty years ago the men who made the French Revolution placed the rights of Jews on the same basis as the rights of all other citizens. In the sight of the whole world the yellow star was torn from Jewish vestments. It has been nobly said that every Jew, having a memory and a heart, is a son of the France of 1791 . . .
>
> Today thousands of French citizens suffer the fate of Dreyfus . . . Marshal Pétain's sore sense of honour does not seem to be provoked when the other devilish practices of Nazism against Jewry are imported into his own land . . .
>
> Let us look on this pitiful scene, but not despair. Let us commemorate the anniversary and take pride that the great tradition of France is in our keeping. And for all their tribulations the Jews, too, have cause for pride this day. They need ask no more of their fellow citizens than that they should be judged by their enemies. They were the first enemies of Hitler. The Yellow Star is an honourable badge in this world where some would outlaw reason and love and pity from the minds of men.

The *Standard* did not confine itself to rhetoric; it also recruited as contributors three Jews with origins in continental Europe and, under wartime rules, the classification of 'alien'. The least alien was Jon Kimche, who had lived in England since the age of twelve but had been born in Switzerland and still had a Swiss passport. His political allegiance was to the ILP and he managed the ILP bookshop in St Bride Street, off

Fleet Street, which had an eclectic stock of political and historical literature and also of rare books. From the day when Michael bought a first edition of Gibbon and a set of Hazlitt in twenty-two volumes, he and Kimche were friends. But Kimche also had something in common with Frank Owen – an expertise in military strategy. From 1940 onward, some of the *Standard*'s leaders were analyses of the state of the war and the discernible threats or prospects, and these were written by Jon Kimche.

Isaac Deutscher's homeland was Poland. An intellectual prodigy, he had acquired the Talmudic knowledge to become a rabbi at the age of thirteen, but had soon turned from religion to Marxism. Although he was too independent in his thinking to put uncritical faith in any leader, he could be described fairly enough as a follower of Trotsky, of whom he later wrote a magisterial three-volume biography. This commended him to Owen, who liked to declare (without much idea of what he meant by it) that he was a Trotskyite. Arriving in England shortly before the war, Deutscher quickly taught himself English, was able by 1940 to write political commentaries for the *Standard* and went on to achieve the same fluency as another remarkable Pole, Joseph Conrad.

Arthur Koestler, Hungarian by origin, already had a reputation as a writer and journalist when he was invited to contribute to the *Standard*. As *News Chronicle* correspondent in Spain during the civil war, he was captured when Malaga fell and sentenced to death by a Franco court martial. Saved by an international protest campaign, he told the story in *Spanish Testament*, one of the most successful Left Book Club choices. His novel *Darkness at Noon*, published in London in 1940, made a deep impression on Michael Foot – among many others – as an explanation of how the Soviet trials were staged and the confessions secured.

The autumn of 1940 was the season of what soon came to be called the blitz. In London, the sirens sounded and the shelters filled on seventy-five nights out of seventy-six. The bombs brought destruction to homes, workplaces, railways, water mains, gas mains, electricity cables. After six weeks, a quarter of a million Londoners were homeless. They moved in with relatives or friends, were billeted in undamaged large houses in the West End or camped in Epping Forest. It was the densely inhabited East End that was attacked first and suffered most heavily. On 13 September, in the first week of the blitz, the *Standard* wrote:

> This is the story of the East End of London. It is a terrible, tremendous story: a story of anger, hate, love, defiance; a story of whole streets where you can see women's eyes red with tears, but women's hearts overflowing with kindness towards their neighbours . . .

Hitler has struck most heavily at the poor people of this country just as in Germany he struck first against the institutions of the poor. He will have men serve no other god but him. In one country after another we have seen him succeed in his foul designs. He will fail now. The blood which he has spilt in the East End of London means that this people will never abase themselves at his footstool.

Among the cities that met with the worst destruction in the blitz were the three in which Michael had lived: Plymouth, Liverpool and London. Plymouth, strange to say, had been regarded as safe. The naval dockyard made it an obvious target, but it was assumed to be out of range of bombers coming from Germany. This was a false assumption in the first place, and the danger was greatly increased when the Germans occupied France and the bombers had only a short journey across the sea. Even then, women and children were not evacuated from Plymouth, as they had been from London. An official report, unpublished until 1976, admitted: 'Plymouth should have been made an evacuation area on the fall of France. Central government had many months to decide on this course of action, in conjunction with the local authorities. But nothing was done – and the city paid the price.'[1]

It did indeed. Pre-war Plymouth was one of Britain's most congested cities, with narrow streets and close-packed little houses. Repeated attacks through the autumn and winter culminated in a devastating assault on the night of 20 March 1941.

Streets became ovens as the air currents sucked the flames from buildings on either side to make ferocious tunnels of heat. Walls cracked and crumbled, glass began to melt. The post office and the county court were gone, along with a host of familiar businesses and houses. The city hospital, struck in previous raids, suffered again, and fourteen newborn babies died with three nurses . . . When Plymouth woke the next morning, the city had changed almost beyond recall.[2]

Six more heavy raids followed in April. At long last, the authorities decided on an evacuation order, but thousands of people had left the city of their own accord to sleep in barns and haystacks in the countryside. The blitz was reckoned to have halved the population. The death toll was over 2,000.

The worst raid on London was on the night of 10 May, when a record total of 1,436 lives were lost. The Tower, St Paul's Cathedral and Westminster Abbey were all hit and damaged. The chamber of the House of Commons was destroyed and the MPs borrowed that of the House of

Lords until after the war. Fire in the British Museum reached the famous reading-room and consumed a quarter of a million books. On a smaller scale, but just as sadly, Jon Kimche lost his bookshop.

Meanwhile, all the war news was bad. The Germans invaded and subjugated Yugoslavia and Greece as quickly as they had overrun Poland. British troops from Egypt were sent to the aid of the Greeks, but the outcome was another Dunkirk, and even Crete was lost. General Rommel's Afrika Korps advanced across Libya, Cairo was threatened, and Jews in Palestine had cause to tremble. But Hitler's main forces were massing for the most ambitious of his enterprises.

Despite the twists and turns of Soviet policy, Michael had never abandoned hopes that Britain and Russia would end up fighting together against Nazism. On 17 June 1940, the day of the French capitulation, a *Standard* leader headed 'ANOTHER ALLY?' reminded readers who felt that Britain was irrevocably isolated: 'Soviet Russia holds the power at any moment of her choice to shift the balance.' Britain had almost blundered into disastrous hostility at the time of the Finnish war, when 'the true blues, the pale pinks, the ex-reds, the yellows, the dull greys, the chocolates, all these schools argued (or rather caterwauled) for action against Russia'. But the Soviet Union, Michael argued in this article, was simply looking after its own interests: 'Stalin did not tell the Russians after the conclusion of his pact with Hitler that he had brought them peace in their time. He called for more vigilant defence measures . . . May it not be, therefore, that his long-range interest lies in the dismantling of German power before being left single-handed against her?'

Unfortunately, Michael overestimated Stalin's wisdom and vigilance. Up to the last moment in June 1941, he turned a deaf ear to warnings, even from his own spies, that a German attack was in the making. Others, however, could read the signs. On 19 June, the *Standard*'s main headline was: 'HITLER EXPECTED TO MARCH ON RUSSIA'. Readers were told: 'The expectation of an early German offensive against the Soviets is growing steadily.' On 21 June the military correspondent – doubtless Kimche – contributed a detailed estimate of Russian strength. His conclusion was that the Soviet armed forces were a formidable opponent for Hitler.

The following day, 22 June, was a Sunday. Michael was one of a weekend house-party at Cherkley. Starting the day early as usual, he switched on the radio and heard that a full-scale invasion of the Soviet Union had been launched at dawn. He ran downstairs, hunted through Beaverbrook's gramophone cupboard until he found a recording of the 'Internationale', and put it on at maximum volume.

The *Standard*'s leader on 23 June read:

We have another chance now beside that of stubborn defence. Our allies are all those who understand the Nazi menace and have the courage to fight it. Since Nazi ambitions are boundless there is no other logic. A world alliance stretching from Asia to the Americas can throw back the flood that would engulf mankind.

And on 24 June: 'Every day Russia fights is a huge gain for us . . . Soviet Russia must be sustained with all our might . . . Soviet Russia's engagement in the war has planted a fifth column in a half a dozen countries now under Hitler's boot.'

This was in line with Churchill's attitude. In a broadcast on the evening of 22 June, he said: 'The Russian danger is our danger, and the danger of the United States, just as the cause of any Russian fighting for his hearth and home is the cause of free men and free people in every quarter of the globe.' Churchill discussed this speech with Beaverbrook and also with Cripps, who was on leave in England at the time, but there was no question of a snap reaction, since he had known for several days, through intelligence sources, that the attack was coming. His lifelong detestation of Communism was set aside as an irrelevance. He is said to have remarked in private: 'If Hitler invaded hell I would make at least a favourable reference to the devil.'

Beaverbrook, too, quickly became an enthusiast for helping Russia in every way possible. A week after the attack, he was made Minister of Supply, and in September he went to Moscow – with Averell Harriman as Roosevelt's representative – to work out arrangements for sending British and American war material to Russia. Beaverbrook got on very well with Stalin, presumably recognising an autocrat of his own type.

For the left, the entry of the Soviet Union into the war was a tonic. The Communist Party was quick to announce that the character of the war had changed and reverted to claiming a place in the forefront of the battle against fascism. Pollitt was reinstated as leader and was soon making the speeches that he would have liked to make during the past two years. In the war factories, a surge of sympathy for Russia went far beyond ideological motives, although it naturally benefited the CP, whose membership shot up. 'Tanks for Russia week', when all production was earmarked to be sent to the Russian front, saw a big increase in output.

There were some, however, who thought that aid to Russia was far from advisable. The low opinion of the Red Army's capabilities, which had been so influential in 1939, was still prevalent. Military experts, except Kimche, expected that Hitler would chalk up another of his easy victories, and in that case sending tanks to Russia would be tantamount to presenting them to the enemy. Political prejudice influenced the argument. Beaverbrook's successor as Minister of Aircraft Production, Colonel J. T. Moore-Brabazon, said on a private occasion that the best policy would be to let the Germans and the Russians fight each other to mutual exhaustion. His words leaked out and he was forced to resign. But *Tribune* reported in 1942: 'It is no secret that but for vast public pressure and a hell of a row in the Government itself the supplies which we have sent to Russia would have fallen far short of their present volume.'

The Germans did indeed achieve great successes. Entire Soviet armies were encircled and had to surrender, and by November the invaders were in the outskirts of Moscow and Leningrad. But in December – luckily, an exceptionally cold December – the offensive was checked. Moscow was successfully defended. Leningrad too, though it was surrounded and had to endure the agonies of a long siege, never surrendered.

Another event, just as enormous in its consequences, occurred on the other side of the world. On 7 December, Japanese bombers attacked Pearl Harbor, the American naval base in Hawaii. The destruction in the American fleet was devastating, and a few days later the Japanese sank two British battleships off Malaya. One disaster followed another. Within four months, the Japanese conquered Malaya, Singapore and Burma from the British, the Philippines from the Americans, and Indonesia from the Dutch.

The blows were heavy, but the significant fact was that the United States was in the war. The potential strength of the world alliance against the aggressor nations outweighed that of Germany and Japan together. Ultimate victory, no more than a matter of faith in Britain since Dunkirk, was now a realistic objective.

In their talks in the Kremlin, Stalin had impressed on Beaverbrook that the only battlefront in the war was on Russian soil. What was needed was the creation of a 'second front' – an Allied landing on the coast of occupied Europe. This was to be the central controversy of 1942.

2

In January 1942, Stafford Cripps returned from Moscow. His job as ambassador was done and he was given credit for forging friendship between Britain and Russia (in reality the credit belonged to Hitler, and then to Churchill and Beaverbrook). Many people in Britain were uneasy about the contrast between the sacrifices being made by the Soviet Union and the relative safety of life in Britain, where air raids were now rare events. In a speech in Bristol, Cripps identified himself with this feeling: 'There seems to be a lack of urgency in the atmosphere of this country.' He called for more effort, harder work and more austerity. This quintessentially Crippsian word, which became a term of abuse after the war, was counted for virtue in wartime. Cripps was thus in a strong political position. Churchill made him Leader of the House of Commons, with a seat in the War Cabinet.

Coincidentally, a change was made in the editorship of *Tribune* (a paper with which Cripps now had no connection). Bevan, the dominant personality on the editorial board, quarrelled with Postgate. According to Michael, 'the difference was much more one of temperament than of policy'.[3] Michael was able to recommend a man with all the qualities of a good editor: Jon Kimche. Bevan and the board approved of Kimche, but there were two problems. Independent though its attitudes were, *Tribune* was a paper associated with the Labour Party, and Kimche belonged to the ILP. Secondly, Kimche was an alien, and in the wartime atmosphere it was thought necessary that the editor should be British. Nye Bevan therefore took over the editorship himself, although he had neither the time (as an MP) nor the professional knowledge to attend to the details of producing the paper. Kimche moved into the office as the working editor.

Within the government, Beaverbrook was becoming discontented. He was encountering powerful resistance to his demands for aid to Russia. To do an effective job as Minister of Supply, he argued that he should have control over the direction of labour, but he was blocked by Bevin, and Churchill supported Bevin on this issue. The rise of Cripps, too, was unwelcome to Beaverbrook. He resigned from the government and went off for a long stay in America.

On 25 March, Frank Owen received his call-up papers for the Army. In principle, all men under fifty were liable to military service, but at this stage of the war a call-up notice for a man of thirty-seven was exceptional. It has been suggested that Bevin, whose full title was Minister of Labour and National Service, arranged for Owen to be called up in order to annoy Beaverbrook. There may well have been another reason: Owen was due to chair a Trafalgar Square meeting on 28 March urging 'more aid to Russia'.

Owen himself was not at all upset by his move from Fleet Street to a barracks on Salisbury Plain. He was an enthusiast for tank warfare and was happy to find that, sent into the Royal Armoured Corps for training, he would be able to drive a tank and fire its guns in person. Also, he had excellent connections with Army high-ups and was unlikely to remain a mere trooper for long; in fact, two years later he was a lieutenant-colonel. Meanwhile, someone had to take over his job on the *Evening Standard*, and that someone could only be Michael Foot. Michael ranked officially as acting editor and Owen was expected to return after the war, but he never did. He went to South-East Asia Command and, as editor of its morale-building paper *SEAC News*, came under the patronage of Lord Mountbatten, who held a notorious place on the Beaverbrook black-list.

Later, Beaverbrook described Michael as 'a very clever fellow, a most excellent boy', but added: 'He was projected into the editorship of the paper before he was ready for it.'[4] This was said, however, to defend himself from accusations that he had sent Michael constant orders on how to run the *Standard*. Kimche, who was in a good position to observe – there was a constant interchange between the offices of the *Standard* and *Tribune* – recalls that Michael was sometimes exasperated by Beaverbrook's authoritative control, and that he had drawers full of articles which he was not allowed to print. On the whole, however, the relationship between proprietor and editor was harmonious.

Nothing indicates the fluidity of the wartime years better than the story of the debate that raged, behind the scenes and openly, over the second front. Its advocates included: Stalin and the Soviet government, working especially through Molotov as Foreign Minister, Maxim Litvinov (now ambassador in Washington) and Ivan Maisky, the capable and persuasive ambassador in London; the American military establishment, notably the Secretary for War, Henry Stimson, the Chief of Staff, General George C. Marshall, and the potential field commander, General Dwight D. Eisenhower; the British Communist Party, the large section of working-class and trade union opinion which followed its leadership, and the Labour left, of which Aneurin Bevan was the outstanding figure; and last but not least, Lord Beaverbrook and the talented journalists who worked for him.

On the opposing side, one can list: the Chamberlainite Tories, still well represented in the government and the Conservative Party, who were impervious to any sympathy with Soviet Russia; the British military establishment, who on this issue had Churchill as an ally; the chiefs of the Royal Air Force, at this period a formidable lobby, who sought the maximum resources for the bombing of Germany in preference to land warfare; and the Labour members of the War Cabinet, Attlee and Bevin, who went along with Churchill as an expression of their general support for him.

At the level of popular and press campaigning, the leading activists in favour of a second front were Bevan, Harry Pollitt and Michael Foot. In the autumn of 1941, they had been active in a campaign to press for aid to Russia. Meetings were held up and down the country, generally organised by the Russia Today Society (*Russia Today* was a magazine devoted to Soviet achievements). Michael spoke at several such meetings, including one in Glasgow on 28 September. The Scottish Committee of the Labour Party observed it with disapproval and informed George Shepherd, the Labour Party's national agent, who wrote to Michael:

> The responsibility for the meeting does not appear but we gather that members of other political parties, including the Communist Party, participated in the gathering . . . If Communist interest can be served in this way under the impression that the National Executive Committee of the Labour Party will take no notice, the number of such gatherings will grow and the steadiness our Party has displayed during the past two or three years on war issues may be broken.

Michael replied:

> I have been addressing several meetings up and down the country. Some of them have been organised by the Russia Today Society, some of them by ad hoc committees, and one or two of them by local Trades Councils. Who organised the meeting at Glasgow I do not know, and I confess that in all these meetings I have not troubled to inquire. I have spoken on platforms with Conservatives, Liberals, Labour Party members and Communists. The sole purpose of these meetings has been to arouse the maximum enthusiasm for the Anglo-Soviet alliance and to attempt to awaken the country to the tremendous implications of the present decisive phase of the war.
>
> At this fateful moment in our history I should not have thought that such activities required any explanation.

The Labour Party refrained from issuing such reproofs in 1942, although Michael, Nye Bevan and a number of Labour MPs or candidates shared platforms with Communists. The demand for a second front was voiced persistently from March 1942. The Russians had survived the winter, to the surprise of many, had gained some ground in limited counter-offensives and were bringing up fresh troops from their hinterland. A front-page article in *Tribune* of 13 March, under the headline 'THE YEAR OF DECISION IS 1942', argued that, if an attack in the West were to divert thirty to fifty Nazi divisions from the East, 'it is not only possible, it is probable that the German military machine will be smashed this summer'.

Beaverbrook, after restoring his health and spirits in Trinidad and Miami, now reached Washington and was heartened by the mood of the American commanders. General Arnold, the top man in the Army Air Corps, expressed the opinion that the way to win the war was to hit Germany 'where it hurts most, where she is strongest – right across the Channel from England, using the shortest and most direct route to Berlin'. Invited to speak at a dinner in New York, Beaverbrook stayed a night at the White House and showed his speech to Roosevelt, who raised no objections to it. Astonishingly – or astonishingly to the upper-crust diners – Beaverbrook not only made a fervent plea for the second front but also lavished praise on the Soviet regime: 'Communism under Stalin has produced the most valiant fighting army in Europe. Communism under Stalin has provided us with examples of patriotism equal to the finest annals of history. Communism under Stalin has won the applause and admiration of all the Western nations.'[5]

In April, a high-level Anglo-American conference in London resulted in a compromise: a limited operation to seize the Cherbourg peninsula as a base for a break-out in 1943. This decision was not, of course, made public, so the political campaign for the second front went on. Two big demonstrations in Trafalgar Square attracted crowds of up to 50,000. Churchill, though irritated by this agitation, made the best of it and hailed it in a broadcast as a proof of 'the militant, aggressive spirit of the British nation'.

The talk of the town in May 1942 was a series of three articles in *Tribune* devoted to a scathing attack on Churchill. Since the heroic days of Dunkirk, the Prime Minister has never been treated to such derision:

> Churchill, the Modern War Lord, has never yet grasped the clear fact that an army is just as good (or bad) as the social foundations on which it rests. The shrilling bugles go to his head! He hears the deep drums – and he is drunk! He sees the proud fluttering flags – and he could weep! He often does! . . . If Winston Churchill saved Britain in June 1940, Britain also did a bit towards saving Winston Churchill and party.

In the second article, Churchill was reproached for the 'Balkan blunder' of sending troops to Greece in 1941. In the third, on 15 May, he was named as 'the responsible person for refusing the Second Front'. Readers must have wondered how the writer knew that Churchill had in fact refused it. The verdict was: 'The concentration of hero-worship in one individual is always full of sinister consequences for the nation which indulges in it.'

The articles were signed by 'Thomas Rainboro''. It was obvious, and was admitted editorially, that this was a pseudonym. A follow-up article supplied a biography of the original Thomas Rainboro', one of the leading Levellers, or radical democrats, in Cromwell's time. The twentieth-century Rainboro' told the readers that some people were so keen to discover his identity that they were opening his letters. 'These inquirers are hired by Mr Churchill's government.' He added generously: 'I cannot believe that these gentry have failed to discover the identity of Thomas Rainboro'.'

Rainboro' was Frank Owen, and the articles were written in his Army camp on Salisbury Plain. If one knew this, the sources of his military knowledge could be guessed. He was on friendly terms with Britain's leading military expert, Captain Liddell Hart, and with General Martel, commander of the Royal Armoured Corps. As Owen was serving in the RAC, the presumption is that his superior officer was aware of these verbal onslaughts on the Prime Minister.

This time, in contrast to the *Guilty Men* episode, Beaverbrook was in on the secret. After three articles appeared, he decided that the dangers were too serious, or perhaps learned that 'these gentry' had identified Owen. He asked Michael: 'When's the next article due from Frank?' Michael was working for the *Standard*, not for *Tribune*, but it was understood that both were covered by the second-front network. He replied that it was due at any moment. 'You'd better stop it – tonight ,' Beaverbrook ordered. Michael drove at top speed to Andover, searched the pubs, found Frank and took the explosive document from him. Unfortunately, he crashed the car on a hump bridge. It was promptly repaired by Army mechanics, who made no inquiries as to what this civilian was doing in the military zone.

Also in May, Molotov visited London and Washington. A statement was issued in London recording agreement 'on the urgent task of a Second Front in 1942'. The ambiguity was noticeable – did Churchill and Molotov agree that it was a task, or that it would be undertaken? And was the ambiguity designed to fool Molotov, to fool the enemy or to fool the British people and the second-front campaigners? *Tribune* kept up the pressure, writing on 14 June: 'The sombre question remains. When is the final attack on the central citadel of the Fascist powers going to open?' On 17 July:

What are we waiting for? . . . Hitler is allowed to hurl all he has at the Red Armies and apparently he does not even bother to look over his shoulder at what we are doing or preparing to do . . . The government must give the Soviet Union a simple, unambiguous pledge that we are going to land in Europe before autumn.

It was another bad summer. The Germans opened their big offensive in the Ukraine and pressed forward, though against determined resistance, towards the Volga. Rommel advanced from Libya into Egypt. The fortress of Tobruk fell. Churchill persuaded the Americans to give up all thought of a landing in Europe, even the Cherbourg plan. The awkward question was: were the Western Allies to do nothing whatever for another year while the Russians poured out their blood? Churchill and his generals produced an idea: a surprise landing in French North Africa, which was governed by the Vichy regime and not occupied by the Germans.

The operation, carried out in November, was a success, and it coincided with Montgomery's victory at El Alamein, which saved Egypt for good and all. However, the Allies were drawn into a lengthy struggle in the Mediterranean. Though they secured Algeria, the Germans rushed to occupy Tunisia and were not defeated there until May 1943. Then came a landing in Sicily, then landings in Italy, and then a slow advance which took twenty months to get from Naples to Milan. The invasion across the Channel, postponed (so everyone thought) from 1942 to 1943, was delayed until 1944.

Nevertheless, the final months of 1942 saw the turning of the tide in the war. The Russians held Stalingrad and eventually forced the surrender of a German army of 400,000 men. Next year, the offensive was Russian, not German. Hitler's armies, which had spread like a plague from Crete to the North Cape and from the Atlantic to the Volga, began the long retreat that ended in the ruins of Berlin.

3

With victory at least on the horizon, men and women in the factories and the Army camps turned their thoughts towards the shaping of the post-war Britain. Sir William Beveridge, a Liberal academic, had been given the task of preparing a comprehensive scheme of social security. His report was leaked before publication to the *Evening Standard*, which gave it a hearty editorial welcome. This displeased Beaverbrook, for the Beveridge philosophy ran counter to his brand of individualism. After the comradeship of the second-front campaign, it was the first rift between the proprietor of the *Standard* and the young editor. But the report, once published, aroused enormous interest. In full or in a shortened version, it sold 635,000 copies.

The vital question was: would it be implemented by a post-war government? Intelligent Tories, such as R. A. Butler and Harold Macmillan, realised that their party must shed its identification with poverty and inequality. Churchill, in Angus Calder's phrase, 'groped his way to the head of the consensus'[6] and made a broadcast in March 1943 promising to lead Britain into new paths with the co-operation of all men of goodwill. His purpose, clearly enough, was to create the basis for a post-war coalition, and there were signs that Labour leaders such as Attlee and Bevin were not averse to that prospect. Aneurin Bevan's *Tribune* took a very different view. A *Tribune* leader in October 1943 declared: ' The coalition is dead. Let us bury it quickly.'

The aspect of coalition which Bevan rejected outright was the electoral truce. By an agreement dating from 1939, the major parties did not oppose each other in by-elections. The loophole was that it was impossible, so long as democracy existed, to prevent a candidate from some other party, or an independent, from standing. In 1942 a new party was formed with the name of Common Wealth, voicing the radical ideas and the outright rejection of Toryism that made an obvious appeal to Labour supporters. The leading figure was Sir Richard Acland, a Liberal who in pre-war days had joined enthusiastically in People's Front campaigning (his book *Only One Battle* had been published by the Left Book Club). Obedience to the truce became increasingly frustrating for people on the Labour left, and they were irresistibly tempted to vote – or even campaign – for any anti-Tory candidate. In the course of the war the Tories lost eight by-elections, three to Common Wealth and five to independents.

One of the by-election winners was a Beaverbrook journalist and therefore well known to Michael Foot and Frank Owen. Tom Driberg had joined the *Daily Express* in 1928 and wrote a Diary under the name of William Hickey. Just as there was a historical Cato and a historical Thomas Rainboro', there was a historical William Hickey, an entertaining diarist in the eighteenth century. Driberg's 'Hickey' Diary was also highly entertaining, and rich both in gossipy anecdotes and in candid opinions. Unlike most other gossip columnists, including those who inherited the Hickey by-line, Driberg wrote it all himself. This gifted and extraordinary man was also a sincere High Churchman, a member of the Communist Party, and a homosexual who, in the days when homosexual conduct was a criminal offence, took hair-raising risks. In 1935 he was arrested and charged with indecent assault. Beaverbrook not only persuaded all the editors in Fleet Street to print no reports of the case, but also paid for a first-rate defence counsel, who secured an acquittal.

In June 1942 a by-election fell due in the Maldon division of Essex, a part of the country where Tom Driberg owned a beautiful Georgian house (bought with money borrowed from Beaverbrook). He came forward as an independent candidate, sharply criticising Churchill's management of the war. A Driberg leaflet told the voters: 'Our sons and brothers fighting in far lands hang on desperately for munitions that don't turn up, while profiteers haggle with the Government at home.' It was *Guilty Men* talk, and equally effective. A Tory majority of 8,000 was turned into a 6,000 majority for Driberg.

The next notable by-election contest came in February 1943. Bristol Central was a marginal seat with a Tory majority in 1935 of only 1,500, and adjacent to Bristol East, represented by Cripps. Jennie Lee stood as an independent with the support of well-known activists in the local Labour Party and the trade unions. Michael went to Bristol and campaigned for her. Normally he spoke off the cuff at meetings, but on this occasion he spoke from a prepared text, presumably for the benefit of the press. He said:

> There are some people who say that holding elections in wartime is dangerous to national unity . . . This is really a very stupid doctrine . . . Every week in Parliament debates are conducted about the war and about plans for after the war . . .
>
> I am a member of the Labour Party. And there are some persons who say that the unity of the Labour Party is being broken up by the defiance of the truce at by-elections. However it is not the defiance of the truce but the truce itself which is dangerous to the unity of the Labour movement. The people of this country are not prepared to go on voting tamely for Conservative candidates . . . If the leaders of the various parties try to maintain this false and dangerous truce they will find that all kinds of candidates in various shapes and sizes will be trying to break it up. Here in Bristol you are very fortunate in having a candidate who has given her life to the Labour movement and to the fight for social reform in this country. The best service you can do to the Labour movement is to return Jennie Lee at the top of the poll.

At the eve of poll meeting, Michael said:

> The good things of this earth – peace and happiness and communities in which men may live in security and freedom – are not to be won

without a struggle . . . We remember what happened after the last conflict. The armies came home, the men were demobilised, but the peace which they had fought for was stolen from them. It must not be stolen a second time.

You can make a start here in Bristol. Tomorrow is the hour. Get up early. Get out your friends . . . Go to that polling-booth tomorrow in the knowledge that in casting your vote for Jennie Lee you will be striking a blow for the soldiers in Tripoli, for the airmen who saved the life of this nation . . .

Unfortunately, the voters to whom Michael was appealing were not there. The centre of Bristol had been devastated by bombing and only 10,000 votes were cast in the by-election, compared to 30,000 in 1935. The Tory majority was again about 1,500.

In 1943, the Foot family was widely scattered. Isaac went on a three-month tour of the United States, preaching to Methodist congregations. Mac was again in the Middle East, on duty in Amman, which he found as desirable as Outer Mongolia, and missing his wife and children, who were in South Africa. Eva was still worrying about Michael's welfare. She had written to him in November 1942:

Sometimes I wonder if you are as free as you ought to be and if you are not paying too big a price for fame. Professor Joad – with whom we lunched on Monday – was saying some very flattering things about you . . . He expects you to be one of the leaders of the future . . . Sometimes I think of what a power you would be with all your gifts of speech and leadership if you could take a decided Christian line.

In a letter for his thirtieth birthday in July 1943, she wrote:

I don't somehow feel you are in quite the job best suited to you; I hope something better is before you, suited to your special genius and traditional idealism . . . I wish I could look forward to settled happiness for you in other ways. Would that you had a settled home and had not to spend so much time in restaurants and elsewhere.

Michael, for his own part, was beginning to wonder how long he ought to stay in his *Evening Standard* job. Beaverbrook had mended his fences with Churchill and was back in the government, holding the decorative post of Lord Privy Seal with no specific duties to absorb his energies. It was predictable that he would keep a closer eye on his newspapers and their editors; it was possible that he would be devising plans to influence opinion in ways that would keep Churchill in power after the war. Whatever Michael might think about Beaverbrook's 'emotional radicalism', there was no denying that in party allegiance he was a Tory. In the same letter in which Michael thanked Beaverbrook for a 'princely bonus' and praised his 'unbounded generosity', he continued:

> I feel it is only fair that in return for such kindness I should tell you exactly what is going on in my mind. I realise that I can never be a satisfactory editor for one of your papers. I am too much of a propagandist politician and I am sure that my political ideas must appear to you stubborn and irritating, a fact which makes your kindness and tolerance towards me all the more remarkable. It seems to me that your political ideas and mine must become more and more irreconcilable . . . The Evening Standard advocates neither your full views nor mine. In consequence its vitality suffers. I begin to feel more frustrated and from your point of view I am a bad investment. I am a Socialist and my convictions or prejudices become stronger every day.
>
> I do not know what is to be done about all this. But I felt that I could not write to you honestly without pointing out these difficulties which I see in the future.

British and American troops had now landed in Sicily, and the Fascist regime was visibly crumbling. Bevan vehemently criticised the Allied command for failing to move quickly into the industrial north of Italy, where anti-Fascist partisans were ready to rise in revolt. Churchill, however, preferred not to take the risk of what (in a letter to Roosevelt) he called 'chaos, Bolshevization or civil war'. On 25 July, Mussolini was deserted by a majority in the Fascist Grand Council, removed from power and arrested. Marshal Badoglio (the conqueror of Abyssinia in 1936) was appointed by the King to take over and indicated to the Allies that he was ready to make peace.

These events gave Michael an idea. With the prospect of victory, there was much talk of bringing Nazi and Fascist war criminals, including the dictators, to trial. Hitler was still well protected in his Berlin bunker or his war headquarters in East Prussia, but Mussolini was under lock and key in a castle not far from Rome. Presumably, he would be handed over to the Allies as part of the surrender terms. There was room for an imaginative description of the anticipated trial. (Actually, before anything of the kind could happen, Mussolini was rescued in a daring operation by German paratroops, to survive until he met a less legalistic fate in 1945.)

Conveniently, Michael was due for a holiday starting on 4 August. On that day, he wrote to Gollancz:

The idea I have is to write a book called 'The Trial of Mussolini'. It would be an imaginative picture of the first great war criminal's trial . . . The whole purpose of the book, of course, would depend on its Left Wing political significance . . . Mussolini's counsel would defend him by putting in the witness box all the persons who have condoned Mussolini's crimes for the past 20 years . . . They would include Chamberlain, Rothermere, Halifax, etc., etc. They would also include Winston Churchill . . .

It seems to me that this is a good propaganda idea; that it would be a clear way of countering the argument now used against the Left by the Tories who suggest that all parties were guilty . . .

I would supply you with the finished manuscript on August 25 . . . I would not want the book to be done under my own name, but, as you may recall in a previous book, this is no disadvantage – in fact it is a great advantage in the matter of publicity.

As with *Guilty Men*, Gollancz indicated his approval without delay, sending a phone message that he was 'very enthusiastic about the book and agreed to lines suggested. He will publish as soon as possible.' Michael, already at Pencrebar, started writing immediately. He chose the pseudonym 'Cassius'; the implication was that he was mercilessly destroying a self-proclaimed Caesar. (A debunking biography of Mussolini, written before the war, had been entitled *Sawdust Caesar*.) He completed the book and sent off the manuscript on 20 August, telling Gollancz with justifiable pride: 'I think I promised it by August 25 so I am a few days early.' The pace of composition was not quite so breathtaking as that of *Guilty Men*, but this time Michael was the sole author. The book was published in October. Confident of success, Gollancz ordered a print of 100,000. The ultimate sale was 150,000 – less than *Guilty Men*, but still a remarkable success.

When one reads *The Trial of Mussolini* today, one may be inclined to think that its defect as a work of propaganda was excessive subtlety and that the case for Mussolini was put with such persuasiveness that he scarcely ended up as a war criminal at all. For example, the defence counsel is given a cogent reply to the accusation of 'treacherous acts of aggression':

The Prisoner has proved himself one of the most consistent statesmen of modern times. From the attack on Corfu in 1923 until the attack on Albania in 1939 the principle of international conduct upheld and acted upon by the Prisoner appears to have been uniform, unalterable, nay, almost monotonous in character. His conduct might compare favour-

ably for instance with the consistency of a person like Lady Astor, who
was violently anti-German in 1919, violently pro-German in 1938, and
violently anti-German again in 1943.

Sardonically, the defence counsel inquires whether Hoare, Simon and
Halifax are to be brought to trial, or whether the mortal remains of
Chamberlain are 'to be dug up like Cromwell's and hurled into a
common pit. If they are guiltless, I cannot see by what standard the guilt
of the Prisoner is to be established . . . Let a small part of the accumulated
mercy required for these persons be allowed for my client.'

Mussolini, when giving evidence, takes a defiant line which must have
given Michael pleasure in the writing. 'Politics is a naked struggle for
power and the only law between states is the law of the jungle . . . It is the
weak who are guilty and the strong who are righteous.' He adduces the
history of England: 'Do you imagine that she became the first power on
earth by the quality of her laws, the tenderness of her manners and the
sweetness of her poetry? England was made great by force.' He admits
only to the mistake of thinking that Britain was defeated in 1940: 'If I had
held my hand at that fateful moment, what prospects would have opened
for me now! What courtings would have proceeded in Rome! What
tributes would have been paid to my statesmanship! . . . Condemn me,
hang me, shoot me for my failure, but spare me the English hypocrisy of
calling it a crime.'

But if the evidence did not damn Mussolini, it damned and shamed his
British admirers, and of course that was the point of the book. In 1927
Churchill visited Rome and, addressing Mussolini in a public speech,
said: 'If I had been an Italian I am sure that I should have been whole-
heartedly with you from start to finish in your triumphant struggle
against the bestial appetites and passions of Leninism.' Ten years later,
Hore-Belisha paid a similar friendly visit and was presented with a
medallion by Mussolini. In 1940, shortly before Italy entered the war,
Lord Halifax wrote a preface to a pamphlet which explained that Fascism
'threatens neither religious nor economic freedom, nor the security of
other European nations'.

The judge, in summing up, speaks with contempt of these British
statesmen: 'When he was merely a Fascist dictator they applauded him;
when he was merely a breaker of international treaties they made new
treaties with him; but as he was ambitious to make war on England they
would slay him.' The jury – that is, the readers – are then charged to give
their verdict. The judge tells them that it will be decisive not only as a
judgement on the past but as a signpost to the future:

It will not do for us to forsake our high resolves when the Armistice is signed, and to abandon the lands which we have liberated to their fate . . . If, having saved Europe in 1940, we were to abandon Europe in 1944, her people would not thank us . . . If you are not to mock those who have fought and died in this war, the whole career of this Fascist dictator is a fitting subject for your verdict.

The book received a two-page review in *Tribune* from George Orwell, who was about to take up the job of literary editor. His comment was that quite a number of similar books could have been written: 'The Left has also been willing to shut its eyes to a great deal and to accept some very doubtful allies . . . The attitude of the Left towards the Russian regime has been distinctly similar to the attitude of Tories towards Fascism.'[7] As for trials of war criminals, he thought that they were a thoroughly bad idea and that it would be best to let Hitler and Mussolini 'settle down as the accredited bores of some Swiss *pension*'.

Beaverbrook, with *Guilty Men* in his memory, could not fail to identify the author of *The Trial of Mussolini*. The distinctive style, the use of the cuttings library as an arsenal, the pseudonym borrowed from Roman history – all pointed to Michael. Sharply, he reminded Michael of his order forbidding his employees to write without his permission. Michael had no defence; he had simply ignored the memo. Memos from the proprietor reached editors in the Express Group in a constant flow and Beaverbrook himself forgot about most of them – but in this case he had not forgotten.

It was becoming clear that Michael could not continue as editor of the *Standard*, but Beaverbrook did not want to lose his services. A feasible solution, he thought, was that Michael should become a feature-writer on retainer, with freedom to write books if he chose. He made this proposal to Michael, who replied on 1 November 1943:

I have considered most fully the proposition you put to me. I would like to say at the start that no more kind or generous offer was ever made in Fleet Street, especially in view of the quite legitimate protests which the management can make against my conduct. The only excuse I can give for it is to say what I hope is evident, that the book was written with a fire in my belly . . . Having written it I feared that if I asked for permission to publish, the book might never appear.

However, that is the past which you have generously offered to forget. As regards the future, I certainly intend to become a politician, if I can, and difficulties are bound to arise since my politics are not the same as yours . . . I therefore suggest one of two courses, either of which would be agreeable to me.

(1) I continue to act as Editor of the Standard on the present basis for a year, assuming no tremendous political upheaval in the meantime, after which the position could be reconsidered. It seems to me that some difficulty would be bound to arise then, since, if there is a General Election, I would like to fight it, and an editor who is not running his paper at the time of a General Election is certainly not much use. I would like during this period to maintain my connection with Devonport, but for the rest I would give an absolute guarantee not to write any books and not to make any speeches for which I had not received prior agreement from the management.

(2) I understand that this first proposition may not be satisfactory to you. I certainly intend, when the war or the Coalition comes to an end, to devote such energies as I possess to the annihilation of the Conservative influence in British politics. If you prefer, therefore, I am perfectly ready to accept your other proposition: that is, to continue to work for the Express Group in such a way as you may decide as a writer on the understanding (which has of course worked in the past) that I am not required to do anything in defiance of my views and that I have freedom to engage in such nefarious activities as I choose in writing books or on the platform. It is certainly not my desire (or my interest) to work for other newspapers, as I know well enough that you have given me opportunities and freedom which I would have received from nobody else . . .

Once more I would thank you for the most magnanimous way you have dealt with the whole affair.

Agreement on the second proposition would have been the best course for everyone concerned. But Beaverbrook decided that he would keep Michael on for as long as possible as editor, probably because rumours of the growing estrangement were getting around Fleet Street, Michael was receiving tentative offers from other papers, and he might be inclined to accept such an offer unless firmly anchored to the *Standard*. So he stayed for a final year, but his position was becoming more and more difficult and the occasions when he was prevented from taking the line that he wanted were becoming more frequent. When he was campaigning in the 1945 election, a questioner at a meeting asked him whether it was true that he had worked for Beaverbrook and edited the *Evening Standard*. As reported in the local press, his answer was: 'It was a very good newspaper when he had power to say what should appear in it. It had since become a very different newspaper. The reason he had left was because someone was trying to interfere with his rights as to what he wanted in that newspaper.'[8]

<h2 style="text-align:center">4</h2>

On 6 June 1944, Allied troops landed on the Normandy beaches and established a firm bridgehead. On the same day, the Germans gave up Rome. The Red Army had freed Leningrad from its siege and driven the invader from almost the whole of the Soviet Union. It seemed more than likely that these advances from east, west and south would secure victory in 1944. The political consequence was that there might be a break-up of the coalition and a general election before the end of the year, or early in 1945. Michael wrote a decisive letter to Beaverbrook:

> Your views and mine are bound to become more and more irreconcilable. As far as this Socialist business is concerned my views are unshakable. For me it is the Klondyke or bust, and at the moment I am doubtful whether I am going the right way to Klondyke. There does not seem to be much sense in my continuing to write leaders for a newspaper group whose opinions I do not share and some of whose opinions I strongly dissent from . . . I am associated with a newspaper group against whose policies (but not against the proprietor) I am resolved to wage perpetual war. Somehow things were different before. The compromise worked and certainly greatly to my advantage. But I do not see how it could work very much longer . . .
>
> From the point of view of my own self-interest as an ambitious and intransigent Socialist I think I could make better use of such talents as I possess. I think I could get on some other paper an agreement to write a column under my own name. I know I would not get complete freedom and certainly I do not wish you to think I don't appreciate the great freedom you have given me . . . But I do not see how your papers could run such a column by me; it would involve you in perpetual anxiety and embarrassment. Meantime at the present I am engaged in writing a great deal of stuff in which I have no particular interest, and I would like to do something different. I have thought the matter over very deeply for a long time. I would therefore ask you to do me yet another favour and release me from my obligations to the Evening Standard, and more still, from my numerous obligations to you . . .

My feeling is that I am wasting my time and there is so much I want to do and accomplish. Your kindness to me has given me great advantages in this world. I do not forget them. But I am sure it is right for me to make a change and I dearly hope you will understand my reasons.

Beaverbrook had no option but to accept the resignation. Michael, without delay, accepted an offer from the *Daily Herald*. The *Herald* was identified with the right rather than the left of the Labour Party, but it was at all events a Labour paper – indeed, *the* Labour paper – and was bound to campaign vigorously against the Tories if and when the general election came. Besides, it was edited at this time by Percy Cudlipp, a man whom Michael found very congenial. The Cudlipp brothers, Hugh and Percy, were working-class young men from the mining valleys of South Wales whose talents and energy had enabled them to scale the heights of Fleet Street; Hugh was with the Mirror Group while Percy edited the *Herald*. Michael was engaged to write a column twice a week. When his first piece appeared on 15 August 1944, he was introduced thus: 'Michael Foot has won prominence as a brilliant young Left Wing author and journalist. He is prospective Labour candidate for Devonport. Now he has joined the staff of the "Daily Herald". He will contribute a column of political comment twice weekly on Tuesdays and Fridays.'

The arrangement suited Michael admirably. He had no routine editorial duties and, given his facility as a writer, producing the column would leave him with time to spare. He would be able to give some of that time to *Tribune*, where a guiding hand was needed as Jon Kimche was leaving to work for Reuters. The new *Tribune* editor was Evelyn Anderson, a German–Jewish woman who had come to Britain before the war. She was efficient, highly intelligent and a dedicated socialist, but she lacked Michael's flair and style as well as his experience of the left and the Labour movement. Even if he won Devonport and became an MP, there would be no difficulty about continuing to write the *Herald* column. True, his salary on the *Herald* would be only about half what Beaverbrook had been paying and there was no prospect of an unexpected princely bonus. But this was nothing to worry about, as he had never – since 1940 – spent anything like all his earnings. He had found a flat at 62 Park Street, a block away from Park Lane, and friends were teasing him about his Mayfair establishment. However, in wartime landlords were glad to find tenants and the rent was the sum that Michael was used to – thirty shillings a week.

His first column struck a characteristic note. Challenging the dictum that the post-war settlement should be based on power and not on mere idealism, he wrote:

Idealism can mean much more than a mere glimmer in the blackout. When it possesses the minds of millions of men it can be the mighty engine for changing world history. The greatest statesmen are those who seek to excite it with the object of elevating the condition of life on this planet . . . The war that now afflicts us, let us not forget, could have been stopped before it really started if the much-scorned idealists who wanted to use power for building a genuine collective security had succeeded in expelling from office the 'realists' who preferred to recognise Mussolini's conquest of Abyssinia, keep the ring for General Franco and assist in the mutilation of Czechoslovakia.

On 25 August he hailed the liberation of Paris, recalled the great days of the French Revolution, and treated readers to quotations from Saint-Just, Danton, Lafayette, Fox, Wordsworth, Hazlitt, Shelley and Babeuf.

Paris means more to us than any other capital city but our own, and the reason is that every street name, every bridge, every monument, every garden can remind us of one of the wondrous epochs in the history of the human race when the French people, almost without leaders, overturned an edifice of old custom and legal crime,[9] an edifice which decreed that all but a gilded few should lead lives of penance and drudgery, should hardly be able to lift their heads to feel the sun. This is the true magic of Paris. This is why they laugh and dance on Bastille Day. This is why the Marseillaise is a universal anthem.

These were articles that might, perhaps, have been *Evening Standard* leaders, but he was writing others that Beaverbrook could never have countenanced. On 20 October, when details were made public of the artificial harbour created on the coast of Normandy, he drew its lesson under the headline 'PRIVATE ENTERPRISE COULDN'T DO IT!':

If we can achieve so much in war, why cannot we do the same in peace? If we can build harbours in this way, why cannot we build cities? . . . No Tory has yet discovered the answers. Their tame economists (and most of them are tame) are puzzling out how it can't be done, and their politicians are protesting that Socialism doesn't work, and their newspapers are chanting that competition is the breath of life, and meanwhile a mammoth army has passed through the harbour which public enterprise built . . . They still talk of the romance of capitalism . . . And they live in the age of the Dnieper Dam, the Tennessee Valley Authority and the harbour that the people of Britain built in a year when the shackles of private capitalism were off.

At the same time, he was working on a book that was certain to give grave offence to Beaverbrook. *Brendan and Beverley* was published in November 1944, again by Gollancz. This time the author was openly identified; it was 'by "Cassius" (Michael Foot) author of *Trial of Mussolini* and part author of *Guilty Men*'.

Unlike the other two books, this one was cast in the form of a satirical novel. It was a pastiche of the less serious parts of Disraeli's *Coningsby* and consisted largely of conversations between two men called Mr Tadpole and Mr Taper, the names of two party hacks in *Coningsby*. A prefatory note assured the reader: 'The two chief characters, Mr Tadpole and Mr Taper, are fictitious.' However, no one was expected to believe this, and readers were told at a neatly chosen point that their first names were Brendan and Beverley.

Brendan was Brendan Bracken, an Irishman who had made a career as a financial journalist, had become a Tory MP and had been Minister of Information since 1941. Beverley was Beverley Baxter, a Canadian, who was editor of the *Daily Express*. Both had the reputation of being skilful propagandists, not over-burdened by scruples or regard for the truth, and were expected to take directing roles in the Tory campaign to retain power after the war. Another man who would have a key role, however, was Beaverbrook. Bracken and Baxter were regular guests at the Cherkley dinner-table; Michael knew them well.

Most observers in 1944 thought that a Tory victory in a post-war election was inevitable, but Michael did not. He paid close attention to the by-elections – notably to a recent by-election in West Derbyshire when an independent (actually a Labour man defying the truce) defeated the Marquis of Hartington. The fictitious Taper reflected: 'There are about two hundred seats which are certainly going to be lost if the rest of the country shows a turnover like the one we saw at West Derbyshire.' This was a highly accurate calculation, for the number of Conservative or Liberal National seats which were lost in 1945 was just 196. But Taper went on to tell Tadpole: 'With Churchill's prestige and a cry of "Thanks for the victory" and a Zinoviev letter or Post Office savings stunt thrown in at the last moment, we can do it.' Another perceptive forecast: as we shall see, the Tory tactics were highly reminiscent of the faked Zinoviev letter which had been successful in 1924.

Essentially, the book was a warning of the hypocritical rhetoric and the dirty tricks that the Tories would employ on the prompting of Taper and Tadpole. But it ended with two speeches, each entitled 'The Speech That Could Win'. The first was clearly a Churchill speech and a good imitation of the Churchill style:

> We look to the past because we know that in our traditions there is so much to revere, so much to preserve, so much to make us noble in sustaining the good causes for which our country has always stood, and never more proudly than today. But we look to the future too; a future in which the renown so dearly bought in these five years of sweat and tears shall be firmly established, amplified, expanded and handed down untarnished to our sons.

The other speech was put in the mouth of a Labour leader, though it was far more eloquent than anything ever uttered by Attlee.

> What meagre lives are we content to live on this most bountiful earth! What niggardly grants are we ready to take as our portion from the gain provided by the soaring genius for science which man is able to display! The time has come, we believe, for the common people to break the power over their destiny of a small financial and industrial oligarchy.

An interesting passage in this speech read: 'The world will soon possess the mechanical apparatus to blow itself to oblivion; at least it will be able, if we allow this apparatus to be employed, to make the life of man on this planet, once again, nasty, brutish and short. We can only forestall that apocalypse by the boldest innovation.'

Michael had no inside information about the atomic bomb, and in 1944 the scientists who were involved in the project were not yet sure whether it would work. He was writing from an inspired guess – and from a memory. H. G. Wells had envisaged the atomic bomb in his book *The World Set Free*, written in 1913; and Michael had met Wells at Cherkley weekends. When *Brendan and Beverley* came out, Michael sent a copy to Wells, who replied with a letter of thanks and congratulations.

As a campaigning pamphlet, however, *Brendan and Beverley* was published too soon. There was no victory in the autumn of 1944, and therefore no election. The Allied armies liberated France and Belgium and advanced into Holland, but they were checked when the attempt to seize the Rhine bridges – 'a bridge too far' – was a costly failure. In Poland, the Russians stopped short of Warsaw and did nothing to help the uprising by the Polish resistance movement, which was ruthlessly crushed.

Disagreement over the future of Poland led to the first sign of antagonism between the Western Allies and the Soviet Union. There was an exiled government in London, anti-Nazi but also strongly anti-Communist, and there was a so-called National Committee in the eastern town of Lublin, sponsored by Stalin as the embryo of a Communist regime. Michael pointed out in his column: 'Not all the follies of the Polish Government can establish the Lublin Committee's claim to be a national administration; for sixty-three heroic days Warsaw took its orders from London and not from Moscow, and no amount of Jesuitical disputation can disguise the fact.'[10] Some *Daily Herald* readers wrote in to protest against his tone, but he defended his attitude:

> Of course, a permanent quarrel with the Soviet Union would be fatal. The Labour movement of this country does not need to be instructed in that fact either by Conservatives or Communists . . . But true friendship with the Soviet Union does not mean that we must accept every policy which she supports as all-wise or all-sufficient.'[11]

A sharper clash developed in Greece, with Michael this time on the side of the Communists. When the Germans withdrew from the country, a resistance movement under mainly Communist leadership took control. Churchill was determined to secure the return of the King of Greece and the right-wing exiled government, which had been based in Cairo, and sent British troops to ensure this aim. He cabled to the general on the spot: 'Do not hesitate to act as if you were in a conquered city where a local rebellion is in progress.' On 4 December, armed police loyal to the King, supported by British armoured cars, opened fire on a left-wing demonstration in Athens and killed twenty-eight people. In the House of Commons, a censure motion was put down in the names of, among others, Aneurin Bevan, Tom Driberg and Richard Acland. Michael wrote: 'Mr Churchill may produce some new facts in today's debate. The facts will have to be powerful indeed to convince us that Britain has not been wantonly and dangerously committed to a battle of intervention against the will of a majority of a brave people, who long to be our friends.'[12]

The official Labour line was to abstain in the debate, but thirty MPs voted for the censure motion. When the party conference met a few days later, Bevin declared in uncompromising terms that the Labour ministers shared the responsibility of their Tory colleagues. Bevan's reply from the floor was: 'Our representatives inside the government should exercise a more decisive influence upon the conduct of our affairs or else leave the Tories to do their dirty work themselves.' Michael was still more emphatic: 'We are fighting a war in Greece which will perjure our name, a war which, if it continues to the bitter end, must mean for all our friends and comrades in Europe a fallen hope, an aching fear, an ideal betrayed. We are drinking poison. A halt must be called.' He took a sombre view of the outlook:

Is this the future and this the world that we are working for and millions fighting for? A Poland ruled by the Lublin Committee . . . A Greece patrolled by British guns and sullenly protesting that every sacrifice since 1941 had been in vain; a starving Italy with those elements which had organised underground against Fascism derided by Churchill as they were once hunted by Mussolini.[13]

But, with the coming of spring in 1945, victory was at last near. Meeting at Yalta in February, Churchill, Stalin and Roosevelt drew the map of post-war Europe and decided on the creation of a United Nations Organisation to replace the defunct League of Nations. The founding conference was to open in San Francisco on 25 April. Michael was to report it for the *Herald* and comment on what he saw in an America which he had last visited in 1934. He landed in New York on 12 April, to spend several days there before crossing the continent by train.

He had his own reasons for the stay in New York. During the last couple of years, he had been greatly attached to Connie Ernst (no relation to Lili), an American who was in London working for the Office of War Information. She introduced him to a lively Anglo-American circle of friends, including Ernest Hemingway and Mary Welsh. According to one story, Hemingway proposed marriage to Mary lying on a bed in the Dorchester Hotel, while Michael and Connie were on the other bed. Connie was a young woman of great charm, wit and vivacity, and Michael's relationship with her was more serious than any of his other wartime affairs. At the end of 1944 she went home to New York (her father was a distinguished liberal lawyer) and he sent her a copy of *Brendan and Beverley* with this inscription:

This book is dedicated to Connie Ernst, without whom it would never have been written, without whom the author would not even have shelter over his head, without whom he would not possess a whole book of clothing coupons, without whom he would never have discovered the 23 bus route, without whom it will be hardly decent to drink an uzo at the White Tower, without whom the Dorchester Hotel is just another joint, without whose gibble-gabble we might just as well resign ourselves to basic English, without whom England will seem to return to the bad days before Lease–Lend, without whom the O.W.I. is likely to make an awful mess of Europe, and without whom the world would be a much poorer, duller and less beautiful place.

Whether or not inspired by Hemingway's example, Michael was urging Connie to marry him, and she promised to give him a definite answer when they met again in New York. The answer was 'Thanks, but no, thanks.' Though she was very fond of Michael, she did not want to make her permanent home in a Britain of shortages and austerity. Not much later, she married Simon Michael Bessie, who had also been in the OWI and had worked with Dick Crossman in Algiers. Bessie went into publishing and founded Atheneum, the firm that published several of Michael's books. Linked by affection for Connie, Michael and Bessie became good friends, although Bessie's marriage to Connie broke down in the 1960s.

While Michael was in New York and San Francisco, his future wife was in his home town, Plymouth. Jill Craigie was planning to script and direct a documentary film about the reconstruction of a badly bombed town. Her enthusiasm for the creation of a better environment for city-dwellers had been aroused first by reading the books of Lewis Mumford and then by meetings with Charles Reilly, a pioneering town-planner and a strong socialist, father of the Paul Reilly who had been Michael's friend at Oxford. After inspecting Coventry and considering other possibilities, she settled on Plymouth. Professor Patrick Abercrombie, entrusted with the reconstruction plan, was making sketches on his drawing-board of a spacious and beautiful new Plymouth, in total contrast to the congested city that had grown up over the centuries.

Jill was interested to learn that the well-known journalist Michael Foot came from Plymouth and would be Labour candidate for Devonport in the post-war election. In March 1945, she was introduced to him by Charles Reilly. They lunched together at the Ivy restaurant and talked about the projected film. By the time she emerged into the street, Jill was in love. As for Michael, he has written this account in an article that can be taken as an autobiographical fragment:

Jill Craigie was a raging beauty let loose on susceptible wartime London . . . Despite her qualifications as the first woman director to work in the British film industry, I could not take my eyes off this original apparition. She had the colouring of an English rose but everything else was a romantic, mysterious addition. She was half

Scottish and half Russian, not a tincture of English reserve in her make-up. She had Celtic and Russian fires and passions intermingled with what seemed an inborn gift for appreciating painting and music.[14]

However, he had much else to fill his mind: the approach of victory in the war, his prospects as a candidate, the forthcoming trip to America – and Connie Ernst. He agreed to appear in the film, and they shook hands.

Jill went to Plymouth and met Michael's parents. She liked them and they liked her. Eva, indeed, liked her so much that she telephoned Michael and told him: 'She'll do for you.' Few men wish to be guided in such matters by their mothers, and Michael responded by pointing out that Jill was a married woman (though he knew that her marriage was finished). He boarded the ship for New York, while Jill took up residence in Plymouth and started filming.

Whereas Michael had been encouraged from boyhood to think that he had a golden future if he only made use of his obvious talents, Jill had been obliged to build her future – and, virtually, her identity – for herself. Her parents, Arthur and Sonia Craigie, were divorced when she was an infant. Sonia then married a man who had a job on a cotton plantation in the Sudan, and she spent her time flitting about Britain and Europe with various lovers. Jill was placed in a sequence of boarding-schools and shifted according to Sonia's finances or those of the current lover. At her last school, a teacher lent her a book which she read avidly: *The Intelligent Woman's Guide to Socialism and Capitalism*, by Bernard Shaw. This teacher also encouraged her to sit for the Oxford entrance exam; she passed, but her mother could not or would not pay the fees.

She took a humble, boring office job. 'A young girl alone in London, with no home and no family,' Jill has written in an unpublished account, 'is regarded by men, fat men, old men, unattractive men, and especially married men as their natural prey. I could not walk to my lodgings or find myself alone in a lift with a man without his making a pass.' At the age of nineteen, seeking relief from this harassment, she married a young sculptor, Claude Begbie-Clench. They soon had a child, a daughter named Julie. Unhappily, Begbie-Clench was a hopeless alcoholic, spent his limited earnings on drink and was heavily in debt. The marriage collapsed. After the divorce, Jill married again, mainly in order to secure custody of Julie, who had been snatched by Claude's parents. Her second husband, a considerably older man, was Jeffrey Dell, who wrote film scripts for Alexander Korda. This marriage too was of brief duration, but Dell did her the service of introducing her to the film world and giving her the idea that she could stand on her own feet as a film-maker. Her outlook was marked by a passion for artistic creativity, a hatred of commercialism – a major cause of disharmony with Dell, who wrote frankly for money – and a faith in the ideals of William Morris, which fused creative fulfilment and freedom into a vision of a better world. She counted herself, and still counts herself today, as a William Morris Socialist. During the war she made a film called *Out of Chaos* about the work of war artists, in which Henry Moore, Stanley Spencer and Graham Sutherland demonstrated their aims and methods. But her ideals also gave her a keen interest in the environment (not, at that period, an everyday phrase) and hence in town planning.

Michael and Jill were close together in age, had the same socialist convictions and shared a capacity for ardent hope and scornful discontent. Where they differed was in education and background; his experience had been of warm security, hers of chilling insecurity. He came from the serious, high-minded, socially responsible English middle class; she from the raffish, hedonistic, irresponsible segment of that class. He was happy at his boarding-schools, while she had hated hers and run away from one of them. He was well read and soaked in history and literature in boyhood, but her education was unsystematic and her knowledge, especially of painting and music, was acquired by her own efforts. He had loving parents whom he loved in return, brothers and sisters, a swarm of cousins, a proud tradition of Devon Foots; she was an only child ready to make the Foots her family. In this spring of 1945, she was thankful that it was Plymouth she had chosen as the subject of her film.

While Michael was 6,000 miles away, the war in Europe was ending in victory. The Russians fought their way into Berlin and hoisted the red flag over the blackened shell of the Reichstag. Unrecognisable corpses, assumed to be those of Hitler and Goebbels, were found in the bunker to which the Third Reich had contracted. Mussolini had already been slaughtered by the Partisans of Milan. On 8 May, German generals signed the terms of surrender at General Eisenhower's headquarters. In London and in Plymouth, the streets were joyous with dancing and singing and the pubs ran out of beer. In San Francisco, to the disgust of British journalists, the effect of declaring Victory Day a public holiday was that the bars were closed.

Attlee was also in San Francisco, representing Britain at the conference in his capacity as Deputy Prime Minister. On his return to London, he met Churchill on 15 May to discuss the future – if any – of the coalition government. Three days later, the Labour Party was due to hold its Whitsun conference. Churchill urged that the coalition should be preserved, at least until Japan too was defeated, perhaps even into the years of peace.

Partly because the war in the Far East had yet to be won, partly because they were pessimistic about Labour's chances in an early election, Attlee, Bevin and Dalton all wanted to keep the coalition going. However, within a matter of days it became clear that this was a non-starter. When the Labour Chief Whip, William Whiteley, was asked about the likely attitude of Labour MPs, he declared emphatically that 'the lads will never agree'.[15] Above all, when Attlee arrived in Blackpool for the party conference, he quickly saw that he could be in danger of a revolt from the delegates. So the Labour leaders notified Churchill that they were leaving the government, thus putting an end to the coalition which had lasted from the Whitsun of 1940 to the Whitsun of 1945.

Churchill formed a Tory government with a few 'National' or Simonite Liberal faces. One of these was Leslie Hore-Belisha, Michael's opponent at Devonport, who became Minister of National Insurance. Brendan Bracken, amid general incredulity, was made First Lord of the Admiralty. The remaining question was the date of the election. Attlee wrote to Churchill proposing October, which would allow time to compile a new register – the existing register was scandalously incomplete and inaccurate – and to get some of the soldiers home from Germany. But Churchill replied that it would be bad for the country 'to live for so long a time under the spell of an approaching general election' and fixed polling day for 5 July.

By the end of May, almost all the candidates of every party were busy in the constituencies, but Michael was still on a ship coming from New York. The Labour agent in Devonport watched anxiously as Hore-Belisha began showing himself in the familiar streets and shaking hands. On 2 June he went to the station to meet his candidate, but discovered that Michael had taken an earlier train and was already at the committee rooms. That was an encouraging start.

Someone else who had been waiting impatiently for Michael's arrival was Jill Craigie.

5

The election of 1945 has been described by some historians as dramatic and exciting, by others as quiet and serious. In different ways, both descriptions are accurate. The air was filled (literally, since radio was the important medium) with well-prepared surprises, 'bombshells', accusations and denials. These, however, passed ineffectively over the heads of the voters, who were calmly considering what a Tory or a Labour victory would mean for them. Three things mattered supremely to the ordinary man or woman: the provision of new homes to meet the acute shortage caused by bombing and by six years without building; an orderly transition to a peacetime economy with full employment; and a socially equitable system of benefits and pensions, as promised by the Beveridge Report. The Labour Party won the election because it was judged most likely to deliver on these three counts.

This is clear enough with hindsight, but it was by no means obvious during the campaign. It was possible – or, some observers thought, practically certain – that Churchill's personal prestige would be decisive, especially by contrast with Attlee's colourless personality and unimpressive oratorical style. Hoardings were plastered with posters showing Churchill's face and the slogan 'Help Him Finish the Job'; he made four of the ten broadcasts allotted to his party (Attlee made one of Labour's ten); and his motorcade tours of the towns and cities brought out the crowds. True, he was more popular than his party. But Tory strategy was to offer a choice of national leader rather than a choice of government, and no one could be sure that this strategy would not prevail.

Besides, while there was evidence that millions of voters distrusted the Tories and feared a return to pre-war conditions, this did not mean that they were attracted by socialism as a political philosophy. Labour's colours were nailed to the mast; its manifesto, *Let Us Face the Future*, announced: 'The Labour Party is a Socialist party, and proud of it. Its ultimate purpose at home is the establishment of a Socialist Commonwealth of Great Britain – free, democratic, efficient, progressive, public-spirited, and its material resources organised in the service of the British people.'

What did that last clause imply? At the party conference of December 1944, Ian Mikardo, the delegate from (and after the election MP for) Reading, moved a resolution embodying a sweeping programme of public ownership. It was carried by acclamation and replaced the cautious statement which had been put forward by the NEC. As the delegates adjourned, Morrison said to Mikardo: 'Well, young man, you've just lost us the election.' Despite Morrison's objections, *Let Us Face the Future* pledged Labour to nationalise the mines, the railways, gas and electricity, the iron and steel industry and the Bank of England. The Tories were confident that British voters would never endorse this economic transformation.

If these voters were enamoured neither of the Tories nor of the socialists, they had another option. The Liberals entered the campaign with high hopes, enhanced by the fact that Beveridge was a Liberal and was among their candidates, so his report could be cited as a Liberal asset. They had eighteen MPs at the dissolution and looked forward to at least doubling this figure, perhaps to holding the balance in the next Parliament. Among the Liberal hopefuls were three members of the Foot family. Isaac was standing for Tavistock, where the Liberals had several times given the Tories a close run and the Labour vote was derisory. John – Major Foot, with the advantage of service in the Normandy campaign – was contesting Bodmin, the constituency where his father had twice triumphed. Dingle was again standing for Dundee, which he had represented for fourteen years. Of the four Foots who were fighting the election, the one with the least chance seemed to be the one who wore the Labour colours.

Indeed, Labour did not appear well placed to win any of the three Plymouth constituencies. In Devonport, particularly, Hore-Belisha was regarded as a safe bet. He had now dropped the Liberal National label and presented himself as the National candidate. Michael announced: 'I propose to fight the election on the assumption that Mr Hore-Belisha is a Tory. If he has any objection, perhaps he will tell us.'[16] Hore-Belisha did object, but was found to be speaking for Tory candidates in the Bodmin division and elsewhere. 'He's as much a Tory in Devonport as he is in Liskeard,' Michael reiterated.

In a speech on 8 June, Hore-Belisha told the voters that the issue in the election was between socialism and parliamentary democracy, and warned: 'Socialism will lead to totalitarianism just as surely here as in other countries.' He was contributing to the political offensive launched by Churchill a few days earlier in his first radio oration:

> Socialism is inseparably interwoven with totalitarianism and the abject worship of the State . . . Socialism is in its essence an attack not only upon British enterprise, but upon the right of an ordinary man and woman to breathe freely without having a harsh, clumsy, tyrannical hand clapped across their mouth and nostrils.

The attack was a blunder, and it developed into a catastrophic howler when Churchill went on to assert that socialism must involve the setting up of 'some form of Gestapo'. Low, in the *Standard*, produced a risible cartoon showing Attlee in Gestapo uniform. Attlee himself suggested charitably that Churchill must have wanted to show the voters 'how great was the difference between Winston Churchill, the great leader in war of a united nation and Mr Churchill the party leader'. Morrison commented: 'Winston was having a night out.' Churchill's allegation was heavily criticised by *The Times* and was described by the *Economist* as 'pernicious nonsense'. The academic historian of the election, R. B. MacCallum, sums up: 'No one took these warnings seriously.'[7]

In the Labour camp, there was no doubt that the planner of these smears and scares was Beaverbrook. As well as giving orders for sensational headlines in his newspapers, he was the star speaker on Tory platforms in a number of constituencies. Attlee, replying to Churchill's 'Gestapo' broadcast, said: 'The voice we heard last night was that of Mr Churchill, but the mind was that of Lord Beaverbrook.' Bevin told an audience: 'I have no quarrel with the Prime Minister, but I have had enough these last five years of Lord Beaverbrook . . . I object to this country being ruled from Fleet Street.'

No vestiges of past affection deterred Michael from joining in the counter-attack. On 8 June, in his *Herald* column, he alluded scathingly to 'a few neolithic monsters still surviving in our midst, such as Lord Beaverbrook'. The *Herald*'s artist added an unflattering sketch of Beaverbrook as some kind of tyrannosaur. On 15 June Michael directed his irony to the cause which Beaverbrook had championed for decades, the British Empire.

> Lord Beaverbrook likes the Empire. He believes in the Empire . . . The only trouble is that the Empire does not believe in Lord Beaverbrook . . . He is the Old Maid of politics, perpetually rejected by the embarrassed beau on whom he has fixed his attentions. Every few years he appears at the church door, decked out in the same old wedding dress of economic nationalism. The trousseau is getting very tattered by now.

On 29 June, with the election campaign in its final stage, Michael summed up:

> The dust and filth are settling amid this dirtiest of all elections, in which the Tories have sought to exploit sacrifice and patriotism in the interests of Big Money and its possessors . . . How pitiable appear the antics of the Beaverbrooks and the Baxters, the Brackens and the Belishas – yes, and the Churchills – in contrast to the forward march of the British people!

Politics is politics, and Beaverbrook could claim no courtesies after he had chosen to sponsor the kind of campaign that the Tories were pursuing. Even so, he must have been wounded when he read these derisive words from the pen of the young man on whom he had lavished so much kindness and generosity. Any links between Beaverbrook and Michael, it surely appeared, had been broken for ever.

But hard hitting in controversy was definitely in the Foot tradition. In the run-up to the election, Michael once mentioned to his father that he had met Hore-Belisha on a social occasion and they had chatted amicably. 'I hope', Isaac Foot said, 'that you didn't promise him a clean fight.'

Definitions of 'clean' or 'dirty' may vary, but Michael certainly gave Hore-Belisha no quarter. At his adoption meeting on 8 June, he took up the question of the rushed election and the inadequate register: 'I should like to know whether the Member for Devonport entered any protest against the plan which is going to deprive so many constituents of the right to vote.' From then onward, he hammered away at Hore-Belisha's record, which was indeed vulnerable enough. There was the medal he had accepted from Mussolini in 1938 – 'I have been an opponent of Fascism ever since it started,' Michael reminded the audience. There was Hore-Belisha's responsibility, when Minister of War, for failing to muster and equip a British expeditionary force. There was a speech he had made as late as July 1939 containing an assurance that there would be no war. By 3 July, Hore-Belisha was complaining: 'My opponent has devoted the whole of his time to personal attacks on me and my political record, and has issued last-minute leaflets containing garbled extracts from speeches.' Michael's response to this complaint was relentless:

> Does he say that Devonport has no right to discuss his votes and actions in the past ten years? . . . I note that Mr Hore-Belisha makes no reply regarding his tributes to Mussolini. I advise Mr Hore-Belisha to continue his silence. I have treated him most tenderly, as he well knows. There are many other skeletons in his cupboard which I have left undisturbed.

Hore-Belisha was also vulnerable with regard to the major local issue in Devonport and the whole city of Plymouth: that of reconstruction after the devastating air raids. Professor Abercrombie had produced a plan which envisaged the creation of a virtually new city. Suggestions for restoring the street-plan of the old Plymouth, put forward by shop-keepers and property-owners, were firmly rejected. Abercrombie's scheme raised very broad issues – social, financial and political. His new avenues and piazzas could come into existence only if the land passed into some form of municipal or community ownership. In an election speech of 24 June, Michael said:

> The real issue has nothing to do with the Gestapo or totalitarianism. It is whether we are going to plan the economic life of our country and

whether we are going to plan the reconstruction of our city. Every acre of land on which our city is going to be built should belong to the people of Devonport and Plymouth.

Abercrombie was the central figure in the film that Jill Craigie was making, entitled *The Way We Live*. He was shown walking through the ruins and meditating (in voice-over) on the opportunities of this *tabula rasa*, and then expounding his ideas to meetings of Plymouth people and countering their objections. The film alternated between these sequences of exposition and the story of a fictional, but typical family – a dockyard worker with a wife and three children, bombed out of their old house and yearning for a new home in improved surroundings.

Abercrombie's concepts were those that were to guide building in Britain over the next two decades, for example in the new towns. Sprawling suburbs would be replaced by self-contained communities. Inner and outer ring roads would segregate traffic from pedestrians. Every unit of between 6,000 and 10,000 people would have its shops, schools, community centre, swimming-pool, cinema and pubs. Thus, the narrator explained, there would be active citizenship – 'not docile people who take their ideas from the wireless and the newspapers'. Abercrombie told a meeting: 'We must make the best use of land in the interests of the community as a whole' and: 'You citizens must own the land.' Enlarged by the camera from a model, clean white building-blocks arose from the rubble. To the sound of inspiring music, grand phrases were enunciated: 'monumental feature . . . vista . . . spaciousness and beauty for all'. The film closed with a Youth March – a real event – with young people carrying banners which read: 'We want the Plan . . . Premises not Promises . . . Holiday Hostels . . . Pools for Schools . . . A Theatre . . . Club rooms.'

The Abercombie plan, incarnating the spirit of the times, was indeed popular and was eventually realised. Today, most people who tramp along the immensely wide new streets and gaze at the standardised five-storey buildings find the effect dull and monotonous and regret the loss of what would now be listed buildings. (To achieve a clean sweep, more buildings were demolished than had been destroyed by the bombs, and only a last- minute defence saved the picturesque Barbican quarter.) But in 1945 no one spoke of conservation; the plan was an inspiring symbol of a better future.

The election campaign figured prominently in the film. Jill was prepared to show meetings by opposing candidates, but Hore-Belisha, who was trying to evade the issue of the Abercrombie plan, refused to appear. The screen, therefore, showed a large poster with the name 'MICHAEL FOOT'. Then Michael appeared, demanding the implementation of the plan with financial help from places that had not been bombed – 'the burden must be shared'. In tones of fervent conviction, he declared: 'We have the right to live in one of the most beautiful cities in the whole wide world.' The next shot was a close-up of a ballot paper on which a pencil was unhesitatingly marking a cross against the name 'FOOT'. That was Jill's declaration of love.

She was following the campaign closely and questioning the Labour activists whom she had got to know. They all told her, with a wry smile and a shrug, that Hore-Belisha was unbeatable. Labour was putting up a good fight, but was unlikely to win any of the Plymouth seats. The only Tory defeat generally predicted was in Bodmin, where John Foot was tipped to achieve a Liberal success. John himself believed that he was going to win and was sorry that Michael was not.

This pessimism regarding Labour's prospects was by no means confined to Plymouth. True, the Gallup poll showed 47 per cent of the voters opting for Labour and 41 per cent Conservative – figures that presaged a big Labour victory and proved accurate to within 1 per cent. Few people in 1945, however, were impressed by this new-fangled American device; subjective judgements were considered more reliable. Alison Readman, co-author of the election book sponsored by Nuffield College, Oxford, visited Newcastle-on-Tyne and found no evidence that Labour might capture any of its four Tory-held seats.[18] (Labour won three of them.) Others were misled by Churchill's reception in the streets; the *Yorkshire Post* declared that no one who witnessed it 'could doubt that he has the wholehearted support of the country'.

The Nuffield authors recorded that political correspondents in the press differed only as to whether the Tory majority would be large or small. 'The only point on which all were agreed was that there would not be a Labour majority.' The *Daily Mail*'s headline on 1 July was: 'EXPERTS TELL PREMIER YOUR VICTORY IS SURE', while the *Express* on polling day headlined simply: 'WE ARE WINNING'. Confidence on the right was mirrored by caution on the left. Kingsley Martin, in his *New Statesman* Diary, forecast 'a close shave'. Ian Mackay of the *News Chronicle*, himself an ardent socialist, took the view that there would probably be a hung Parliament.

When the polls closed, the ballot-boxes were taken to police stations to be kept under lock and key for three weeks. To allow time for the servicemen's ballots to be flown home from as far afield as Burma, the count would take place only on 26 July. In Devonport, it was clear that there had been a heavy poll, normally seen by Labour supporters as a good sign. However, the *Western Morning News* reported confidence in the Hore-Belisha camp.

On 26 July, since all the boxes were ready for opening, the count proceeded promptly and simultaneously everywhere in Britain, starting at nine in the morning. Within two hours, the Tories were startled by the defeat of two members of the Cabinet, Brendan Bracken at Paddington and Harold Macmillan at Stockton-on-Tees. By lunch-time, big swings in Birmingham and in outer London made a Labour victory certain. At seven o'clock, Churchill drove to Buckingham Palace to hand in his resignation to the King. He was closely followed by Attlee, the incoming Prime Minister. The complete figures showed that 393 Labour MPs had been elected (or 397 if we include ILP and Common Wealth members who subsequently took the Labour whip). It was a landslide of dimensions matched only by the Liberals in 1906 and the Tories in 1931.

For Labour campaigners, this was a day of wonder and delight, and nowhere more so than in Plymouth. All three constituencies yielded Labour victories. The result in Devonport was:

Michael Foot, Labour	13,395
Leslie Hore-Belisha, National	11,382
Labour majority	2,013

Against all apparent probabilities, he was the only Foot elected. Dingle was ousted by a Labour victory at Dundee. Thanks to a surprisingly strong Labour vote, the Tories held on to Bodmin and Tavistock. The 1945 election, disastrous for the Tories, was shattering for the Liberals; they won only eleven seats.

Hastily, the Plymouth Labour Party organised a victory celebration at the Corn Exchange, a hall which had luckily survived the bombing. Hundreds of people gathered, filled the hall or stood outside despite an evening of rain. According to the local paper, the most enthusiastic reception was given to Michael Foot, who was carried into the hall on the shoulders of two Navy bluejackets and was 'cheered to the echo'.

— Chapter 5 —

COLD WAR YEARS

I

The House of Commons elected in 1945 was the first in history with an unchallengeable Labour majority. On 1 August, when Churchill took his place on the Opposition front bench, the depleted Tories welcomed him with 'For he's a jolly good fellow'. As the song died away, a voice from the Labour side rang out with: 'The people's flag is deepest red . . .' It was the voice of a Yorkshire miner, George Griffiths, who represented Hemsworth with a majority of 26,000, the largest in Britain. Almost 400 Labour members, in accents from Cornish to Aberdonian, joined in the triumphant singing of 'The Red Flag'.

Normally, the House that emerges from a general election contains somewhere between 100 and 200 new MPs. This time, the 343 newcomers outnumbered the 297 re-elected members of the old House. The renovation of the Parliamentary Labour Party was still more striking. At the dissolution, there had been 166 Labour (including ILP) members. Twenty-nine retired, two were defeated – one by a Liberal, the other by a Communist – and two were re-elected but immediately sent to the House of Lords. That left only 133 Labour MPs who had sat in the last Parliament, to be joined by 263 newcomers. Among these newcomers were the four men who would lead the party over the years from 1955 to 1983: Hugh Gaitskell, Harold Wilson, James Callaghan and Michael Foot.

As in earlier years, the Labour Party had its left-wingers, ready to watch Attlee's government with vigilance and advance criticisms if necessary. Newcomers answering to this description included Geoffrey Bing, Raymond Blackburn, Donald Bruce, Barbara Castle, Dick Crossman, Hugh Delargy, Michael Foot, John Freeman, Benn Levy, J. P. W. (Bill) Mallalieu, Ian Mikardo, Stephen Swingler, Woodrow Wyatt and Konni Zilliacus. Here was a considerable store of talent, ideas and polemical force. (Not all of them remained on the left, or even in the

Labour Party, throughout a political lifetime.) To these names, we should add Sydney Silverman, who had been in the House since 1935, and Emrys Hughes, who arrived after a 1946 by-election.

In general, the left-wing MPs who were new to the House were not acquainted with one another. Crossman – who had been a *New Statesman* journalist, a lecturer at Oxford, leader of the Labour group in Oxford City Council and a planner of wartime Allied propaganda – was the best equipped to be the co-ordinator of a future left group. Before organising anything else, he organised a lunch party at the Savoy Grill on the first day of the session. Michael Foot, of course, was among those present.

One more fact may be noted. This Labour Party, dedicated to the overthrow of the old Tory ruling class and to the primacy of working-class interests and needs, was in its composition less proletarian than any of its predecessors. About a quarter of the Labour MPs were university graduates; a list would include some of the leaders, notably Attlee and Dalton, but also many of the newcomers. The middle-class orientation applied to the left as much as to the right, if not more so. Of those on our left-wing list, Michael Foot, Barbara Castle, Dick Crossman and Bill Mallalieu were graduates of Oxford, and Zilliacus of Yale. Bing, Blackburn and Wyatt had been called to the Bar. The Army ranks were Captain Bing, Captain Blackburn, Major Bruce, Captain Delargy, Major Freeman, Captain Swingler and Major Wyatt, while Levy and Mallalieu had been officers in the Navy.

On his first morning as Prime Minister, Attlee appointed Dalton as Foreign Secretary and Bevin as Chancellor of the Exchequer. In the afternoon, he switched them round. It is still an open question why he changed his mind, but there is some evidence that senior Foreign Office officials indicated that they would find it difficult to work with Dalton.[1] Bevin, at all events, soon satisfied these mandarins, who ranked him as a Foreign Secretary in a class with Canning and Palmerston, and correspondingly alienated the left. 'We are appalled', *Tribune* complained, 'to find that Mr Bevin relies for advice on the same Foreign Office experts who used to advise Eden and Halifax.'[2] Indeed, Halifax himself was kept on at the Washington embassy although he had gone there as a political appointee and had fully expected to be replaced by a Labour government; Sir Rex Leeper was retained as ambassador in Athens, where he had enthusiastically carried out Churchill's instructions to act as a proconsul; Sir Alexander Cadogan, head of the Foreign Office since the time of Munich, was asked by Bevin to stay on after reaching the normal retiring age.

On the face of it, Bevin was an improbable Foreign Secretary. He had little knowledge of other countries except through international trade union conferences. When conducting negotiations, he was blunt of speech, undiplomatic and often tactless. His undisguised personal hostility to Molotov was a factor, though of course a minor one, in future rifts with the Soviet Union. As these rifts widened, the comment that went the rounds was that he treated the Russians as a breakaway from the Transport and General Workers' Union.

Partly because Bevin was at the Foreign Office, criticism from the left arose from issues of international rather than domestic policy. There was little reason to doubt that the government was at least laying the foundations of a socialist Britain. The structure of the welfare state was replacing the old Poor Law, Bevan was designing a free and comprehensive National Health Service, one measure of public ownership succeeded another. Nationalisation of the mines, a reform which had unequalled emotional significance for the Labour movement, was made the first priority and entrusted to a known left-winger, Emanuel Shinwell. By contrast, Attlee and Bevin seemed to subscribe to the Tory belief that British national interests, not ideological sympathies, should be the mainspring of foreign policy. By maintaining the coalition policy of anti-Communist intervention in Greece, Bevin angered the left as he had before 1945. Resolutions from the constituencies regularly demanded 'a socialist foreign policy' and *Tribune* enunciated the doctrine: 'You cannot plan Socialism with Liberal economists to advise you, and you certainly cannot conduct a foreign policy divorced from Socialist objectives.'[3]

Such was the basic divergence; but there was also a divergence within the divergence – that is, within the left. For many Labour activists and for some MPs, adherence to 'socialist objectives' meant primarily friendship with the Soviet Union. Indeed, the Labour leaders had given this impression in the election campaign. Cripps had promised that a Labour government would be 'in broad sympathy with the views of the Russian people'. Bevin's oracular pronouncement: 'Left understands Left, but the Right does not' was widely quoted, and soon quoted against him. Few people remembered the context, which showed that he was talking about relations with the France of Léon Blum, not with Russia. For those who saw a comradely relationship with the Soviet Union as the litmus test of a 'socialist foreign policy', the assumption was that there were two, and only two, political forces in the world of 1945, one seeking the maintenance of capitalism and the other aiming to abolish it. In the latter, the most important element was obviously the huge nation in which capitalism had been abolished since 1917.

Distinct from this outlook – and more distinct than was generally perceived at this time – was the view taken by Michael Foot. For him, there were crucial differences between Communism and the socialism that could be achieved in Britain and other European countries. It followed from this stance that Communism had to be frankly criticised and, when necessary on specific issues, opposed. Rather than two competing forces on the world scene, there were three; the third, which Labour Britain should champion, was democratic socialism. 'Third force' became a familiar expression, in France and other West European nations as well as in Britain.

The first full exposition of this theme was made in Michael's maiden speech in the House of Commons on 20 August 1945. He began with a robust attack on Churchill, who had pointed to the creation of 'police governments' in Soviet-controlled nations and demanded free elections. Michael's retort was:

> I agree with a good many of those sentiments, but I cannot help feeling that honourable members who applauded him so lustily on those points have left the mass journey to Damascus a little late. The right honourable gentleman himself was once an avowed supporter of the police government of Signor Mussolini, and when General Franco raised his rebellion in Spain against the ballot box, where were those honourable gentlemen? . . . We think we have no reason to submit to instruction on the principles of democracy from that side of the House . . . There were very few friends of Hitler to be found in the workers' homes in Europe, and there were very few friends of democracy to be found in the precincts of the palaces and the offices of big business.

It would have been easy for Michael to leave it at that, to the sound of lusty applause from the Labour side, but he added: 'Men have had their freedom taken from them and worse, merely for expressing their opinions and for being suspected of holding certain opinions, in Poland and many other parts of eastern Europe. I protest against that . . . We must establish our right to criticise the Soviet Union just as the Soviet Union exercises its right to criticise us.'

Then came the positive message:

> We do not wish to play the part of Lepidus in this triumvirate of great nations. Britain stands today at the summit of her power and glory, and we hold that position because today, following the election, we have something unique to offer. We have a conception of political

liberty which our friends in Russia unhappily have not been blessed with. We have at the same time a conception of economic democracy . . . which is unhappily not yet shared by the people of the United States . . . It is this unique combination of treasures . . . which gives to us the commanding position of leadership if we choose to exercise it . . . As we look out across this stricken continent and as we seek a new hope in the struggle to be born across this wilderness of shattered faiths, may it not be our destiny as the freest and most democratic and a Socialist power to stand between the living and the dead and stay the plague?

This appeal evoked a response from many in the Labour Party, but not from the Prime Minister. Recalling this period in later conversation with his biographer, Attlee remarked with his customary terseness: 'Some people . . . thought we ought to concentrate all our efforts on building up a third force in Europe. Very nice, no doubt. But there wasn't either a material or a spiritual basis for it.'[4]

When Bevin replied to the debate, he made no concessions to the left and endorsed Churchill's strictures on the Soviet Union. His biographer records that his speech met with 'a noticeable lack of enthusiasm on the Labour benches'.[5]

In September, Bevin, Molotov and James Byrnes, the US Secretary of State, met in London. The meeting was designed to take the first steps toward peace treaties with the ex-enemy nations, but it ended in complete deadlock. Bevin told MPs: 'Our arrangements in economics and defence must be such that we are ready to stop aggression should the occasion arise.'[6] He could only have been alluding to a possible Russian aggression; was the Soviet Union now seen as an enemy, six months after the handshakes on the battlefields? A still more ominous question was: what could be the future shape of a Europe divided into hostile blocs? George Orwell, writing in *Tribune*, prophesied: 'We may be heading not for a general breakdown, but for an epoch as horribly stable as the slave empires of antiquity'[7] – a suggestion that foreshadowed the vision of *1984*.

Meanwhile, Europe from Russia to Italy was in the grip of hunger bordering on starvation. In the British and American occupation zones of Germany, small children begged or died, Army units posted sentries to check pilfering from their dustbins, and the only valid currencies were cigarettes or women's bodies. To make matters worse, millions of Germans had fled westward before the advancing Russian armies and millions more had been expelled from Poland and Czechoslovakia, an action which Michael denounced in his second speech in the Commons. It was Victor Gollancz who reacted most speedily to this human tragedy. He started a campaign with the name of Save Europe Now; the committee included Michael, Bertrand Russell and the Independent MP Eleanor Rathbone. The organiser was Peggy Duff, a war widow who dedicated herself to campaigning for good causes. She was unsystematic in her way of working and dismissive of conventional office routine, but a brilliant improviser and ideally suited to an urgent campaign in which every day counted. As Michael said: 'A terrible and frightening winter faces us in Europe, but it can also be a winter in which our country has the honour to speak with the voice of reason and of pity.'[8]

Not everyone saw it thus, for Germany was still an enemy nation. When 100,000 people responded to an appeal to surrender ration coupons so that the equivalent on food could be sent abroad, the government refused to operate the scheme. Save Europe Now then proposed that people should be allowed to send parcels of food or medicines to Germany. John Strachey, as Minister of Food, favoured the idea, but it was vetoed by the Cabinet and ultimately accepted, after a campaign of pressure, only at the end of 1946.

Britain was not starving (though rations were very tight) but was facing acute economic difficulties. The Lease–Lend scheme, whereby the US had supplied vital commodities to Britain on deferred payment, was abruptly terminated within a week of the end of the war with Japan. The government was obliged to ask for a substantial American loan. Negotiations, described by Dalton as 'hard bargaining', took three months, but Britain had to yield to the American demand for the scrapping of protective tariffs. Bevin told the Cabinet that he 'felt the most profound reluctance to agree to any settlement which would leave us subject to economic direction from the United States'; but he could not advise rejection, which 'meant asking the British people to endure for perhaps another three years standards of living even lower than those to which they had been reduced at the end of six years of war'.[9] When the hard decision was made, the only dissenters in the Cabinet were Bevan and Shinwell.

The argument over the loan created fissures in both parties. Robert Boothby, who called it 'an economic Munich', led seventy-one Tories in voting against acceptance, though the official Conservative line was to abstain. On the Labour side, twenty-three MPs voted against, twenty-seven abstained and the great majority backed their government. The unhappiness of the left was reflected in a *Tribune* editorial headed 'A SAVAGE BARGAIN', which admitted that 'the dilemma is cruel' and came down for rejection in a tone which hinted at painful disagreements among friends. While Michael Foot, Barbara Castle, Jennie Lee, Hugh Delargy and Benn Levy voted against the loan, Crossman, Driberg, Mikardo, Swingler and Zilliacus voted for it, as did the two Communist MPs.

The decision to accept the loan can be judged, in historical perspective, as committing Britain to an economic reconstruction on predominantly capitalist lines and to choosing the American side in future political conflicts. Michael, who failed to catch the Speaker's eye in the debate, used his *Daily Herald* column to warn: 'American capitalism is arrogant, self-confident, merciless and convinced of its capacity to dictate the destinies of the world.'[10] In Plymouth at the weekend, he told a reporter for the local paper: 'I have a deadly fear that we shall awake to find ourselves in chains to American capitalism, which is the most evil force in the world today.' What he did not foresee was that, within a couple of years, he would identify another force as more evil than capitalism.

2

These were busy days for Michael. Nye Bevan, *Tribune*'s editor during the war, and George Strauss, who had been chairman of the board, became ministers when the Labour government took office and had to terminate their direct connection with the paper. Their wives, Jennie Lee and Patricia Strauss, replaced them as members of the board. The third board member was Michael (in 1946, Ian Mikardo joined it and Patricia withdrew). Michael took over Nye's role as the political director of *Tribune*, with the decisive voice in shaping its line. He wrote the front-page editorial more often than not, as well as signed articles from time to time. His relationship with Nye continued to be close; to cite the phrase that he used to describe a similar relationship when he was on the *Evening Standard* and Beaverbrook was in the government, 'telepathic communication was fully maintained'. The Minister of Health knew that he could trust the discretion of his friend and disciple, and Michael did not recount the inside stories until he wrote the second volume of his Bevan biography in 1973. However, *Tribune*'s criticisms of Attlee and Bevin tended to reflect what Nye had been saying at restaurant dinners or on weekend country walks.

Although Michael was effectively the editor of *Tribune*, he was reluctant to take on the position of editor officially because it had been held by Evelyn Anderson since the departure of Jon Kimche in 1944. But Anderson, as we have seen, had her limitations, and at the beginning of

1946 Michael persuaded Kimche to leave his job at Reuter's and return to *Tribune* as editor.

Another change involved George Orwell, who had been literary editor since 1943 and had also written a weekly column, 'As I Please'. His trenchant attacks on Communism and the Soviet Union had scandalised many readers, but Bevan defended him and sympathised with the Orwell motto: 'Liberty is the right to tell people what they don't want to hear.' In 1945 Orwell handed over as literary editor to his friend Tosco Fyvel and also handed over the 'As I Please' column – to the relief of some on the *Tribune* left – to Jennie Lee. He was still associated with the paper, however, as a book reviewer and occasional contributor.

In addition to his work for *Tribune*, Michael had to write his twice-weekly column for the *Daily Herald*, and he was determined to be a good constituency MP. At that period, the MP's 'surgery' was not yet an established institution, and there were many members of the House – mostly Tories, but also Labour MPs with safe seats – who appeared in their constituencies only to make platform speeches at longish intervals. Michael, from the start, made himself regularly accessible to Devonport people who had individual problems – and there were plenty of these, especially because of the desperate housing shortage. In any case, he liked to spend weekends in his home town in order to see his parents, his brothers John and Christopher (both working for Foot and Bowden), and above all his beloved sister Sally.

Plymouth was the first of the bombed cities to be ready with a redevelopment plan, but in the early months after the war it sometimes seemed that nothing would ever happen. Property-owners used legalistic devices to hold on to every patch of rubble, while the building industry was hampered by shortages and competing demands. Fortunately, the city's three Labour MPs and the Labour-dominated City Council exerted constant pressure and had an ally in Lewis Silkin, the Minister of Town and Country Planning, who pushed through legislation enabling Plymouth to get round delays and formalities. Sometimes money was spent and projects were started without strictly correct legal sanction, but Michael could get assurances from Silkin that there would be no penalties.

Michael's relationship with Jill Craigie was developing into a firm commitment. They became lovers in the autumn of 1945, but they did not decide on marriage, nor did they start living together. In the 1940s, a domestic partnership without legal sanction was likely to raise eyebrows even among the liberal-minded. There were also practical considerations. His flat was small and space was further limited by an accumulation of

Right Michael as a child.

Below Oxford University debating tour in the USA, 1934. Michael (left) and John Cripps with Smith College students, described by Michael as 'more notable for their beauty than their speaking'.

Below With the Cripps family on holiday in the Scilly Isles, 1933. Michael is on the right; Stafford Cripps is second from left.

From Michael's election address as Labour candidate for Monmouth, 1935.

The Foot family in the late 1930s. Standing: Christopher, Michael, Mac, Dingle, John. Seated: Sylvia (Mac's wife), Anne (John's wife), Isaac, Eva, Sally, Dorothy (Dingle's wife). (*Tribune*)

Michael speaks at a Second Front meeting, 1942. From left: Aneurin Bevan, unidentified, Harry Pollitt.

Michael, photographed by Jill, in his Park Street flat, 1946. (*Pictorial Press*)

Jill Craigie, film-maker.

Michael, while on holiday
with Jill in Rome, 1947.

Candidates for Plymouth constituencies and their spouses, 1951. Left to right: Jim Middleton, Lucy Middleton (Labour candidate for Sutton), Chiquita Astor, John Jacob Astor (Tory candidate for Sutton), Jill Foot, Michael Foot (Labour candidate for Devonport), June Churchill, Randolph Churchill (Tory candidate for Devonport).

Right, above Michael listens to Bevan speaking in Ebbw Vale, 1947. (*R. L. Jenkins*)

Right, below The 'Free Speech' team on Independent Television, 1954. Left to right: W. J. Brown, Robert Boothby, Kenneth Adam (chairman), Michael, A. J. P . Taylor.

Above At Paddock Cottage, 1957. Julie Hamilton, Jill, Michael. (*Michael Ward*)

Left Out! *Tribune* v. *New Statesman* cricket match, 1950s.

books which Michael, like his father, was unable to check. There would not have been room for another person – let alone a woman with a child, for Jill's daughter Julie was with her when not at boarding-school. Jill was more amply housed; she lived in a house in Hampstead, which had belonged to Ramsay MacDonald and was now owned by his son Malcolm. Malcolm was in Canada as High Commissioner and Jill was looking after the house in his absence. Michael was also friendly with Malcolm, but there might have been trouble, or at least undesirable publicity, if he had moved in with Jill while the owner of the house was serving His Majesty as a High Commissioner.

Publicity threatened, in fact, when they flew to Nice for 'ten delirious days and nights' and stayed at the luxurious Hotel Negresco. In Michael's account:

> It seemed eerily empty. But we still thought we'd better order separate rooms . . . Diffidently, we made our excursions, first along the Negresco corridors and then along the beautiful French coast . . . Every resort was a desert; we were among the very first English post-war visitors . . . We did not hear a single English voice or suffer a single investigative intrusion.[11]

However, a vigilant newspaper stringer caught sight of the MP and his attractive companion, and when Jill got home she found reporters clustered at the front door. She managed to push her way into the house and phoned Michael for advice. 'Just tell them', he instructed her, 'that next week's *Tribune* will carry a supplement on the private lives of their proprietors.' Jill did so, and in a few minutes the street reverted to its normal tranquillity.

She faced a more alarming problem when she found herself pregnant. Abortion in those days was illegal and expensive, but there were also strong arguments against keeping the child. She was afraid that Michael might think that she was trapping him into a permanent relationship or marriage; the career of a new MP, with a small majority and a Methodist tradition in the constituency, could well be injured; and Jill's own career – she was planning another film – would be at least interrupted. Michael assured her that he loved her, he would go on loving her in any case, and the decision was hers. She had the abortion, but she might have decided otherwise if she had been able to foresee the future. A few years later, Michael and Jill were married and were eager to have children, but Jill never became pregnant again.

Jill was a convinced feminist and directed a film, commissioned by the Equal Pay Campaign, which forcefully put the case for women's rights.[12] In the 1940s, masculine predominance prevailed with little effective challenge in the film industry – 'cameramen' were automatically of the male gender – in most of the professions and in the political world (there were twenty-four women MPs). The Labour government was stalling on demands for equal pay, which was introduced in the Civil Service only in 1956 and became the law of the land – thanks to Barbara Castle as Secretary for Employment – only in 1970. Michael was a firm believer in women's rights as a matter of principle and as an essential element in his socialism, but Jill found that he had not altogether overcome the assumptions that had been taken for granted in the Foot family in his boyhood. To this day, friends are sometimes amused and sometimes embarrassed by his habit of addressing Jill as 'my child'. However, life with Jill made him better prepared than most men for the new surge of feminism in the 1970s, or at least he recognised his limitations. In a welcoming review of Kate Millett's *Sexual Politics*, he wrote:

Countless females, I suppose, will read these pages with rising excitement and every male will feel a touch of the lash. I write, it should be explained, as a strong theoretical feminist, but also – my wife most properly and charmingly insists – as an incorrigible patriarchist in practice who has never had the foggiest idea what equality truly means.[13]

In 1946, Jill wrote and directed a film called *Blue Scar*. Her subject was the mining industry; the blue scar is the mark that thousands of miners carry somewhere on their bodies as the indelible aftermath of an accident. She lived for several months in Abergwynfy, a mining village in the Welsh valleys, and made herself at home in the community. Both she and Michael now had bonds of sympathy with South Wales – bonds that became stronger in future years.

Michael's father, Isaac Foot, was living through what should have been the happiest year of his life. After long service as a Plymouth councillor, he was Lord Mayor of his native city, with a term of office from November 1945 to November 1946. Wearing his ceremonial robes, he visited every school in Plymouth and treated the children to a rendering of his 1940 broadcast on Drake's drum. The 400th anniversary of Drake's birth came round in 1946 and was the theme of two weeks of celebrations. In this year, too, Isaac made a carefully researched comparative study of the lives of his two heroes, Cromwell and Lincoln, which was delivered as a lecture and then printed as a pamphlet. But this year of achievement was also a year of deep sorrow. On 17 May 1946, Eva Foot died.

She was due to have an operation which did not appear to be very serious, and which was performed at a nursing-home in East Grinstead. Isaac accompanied her there and started his journey home. He was intercepted at Reading station by a message which advised him to return to East Grinstead. By the time he got there, she was dead. They had been married for forty-four years and had become as mutually dependent as any couple can be; she had shared his unshakeable faith in Liberalism and Methodism, rejoiced in his successes and sustained him in his defeats; they had seen seven children grow up. Michael had loved his strong-minded mother deeply, despite their disagreements, and he too felt her death as a grievous loss.

3

The year 1946 brought Michael Foot and his friends increasingly into conflict with Bevin – not, however, over major issues of foreign policy so much as over the problem of Palestine. The demand for a national home for the Jews had been supported by Labour Party conferences ten times since 1917, most recently at the pre-election conference in 1945. Moreover, the best-known leaders of the Zionist movement were also socialists. They were, as Michael put it, 'men we know well, men who have come to Socialist conferences and are colleagues of ours'.[14]

The generally accepted view in the Labour left was that the British mandate should be wound up and Palestine should be partitioned between Jews and Arabs. This would enable the survivors of the holocaust, who were living in comfortless camps in Germany and Austria, to go to Palestine, where the Jewish community was of course eager to receive them. Bevin, however, was firmly opposed to partition and to the concept of a Jewish state, and was trying to keep the mandate alive as long as possible. He sought to check unauthorised Jewish immigration, which the Zionists were organising by means of an 'underground railroad'. British troops had orders to disarm and suppress illegal organisations, a term which covered not only Irgun Zvai Leumi and Lehi, already opposing British rule by force of arms, but also the Haganah, the defence force of the Jewish community. 'If I were a Jew in Palestine,' Michael declared in the House of Commons, 'I should certainly be a member of the Haganah.'

These Bevin policies were unpopular not only in his own party but also in the US, especially in the Democratic Party. Hence, in November 1945 he agreed to set up a commission of inquiry into Palestine with six British and six American members. One of the British members was Dick Crossman, described by an American who knew him as 'the brainiest of the lot, the most sophisticated, the most intelligent'.[15] He was not selected by Bevin because of these qualities, but because he regarded the idea of a Jewish national home as 'a deadend out of which Britain must be extricated'.[16] But, with his characteristic facility for changing his mind, he came round to favouring the Zionist programme after talks with his American colleagues in Washington. Bevin, infuriated, asked him whether he had been circumcised (the Foreign Secretary was presumably unaware that this was a Moslem as well as a Jewish custom).

After taking evidence from Jews and Arabs in Jerusalem, the commission drew up its report in April 1946. Crossman pressed the other members to agree to a unanimous report because Bevin had promised to implement any unanimous recommendations. As the members had reached no agreement on the future of Palestine, they could recommend only a rather vague 'condominium' structure under continued British supervision. However, they also recommended the admission in 1946 of 100,000 Jews 'who have been the victims of Nazi and Fascist oppression'. This, inevitably, was the recommendation that captured the headlines. It was at once accepted by President Truman, but rejected by Attlee and Bevin. Now it was Crossman who was furious – 'it was Ernie who had double-crossed me', he wrote in his diary. His conclusion was that Bevin had yielded to pressure from Arabs, from his Foreign Office advisers and from the military hierarchy. This charge was forcefully expounded in a pamphlet called *A Palestine Munich?*, signed by Crossman and Michael Foot, actually written mainly by Arthur Koestler, and published by Gollancz.

Bevin was now the public enemy of Jews throughout the world, especially in America. Whether or not he was personally anti-Semitic is still an open question – Michael thinks that he was not – but he had only himself to blame if he gave that impression. The Americans, he said, had urged the admission of Jews to Palestine because 'they don't want too many Jews in New York'.

On 29 June, raids were made on the Jewish Agency head office and on twenty-five kibbutzim, and 2,700 Jews were detained without trial. 'The Jewish leaders now arrested', *Tribune* reminded Attlee and Bevin, 'have shared that honour with the present Prime Minister of Eire and Pandit Nehru.' Michael predicted that, if the vicious spiral continued, 'we shall be engaged in a long, wretched and miserable war, a war that will leave a black and indelible stain on the record of this great government.'[17] Kimche, reporting from Jerusalem on 19 July, wrote: 'Everything is set for the explosion.' Three days after his article appeared, the Irgun blew up the King David Hotel, which was used as an administrative office, and killed ninety-one people. The next *Tribune* headline was, irresistibly: 'AFTER THE EXPLOSION'. The comment was: 'Repression in Palestine is as little a substitute for a constructive policy as it has been in India or Ireland.'

By the end of 1946, partition of Palestine was the policy favoured by four members of the Cabinet (Bevan, Dalton, Shinwell and Strachey); by the High Commissioner, General Cunningham, who reported that he had not enough troops to restore order; and by the United States. Yet it was still resisted by the Prime Minister and the Foreign Secretary.

A by-product of the conflict was a change in the editorship of *Tribune*. In December 1946, Kimche vanished from the office and was not seen for a week. Responding to an appeal from the Zionist underground, he had flown to Istanbul to negotiate the release of a ship held in the harbour with thousands of Jews aboard. The *Tribune* board, regardless of Zionist sympathies, took a stern view of the unauthorised disappearance of the editor. Kimche was dismissed; Michael Foot and Evelyn Anderson were listed in the paper as joint editors.

In this year of 1946, international relations were settling into the mould that remained rock-hard for the next forty years: the mould of the cold war, with America and the Western European nations opposed to the Soviet Union. Bevin told the Cabinet: 'The danger of Russia has become as great, and possibly even greater than, that of a revived Germany.'[18] The charge levelled against the Foreign Secretary by the left was that, just as he had faithfully supported Churchillian policies during the coalition – notably over Greece – he was still behaving as though the coalition had never come to an end. At the New Year, *Tribune* urged: 'The decisive political event of 1946 must be to disenthrall ourselves from the legacies of the coalition . . . At the election we shot the albatross . . . But how long are we to allow the dead bird to hang round our necks?'[19] Six months later, *Tribune* had to repeat: 'The spell of the coalition still operates . . . The campaign which the Soviet Union conducts against us is not a reason for abandoning our Socialist objectives.'[20]

By that time, Churchill had made the speech which is remembered as the initiation, or at least the open declaration, of the cold war. Speaking on 5 March at Fulton, Missouri, with Truman by his side, he denounced the 'iron curtain' and the oppression fastened on Eastern Europe, and called for a firm Anglo-American alliance buttressed by the possession of the atomic bomb. Attlee and Bevin, as subsequently published papers have shown, agreed with the Fulton speech – off the record. But *Tribune*, under the headline 'NO, MR CHURCHILL!', declared: 'The people of Britain will not sell out to American capitalism'; and Michael warned that a Western military alliance would be 'the most certain and shortest way to create the gulf across which the next war will be fought.'[21]

A possible flashpoint in the developing conflict was Iran (then generally called Persia). The Foreign Office ranked that country as crucially important, both because it contained a major oilfield owned by a British company and because it stood on the route between the Mediterranean and the Asian territories of the Empire. During the war, the pro-Nazi Shah was put under arrest and deported and an Allied occupation was enforced, with a Soviet zone in the north and a British zone in the south. The occupation was due to end on 2 March 1946. The British withdrew ahead of time, but the Russians remained firmly established in Azerbaijan, Persia's northernmost province (ethnically related to a neighbouring Soviet republic with the same name). On the eve of a Foreign Ministers' meeting in December 1945, the formation of an autonomous government in Persian Azerbaijan was announced. It was dominated by the Tudeh Party, which was also active in the rest of Persia, and fears arose that the whole country might come under the control of Tudeh – that is, effectively, of Soviet Russia.

Bevin showed his concern but moved cautiously. He asked two MPs to go on a fact-finding mission. One was Michael Foot; the other was a Tory who had been a wartime brigadier, Anthony Head. The bipartisan mission looked suspiciously like a coalition legacy, but Michael accepted the task and the two men worked happily together. Head, in fact, was a quite moderate Tory and his outlook was influenced by his wife, who was a socialist and an admirer of Aneurin Bevan.

Arriving in Teheran, the visitors met the Prime Minister, Ghavam Sultaneh, who told them: 'Our frontiers are indefensible. Our army is weak. Our people are poor. But we have one secret weapon: we are very good double-crossers.'[22] Ghavam, evidently, was keeping the Russians at bay through profuse expressions of friendship. The first message for Bevin was not to assume that Ghavam was a Soviet stooge. Foot and Head moved on to Azerbaijan. Bevin wanted them to test whether foreigners could gain entry and, if so, to see whether the province really was full of Soviet soldiers. The two Englishmen made the journey without any trouble, stayed in an empty luxury hotel, observed that the coast of the Caspian Sea was as beautiful as the French Riviera, were politely received by Tudeh leaders and saw no Soviet uniforms; apparently the Russian soldiers were confined to barracks for the duration of the British visit.

Back home, the MPs reported to Bevin, and Michael emphasised his impression that Tudeh was a political force with considerable popular support and should not be dismissed as a mere Soviet fifth column. Bevin didn't seem to be listening; Michael saw that he already knew as much as he wanted to know, from his officials and from his hunches. In his *Daily Herald* column, Michael stressed the appalling poverty which he had observed in Teheran, and explained: 'The root of much that has happened in Persia lies deep in the past, in the fear of Russia for her security, in the pitiable social backwardness of the Persians, in the failure of British diplomacy to display its interest in reform, in the support given by past British governments to a decadent feudalism.'[23]

At the same time, he made it clear that the Soviet Union had 'quite deliberately and shamelessly' broken the agreement on military withdrawal. To the general surprise, the Soviet troops were withdrawn in May and the potential crisis simmered down. However, Michael was now convinced that Stalin was aiming to achieve political domination of other nations – Persia or Poland, perhaps even France or Italy – wherever it was a feasible goal and by any available means of pressure; and that this pressure would have to be resisted if democracy or democratic socialism were to have a chance of survival.

These views were not acceptable to everyone on the left. One Labour MP, Will Cove, wrote to *Tribune* to say that he found its political evolution 'deeply disturbing' and to complain of its 'jaundiced prejudice against Russia'.[24] Those who shared Cove's attitude were still further disturbed later in 1946 when Michael began, reluctantly but definitely, to suggest that the defence of democracy might require the aid of a distinctly anti-socialist world power – the USA. A *Tribune* leader on 25 October contained a sentence that could not have appeared a year earlier: 'Faced with continued hostility on the part of Soviet Russia, it is the most natural thing in the world that this country should lean on friendship with America.' For some, that was very far from natural and was indeed a shocking proposition.

There was not much sign, it had to be admitted, of a socialist foreign policy. Besides, the military commitments that Britain was shouldering were slowing down demobilisation, absorbing heavy expenditure and diverting resources from social needs. Looking back on 1946 when he wrote his autobiography, Ian Mikardo told younger readers: 'It's difficult now to recapture the deep disappointment and disillusion which afflicted many of the new young Members as we saw our government moving rapidly away from the Party's Socialist philosophy and principles.'[25]

These new young MPs often gathered round a large table in the smoking-room of the House to discuss events and exchange opinions. On 29 October, twenty-one of them signed a letter to be sent, privately and without publicity, to Attlee. Among the names were those of Michael Foot, Dick Crossman, Jennie Lee and Donald Bruce. As Jennie was Nye Bevan's wife and Bruce was his PPS (parliamentary private secretary), the move could scarcely have been made without his knowledge. The letter repeated the third-force doctrine of a 'genuine middle way' between America and Russia, suggested that democratic socialism in Britain would 'encourage the Soviet Union in extending political and personal liberties', and warned the government against 'being infected by the anti-Red virus which is cultivated in the United States'. It ended: 'Believing that the future of Britain and of humanity is at stake in these matters, we cannot continue to remain silent and inactive.'

Attlee made no response beyond a routine acknowledgement, so the group tabled an amendment to the government motion to be debated in the new session of Parliament. Signed by fifty-seven MPs, it urged the government 'to affirm the utmost encouragement to and collaboration with all nations striving to secure full Socialist planning and control of the world's resources, and thus provide a democratic and Socialist alternative to an otherwise inevitable conflict between American capitalism and Soviet Communism'. At a party meeting ahead of the debate, Herbert Morrison demanded the withdrawal of the amendment. The sponsors decided to keep it on the order paper but promised not to press it to a vote. Bevin, who was in Washington, wired to Attlee that the government should insist on a vote even if the rebels did not: 'The element of treachery in it ought to be brought to a head.' There were no votes for the amendment but probably, after allowing for absences, about 130 deliberate abstentions. It was a clear sign of discontent on the back benches.

As a salaried member of the staff of the *Daily Herald*, writing a regular column and occasional leading articles, and as an (unpaid) editor of *Tribune*, Michael was still very much a working journalist. In his column, he called attention to two dangers. One was the unfair reporting and misrepresentation of Labour policies in the Tory press, which went beyond acceptable partisanship. The other was the growth of chain ownership, which meant that the only local paper in a provincial city – Plymouth was an example – was owned by a centralised management. 'London ownership has invaded the provinces,' Michael wrote, 'and there is a steady growth of the syndicated leading article, the foulest abortion in journalism.'[26] On both these issues, his target was most often Lord Kemsley, owner of the *Sunday Times*, the tabloid *Daily Graphic* and a nation-wide chain of local afternoon papers. Examples of dishonest journalism criticised by Michael in the *Herald* or in *Tribune* were sometimes taken from the Beaverbrook or Rothermere papers, but generally from the Kemsley press, and Kemsley was also the outstanding monopolist.

The National Union of Journalists proposed that a Royal Commission should be set up to examine the state of the press. The press lords vehemently denounced the idea as an entering wedge for control of the press on Nazi or Communist lines, but the government, after some hesitation, gave its support. Michael seconded the motion to set up the Royal Commission when it was debated on 29 October 1946. He attacked the trend to monopoly, giving an outstanding example: 'No one can really imagine it is by the democratic choice of the people of South Wales that they read the *Western Mail*' – a Kemsley paper. A democratic government had a right to intervene, he asserted, 'as the protector of freedom and the enemy of monopoly'.

He went on to say that there had been a serious decline in the quality of journalism, ascribing it to 'the decline in the power of the editor and the encroachment of the authority of the newspaper proprietor'. The trouble was that 'megalomania is an occupational disease among proprietors'. He did not name the proprietors he had in mind, nor the latter-day editors whom he described as 'stooges, cyphers and sycophants', but the speech cannot have made him popular in managerial circles.

The Royal Commission held hearings over the ensuing two years. Michael gave evidence on 12 November and 18 December 1947. He attacked the Kemsley chain as 'the biggest and the most disgracefully conducted', guilty of the most frequent and flagrant exercises in misrepresentation. Naturally, he was asked about his own experience as an editor. He gave this account:

> I had a tacit agreement that I didn't publish anything that I knew the proprietor would be opposed to publishing, and he never required me to publish anything I was opposed to publishing, and on the whole it worked, but I left because the strains became too great . . . I got a series of directives all the time . . . The arguments became so frequent that it was impossible.

He gave details, too, of the black-list of people who were never to be mentioned in the Beaverbrook papers, including Paul Robeson, Noël

Coward and Sir Thomas Beecham. Few people outside Fleet Street had realised that such black-lists existed. These disclosures, on top of the attacks on Beaverbrook that Michael had made in the 1945 election campaign, seemed to rule out any possibility of a renewal of friendship between the two men. Michael wrote later: 'My association with the old man became bruised almost beyond recognition or repair.'[27] The significant qualifying word, however, was 'almost'.

4

The Keep Left Group of Labour MPs, growing out of the smoking-room gatherings, came into existence in the early weeks of 1947. Ian Mikardo, overcoming some disagreement, suggested regular meetings with an agenda and minutes; he normally took the chair and the minutes were written up and circulated to members by his efficient young secretary, Jo Richardson. The Group now met away from the House of Commons, either in someone's home or in the upper room of a pub. At this period, the party leadership did not frown on the formation of what was later called 'a party within a party'. However, membership of the group was by invitation and was kept deliberately small. One reason – and this had something to do with the tolerance shown by Attlee and Morrison – was that it was thus possible to exclude MPs who could be regarded as Communist fellow-travellers.

There were three Labour MPs – John Platts-Mills, Leslie Solley and Lester Hutchinson – who, whether or not they actually held CP cards, consistently followed the Communist political line. In a slightly different category was D. N. Pritt, who had been expelled from the Labour Party in 1940 and never readmitted; he had been triumphantly returned as Independent MP for Hammersmith in 1945. There were several others who were prepared to write articles for the *Daily Worker*, attend Communist-sponsored peace conferences or tour East European countries as honoured guests. A unique position belonged to Konni Zilliacus (always addressed as Zilly, even by his wife). A cosmopolitan figure and a champion linguist, he had improbably entered the Commons as MP for Gateshead. Between the wars, he had worked in the Secretariat of the League of Nations, acquired a vast stock of diplomatic knowledge, and denounced appeasement (writing under a pseudonym) in *Tribune* articles and Left Book Club books. One of his books, *The Mirror of the Past* – written under his own name in 1944 – had appeared with a laudatory preface by Michael Foot.

Zilly was never a Communist (though Bevin regarded him as one) but he was a socialist who did not accept Michael's distinction between democratic socialism and Communism. He argued that British Labour should be on the side of the workers and peasants of Europe and of the countries where, as he saw it, they were in power. Dictatorial tendencies in these countries, he maintained, were the fault of hostility from the West and would melt away if that hostility was relaxed. Michael reproached him for his reluctance to protest when socialists in Eastern Europe were victimised or imprisoned, since such protests, coming from a friend, might have had some influence. The editors of both *Tribune* and the *New Statesman* gave up accepting Zilly's articles, which were prolix in the extreme and always reiterated what he had said before. Orwell accused him of being either an undercover Communist or, at best, 'reliably sympathetic' to the Communists in all circumstances.[28] Zilly denied the charge; through a long and bitter exchange of letters, Orwell refused to withdraw it. Later, when Zilly was facing expulsion from the Labour Party, Mikardo defended him and wrote: 'He forms his views quite independently of the Communists or anyone else and holds them with complete and selfless sincerity.'[29]

On the Palestine issue, *Tribune* kept up the attack. On 7 March, its verdict on Bevin was: 'tough and rough and wrong'. It saw a 'disastrous attempt to ignore the strength of Zionism and the needs of Jewish survivors after Hitler's massacre of millions'. Another article demanded of the government: 'Must you complete the bloodstained circle of revenge and terror and murder? . . . The end is always the same. The terrorists always lose the battle and their cause almost always wins.'[30] In August, a ship renamed the *Exodus*, carrying thousands of Jews who had embarked at Marseille, was boarded by the Royal Navy off the Palestinian beaches and forced to return. The French refused to accept the Jews unless they landed voluntarily, so – in a record heat-wave and in appalling sanitary conditions – the ship made its way to Hamburg, in the British zone of Germany. Amid a chorus of horror from world-wide Jewry and from American opinion, British troops forced the unhappy survivors back to the heartland of the holocaust. This was the breaking-point; the United Nations, with America and Russia in agreement, decided on partition and the admission of 150,000 Jews. Bevin, complaining that this was 'manifestly unjust to the Arabs', refused to implement the decision and announced that the British mandate would be wound up by May 1948. Under the headline 'BEVIN'S WATERLOO', *Tribune* lamented that there was 'no way out except inglorious withdrawal and admission of failure'.[31] Bevin was always the evil genius in the eyes of the left, while Attlee was regarded more favourably. It was Attlee who made the decision, overruling objections from Bevin, to order a rapid transition to independence for India, thus averting the kind of hopeless war that France fought in Vietnam.

The British economy was coming under severe strain. Freezing weather in February 1947 led to a breakdown in fuel supplies, power cuts, shivering homes, factories made idle by lack of materials and a suddenly zooming, though temporary, total of two million unemployed. It was unpredictable bad luck, but it revealed the underlying weaknesses. Overseas commitments had to be cut somewhere, and Attlee decided that Britain could no longer prop up the regime in Greece, which was facing full-scale civil war against Communist forces in the north of the country. Truman took up the burden, sending an American general to direct operations and lavish American supplies of weaponry. In a major speech, he enunciated what was called the Truman Doctrine, promising that the US would sustain any nation menaced by Communism.

The left MPs watched this intensification of the cold war with foreboding. They decided to set out their views in a pamphlet called *Keep Left* and entrusted the writing to Michael Foot, Dick Crossman and Ian Mikardo, who spent the Easter weekend at Crossman's country home near High Wycombe. As Mikardo recorded: 'We worked through the rest of Friday, all day Saturday and Sunday, non-stop through Sunday night, and on until we completed *Keep Left* by Monday tea-time.'[32] It was published by the *New Statesman*, of which Crossman was an assistant editor.

Read in the light of later conflicts in the Labour Party, *Keep Left* is notable for its studious moderation. A long section was devoted to praising the government's achievements, and the Communist analysis of the cold war was explicitly rejected. But *Keep Left*'s own analysis – written by Dick Crossman with, Mikardo remembers, 'considerable input from Michael' – rejected the idea that the Russians were planning for aggressive war and that the situation was a repeat of the 1930s. It urged: 'Let us get rid of the analogies between Stalin and Hitler . . . The Russians have every reason for many years to avoid war and concentrate on reconstruction at home.' It continued: 'By accepting the American lead in a world alliance against Russia, we shall merely ensure that every small people has to choose between the bleak alternatives of anti-Communism and Communism.' In fact, the policy of the left was still that of the third force. 'The security of each and of all of us depends on preventing the division of Europe into exclusive spheres of influence . . . The goal we should work for is a federation which binds together the nations now under Eastern domination with the peoples of Western Europe.' The first step was to forge closer political and economic links with Britain's neighbours, particularly France.

The government's record in foreign policy, according to *Keep Left*, was mixed, but there was 'one disturbingly consistent note – a readiness to follow American strategic thinking and consequently to accept commitments, far beyond our economic strength, which may increase American security but certainly decrease our own'.

Mild though this criticism was, it angered Bevin. What he wanted was unquestioning loyalty, and he demanded it when the party conference met at Whitsun. In the foreign policy debate, he had to listen to critical speeches from Crossman, Mikardo and Zilliacus. He replied with a hammer-blow speech. He had neither forgotten nor forgiven the 'treachery' of the critical amendment to the address in November 1946, which had unfortunately occurred while he was in Washington in a quest for economic aid. Now he thundered: 'On the very day I was trying to get the agreement with the Americans to prevent the bread ration from going down – on that very day I was stabbed in the back.' This recurrent metaphor cast a revealing light on Bevin's obsession with dissent from the left, especially 'left intellectuals'. At the moment of the election triumph of 1945, he growled to Kingsley Martin: 'I give you about three weeks before you stab us all in the back'.[33]

Bevin won an ovation at the conference and his position was clearly unchallengeable, but Michael was not alone in observing that he achieved this by force of personality and not by reasoned argument. In a signed *Tribune* article headed 'THE UNANSWERED QUESTIONS', Michael gave his own version of events: 'At a vital moment St. George is stabbed in the back. But he still kills the Dragon . . . What has happened to the maiden is more obscure.' The prospect was: 'a long vista of oratorical victories for the Foreign Secretary at home and moral and material defeats for British Socialism abroad'.[34]

However, on the day when Bevin may or may not have read this article, he was excited by reports of a speech made by General George Marshall, the US Secretary of State. Marshall's theme was a revival of the economies of European nations, nourished by American assistance. He made no concrete proposals, but Bevin seized on one sentence in the speech, 'The initiative, I think, must come from Europe,' and hastened to Paris to urge French participation in such an initiative. Fourteen nations were invited to a conference which met in Paris on 12 July. It was a success, and led to the foundation of the Organisation for European Economic Co-operation, which proved to be the driving force in the building of a prosperous (western) Europe in succeeding years. The Americans weighed in with a promise of four billion dollars for the 1947–8 period and the appointment of Paul G. Hoffman as head of their European Recovery Program, which was in effect an American aid mission based in Paris and working closely with the OEEC.

To avoid charges that the Marshall Plan was simply part of the cold war and the strengthening of an anti-Communist bloc, invitations to the Paris conference were addressed to the Soviet Union and the nations of Eastern Europe. But Jefferson Caffery, the US ambassador in Paris, reported to Washington: 'The British feel that Russian participation would tend greatly to complicate things and that it might be best if the Russians refused the invitation.'[35] Molotov, caught on the hop, came to the conference but soon walked out, denouncing the scheme as an infringement of national sovereignty. The Soviet Union and the nations under its control did not join the OEEC – an outcome which, Bevin told Caffery, he had 'anticipated and even wished for'.

The Labour left, in general, welcomed the Marshall Plan and especially the creation of the OEEC, which presaged the tightening of European links urged in *Keep Left*. However, *Tribune* expressed acute regret over the Russian refusal to participate: 'A final and irrevocable division of Europe would be the greatest calamity for all its people.'[36] A clearly predictable calamity was an irrevocable division of Germany, since the economy of the Western zones would be managed and rebuilt in the OEEC framework while the Soviet zone faced an entirely different future. At the end of the year, when another and final meeting of Foreign Ministers broke down, *Tribune* concluded: 'The Western powers will now have to go full speed ahead with the task of restoring West Germany.'[37]

The material benefits of the Marshall Plan were undeniable, but all the projects financed or aided by it had to be approved by Hoffman's office, and those which had a socialist coloration were likely to be regarded as unsound. Hoffman explained: 'What they do with their economy is their business, and what we do with our dollars is our business, and if they start playing ducks and drakes with their economy to such a point that they cannot recover and our investment is not worth while, we are going to hold up the investment.'[38] The Soviet Union, certainly, could not welcome a revival of Europe's most advanced nations – including West Germany – on capitalist lines, and the autumn of 1947 saw a sharp stepping up of Russian hostility to the West. The Communist Information Bureau, or Cominform, was created as a successor to the Comintern; its membership covered the ruling parties of Eastern Europe and also the strong Communist parties of France and Italy. An initial statement made a ferocious attack on American imperialism and had special words of condemnation for 'the treacherous policy of the right-wing Socialists like Attlee and Bevin . . . the faithful accomplices of the imperialists'. On both sides of the developing cold war, 'imperialism' was a term of abuse. In a broadcast on 3 January 1948, Attlee defined Communism as 'a new form of imperialism'. Following up in a *Daily Herald* article, he wrote that the Communists were 'like those other totalitarian fanatics, the Hitlerites'. His conclusion was: 'This great fight is on and we are all enlisted in it.'[39] Whoever was or was not enlisted, there was no doubt that the fight was on.

5

By 1948, Michael was more convinced than ever of the view he had formed on his visit to Iran: that the Soviet Union was bent on imposing Communist domination on vulnerable nations. The further development in his thinking was that, although the Russians probably did not want a full-scale war, their pressure would lead to war unless it was resisted. Under the front-page headline 'WILL THERE BE WAR?', *Tribune* warned on 26 March 1948: 'No other issue counts beside the struggle to save the nations from a third world war . . . That issue appears now more stark and challenging than at any time since the armistice with Nazi Germany was signed.' The conclusion was that the Western nations 'should state their will to resist as emphatically as possible'.

This was not, of course, the doctrine presented in *Keep Left* a year earlier, and was greeted with dismay by some of those associated with *Tribune*. Frederic Mullally remembers the office secretaries, Sally and Dotty, asking tearfully: 'What's happened to *Tribune*?'[40] Indeed, *Tribune* admitted:

> A part of the Movement remains unconvinced that the overwhelming responsibility for the breakdown of Great-Power relations rests with the Russians. Some are still gulled by the monstrous delusion that the Russians are the friends, not the enemies, of democratic Socialism . . . If they prefer the world view of the Communist Party, let them clear out and no longer seek cover in our ranks.[41]

The harshness of this concluding sentence was liable, no doubt, to make Sally and Dotty yet more unhappy. Michael had come to treat those whom he regarded as 'gulled' – notably Zilliacus – with ruthless contempt. At this time, Zilly directly challenged *Tribune* to print an article stating his views. It appeared on 12 March with an editorial note: 'We are glad to afford him a facility for criticising the policy of the government – a facility which is denied to Socialists in all the countries of eastern Europe.'

Personal influences, as well as the course of events, had steered Michael toward this intense hostility to Communism and 'softness' on Communism. Arthur Koestler was always ready with shocking inside stories drawn from his Communist past and was nurturing the project of a book of essays by distinguished ex-Communists. (Edited by Dick Crossman, and entitled *The God That Failed*, it appeared in January 1950.) More directly, Michael was in daily contact with Evelyn Anderson, the other joint editor of *Tribune*. She had come to Britain from Nazi Germany in pre-war days, and her formative memory was of the part played by German Communists in easing Hitler's path to power by venomous attacks on the Social Democrats. Now, she visited East Germany as a reporter and witnessed the destruction of an independent Social Democracy under Soviet rule. Michael had his own memories of Communist untrustworthiness, notably the takeover of *Tribune* in 1938 and the opposition to the 'imperialist war' in 1939–41.

The crucial change in his thinking was that he no longer believed, as he had in the *Keep Left* period, that Communism could be held at bay simply by the shining example of a successful democratic society. The event that forced him to renounce this comfortable belief was the Czech coup (as it was at once called) in February 1948. The non-Communist ministers in Czechoslovakia's coalition government, faced with a Communist demand for control of the vital Ministry of the Interior, resigned, hoping to bring about the formation of a new government from which Communists would be excluded. They miscalculated; the Communists mobilised armies of factory workers and kept up intense pressure on the ailing President Beneš. The new government that emerged from the crisis gave the Communists a monopoly of power. Unlike Hungary and Romania, where a similar monopoly was being enforced, Czechoslovakia had a democratic, not a fascist or reactionary, record and had been an ally, not an enemy, of the Soviet Union in the war.

In the week of the coup, *Tribune* declared:

Democracy in Czechoslovakia is being murdered by the same brutal methods employed in other lands . . . If they are finally resolved to stamp out all opinions and political activities except those of their own partisans . . . then the result in the end will be war . . . Let them pause before they persist in such a course of folly for themselves and crime against all mankind.

The leading article a week later stated: 'Communist deeds in Prague . . . have confronted us with one of the great Rubicons of history . . . The unavoidable deduction is that all which applies in Czechoslovakia applies equally in Britain.'

The Czech coup produced swift and strong reactions in Washington and London. Marshall telegraphed to Bevin on 12 March: 'We are prepared to proceed at once in joint discussions on the establishment of an Atlantic security system.' The outcome of the discussions was the formation, a year later, of the North Atlantic Treaty Organisation (NATO).

In this dangerous spring of 1948, the most likely flashpoint was Berlin. As part of the return to economic stability, two currencies had been introduced in Germany: the mark in the Soviet zone and the Deutsche mark in the Western zones. The Russians demanded the use of the mark in Berlin; the Western powers refused, and introduced the Deutsche mark in their occupation sectors of the city. In March, the Soviet authorities began to close the road, rail and canal routes between West Germany and Berlin, on the pretext of carrying out repairs. It was soon clear that this was a blockade. Truman and Attlee were prepared to meet the challenge by a confrontation, although less ferociously than Churchill, whose attitude was summarised in a report by the US ambassador in London, Lewis Douglas:

> He believes that now is the time, promptly, to tell the Soviets that if they do not retire from Berlin and abandon East Germany, with-drawing to the Polish frontier, we will raze their cities. It is further his view that we cannot appease, conciliate or provoke the Soviets; that the only vocabulary they understand is the vocabulary of force; and that if, therefore, we took this position, they would yield.[42]

While the antagonists were squaring up in Germany, a political trial of strength was approaching in Italy, where an election was due on 18 April. The three major parties were the Christian Democrats, the Socialist Party and the Communist Party. In the first post-war election, in 1946, the parties of the left had secured 39 per cent of the votes, while the Christian Democrats won power with a narrow majority. This time, the Socialists and Communists made an electoral pact and offered the voters a joint list of candidates. A minority of Socialists broke away to form a Democratic

Socialist Party, in which a leading figure was Ignazio Silone. He was a brilliant novelist, an ex-Communist and contributor to *The God That Failed*, and one of Michael's heroes.

Although the Labour Party was linked with the Italian Socialist Party in the Socialist International, the Labour leaders gave their support to Silone's party. They did not say explicitly that a Christian Democrat victory would be preferable to a success for the Socialist–Communist coalition, but Michael, as usual, was ready to bite the bullet. A *Tribune* article explained that, while a victory for clerical reactionaries was a depressing prospect, the alternative could only be 'the extinction of democracy by the same methods recently employed in Czecho-slovakia'.[43]

This view was not universally accepted in the Labour left. Two days before the Italian polling-day, thirty-seven MPs signed a telegram to Pietro Nenni, leader of the Socialist Party, which read: 'Greetings to our Italian Socialist comrades and warm hope for your triumph in the election.' The message can have had little impact on the voters, who gave the Christian Democrats a comfortable majority, but Herbert Morrison accused the offending MPs of contravening Labour Party policy. *Tribune*, too, charged that the telegram was designed 'to give the impression that large sections of British Labour favoured what would in effect have been a Communist victory' and stigmatised 'an act of sabotage against the declared policy of the Party'.[44]

Faced with the threat of expulsion, some of the MPs recanted at once and others, after two weeks of intricate manoeuvring, conceded that 'expression of disagreement be confined within the limits set by the party constitution'. *Tribune* did not advocate expulsion, but commented that some people would be behaving suitably if they transferred their membership from the Labour Party to the Communist Party. In the end, only John Platts-Mills was expelled; he was the unlucky man who had actually taken the telegram to the post office.

After this storm in a very British teacup, serious attention reverted to Berlin. By June, the blockade was total. Bevin declared: 'We cannot abandon those stout-hearted Berlin democrats who are refusing to bow to Soviet pressure.'[45] *Tribune*, scouting the idea of a retreat from Berlin in exchange for concessions elsewhere, wrote that this would be 'an unforgivable betrayal of many thousands of Berlin's Socialists and democrats who have stoutly resisted all acts of intimidation, trusting that we shall not abandon them to their fate'.[46]

Berlin had stocks of food and fuel sufficient for only five or six weeks. As there were airfields in the Western sectors, the decision was made to extend these supplies by a continuous airlift. However, technical advisers warned that this could not conceivably meet the needs of a population of two million, certainly not when winter came. General Lucius Clay, the US High Commissioner in Germany, said that he was willing to try the airlift but would prefer sending a convoy along the Autobahn with an armed escort, defying the Russians to stop it if they dared. When this hazardous project was discussed, it had an unexpected supporter in London – Aneurin Bevan. As Michael recorded: 'This was the alternative Bevan preferred and argued for powerfully in the Cabinet. He was convinced that the Russians were as war-weary as everyone else and, once their challenge was rebuffed, would take no action which risked war.'[47] Presumably after some telepathic communication, *Tribune* agreed. The leading article on 9 July rejected three possible policies – to allow Berlin to sink into chaos and starvation, to evacuate two million people or to give in to Russian demands – and concluded that the only remaining choice was to 'drive a land passage through the Russian zone against Russian resistance and if necessary by force of arms'. Fortunately, the airlift was more successful than anyone had expected and equipped the city to withstand the blockade indefinitely; the Russians called it off in March 1949.

It was Dick Crossman, with his customary embarrassing candour, who drew the conclusions. A *Tribune* reader inquired 'why the Keep Left group faded out', and Dick was ready to explain. 'Most of our proposals are now Government policy . . . The Harvard speech, the Marshall Plan, and the Russian refusal to co-operate in it . . . completely outdated our proposals for an independent Third Force between Russia and America . . . There is now no difference of principle between the Foreign Secretary and those of us who were criticising him.'[48]

In the politics of the Labour Party, the cold war had done its work.

6

The North Atlantic Treaty was signed in Washington on 4 April 1949. Presenting it to the House of Commons, Bevin said: 'The real purpose of this pact is to act as a deterrent. Its object is to make aggression appear too risky to those who are making their calculations.'[49] *Tribune* concurred: 'It enhances the security of those who are sheltered beneath the pact. It is therefore a pact for peace.'[50]

The lack of enthusiasm in the Labour Party could not be disguised. While only five Labour MPs voted against British membership of NATO, 112 abstained. One of these was Ian Mikardo, who emphasised his attitude by resigning from the editorial board of *Tribune*. The episode did not injure the close personal friendship between Mik (as he was generally called) and Michael, but it was a serious political divergence.

The argument centred on *Tribune*'s view that, despite the ending of the Berlin blockade and the prospect of another Foreign Ministers' meeting, there could be no valid agreements between the West and the Soviet Union. In the words of a *Tribune* leader: 'If an agreement to disagree means a general undertaking that both sides would refrain from interference in defined areas of the other, it should be obvious that the Soviet Government cannot genuinely give any assurance of this nature.'[51] Mikardo, in an article headed 'WHY I DISAGREE', declared that this was 'painfully, pathetically, dangerously wrong'. The attitude that 'whatever the Russians say or do, we mustn't believe them and mustn't trust them' could, Mik wrote, 'only increase their intransigence'. Michael replied: 'Would Stalin have left the challenge undelivered altogether if Britain had pursued a more Socialist policy or the Third Force policy to which Mikardo refers? . . . Mikardo may believe it, but I don't.'[52]

These arguments among friends did not harm Michael's popularity with the Labour rank and file. Standing for the constituency section of the NEC, he was a near runner-up in 1948 and an easy winner in 1949, coming second only to Nye Bevan. One decision that came before the NEC was the expulsion of Zilliacus, who had survived the 'Nenni telegram' episode but was in trouble for speaking at a (patently Communist-controlled) peace congress in Paris. Michael, with Laski and Shinwell, voted against the expulsion, but Zilly was duly cast into the outer darkness.

For a couple of years, Michael and Jill had been openly living together, or as openly as anyone did at a time when such liaisons were not mentioned in the newspapers. They had a short lease of a house at 33 Rosslyn Hill, Hampstead, which was the property of the Ecclesiastical Commissioners. Neither he nor she attached any importance to the sacrament of marriage, but in 1949 they decided to become husband and wife, partly to avoid trouble with the landlords and partly to give pleasure to Michael's father. Connie Ernst, now Connie Bessie, wrote from New York: 'Your wonderful letter arrived last week and it has taken me all this time to make sure I wasn't misled by the famous scrawl. We think it said you were going to be married, we know her name is Jill Craigie, and we couldn't miss the fact that you were in love. Dear Mike, how wonderful!'

On 21 October 1949, Michael and Jill walked the short distance to the registry office in Hampstead Town Hall. Isaac Foot came from Cornwall for the occasion, but did not join in the ensuing drinking session with Michael's old friends, Frank Owen and Paul Reilly. Jill wrote to thank the old man for being present – 'it looked better for Michael', she said – and wrote a little later to tell him that she would be making a broadcast in the Light Programme. She hoped he would listen 'if no other member of the Foot family is monopolising the Home or Third programme, and if there is no Mozart symphony, football commentary or other distraction'. Isaac Foot must have replied with a good letter, which regrettably has not survived. On 20 November 1949 he received a telegram reading: 'A CLASSIC LETTER. HAZLITT APPLAUDS. SWIFT REJOICES. EVEN THE MARTYRED MARAT FINDS COMFORT FOR HIS WOUNDS. MICHAEL AND JILL.'

A few months later, Michael and Jill were repaying the compliment by travelling to Callington for Isaac's wedding. He was marrying a lady called Kitty Taylor (originally Kitty Dawe) who was the widow of a Mr Taylor of Liskeard. He had proposed to her, just as he had proposed fifty years earlier to Eva, practically as soon as he met her. Jill suggested that they might wait until they knew each other a little better, to which Isaac replied: 'I can't wait. I'm only flesh and blood.' He was just seventy years old and, clearly, in vigorous good health. Kitty did not have Eva's forceful character, nor did she share Isaac's intellectual interests – she appears to have been a fairly ordinary woman – but she was devoted to him and gave him real happiness in the final decade of his life.

Among Jill's other talents, she had the gift of delighting and charming men of the older generation. Another old man with whom she got on famously from the day of their first meeting was Lord Beaverbrook. Unexpectedly, despite the hard words that had been spoken and written, Michael and his former boss were now reconciled. Michael had been invited to attend a dinner at the Savoy Hotel to celebrate Beaverbrook's seventieth birthday. It was perhaps risky to go, but churlish to refuse. The man who presided, an Express executive, called on Michael to speak. Having prepared nothing, Michael resorted to a trick learned from his father and recited some lines from *Paradise Lost*:

> Deep on his front engraven
> Deliberation sat, and public care;
> And princely counsel in his face yet shone,
> Majestic, though in ruin; sage he stood
> With Atlantean shoulders, fit to bear
> The weight of mightiest monarchies.

The trick was the revelation that the subject of this respectful, even admiring, portrait was Beelzebub. Everyone present roared with laughter, including Beaverbrook, who was accustomed and even pleased to have a diabolical reputation. He realised that he had missed the company, the wit and the ingenuity of his surrogate son, and let Michael know it. Towards Christmas of 1948, Michael wrote expressing a hope that they could let bygones be bygones. Beaverbrook replied (evidently from his Jamaica residence) on 19 January, 1949:

> My dear Michael,
>   This is my thanks for your letter. The separation that has lasted so long has distressed me. The reunion will give me joy. When I get back to England, let us meet.
>   Yours ever,
>   Max

Soon, Michael was again a guest at Cherkley, accompanied by Jill. She was as dazzled, or in the non-sexual sense as readily seduced, by the old man as Michael had been ten years before, and he made her a favourite. Michael wrote later: 'Jill, my wife, knew how to deal with him from the very first meeting, how to awaken and sustain his curiosity, how to appreciate all the human sides of him which the outside world believed not to exist . . . Jill was one of the very few who knew best how to deal with him in every mood and extremity.'[53]

The reconciliation might have been imperilled when the Royal Commission on the Press reported in June 1949. The report, described by *Tribune* as 'a tepid and unimaginative document', made no worthwhile proposals except for the establishment of a Press Council to rebuke unfairness and misrepresentation, and *Tribune* rightly predicted that it would be useless if all its members were drawn from the press itself. The *Tribune* comment claimed, however, that the mere existence of the Commission had done some good: 'The press lords have been compelled to take precautions . . . to introduce an element of apparent fairness into their political reporting.'[54]

On the question of concentration of ownership, the Commission took a complacent view and proposed no action. When the report was debated in the Commons on 28 July, Michael spoke angrily:

> Is it a crime to fight this peril, that great owners from London should be able to stretch their control wider and wider across the country and subject and subdue local pride, local initiative and local power? It is damnable that such a thing should go on . . . That is the real reason why we started this fight and why we are intending to go on with this fight.

Beaverbrook can scarcely have been gratified by these sentiments, but the main target of Michael's denunciations was the Kemsley chain.

Moreover, when Beverley Baxter – now a Tory MP – interrupted to suggest that Michael was showing ingratitude to Beaverbrook, Michael replied: 'I have great personal affection for Lord Beaverbrook, who has done great service to me. I have never made any personal attacks on him, but I have made many political attacks, which I intend to continue with increasing momentum as the general election comes nearer. I have never had any complaint from Lord Beaverbrook.'

One other Michael Foot foray belongs to the year of 1949. A bill to abolish the censorship of plays – exercised since the eighteenth century by an anachronistic dignitary, the Lord Chamberlain – was introduced by two playwrights, the Tory MP E. P. Smith (who wrote under the name of Edward Percy) and Benn Levy. Seconding the bill, Michael treated the House to a declaration of faith:

> We prefer the laws of England to the whims of any individual, whether he be the Archangel Gabriel or even the Archangel Michael . . . These are cruel times in which we live. Freedom is being suppressed in one land or another . . . The most evil thing in the world today is censorship, which divides nation from nation and people from people on a scale not previously considered possible . . . It would be a splendid thing if at this time, when new and more barbarous forces are being unleashed upon the world, we took steps to enlarge the empire of the human mind and to widen the territory where heresy and inspiration can bring new life to the people.[55]

But the issue was of no great interest to Herbert Morrison, who controlled the parliamentary time-table, and no facilities were provided for this private members' bill. Censorship survived, amid increasing derision and discredit, until 1968.

The next general election was indeed coming nearer; the latest possible date was July 1950. It was inevitable that Labour would lose seats, if only because of the redistribution which had wiped out small inner-city constituencies. Besides, the government had been forced into strategic retreats which had brought disappointment to working-class Labour supporters. Since replacing Dalton as Chancellor of the Exchequer in November 1947, Stafford Cripps had insisted on rigorous caution in the economic sphere. Bevan, who was responsible for housing, was forced to accept cuts in the building programme which meant that only 217,000 homes, instead of the planned 280,000, were provided in 1949. To check the threat of inflation, Cripps demanded a freeze on wage increases which was only reluctantly accepted by the trade unions. Cuts in capital investment halted some cherished projects. In September 1949 the pound had to be devalued from $4.00 to $2.80 – a humiliating necessity, resisted by Cripps himself until the last moment. Meanwhile, after tense arguments in the Cabinet between Morrison and Bevan, the nationalisation of steel had been delayed for a year, which meant that it could not be implemented until 1950 and might be reversed by a Tory government. More and more, differences between left and right in the party involved economic issues rather than foreign policy.

Still, Labour had much to be proud of. Thanks to American aid under the Marshall Plan, but thanks also to the government's positive planning and decisions on priorities, production was booming. Exports were well ahead of pre-war levels and the balance of payments deficit had been wiped out. Full employment had been maintained and was confidently seen as a permanence. In Michael's constituency, for example, the use of the Devonport dockyard for civilian as well as naval repair work checked redundancies, making a contrast with the aftermath of the First World War when 3,000 men were sacked. In a *Tribune* article, Michael could claim: 'Whole towns in South Wales and Durham which were once dead and derelict are now pulsing with life.'[56] He was infuriated by the unfair picture of Britain under Labour, with lazy workers, industry paralysed by trade union restrictions, and families groaning under ruthless taxation, drawn in Tory papers and in the American press. It was, he wrote in a signed article in *Tribune* of 12 August 1949, 'the most shameful lie-campaign ever engineered by yellow journalism and backed by yellow politicians.' What roused him to yet shriller anger was to find these misrepresentations echoed in the *Manchester Guardian*. 'Do they know what they are doing, these pious, pigeon-livered, chicken-hearted Liberals?' he demanded.

He drew the conclusion that the best course for the government was a fresh appeal to the people. He urged an autumn election and asserted: 'We do not doubt the result.'[57] Disraeli was quoted: 'A majority is the best repartee.' The case presented by *Tribune*, under the headline 'LET'S HAVE AN ELECTION NOW!', was strong. The Tory attacks were damaging Britain, especially in American eyes, and this was the underlying reason for devaluation; civil servants, hedging their bets, were no longer helping ministers as they should; there was 'an atmosphere of unrest and uncertainty in the country'. Whether a 1949 election would have been better for Labour than the actual 1950 election, one cannot say. At all events, Attlee decided against it.

7

As 1950 began, the political world expected a May election. To general bafflement, Attlee decided on a January dissolution and polling on 23 February – on a stale register, since the new one came into effect on 15 March. Labour candidates and agents feared that freezing weather might bring disaster, but polling-day, by good luck, was mild and sunny.

Michael was optimistic. *Tribune* on 13 January predicted: 'Labour will win despite the redistribution of seats, despite the so-called opinion polls, and despite the fact that the press, both London and provincial, is heavily against us.' The polls were dismissed as 'grossly inaccurate and mostly material for reactionary propaganda'. (The result showed that, as in 1945, they were accurate enough.) The *Tribune* article even ventured a precise forecast that Labour would lose no more than forty-five seats and would have a majority of ninety-seven in the new House.

This optimism was based primarily on the belief, which Michael has always held firmly, that most people are swayed by their direct experience more than by what they read in the papers. Full employment and the free Health Service, Labour's most popular achievements, were facts, and the danger that they would be at risk under a Tory government was a potent fear. In strictly electoral terms, the good news was that the Liberals were fielding 475 candidates, a much larger number than in 1945. It was credibly reckoned that a Liberal, even when he had no chance of winning, took three votes from the Tories for every two taken from Labour. The Tories were naturally furious over what *The Times* called this 'irresponsible spattering of the electoral map', and tried to limit the damage by labelling their own candidates as 'Conservative and National Liberal', or even 'Conservative and Liberal'. In Devonport, Michael's main opponent, Randolph Churchill – although he was the son of the Tory leader and had been a Tory MP from 1940 to 1945 – was presented as 'Conservative and National Liberal'. The real Liberals, of course, denounced this deception but their own candidate, Alfred Cann, had been a Tory until he underwent a conversion in 1947. Michael could claim to be the only candidate whose political identity was unambiguous.

Thanks to the redistribution, Plymouth now had only two constituencies: Devonport and Sutton. Lucy Middleton, who had won Sutton in 1945, was opposed by the youngest son of Lord and Lady Astor, John Jacob (known as 'Jakie'). As usual, the Foot family was in battle on several fronts. John was fighting Bodmin again, and Dingle was Liberal candidate for North Cornwall. Isaac, no longer a candidate himself, spoke for both of them and looked forward zestfully to polling-day, which was also his seventieth birthday. Victory for his three sons would be a magnificent present, but even the ever hopeful Isaac can scarcely have thought it likely.

Michael had little doubt that he would hold Devonport – partly because he knew Randolph Churchill. Both men had worked for the *Evening Standard* and both had been among the company at Beaverbrook's dinner-table. Randolph was one of those men whose good qualities were perceptible only to those who knew him well, while his faults were obvious on casual encounter and became notorious. Martin Gilbert, who assisted Randolph with the multi-volume biography of his father and went on to complete it, quotes Michael as saying to him: 'You and I belong to the most exclusive club in the country – Friends of Randolph Churchill.'[58] Randolph could be an entertaining companion and, at his best, a fascinating talker; he shared with Michael an innate sense of history and a love of literature. But he could be arrogant, undisguisedly impatient with people who bored or annoyed him, sometimes rude and boorish, sometimes (the wrong times, generally) very drunk. Generously (years later, when Randolph was a sick man) Michael paid him this tribute: 'His three principal qualities were also much larger than life: his honesty, his candour and his courage.'[59] Whatever his qualities, they did not make him popular with the businessmen, estate agents and Methodist lay preachers whom he met in the Devonport Conservative Association. They were not, in any case, disposed to welcome him with open arms, for they had been grooming a local man as Tory candidate until the great man's son was imposed on them by Conservative Central Office. Jill noticed that Randolph was at a loose end after his evening meetings and no one was inclined to buy him a drink. She mentioned this to Michael; the result was that the Labour and Tory candidates, with their wives, ended the evening discreetly at a remote pub on Dartmoor, unobserved by their supporters. As a candidate, Randolph had a distinctly out-of-date approach to contesting a marginal constituency, and was much more ready to address meetings than to undertake the humble and demeaning work of canvassing. Michael commented: 'He thought it was the Midlothian Campaign or something.' Hence, the willingness of the Labour rank and file to work to the point of exhaustion for Michael was far from being matched by a corresponding dedication on the Tory side.

The big day in the campaign was 9 February, when Winston Churchill spoke for his son at the Forum cinema in Devonport and Aneurin Bevan spoke for Michael in the Exmouth Hall. Both these celebrated orators drew the crowds, with hundreds of people standing outside listening to amplifiers, but the day was a success on points for the Labour side. Churchill *père* recommended Randolph as 'a mature, formidable and experienced politician' – a valuation that might more wisely have been left to the voters and that did not, as insiders were aware, represent the old man's real opinion. The real error, however, was to schedule the Churchill meeting for the afternoon, which enabled the Labour side to retort without delay (and in the same issue of the *Western Morning News*). Thus Churchill claimed that the National Health Service had been planned before Labour took office, so Bevan challenged him to give details of the kind of service that he would have introduced, and pointed out that the actual NHS had 'been launched against bitter opposition from the Tories'. Worse still, Churchill asserted that Plymouth was suffering from the poor housing record of the socialists, who produced 'not bricks and mortar but venom and spite'. At the Exmouth Hall, Michael reproved Churchill for sneering at Plymouth, cited the figures (6,400 houses built since the war) and declared without fear of contradiction: 'I don't believe there is one person in Plymouth who says we've not done a good job.' Large-scale reconstruction had been made possible by the Town and Country Planning Act passed in 1947, but the Tories had voted against it, Churchill had been absent and, Michael wound up, 'he hasn't the foggiest notion what a Town and Country Planning Act is'.

Scorning these humdrum details, Randolph blurted out at a meeting on 13 February: 'The reason I haven't talked about Plymouth housing is that I don't know much about it, but I'm trying to find out.' Michael pounced on this admission to ask the voters: 'Do you think these people are the right people to get on with the housing drive in the future?' Randolph knew little, either, about the Devonport dockyard and the strategies whereby the Labour government had prevented mass redundancies. The *Western Morning News*, though a Tory and in fact a Kemsley-owned paper, had to pay Michael a grudging compliment: 'His has been no mean record, especially on behalf of the dockyard and the Navy.'

As polling-day approached, the assistant editor of the mass-circulation weekly paper *Picture Post* – he was Ted Castle, Barbara's husband – invited Michael and Randolph to contribute articles on the subject of 'What I think of my opponent's campaign'. Encouraged by Ted to be as nasty as he pleased, Michael wrote:

Mr Randolph Churchill is a politician with plenty of guts, an agreeable overdose of pugnacity and as much knowledge of the real political and economic issues facing the British nation as the man in the moon. He is a throwback to the nineteenth century. He thinks that politics is a matter of stunts, scares, handshakes and synthetic smiles for the ladies. It is perhaps more his misfortune than his fault that he picked on the city of Plymouth for his latest political escapade. For the people of Plymouth do not regard politics as a game . . . It remains to be seen whether before polling day Mr Randolph Churchill will spend sixpence at His Majesty's Stationery Office and risk stunning himself with the discovery of figures which are available to every citizen.

Jill, meanwhile, was making speeches in support of her husband and telling the voters that nearly everyone in the film industry was a socialist 'because we get around the country'. Randolph voiced his annoyance over a report that she had called him 'a Mayfair playboy'; the Foots, he riposted, lived in Mayfair themselves. His information was wrong again. The Foots now lived in Hampstead and the report was inaccurate. Jill wrote to the *Western Morning News*: 'I have made no personal references in this campaign, although I have referred to the "circus" tactics which I regard as insulting to the intelligence of women.' She added that Randolph was wrong, furthermore, in statements he had made about coal production – 'I do know something about coal, having spent a year just recently in the mining areas.'

Near the eve of poll, Randolph told the local paper that the election in Devonport would be 'a close thing' and he expected a narrow majority – a forecast that no candidate should ever make. Observers drew the conclusion that he had written off his chances. The *Morning News* expressed the view that Michael 'seems to be on the Left road back to Westminster', although it added that Jakie Astor would probably beat Lucy Middleton in Sutton.

At a national level, the surprise of the campaign was a speech made by Winston Churchill at Edinburgh on 14 February. He urged the advisability of 'another talk with Soviet Russia upon the highest level', and told his audience: 'The idea appeals to me of a supreme effort to bridge the gulf between the two worlds, so that each can live his life, if not in friendship, at least without the hatreds and manoeuvres of the cold war . . . It is not easy to see how things could be worsened by a parley at the summit.'

Thus 'summit talks' entered the vocabulary of politics. The speech was fairly breathtaking, coming from the man who had inaugurated the cold war at Fulton. However, he had undoubtedly stolen the Labour Party's clothes. Bevin, in a broadcast next day, could only say that serious problems could not 'be solved by any stunt proposals'. But an appeal for the relaxation of the cold war struck a chord with many ordinary people and uncommitted voters. Michael had to ask himself whether he had been altogether right in his argument with Ian Mikardo.

On 23 February, the voters of Plymouth turned out to produce an 86 per cent poll in both constituencies, an astonishing figure on a stale register. At half-past one next morning, a big crowd heard the reading of the Devonport result:

Michael Foot, Labour	30,812
Randolph Churchill, Conservative	27,329
Alfred Cann, Liberal	2,766
Labour majority	3,483

The cheering went on for several minutes before Michael could speak. He said: 'It has been a hard, stiff fight, but no heads or bones have been broken.' Randolph accepted the result with the words: 'No complaints and no excuses.' The two men shook hands. Soon, there was more good news for Labour. Lucy Middleton had held the Sutton seat with a majority of 924.

But, as results came in on 24 February and millions stayed glued to their radios, it was clear that the contest – nationally if not in Devonport – was a very close thing. Not until eight in the evening was Labour able to claim an absolute majority in the House of Commons. The final tally of seats was: Labour 315, Tories and associates 298, Liberals 9.

With 315 lost deposits, it was a disaster for the ailing Liberal Party. The two Communist MPs vanished from Westminster. So did the left-wingers who had been expelled from the Labour Party, although they had considerable support from Labour activists in their constituencies and polled reasonably well; Pritt had 8,000 votes, Platts-Mills 7,000 and Zilliacus 5,000. The real victor in the 1950 election was the two-party system. For the next quarter of the century, Labour and the Tories would confront each other as the sole serious contestants in any election.

This thought, however, was of no great comfort to Attlee and his colleagues. The question before them was: how – and for how long – could they govern without what was generally reckoned to be a proper majority? And the question for the left was: in a situation that made it easy for any criticism to be depicted as treachery, what were the possible limits of dissidence?

— *Chapter 6* —

THE BEVANITES

I

Few people – apart from Jill, of course – have seen more of Michael Foot at close quarters, or over a longer period, than Elizabeth Thomas. She worked in the same office with him for ten years in the 1950s, first as his secretary and then as literary editor of *Tribune*. Later, for three years in the 1970s, she again worked in his office, this time as political adviser to a Cabinet minister. She and her husband, George, who became director of a polytechnic, were always among Michael's closer friends. Her impressions of him are the best possible starting-point for a description of his complex personality.

Elizabeth began working for Michael after the 1950 election, having previously been secretary to a Labour MP who lost his seat. With a first in classics from Cambridge, she was a highly educated young woman – certainly by comparison with most Westminster secretaries – and well equipped to share Michael's literary interests. She was a socialist of the *Tribune* persuasion, and she felt that being secretary to Michael Foot was the ideal job. At first, however, she found it difficult to come to terms with him. He had a tense and anxious air, especially during his bouts of asthma, and this was accentuated by his constant cigarette-smoking. He was not, she realised, a man who moved easily from formality to friendship. Once they knew each other well, a process which took a few months, the confidences and the jokes began to flow and she saw him in an entirely different light.

Newcomers to the *Tribune* staff had the same experience. 'He was kind and helpful, but hard to get to know,' Robert Millar recalls. When I joined the paper in 1955, my first meeting with him was not at all what I expected. As soon as we had agreed on the terms of employment, he said abruptly: 'Good – that's all right,' and then retreated into silence and concentrated study•of some document on his desk. This Attlee-like performance, utterly in contrast with his scintillating reputation, was most confusing. I wondered whether it arose from wariness or suspicion; shyness was an explanation that did not come to mind. But Geoffrey Goodman, who also came to know Michael extremely well, has described him as diffident – a word that Tories scorched by his derision in the Commons would scarcely have credited. Many years later, Jill told me what most surprised her when they first met for lunch. 'He was', she said, 'the first reticent man I'd ever encountered.' I had some idea of how she felt .

There are, indeed, two contrasting aspects to Michael Foot's personality, or one might almost go so far as to say 'two Michael Foots'. There is an ebulliently self-confident Michael, highly entertaining in company, emphatic in his opinions, a fluent and fascinating talker, apt to raise his voice and disregard interruptions. He gives a splendid performance, without the calculation or artificiality that the word might imply. Many have benefited by this performance, in the leisure rooms of the House of Commons, at dinner-parties or in hotel lounges after public meetings, and they include fresh acquaintances as well as established intimates. There is also a Michael who speaks quietly and tentatively, resists efforts to draw him out, retires into abstracted reflection and might be set down as a reserved academic, unsure of himself and content to defer to others. However, to ask which is the 'real Michael' is to pose an unreal question. His friends have seen both and have learned not to predict which will appear on a given occasion. It would be truer to say that both are necessary components of the man; and perhaps that, when either comes uppermost, it is in compensation for the other.

These aspects of Michael have always alternated, even in boyhood (by such accounts as I have gleaned), and at any period of his life. But it seems that, by and large, the shy and hesitant Michael tended to predominate before the mid-point of his life and the self-confident Michael thereafter. For example, his earlier speeches in Parliament, though they read well, were not very well delivered and did not command the full attention of the House; they were the over-prepared speeches of a writer. It was only after 1960 that he spoke easily without notes and developed into an outstanding parliamentary orator.

Several reasons for this gradual pace of growth can be suggested. One must surely be the long ordeal, and the embarrassment, of the eczema and asthma which lingered into middle age. Another might be that he did not achieve a secure and durable relationship with a woman until he was in his thirties, after Lili Ernst had rejected his love and Connie Ernst had declined to marry him. Then, a repeated pattern in earlier years was that he offered a modest admiration to older men of powerful personality: his father, Bevan and Beaverbrook. In the ranks of the left, he was Bevan's disciple or lieutenant, and Bevan could behave roughly and intolerantly even towards followers of whom he was genuinely fond. There may have been an element of liberation, as well as loss and sincere grief, when Isaac Foot, Bevan and Beaverbrook all died within a few years. Freud, after all, teaches that the most important event in a man's life is the death of his father.

It was in the 1950s that Michael made some friendships which endured, unless ended by death, for the next forty years. James Cameron, Tom Baistow and Geoffrey Goodman were journalists working for the *News Chronicle*. The most forthright anti-fascist paper in the 1930s, the *News Chronicle* was now timid and vacillating in its political line, but people on the left still read it in preference to the *Herald* because of the quality of its outstanding writers. Cameron, who was a man of rare integrity and had twice given up a good job on a point of principle, was also a stylist who could be read for sheer pleasure, and whose most hurriedly filed despatches never contained a clumsy sentence or a stale cliché. Yet the chief reason for reading the *News Chronicle* was always the cartoon by Vicky. He was the most brilliant cartoonist of his time, and ranks with no more than half a dozen others in the history of the art.

It would not be enough to say that Michael and Vicky were friends; Michael felt a warmer affection for this man than for anyone else in the world except Jill, his father and his sister Sally. Vicky, whose real name was Victor Weisz, was a Hungarian Jew (like Koestler). He arrived in London from Berlin in the 1930s and proceeded, systematically and with astonishing thoroughness, to anglicise himself. He acquired an extraordinary knowledge of the idioms, characters, quotations and allusions that English people might recognise; indeed, very few English people had Shakespeare, Dickens, Lewis Carroll and Edward Lear at their finger-tips so comprehensively. Such a man, clearly, was bound to be dear to Michael's heart. However, Michael's affection for him was generated by more than admiration.

Vicky, who was a small man with a big, domed forehead and black-framed spectacles, liked to draw himself in a corner of his cartoons. He made himself even smaller than he really was and gave himself an expression of melancholy bewilderment at the follies of the powerful. The bewilderment was assumed as a medium of comment – he was exceptionally clear-minded – but the melancholy was real. For him, a political disaster was as wounding as the loss of a friendship or the break-up of a love affair is to the average person. He was capable of wild outbursts of laughter or comic mockery, but also of almost unbearable sadness. Cameron, who shared this temperament enough for empathy, wrote of him as 'the gentle and beloved Vicky with whom I was to plod in hilarious despair through twenty years of mutually hopeless exhilaration'.[1] This, indeed, was why Michael and others who were close to Vicky cherished him with an affection darkened by anxiety. If one knew anything about Vicky, one knew that he was a potential suicide.

These friends – Michael and Vicky with Cameron, Goodman and Baistow – made up an informal lunching club. They met about once a fortnight at the Forum restaurant in Chancery Lane, or later at the Gay Hussar in Greek Street; it was generally Michael who made the phone calls. The lunches were for pleasure and gossip, but *Tribune* was also an outlet for stories that the *News Chronicle* would not touch. Goodman and Baistow, using pseudonyms, were regular *Tribune* contributors.

Most of the political articles in *Tribune* were written by Michael and other left-wing MPs, but he was building up a team of promising young journalists. Robert J. Edwards, who came from Berkshire, had produced a Labour propaganda sheet while doing his National Service in the RAF and then worked for the *Reading Mercury*. In 1949, Mikardo, who was MP for Reading, spotted his talents and recommended him to Michael. After a spell on *Tribune*, he moved on to the *People*, a Sunday paper which he later edited, but in 1952 Michael asked him to return to *Tribune* on a salary of £50 a week and added casually: 'You can be the editor if you like.' Edwards' name duly appeared on the masthead, but he prudently considered that Michael was the real editor. Ian Aitken joined *Tribune* as industrial reporter; there was increased coverage of union activities and strikes, and also of the role played by union leaders in the politics of the Labour Party – a coverage that, accurate and frank as it was, led to plenty of trouble. Bruce Bain joined as literary editor and wrote theatre criticism under the name of Richard Findlater. There was also a new business manager. Peggy Duff, formerly of Save Europe Now, was appointed in 1949 but sacked a few years later because of her rather slap-happy bookkeeping methods, or perhaps because of her failure to win the confidence of wealthy backers ('I was never very good with millionaires,' she admitted).[2] Robert Millar took on the job and also wrote a facts-and-figures column, thus justifying his journalistic status (Michael had helped him when he had difficulty in getting an NUJ card).

2

The cold war was still generating a mood of panic, heightened by sensations about Russian spies. The Soviet Union had produced its own atomic bomb, a feat that was ascribed to the role played by Klaus Fuchs, a nuclear scientist of German origin, who was convicted at the Old Bailey of passing secret blueprints to Moscow. On 5 March 1950, shortly after the trial, readers of the *Evening Standard* were startled by a banner headline: 'FUCHS AND STRACHEY: A GREAT NEW CRISIS'.

John Strachey was at this time Secretary of State for War, and the smear was tenuously based on the failure of MI5 to unmask Fuchs in good time. In fact, MI5 reported direct to the Prime Minister on security matters, so it was nothing to do with Strachey. The *Standard*'s second headline, 'WAR MINISTER HAS NEVER DISAVOWED COMMUNISM', was blatantly false, since Strachey had disavowed Communism very explicitly in a book called *The Betrayal of the Left*, written with Gollancz and Laski in 1941. As James Cameron wrote: 'The association of these events could have had a relevance only for the sickest of minds, but such a one was available. It belonged to Herbert Gunn, the editor of the *Evening Standard*. More properly it should be said that Mr Gunn's mind belonged, like the *Standard*, to Lord Beaverbrook.'[3] It was on this occasion that Cameron resigned in protest from the *Daily Express*, earning the accolade in *Tribune*: 'Thousands of journalists all over the country will wish to pay honour to Mr Cameron for this splendid act of courage.' But *Tribune* had already, on 10 March, denounced 'the foulest piece of journalism perpetrated in this country for many a long year.'

Such a phrase might well have endangered Michael's reconciliation with Beaverbrook, or might indeed have brought a writ for libel. However, Beaverbrook disapproved of the smear and dismissed Gunn soon afterwards. The libel writ came from another quarter. Michael had used the headline: 'LOWER THAN KEMSLEY'. This was an echo of a speech made in 1948 by Nye Bevan, which had caused considerable uproar; he had described the Tories who inflicted human suffering on South Wales in pre-war years as 'lower than vermin'. Since Michael had said several times that he rated the ethical standards of the Kemsley press as the lowest in Britain, he wrote his headline as a suitable description of a piece of dirty journalism. But, when he took legal advice, he was told that it could be judged to be defamatory.

It was obvious that Kemsley's aim, as *Tribune*'s solicitor put it in his brief to counsel, was 'to obtain heavy damages against the defendants and force them into bankruptcy'. Jill suggested that there was one man who might be sympathetic enough, and was certainly rich enough, to come to the rescue – Beaverbrook. Michael had a certain moral claim on him, having never received (nor requested) any golden handshake when he left the *Standard* in 1944. With considerable trepidation,

Michael went to ask for his help. Beaverbrook immediately handed over £3,000.[4]

Kemsley won the first round by means of a technicality which enabled a judge to hear the case in chambers, without a jury. The judge ruled in Kemsley's favour, so *Tribune* took the case to the Court of Appeal. This round went to the defence after one of the judges, Lord Birkett, who was a Devon man and an old friend of Isaac Foot, laid down: 'The defence of fair comment is recognised to be one of the most valuable parts of the law of libel and slander. It is an essential part of the greater right of free speech.' Kemsley opened a third round in the House of Lords, but *Tribune* – after an agonising delay until May 1952 – won that round too. With some restraint, Beaverbrook advised Michael to be more careful in future. Michael replied: 'I am sure your advice to me is wise and I am resolved not to get into the same scrape again.'

On 26 May 1950, Michael appeared on the television screen for the first time in a programme called *In the News*. It was to be a weekly discussion of topical issues, launched after considerable reluctance by the BBC. John Irwin, the producer, and Edgar Lustgarten, the editor, placated a nervous board of governors by describing it as 'an entertainment programme'. Michael was a natural choice as a member of the panel, as he had often been heard on the radio in *Any Questions?* The other participants were Robert Boothby and W. J. Brown. Boothby was a far from orthodox Tory and Brown, who had won a wartime by-election as an Independent, was a member of no party, but they belonged to the right rather than the left, so Irwin soon decided to even up his team in the interests of balance (always an anxious matter of concern for the BBC) and recruited the historian A. J. P. Taylor to reinforce Michael. He was a man of deep-rooted radical convictions, mitigated by quirkiness, playfulness and a delight in saying the unexpected. Michael had made another enduring friendship.

Taylor, who had hitherto led a somewhat cloistered life in Oxford, gave this account of his new experience:

> We met at Edgar Lustgarten's chambers in the Albany and drank champagne while we surveyed possible subjects. Then we moved to the Ecu de France where we dined richly in a private room . . . Limousines swept us to Lime Grove where the BBC had started to produce television in unconverted film studios. Here the amenities were less, but this, in our exhilarated state, we hardly noticed.[5]

By 1952, *In the News* was watched by 48 per cent of people who had television. Grace Wyndham Goldie, an influential figure in the BBC hierarchy, commented that the team 'seemed in combination to provide a remarkable effervescence of wit, common sense, intellectual honesty and political passion'.[6] Taylor recalled: 'We never worried about what people would think of us. We let our minds run.'[7] Over late-night drinks, they looked back on their polemical display as sportsmen might look back on a strenuous, hard-fought game. The viewers would have been surprised by the off-screen camaraderie, for the arguments appeared to be savage and powered by real hostility. Michael, who did not joke or smile and attacked his opponent with relentless insistence and a fiercely jabbing finger, contributed most of all to this impression. Reports from the BBC's sample of viewers showed that he was the least popular member of the team. He was seen as intolerant, humourless and fanatical, an 'image' (to use the deplorable TV word) entirely at odds with his character as understood by those who knew him. It is strange to reflect that, thirty years later, the distorting mirror of the screen showed him as an indecisive waffler.

In the News was never much loved by the apparatchiks of the BBC and was much disliked by the political party machines. A BBC memo warned: 'Michael Foot's continued appearance has made the Labour Party feel that the solid core of the party is overshadowed. Similarly on the Conservative side the continued appearance of Boothby has not been acceptable to all Conservatives.'[8] From the autumn of 1951, the team was diluted by such 'acceptable' faces as Lord Hailsham, James Callaghan and Hugh Gaitskell. Once in three months there was a 'ladies' night', featuring Barbara Castle and Lady Astor. After Independent Television came into existence, Lustgarten moved to the commercial channel and took the *In the News* team with him, to appear in a virtually identical programme called *Free Speech*. But it was not really to the taste of the top men in ITV, whose main concern was to attract advertising, and within a few more years it was wound up too.

Michael was also much concerned over the future of the film industry. Jill was more directly concerned; films were her career and her livelihood. Even after they were married, she was averse on principle to taking money from Michael. The great age of documentary was over and she was working as a script-writer in feature films. Her greatest success was *The Million Pound Note*, directed by Ronald Neame with Gregory Peck as the star. It was based on a short story by Mark Twain, only six pages long, which Jill had to extend and elaborate.

Harold Wilson, President of the Board of Trade, set up the National Film Finance Corporation to back British projects with public money, thus helping the industry to survive in face of the vastly greater wealth and productive capacity of Hollywood. Michael, briefed by Jill for a speech in the Commons, suggested NFFC loans for script-writing as well as production and declared that it was 'absolutely fantastic to say there is a shortage of ideas or talent'. He diagnosed the ailments of the industry as: 'dictatorial powers exercised by distributors, a near-monopoly of exhibition and distribution, the reduction of artists and technicians to a position of complete subordination'.[9] The British film industry survived, but only by the skin of its teeth. The irony was that it was making films still prized as classics by television viewers.

3

In view of the government's narrow majority and the fiercely harassing tactics employed in the House by the Tories, it was clear that there would have to be another election before long. The problem was: what should Labour's appeal be? A private conclave at Beatrice Webb House, near Dorking, in May 1950 brought together Cabinet ministers, members of the NEC and trade union leaders. For Morrison, the right strategy was to capture the 'middle ground' of voters with no fixed loyalties. Attlee remarked: 'We must not over-emphasise class solidarity. Lots of people want to climb out of the class in which they are.'[10] Michael spoke next and asserted: 'Our main task is to increase our hold over the working class.' The central argument was on whether Labour's programme should include further measures of public ownership. Morrison saw, among undecided and even Labour voters, 'a desire for a temporary pause in further nationalisation'. In his winding-up speech, he said: 'The people want a Labour government, but they want to put the brakes on . . . We don't want to sully our principles, but we've got to win.' This contrasted with Michael's prescription: 'We have shown by deeds that socialism works. We must maintain the impetus of the advance.' The issue was never clearly resolved and no votes were taken at Dorking, but Morrison was the winner by default. The policy document for the next election, presented at the party conference (which now met in October instead of Whitsun) did not include the nationalisation plans which had been under debate. Morrison explained that they were 'within the field of eligibility for consideration'.

Strong criticisms of the Morrison line were appearing in *Tribune* and were assumed, rightly, to be written by Michael. He felt that he was in an awkward position; he was listening at NEC meetings to remarks which furnished him with material for his attacks. At the conference, he did not stand again for the NEC. The constituencies elected Bevan, Mikardo and Driberg as standard-bearers of the left.

Bevan was finding it hard to contain his disquiet at the way things were going. A few weeks after the conference, Stafford Cripps, who had suffered a severe stroke during his summer holiday, resigned. Attlee's choice as the new Chancellor was Hugh Gaitskell, then forty-four years old. In Bevan's opinion, he had no standing in the Labour movement and had been unjustifiably pushed forward by senior patrons (primarily by Dalton). Nye therefore wrote to Attlee to express his 'consternation and astonishment' over this promotion. Attlee agreed to listen to his views, but the meeting developed, as Nye told Michael, into 'a tremendous row'.[11]

The battle between Bevan and Gaitskell, which was to dominate Labour politics through the 1950s, was now inevitable. But the slow-burning fuse that ignited the explosion in 1951 was lit on the far side of the globe – in Korea, of all places.

War between Communist North Korea and anti-Communist South Korea broke out on 25 June 1950. As the North Korean forces advanced rapidly, the general assumption was that they were the aggressors. Truman immediately ordered American troops, based in Japan, into action to help South Korea. The commander was General Douglas MacArthur. The Security Council of the UN – without the Soviet representative, who had withdrawn from its proceedings six months earlier in protest against the occupation of the Chinese seat by the discredited Chiang Kai-shek regime – called on all UN members to give their support. In Britain, both Attlee and Churchill endorsed this policy. So did *Tribune*, which denounced North Korea for 'an act of flagrant unprovoked aggression', considered that the US had 'taken the correct and inevitable course', and added: 'The West has shown it is prepared to fight if needs be and that is a lesson that will not be lost on the Russians.'[12]

Others were not so sure. If North Korea had indeed launched what *Tribune* called a 'carefully premeditated attack', it was curious that the Soviet delegate had not stayed at the UN to veto the American-backed resolution. It was possible that the North Koreans had reacted to a challenge or provocation from the Southern side. A sharp American journalist, I. F. Stone, after pondering the evidence, asked: 'Was the war Stalin's blunder? Or was it MacArthur's plan?'[13] In the Commons, Tom Driberg said that he had 'many misgivings' and that 'many people are intensely disturbed and alarmed'. Sydney Silverman put down a motion calling for the withdrawal of US forces, a ceasefire and mediation under UN authority. *Tribune*, in an article headed 'A MISTAKEN MOTION', rebuked him: 'Such a course would be to condone aggression.'[14]

Equally worrying was the fact that Truman's order had also authorised the use of US forces to protect Taiwan, stronghold of the Chiang Kai-shek regime which was still recognised by the US – though not by Britain – as the government of China. MacArthur, evidently preparing for a counter-attack, issued a statement couched in terms of limitless confrontation between his armies and the Communist world. He was known to be a man of great arrogance and self-righteousness, who made his own policy without caring about the approval of Washington, let alone other nations. *Tribune* was now more critical: 'The whole of his statement reeks of an out of date imperialism which would have shamed the worst of British Blimps . . . It is hard to see how President Truman can retain MacArthur as US Commander much longer.'[15]

The counter-attack quickly regained the whole territory of South Korea; aggression, presumably, had been repelled. But in October MacArthur sent his armies on a further advance northward, overran all of North Korea too, and reached the frontier of China. Thus the Chinese were drawn into the war. Kingsley Martin took the lead in organising a Peace with China Campaign, and Michael spoke at a crowded public meeting. *Tribune* warned: 'The world is living on the edge of full-scale war between American or UN forces and Communist China. That would be a disaster – a crime – of incalculable magnitude . . . British involvement in such a war would split the Labour movement in this country to fragments.'[16]

There was another terrifying danger. MacArthur controlled Amercian air forces based on Japan, whose weapons included atomic bombs. A report from Washington told British readers that Truman 'may be under pressure to keep his and General MacArthur's hands free to use all weapons to redeem what some people here believe to be approaching military disaster'.[17] Attlee, at short notice, flew to Washington for a talk with Truman. His message was that Britain had agreed to a defence of South Korea, not to an assault on China from Taiwan or anywhere else. Truman, caught between contending pressures, responded only with vague promises of consultation, but Attlee felt reassured that his mission had tipped the scales. MacArthur, however, was unrepentant and in April 1951, in a letter to a Republican Congressman, declared that he was in favour of 'meeting force with maximum counter-force'. This time, Truman screwed up his courage and dismised the vainglorious general. MacArthur's departure cleared the way for a truce in June 1951 and ultimately to a peace agreement in 1953.

However, the Korean war had increased the risks of a general war between the West and the Communist world. General Eisenhower, as Supreme Commander of NATO, called on its member nations to step up their military spending. The British government responded with loyal pledges, but the hard decisions would have to be embodied in the 1951 budget, to be prepared by the new Chancellor, Hugh Gaitskell.

The government was now in a visible state of decline. Bevin was clinging to the Foreign Office in a state of gravely declining health; he was away sick for 85 of his last 150 days in the job and played little part in the crises over Korea. In March 1951 Attlee told him tersely that it was impossible for him to carry on. He died a month later. Attlee gave the job to Morrison, whose expertise was entirely in domestic affairs and party management and who was never at ease as Foreign Secretary. Bevin, in his last days, had told Attlee that Bevan would be a better choice, but Bevan had been moved in January to the Ministry of Labour, a position which he found unattractive. Attlee himself was in indifferent health. The one man in a senior Cabinet post who was in full health and vigour and holding a job he enjoyed was Gaitskell.

4

The Keep Left Group had been revived, and Michael rejoined it when he left the NEC. Its meetings were attended by three Oxford academics with socialist sympathies, Thomas Balogh, Dudley Seers and David Worswick. The first task was to examine the rearmament programme which the government had accepted, involving an expenditure of £4,700 million over three years. This was a modification of the original American demand for £6,000 million, but it would still be almost double the existing defence budget and would amount to almost 14 per cent of gross national product. The Oxford economists advised that even if the money was voted, at dire cost to other forms of expenditure, it could not actually be spent. The industrial resources, in particular the machine-tools, to support such a rearmament effort did not exist. From August 1950, when the proposals first came before the Cabinet, Bevan voiced his strong opposition.[18]

When Gaitskell drew up his plans for the 1951 budget, he proposed to raise some of the extra revenue required by imposing charges on dental treatment and spectacles. The amount raised would be a mere £13 million (or £30 million in a full year). But the issue of principle was vital: free treatment on a basis of need was the cornerstone of the National Health Service, and Gaitskell's plan was a challenge to its architect – Aneurin Bevan. Gaitskell was seen by Bevan's friends, in Michael's words, as 'the most pedantic spokesman of the Treasury's most arid doctrines'. The Treasury had, from the start, disliked the Health Service because its costs rose according to demand and could not be reduced at will. Bevan had put his position on record in a letter to Cripps in 1949:

> I have made it clear to you, the Prime Minister and Gaitskell that I consider the imposition of charges on any part of the Health Service raises issues of such seriousness and fundamental importance that I could never agree to it. If it were decided by the Government to impose them, my resignation would automatically follow.[19]

As the clash over the budget drew nearer, Michael was dealing with another crisis: *Tribune* was in heavy trouble, had been forced to go down from weekly to fortnightly publication, and was even in danger of extinction. Peggy Duff, the business manager, recalled:

> We were in desperate financial straits. I talked about it with Michael and for the one and only time he put into words the dreadful thought that was always in mind – that we might have to call it a day and close the paper down. A few days later he sent for me and took me into the far west room which was empty. He told me, in confidence, that he expected that as a result of the Budget some ministers would resign. This would give *Tribune* new opportunities, a new lease of life.[20]

Three members of the Cabinet were considering resignation: Bevan, Wilson and Strachey. Gaitskell faced the prospect with equanimity and told Dalton: 'We'd be well rid of the three of them.'[21] But Jennie Lee thought, correctly, that Strachey would never resign.

Budget day was 10 April 1951. At the final Cabinet meeting, Gaitskell stated that he would be the one to resign if the Cabinet did not back his proposals. He got his way, and the Health Service charges duly figured in his budget speech. Bevan still hoped for a compromise – for instance, the charges could be announced in principle but the legislation to implement them could be deferred (there was a precedent for this with regard to prescription charges in the 1949 budget). In the ten days that followed the budget, Bevan was listening to friends who begged him to see if something could be worked out.

But, whereas Nye could put off his decision (within limits, at least), Michael was editor of *Tribune* and had a deadline to meet. The front-page comment, headed 'A DANGEROUS BUDGET', was a categorical condemnation of the Health Service charges: 'There is no case whatever for this proposal on the grounds of merit . . . a fundamental blow at the essential principle of the Health Service . . . Mr Gaitskell has delivered a frontal attack on the Health Service.'[22]

This article has been interpreted in various ways. One theory was that 'it obviously bore the stamp of approval from Bevan himself';[23] the Minister of Labour, who had not yet resigned, was attacking the Chancellor in the only way open to him. An alternative theory was that Michael wrote in such forthright terms in order to force Nye's hand and curtail his hesitations. Actually – and simply – he was writing for his readers, who expected a clear line. However, one passage in the article infuriated the right-wingers in the party and the government. It read: 'Must it be 1931 over again? We have had to wait twenty years for a Labour Chancellor to win such warm approval in Conservative quarters.' The analogy seemed to imply that the Labour leaders of 1951 were about to repeat the 1931 betrayal, a source of shame in the party's collective memory. In the tense and heated atmosphere of those April days, it was a paragraph that could prudently have been omitted. Soon, a right-wing MP, Stanley Evans, was describing Bevan's supporters as 'an uneasy coalition of well-meaning emotionalists, rejects, frustrates, crackpots and fellow-travellers'.[24]

At all events, Bevan sent his letter of resignation to the Prime Minister on 21 April. Wilson and one junior minister, John Freeman, also resigned. Bevan's resignation speech in the Commons, while presenting a forceful and cogent case on the issues involved, also attacked Gaitskell in such biting and wounding terms that the two men were cast – so it seemed at the time – as enemies who could never be reconciled. Michael, in his biography of Bevan, recorded that 'no single cheer greeted his peroration' and that 'even most of those reckoned as his friends were dubious about or, more usually, bitterly critical of his tactics'.[25]

However, the friends gathered to take stock of the situation and chart their next steps. The organiser, as usual, was Ian Mikardo, who sent out a circular letter in these terms: 'A little dinner party is being thrown on 24 April . . . for the purpose of having a discussion on the subject of Chinese art in the Fourth Ming dynasty.' A list of those who had accepted the invitation included Michael, Dick Crossman, Jennie Lee, Harold Wilson and John Freeman. Nye Bevan's name was typed in, but crossed out. The Keep Left Group was developing into what inevitably came to be called the Bevanite Group, but not on Bevan's initiative. A generally hostile journalist conceded: 'It was not Bevan who led a crusade and gathered round him a band of disciples.'[26]

In July, the policy of the left was expounded in a *Tribune* pamphlet, *One Way Only*. It was unsigned, but had a foreword in the names of Bevan, Wilson and Freeman. According to Peggy Duff, 'Michael Foot wrote most of it, though Dick Crossman was responsible for the foreword, signed by the three ministers. A meeting at *Tribune*'s office agreed the final text.'[27]

At the outset, the pamphlet emphasised: 'War is not inevitable, but will certainly become so if the rearmament race continues unabated. For that reason, a supreme effort must be made to negotiate a settlement with Russia.' Michael's thinking had made a notable recovery from 1949, when he thought that a settlement was impossible. *One Way Only* argued: 'The policies of the West are based on a gross over-estimate of Soviet strength and a cringing inferiority complex about Soviet political warfare.' However, the tone was moderated:

> We are not opposed to a strong defence: we do assert that breakneck Atlantic rearmament can destroy our ability to win the peace . . . We do not, of course, suggest that the alliance should be broken. We do propose that over the coming months a series of British initiatives should be taken to rectify the lop-sided nature of the alliance.

Such qualifications could not appease the dedicated warriors of the cold war, for whom Michael was an incorrigible extremist. One journal catering to readers in the City, the *Statist*, discerned: 'The true mind behind the fat facade of Mr Bevan is the Robespierre mind of that sea-green, incorruptible, febrile, class-conscious agitator, Mr Michael Foot.'

Michael did not mind the attacks, but fumed when the weapon of suppression was employed. W. H. Smith, the chain which in 1940 had boycotted *Guilty Men*, declined to order more than 5,000 copies of *One Way Only*, and Wyman's (which then owned all the railway bookstalls) stocked only 1,000. Finding the pamphlet unobtainable, people made their way to the *Tribune* office to track it down; 800 copies were sold there in a day. Furious phone calls from Jennie Lee compelled Smith's to take another 40,000 copies. Peggy Duff added up the total: 'Altogether we sold over 100,000. We could have sold double that if the trade had co-operated.'[28] Still, it was the success of *One Way Only* that saved *Tribune* from the threat of closure.

The Keep Left Group (it retained that name until 1954, when it became the Tribune Group) was vulnerable to charges of being a secretive conspiracy. The membership was therefore broadened from the original dozen to include anyone in general sympathy with Bevanite ideas, but the meetings were still private. In 1951 twenty-six MPs were listed as members, plus one peer, Lord (Gavin) Faringdon. His beautiful house in Berkshire, Buscot Park, was useful for weekend conclaves and he sometimes ferried MPs to meetings in his roomy Rolls-Royce.

Most of the public meetings were announced as *Tribune* Brains Trusts. A 'brains trust' – the name was taken from a very popular radio programme launched during the war – was a meeting with a panel of three or four MPs, who answered questions from the audience instead of making speeches. It was a well-timed innovation in politics, coming at a period when formal meetings in the traditional style had lost their appeal. The team could travel together and appear in various places between Friday evening and Sunday. For example, Michael, Barbara Castle and two other MPs, with Mikardo as question-master, spoke on 27–29 April – the weekend after the resignations – in Plymouth, Exeter, Taunton and Bristol. The itinerary was organised by Elizabeth Thomas, Michael's secretary, but it was a rule that the invitation had to come from the local Labour Party. Since most of the constituencies were Bevanite, and a successful public meeting was a bonus for them, this was rarely a problem. The brains trusts were almost always well attended, it was generally possible to charge for admission, and dozens of copies of *Tribune* were sold.

Although the members of a panel sometimes disagreed with each other – which made for liveliness and was part of the attraction – the general effect was, of course, to put across the Bevanite view. A senior Labour Party dignitary like Herbert Morrison was naturally far from delighted when he returned from addressing an audience of 50 and learned that the Keep Left team had drawn 200 in a nearby town. The staff of Transport House, too, considered that the proper task for a constituency was to organise an official party meeting with a member of the NEC as the speaker, not to play host to a bunch of rebellious back-benchers. who devoted the evening to criticising official policy. Moreover, the effect of a brains-trust visitation was to give extra prominence to the local MP if he was a Bevanite (such as Michael in Plymouth or Mikardo in Reading) or to embarrass him if he was a right-winger. The accusation that the Bevanites were setting up 'a party within a party' was voiced more and more angrily.

Angriest of all were the trade union leaders for whom – as for Ernest Bevin in his day – loyalty was the supreme virtue and any dissidence was a stab in the back. Bevin's successor at the head of the Transport and General

Workers' Union was Arthur Deakin, a man who had inherited all of Bevin's intolerance and ruthlessness. Shoulder to shoulder with him stood a group of union bosses – the word is fair, considering the absence of democracy in their organisations – including Sir Tom Williamson of the General and Municipal Workers, Sir Will Lawther of the miners, Sir Lincoln Evans of the steelworkers and Sir Tom O'Brien of the cine-technicians. (Equestrophilia was well developed in the higher ranks of the union hierarchy.)

When Gaitskell introduced his Health Service charges and Bevan raised his objections, the NEC passed a resolution supporting the Gaitskell budget. It was criticised in *Tribune* on the grounds that the NEC was responsible to the party conference, not to the parliamentary party or the Cabinet. The Bevanites – presumably Michael, the regular pamphleteer – returned to the episode in *Going Our Way*, a *Tribune* pamphlet produced as a follow-up to *One Way Only*. The resolution had been opposed only by four constituency members (Bevan, Castle, Driberg and Mikardo) and supported by all the trade union members of the NEC. But these included eight men whose own unions had, in varying terms, objected to the budget. For example, the National Union of Railwaymen had submitted a resolution to the 1951 TUC that 'this Congress strongly disapproves the policy expressed in the statements of the Chancellor of the Exchequer' – but its man on the NEC, Bill Potter, had voted for the resolution describing the budget as 'fair and reasonable'. The comment in *Going Our Way* was: 'When the Government called for a bang on the rubber stamp, these trade union leaders rushed to give it . . . The men who did it may have been speaking for themselves; they were assuredly speaking for nobody else.' Stung by this, the NEC (with its trade union majority) passed a resolution deprecating personal attacks and in particular objecting to revelations of the way its members voted.

By the autumn of 1951, Attlee felt that he could not face another session with a tiny majority, constant harassment from the Tories and disunity in the Labour Party. He called an election, with polling on 25 October. The party conference was cut down to the two days needed for the adoption of a manifesto and essential constitutional business. The headlines went to Bevan's speech at the *Tribune* fringe meeting:

What I object to, and always have, is the assumption that every new and vital growth in the party must be smothered in a demand for unity . . . There is also an obligation on public men when they disagree on certain policies to make the disagreement known . . . because our movement has been built up by lions and not by sheep.

For the men who dominated the NEC, this was bad enough, but they were still more angered by the voting for the constituency section. Bevan topped the poll as usual, Barbara Castle won second place, and Driberg and Mikardo were elected. Shinwell, a former left-winger who had moved to the right and taken the unpopular post of Minister of Defence, lost his seat.

A few hours after the results were declared, three trade-union potentates – Deakin, Lawther and Williamson – met at a Scarborough hotel and pledged themselves to restore order in the party. Deakin told Leslie Hunter of the *Daily Herald*: 'There's five or six, like Bevan, who are out to wreck the party and unless we deal with them now, the party's done for.'[29] Hunter also noted a conversation with Sir Tom O'Brien: 'He told me they had decided that as soon as the election was over they were going to take steps to squash the Bevanite movement and expel its leaders from the party.'[30]

In this spirit of fraternal comradeship, Labour's stalwarts dispersed to confront the Tories at the polls.

5

It would be, most commentators anticipated, another close election with another unpredictable result. Nevertheless, two factors favoured the Tories. The open dispute between the Labour leadership and the Bevanites made it easy to depict the Labour Party as hopelessly disunited and to frighten wavering voters with warnings that Bevan might seize control and become the next Prime Minister. The other factor was that the Liberals, or most of them, were now far more anti-Labour than anti-Tory. Pacts between Tory and Liberal candidates were in operation in two towns, Bolton and Huddersfield; Lady Violet Bonham Carter, contesting Colne Valley, had no Tory opponent and Churchill spoke from her platform. Also, the catastrophe of the 1950 election had bankrupted the Liberal Party and it put up only 109 candidates in 1951. Where they were stranded without a candidate, Liberal voters were inclined in these circumstances to veer towards the Tories. One constituency that the Liberals did not fight again was Devonport. Michael was not too worried; his 1950 success had given him a clear majority over the combined Tory and Liberal vote.

The Tory candidate, again, was Randolph Churchill. Two days before polling, he made an unexpected attack on Michael's record. He announced at one of his meetings: 'Michael Foot was one of those misguided men who sought to stampede the British Government and the High Command into launching a Second Front in 1942. He did not, I gather, intend to take part in this expedition himself.' Randolph, of course, knew perfectly well that Michael suffered from asthma and eczema and had been classified as unfit for military service. Labour activists found some evidence that the canard was being used by Tory canvassers on the doorstep. Michael would have preferred to ignore it, but Jill was up in arms. Speaking at a Labour meeting, she said: 'Let's have this out in the open. Michael Foot volunteered for the Army, he was rejected because of his asthma, and he was on the rooftops of London during the blitz, but he never talks about it . . . The people who have achieved the most are those who talk the least.' She even added, not altogether convincingly: 'Michael is the personification of British understatement.'

The *Western Morning News*, although a Tory paper, had a political correspondent, L. K. Way, who was capable of objectivity and shrewdness and whose electoral forecasts were seldom wrong. He wrote on 23 October that 'the delicate balance of the scales' was tilted in Michael Foot's favour. The actual result gave Michael a more emphatic victory than anyone predicted. The figures were:

Michael Foot, Labour	32,158
Randolph Churchill, Conservative	29,768
Labour majority	2,390

When the result was declared, the scene in the street was so noisy, with Labour and Tory supporters yelling fiercely at each other, that both Michael and Randolph had to cut short their inaudible speeches. Michael went on to Victory Hall, the Labour headquarters, to receive an ecstatic reception. Randolph, arriving at the Embassy Ballroom to say farewell to the Plymouth Tories, had tears in his eyes. They were tears of emotion, he explained, 'for the kind and generous way you have received me after defeat'. He must have realised, however, that they were glad to see the last of him and he would never be invited to contest Devonport again. When he caught the London train in the morning, no one came to the station to see him off.

Examining the results, *The Times* commented: 'Almost as remarkable as the virtual extinction of the Liberal Party – and as full of significance for the future – has been the triumph of Mr Bevan and his associates. Mr Foot, Mr Driberg, Mr Freeman, Mr Wilson and Mrs Castle were all defending marginal seats and all succeeded in holding them. It cannot be just a coincidence.' Had the voting in these constituencies gone in line with the national swing, *The Times* pointed out, at least three of the five would have been lost. While Michael held Devonport, Lucy Middleton, identified as a right-winger, lost the Sutton division of Plymouth to Jakie Astor.

When all the results were in, the Tories had 321 seats, Labour 295 and the Liberals 6. Michael was justified in claiming that 'the voting figures testify to the inherent robustness of the British Labour movement,'[31] for Labour polled almost fourteen million votes, 224,000 more than the Tories, and more than any British party before or since. The oddities of the first-past-the-post system, however, made the Tories the winners. Churchill was back in Downing Street, and Michael was an opposition MP for the first time in his life.

One unexpected result of the Tory victory was to settle the argument over the rearmament programme. Churchill ordered a fresh scrutiny of the commitments for which, having been in opposition when they were made, he was not responsible. The plan adopted by Gaitskell called for an expenditure of £1,250 million in the first year of the rearmament effort. Almost casually, Churchill told the House of Commons that spending this amount was impossible. He added – perhaps generously, perhaps mischievously – 'The point was, I believe, made by the right honourable member for Ebbw Vale [Bevan] after his resignation.'

Naturally enough, *Tribune* crowed: 'What Socialist will now declare that our view has not been vindicated?'[32] To tie up all the loose ends, the editors offered Gaitskell space for comment. He made the best of his indefensible position, claiming that the projected £4,700 million was merely 'the best estimate in round figures' and that: 'We knew the programme might be modified in substance as time went on.' Michael, replying in the same issue of *Tribune*, wrote: 'The more he insists that the estimates must necessarily be vague and uncertain, the more incomprehensible becomes his attack on the Health Service . . . There were many millions available for protecting the Health Service which the Chancellor was devoting instead to an unrealisable arms programme.'[33]

The whole episode could bring the Tories nothing but benefit. The acrimony within the Labour Party was as sulphurous as ever, while Gaitskell's reputation for economic expertise was dented. Moreover, Labour was faced with the awkward problem of deciding its attitude to the Defence White Paper presented by the government in February 1952. In essence, Churchill maintained the rearmament project demanded by the Americans in the framework of NATO. Since the outgoing government had accepted this project, it was difficult for Labour in opposition to attack it. However, a quite large number of Labour MPs had never liked it in the first place and wanted to be free, now that there was no Labour government making claims on their loyalty, to repudiate it. The Shadow Cabinet, resorting to the rather inglorious strategy that appears useful in such circumstances, called on Labour members to abstain when the vote on the White Paper was taken. Fifty-seven MPs, led by Nye Bevan, defied this decision and voted against the government. The outcome was that the party's disciplinary standing orders, which had been in abeyance since 1945, were reimposed. It was an ominous prelude to future conflicts.

The year 1952 saw the Tories settling in nicely. The saving, or rather non-spending, in the rearmament programme enabled the new Chancellor, R. A. Butler, to make popular tax cuts in his budget. The economy regained its balance and inflation dropped almost to zero. Churchill prudently ruled out a return to the policies of the 1930s; there was no mass unemployment, no vengeful assault on the welfare structure. The last vestiges of wartime rationing were swept away. A tactful Minister of Labour, Sir Walter Monckton, established friendly relations with the trade unions. It was the beginning of a period of Conservative government that lasted for the next thirteen years.

In October 1952, delegates gathered for a conference that no one expected to be harmonious. The scene was Morecambe, an undistin-guished seaside resort never patronised by Labour before or since. One journalist recalled: 'The weather was vile – squally rain and high wind. The hall was too small and was badly lighted. Hotel accommodation was inadequate.'[34] Few people who endured that supremely unenjoyable week ever forgot the atmosphere of hostility amounting even to hatred, in which adherents of the rival factions glared at each other before marching off to different cafés or pubs. The sessions, as Michael wrote, were 'rowdy, convulsive, vulgar, splenetic; threatening at moments to collapse into an irretrievable brawl'.[35] Arthur Deakin, as it happened, had what was the normally anodyne task of bringing the 'fraternal greetings' of the TUC. He delivered an ultimatum to what he called 'this dissident element' – 'Let them cease the vicious attacks they have launched upon those with whom they disagree, abandon their vituperation, and the carping criticism which appears in *Tribune*.' As for Lawther, when he was interrupted while at the rostrum he bestowed on the rash delegate a retort straight from his native Northumberland: 'Shut your gob!'

As at Scarborough the year before, the left showed its strength in the voting for the constituency section of the National Executive. Wilson and Crossman were elected to join Bevan, Castle, Driberg and Mikardo, leaving James Griffiths – a veteran Welsh miner who enjoyed general popularity – as the only winner not clearly identified as a Bevanite. Morrison and Dalton were defeated, following Shinwell into humiliation. Dalton by this time saw himself as an elder statesman with no ambitions, but the rejection was a bitter blow to Morrison. He had been on the NEC for thirty years, had made a bid for the party leadership in 1935, was at this time deputy leader (elected to this position by MPs), and cherished hopes of winning the leadership when Attlee retired. He was reduced to the expedient of getting the constitution amended in 1953 so that the deputy leader, like the leader, had an automatic seat in the NEC.

A few days after the end of the Morecambe conference, Gaitskell made a speech voicing his irritations. 'It is time', he declared, 'to end the attempt at mob rule by a group of frustrated journalists and restore the authority and leadership of the solid, sound, sensible majority of the movement.' Since Michael had a column in the *Daily Herald*, Dick Crossman in the *Sunday Pictorial* and Tom Driberg in *Reynolds' News*, 'frustrated' was a curious adjective. But the most widely quoted passage in Gaitskell's speech was: 'I was told by some observers that about one-sixth of the constituency party delegates appear to be Communist or Communist-inspired . . . If it should be one-tenth, or even one-twentieth, it is a most shocking state of affairs.' In calmer mood, Gaitskell could scarcely have been proud of his reliance on anonymous sources, nor his hazy statistics, nor his blurring of the distinction between Bevanites and Communists. Gaitskell's sympathetic biographer, Philip Williams, has written that the speech was a blunder, that the 'one-sixth' was a 'very exaggerated estimate', and that Gaitskell himself did not believe it when he cited it.[36]

The right was on somewhat stronger ground in attacking 'the party within the party'. Membership of the Keep Left Group had risen to forty-seven and it was a standing challenge to the conformist majority. Attlee was persuaded to move a resolution in the Parliamentary Labour Party calling for the disbandment of all unofficial groups. Validated by the authority of the party leader, it was carried by 188 votes to 51, and there was no alternative to obeying it.

The effect was to push the Bevanites back into small private gatherings. Every Tuesday, Crossman's house in Vincent Square was the venue for a lunch attended by the six left-wingers on the NEC, plus Jennie Lee, Michael Foot, John Freeman, Bill Mallalieu and Thomas Balogh. The sessions gave opportunity for lively discussion, but not always for agreed decisions. One respect in which Bevanites differed from Communists was that they were not believers in 'democratic centralism'. Those who knew Nye Bevan well realised that, at moments of crisis, he would decide for himself what choices to make – and that his 'followers' would not always follow him.

6

On 6 March 1953, Joseph Stalin died. Both inside and outside the Soviet Union, there were many who hoped that an ice age had come to an end; Ilya Ehrenburg, a Russian writer with sensitive antennae, hastened to produce a short novel entitled *The Thaw*, and it was legally published. A milder climate might allow the growth of the genuinely humane and democratic socialism that pilgrims had tried to see ever since 1917.

Michael's immediate response came in an article in *Tribune* of 13 March 1953 headed 'NOW LET'S BURY THE STALIN MYTH'. He wrote:

> Stalin, the man, is dead. What about Stalin, the myth? . . . He was acclaimed as the most far-seeing of statesmen, the most perspicacious interpreter of Marxist philosophy, the most brilliant of military commanders, the final arbiter of truth in the realms of science, music, art and every other conceivable human activity . . . Strangely, the Communists were powerfully assisted in building the legend by their most raucous opponents . . . By them, hardly less than by the Communists, he was made to appear infallibly wise in pursuit of his own devilish interests, remorselessly successful in marching towards the triumph he had planned. There he sat in the Kremlin at the centre of the web, smiling and self-confident, jerking his puppets as he willed across half the globe, watching his enemies scurry to their appointed roles in obedience to his grand design.

But, Michael recalled, Stalin had invited the Nazi onslaught by his 'frightened sycophancy' to Hitler. 'No politician in a democratic country would have survived such a debacle.' After the war, the course of social revolution, especially in the Third World, had been retarded by 'the stolid, brutal determination of Stalinism to fit every social and national uprising into the same harsh, fixed pattern'. Notably, Stalin had failed to foresee the Communist victory in China. Within Russia, 'he distorted the Socialist aim in a manner which would have horrified both Lenin and Marx.' The indictment concluded: 'The question remains open whether Stalin's dictatorship has been sufficient to destroy the constructive momentum of the Revolution which gave him the real sinews of Soviet strength . . . But it may be that Socialist regeneration in Russia itself is just another of the world developments which the infallible Stalin could not foresee.'

Internationally, the death of Stalin opened a window to a prospect which ultimately became a reality in 1990: the end of the cold war. The new rulers, it could be guessed, understood the fact which had been concealed both by loyal Communists and by fanatical anti-Communists, but had been grasped by Aneurin Bevan and Michael Foot – that Soviet strength was unequal to the risks of war. The moment had come for an effort to lay the foundations of 'peaceful coexistence' (a phrase which, it is only fair to recall, had been coined by Stalin towards the end of his life). Churchill, the old warrior, saw the opportunity. He was in a position to influence his friend of wartime years, Dwight Eisenhower, who was now President of the United States. A meeting in Bermuda was arranged, at which Churchill intended to secure Eisenhower's co-operation in an overture to the Soviet leaders. Sadly, Churchill was struck down by a severe stroke, from which he never made a complete recovery, and the Bermuda meeting was cancelled. No one else in London or Washington was keen on the project – certainly not the Foreign Secretary, Anthony Eden, nor the US Secretary of State, John Foster Dulles.

Dulles, a rigorous and blinkered anti-Communist, was pursuing a very different project: the construction of a world-wide chain of alliances on the model of NATO. France was engaged in a colonial war against the (largely Communist) National Liberation Front of Vietnam, and was visibly about to lose it. Intensely alarmed, Dulles was preparing the ground for America to carry the baton. Meanwhile, he was trying to enlist Britain, Australia and any other possible candidates in creating a South-East Asia Treaty Organisation (SEATO). By April 1954 the plan was making headway, and Eden informed the Commons that Britain was co-operating in it. Attlee, speaking from the Labour front bench, voiced no opposition, but merely observed that Asian as well as Western nations should be invited to join. Bevan then intervened to denounce SEATO as 'establishing a NATO in South-east Asia for the purpose of imposing European colonial rule'.

Attlee, naturally, was ruffled. Bevan had spoken from the front bench too and had thus assumed the role of leader of the Opposition, plainly implying that Attlee was failing to perform it adequately. Next day, he resigned from the Shadow Cabinet. This body, with twelve members, was elected by Labour MPs and Bevan was the only left-winger who had won a place in it, but Wilson had been placed thirteenth. The rule was that, if a vacancy occurred for any reason, the runner-up moved on to the front bench. However, Wilson was free to decline to do so and the unanimous view among the Bevanites (according to Dick Crossman's biographer, Anthony Howard) was: 'it was unthinkable that any of their number should weaken their leader's protest'.[37] It need hardly be said that this was Michael's view. But Wilson, although aware of this feeling, blandly took the vacant place. Bevan was furious; Mikardo, for one, was not greatly surprised. His portrait of Wilson was: 'He had eyes for nothing but the goal, and his goal was to become leader of the Party; every thought and action, every word he said or wrote, every contact he made was all directed single-mindedly to that end.'[38]

Fortunately, a new French Prime Minister, Pierre Mendès-France, agreed to peace terms in Vietnam. The United States eventually took the burden of this unwinnable war on its shoulders, but not yet. The great controversy that raged in the remaining months of 1954, particularly in the Labour Party, was over a different question: German rearmament.

The project of rebuilding the German Army (which of course had ceased to exist after the defeat of Hitler) to take part in the defence of Europe against the Russian menace had been mooted since 1949. It met with intense opposition in Britain, in France and indeed in Germany itself, and hung fire until 1954, but the Tory government was now ready, under American pressure, to fall into line. The question was whether the Labour Party would fall into line too. The leaders – notably Morrison and Gaitskell – were firmly in favour of it, but aware that the vote at the 1954 conference would be touch and go. German rearmament – so the left, and some who were not normally on the left, argued – would strengthen reactionary and militarist elements in German society, would intensify the cold war and would threaten the hopes of conciliation with the Soviet Union which had risen since Stalin's death.

The NEC, obedient as usual to the big trade unions, adopted a resolution in favour of German rearmament. One small union which, at its own conference, demanded 'the reversal of this tragic decision' was the Amalgamated Society of Woodworkers. But at the party conference the ASW delegation, as a result of ferocious arm-twisting by Deakin, defied this mandate and voted with the NEC. The motion accepting German rearmament got a majority of 3,270,000 votes against 3,022,000.

By the end of the year, German rearmament was pushed through the House of Commons. The official Labour line was abstention, but six MPs voted against it – they included Sydney Silverman and Emrys Hughes – while one enthusiast voted for it. The seven were punished by the withdrawal of the Labour whip. Michael wrote that the Bevanite MPs had been faced with 'an agonising choice'. If forty or fifty MPs had followed Silverman and Hughes, courting mass expulsions at a time when another general election was not a remote prospect, 'the Party would have been plunged into a major crisis'.[39]

Another deep anxiety was weighing on his mind. By 1954, the menace of the atomic bomb had been multiplied by the development of the hydrogen bomb. One bomb tested by the Americans in the South Pacific attained an explosive power of fifteen megatons, and the radiation killed a Japanese fisherman who was eighty-five miles away. This terrifying weapon made German rearmament appear more reckless than ever. Although even Dulles did not propose to equip the new German forces with a nuclear arsenal, unlimited destructiveness might be the consequence of a war in Europe. In any case, the new weapons demonstrated the irrelevance of old concepts of warfare and 'defence'. Michael wrote in *Tribune* of 7 January 1955:

> Historians will find it utterly incredible that all the wise men of the West could find nothing better to do in the year 1954 than to press obsolescent arms into the hands of unwilling Germans to be commanded by ex-Nazis – this is the year when man's final capacity to destroy civilisation was at last revealed in unmistakable language.

In that year of 1954, while the Bevanites were fighting against what they regarded as disastrous policies, they were engaged in another – though related – battle against the intolerance of those who controlled the party machine. The NEC issued another threatening edict against 'personal attacks', and the implications were obvious. Morrison, as it happened, penned an attack on Nye Bevan in *Socialist Commentary* which was quite as personal as anything written in *Tribune*, and Michael retorted with a front-page headline: 'DON'T DISCIPLINE MORRISON'. 'Why not carpet him? The idea has its comical appeal. But we trust that no action so foolish will be taken.' He continued:

> Are we to set up a panel of judges to determine the precise point when a whip becomes a scorpion? How much of the great political literature of the past must be burnt lest the modern generation becomes infected? . . . A healthy dose of liberalism is sorely needed to loosen the hardened bureaucratic arteries which a too conservative leadership has induced.[40]

A few months later, the NEC turned its attention to a paper called *Socialist Outlook*, which was the mouthpiece of a Trotskyite group. The NEC ruling was that 'persons associating' with the paper were ineligible for Labour Party membership. Michael denounced this 'stupid, cowardly and totalitarian edict'. He wrote: 'Such a decree might fittingly be issued within a Fascist or Communist party. But that it should be issued by the leaders of a democratic party is an outrage.'[41]

The next episode involved *Tribune*'s arch-enemy, Arthur Deakin. Deakin had forbidden TGWU members in the London and Liverpool docks to support a strike which had been called by a smaller union to which a considerable number of dockers belonged. Within a few weeks 40,000 dockers were on strike, with members of both unions standing shoulder to shoulder. *Tribune* pointed out that Deakin did not represent his own members. Determined to discipline *Tribune* at last, Deakin persuaded the NEC to write to Michael, Jennie Lee and Bill Mallalieu demanding an answer to the question: 'How do you reconcile your attack on the leadership of the TGWU with your membership of the Party?'

Michael threw himself willingly into writing the reply. It ran to 6,000 words and appeared in an enlarged issue of *Tribune* on 12 November 1954:

Where and when, we would like to know, was it ever decreed or even tentatively suggested that members of the Labour Party have no right to criticise or attack the leadership of the TGWU or any other union? . . . Ernest Bevin was often attacked; he exercised his right to reply, often in unparliamentary language, but even in his most explosive moments we do not recall that he ever demanded the suppression of criticism . . .

Goliath was overthrown by David with his sling. Small newspapers and small unions and all who challenge the big battalions naturally find the story agreeable. But . . . no one has suggested as the proper moral to be deduced from the tale that the monopoly of all weapons, coat of mail, helmet of brass, spear *and* slings should henceforth be retained by the Goliaths . . .

Trade union leaders are not a special breed of humanity, always to be shielded from the rough breezes of democracy, rare birds to be protected by special game laws . . . If they expect to be praised – as most public men do – they must also expect to be criticised . . .

The opposite theory – that leaders must decide what arguments are fit for the rank-and-file to hear – implies three doctrines which no democrat can accept. The theory implies, first, that the few possess a wisdom which the many cannot be expected to share. It implies, second, that society or the party has no need for the awkward, unorthodox, challenging minority . . . It implies, finally, that the established ruling few possess infallibility; for if the leadership of a nation, a party or a trade union is never to be attacked, how can errors be exposed or the process of education go forward? . . . A real understanding of freedom means a willingness to tolerate, not only the views of the majority or those which have won considerable favour, but the irritating, defiant, even ill-expressed and outrageous opinions of the minorities which may still contain the essential grain of wisdom as small as a seed of mustard . . .

We shall continue to print the truth as we see it. We trust that others will do the same. We ask no more and we expect no less than the freedom which the men and women who built the Labour movement exercised themselves and struggled to make possible for their heirs of every nation and race.

7

When Michael and Jill went to Plymouth, they generally stayed at Pencrebar, where Isaac Foot was living with his wife Kitty and his daughter Sally. Sally, with her passion for horses and dogs, was making good use of the land belonging to the house, while Isaac filled one room after another with books. He had written to Michael in 1949: 'The laundry has now been appropriated as a supplementary library and looks lovely. I would like to have my old bedroom but Sal demurs. I may bribe her with another horse!' He had borrowed a thousand pounds, a considerable sum in those days, from Michael, and repaid the last instalment in October 1954. 'In accordance with your wish I am making out the cheque in favour of Jill,' he wrote. He had owned several farms in the neighbourhood, but in the 1950s he sold the freehold to the tenants. 'I shall soon have no land,' he told Michael regretfully. In later life, he was still recklessly extravagant and unfailingly generous. When a nephew had a spell of illness and asked for a loan of five pounds, Isaac sent him a cheque for fifteen by the next post.

Dingle Foot fought North Cornwall as a Liberal in 1951, but was increasingly unhappy about the Liberal Party's drift to the right. He and his friend Megan Lloyd George, who lost her seat in 1951, spent the next few years hesitating over whether or not to move to the Labour Party. In May 1955 Dingle announced that he would vote Labour at the next election. Isaac wrote: 'I am more fortunate than my son Dingle, in that I have a Liberal candidate to vote for in the Bodmin division, and that I can work day after day in support of our gallant West Country candidates.' What most concerned him was the unfair electoral system. 'As long as this injustice remains unrecognised and unremedied, neither of the two parties deserves a Liberal vote. Certainly they will not get mine.'[42]

Mac, pursuing his career in the Colonial Service, had spent some years in Nigeria, and in 1951 he became Governor of Jamaica.[43] In Nigeria he was narrowly saved from being stabbed (perhaps by a militant opponent of imperialism) and in Jamaica, in 1954, he was thrown from his horse during a game of polo and suffered severe concussion. Sylvia wrote to remind Isaac that he had forgotten to send money to pay for a secretary for the Methodist deaconess. 'Do pull yourself together and write to me as soon as you get this letter *with absolutely not a second's delay*.' But she added: 'Although you do not deserve it I still love you to extinction.' Isaac, at the time, was still in debt to Michael. The finances of the Foot family were always complicated. In June 1958 (to anticipate) Dingle wrote to tell his father that he had not been paid on time by solicitors and asked Isaac to guarantee a £5,000 overdraft. Isaac cheerfully complied although he was being pressed by his bank manager – a different bank, fortunately – to reduce his own overdraft of £4,000.

Michael was the only Foot who lived within his income, but he had other problems. The Church Commissioners refused to renew the lease of the house in Rosslyn Hill, and Michael and Jill were forced to move out at short notice. They stayed with friends here and there, and on one occasion were reduced to sleeping in a car. In a letter written on 33 Rosslyn Hill notepaper, but sent from Pinewood film studios, Jill told Beaverbrook: 'We are having a frustrating time trying to find somewhere to live and seem to spend all our free time looking at flats and houses with inadequate heating and decorated in cream and brown.' Michael has described what happened next:

> Beaverbrook, hearing of our plight, rang up to say that he could offer us a roof for our heads; he had especial sympathy for refugees from the English Church. So we turned up at Cherkley in the late afternoon, supposing we had been offered a bed for the night. Instead we were taken on a tour of four derelict cottages on his estate, each more dilapidated than the other and none of them conceivably habitable on the spot . . . 'Choose which you like,' he said.[44]

The Foots stayed for the next six months with Bill and Rita Mallalieu, but they remembered Paddock Cottage, the most attractive and least derelict of the four that Beaverbrook had offered. Michael wrote to him:

> It was extremely kind of you to make the suggestion about your cottage and both Jill and I would very much like to accept . . . and we

are certainly very excited about it . . . I am sure Jill could make it look very nice. I am not sure what would be the best way to go about it in making the required arrangements. Perhaps one day she might call at Cherkley and pick up the keys and then see some decorator in Leatherhead.

After a year of living, as Michael put it, like gipsies, they bought a house at 32a Abbey Road for £12,000. The purchase was a mistake. It was a modern house with no particular character, there was not enough room for Michael's books, and St John's Wood could not compare with Hampstead as a neighbourhood. Although Michael and Jill kept the house for ten years, they never became fond of it. They did, however, become very fond of Paddock Cottage after Jill had made it habitable as a second home. Michael recorded: 'She painted the cottage white, introduced calor gas, and made it into a marvellously convenient hide-out for a writer.' She wrote to Beaverbrook on 1 January 1956: 'I am embarking on the cottage at last, it will be ready well before you return. You really must not think we don't appreciate this, it is going to give us enormous fun.' A year later, on 27 December 1956, she was writing (now on Paddock Cottage notepaper with a Leatherhead telephone number):

> More and more we stay at the cottage, recently groping our way through the field in the fog to get there. We've installed heating and have cleared the garden preparatory to making an orchard and putting down hundreds of bulbs. It's a fine place for work, and I think too Mike is much healthier than in town.

Paddock Cottage needed a great deal of work, including wiring for electricity, for which Michael and Jill paid. Beaverbrook would gladly have taken care of the bills, but Jill consulted Michael's father as an ethical authority and he advised her that paying for the modernisation was a fair exchange for getting the cottage rent-free.

The cottage was not the only benefit bestowed by Beaverbrook. Two or three times a year, Michael and Jill were his guests at Capponcina, his villa at Cap d'Ail on the French Riviera. The air tickets were at Beaverbrook's expense and on one occasion in 1961, when Michael was working hard and had to take a load of books and documents, a letter to the duty officer at London airport put the excess baggage on the Beaverbrook expense account. Unexpected cheques revived the 'unbounded generosity' of the 1940s, with the difference that Michael was not working for Beaverbrook's papers. On 29 December 1957, Jill wrote: 'Thank you, thank you for your munificent gift which made our Christmas all the things they say it should be on the Christmas cards.'

In the eyes of the left, Beaverbrook was just as much of an enemy in the 1950s as in earlier years. When I was on the staff of *Tribune* between 1955 and 1960, I had some awkward conversations with Bevanite activists who inquired anxiously whether it was true that Michael had the use of a cottage on the Beaverbrook estate. More critical comment was aroused by the constant recruiting of *Tribune* journalists by the Beaverbrook papers. Ian Aitken, after leaving *Tribune* for a brief stint on *Reynolds' News*, moved on to the *Daily Express*. In 1955 the editor of *Tribune*, Bob Edwards, received an offer from the *Evening Standard*. Michael wrote to Beaverbrook: 'Naturally we don't want to lose him and I am most grateful to you for saying that you would not make the approach to him if I didn't want you to do so. I am entirely satisfied that the only fair and proper course is for any choice in the matter to be entirely made by Bob Edwards himself.' Bob's choice was to accept the offer. 'This job was a little difficult for my friends to understand,' he commented modestly in retrospect.[45] His pro-Tory articles in the *Standard* (under an easily detected pseudonym) evoked some hilarity in Fleet Street when compared with the opinions he had expressed in *Tribune*. After he left, three newcomers joined the *Tribune* staff: Dick Clements, Bob Millar and myself. A few years later, Michael encouraged Beaverbrook to offer Millar a job, and he took charge of the campaign against the European Community in the *Express* papers. Bob Pitman (not a member of *Tribune*'s staff, but a frequent contributor) also took the Beaverbrook shilling. These cumulative transfers of allegiance caused considerable disquiet, or even disgust, on the left, as I was made aware on various occasions while I worked for *Tribune*. I realised, however, that Michael did not share the disquiet nor see any reason for it.

8

During 1954 and the early months of 1955, there were signs of protest against a Western policy of reliance on nuclear weapons, and particularly against British intentions to make a hydrogen bomb. Mikardo and Silverman addressed a meeting in the Albert Hall, unfortunately drawing only a small audience. The Coventry City Council refused to implement its Civil Defence duties. Richard Acland gave up his seat in the Commons and proposed to fight a by-election on the issue. (To his chagrin, the gesture was nullified when the 1955 general election was called.) The

Labour Party leadership steered a cautious course, urging new summit talks in the hope of reaching a disarmament agreement, but accepting the nuclear strategy as a deterrent to aggression. When the Commons held a defence debate on 2 March 1955, this was the line expressed in the Labour amendment to the motion approving the government's White Paper. It was not a line that satisfied Bevan or the Bevanites. For Bevan, the crucial question was whether Britain should be committed to 'first use' of nuclear bombs in response to a non-nuclear attack. Speaking in the debate, he condemned such a commitment as 'recklessness'. He went on: 'We want from . . . the leaders of the Opposition an assurance that the language of their amendment, moved on our behalf, does not align the Labour movement behind that recklessness.'

Here was a direct challenge to Attlee, who was to wind up for the Opposition. Characteristically, Attlee met the challenge by ignoring it and completed his speech without an answer to Bevan's question. Bevan repeated it. Attlee's colleagues were scandalised – the leader was being cross-examined from his own side of the House. Cornered, Attlee said that he did not support the Tory White Paper but did support the 'general thesis' that deterrence was the best way to prevent war. Sixty-three Labour MPs, led by Bevan, abstained from voting for the Labour amendment. Wilson and Crossman, however, did vote for it.

In the eyes of the right-wingers, Nye Bevan had committed an unpardonable offence and given them the opportunity to drive him into the wilderness. Herbert Morrison – strongly supported by Edith Summerskill, Chuter Ede and James Callaghan – demanded that Bevan should be deprived of the party whip. Gaitskell (according to his biographer) at first demurred, but was talked into backing the move by Ede and Callaghan. It was, he confessed later, his 'worst blunder'.[46] *Tribune*, naturally, came to Nye's defence with a banner headline: 'HIS CRIME: HE SPOKE FOR THE MOVEMENT'.

Awkwardly for the executioners, the man who showed least enthusiasm for drastic action was the man who had been personally challenged. Attlee, reluctantly, voted for the withdrawal of the whip in the Shadow Cabinet and proposed it in a meeting of the Parliamentary Labour Party, where it was carried by 141 votes to 112. But his heart was not in it, and he would probably have admitted the truth of *Tribune*'s next headline: 'ATTLEE UNDER FIRE'. He knew that Bevan did indeed speak for a large part of the movement; he also knew that Churchill, now over eighty years old, was about to retire and Eden, the heir apparent, was likely to hold an election. He said later, referring to Morrison and Gaitskell: 'What they were really concerned about was their own future. Each of them thought that one day he might succeed me as leader and . . . wanted Bevan brought to heel well in advance.'⁴⁷

At all events, he told the Shadow Cabinet that he was opposed to the ultimate punishment – the expulsion of Bevan from the party itself by a vote of the NEC. When it became known that this was being demanded, pleas that the fatal step should not be taken poured in from all over the country. Attlee, it appears, said to Gaitskell crossly: 'You wanted to expel him, I didn't, I was against it from the first, and now look at the mess we're in.'⁴⁸ He proposed a compromise: Bevan should be interviewed by a sub-committee and required to make a promise of future good behaviour. The question now was whether the compromise could get a majority in an NEC largely composed of bitter enemies of Nye Bevan. Anyone who added up the votes knew that it was touch and go.

At this point, Ruth Mikardo played her part in political history. She was Ian Mikardo's daughter and was about to be married in Israel, where she lived. Her father was there to attend the wedding. The bride gallantly volunteered to bring it forward by twenty-four hours, Mikardo flew home in time to be present when the NEC met, and Attlee's proposal went through by a vote of 14 to 13.

For Labour MPs with marginal seats to defend, it was a distinctly unpromising prelude to an election. Eden dissolved the House as soon as he moved into Downing Street and fixed 26 May as polling day. All the newspapers had been on strike for five weeks; they began to publish again only after the campaign started. Next came a railway strike called by the engine-drivers' union. The stoppage was partial, but more effective in the West Country than elsewhere. A miners' strike in Yorkshire spread until 60,000 men were out. Just before polling day, the 'blue union' called another dock strike. Deakin would have been angry, but he had dropped dead after addressing a May Day meeting. Resentment over the inconveniences arising from this strike wave, combined with apathy in the political arena, made bad news for Labour.

Michael's Conservative opponent this time was Joan Vickers, who came to politics from a career with the Red Cross. Unlike Randolph Churchill, she did not rely on oratory, but canvassed the streets tirelessly, chatted with women about their shopping problems and introduced herself to people in cinema queues. L. K. Way in the *Western Morning News* reported that she brought, 'after the tub-thumping campaigns of the past, a more subtle approach which has won by charm and resolution many new adherents'. The Plymouth Tories respected her hard work and liked her personally; if Randolph had been a dubious gentleman, she was distinctly a lady. She made no blunders and refrained from personal hostilities. Her only departure from good manners came after the election, when she told a journalist that Michael 'went so far as to walk down some of the poorer streets, wearing a dirty jacket and split shoes, telling people: "You'll be reduced to this if the Tories get in again." '[49] Michael wrote to tell her that the story was 'completely untrue' and demanded a retraction. She replied blandly: 'Nobody should know better than you how press interviews can become garbled and I think it is a mistake to pay too much attention to stories of this kind.' How the story started, it is impossible to say. The sly (and, for that matter, ridiculous) stratagem is utterly uncharacteristic of Michael; on the other hand, he was – despite Jill's efforts – always careless about clothes and capable of walking around in a dirty jacket and split shoes without being aware of it.

Joan Vickers was standing as a Conservative and National Liberal candidate, although her record as any kind of Liberal was as non-existent as Randolph Churchill's. There was a Liberal candidate, a man named A. Russell Mayne, in the field. He made some telling references to the intolerance that prevailed in the Labour Party and urged Michael to join (or rather rejoin) the Liberals because he was 'unable to act freely in his own party'. Mayne appears to have belonged to the radical wing of the Liberal Party, and had the potential capacity to take votes from Labour rather than from the Tories.

In Plymouth as much as in London, the danger of nuclear war was always present in Michael's mind, as reports of his speeches show. He was seeking to raise the level of the campaign above the parochial, and also to inject some drama into the lifeless atmosphere. He declared: 'I want our representatives to go to the table to pull down the Iron Curtain which is dividing the world and end this armaments race. Nothing less than that should be our aim.' But considerations of war and peace had little influence on the voting in 1955, whether in Michael's constituency or nationally. Way observed: 'The H-bomb issue has exploded like a damp squib.'

His summing up was: 'Michael Foot may get in by his finger-tips. Devonport is a bit of a poser and the result may very well hinge on a few hundred votes one way or the other . . . Such portents as there are suggest a slender advantage to the defending Socialists.' Michael would have concurred with this cautious forecast. He was aware that a swing towards the Tories was inevitable, that Joan Vickers was an excellent candidate, and that he could not expect a majority of the size that he had chalked up in his three previous battles. Nevertheless, he believed that he was winning.

Polling-day, however, brought bad luck to the Labour cause. There was a thick mist in the morning, then fine weather during the hours when people of leisure go to the poll, and – disastrously – heavy rain in the late afternoon and the whole evening. The weather and the lack of excitement that characterised this election combined to reduce the poll to 77 per cent, a crucial reduction from the 84 per cent of 1951. After a recount, the result was:

Joan Vickers, Conservative	24,821
Michael Foot, Labour	24,721
A. Russell Mayne, Liberal	3,100
Conservative majority	100

Miss Vickers said gracefully: 'I hope to represent Devonport as well as Michael Foot did. After his ten years of service, I'm sure that many will miss him.' Michael said: 'I'm naturally disappointed, but it was a fair election and I congratulate my opponent.' While he had been unlucky, most of his friends had been lucky. Barbara Castle held her seat with a majority of 489, and Mikardo held his with a majority of 238.

The poll was down everywhere, with only 76 per cent of the electorate voting, but it was mainly the Labour voters who stayed away. By comparison with 1951, Labour lost a million and a half votes, while the Tories lost 400,000. In terms of seats, the Tories had a net gain of twenty-four and were assured of a comfortable majority in the new House.

The distress among Michael's supporters went far beyond the normal disappointment of the losing side. Ron Lemin, the Labour agent, refused to believe that Michael had really lost, and maintained ever afterwards that he would have won if he had pressed for a second recount. Lemin recalled: 'Jill sat there transfixed and I was shattered. If they'd said: "Let's all get in our cars and go and jump off the Tamar Bridge," I'd have been the first. I cried all night.'[50]

Isaac Foot sent Michael a first edition of one of Jonathan Swift's books and wrote on the flyleaf:

This book (from my library at Pencrebar) is given, with my love and some reluctance, to my son Michael, as a token of consolation on his defeat at Devonport in the General Election, May 26, 1955. I recall defeats at Totnes, Plymouth, Bodmin, St Ives and Tavistock, in the years 1910, 1918, 1924, 1935, 1937 and 1945. On the whole, these defeats were more honourable than my five victories.

Swift, always one of Michael's heroes, was much in the minds of both father and son. Isaac had been urging Michael to write a book about him, but much of Michael's time was devoted to the House of Commons and to his constituency, so the idea had been regretfully shelved. But, on the morning of 27 May, he said to Jill: 'Now I can write that book.'

— *Chapter 7* —

THE CLASH

I

The book that Michael wrote in 1955–6, *The Pen and the Sword*, was devoted to the achievements of Jonathan Swift, whom Michael ranked as the supreme practitioner of his own craft of journalist and pamphleteer. The narrative covered a fairly short period, from October 1710 to January 1712. In that time, Swift made a vital contribution to ending a long and costly war against the France of Louis XIV, and to destroying the reputation and power of the greatest Englishman of the age, the Duke of Marlborough.

For the first time since his abandoned life of Fox, Michael was writing as a historian. But he was a historian closely involved in the politics of his own time, and similarities came continually – if sometimes only half-consciously – to his mind. He was aware, in particular, that human character and historical conditions are intertwined. He had certainly read the passage in Trotsky's *History of the Russian Revolution* in which that politician–historian delineated the strikingly similar personalities of Charles I of England, Louis XVI of France and Czar Nicholas II.

The architecture of *The Pen and the Sword* was masterly. In his first chapter, Michael introduced the Swift of 1710 – a man of forty-one, who had risen no higher than the vicarage of a poor Irish village with a tiny Protestant congregation. This Swift was a man of frustrated ambition, with a burning sense that his talents far exceeded his rewards. (Michael, aged forty-two, was still a secondary, though valued, member of the Bevanite team and had just lost his seat in Parliament.)

Swift, wrote Michael, 'hated lies and sham and every form of pomposity and imposture. He unsheathed his pen to rescue a friend, to savage an opponent, to serve an immediate cause.'[1] As yet, however, his themes were chosen from intellectual life and religious debate rather than directly from politics (though, in his time, politics and religion were in constant interaction). His greatest success to date was *A Tale of a Tub*, but he gained no credit because he prudently published it anonymously. Like *Guilty Men* in 1940, *A Tale of a Tub* in 1704 caused considerable stir and evoked numerous wrong guesses as to the authorship. Swift remarked: 'The world, with all its wise conjectures, is yet very much in the dark; which circumstance is no disagreeable amusement either to the public or himself.'

With Chapter 2, the main characters of the drama take their places on the stage. We meet Queen Anne, a woman of limited intellectual capacity but considerable obstinacy (like Queen Victoria). Despite the constitutional settlement (or 'Glorious Revolution') of 1688, she retained extensive powers, including the power to select or dismiss ministers. The principle of monarchical impartiality was still unborn, and Anne – like most occupants of the throne up to and including George VI – was in her own creed a Tory.

We meet another woman who might, had birth so destined her, have been a great queen – Sarah, Duchess of Marlborough. Michael dissected her faults but warmed to her irresistibly. He portrayed her as 'a source of boundless vitality and intrigue, insatiable in influence and ambition, masterful, outspoken, restless, an aggressive Whig, and, with it all, a wonder of loveliness'. It could have been a sketch of Barbara Castle (that aggressive socialist) or at least of Barbara as seen by the young Michael Foot.

We also meet the dominant politicians of the period – Lord Godolphin, Henry St John and Robert Harley, who was the first to win the appellation of Prime Minister. Harley was a man of phenomenal subtlety and sophistication, always a jump ahead of his rivals. In Michael's fascinating but also fascinated analysis of Harley's twists and turns, we can detect the first sign that Michael himself, always anchored to his principles, could nevertheless relish the politics of the private deal and the balancing act, which he eventually relished in action in 1976–9. St John was also a skilful politician, but more impatient and strong-willed. Michael defined his characteristics as 'energy, audacity and duplicity'.

However, pride of place in this gallery was given to John Churchill, Duke of Marlborough. The comparison with his descendant, Winston Churchill, was inevitable (though never explicitly made by Michael). Like Winston, the Duke received credit and even adulation as 'the man who won the war' – but Swift pointed out, as did Michael in 1945, that every war leader is impotent without the bravery and self-sacrifice of his soldiers. At the zenith of the Duke's career, his prestige and popularity were enormous. To cut him down to size, as Swift essayed, was a task as venturesome, and to some as shocking, as the task undertaken by Michael

Foot and Frank Owen of performing that operation on Winston in the Second World War.

Most historians have assumed as an axiom that the Duke's war, like Winston's, had to be fought and won. The France of Louis XIV was Europe's most populous, most cohesively governed and most militarily formidable nation. Its domination of Europe, with the reduction of England to impotent servility, was as real a menace as any presented later by Napoleon and by Hitler. A defeated England in 1704 might have resembled a Britain governed by Oswald Mosley in 1940. Yet the parallel cannot be pushed too far. Despite Marlborough's victories, a negotiated peace was at some point inevitable. It was never possible, or contemplated, to destroy Louis as Napoleon and Hitler were destroyed.

Moreover, at the height of his fame Marlborough aroused suspicions. In Swift's view, 'he is covetous as Hell, and ambitious as the Prince of it'. He had made the blunder of asking the Queen to appoint him as General (that is, Commander-in-Chief) for life. Swift warned: 'By these steps a General during pleasure might have grown into a General for life, and a General for life into a *King*.' The word was electrifying. Only sixty years had passed since the transmutation of Cromwell from General into Lord Protector. Marlborough's motive for intruding into politics could be, Swift hinted, 'that of Caesar or Cromwell, of which, God forbid, I should accuse or suspect any body'.

In reality, the Duke cherished no ambition for supreme power; but he had the soldier's contempt for quarrelling politicians and angrily resented any criticism of himself. In particular, he scorned and tried to ignore attacks in the printed press. 'This foolish disdain', Michael commented, 'was his real Achilles heel.' He never grasped that he was living in the primordial era of Grub Street – that imaginary thoroughfare pulsating with talent, energy and malice. As Michael wrote:

> The Duke understood nothing of Grub Street; he despised the public opinion which the Grub Street writers so largely dictated . . . Probably the Duke and Queen Anne herself were the only two eminent figures of the time who still regarded the printing press as an invention of the devil, a wretched encumbrance on the political scene . . . Public opinion with the press as its main engine, in the country at large and particularly in the London coffee-houses, was now a considerable force. It could help sway votes in Parliament, settle elections, sink the public credit or raise a mob in the streets.[2]

Hence Michael's Chapter 3 was an affectionate description of Grub Street, its workings, its powers and its outstanding citizens. But he was especially concerned to stress that Grub Street had to fight for its freedom against an array of outraged ministers, courtiers, bishops and judges. Any journalist who offended too riskily could find himself in prison or in the pillory, and Swift at times feared such a fate. In 1710 the House of Lords demanded ruthless measures against any writings likely to 'disturb the Peace and Quiet of the Kingdom'. The public, it was contended, had no business to know of the privileged debates or the unwary utterances of MPs and peers. A sequel in our own times has been the struggle, waged among others by Michael Foot and Dick Crossman, for the televising of Parliament – a battle that ended in victory only in 1988.

Against this background, Michael proceeded to relate the political events and conflicts of 1710–11 and especially the role played by Swift. Arriving in London from Ireland with no plan for his future and no fixed political loyalties, Swift was soon spotted or 'head-hunted' by the Tory leader, Harley. Hitherto, he had been if anything a Whig, and his friends were as disturbed by his acquisition of Harley as a patron as Michael's friends had been when he took employment under Beaverbrook. Like Michael, Swift was unrepentant. He wrote to his Stella: 'Who the Devil cares what they think? Am I under obligations in the least to any of them at all? Rot 'em, for ungrateful dogs.'

Michael conceded that Swift was motivated by personal ambition and by the desire for an outlet for his gifts. But Swift could truthfully have claimed, as Michael claimed when on the *Evening Standard*, that he wrote nothing which he did not believe. The aim of Harley and St John was a peace treaty, which a Whig administration had rejected in 1709. The war had lasted for ten years; the weariness in England was real and deep. What spurred Swift, so Michael asserted, was 'his blazing hatred of war – a hatred which still scorched when some twelve years later he wrote the Voyage to the *Houyhnhnms*'.

What inspired Michael, as much as this justification, was his professional admiration for Swift's abilities. 'He could persuade, mock, instil passion or incite to action, and whichever faculty he chose to employ for particular occasions he spoke always as one having authority.' Michael noted too that 'he addressed himself – as only supreme controversialists will do – less to the weakness of his opponent's case than to its strength.' That had been the principle followed in debate by Nye Bevan, and learned from him by Michael.

Always writing anonymously (but in time quite widely identified), Swift expounded the case for peace between November 1710 and June 1711 in his journal, the *Examiner*, which he had started under Harley's patronage. It was read, like the *New Statesman* in its heyday, by everyone concerned to follow political events or debate political opinions. Incontestably, it was of crucial importance in extending and crystallising the sentiment for peace. Whig journals attempted to contend with it, but were utterly outclassed. The national mood swung towards the Tories. The Queen dismissed her previous ministers and appointed Harley and St John to leading positions. In elections in November 1710 (held, of course, on a limited franchise which favoured those most open to the influence of a paper like the *Examiner*) the Tories won an overwhelming majority in the Commons. This was not conclusive, as it would be today; the Lords, with a Whig majority, held equal power. But, as things turned out, it was the vital breakthrough.

A further effort, however, was needed. Swift rose to the occasion by writing one of the cleverest, most eloquent and most influential pamphlets of all time: *The Conduct of the Allies*. Michael quoted from it extensively and described its technique enthusiastically. Its success, relative to the possible readership, matched that of *Guilty Men*. The first edition of 1,000 copies sold out in two days; within a week, four more editions followed.

The *Conduct* gained its effect by convincing readers of two propositions. One was that the Duke of Marlborough – because of his ambition, his avarice for wealth and his determination to keep his job – was the main obstacle to peace. If peace were to be secured, this obstacle must be removed. That argument was advanced, not only by Swift, but by Harley, St John and the Tories in general. But the second proposition was Swift's alone – the proof, Michael considered, of his genius – and there is no evidence that it was suggested to him by Harley or anyone else. Until now, advocates of peace had been content to argue that the war had gone on too long. Swift astounded his readers by declaring that the war had been wrong from the beginning. 'We began this war contrary to reason' – simply for the benefit of the Duke and Duchess. 'The true spring or motive of it was the aggrandising a particular family.' It had been 'a war of the General and the Ministry [that is, the previous Whig ministry] and not of the Prince or People'.

This came as a blinding revelation, making sense of everything that had been obscure, to thousands who were ready for it. The achievement was the equivalent of convincing Americans in 1968 that the Vietnam war had been wrong all along.

So the story moved on to its climax. The Queen was persuaded to eliminate the Whig majority in the Lords by creating new peers. The final weeks were a cliff-hanger, in which the campaign almost foundered. But the essential victory was won when the Queen dismissed an outraged

Duke from his generalship. The peace treaty followed with the force of irresistible logic. Michael summed up:

> The crash sounded milder than all had expected. The heavens did not fall. The sun still kept its course. No sudden alarm swept the country. The coffee-houses, the country gentlemen, members of the House of Commons, men of opinion everywhere had been prepared for the event. *The Conduct of the Allies*, the most deadly pamphlet in the English language, had done its work.[3]

The book was written between the summer of 1955 and the autumn of 1956. It was a long book – about 120,000 words – and the most substantial work of research and composition that Michael had ever undertaken. Most of the writing was done at Paddock Cottage. Michael had no other duties except his *Daily Herald* column and *Tribune*; and after 1955 he ceased to be officially the editor of *Tribune* and preferred to say that it was edited by a collective. In practice, I wrote some of the political articles and Dick Clements took charge of the layout and sub-editing and saw the paper through at the printers. This year was indeed the most relaxed and tranquil of Michael's life so far.

The publisher of *The Pen and the Sword* was MacGibbon and Kee. This firm was owned by Howard Samuel, a property tycoon who, though he had no strong political convictions, was a friend of Nye Bevan and Jennie Lee. Because of this friendship, he put money into *Tribune* and became a director. When he diversified into publishing, he let it be known that he would gladly publish any book that Michael wanted to write; Michael took the hint and offered his book to MacGibbon and Kee rather than to Gollancz. The editor was Reginald Davis-Poynter, a Bevanite activist who soon became a friend.

Michael dedicated *The Pen and the Sword* to 'my father and Jill'. It was Isaac Foot who had suggested Swift as a fruitful subject, and he was delighted with the result. He made this clear in a phone call to Mac, who was then Governor of Cyprus. In an interview, the father of the Foots said: 'I told Mac on the telephone today that anyone can be an MP or Governor of Cyprus. But this is the summit of the Foot family's achievement – an historical work that will be read in fifty years' time.'[4] More enthusiasm reached Michael in a letter from John:

> It is magnificent . . . The story grows in excitement as you go along until, if one's ignorance of the period is as abysmal as mine, you are sorely tempted to turn to the Epilogue in advance to see how it all

works out. The two outstanding features to my mind are the unravelling of the political intrigue and the character studies . . .

Mind you, Swift – when all is said – is a disgusting fellow, an appropriate progenitor of British journalism. I hope you realise that the book is a devastating indictment of the political animal, and nest-fouling on an eagle scale.

Confining himself to the political theme, Michael had not written about Swift's much debated private life; but he was convinced that Swift genuinely loved the two women who figured in it, known as Stella and Vanessa. Just when *The Pen and the Sword* was completed, Jill's daughter Julie gave Michael and Jill a dog. The name chosen for this charming bitch was Vanessa.

There was much more to be said about Swift. Michael became friendly with a Swift scholar, Kathleen Williams, whose important book he reviewed in *Tribune* in 1959. She wrote to him: 'What I find fascinating in Swift's political thinking is the humane basic attitude underlying it, and how that is reflected in *Gulliver's Travels* and the rest. I think that attitude is best expressed in the Irish political period.' Michael was stimulated to give close attention to *Drapier's Letters* and *A Modest Proposal*, and to the development of the Tory pamphleteer into the champion of the Irish poor. He wrote later:

War, poverty and oppression, which he knew at first hand, broke his heart and maybe also his faith, but not his reason. Ireland changed his temper, his style and his political vision. He had equipped himself to enter the battle to help his stricken people and he raised his art to a new height.[5]

2

Clement Attlee, now distinctly past his best as Labour Party leader, was under pressure to resign but was reluctant to go. It was an open secret that he wanted to stay long enough to rule Herbert Morrison out of the succession. But the *Daily Herald* forced his hand by stating as a fact that he would retire before his next birthday, and on 7 December 1955 he announced his resignation.

At the party conference in October, Gaitskell had strengthened his position by making an effective speech and by defeating Bevan – for the second time, and by an overwhelming majority – in the election for the post of party treasurer, which was effectively decided by the block votes of the big trade unions. It was clear that the right wing in the party, and many in the centre, wanted him as the next leader. When Attlee resigned, Gaitskell informed Morrison that he intended to stand. Morrison, living in a fool's paradise, replied: 'Of course, my boy, you go ahead if you want to. You'll be out on the first ballot.'[6]

Taking pity on Morrison, Shinwell and a group of Labour elder statesmen proposed that he should be elected without a contest. Bevan, who hoped to avert or at least postpone the ascent of Gaitskell, accepted the suggestion, but Gaitskell – not surprisingly – rejected it. Instead of being 'out', he was elected on the first ballot, with the votes of 157 MPs against 70 for Bevan and a mere 40 for Morrison. For Morrison, it was a devastating humiliation. Bevan's vote was not bad, considering how few Labour MPs could be listed as genuine left-wingers, but he was depressed by Gaitskell's triumph; it was, as Michael wrote, 'a galling moment'.[7] Bevan thought Gaitskell quite incapable of leading the party to victory – a judgement which was to be proved sound in 1959.

His reaction was to resolve to stand again for treasurer in 1956. There was no obvious right-wing candidate, and any opponent was bound to be less formidable than Gaitskell. However, the prospect did not cheer him. Among friends at the weekly *Tribune* staff lunch, he said: 'The danger is I might be elected. There's the bloody agony of being trapped in the annual conspiracy.' On the same occasion, commenting on plans to celebrate the party's fiftieth anniversary, he remarked: 'We're celebrating the jubilee as the decay sets in.'[8]

Meanwhile, Eden was winning no laurels as Prime Minister. The *Daily Telegraph* noted that his favourite oratorical gesture was to bring one fist down into the other hand, but no sound was audible. What was missing, the article pointed out, was 'the smack of firm government'. Coming from the most orthodox Tory paper, the criticism was deadly. Michael, writing in 1955, had diagnosed his limitations: 'With mock bravado, he lets out his war-whoops, mounts his charger, and hurls himself upon his victims with all the devastating effectiveness of a fancy-dress warrior in a tea-party charade.'[9]

Thin-skinned and irritable, Eden was looking for a chance to prove that he was really a strong man. The opportunity came in July 1956. Gamal Abdel Nasser, President of Egypt, was planning the construction of a huge dam on the Nile at Aswan, to be financed mainly by an American loan. On 12 July, Dulles informed an incredulous Egyptian ambassador that the deal was off.

Nasser's response was swift. In a speech at Alexandria on 26 July, he announced the nationalisation of the Suez Canal Company. This company, with headquarters in Paris and British and French directors, had been managing the canal since its completion in 1869. Overnight, its installations were taken over, the staff and pilots were told that they must work for a new authority on pain of imprisonment, and shipowners were notified that this authority would collect the passage tolls.

Eden heard the news, that Thursday evening, while hosting a dinner for the King of Iraq. One of the guests was the Leader of the Opposition, Hugh Gaitskell, whose reaction was made clear by his subsequently published diary: 'I said that I thought they ought to act quickly whatever they did and that, as far as Great Britain was concerned, public opinion would almost certainly be behind them.' With this assurance, Eden called Army, Navy and RAF chiefs to a midnight meeting and asked them to make plans for a quick landing at Port Said, northern terminus of the canal.

No secret information was required to arouse suspicions of Eden's intentions, and on Monday morning the staff of *Tribune* – although Michael was on holiday, staying with Beaverbrook at Capponcina – soon decided to take a line of forthright opposition. Under the headline 'STOP THIS SUEZ MADNESS!', the front page declared: 'Labour's duty is clear. It must oppose the hysterical campaign against Nasser and his nation . . . It must protect Britain from being hustled into the use of force.'

On 2 August the House of Commons debated the crisis. The 'hysterical campaign' was well under way, at Westminster as well as in the press. A Tory MP, Hugh Fraser, demanded: 'Who will chain the mad dog in Cairo?' On the Labour side, Morrison said that he would support the use of force: 'I therefore say to the government that I wish them luck in solving this problem.' Gaitskell was more cautious: 'There are circumstances in which we might be compelled to use force.' But he added: 'We must not allow ourselves to get into a position where we might be denounced in the Security Council as aggressors.' His verdict on Nasser's action was: 'It is all very familiar. It is exactly the same that we encountered from Mussolini and Hitler.' This comparison was quickly becoming popular. In a broadcast on 8 August, Eden said: 'The pattern is familiar to many of us, my friends. We all know this is how fascist governments behave.'

Nye and Jennie spent the next weekend with John Mackie, a Scottish farmer and an old friend, at his beef-fattening farm in Essex. Ian Mikardo joined them for dinner. He remembers Nye saying emphatically: 'Nasser's a thug. He needs to be taught a lesson.'[10] No one else round the dinner-table agreed with this attitude, and three days later Mikardo found that Nye had changed his mind.

The curious feature of this period was that a general approval of the use of force was combined with a general disbelief that it would actually come about. Michael wrote later:

It was true – unbelievable though it first appeared to both Gaitskell and Bevan and most others – that the British Cabinet was contemplating a resort to force in defiance, if need be, of the United Nations . . . For once, Bevan's antennae had not immediately diagnosed the symptoms . . . Bevan posed the question but he still found it inconceivable.[11]

Eden, in fact, was obliged to hold his hand for two reasons. General Templer, the Army Chief of Staff, reported that an invasion of Egypt could not be mounted in less than six weeks; and the Americans required an international conference of the parties concerned, which met in London on 16 August.

Michael rounded off his holiday with a week at Paddock Cottage, working on Swift. In a thank-you letter to Beaverbrook, he wrote on 9 August:

I have just returned to the Tribune office after a fine week at Paddock Cottage. Yesterday the sun shone, Cherkley is looking very beautiful, if not quite so beautiful as Capponcina . . . Back in London, just at the first glance, the political situation looks tougher than any time since the war. Eden's speech last night was extremely effective as a speech. But I believe he is sunk. If he wanted to take any action, his only chance was to do it before the conference. Now, I believe, he has stymied himself.

Nevertheless, British and French military men were working intensively on plans for an invasion of Egypt. Guy Mollet, the French Prime Minister (nominally a Socialist) was as enthusiastic as Eden. But the Americans did not approve; Eisenhower told his press conference: 'I can't conceive of military force being a good solution.' Gaitskell made it clear that Labour would not support the use of force unless it was authorised by the UN. As early as 14 August, a hastily formed Suez Campaign Committee drew an audience of 500 to a London meeting, with Michael and A. J. P. Taylor among the speakers.

Through September, the invasion plan was delayed by various attempts at a compromise. October began with the Labour Party conference and a virtually unanimous denunciation of Eden's policy. Bevan was standing for the treasurership again. His opponent was George Brown, who had first made his mark by ferociously demanding the expulsion of Stafford Cripps at the 1939 conference. Since Brown had the backing of the biggest trade unions, it looked as though Nye might suffer a third defeat. The night before the voting was described in my diary:

> Michael kept Bob [Millar] and me up over the teacups till about three, I suppose because he was so worried about the treasurership he didn't expect to sleep. He had it worked out that Brown had won . . . I realised later his arithmetic was decidedly peculiar (so was Brown's) and he was really protecting himself against disappointment.

Bevan won by a majority of 274,000 votes in a poll of over six million. I recorded: 'The delegates let a moment go by before the applause broke, a moment of sheer relief. All day Michael was simply walking on air.'

The victory came at the right time, for Gaitskell had no choice but to accede to urgings from all sides (or most sides) of the party that Bevan should become the front-bench spokesman on foreign affairs. Two crises were nearing explosion points: one in the Middle East, the other in Eastern Europe. In the wake of Khrushchev's denunciation of Stalin, riots broke out in Poland and Wladyslaw Gomulka – a man who had been reviled as a deviationist and spent years in prison – emerged as Communist Party leader. In Hungary too, while crowds surged through the streets of Budapest and demolished a statue of Stalin, Imre Nagy, expelled from the party the year before, was hastily installed as Prime Minister on 23 October. But here the outcome looked more perilous; the hated security police opened fire on an unarmed crowd, Russian tanks were deployed to restore order, and a week of street-fighting followed.

The Suez war began on 30 October with an attack on Egypt by Israel. Britain and France sent an ultimatum ordering both Israeli and Egyptian forces to keep clear of the canal. Failing compliance within twelve hours, Britain and France would send troops to occupy and 'protect' the canal zone. Egypt naturally rejected the ultimatum. As the world now knows, the whole plan had been worked out ten days beforehand at secret meetings in a Paris suburb between British, French, and Israeli ministers. Eden denied in the House of Commons that he had any foreknowledge of the Israeli advance, but on 31 October a British correspondent in Washington reported: 'There is no longer any doubt in the minds of American officials that Britain and France were in collusion with the Israelis from the beginning, and sanctioned the invasion of Egypt as an excuse to reoccupy the canal zone.'[12] Eisenhower and Dulles were furious at the deception and determined that the Anglo-French aggression – it could be called nothing else – should not succeed.

The headline in *Tribune* of 2 November was 'A CRIME AGAINST THE WORLD'. Michael wrote:

Eden's government must be destroyed. The crime done in our name must be expiated. Only thus can Britain recover its reputation as a friend of peace and human decency . . . Not since Neville Chamberlain presented Hitler's terms to the Czechs in 1938 has a powerful Western nation treated a small nation with such brutal contempt.

But the aggression was a fiasco, and something of a farce, as well as a crime. To sustain the structure of lies, the invasion forces set out by sea from Malta only after the ultimatum was sent. The only action in the intervening days was the bombing of Egyptian towns. By the time the troops went in on 5 November, the Israelis had reached their objectives and stopped fighting, Egypt as well as Israel had accepted the ultimatum, Britain and France had been condemned as aggressors, and the UN had acted swiftly to assemble an international peacekeeping force.

Everything was coming unstuck. The Russians, who had promised a withdrawal from Hungary, reversed engines and crushed the popular uprising; it could well be argued, though without clinching evidence, that the uncertainties arising from the Suez aggression were the fatal influence. Gaitskell and Bevan, working as a team, subjected Eden to merciless fire in the House of Commons. After a huge protest rally in Trafalgar Square, addressed by Bevan, demonstrators battled with police at the corner of Downing Street. The government lost the support of *The Times* and the *Observer*, which printed an outspoken leader written by Dingle Foot, a member of the board. Reactions all round the world were hostile and India was on the verge of leaving the Commonwealth. Harold Macmillan, Chancellor of the Exchequer, who had been one of the most determined enthusiasts for the attack, had to admit that a disastrous run on the pound had set in, the Americans would offer no support and the UN was about to order an oil embargo. 'That finishes it!' he exclaimed.[13] On 6 November, with the troops still only halfway along the canal, Eden and Mollet had to order the ceasefire. As a cruel postscript, Eden's health, which had been precarious throughout the crisis, collapsed, and on 21 November he had to fly to Jamaica for a complete rest.

Victor Gollancz, as outraged by Suez as anyone, had not forgotten Michael's polemical and investigative talents. He asked Michael to write a book, to be titled *Guilty Men 1957*. (The date of the crime was 1956, but the book could not be completed until the New Year.) The urgency was obvious, so Michael enlisted me as co-author.

Two chapters were devoted to a chronology of the crisis from July to the week of the aggression. Three other chapters were concerned with the history of British imperialism in Egypt (this one was written by Michael, and he quoted from Wilfred Scawen Blunt and from Shaw's preface to *John Bull's Other Island*); with Cyprus, which was then in revolt against British rule and was the base for the bombing of Egypt; and with Algeria, which supplied the motive for French complicity. 'Was There a Plot?' marshalled the evidence for collusion. 'Break with the Past!' was the concluding chapter in which Michael drew the lessons. We had several cartoons by Vicky, some reprinted from the *New Statesman* or the *Daily Mirror*, some drawn specially. And the epigraphs to head the chapters were contributed by Shakespeare, the Bible, the French Declaration of the Rights of Man, Burke, Paine, William Morris, Lewis Carroll, Joseph Conrad and Winston Churchill.

Following the system employed by the authors of *Guilty Men*, we read the entire text aloud to each other and agreed on corrections or emendations. It took all night. In the morning, we set out to drive from Michael's house in Abbey Road to the *Tribune* office. I was at the wheel, I was not at my most alert and we had an accident. As there were no seat-belts in 1957, Michael cut his forehead on the windscreen. Blood dripped on to the manuscript, which he was holding on his lap, and Elizabeth Thomas had to retype forty pages. In view of the subject, this was not inappropriate.

While the book was in the press, Eden resigned. Most people expected that Butler would succeed him, but Randolph Churchill pulled off a scoop by telling *Evening Standard* readers that the Queen, advised by Tory grandees, would send for Macmillan. Michael dashed off a new introduction pointing out that Macmillan had been an eager supporter of the Suez adventure until he saw its disastrous consequences, whereas Butler had been 'lukewarm and equivocal about the whole enterprise'. In narrow political terms, the Tories were making the right choice. Macmillan was rated as a successful Prime Minister, at least for the next five years.

Our book was, not surprisingly, condemned by the *Economist* as 'an arid and one-sided tract'. The Tory historian Robert Blake conceded: 'Although much of Mr Foot's book is partisan and tendentious, many Tories will agree with him in deploring the prevarication and evasiveness of Government spokesmen.' Anxiously, he asked: 'Where are our pamphleteers of the Right?' Another Tory, Ian Gilmour, wrote in the *Spectator*: 'A juster and more charitable verdict than that passed by Mr Foot would be "guilty but insane".' When he read this, Michael said to me: 'Damn it – there was our title.'

3

Suez and Hungary had diverted the thoughts of people on the left from the issue that came to dominate the political scene in 1957: the issue of nuclear weapons or, in the phraseology of the time, the H-bomb (or simply 'the bomb'). The Attlee government had authorised the making of a British atomic bomb (without consulting Parliament, the Labour Party or the people at large) and the Tories took the further decision that Britain should follow America and Russia with possession of the hydrogen bomb. The first British H-bomb was due to be tested in the early summer of 1957 at Christmas Island, a fragment of empire whose name suggested ironic reflections on peace and goodwill.

The files of *Tribune* show that the tests were the sole preoccupation through the first six months of the year, and the question of the manufacture or possession of the bomb was not argued out until July. In retrospect, this may seem strange; but the fact that the tests were harmful to health was a new and horrifying discovery. Radiation would cause cancer and leukaemia, and would be responsible for genetic mutations and the birth in future generations of defective children. For the first time in history, death and suffering were being inflicted, not in war but in peacetime in the process of experiment.

On 5 April a narrow majority of Labour MPs, at a party meeting, voted for a postponement of the Christmas Island test – a compromise between endorsement, advocated by George Brown among others, and clear opposition. Barbara Castle and Donald Soper (a popular Methodist preacher and friend of Michael's) addressed a crowded meeting, which was followed by a Trafalgar Square rally. Two public-spirited women in Hampstead, Sheila Jones and Ianthe Carswell, founded the National Committee for the Abolition of Nuclear Weapon Tests, which received a thousand letters of support in a week.

Yet the fact had to be faced that the bomb, like any other weapon, could not be credible without being tested. To oppose the tests and accept the bomb was a logical impossibility. One distinguished man who thought his way through to the crux of the matter was Bertrand Russell, whose humanist philosophy had attracted Michael since the 1930s and who was now eighty-five years old. In a contribution to a book entitled *Fallout* (edited by a scientist, Dr Antoinette Pirie), he urged that, with or without an international agreement, Britain should 'explicitly and emphatically abandon H-bomb tests'. But he also wrote: 'I should rejoice if the British government were to abandon not only the projected tests but also the manufacture of the H-bomb . . . I do not wish to be an accomplice in a vast atrocity which threatens the world with over-whelming disaster.'

Tribune reprinted these words on 2 August 1957. Russell was lending his vast moral and intellectual authority to a policy line on which Michael and the *Tribune* staff were fully agreed. We wrote on 30 August: 'Let us dismantle our petty arsenal of nuclear bombs and make no more.' And on 27 September: 'The H-bomb excludes both victory and defeat. After suicide, there can be no slavery. The end and the means are one, joined in a split second of annihilation.'

The moral imperative was clear, but other questions presented themselves in the – never purely moral – world of politics. Was a British rejection of nuclear weapons necessary, or indeed desirable, if there was a chance of disarmament by international agreement? Would a Britain which acted unilaterally be better, or worse, placed to influence other nations? These questions were posed most acutely and personally for the man who, since the Suez days, had become Shadow Foreign Secretary: Aneurin Bevan.

A study of his speeches and writings in 1957 does not reveal any complete resolution of the problem. As Michael observed: 'Sometimes in a speech he would argue with himself . . . He ran the risks of exposing himself to the misinterpretation which might be placed upon some uncompleted, tentative judgment.'[14] Yet he came close to saying that rejection of 'the bomb' should be absolute and unqualified, and his followers could not be blamed for thinking that he had made a firm commitment. In one speech, he proposed: 'If Britain had the moral stature she could say: "We can make the H-bomb, but we are not going to make it." . . . Tens of millions of people all over the world would once more lift their eyes to Britain.' In a *Tribune* article: 'The existence of nuclear weapons can no longer be regarded as a deterrent to war, but as making war a certainty . . . We must apply our minds to the destruction of nuclear weapons before they have a chance to destroy us.'

The party conference was to be held in Brighton in the first week of October. A debate on the nuclear issue was inevitable, since no fewer than 127 resolutions were submitted and listed in the agenda under 'Disarmament'. Some simply pressed for a new effort towards a disarmament agreement and some were limited to the question of nuclear tests. But Sunderland demanded that a Labour government 'shall not under any circumstances produce or use any form of nuclear weapons'. Huddersfield proposed: 'Britain should give a lead to the world by unilaterally renouncing the manufacture and use of the hydrogen bomb.' With Welsh fervour, Ogmore declared: 'The Labour Party and the next

Labour government must be the advocates of the right of mankind to survive.'

Very regrettably – in the light of what happened later – Michael never discussed the crucial question with Nye. A dinner at the end of July was devoted to matters of economic policy and 'no more than a few minutes were left to talk about the bomb'.[15] The two people who were closest to Nye, Michael and Jennie, were both convinced of the rightness of the unilateralist line, but both refrained from pressing him to commit himself to it. Michael has written: 'I believed, and I think he believed, that however awkward the corner to be turned, he would be able to do it in a major speech covering the whole perspective of foreign policy and setting the issue of the British bomb in its proper place within it.'[16]

In the days leading up to the conference, Nye was – in Barbara Castle's words – 'twisting and turning, playing with different ideas'.[17] At a meeting of the NEC on the Friday before the conference, he was faced with a statement drafted by Gaitskell which offered no concessions other than the already agreed suspension of tests. Bevan declared that he could not support it; someone else would have to speak for the NEC. Presumably, he was hoping to bring Gaitskell and the majority to a compromise. Of this, it was soon apparent, there was no hope.

There was another chance: perhaps the unilateralist resolution, a composite emerging from the many submitted, would be acceptably ambiguous. That hope too vanished on the Saturday; it was categorical, and it was to be moved by the delegate from Norwood, Vivienne Mendelson, a highly determined young woman adhering to the most rigorous part of the left. The final slender hope lay in a suggestion, advanced by Barbara, that Norwood should be asked to remit the resolution for later consideration instead of pressing it to a vote. But the NEC majority would have none of this, and in any case Vivienne Mendelson would not have agreed.

That Saturday, Nye conferred earnestly with Sam Watson, leader of the Durham miners and an influential member of the NEC. Although generally regarded as a right-winger, Watson was no enemy of Bevan's; they liked and respected each other and were linked by the camaraderie of the mining background. Watson's appeal was: 'We need you as Foreign Secretary.' The same day, Nye went for a long walk with Ian Mikardo and explained that he had decided to speak on behalf of the NEC and oppose the Norwood resolution. Mik recalled later: 'He honestly felt that he could bring the cold war to an end, and that no alternative Foreign Secretary would even try. But he was agonised. He knew he would be violently attacked by people who had followed him.'[18] Mik was sure that Sam Watson's influence had been decisive.

Michael, detained in London until after the start of the conference, was able to talk to Nye only when the decision had been taken. The time for argument was past, but he persuaded Nye to include in his projected speech a passage to the effect that unilateral action was not ruled out for the longer future. Nye did say this, but in the sensation provoked by his speech the proviso received little attention.

The debate on the next Thursday was tense and dramatic. Judith Hart, supporting the unilateralist resolution, said with uncomfortable logic: 'Everyone here firmly believes that the bomb is an evil thing. The only difficulty arises from the Labour government's wrong decision which created the British atomic bomb.' Harold Davies, in an outburst of true Welsh *hwyl*, shouted: 'If we fail now, the last child that dies in a radioactive England will curse the movement that hadn't the courage to give a political and moral lead.' But Anthony Wedgwood Benn, the young MP for Bristol South-east, said: 'I plead with this conference not to run round chasing after moral leadership.'

Then Frank Cousins, general secretary of the TGWU, came to the rostrum. He was an unknown quantity, having been recently elevated to this position as a result of two unexpected deaths. What he had to say was: 'I am proud to be emotional. I have a six-year-old daughter and I will not compromise with anybody on the future of that child . . . We must say that this nation . . . does not approve of the maintenance and manufacture, by ourselves or by anyone else, of this idiot's weapon.'

The hall was electrified, not only by Cousins' sincerity and passion, but by the amazing possibility that the old union of Bevin and Deakin would swing its weight against the platform and the resolution might actually be carried. But Cousins was compelled by the TGWU delegation to ask for a postponement of the vote, he had to back down in a lunchtime consultation, and the block vote was cast as it always had been.

Bevan then rose to make the speech that put an end to Bevanism. He had always been able to count on applause from the constituency delegates who had the majority in voices (no matter how heavily the majority in votes went the other way) and for the first time they were against him. His best speeches had been memorable for effective phrases, but this one was remembered – alas, bitterly and for years – for two phrases that were disastrously ill-chosen. Making the argument that a unilateralist Britain would have no diplomatic leverage, he said: 'You will send a Foreign Secretary, whoever he may be, naked into the conference chamber.' The context shows that 'naked' meant 'without allies', but it was endlessly interpreted to mean 'without the bomb'. A little later, he declared that unilateralism represented 'an emotional spasm'. I was sitting beside Michael in the press gallery and saw him wince as though he had been stung by a wasp. Describing the effect, Michael wrote: 'He was caught in a frontal clash with a great section of the audience, and if many had not been nearer to tears, the whole place might have broken into uproar.'[19]

In the evening, Michael had dinner with Vicky, James Cameron, Geoffrey Goodman and Ian Aitken. Ever afterwards, the friends referred to this dinner as the 'wake'. The unilateralist resolution had of course been heavily defeated, there was no clear way ahead for the cause, the Bevanite left was in ruins and there was not even the consolation that Nye himself had emerged with credit or respect. Cameron and Vicky were scathing in their condemnation – 'I'm finished with him,' Vicky said. Michael attempted a defence, but with little spirit. Goodman remembers: 'He was obviously under great stress. It was a soul-searing wound.'[20] Already, in the bar of the Bedford Hotel which was the gathering-place of the left, he had heard his friend and hero accused of all the offences that ranked worst in the Foot scale of values: hypocrisy, betrayal, personal ambition. Michael rejected those charges, but he was certain that Nye had made an utterly wrong choice and a fatal blunder. In more than twenty years of happy comradeship, they had never disagreed on more than tactical matters. Now, the comradeship was nullified and the friendship itself was painfully damaged.

The letters that *Tribune* had to print next week rubbed salt in the wounds. 'I hope that Labour Party members who saw Bevan as the champion of the Left wing now realise their error' . . . 'Nye Bevan, our stormy petrel, has turned out to be a very tame duck indeed.' And from Nye's home town, Tredegar: 'We are naked, without H-bombs, but fully clothed in morality.' However, the voices were not unanimous. Another reader wrote: 'Our trust in Aneurin Bevan will never be displaced, with his unequalled courage, sagacity and brilliant thought.'

Jennie Lee, too, had gone through some painful hours, but by the time when Nye rose to make his speech she had decided that he was right and in any case her place was at his side. Later, she explained: 'I had come round to accepting Nye's point of view . . . Nothing could have done more to damage the prospects of winning the general election we then thought was due very soon than Nye going off once more into the wilderness.'[21]

In the aftermath of Brighton, there had to be a clash, and it came when Nye, Jennie and Michael met in the *Tribune* office on the Monday after the conference. In Michael's account:

I proposed writing an article in which I would try to reply to the Brighton speech while disowning the scandalous misinterpretations of it, but, to my astonishment, Bevan suggested that *Tribune* should carry no comment at all for a week or two; report the proceedings, let readers write, and let the dust settle. It was the first of several awkward editorial arguments which were to engage us in the subsequent weeks . . . What amazed me most about that conversation, the first I had had with him since the Conference, was that he did truly seem to underestimate the nature of the wrench which had occurred with so many of his followers. [22]

Nye and Jennie continued to demand, not just for 'a week or two' but through the ensuing months as the gulf widened, that *Tribune* should adopt a posture of neutrality and take no editorial line on the great issue. The idea was impossible; *Tribune* had never been, least of all under Nye's editorship, that sort of paper. Had Michael accepted the demand, he would have lost his staff and most of his readers, to say nothing of his own self-esteem.

Michael's comment on this bitter experience, written fifteen years later, conveys the sympathy that he felt for his friend, but also his own distress:

There was no doubt about the torment which his courage had invited. At his meetings in the country he had often to face a quite new kind of hostility from a new quarter . . . As the days passed, it became evident that his relationship with the Left of the Party and therefore with the Party itself was profoundly altered . . . Everybody who knows anything knows that politics can be cruel, but no man ever felt that cruelty more than Aneurin Bevan in the autumn of 1957. [23]

Nevertheless, Michael lost no time in writing the article that his readers expected. Under the headline 'BEVAN AND THE H-BOMB', it appeared in *Tribune* of 11 October. The first point he made was that the conference had produced some worthwhile resolutions, notably a unanimous demand for a halt to nuclear tests. His next point was: 'It is not, of course, an argument about whether anyone likes or dislikes the bomb. Aneurin Bevan loathes the hideous weapon as passionately as anyone else.' Then he turned to the 'crux of the argument':

Consider, first, the simple question whether the possession or non-possession of the bomb decides the issue of which alliances we may join or retain. The flat answer is that it doesn't settle the matter one way or the other. Why, Britain has only had a tested H-bomb for a matter of months. If not having the bomb puts us into diplomatic purdah [this was one of the phrases used in Bevan's speech] that's where we've been for years. Were we not members of all these alliances before we had the bomb? And does not the same apply to many other nations who, fortunately for the world and wisely for themselves, have no intention of attempting to make one? . . .

It would be hypocritical to surrender our own bomb and merely be content to shelter behind somebody else's. But it would not be immoral to abandon our own bomb and seek the best diplomatic means to ensure that others did the same. The power of example might be one of the best ways of securing that end . . .

Nothing I have heard persuades me that the possession of a few bombs which can never be used except as an act of national suicide and which as long as we produce them will impose enormous burdens on our economy will assist in making Britain's voice more powerful in the world. Indeed, I still believe – as I am convinced a growing number of people throughout the country will believe – that Britain's readiness to renounce the weapon which we all regard as an invention of the devil could capture the imagination of millions of people in many lands.

4

The Brighton decision was unlikely to be reversed through the formal processes of the Labour Party, in view of the weight of the union block vote and, moreoever, of the new amity between Bevan and Gaitskell. The idea of an independent campaign for nuclear disarmament arose as a natural reaction. A foundation existed in the form of the National Council against tests, which had acquired thousands of supporters, an office in central London and an organising secretary with an impressive campaigning record, Peggy Duff. Another fountain-head of activity, the Direct Action Committee against Nuclear War, had come into existence in April 1957. Its members were pacifists, and it aimed at challenging the war machine through civil disobedience in the Gandhian tradition. One of its first activists was a young woman named Pat Arrowsmith.

There were also 'texts' which struck a chord. J. B. Priestley, well known as playwright and novelist and also as a columnist in the *New Statesman*, wrote:

The British of these times, so frequently hiding behind masks of sour, cheap cynicism, often seem to be waiting for something better than party squabbles and appeals to their narrow self-interest, something great and noble in its intention that would make them feel good again. And this might well be a declaration to the world that after a certain date one power able to engage in nuclear warfare will reject the evil thing for ever.[24]

The *New Statesman* also published an 'Open Letter' to Khrushchev and Dulles by Bertrand Russell. He appealed to them to recognise that the perils of a historically new situation must take priority over the national interests even of a superpower. Much to Kingsley Martin's astonishment, a messenger appeared in the *New Statesman* office with a lengthy reply from Khrushchev. Agitated cables from Grosvenor Square persuaded Dulles that he too had to make a response. Both letters were, of course, justifications of Soviet or American policy, and Russell wound up the correspondence by telling them with dry irony that they had completely missed the point.

All this ferment proved to Kingsley Martin that there was a widespread mood which ought not to be allowed to melt away in frustration. He convened an informal meeting at his flat to discuss the possibilities. Michael was not invited. It is possible, though the point must be left in doubt, that Martin did not want a confrontation between unilateralists and others; among those present were the American George F. Kennan, Bertrand Russell, the physicist P. M. S. Blackett and Denis Healey, who were all deeply concerned about the nuclear threat but could not be classed as unilateralists. (Russell was putting the emphasis on the need for new thinking in Washington and Moscow.) Still, this meeting planted the seed that flowered as a mass campaign, and Michael gave Martin full credit for his initiative:

> He could seize the moment to inspire a new departure. It was his flair – against the advice of most of his *New Statesman* colleagues – that made possible the conjunction of people and ideas which launched the Campaign for Nuclear Disarmament . . . No doubt he regarded himself as a leader of a great crusade, but mingled with the deed was the matchless timing of the journalist born and bred.[25]

One man who responded was Canon L. John Collins of St Paul's Cathedral, a veteran of campaigns against capital punishment and against apartheid. His grace-and-favour residence in Amen Court, close to the cathedral, was the scene of a second and larger meeting on 15 January 1958. About fifty people attended, including Russell, Priestley, Michael Foot, James Cameron, Richard Acland and Ritchie Calder.

Kingsley Martin took the chair. As Duff records: 'It was not a difficult meeting. There was no dissension. Everyone agreed that a campaign was needed.'[26] The discussion turned mainly on the name of the campaign and on the personalities to head it. The name arrived at was Campaign for Nuclear Disarmament, which left conveniently open the question, not yet firmly decided, whether it was a campaign for unilateral action by Britain or for a disarmament agreement. On Martin's suggetion, Russell was appointed as president and Priestley as vice-president. Canon Collins was chosen as chairman, with the duty of presiding over meetings of the Executive Committee. This committee was constituted without any suggestion that the Campaign should enrol members and entrust them with an election. Its members were James Cameron, Ritchie Calder, Howard Davies (of the United Nations Association), Michael Foot, Kingsley Martin and a distinguished scientist, Professor Joseph Rotblat. In addition, Arthur Goss (publisher of the *Hampstead and Highgate Express*) and Sheila Jones were included as representatives of the anti-test National Council, which nobly dissolved itself and placed its resources and files at the disposal of CND. Peggy Duff was appointed as secretary and got down to work at once.

The next step, on 17 February, was to hold a public meeting at the Methodist Central Hall in Westminster. The only publicity was in the classified columns of *Tribune*, the *New Statesman* and *Peace News*, so fingers were crossed as to the prospects of filling a hall with 2,500 seats, especially as there was an admission charge of sixpence. But the advance demand for tickets was so large that Peggy had to hire five other halls for overflow meetings and the speakers shuttled to and fro, addressing a total of 5,000 people. With Collins in the chair, the speakers were Russell, Priestley, Sir Stephen King-Hall, Michael Foot and Alan Taylor. Michael was expected to be the oratorical star of the evening, and in fact he gave one of his best performances, but it was Taylor who roused the audience to stampeding enthusiasm. After a blood-curdling description of the effects of nuclear bombs, he shouted: 'Any man who can prepare to use those weapons should be denounced as a murderer!' At the close of the meeting, Collins' appeal for membership and donations was interrupted by cries of 'March to Downing Street!' Taken aback, the Canon said that people would have to do what they felt right and himself went home in a taxi. Scores of people made their way to Downing Street (which in those days had no protective gate), a panic call brought police with horses and dogs, and several people were arrested. This ensured a publicity which the meeting itself might not have received.

After the Central Hall meeting, there was no doubt that CND was a campaign for unilateral nuclear disarmament. All the speakers (except King-Hall, who later left CND) had taken a unilateralist line, and the mood of the audience showed that nothing less would meet expectations. The Campaign's original policy statement was hastily rewritten. It still recommended that Britain should try 'to bring about negotiations at all levels for agreement to end the armaments race', but this clause came second to the key sentence: 'We shall seek to persuade the British people that Britain must renounce unconditionally the use or production of nuclear weapons and refuse to allow their use by others in her defence.'

Michael was fully and enthusiastically committed to the CND cause. So, of course, was *Tribune*. Dick Clements had the idea of putting a strap-line which read: 'The Paper that Leads the Anti-H-Bomb campaign'. There it stayed for the next five years. Nye Bevan, Michael has written, 'hated our slogan' and regarded it as 'a calculated affront to himself'.[27] He and Jennie, but particularly Jennie, kept up their protests against Michael's insistence that he and his staff should decide the paper's policy. A further exacerbation was the fact that Howard Samuel, who made a vital contribution to *Tribune*'s finances, was a director of Tribune Publications Limited. In Michael's words: 'Theoretically, Jennie Lee and Howard Samuel, the two other directors of the paper with myself, could outvote me, but we had never dreamt of conducting our business on that basis.'[28] Failing to get Michael to yield, Jennie urged Samuel to stop his subsidy and thus kill the paper. Michael chose not to reveal this in his biography of Nye, but Jennie never made any secret of it.[29] Nye, however, vetoed the plan. For him, despite his anger over *Tribune*'s conduct, it was not a legitimate weapon.

Jill, acutely unhappy over these developments, relieved her feelings in letters to Beaverbrook. (She was able to ignore the fact that Beaverbrook's papers vilified CND and that the *Daily Express* hailed the Christmas Island test with the exultant headline 'OUR H-BANG!'.) Writing to Capponcina on 16 December 1957 to thank him for a 'wonderfully generous' Christmas present, she said: 'I wish you were here. I particularly wished it when Nye said goodbye to the left and, as it seemed to me, though Michael denies it, to Michael in particular.' In another letter (29 December) she confided:

Michael seems to me to be becoming more and more isolated politically. Not that this matters; but old friends are far from friendly. Nye is just bloody. His soul mate is Howard Samuel. And Howard has two topics of conversation: what he can do with his money and how he, as opposed to Michael, is a real socialist. This wears thin. I shouldn't write that, I suppose, but as it is what Howard himself tells everyone he meets when he is drunk, which is often, I don't see that it matters.

Within a couple of weeks, there were over a hundred active CND groups in a network that covered England, Wales and Scotland. Their first task was to mobilise support for an enterprise that caught the imagination of many – particularly young – people: a four-day march over the Easter weekend from London to the gates of the Atomic Weapons Research Establishment at Aldermaston, a distance of forty-five miles. Michael spoke at the send-off rally in Trafalgar Square, on the morning of Good Friday. The column was pitifully thin on the Saturday, marked by bitterly cold weather and even a snowstorm, but on the Monday 4,000 people covered the final miles.[30] The march – reversed from 1959 to go from Aldermaston to London – was repeated every year up to 1964 and the numbers steadily grew. In affectionate memory, the Aldermaston march has passed into the folklore of a generation.

Meanwhile, *Tribune* was pressing the argument. The centre pages on 4 April (the issue sold on the march) were devoted to a long question-and-answer feature, which formed the basis for the Campaign's first pamphlet, *Sanity or Suicide*. Readers were told:

> No cause can justify the slaughter of millions all round the world, the maiming of the children of the future, the spreading of disease and hunger, the risk of wiping out the human race . . . To renounce the bomb means to break through the haggling with a declaration, proven by deeds, that the threat to the human race outweighs any advantage or sacrifice affecting any nation.

While CND held well-attended and enthusiastic meetings all over Britain, Labour Party meetings organised to stem the tide were failures. In Birmingham, Gaitskell was told from the floor: 'You think you're leading public opinion, but you're tagging behind it.' When Bevan spoke to delegates from London constituencies and tried to counter the unilateralist case, he was met by shouts of 'We are the majority!' Infuriated, he exclaimed: 'There you are! These are the moralists. These are the pure saints.'

Between Michael and Nye, arguments raged whenever they met, with tempers barely restrained or sometimes lost. It was, more often than not, Nye who wanted the argument. Apparently, he could not believe that it was beyond his power, for the first time in their long association, to bring

Michael round to his way of thinking. On one occasion he stormed out of the *Tribune* office, slamming the outer door, which had a frosted-glass panel, with a clang that reverberated throughout the building. The worst clash occurred, Michael recalled, 'one terrible evening in July when I met him and Jennie accidentally at the Polish Embassy and they both returned to our house to drink a few reconciling nightcaps'.[31] Far from reconciling, the nightcaps removed all inhibitions and the pros and cons of the bomb debate 'were thrown like faggots onto a blazing bonfire of a row'. It ended with Nye, whose rich vocabulary of invective seldom descended to the crudities of his Tredegar youth, bellowing at Michael: 'You cunt! You cunt!' To Michael's horror – and still more to Jill's, for she prided herself on her taste as a collector – he then seized a Sheraton chair and crashed it violently down on the floor, breaking the slender legs. Next day, Jill succeeded in making peace between the two men, but Nye never ceased to insist that he was right on the great divisive issue.

The strength of CND – the secret of its vitality and also of the breadth of its appeal – was that it enlisted thousands of people who thought of themselves as non-political and who could not be mobilised by the established parties. Quite simply, they felt that they were confronted by a measureless evil and that indifference was a complicity in this evil. They believed that nuclear war might break out at any moment; they could not have imagined that they, or their children, would still be campaigning a generation later. Given this belief and this mood, it was useless to argue about whether CND should be unilateralist or not. The demand for renunciation of the bomb without guarantees, without calculation, *because it was right*, was what evoked their commitment.

If CND had evaded the commitment to unilateralism, Michael wrote, 'the Archbishop of Canterbury would doubtless have bestowed his blessing from the outset and might even have marched from Aldermaston in such a respectable cause – if there had been any marches'. In this summing up, made in 1964 when the Campaign was going into decline, Michael's defence of its record was:

CND forcefully intruded into the debate an element which almost everybody else wanted to keep out . . . CND insisted that, whatever else the question also was, it was a *moral* one. And who will dare say that this emphasis was wrong? How debasing and dishonourable to the human species it would have been if the question of massive extermination on a scale far exceeding anything known even in Hitler's death camps had been permitted to continue being discussed without the issue of moral responsibility arising . . . CND developed differently from the campaigns that had gone before, provoked furious enthusiasms and enmities, and made a spectacular appeal particularly to the young, precisely because it did not take refuge in vague generalities, precisely because it did urge that something could be done.[32]

5

In these difficult times, Michael was at least enjoying his holidays. In 1957, he and Jill went to Venice for the first time and stayed at the luxurious Danieli Hotel. Jill informed Beaverbrook: 'Here could be seen the diverting spectacle of Michael setting off for his morning bathe in the hotel motor launch in the company of Sir Oswald Mosley, Profumo, a Conservative minister whose name I've forgotten, I think it was Maud,[33] George Strauss and various Italian starlets.' Some *Tribune* readers might have found the spectacle less than diverting; they might have reacted in stern condemnation to the thought of Michael giving a polite good-morning nod to Mosley. But Michael's principle was always that, so long as he did not soften his political attacks on political enemies, there was nothing culpable in friendly personal relationships.

Venice, for Michael, was 'the immortal city, beloved of Rossini and Hazlitt and Stendhal and Casanova'.[34] This list does not include Byron (nor, for that matter, Baron Corvo), but he was of course aware that the great poet ranked high among those who had reclined in the gondolas. It may have been in Venice that Michael's enthusiasm for Byron was first implanted; he had hitherto been more interested in Wordsworth and Shelley. At all events, he and Jill both fell in love with the 'immortal city', and they spent many September holidays there until, in the 1980s, they transferred their affections to Dubrovnik.

But for Michael, as for so many others, the city beyond compare was Paris. He had been brought up to revere its revolutionary tradition; he had agonised over the shameful capitulation to the Nazis and rejoiced over the liberation. He was pleased, therefore, when the editor of the *Daily Herald*, Douglas Machray, asked him to go to Paris as a special correspondent in May 1958. However, the reason for this assignment was a formidable crisis.

The Fourth French Republic, which had replaced the defunct Third Republic after the war, had never functioned well and now seemed doomed to expire in its turn. One shaky coalition had succeeded another since de Gaulle, in 1946, had retired to his village home at Colombey-les-Deux-Eglises. But the retirement was never meant to be final; he was waiting, patiently and vigilantly, for the moment when a return to power would appear to be the response to an irresistible call. Now, the National Assembly was about to vote its acceptance of yet another patched-together government, headed by a mediocre centrist politician, Pierre Pflimlin. Suddenly, news came that a group of generals in Algiers had seized power and set up a Committee of Public Safety. They appealed to de Gaulle to put himself at the head of a similar committee in Paris – an authority that would sweep away the Fourth Republic and what de Gaulle himself had scornfully called 'the regime of parties'. Who could bar the way to de Gaulle? Not Pflimlin, who did get a favourable vote and form a Cabinet, but who was sadly incapable of decisive action. Certainly not the aged and feeble President of the Republic, René Coty.

British newspapers, in general, were writing off the Republic and taking the line that a de Gaulle regime was inevitable and the best way out of the mess. The exception was the *Daily Herald*, edited by Machray, who had shocked Gaitskell and the Labour leadership by coming out in favour of unilateral nuclear disarmament, and who was a good friend of Michael's. The *Herald* gave trenchant warnings of the Gaullist threat, both in reports from its Paris correspondent, David Ross, and in Michael's column, which wound up on 23 May: 'As on so many previous occasions, the Frenchmen who still defend freedom in France uphold that cause for multitudes of other peoples besides themselves.'

The press attaché of the French Embassy in London, a thoroughgoing Gaullist, telephoned Machray to say that 'it would be more politic in the interest of future Franco–British relations to be more prudent'.[35] Machray's reaction was to stick to his guns and send Michael to Paris to reinforce Ross. Accompanied by Jill, Michael flew to Paris on 26 May. In his first report, telephoned that night, he described the Pflimlin government as 'mustering its last energies for the strange purpose of cutting its own throat'.

On the morning of 28 May, Pflimlin resigned. In the afternoon, thousands of Socialist and Communist demonstrators marched through Paris. Everyone knew that it was too late. Michael reported: 'It was a wonderful sight, but in another sense a spectacle too tragic for tears.' President Coty recommended the National Assembly to vote for a government headed by de Gaulle, and the necessary majority was forthcoming.

For the *Daily Herald* of 30 May, Michael wrote:

De Gaulle scrambles in . . . His road to power has been prepared by some of the most sordid episodes in the history of the Fourth Republic . . .

Coty stands for little. He is the Great Nothing of the Fourth Republic. All he has in his power to bestow is the flimsy camouflage of legality. And this miserable blessing he has bestowed on blood-red illegality . . .

The men responsible are those who insisted on pursuing the Algerian war to its bitter, unending conclusion and who, when driven frantic by their failure, turned to destroy freedom in France as they have dishonoured it among the Arab peoples. Men with famous names came forward to give their sanction to this conspiracy . . . But the President was the man who gave the final sanction. All the perfumes of Arabia will not sweeten the name of Coty.

Almost certainly, the men who pounced on this article were the Gaullists in the French Embassy in London. They alerted the authorities in Paris, who decided to make use of a 1945 law providing for the immediate expulsion of a foreigner whose presence was 'of a nature to compromise public order'. An expulsion order naming 'Foot Michael, né le 23 juillet 1913 à Plymouth' was drawn up and signed the same evening by the Minister of the Interior in the collapsing Pflimlin government.

Michael was told when he arrived at the *Herald* office at 11.30 p.m. The police were expected at any moment, but did not appear, so Michael had time to compose another piece, printed on 31 May as 'My Last Crisis Commentary':

I understand I have been expelled from France for offending the President of the Republic, although nobody has approached me officially yet, not even a paratrooper . . .

Have not Englishmen in Paris, then, the same right to speak and write as Frenchmen? That would be a novel doctrine. It was a great Englishman, Tom Paine, who was once welcomed in France precisely because he always dared to speak the truth as he knew it . . . I have no doubt that if Tom Paine had been in Paris during these tremendous days he might have been expelled too . . . I hope and pray that this minor and insignificant act of suppression directed against me is not a sign that the liberties of Frenchmen are to be attacked.

After a late meal with some French journalists, Michael and Jill reached the Hotel Castiglione at three in the morning. There was still no sign of the police, so they went to bed. David Ross recalled in a later account:

'Next morning, I rang Michael first thing. Jill answered. The police had burst in early. They had ordered him to dress. He wore no pyjamas but they refused to leave while he dressed. Then they had taken him away, refusing to say where they were going.'[36]

Jill and Ross went to the British embassy to seek the 'assistance and protection' to which any British subject was, in theory, entitled. No senior officials were available, and a press attaché whom Ross knew said that the French were implementing their laws, any protest was out of the question and the embassy did not even feel able to find out where Michael had been taken. Ross, exercising some ingenuity, pointed out that Jill would be leaving Paris too and she could not pay the hotel bill, as Michael had their travellers' cheques in his pocket. The press attaché, alarmed by the prospect that the embassy might have to meet the bill (the Castiglione is a first-class hotel and there had been lengthy telephoning) hurried off to make inquiries and returned with the news that Michael was being held at the Préfecture de Police (the French Scotland Yard). Jill and Ross then went to the Préfecture with a British vice-consul, William Atkinson. Michael had been fingerprinted and photographed, and had been allowed to phone the British embassy, but got no help from them. Ross goes on:

> Michael was looking pale and drawn but that was nothing new; in those days, he always was . . . As for Jill Foot, she was equally in command of herself. I cannot recall a single instance in which she said a word of dismay at their misfortunes . . . While Jill and Michael were reunited, and travellers' cheques were being handed over, I discussed the situation with the police . . . I said that the police were holding him illegally in 'this prison'. That upset them. The préfecture, they said, was not a prison . . . My case was certainly not helped by Mr Atkinson who joined the police in demurring at my description of their rat-warren as a prison.

Having ascertained that Michael would be put on a plane leaving at nine in the evening, Jill went back to the hotel to pay the bill and pack. She had to make her way separately to the airport, while Michael went there under guard. A spokesman for the French Foreign Office was able to tell a press conference that the British embassy had been in complete agreement with the action taken. The junior minister at the British Foreign Office, David Ormsby Gore, replied to critical questions in the Commons with the remark: 'The new self-styled heirs of Tom Paine seem to be unduly sensitive in this generation.'

Michael never regretted what he had written, but his punishment was a nasty blow. In the *Tribune* office on the Monday morning after his return, he said to me: 'Expelled from France! It's like being shut out of heaven.' Later, he wrote to Beaverbrook: 'It's sad to be excluded from beautiful France and I hope this is not going to last for the rest of my life.'

Beaverbrook was one of several influential people who made representations on Michael's behalf. (Given the scale of entertainment at Capponcina, he was no mean contributor to the French economy.) After a waiting period to let things calm down, the matter was taken up by Edward Heath, Lord Privy Seal in the Macmillan government. Michael's expulsion order was never formally revoked, but on 7 March 1961 Heath wrote to him: 'I am glad to say that I have now been assured orally that there will be no objection to your travelling to France. The whole matter will be allowed to drop quietly and there is no need for any formalities. The French immigration authorities have been informed accordingly.'

At this time, while Michael was out of the House of Commons, his brother Dingle was in. Despairing of the Liberals, he joined the Labour Party and won a by-election at Ipswich in October 1957. Mac had finished his term in Jamaica and was Governor of Cyprus, where he had served earlier in his career. The Greeks who made up 80 per cent of the population sought freedom from colonial rule and union with Greece; guerrilla warfare (or terrorism, according to the vocabulary preferred) had cost the lives of eighty British soldiers by the end of 1956. Methods of suppression – hangings, collective punishments, the deportation of Archbishop Makarios, who was the spiritual and political leader of the Greek community – proved unavailing. Macmillan hoped that the liberal-minded Sir Hugh Foot would find a way to resolve the problem.

The problem of the Foot family, now as in earlier years, was Sally. With her passion for horses, she had found work as the riding teacher at a school near Bampton in Devon, but in December 1956 it went bankrupt. This left Sally living in a caravan, parked in a field near the village of Oakford, and responsible for feeding her own horses and dogs, as well as herself, with no income. Michael came to her aid as much as he could, although he had to watch his own finances now that he was out of the House and had only his *Daily Herald* salary. She was isolated and unhappy, and had recourse (intermittently, depending on the available funds) to alcohol and to heavy tranquillisers. Her native intelligence never deserted her, nor did her political sympathies, which were always in tune with Michael's, but her letters to him make pathetic reading. In May 1957:

I got very deeply into debt at the school – and have cashed in on everything, insurance etc. . . . Selling horses is a miserable business –

selling in a hurry is absolutely bloody, quite apart from losing close
personal friends you sell at a loss . . . The school where I taught went
bankrupt before Christmas and naturally people feel I am involved in
that . . . I am particularly anxious that Dad should not be troubled any
more on my behalf . . . I have advertised now for temporary work of
any sort . . . I have *also* advertised for London misses for riding
holidays here . . . *Also* I have four tickets for a draw in the Royal Hunt
cup to be run on 19 June and I am COUNTING on this! So, as I say, this is
not a plain begging letter. Long, *long* ago I lost my self-respect, but
begging from one's nearest and dearest is worse than anything – I
suppose Lord Beaverbrook wouldn't like to lend me a hundred or two
without security or interest?

In January 1958:

Roll on the election . . . Quite time you were back in your true milieu.
Don't ever be anything but a back-bencher. Not for you the fruits of
office. Dear Mike, come and see me some time, only small detour with
car . . .

P.S. I would just like to add that, although I haven't stopped smoking,
I do not drink now. I certainly couldn't afford it and I can't get any
credit these days.

In October:

I seem to be pressed by unpayable bills once again – and am at my wits'
end of how to pay them. I shall have to get rid of all the ponies – but am
always hoping a suitable job in which I can use them will turn up or
manna will fall from heaven. Anyhow if you can spare anything I shall
be more than grateful – you cannot think how it sickens me to have to
ask you again.

About this time, Sally wrote: 'I was so glad to hear your views on the
bomb. I am hoping you didn't find Bevan's defection too bitter. If you
have one fault, dear Mike, it is a dangerous loyalty capacity, an inability
to criticise your friends.' Her most alarming letter (undated) gave the
impression that it was written in her own blood. As it is still red, and not
brown, many years later, we can feel reassured that it was actually red
ink, but Michael must have been shaken when he received it:

Biro run out, just one more frustration. So this is written with
sharpened finger nail dipped in opened artery. I must find some outlet
or burst!

Have been listening to news and I can't bear it . . . In my eyrie (caravan moved into fastnesses of woods) I hear these horrors over radio – I have no one to let off steam to . . . If it weren't for Hungary and Nagy[37] I'd go straight off to Russia, dogs and all, but that made me properly, physically sick . . .

I must stop and I shall put this into envelope if such is available and it will go at some future date when I have saved money for stamp. Don't bother to answer. Thank Heaven you feel like me about atom bombs. Macmillan is a horrible cringing TOAD – or rather toads are nice, solitary creatures – living on their own, making their own decisions . . . How far, far better to be right alone, not waste money on these bloody bombs.

6

When Will Cove, MP for Aberavon, announced that he would retire at the next election, the constituency Labour Party invited Michael to succeed him. It was a rock-solid Labour seat, with a 16,000 majority provided by miners and steelworkers; besides, Michael had been fond of Wales since his youth and the thought of a Welsh constituency was attractive. However, he had accepted renomination for Devonport and felt that it would be dishonourable to abandon it midway through a Parliament. In the aftermath of Suez, Labour was ahead in the polls and winning by-elections, so Michael could reasonably hope to reverse a defeat which had been very narrow and could be attributed to bad luck and rain. So he turned down Aberavon and other constituencies which made approaches to him. He said later: 'My primary interest in life is not to get into the House of Commons. If that were so, I would have accepted one of the safe seats offered to me.'[38] The truth was that it would have caused him no great unhappiness to spend the rest of his life preaching socialism, editing *Tribune* and writing books like *The Pen and the Sword*. Jill once wrote to Beaverbrook: 'I think Michael's heart is in writing and newspapers and something of a tug of war goes on in him as to which he should do most wholeheartedly. He is not really cut out for political intrigue.'

From 1958, Michael realised that he was unlikely to win back Devonport after all. Harold Macmillan was rebuilding Tory morale and confidence more effectively than anyone could have predicted. Beneath his air of languor, he was a very shrewd politician. Besides, everything seemed to go right for him. Industrial production rose, jobs were easy to find, new universities were built, motorways were opened, and always Macmillan managed to take the credit. Vicky satirised him as 'Supermac', a poseur pretending to work miracles in Superman style; but, greatly to Vicky's chagrin, the miracles were plausible and the Supermac cartoons benefited Macmillan too. Working-class families were being introduced to what were then novelties: house ownership with the aid of a mortgage, car ownership, holidays in Spain. 'Affluence' became a catchword.[39] Macmillan annexed the phrase 'You never had it so good', which had won Truman the US election in 1948, and made it his own.

Abroad, too, the government was able to claim successes. In Cyprus, the Governor recorded with satisfaction: 'I called on the surprised Greek mayor of Nicosia, Kiki Dervas, at his home; walked through the streets of Nicosia; saw the Turkish leaders repeatedly; rode through the villages; visited the detention camps on Christmas morning.'[40]

Makarios was released from exile and Mac negotiated with him in a hotel in Athens. He was persuaded to drop the demand for union with Greece in favour of an independent Republic of Cyprus. In February 1959, an agreement was signed on terms accepted by both Greeks and Turks. Peace returned to the island.

In March, Macmillan made a flamboyant visit to the Soviet Union, had himself photographed in a white fur hat and presented himself as the peacemaker between Washington and Moscow. In September, Eisenhower came to London and joined Macmillan in a televised after-dinner chat, in which both proclaimed their devotion to peace. Whether Eisenhower realised it or not, it was the opening broadcast in the British election campaign. Arrangements for a summit meeting were announced, and Macmillan did not omit to point out that this would not have happened 'if I hadn't decided to break the ice and go to Moscow'.

Macmillan's dedication to peace was in contrast to his uncompromising reliance on nuclear weapons; but, although CND was gaining strength and the second Aldermaston march was much bigger than the first, this caused the wily Prime Minister few anxieties. While the more bone-headed Tories denounced nuclear disarmers as tools of Moscow, Macmillan treated them as naive idealists and listened courteously to deputations of concerned women. He benefited, too, from the fact that the argument was raging most fiercely, not between the government and the Opposition, but between the left and right of the Labour Party.

In June 1959 the conference of the General and Municipal Workers' Union, the most conformist and disciplined of the big right-wing unions, voted for unilateral nuclear disarmament. Sir Thomas Williamson organised a recall conference and got this stand reversed, but the damage had been done. If the Transport and General, with Frank Cousins at its head, went the same way, unilateralism could well triumph at a Labour conference. Suddenly, Gaitskell and Bevan were fighting a rearguard action. The Tories were in a position to rub their hands. They repeated at every opportunity that a party aspiring to form a government was split wide open on a life-or-death issue.

Thus, Macmillan's mood was one of serene confidence when he fixed the election date for 8 October 1959. Gaitskell too was confident, went into the campaign energetically and believed that he would win. Bevan, however, thought otherwise. On the eve of poll he told Geoffrey Goodman, who accompanied him to his meetings, 'that Gaitskell was a Jonah; the Party would never win with him'.

Michael was equally pessimistic. He gave himself little chance of regaining Devonport unless he could defy what he perceived as a nation-wide trend towards the Tories. But Joan Vickers had shown herself to be a capable and hard-working MP; moreover, Devonport had lost 4,000 voters who had been rehoused in other parts of Plymouth.

Michael and Jill arrived in the constituency on 20 September. In his first speech, he came out boldly for renunciation of nuclear weapons: 'The response throughout the world would be enormous.' Khrushchev had just put forward sweeping proposals for general disarmament. In his next speech, Michael said: 'We should welcome Khrushchev's pro-posals . . . I personally would rather believe he is sincere. A nuclear war could well destroy us all. We are alarmed by the thought of it, and so are the Russians.'

Nye Bevan had come to Plymouth and spoken for Michael in every election since 1945, and he was billed to do so again on 2 October. But, although he was making an extensive election tour, he was in seriously bad health. His fatal cancer, though not yet diagnosed, must have taken hold by this time. Michael wrote later: 'He should never have taken part in the election at all; he was already deeply sick.' At Coventry on 26 September, Goodman wrote in his diary:

> He was in one of the strangest moods. Tired, obviously quite fatigued by the whole business. His eyes a curious green/blue and ablaze in a strange half madness, which seemed to sear through you in anguished contempt . . . He spoke with immense irritation about everything. The meetings were plainly becoming burdensome.

On 2 October, Nye woke up at his London home with a high temperature, and had to admit that he was not fit to travel to Plymouth. In a message to be read out at the meeting, he said: 'I am depressed beyond expression at not being able to be with you tonight.' He had to cancel his remaining meetings, except for the eve of poll in his own constituency.

On 5 October, with Donald Soper as supporting speaker, Michael urged: 'Let's be bold and adventurous. That's what this age needs. Let's be done with Tory timidity.' And on the eve of poll, speaking to an audience of 1,500 in the newly rebuilt Plymouth Guildhall, he wound up: 'The Tories haven't got any dreams or ideals for the future. They want the nation to stay as it is. They don't want anything better. But that has always been the cry of the Tory dismal Jimmies . . . The Tory Party accuses us of being dreamers, but then many great things come from dreams.' It was stirring stuff, but it was an appeal that evoked few echoes in 1959, when too many of the voters did want the nation to 'stay as it is'.

L. K. Way of the *Western Morning News*, still in business as a political tipster, told his readers: 'On the eve of poll, nobody can be sure about anything in Devonport.' Michael, Way found, 'has been catching up gradually over the last three weeks on the tentative lead established by the sitting tenant, Joan Vickers . . . [but] I think the course will prove just too short for him.' Dockyard men, Way reported, were betting on a Tory majority between 800 and 3,000.

But the dockyard men, and Way himself, were estimating Michael's prospects too favourably. The result was:

Joan Vickers, Conservative	28,481
Michael Foot, Labour	22,027
Conservative majority	6,454

To the crowd that heard the declaration, Michael said: 'I have no complaints to make, no excuses to offer, because we have fought this election on our principles.' He added that he would go on fighting for the abolition of the H-bomb. He went on to meet his supporters, with Jill near to tears and his arm round her. He was still defiant: 'We can hold up our heads to anybody. I'm more than glad at this moment that I fought again.' But when he was asked whether he would contest Devonport yet again after this severe defeat, he could only say: 'I'll have to think about it.'

If Michael that night was a disappointed man, the same was true of Hugh Gaitskell. Except in Scotland, there was a marked swing towards the Tories. The Tories had a net gain of twenty-three seats. 'Supermac', winning his first election as Prime Minister, appeared set for another five years of power. One Tory minister, Iain Macleod, predicted that Britain would never again elect a Labour government, and there were many to agree with him.

Such was the background when Labour delegates gathered in Blackpool in November for a special conference. Unlike the customary annual conference, which had been cancelled because of the election, it lasted only two days, there were no resolutions to be voted on and it was entirely devoted to an inquest on the defeat.

The air was thick with recipes for recovery, emanating from Douglas Jay and others known to be close to Gaitskell. The Labour Party should change its name; it should merge with the Liberals; it should (like the German Social Democratic Party a few years earlier) explicitly renounce its doctrinal inheritance.

To this school of thought, Barbara Castle – who, thanks to the party's rotation system, was in the chair – made a robust reply in her opening speech. She said: 'The fallacy is that you can separate moral issues from economic issues . . . Radicalism without socialism is an also-ran. The objection to the reformist argument is a practical one: it just won't win elections.'

Gaitskell then made a long speech in which, while dissociating himself from the wilder suggestions of the Jay group, he endorsed their central thesis. 'Our object', he said, 'must be to broaden our base, to be in touch always with ordinary people, to avoid becoming small cliques of isolated doctrine-ridden fanatics.' He proposed the rewriting of Clause Four of the party constitution, which set out the aim: 'to secure for the workers by hand or by brain the full fruits of their industry . . . upon the basis of the common ownership of the means of production, distribution and exchange'. These words, drafted by Sidney Webb in 1918, appeared (and still appear) on every party membership card. Gaitskell's objection was: 'We don't aim to nationalise every private firm or to create an endless series of state monopolies.'

The delegates were startled and puzzled. Nobody imagined that it was Labour policy to 'nationalise every private firm'; Bevan, at the party conference in 1949, had made it clear that socialists envisaged a mixed economy in which 'we shall have for a very long time the light cavalry of private competitive industry'. To propose a revision of Clause Four, which few people could have accurately quoted, was to raise an irrelevant, divisive, almost Talmudic argument. But was Gaitskell really attempting a retreat from the whole concept of common (or public) ownership?

The debate was now open to the floor. In those days, glaring television lights made it difficult for the chairman to see the ranks of delegates. One journalist reported that Barbara 'peered theatrically into the murk and cried "Michael!", whereupon Foot emerged coincidentally from the blackest and most invisible quarter'.[41]

Whether in a spirit of gratitude or otherwise, Michael began by praising Barbara's 'masterly statement'. He went on:

> If that statement from Barbara Castle were spread all over the country . . . we should win thousands and millions of people as converts to socialism . . . I don't believe that Hugh Gaitskell made the same sort of speech . . .
>
> What is this philosophical argument Hugh Gaitskell makes about ends and means? Many of the ends that Hugh Gaitskell described at the end of his speech are in such general terms that the Tories would agree with them too . . . They say they believe in social justice, they believe in freedom . . . Therefore, it is a fallacy to try to separate the ends and the means because socialism, in my view, is a doctrine which reveals how only by mobilising the resources of the community, can you achieve the ends. That's what socialism is . . . If Hugh Gaitskell had stated the case for public ownership in the terms that Barbara Castle did this morning, this party would be much more united than it is after Hugh Gaitskell's speech.

Michael's speech was greeted by an ovation. A riposte, however, came from Denis Healey: 'Hugh Gaitskell was absolutely right when he said that what gets cheers at conference does not necessarily get votes at elections. If it did, we would have won Devonport.'

To wind up the debate, Bevan conquered his worsening health to make an eloquent and ingenious speech. There were differences within the party, he conceded, but 'those differences are not really fundamental differences of a character that should divide this movement permanently'. His formulation – that socialism meant 'the conquest of the commanding heights of the economy' – had been quoted by both Hugh Gaitskell and Barbara Castle, which showed that there was a basic unity beneath the variety of approach. The delegates dispersed, despite the continuing arguments and suspicions, in a mood of relief; there had been no explosion.

But Bevan's Blackpool speech – the last time that his voice reached an audience of his comrades – did not reveal the conclusions that he had reached. He had restrained himself, and had not chosen a party conference as a fitting occasion for a declaration of war. A declaration of war, however, was what he intended. Two years of vain efforts at co-operation with Gaitskell, culminating in the loss of the election through Gaitskell's defective leadership, had snapped his patience. Years later,

Michael put on record what Nye had said in December 1959 at a lunch at the Café Royal:

> What he had seen and heard and felt and smelt at Blackpool convinced him that the Clause Four controversy marked a deliberate design to alter the nature of the Labour Party . . . 'We are living in the presence of a conspiracy,' he said . . . There was no disguise in what he described; no relish and little malice but plenty of bitter invective. He saw Gaitskell and Gaitskellism as more of a threat than ever to the kind of Socialism he had dreamed of and fought for all his life, and he said that great upheavals would have to be faced if the Party was not to be twisted into a caricature of what a Socialist Party should be. [42]

Whether Nye Bevan could have resumed his struggle against Gaitskellism with any hope of success, and whether he could have regained the loyalty of the thousands on the left whom he had alienated in the past two years – these are questions that must for ever remain unanswerable. A few days after Christmas, he went into the Royal Free Hospital for an urgent operation. Cancer had been diagnosed, and the doctors realised that he was in grave danger. He was not told, and Jennie wrote later: 'We managed to deceive him.' It is more likely that, in supposing that Nye was ignorant of the truth, she deceived herself. Michael went to the hospital to see him on the day before the operation. Nye reproached him affectionately for his 'quixotry' in standing for Devonport again, and said: 'Now you'd better look properly for another seat. Perhaps you needn't look further than Ebbw Vale.' Ebbw Vale was the constituency that Nye had represented, without serious challenge, for thirty years.

Chapter 8

EBBW VALE

I

In that anguished Christmas week at the end of 1959, Aneurin Bevan's friends knew two things. One was that he had cancer; but, for a man of sixty-two with a strong physique, it was possible that the cancer could be held at bay and could allow him an extended period of active political life. On New Year's Eve, Jill wrote to Beaverbrook in this sense; she hoped that it was a 'slow cancer' and cited someone she knew who had been living with cancer for twenty years. Nye's friends also knew – though the outside world did not – that he had made up his mind to renew the battle against Gaitskell. As seen by Nye and Jennie, and likewise by Michael and Jill (whatever their other differences, they were at one in this), the situation was both depressing and dangerous. In her New Year's Eve letter, Jill told Beaverbrook:

> The present editor of the *Herald* [this was John Beavan, since the left-wing Machray had been eased out] is having tremendous pressure put on him by Gaitskell and Gaitskell's associates to replace Michael on the *Herald* by Dick Crossman . . . The Gaitskell clique is exceedingly active and the editor of the *Herald* is a very weak man . . .
>
> Many people are now saying that if the worst happens to Nye, Michael must step into Nye's shoes . . . If he doesn't, he must sit back and watch the complete disintegration of the Labour Party. And the trouble really is Gaitskell, quite apart from the public mood . . . Only the job hunters rally round Gaitskell and people see through them. Even ambitious characters like Dick Crossman and Barbara Castle become disgusted with him . . . Harold Wilson is playing a kind of early Stalin game and he might well oust the leadership from Gaitskell, but Harold is so pompous, conceited and such an uninspiring character that he won't do the party much good either. And now . . . the party is about as effective as an unarmed I.R.A.

Up to the spring of 1960, there were hopes of an improvement in Nye's health. Then, however, he was attacked by a thrombo-phlebitis which proved fatal. On 6 July, he died.

Michael's grief was profound and irremediable. 'The wound is still open,' he said when he returned to the House of Commons six months later. For more than twenty years, he had loved and hero-worshipped Nye, had rejoiced in his friendship and been inspired by his example. To make matters worse, the grief was heavily tinged with bitter regrets, for they had parted company on a fundamental issue and had indeed quarrelled violently. Although the arguments ceased when the illness began and their last meetings were softened by renewed affection, Michael knew that this wound too was still open; Nye considered him guilty of disloyalty and could not forgive him. Moreover, there was a final, cruel twist to the bitterness. The interrelationship between mind and body, and in this case between the clashes since 1957 and the onset or aggravation of cancer, is a subject on which nothing can be proved, but Michael had to conclude: 'It seems almost certain that the political agonies he had endured contributed to his physical destruction.'[1] Jennie made the accusation more categorically: 'Spiritually he recovered from the wounds inflicted by the unilateral disarmers in 1957 and 1958, but they had done their deadly work. Until their attacks began, he never had so much as a stomach ache . . . He did not die, he was murdered.'[2]

When Nye's ashes were scattered on a wild mountainside above Tredegar, Jennie spoke to the mourning crowd. 'Nye was a fighter,' she said. 'He gave blows, he took them, and he didn't whine. Don't think, because he held his head high, that he didn't feel the blows and insults.'[3] Many of her listeners were unilateralists: Michael, some left-wing MPs, Donald Soper, the staff of *Tribune*. It was not an occasion for debate, but it was an occasion for acute unhappiness.

It was also true, however, that this death inevitably marked a turning-point in Michael's life. Until 1957, he had been Nye's helper and lieutenant, and content with that role. After 1957, he had been obliged to strike out on his own, but had hoped – especially in the autumn of 1959 – that Nye would resume his position as leader of the left. Now, there was a vacancy in this position and there was no one – except, potentially, Michael – equipped to fill it. Wilson had moved away from the left, Wedgwood Benn was not yet considered to be on the left, Anthony Greenwood did not quite have the personality, Ian Mikardo's role was that of planner and organiser.

The new factor in the situation was that, for the first time since the early 1930s, there was a chance that the left might actually win control of the Labour Party. Gaitskell's divisiveness and capacity for alienating people, the success of CND, the continuing swing to the left in the constituencies, and the rise of Frank Cousins, which robbed the right of its praetorian guard in the big unions: all these presaged an upheaval. One journalist, venturing a long-range bet on Michael, wrote: 'Some of his admirers think that, in the course of time, if the Labour Party moves to the Left, he might become its leader.'[4] Michael himself, however, was not attracted by this speculation. When his friend Alan Brien put the question: 'If Gaitskell goes, is there anybody who is an alternative leader?', Michael's instant reply was: 'Yes – anybody.' Brien pressed: 'What about you?' Michael was dismissive: 'No, no, it's not my role, I'm not a leader.'[5]

Nevertheless, he was deeply concerned about the state of the party and wanted to play a part in its affairs. The difficulty was that he was not an MP. Friends were urging him to get back into the House of Commons as soon as possible. He had fulfilled his duty to Devonport and no one could blame him for seeking another constituency. He was now forty-seven years old; if he was out of Parliament much longer, he might be seen, in the cruel phrase that haunts politicians, as 'a man with a great future behind him'.

The next forthcoming by-election was at Ebbw Vale. Various people in the constituency – such as Bill Harry, a miner who had been a close friend of Nye Bevan – were keen to nominate Michael as Labour candidate. He accepted at once. He was entitled to feel that he was obeying Bevan's valedictory injunction, and to follow in Bevan's footsteps was cause for pride. He was glad of the prospect of representing working-class people, especially Welsh people, with whom he already felt an affinity. Besides, there could be no better forum than a by-election for arguing the case for nuclear disarmament.

The constituency covered three valleys: the Ebbw valley itself, the Sirhowy valley – which includes Tredegar, Bevan's home town – and the Rhymney valley. A dozen of these valleys, with rivers steeply descending from the mountains to the sea, form the landscape of industrial South Wales. It is a landscape of dramatic contrasts. Within each valley, street after street of small terraced houses produce a density of population, and a traditional neighbourliness, which equals that of the working-class quarters of a big city. Between the valleys, the mountainsides are the preserve of sheep and wild ponies; a chilling solitude still pervades the Waun-y-Pound, where Nye Bevan wandered and brooded as a boy and where stand the rough-hewn rocks that are his monument.

The history of these valleys was that of South Wales in general. The coalmines, opened up in the nineteenth century to meet what seemed to be a limitless demand, declined in the 1920s and 1930s to bring the scourges of mass unemployment and stark poverty. Ebbw Vale was unusual in only one respect: while most of the valleys were entirely dependent on mining, it had a large-scale steel industry and there were rather more steelworkers than miners. But the steelworks was antiquated and uncompetitive, and was closed down in 1929.

The revival of Ebbw Vale was the work of Sir William Firth, a very unusual capitalist, much admired by Aneurin Bevan, who strove for expansion when destruction of 'surplus capacity' was the accepted doctrine. His company, Richard Thomas and Baldwin, rebuilt the plant in 1938 and gave Ebbw Vale the first continuous strip mill in Europe (the process, vastly more efficient than older methods, was pioneered in America). Firth, in the words of his chief assistant and heir, Henry Spencer, 'did this against the wishes and against the bitter hostility of the whole of the steel industry . . . When money ran short, both industry and the banks combined to try to ruin him and his company.'[6] In fact, denial of bank credit drove Firth to bankruptcy; but the post-war Labour government nationalised the RTB steelworks, along with the rest of the industry, and assisted its development. The Tory government of the 1950s, which reversed nationalisation, nevertheless left RTB as a publicly owned concern. In 1960 it was operating to full capacity, the six pits in the constituency were busy too, unemployment stood at a minimal 2 per cent, and the three valleys were reckoned to be the most prosperous part of South Wales. This heightened, rather than diminished, the socialist consciousness of the people of Ebbw Vale. They knew that their well-being was the product of public ownership and planning, and they were determined to defend it.

Eleven men (no women, for this was still 1960) were nominated as possible by-election candidates. Among them, the front-runners were Michael Foot and Frank Whatley. Whatley, a miner and a well-known local personality, was the official nominee of the National Union of Mineworkers; the MP for Ebbw Vale had always been a miner ever since it was first won for Labour, the miners' lodges made the largest financial contribution to the constituency party, and Bevan had been an NUM-sponsored MP. However, Michael had the support of other unions (including the Electrical Trades Union and the Transport and General) and of several ward Labour parties. Ron Evans, a steelworker who had been Nye Bevan's election agent, was supported by the steel unions.

When the constituency Executive Committee met to examine the nominations, it produced a short-list that included neither Michael nor Whatley. It did include Ron Evans, and there were suspicions of a coup by the steel union, whose national leadership was right-wing and

Gaitskellite, but this curious short-list was probably the outcome of sheer muddle. At all events, it caused an uproar. When the General Management Committee met on 19 September, it was faced with a motion of no confidence in the Executive. Ivor Parton, who was presiding as party chairman, declined to accept the motion and suggested a simple way out – adding Michael Foot and Frank Whatley to the existing short-list. This met with unanimous agreement.

The selection conference followed five days later. In accordance with Labour Party practice, the candidates in alphabetical order spoke and answered questions. Parton, who was again in the chair, recalls that Michael was nervous when he entered the hall. However, he made what in Parton's opinion was far and away the outstanding speech.[7] He laid stress on the H-bomb issue and made it clear that he was a unilateralist. On the first ballot, he received 67 votes against 27 for Evans, 23 for Whatley and a scattering for other candidates. On the third ballot, he won an absolute majority. Ron Evans immediately offered his warm congratulations, took on the job of election agent as on earlier occasions and worked hard in the by-election campaign. Up to his death in 1991, he was Michael's best friend in the constituency.

The by-election could not take place until after the reassembly of Parliament. Meanwhile, in the first week of October, the Labour Party conference met at Scarborough.

2

The great and unavoidable issue at Scarborough was that of nuclear disarmament. Since the unilateralist resolutions were proposed by the Transport and General Workers' Union and the Amalgamated Engineering Union, they were sure to be carried. The question was: what would happen afterwards?.

The spokesman for the NEC at the outset of the big debate was Sam Watson. His argument repeated Bevan's in 1957: 'You will be asking the party to abdicate its role and responsibilities in international affairs.' Denis Healey made the same point: 'Our friends all over the world are watching us, appalled at the idea that we might decide to leave the Western alliance and starve ourselves of our defences.'

Wedgwood Benn, who had resigned from the NEC in protest against the polarisation that was threatening a party split, pleaded: 'We have got to begin a regeneration of this movement . . . That means we need everybody in the movement – we need Hugh Gaitskell and Frank

Cousins, Tony Crosland and Michael Foot.' But the likelihood of these four linking hands in amity was remote.

Michael spoke in the debate:

> If a war did come, this country would be utterly obliterated . . . We have undertaken enormous, almost incalculable risks . . . If you tie up the whole of your military machine with that of a much greater military power . . . then you lose a part of your independence and you lose a great deal of your influence.

Gaitskell wound up with a defiant speech: 'There are some of us who will fight and fight and fight again to save the party we love.' When the vote was taken, the unilateralist resolutions were duly carried. George Lansbury in 1935 – to cite a precedent often recalled at this time by the left – had resigned the leadership because the conference adopted a policy that he could not support. Gaitskell did not propose to resign because he had the backing of a majority of the Parliamentary Labour Party, a base in the coming fight. The unique constitution of the Labour Party had created two power centres: the conference, which in principle was the supreme policy-making body, and the PLP, which had the task of conducting day-to-day opposition to the Tories. Years later, when Michael was the party leader, he argued that neither of these bodies should demand the subordination of the other and that their duty was to find a way to harmonise their attitudes. But in the crisis of 1960 he firmly took the line that conference decisions were binding on everyone, including Gaitskell. In any case, Gaitskell had rejected suggestions for a compromise on disarmament policy put forward by Crossman and others.

The first necessity for Gaitskell was to retain the leadership. When the Commons reassembled, Tony Greenwood was nominated to oppose him as a declared unilateralist, but stood down in favour of Wilson, who had carefully avoided taking a stand on the issue. Among the Gaitskellites, there was some anxiety lest Wilson should attract the votes of middle-of-the-road MPs who feared the prospect of civil war in the party. Tony Crosland, who was personally very close to Gaitskell and was encouraging him to stand firm, wrote in a letter to him: 'We have one single over-riding object: to make sure that his [Wilson's] vote is as low as possible and yours as high as possible . . . To achieve this we must resort to any degree of chicanery, lying, etc., etc.'[8] As it turned out, the chicanery and lying were superfluous. Gaitskell was re-elected as leader and George Brown as deputy leader by two-to-one majorities over Wilson and the left-winger Fred Lee. This was followed by the election of a Shadow Cabinet in which known Gaitskellites held ten of the twelve places.

However, this was only the first step. Gaitskell could not afford to be defeated at another conference and to remain permanently at loggerheads with the men and women from the grass-roots. It was in the trade unions and the constituency parties that he had lost vital support in 1959–60; it was here that he must regain it in 1960–1. To this end, his supporters – the most active were Roy Jenkins, Denis Healey and Tony Crosland – formed an organisation called the Campaign for Democratic Socialism.

A key argument for the Gaitskellites was that, if anchored to unilateralism, the party could not win elections. Gaitskell himself, speaking in Cardiff on 24 October, said: 'To fight an election on unilateralism and neutralism would be literally fatal for our party.' This belief was now to be put to the test in what, short of a general election, was a clear proving-ground. Seven by-elections were pending, with polling on 16 or 17 November. In normal circumstances, a by-election is a contest between government and opposition, but it happened that six of these by-elections were in Tory seats (some of them very safe Tory seats) and the seventh was in Ebbw Vale, which was safely Labour. The question, therefore, was: how would anti-Gaitskell candidates fare by comparison with Gaitskellites? Gaitskell could not avoid sending all the Labour candidates, including Michael, the conventional 'good luck' letter, but no one had much doubt that he would be gratified if Michael came out with a poor result.

The Tories were able to watch contentedly while the antagonisms in the Labour ranks made the headlines. In the first week of November, marchers in Glasgow protested against plans to base Polaris nuclear submarines at nearby Holy Loch; the Shadow Cabinet nevertheless gave its backing to the Polaris project; and Gaitskell was shouted down by hecklers in Manchester and Liverpool. On 14 November James Callaghan, Labour MP for Cardiff South-east, spoke at a Labour campaign meeting in Ebbw Vale but dissociated himself from Michael's unilateralism. The Guardian reporter wrote that Callaghan had 'torpedoed (or Polarised) Michael Foot's defence policy'.

Bevan's majority in 1959, in a straight fight with a Tory, had been 20,922. At the by-election there were four candidates; the Liberals contested the seat for the first time since 1929 and Plaid Cymru for the first time ever. The Liberals were enjoying a revival and their candidate was a CND supporter. Thus Michael could scarcely hope to match Bevan's impressive score. The Guardian reported: 'Everyone one hears suggests a number of Labour abstentions' and doubted whether Michael could win 50 per cent of the votes (Bevan had won 81 per cent). The *Western Mail* put Michael's probable majority at 10,000.

There was another reason to fear abstentions: the record of the Ebbw Vale borough council. In a letter to Beaverbrook when the election was over, Jill described it as 'about the worst in the British Isles' and explained:

> The councillors have been unopposed for about forty years and mostly ignore any applications for membership to the Labour Party to ensure that they will remain unopposed. But the townsfolk are sick of them. We heard of such hair-raising grievances that we doubted whether we were fighting a safe seat. Many refused to vote because of their anger with the council. The first ones I met in this category said that they wouldn't vote because the potholes in the pavement resulted in their front room being flooded every time it came on to rain.

Michael, perhaps, benefited in this context from being a newcomer. He based his campaign on two issues: renunciation of nuclear weapons and public ownership. To his mind, both were linked with his conception of socialism. Gaitskell, in his official letter, wrote: 'You and I differ strongly on some important issues of defence and foreign policy, and neither of us would wish to gloss over these differences,' but he added that they were 'relatively narrow' and went on: 'I understand that much of your campaign has been fought on home affairs.' It was true that Michael spoke at most of his meetings about the threat to the steelworks, and declared that it would be 'an absolute outrage to sell off this great industry, on which the well-being of Ebbw Vale is founded'. But he spoke with just as much emphasis and persistence about nuclear disarmament, arguing the unilateralist case just as he had argued it on CND platforms, in *Tribune* and at the conference. In a final appeal, he told the voters:

> The first duty of a political candidate is to say what he thinks and give every elector a chance of questioning him about his views . . . If a candidate fails to perform this duty, if he conceals his views or dodges the questions, he is injuring the process of democracy . . . The most important is the whole question of how we are to get a real peace in the world . . . At all our meetings and in every discussion this paramount question has been persistently raised.

And, after the polls closed, he claimed: 'We have fought this campaign on a clear policy of socialism. It repudiates the nuclear strategy and we've not tried to disguise our views in any way.'

At the same time, he was angered by attempts to contrast his political outlook with that of Nye Bevan. Sir Brandon Rhys-Williams, the Tory candidate, told a meeting that Bevan 'was respected and loved here because he gave a picture of hope', whereas Michael Foot 'comes before the Welsh public with an uncongenial armoury of hatred and malicious propaganda'. Michael retorted that Rhys-Williams was revealing his 'patronising snobbery and pin-headed intellectual capacity'. He said: 'When Nye was alive the Tories lied about him, vilified him and did everything in their power to destroy him. He doesn't need their praise.' And he pointed out: 'Nye came to speak for me at every election I fought because our approach to politics was so similar.'

It was soon evident that Michael's campaign was acquiring a healthy momentum. He was winning friends through his frank statement of his beliefs and principles, and also thanks to a brand of eloquence that was in tune with Welsh traditions. The *Western Mail* reported: 'The atmosphere at many of these crowded meetings had almost a religious fervour. One speaker was wildly cheered by an audience of five hundred when he said that no Christian could defend himself with the H-bomb.'

On his side, Michael was at the beginning of a long love affair with Ebbw Vale – and this was equally true of Jill. Critics, aware of his emphatically middle-class background – a comfortable home crammed with books, fee-paying schools and Oxford – have accused him of inverse snobbery and of idealising the working class. It is true that he delighted in the comradeship of the dockyard workers of Devonport and then of the miners and steelworkers of Ebbw Vale. Shortly after the by-election, he wrote in the *Daily Herald*:

The people of industrial Wales are proud of their working-class tradition, proud of their working-class achievements and still as proud as ever of *being* working-class. Against this rock all the prissy values preached by the BBC, all the tinsel tuppenny-halfpenny ideas filtered through television, all the snobbery and smug complacency associated with a Tory-directed affluent society beat in vain . . . Men and women still believe that it is better to live in a real community than to set before themselves the idea of rising out of their class, spurning their great ancestry and kicking away the ladder . . . The Ebbw Vale election was for me more exhilarating than any political experience in my life precisely because it revealed how strong and indestructible are the sinews of British democracy.

Hundreds of Ebbw Vale people – it would be true to say thousands – came to Michael's meetings, and many who had considered abstention or voting for other candidates must have been won over. As for the activists of the Labour Party, they threw themselves into the campaign with fervent energy. One of them was Neil Kinnock, a student at University College, Cardiff; he was a native of Tredegar, and his father was a steelworker who had been forced to change his job through industrial illness. Young Kinnock canvassed indefatigably, but his main contribution (and pleasure) was inspired heckling at Tory meetings. Michael spotted his political talents and decided to keep an eye on him. When fine weather came next summer, Neil Kinnock and his girlfriend, Glenys Parry, were invited for a day's walking in the mountains.

On 17 November, 76 per cent of the electorate voted – a remarkable figure for a by-election in a safe seat, and one that triumphantly belied the predictions of heavy abstentions. The result was:

Michael Foot, Labour	20,528
Sir Brandon Rhys-Williams, Conservative	3,799
Patrick Lort-Phillips, Liberal	3,449
Emrys Roberts, Plaid Cymru	2,091
Labour majority	16,729

It was a sweet revenge for the saddening defeat at Devonport the year before. Rhys-Williams, in spite of (or because of) his smear tactics, had done very badly, losing more than a third of the 1959 Tory vote.

For Hugh Gaitskell and for the Transport House machine, the bad news was the contrast between Ebbw Vale and the results of the six other by-elections. In four of the six, the Liberals pushed Labour into third place. Dick Crossman, writing in the *Guardian*, summarised the results as 'one great victory and six humiliating defeats'. What hardly needed stressing was that the victory had been won by an uncompromising left-winger and unilateralist. Vicky's cartoon showed Gaitskell reading the news and saying: 'Oh dear, we've won.'

As soon as he could get away from the celebration with Ebbw Vale comrades, Michael telephoned his father to give him the news. It was the last time that they spoke together. On 13 December 1960, Isaac Foot died. In the summer, when the family had gathered for his eightieth birthday, it had been evident that his powers were failing, but he had no specific illness and his death from heart failure came as a surprise. Michael, on this very day, was making his first speech in the Commons since his re-election. When the next speaker, observing parliamentary courtesies, offered condolences, it was noted that 'he bit hard on his lower lip and his eyes glistened over'.[9]

Michael and Jill went to Pencrebar for the funeral, the reading of the will and a sad family Christmas. Jill wrote to Beaverbrook:

Isaac Foot's estate is in about the greatest muddle that could ever be left by a solicitor. He owned farms and a good bit of land around Callington, but it is all heavily mortgaged and the debts are tremendous, since he used every penny he could lay his hands on to indulge his passion for books. . . . Michael, as might be expected, would rather hang on to the books than get any money; but the proposition is to sell them off . . . It seems to me a pity to disperse a library where each book has been added with so much loving care and purpose, so I am wondering whether Harvard or Yale Universities might not be interested. I wonder what your advice would be.

Beaverbrook, picking up Jill's hint, expressed an interest in buying the collection for the University of New Brunswick in his native province of Canada. His letter to this effect (a copy is in his papers) seems to have been ignored. Dingle Foot, as the eldest son, took charge of the disposal of the library and arranged a sale to the University of California. The purchase price was £50,000 – an astonishing bargain, since it amounted to slightly under a pound for each of the 52,000 books, of which some, notably the Bibles, were extremely valuable. Beaverbrook would certainly have paid much more. Michael was very annoyed, not so much because of the financial sacrifice as because California was a long way away and the books were dispersed among five campuses.

But in the early months of 1961 Michael had many preoccupations. He was determined, in spite of his unassailable majority, to be a hardworking constituency MP for Ebbw Vale, as he had been for Devonport. (In this respect he compared favourably with Bevan, who had neglected the constituency and shown his face there only once in two or three months.) He was buying, for £300, a dilapidated little house at 10 Morgan Street, in the centre of Tredegar; Jill planned to repair and modernise it, like the cottage at Cherkley. He was a central figure in the struggle for the control of the Labour Party. Last but not least, he was – while being as dedicated and enthusiastic as anyone else – the most politically experienced among the leaders of CND.

3

The triumph of unilateralism at the Labour Party conference did not produce undiluted satisfaction within CND. Many of its activists looked with suspicion on the strategy favoured by the Executive Committee, most of whose (self-appointed, let us recall) members – Canon Collins, Michael Foot, Kingsley Martin, Benn Levy – were also members of the Labour Party. That strategy, in brief, was first to wrest control of the party from Gaitskell, and secondly to win a majority in Parliament for a Labour Party with nuclear disarmament in its programme. The sceptics argued that a Labour Cabinet would always be controlled either by right-wingers or by compromisers who had no clear stand on the great issue, such as Harold Wilson or Dick Crossman, and any promises would inevitably be broken. Hence, CND must be a mass movement free from contamination by the dirty world of 'politics'. In 1959, this trend of thought was strong enough for the *CND Bulletin* to give space to a debate between Michael Foot and an activist named Michael Craft, who was sponsoring a campaign-within-the-campaign called 'Voters' Veto' – that is, for abstention in the general election. Michael Foot wrote: 'Only through the election of a Labour Government and the political pressure which we may exert afterwards can we succeed . . . To refuse to take any of these factors into account in deciding how to vote would in my view be an act of complete irresponsibility.' Craft's view was: 'The greatest tragedy for the Campaign would be the return of a Labour Government with its policy unchanged. It is pious to hope that we could change their policy in office and disillusion would spread in the Campaign.'[10]

By 1960, the good news was that Labour policy could be changed. But the bad news was that the Tories had won the election and would probably hold power for the next five years. In that period, nuclear war might render all political calculations irrelevant. The only hope and the only way forward, some concluded, lay in the methods of civil disobedience. One advocate for these methods was a young American, Ralph Schoenman, who was in Britain on a student visa but had become Bertrand Russell's secretary. He exerted a commanding influence over Russell – nearly ninety by this time – and persuaded him to give his blessing to a new organisation, dedicated to civil disobedience, called the Committee of 100. (The idea behind this curious name was that the police and the authorities would be unable to identify the directing spirits.) The plans were made in secrecy, so that Collins and other members of the Executive learned of them only through an accidental leak on 28 September. Horrified – and fearing that votes at Scarborough might be scared off – the few members of the Executive who could be gathered for an emergency meeting issued a statement reaffirming their faith in 'legal and democratic methods of argument and persuasion'.

The immediate sequel was a lamentable exchange of verbal hostilities between Russell and Collins.[11] Russell resigned the presidency; the Executive accepted the resignation and voted confidence in Collins as chairman. Russell, according to Peggy Duff, 'probably expected and hoped that the Executive would repudiate the chairman and beg the president to come back'. Michael, who had made the humanist philosopher one of his heroes in his Oxford days, was saddened by the rift, but stood by the 'legal and democratic' strategy.

In the Labour Party, there was open warfare between Gaitskell and the left. Attending a meeting of the PLP for the first time since 1955, Michael demanded that unilateralists should have equal representation when defence policy was discussed by the National Executive and the Shadow Cabinet. The meeting degenerated into uproar and Gaitskell closed it after twenty minutes. (In those days, the leader was also chairman of the PLP.) In a defence debate in the Commons on 13 December 1960, the Labour front bench supported a motion which, while deploring 'undue reliance on nuclear weapons', endorsed the strategy of deterrence. Michael, speaking with vigour despite the news of his father's death, pointed out that the leader of the party 'knows perfectly well that the proposal he is putting is that which was defeated at the Labour Party conference'. He went on: 'Fortunately for the honour of this country there is a great and growing number of people who are protesting against the policies pursued by the government, sometimes supported by the official Opposition – who are protesting against the suffocation of democratic responsibilities.'

Gaitskell and the majority of Labour MPs listened to this speech with resentful indignation. Michael had committed the same offence as Bevan in 1955: he had attacked his own front bench, while the Tories smiled at the spectacle of Labour disunity. Onslaughts in *Tribune* compounded the offence. Michael wrote sardonically:

The designs of an immaculate leadership have been upset by the wicked, irresponsible, obstreperous activities of a minority which engineered the final affront at Scarborough by turning itself into a majority. In short, it is the rank and file of the movement, or a very bulky section of it, which is the source of all the trouble. Now anyone who believes that will believe anything . . . We tried it out at Ebbw Vale. We fought openly and proudly on the basis of the Scarborough decisions about peace and public ownership . . . And we had a wonderful victory.

The Gaitskellites, never very strong on tolerance, were now determined that discipline must be restored. The left in the Parliamentary Labour Party was hopelessly outnumbered and regularly outvoted, but Crosland, for one, took the view that 'our Left is clearly too numerous'. Identifying twenty of the 'hard-boiled', he advised Gaitskell: 'This is the crucial group which must be expelled.'[12] All that was needed was a suitable opportunity.

This presented itself in March 1961 when the House had to vote on estimates for the armed forces. The Shadow Cabinet decided on abstention. For the minority who objected to the nuclear strategy, it was unthinkable to let the occasion pass without a protest. In the debate on the Army Estimates on 8 March, Michael said:

> Service ministers are very good at grinding axes. Indeed, these axes seem to be about the only conventional weapons which are now in full supply . . . The truth is that this country is more defenceless now than it has ever been in history . . . Historians will wonder about the sanity of the rulers of such a country as this, the most vulnerable country in the world, who decided to make their country the most obvious and immediate target if nuclear war should come.

He was denouncing the Tory government, but his words stung the Labour front bench, which had refrained from mounting an attack. Twenty-four Labour MPs disobeyed the Shadow Cabinet and voted against the Army Estimates. The whips spread the word that a repetition of this behaviour when the Air Estimates came before the House a week later would be frowned on, but no formal warning was issued. Five MPs voted against the Air Estimates. They were Michael Foot, his long-standing friends Sydney Silverman and Emrys Hughes, the maverick and perpetually rebellious S. O. Davies and a Scottish member, William Baxter, who was not on the left in his general outlook but was a pacifist. Normally, a 'conscience' vote against armed defence by a pacifist would have been condoned, but Baxter had made the mistake of getting into the same basket as Michael and Silverman.

George Brown, acting as leader because Gaitskell was away, summoned a party meeting next day and called for the withdrawal of the whip from the offenders. All five spoke and refused to back down or apologise. Brown got his way by a majority of 90 votes to 63, with about a hundred abstentions; there was a fairly widespread feeling that the blunderbuss was being unwisely employed.

Being deprived of the whip was a mixed curse, or even a mixed blessing. The five were unable to take part in PLP meetings, which were the forum for vital debates leading to important decisions on political strategy, and indeed on matters of principle. On the other hand, they now had complete freedom in the House of Commons itself, without any obligations to distasteful conformity. Often, they put up a more effective opposition to the Tories than did the Labour front bench. On one occasion, when Baxter declined to follow the same left-wing line as the other four, Hughes warned him: 'If you don't behave, we'll throw you back into the Labour Party.'

Michael used his freedom, in particular, to expose and attack the restrictions imposed by party discipline on the freedom of all the other MPs. For him, this had become a major concern. In 1959, while out of the House, he had written three articles for the *Observer* which were republished as a pamphlet entitled *Parliament in Danger!* In the first article, he deplored the erosion of real distinctions between the parties (this was the time when the *Observer*'s political correspondent coined the word 'Butskellism' to describe the underlying agreement between Butler and Gaitskell). He asked: 'Could there be a more pitiful irony than that Britain, in the midst of her engagement in a world-wide propaganda struggle against the evils of the one-party State, should smugly countenance the growth at her heart of one or other or both of the twin dangers which could destroy her case – a one-party State approved by apathetic consent and the decay of party politics?' In the second, he turned the spotlight on the removal of real argument and real decision-making from the House to the private, unreported party meeting. 'The higher the party meeting rises on the see-saw the lower sinks the Commons.' The problem was:

> If the outside public chooses to study the division lists . . . it will be discovered that an M.P. voted loyally with his party. But how did he speak and vote in the critical, binding debate in the private meeting upstairs? Nobody can discover that except by rumour or leakage or on those infrequent occasions when an individual M.P. kicks over the traces.

Given the sanctions in the hands of the party leadership, controlling an obedient majority, 'the procedure may resemble a kind of liberal form of lynch-law'. It was this, indeed, that Michael was subjected to in 1961. He concluded in his third article:

> The enforcement of ever more rigid party discipline is . . . an engine for suppressing or at least hiding the very questions which need most to be discussed. Are we to tolerate a situation where the major parties become more and more monolithically united to fight about less and less? Here certainly would be an infallible recipe for deepening public boredom with the contest.

Indeed, the voting lobby had become 'a corridor of humiliation where the M.P. must wear the badge of his tribe instead of carrying the banner of his convictions'.

Back in the House from 1960, Michael found that the debilitating processes had gone quite as far as he had feared, with the supine consent of most MPs. In one speech, he reminded the House that the two men who had made the greatest mark on parliamentary history, Winston Churchill and Aneurin Bevan, 'were in perpetual quarrels with their party machine'. He protested:

> We were sent here to be accountable to the public, but we cannot be accountable to the public if real decisions are made in private . . . We must take every precaution to ensure that discussion in the House is real and not fake . . . I am opposed to this state of affairs. It's not a popular view. Apparently, most honourable members prefer to be herded. It seems a strange desire but apparently it is their wish, for whatever reason.[13]

By the spring of 1961, Gaitskell's determination to 'fight and fight again' was being vindicated. The AEU and other unions changed sides; it became predictable that the Scarborough vote would be reversed at the next party conference. *Tribune* admitted as much, and Michael wrote on 9 June: 'Unlike Mr Gaitskell, we have never claimed that Conference decides only when it happens to agree with us . . . We shall exercise the democratic right which we have never denied to Mr Gaitskell but which he has so often sought to deny to others: the right to continue the argument in favour of what we believe.'

Many of the rank and file of CND drew the conclusion that reliance on capturing the Labour Party was a futile policy, and support for the Committee of 100 grew through 1961. On 29 April, 800 people obeyed its call to sit down in Trafalgar Square and were peacefully, if laboriously, carried away to waiting police vans. A repeat of this action was set for 17 September. In an attempt to forestall it, the authorities made use of a law dating from 1361 and ordered the known leaders to promise to keep the peace. Those who refused were jailed for two months and even Russell had to serve a sentence of seven days, which raised his status as a venerable martyr to new heights. The comment in *Tribune* was: 'The government has panicked in the face of the gallantry and initiative shown by the Committee of 100.' The sit-down was a success, with about 10,000 people in the Square and 1,314 arrested (including Canon Collins, who had gone simply to take a look).

The Labour conference in October brought the predictable defeat for unilateralism, though it also voted against the Polaris nuclear submarine project and against a resumption of nuclear tests. Michael warned: 'The reversal of the Scarborough decision could have the most dangerous consequences in spreading the belief – understandable but still hopeless – that real political action can be bypassed in the struggle for peace.'[14] His attitude to the sit-downs, though not ambiguous, was somewhat ambivalent. With the rest of the 'old guard' of CND, he was opposed to switching the Campaign's strategy from political pressure to civil disobedience and was well aware that hopes of forcing a Tory government to scrap nuclear weapons by such methods were illusory. At the same time, he shared the feeling of the activists that legal niceties were immaterial in face of the menace of nuclear war, and he drew on a stock of examples – the Chartists, the suffragettes, Gandhi in India – to show that law-breaking was justified in a good cause. He could even assert (perhaps to shock the complacent ranks of Tories in the Commons): 'Most of the freedoms which we possess have been secured by riots.'[15] When Sydney Silverman protested in the House against the neutron bomb (a weapon which was devised to kill people without destroying buildings) and the Minister of Defence failed to put in an appearance, Michael exploded:

The Minister of Defence complained because some people sat down outside his Ministry. The Minister won't even come and sit down on the front bench of the House of Commons, so he must not complain if people outside the House take extraordinary measures . . . The best thing I could recommend would be for somebody to throw a brick through a Ministry of Defence window.[16]

In support of Silverman, he demanded:

Are these the terms of our alliance with the United States, that they can go ahead with the manufacture of bombs of this mammoth grotesque nature without our even having any say in the matter? . . . One of the horrors of the whole business of nuclear weapons is the bovine fatalism which seems to have settled on so many people . . . Once we start applying the most elementary moral principles, Christian or otherwise, the whole process in which the world is engaged is exposed as a crime of such monstrous proportions that it is impossible to find language with which to describe it . . . The government may not be concerned, the official Opposition may not be concerned, but growing numbers of people outside are concerned.

In the wake of the September sit-down, Ralph Schoenman was among those sent to prison, and the Home Secretary, R. A. Butler, took the opportunity to decree that his visa would not be renewed. Canon Collins and the CND leaders would have been privately delighted to see Schoenman escorted on to a westbound plane, but Michael protested in the Commons:

> His civil disobedience activities are run by a body with which I disagree, but that makes no difference to the argument . . . Many of the freedoms in both countries [Britain and America] were built up by people who were exiled from one country to another. We probably wouldn't have the Anglo-American alliance had it not been for Tom Paine, who went to America and stirred up trouble there.

A reactionary Tory, Lord Hinchingbrooke, intervened to suggest that foreigners who benefited from political asylum (actually, this was not the case with Schoenman) should keep quiet. Michael was outraged:

> It would be a monstrous derogation of the principle of political asylum if we said we were prepared to let people come to this country so long as they kept their mouths shut when they got here . . . Does the noble Lord think that Garibaldi came here to keep his mouth shut or Mazzini came here to be absolutely silent? . . . They came here to say things they were denied the right to say elsewhere. That's the glory of this country. That's the glory of the principle of political asylum. [16]

Butler relented, and allowed Schoenman to stay in Britain if he confined himself to working as Russell's secretary. However, there was a renewal of the argument a few months later when Butler was steering his Commonwealth Immigration Bill through the Commons. One clause authorised magistrates to order the deportation of immigrants convicted of an offence, and an amendment moved by David Weitzman and Barbara Castle sought (in vain) to ensure that this should not apply to political offences. Michael spoke in support:

> The political offences regarded as most reprehensible in one period become the most honoured in the next . . . Almost the last British citizens deported from this country were the Tolpuddle Martyrs . . . It would be absolutely outrageous if a student who came to this country, participated in the activities of the Committee of 100 and was sent to prison, were to be deported on that account. It would be an advertisement of the abandonment of liberal principles by this country. [17]

By the end of 1961, the civil disobedience campaign was only an emotionally evocative memory. A sit-down was planned for 9 December at Wethersfield, a US Air Force base in Essex. Again, the authorities made a pre-emptive strike by arresting the organisers. Two of them, Michael Randle and Pat Pottle, were sent to prison for eighteen months (they served the sentences in Wormwood Scrubs and helped the KGB agent, George Blake, to escape). A rash statement claimed that 50,000 people had promised to be at Wethersfield. For one reason or another – the deterrent effect of the sentences on the leaders, the distance from London or the cold weather – only a few hundred showed up. It was the Committee of 100's last effort. For Michael, it proved that 'real political action' could not be bypassed.

4

'We must condemn the resumption of nuclear tests, no matter who resumed them,' George Brown had declared from the platform at the 1961 party conference. The Russians were the first to resume them, with the explosion of a fifty-megaton bomb of an appallingly poisonous nature. In February 1962, President Kennedy announced that the US would resume testing too and Gaitskell, on a visit to Washington, voiced his approval. Michael protested: 'Mr Gaitskell has no authority on behalf of the Labour movement to express support for Kennedy's proposed action . . . It is hard to conceive of any action more likely to spread cynicism about the Labour Party and its claim to be a democratic party. Mr Gaitskell has struck a most damaging blow at the party he is elected to lead.'[18]

When the annual defence estimates came before the House of Commons again, the Labour leadership pursued its policy of abstention and the only MPs to vote against were those who had been deprived of the whip. Michael moved a cut in the Air Force Estimates:

The operations in which the RAF would be engaged would be operations of mass murder . . . If the opposition think that [the missiles on RAF bases] are provocative first-strike weapons, they should vote against them . . . They would have the benches in this Chamber full and people would think this was a serious debate, but as long as the Opposition front bench treat a matter of this kind in derisory fashion nobody will take their defence policy seriously, and after that nobody will take the House of Commons seriously . . . That is why some of us will vote against this utterly evil, lunatic and dangerous policy.

Silverman moved a cut in the Navy Estimates, which involved the important issue of the Polaris submarines, but the Chairman of Committees refused to allow time for a debate. Michael protested against this 'further derogation from the rights of the independent members and back-bench members'.

Easter came round again. Every year since 1959, Michael had been in the front rank of the march from Aldermaston to London. He had always been fond of walking (though preferably not on main roads like the A4) and he enjoyed the company of old and new friends, the sound of guitars and singing, the picnic lunches. He was able to claim: 'This year the march from Aldermaston was bigger, stronger and more nationally representative than ever. No other political movement in the country could assemble so vast a concourse of dedicated people. In particular, none of the political parties could win the allegiance of such a company of young people.'[19]

This was true enough, but he was worried by the growth of anti-political feeling in the Campaign. Pointing to 'a new mood of desperation and urgency', he warned: 'If it provoked CND to tear itself apart in a frenzied search for new forms of activity, it could also be a source of weakness.'[20] Some people on the left were tearing up their Labour Party cards; *Tribune* told them: 'Every resignation from the Labour Party is a victory for Mr Gaitskell.' Comrades were urged to soldier on, even if they were 'sick of the leadership's arrogant cynicism'.[21]

Gaitskell, for his part, was sick of the persistent rebellions in the party. He secured the reimposition of the strict standing orders in the PLP which had been in abeyance since the days of the Attlee government. Speaking in Glasgow on May Day, he attacked the dissidents: 'Either they choose to go on wrecking our chances, in which case they ought not to be in the Labour Party at all, or they must agree to accept the official policy of the party.' He was shouted down by a crowd of young people waving CND banners, and was goaded into shouting back: 'When it comes to the ballot and to voting in elections these people are not worth a tinker's curse. They are peanuts. They don't count.' But Michael had a different view of what was permissible at public meetings: 'Heckling contributes a great deal to the political scene and most public speakers would be improved when heckled. Indeed, some should be heckled much more ferociously than they are.'[22] He went further: 'There are occasions when it is appropriate for speakers to be howled down . . . and when a well-aimed tomato or a well-matured egg should not be regarded as an entirely improper feature of the political scene.'[23]

There were certainly few people whom Michael disliked more than Gaitskell, and the animosity was amply returned. In the summer of 1962 Michael and Jill, after a visit to Capponcina, went to a hotel at Portofino. Jill wrote to Beaverbrook:

> Would you believe it, the second night after we left you, we found ourselves within two tables from Gaitskell and party . . . We had drunk quite a bit and eaten marvellously in a fish restaurant . . . Did Gaitskell give us a nod? Did he smile? Did he invite us over? Not at all. He cut us dead. And I am sorry to report that your dear Annie Fleming did likewise. Only Maurice Bowra left Gaitskell's table to speak to Michael and was afterwards, so he told us, reproved for disloyalty. So how's that for magnanimity on Gaitskell's part? I was quite sorry that one of your reporters was not lurking about.

Michael had just finished writing the first volume of his massive and detailed biography of Aneurin Bevan. The decision to make it a two-volume project gave the author plenty of elbow-room, and Bevan's life divided neatly in 1945, when he became Minister of Health. It also had the advantage that the story of the clash in 1957 would fall into the second volume and could be deferred until passions had cooled. The book was published in Britain by MacGibbon and Kee and in America by Atheneum, the firm launched by Michael's friend Simon Michael Bessie. Editing and production were the responsibility of Reginald Davis-Poynter, general manager of MacGibbon and Kee. But, as he has said, 'You don't edit Michael.'

The main difficulty for the biographer was that Bevan had been very casual about keeping letters and other papers, and had written few letters himself. (Bevan had been a left-handed child forced at school to write right-handed, which led to his dislike of writing and perhaps caused his stammer.) This handicap was greatly outweighed by the advantage that, since Nye had died at the age of only sixty-three, many people who had known him – some, indeed, who had known him in youth – were available to contribute recollections. These included, in the first place, members of the Bevan family, especially Aneurin's younger sister, Arianwen; they had a relationship as close as that of Michael and Sally Foot. Then, as MP for Ebbw Vale and inheritor of Nye's mantle, Michael could consult the activists of the Miners' Union and the Labour Party. Foremost among these was Archie Lush, Nye's closest friend in the valley ever since they were boys.

Jennie Lee, of course, fully supported the project. Michael wrote in his preface: 'Jennie Lee has given me invaluable assistance and guidance. But she has imposed no limitations on what I wished to write and the responsibility for any errors or misjudgements is mine, not hers.' As Davis-Poynter recalls, this was not precisely true. Michael narrated an episode of the 1920s, when Nye fell passionately in love with a young woman – a cellist – and was ready to sacrifice his incipient political career for her sake. At Jennie's request, the account was removed at the page-proof stage.

In his first three chapters, Michael described Nye's early experiences at the coal-face and in the unemployment queue, and then his activity in the union and in local politics. He was chairman of a union lodge at nineteen, the youngest on record, and a borough councillor at twenty-five. As well as tracing Bevan's political development, these chapters make a significant contribution to the history of the South Wales Labour movement between 1918 and 1929. The rest of the book was the story of Aneurin Bevan as a rebellious and iconoclastic MP, as an increasingly prominent standard-bearer of the left in the 1930s, and as the boldest of Churchill's critics in wartime. From the time of his own first meeting with Nye in 1935 onward, Michael was able to write from memory and from intimate personal knowledge.

Obviously and overtly, the biography was a labour of love. In a disarming footnote, Michael admitted that he was a hero-worshipper. In his preface, he wrote of Bevan: 'I cannot claim to have portrayed the richness of his personality. Such an achievement is beyond my powers. In any case, no printed words can repair the loss of the voice, the gestures, the mind and vitality of the man.'[24] However, Chapter 6 – headed 'The Man' – is a rounded portrait of Bevan at the time when he began to make headway in politics, and an exposition of the very individual workings of his thought and his character. There are passages that would be noteworthy in any biography:

He had come to London to help change the world, with the cries of his own people drilling in his ears. He never forgot and he never betrayed. He had seen the harshness and squalor of the world before he was in his teens. But he grew younger in zest and spirit. It was the youth partly denied him he wanted to experience, not the ways of the London world . . . The most precious possession of a politician is time; to squander it on apparently unassociated pursuits looks too lighthearted and wayward . . . But he knew that his real treasure was his mind; he was resolved to keep it fresh and young and never to bury it in a cemetery of blue books and committee meetings.[25]

Michael certainly did not squander his time. The book, with a length of 510 pages, was written in fifteen or sixteen months – months when he was a conscientious constituency MP, a frequent speaker on a variety of subjects in the Commons, a platform speaker and Executive Committee member of CND, still the guiding hand of *Tribune* and a columnist for the *Daily Herald*. (The only lightening of the load was that he now wrote the column once instead of twice a week.) The speed, the energy and the quality of the achievement are all extraordinary.

The advance from MacGibbon and Kee was only £500, but the *Sunday Times* bought the serial rights for £10,000 – about £110,000 in today's money value – published four extracts on the front of its review section, and plastered London with big advertising posters. The hardback sale was 15,000 and the paperback sale about the same.

At the party conference of 1962, the main issue was no longer nuclear disarmament but the European Community, or the Common Market as it was then generally called. Macmillan had made an application for British membership; Gaitskell was strongly against it, as he made clear in his conference speech. This brought him into clear disagreement with friends such as Roy Jenkins and Tony Crosland, who had fought by his side after Scarborough but who favoured EC membership. As Michael wrote in *Tribune* after Gaitskell's death, only a fool could deny his strength of character. Gaitskell was chiefly motivated by a deep attachment to the Commonwealth, which had also led him to oppose the Immigration Act of 1961, when a limit was placed on immigration from the Commonwealth for the first time, despite the mutterings of some nervous Labour MPs. Denouncing the overture to Europe, he declared: 'We do not propose to forget Vimy Ridge and Gallipoli'[26] – an appeal which Michael, though on the same side on this issue, considered to be pitching it a bit too strong. But he was delighted to see, at long last, clear opposition to the Tories on a major issue. Under the headline 'A GREAT WEEK FOR DEMOCRACY AND SOCIALISM', he wrote optimistically: 'A new hope has arisen and great expectations can legitimately open before us.'[27]

It was an issue that already roused strong passions, but Denis Healey took a shrewd view: 'I saw the whole issue as a futile distraction, since it was certain that de Gaulle would veto Britain's entry.'[28] He was soon proved right. In December 1962 Macmillan, in a meeting with Kennedy, agreed to a virtual integration of the British and American nuclear-weapons systems, and de Gaulle pronounced that Europe could not accept an applicant whose real loyalties were across the Atlantic. The reaction in Britain was an explosion of hurt feelings and fury, reviving all the enmities aroused by Louis XIV and Napoleon, if not Joan of Arc. Having been excluded for three years from a France ruled by de Gaulle, and having forcefully attacked de Gaulle's authoritarian style of government, Michael might have been expected to join in this chorus. But his comment was more reflective:

> De Gaulle is a rebel against American leadership. Some of us who are also rebels have some sympathy with him on that account . . . One of his long-term aims is to secure a settlement between East and West . . . The whole situation is altering between East and West. The planet is trembling with alterations and differences in alliances and arrangements. I don't believe in the old configuration of the cold war . . . It is five years, even ten years out of date . . . We may, whatever his motives and reasons, thank President de Gaulle for doing for us what the British government had not the courage and energy to do for themselves.[29]

Hugh Gaitskell did not live to see this vindication of his hostility to Macmillan's application. He had been suffering since the autumn from a rare immunological disease – so rare that there were persistent rumours that he had been poisoned by the KGB – and on 18 January 1963 he died. In *Tribune*, Michael paid tribute to his 'rich combination of qualities', but added: 'The supreme quality of political imagination – of combined imaginative sympathy, wisdom and power – was the one which Hugh Gaitskell, I believe, most lacked.' Gaitskell, he recalled, had divided the party by his 1951 budget, his attempt to expel Bevan in 1955 and his Clause Four enterprise in 1959 – 'Not Gaitskell but the rank and file restored the unity so severely damaged.' But the story ended well with Gaitskell's last conference when 'to his delight if not astonishment, he found himself the leader of a much more united, robust party'. Michael concluded: 'The last legacy he left may outweigh all the rest. For the door to the future which he unlocked is still open.'[30]

There were three candidates for the succession to the leadership: George Brown, Harold Wilson and James Callaghan. Callaghan was the outsider, putting down a marker for the future. Brown was obviously the leading candidate of the right. Wilson, with his mixed record, was scarcely the candidate of the left, but in their eyes he was certainly preferable to Brown. Michael, being still deprived of the whip, had no right to vote; Wilson was short of five left-wing votes which might, in a close contest, come in very useful. However, the contest was not so close as most observers expected. In the first ballot, Wilson was ahead of Brown and near to an absolute majority, and Callaghan was eliminated. The second ballot gave Wilson a comfortable win, with 144 votes to Brown's 103.

Michael responded with a generous listing of Wilson's good qualities: 'A coherence of ideas, a readiness to follow unorthodox courses, a respect for democracy, a rooted opposition to Toryism and all its manifestations. Above all, a deep and genuine love of the Labour movement.'[31] Admittedly, Wilson was 'canny, ambitious, often cautious, always cool, usually calculating' – but in a figure such as Kennedy, Michael pointed out, these characteristics were counted as virtues. Still in the optimistic mood generated by the last conference, he concluded: 'Another 1945 could be in the making.'

Easing himself into the leadership, Wilson had to tread with all his habitual caution. Ten of the twelve members of his Shadow Cabinet were definable right-wingers and had voted for Brown as leader. Wilson remarked to his friends that his task was 'like making a Bolshevik revolution with a Czarist Central Committee', and perhaps he saw it thus, although the vision of Wilson as a revolutionary must have made some of them smile.

Still, the five rebels were hopeful enough to apply for a restoration of the Labour whip, and wrote to this effect to the Chief Whip, Herbert Bowden, on 18 February. Bowden replied that they would have to apply individually, not collectively, and accordingly Michael wrote to him: 'I am anxious to resume my place in the Parliamentary Party and to play my part in securing a Labour Party victory at the next election and a new Labour Government, and of course recognise that this would mean accepting the same obligations as other Labour MPs.' There was no response until 22 May, when Bowden wrote frostily:

> The Parliamentary Committee [that is, the Shadow Cabinet] have considered your application for the restoration of the Whip. I am to advise you that on the basis of your letter, which they consider does not give the unqualified assurances sought, they are unable to recommend to the Party Meeting on Wednesday next that the Whip be restored to you. You will not, of course, be entitled to attend this meeting.

A week later, after Michael had written another letter repeating his assurances, the Shadow Cabinet relented and he was readmitted; so were the other four rebels. It can be presumed that Wilson overcame the objections from the Czarists.

Michael was undoubtedly eager to be readmitted, especially in the more open situation created by Wilson's leadership. He had protested against the system whereby the real policy decisions were made in the party meeting 'upstairs', rather than on the floor of the House, but this made it more desirable for him to have a voice in the PLP. At the same time, he knew that when he got the whip restored he would miss the advantages of independence. On one occasion, when he had delivered yet another denunciation of 'the whole folly and madness' of the policy of nuclear deterrence, a Tory MP remarked: 'I can understand some of the concern felt by the leaders of the party opposite lest by any chance he should get the whip back and perhaps apply it to their backs.'

His next speech was on a government bill to allow peers to renounce their titles and thus become eligible to sit in the Commons. Wedgwood Benn, after reluctantly acquiring a peerage on his father's death, had won the ensuing by-election in Bristol South-east, been refused admission to the Commons, won another by-election, and thus made a change in the law irresistible. Lord Hailsham (Quintin Hogg, a former Tory MP) suggested that it would be wrong for a title to be 'extinguished' for good and that provision should be made for a resumption. Michael attacked Hailsham for being 'not faintly interested in how the country is to be governed, or what is the proper and democratic way of doing it'. It was extraordinary 'that the House of Commons should have to meet to discuss such a piece of tomfoolery as this'. There was a danger, he warned, of a so-called reform of the House of Lords involving the appointment of peers by the parties – a scheme with 'enormous capacities of patronage'. Michael did not foresee that, within four years, just such a plan would be advanced by a Labour government, but he was rigorously against anything that would preserve the Lords from its proper fate – abolition. He wound up: 'As the Tory Party is about to lose the general election, this is the moment when it needs the House of Lords most of all.'[32]

The Aldermaston march of 1963 was significantly smaller than in earlier years, and the CND Executive decided that it should be the last. It had to be admitted that the rising tide of the Campaign was on the ebb. The Cuba missile crisis in October 1962, when the world trembled for thirteen days on the brink of nuclear war, might have been seen as a vindication of CND's warnings, but apparently it had the opposite effect. Most people drew the lesson that Kennedy and Khrushchev were soberly aware of the dangers of a confrontation and would always stay their hands at the last moment. The feeling of safety was reinforced when a treaty to ban nuclear tests (above ground, at least) was signed in Moscow in August 1963. The tests, with their horrifying effects, had given the protest movement much of its emotional driving-power ever since 1957. Michael wrote: 'The Moscow test ban may be the greatest event since Hiroshima – the first sign that the popular will for peace is penetrating the councils of the statesmen.'[33] The weary footsoldiers of CND could be forgiven for feeling that they could honourably rest from their labours.

As CND became smaller and less concerned with persuading the millions, it came to be dominated by people who had few links with the traditional left. It was a sign of the times when, from 30 August 1963, *Tribune* ceased to carry the 'anti-H-bomb' strap-line and reverted to the old heading: 'Labour's Independent Weekly'. In 1964, Collins resigned from the chairmanship of the Campaign and Michael withdrew from the Executive Committee; Alan Taylor and Kingsley Martin had already dropped out. By the mid-sixties, the men and women for whom campaigning was a way of life were mostly devoting their energies to other causes: opposition to the Common Market, boycotting South Africa and above all the struggle that meant more to a generation of the left than anything since the Spanish Civil War – Vietnam.

During 1963, the Labour Party was regaining its unity and confidence, while the Tories were in trouble. The magic of 'Supermac' was gone; Macmillan looked like a tired old man. Everything went wrong for the government: the rebuff from de Gaulle, economic downturn and then the Profumo scandal. In October, on the eve of the Conservative Party conference, Macmillan had to go into hospital for a prostate operation, was told (incorrectly) that he would need months of convalescence, and resigned. The Tories then had no recognised procedure for electing a new leader, and were plunged into a week of undignified and discreditable jostling. Butler, the obvious front-runner, failed to win the prize for the second time. Among the contenders were Lord Hailsham and the Earl of Home, who were able, ironically enough, to avail themselves of the option to renounce their titles and return to the Commons which had been fought for by Wedgwood Benn. In the end, the new Prime Minister was the Earl of Home, reborn as Sir Alec Douglas-Home, a figure unknown to most of the public. Michael commented:

A new Prime Minister is being selected by methods which, if they were ever used by a trade union in choosing a general secretary, would be the subject of criminal investigation . . . Even they will never dare to repeat the exhibition. In their own interests, they may begin to realise that, compared with the recent public indignities, the Profumo affair exudes the sweet smell of success.[34]

Harold Wilson looked forward to an election – it had to come in October 1964 at the latest – in which the Tories would be crushed. Michael looked forward to it just as eagerly.

5

Michael never became a father, but he was a stepfather. Jill's daughter by her first marriage, Julie, was eleven years old when Michael and Jill met and fifteen when they were married. During the war she had been sent to a boarding-school in the country to escape the bombing, and she completed her education at another boarding-school. She then went to a finishing-school in Switzerland and learned to speak fluent French. Like her mother, she showed clear signs of artistic creativity.

At first, Julie was strongly antagonistic towards Michael. Understandably, she resented the man who was obviously the most important person in her mother's life. Besides, she was repelled by his eczema and asthma and could not understand how Jill could bear to be close to him, physically or otherwise. Michael, sensing her attitude, took the line that she was Jill's responsibility, not his, and did not try to assume any quasi-paternal authority nor to intervene in decisions concerning her. 'He was there, that was all,' Julie recalls.[35] She had a room in the house in Rosslyn Hill and later in the house in Abbey Road, but spent as much time as she could with her own friends.

Gradually, Julie says, 'I became fond of him as I became an adult.' He recommended books for her to read; they liked the same American films of a light, entertaining kind; he took her to the opera and infected her with his passion for Rossini. By the 1950s, Julie was a highly attractive young woman, fond of fun and amusing company, and popular with the younger men in Michael's political–journalistic world. Ian Aitken, when working for *Tribune*, was one man whose attentions were viewed favourably by both Michael and Jill, but he was by no means Julie's only boyfriend.

She trained for the stage and took the name of Julie Hamilton, having inherited from her father the impossible surname of Begbie-Clench. She was fairly successful, finding work with repertory companies and at the Open Air Theatre in Regent's Park, and even playing the lead in a musical comedy (admittedly, a boyfriend wrote the lyrics). Then she decided on a change of career and studied photography at a polytechnic. Michael advised her to show her portfolio to Bob Edwards, then editor of *Tribune*, and he employed her. At Labour Party conferences, the slender blonde in eye-catching clothes was often the focus of attention and was even known to put the more susceptible platform speakers off their stroke. She moved on from *Tribune* to the *Sunday Dispatch* and was also under contract to the Royal Court Theatre for programme and foyer photographs.

Julie's free-ranging personal life sometimes caused Michael a certain amount of concern. At one time, she was friendly enough with Spike Milligan for marriage to be talked of. Michael was friendly with Spike Milligan too and a fan of the *Goon Show*, but he was aware of the comedian's unstable character and warned Julie that he would not do as a husband. In the week after a party conference, Michael summoned Julie to tell her that he had overheard a conversation in El Vino's; the Labour MP Wilfred Fienburgh was boasting of a night in bed with Julie and speaking of her (so Michael put it) 'as no man should speak of any woman'. In fact, he was lying as well as boasting; he had burst into her hotel room and she had managed to get rid of him. Michael never spoke to Fienburgh again, at Westminster or anywhere else. (Anyway, Fienburgh was a Gaitskellite.)

The man with whom Julie had a real love affair – they lived together for some months – was a young actor who had small parts at the Royal Court named Sean Connery. It was Jill, this time, who considered him unsuitable, apparently because of his selfish behaviour toward his girlfriend. Eventually, in 1960, Julie married Victor Lehel, an architect. Next year they had a son, who was named Jason. Still under the age of fifty, Jill was a grandmother.

Mac (Sir Hugh Foot) had found himself at a loose end after finishing his term as Governor of Cyprus. He thought of going into politics and wrote to Michael in 1960: 'What chance of a Labour constituency? I might get anything you discard.' But, much to his own surprise, Mac was appointed by the Tory government as a member of the British delegation to the UN, with the rank of ambassador and special concern for 'emergent and newly emerged countries'. Mac set up a new home in New York and soon made friends among the African and Asian delegations.

His elder son, Paul, twenty-four years old in 1962, had been to Oxford and started a career in journalism. Working as a reporter on the Glasgow *Daily Record*, he was also active in the Young Socialists and in CND. Experience in Scotland pushed him further to the left, and he wrote in a two-page article for *Tribune*: 'The Labour Party has a mass support in Scotland. But the support is cynical, disinterested, contemptuous of all things political. The answers churned out by Labour are no longer applicable.'[36]

He had been approached by a constituency Labour Party when he had only just left Oxford, and in Scotland the party organiser gave him a list of seats looking for candidates. Michael encouraged his nephew – who was, people often remarked, the son he never had – to join the ranks of the Labour left in Parliament. But Paul saw this as a pitfall, not an opportunity. As he said later: 'You want to change society, but what happens is that you get changed yourself.'[37] This, to his mind, is the fate that has overtaken his uncle. He joined a nascent political group called International Socialism, which developed into the Socialist Workers' Party. Michael was emphatic that Paul was heading into a blind alley and there were some warm arguments in the hard-hitting Foot style, in which neither of the two ever convinced the other of the wrongness of his ways.

In the Foot family, Sally was still the main problem. Michael saw little of her, as he had no time to go to North Devon, while she was daunted by London and quite unable to find her way on the tube. However, in March 1962 she ventured to spend a day in the big city and lunched with Michael and Dingle at the House of Commons. By good luck, Mac was on leave from the UN and was there too. Sally wrote after returning to her caravan:

Dearest, darling angel Mike,

I told you that March 16th was to be the highlight of 1962 and it was true. It was an absolutely wonderful heavenly day, blissful from the moment I saw you and Vanessa [Michael's dog] at Paddington . . . I was glad to see the House of Commons again and more than glad – overjoyed to see dear Dingle. *I love him dearly*. He seemed a little hurt to think I had come up to see you without letting him know and that Mac was there unbeknownst too . . . Thank you for the ten pounds, dearest Mike, I *didn't* come to cadge money off you, and what with lunch and time and then *ten pounds* it seems too much . . .

Dear Mike, I too am a reluctant agnostic. Sometimes, like now after being ill I get terribly Quo Vadis – and derelict and clutch rather desperately at the people I love for reassurance. Well, I *am* reassured now. That perfect day is a nice bit of firm ground. Bless you and thank you, darling Mike.

In October 1963, Michael and Jill undertook to look after Jason, Jill's two-year-old grandson, for a few weeks while Julie was convalescing after an operation. They went to Ebbw Vale for a constituency weekend and took Jason with them. On Monday, 21 October (their wedding anniversary) they set out to drive back to London. Jill was at the wheel with Michael beside her; Jason and the dog Vanessa were in the back. They took a picturesque B road leading from Abergavenny to Ross-on-Wye, which crosses the A road from Hereford to Monmouth at St Owen's Cross. Jill failed to stop at the junction. A lorry coming from the Hereford direction struck the side of the car, where Michael was sitting. It had a cargo of Lucozade, a drink that still has unpleasant associations for them. Michael and Jill were thrown out of the car, and the lorry, before it could stop, ran over Jill's left hand as she lay in the road. The driver managed to find a telephone and call an ambulance. Jason was still in the car, or rather the wreckage, and unhurt. Vanessa jumped out, and it was some time before anyone collected the dog and realised whom she belonged to.

Michael and Jill were taken to Hereford General Hospital, eleven miles from the scene of the accident. When he was lifted out of the ambulance, Michael was able to say: 'Mind you don't put me in a private ward.' He urged the doctors to attend to Jill first, while she urged them to attend to him first. But they both needed urgent attention, for they were seriously injured. Michael's left leg and all his ribs were broken. Worse than this, his lungs were pierced; the doctors saw that his life was in the balance. Jill had a broken pelvis as well as a hand shattered to fragments. Both were operated on during the night. The first statement given to the press was that Michael's condition was 'still very serious'.

He recovered consciousness after the operation just when a Salvation Army band in the street outside the hospital was playing 'Beulah Land, Sweet Beulah Land', a hymn that he had often heard in his Methodist boyhood. He knew the lines:

> I look away across the sea
> Where mansions are prepared for me.

Later, he described the experience:

I thought for a few seconds, in my half-dreamy state, that the rendering was being given by a more celestial choir. Then the mists faded; someone arrived with the bedpan; and I knew I was restored to the care of earthly angels . . . Hereford General Hospital is an institution devised by man; yet it came nearer to revealing supernatural powers than a confirmed rationalist like myself chooses to admit. Miraculously, the latest skills and contraptions of modern science were there on the spot, ready to be used at the shortest notice. Mansions *were* prepared for me.[38]

The latest skills were indeed necessary. He was told by the doctors, and stressed in his account: 'Less than a decade ago, survival from such an accident would have been considered inconceivable.'

Julie hastened to Hereford and saw Michael and Jill on the morning after the accident. Michael had been told not to try to speak because of the condition of his lungs. He wrote two questions on a pad: 'How is Jason?' and 'Do you need money?' Julie assured him that Jason was perfectly all right and had spent the night at a policeman's house. She found a room in the town. Elizabeth Thomas, Michael's secretary, arrived and saw him briefly, but other visitors were turned away; the outcome of the battle for his life was still in doubt. Two days later, inquirers were told: 'No improvement can be expected yet.' It was only on 26 October, five days after the accident, that he was described as 'much improved'. Better statements followed. On 28 October: 'his condition no longer gives rise to anxiety'. And on 29 October: 'no more bulletins will be issued'. On 31 October Elizabeth wrote to Ron Evans, the party secretary in Ebbw Vale: 'The hospital is quite staggered by his powers of recovery.' But Michael wrote to Evans regretting that visits were still banned because his breathing was at times much impaired.

Beaverbrook, from Capponcina, wrote to Jill on 28 October:

> You are meeting your dreadful calamity with courage. You have much to do in nursing Michael back to health when he escapes from the hospital. Do not, my dear Jill, dwell on the past. The circumstances of your accident should not – must not distress either of you. There is no use in saying it might have been different if only &c. Remember the song 'Che sera sera.'

It was impossible, however, for Jill to forget that she had been the driver and had not halted at a major road. Michael wrote to Beaverbrook: 'Poor girl, she suffered much anguish.' Beaverbrook's next letter to the hospital struck a practical note; he advised them to get seat-belts (which in 1963 were not compulsory).

They were in the hospital until 19 November. Michael had refused, not only to be given privileges (he was in a ward with four beds), but even to be transferred to a London hospital. He wanted to demonstrate that the National Health Service worked well, not only in a prestigious teaching hospital, but also in an average general hospital. After his recovery, he drew the political lessons:

The ministering angels . . . supplied every form of available comfort, including a fabulously diverse assortment of drugs only recently discovered. And, of course, this modern miracle is repeated for multitudes of others every day of the week all over the country . . . Compared with the situation in the 1940s and the 1930s the development is prodigious . . .

Had we trusted to the old ways and the time-honoured means of distributing medical care, the cost of new discoveries would have removed them far beyond the reach of most people. All the new inventions and all the most expert practitioners would have been concentrated more than ever . . . in a few hospitals, mostly centred round London where the few select patients could afford to pay . . . This was the fatal trend which Aneurin Bevan broke when he introduced the National Health Service. The Socialist cure of making the best available for everyone was not only the most humane; it was also the most practical and efficient . . .

Like many others, I owe my life to the change. Had it not been for the Health Service, heavenly or hellish mansions would have been prepared for me prematurely. Moreover, I would be bankrupt as well as dead . . . So, alive, solvent and almost kicking, I have a strong prejudice in favour of the Socialist principles which make this fresh start possible.[39]

The spell in hospital was not entirely a loss. Michael read a newly published book which made a strong impression on him, E. P. Thompson's *The Making of the English Working Class*, as well as some Montaigne essays in a new translation and four Joseph Conrad novels. Also, as he had been forbidden to smoke while under treatment, he decided never to start again – and kept to the decision.

He left the hospital free from asthma. His eczema had dwindled away and finally disappeared in the 1950s; it had been treated, on Nye Bevan's advice, by Vitamin C transmitted through a sun-lamp. The asthma, however, had persisted, and in December 1960 Jill wrote to Beaverbrook: 'Michael has had the worst attacks of asthma ever.' After 1963, there were no more attacks. Whether this should be ascribed to giving up smoking, to the shock of the accident or simply to the passage of time (as we have noted, it is very exceptional for asthma to persist into middle age), it is impossible to say.

On the other hand, the negative effects were serious and lasting. As a result of the broken leg, he was left with a lopsided walk. After his recovery he still walked for hours on Hampstead Heath or the Welsh mountains, but he walked with a stick. Although the stick became a trade mark like Chamberlain's umbrella or Churchill's cigar, it contributed when he was leader of the Labour Party to an impression of declining strength.

Jill's hand never mended perfectly. While she and Michael were convalescing in Morocco, it became very painful and she had to buy antibiotics – which, in the absence of a health service, cost the then considerable sum of ten pounds, as Michael did not fail to tell *Daily Herald* readers. After returning home, she had to go into hospital for another operation. To this day, the hand still gives trouble.

In January 1964, the Foots were able to travel and went to Capponcina. In February they went to Morocco, having been advised that it was the nearest place for winter sunshine. 'The sun is doing us an immense amount of good,' Michael wrote to Elizabeth Thomas from Mohammedia. One day, to their surprise and pleasure, Randolph Churchill turned up there. He was suffering from lung cancer, but still smoking his habitual eighty cigarettes a day; the two Devonport veterans had some enjoyable evenings of reminiscence, argument and drinking. On 23 February Michael and Jill moved on to Marrakesh, and Michael told Elizabeth: 'I walked six miles yesterday so that's pretty good.' They were back in London on 28 February. On 9 March, Michael wrote to Beaverbrook:

> This afternoon I returned to the House of Commons and had a kind reception. Jill and I returned a few days ago from Morocco and then went to Ebbw Vale for the weekend. I have continued steadily to improve in health, without any setbacks . . . Jill, unhappily, has had a more difficult time . . . It is hard that she has had all these trials while I have been so lucky.

Jill's account was:

> Michael, I assure you, has never been fitter, nor has he ever looked so well. Bronze, brown with his face filled out, not nearly so drawn, since he eats rather more having given up smoking. As for myself, despite ghastly picture in the Express, I am as fit as can be, feel and look, so I am told, years younger.

As well as returning to the Commons, Michael returned to the *Daily Herald* office, where his reception was less than kind. Within a couple of hours, he was back home and telling Jill: 'I've been fired.' Now owned by the Mirror Group, the paper was being relaunched with the new name – the *Sun*. Clearly, the purpose was to make it less politically identifiable in the interests of popular appeal. In a *Tribune* article before his accident, Michael had deplored the change. Now, the editor of the expiring *Herald* informed Michael politely but firmly that there would be no place for his column in the *Sun*.

Beaverbrook, as in 1938, came to the rescue. He had just dismissed Malcolm Muggeridge as the *Evening Standard*'s chief book reviewer, and offered Michael the job. Michael was delighted; he had his pick of the new books on politics, history and literary criticism and could add them to his library without buying them. He continued to review for the *Standard* for the next ten years, until he became a Cabinet minister in 1974.

Another gratifying fact was that the management of the *Herald* had made a miscalculation. They had assumed that Michael was writing his column as a freelance contributor, but in reality he had been on the staff since 1944, occasionally writing leaders and going on reporting missions, and had received a salary. Under trade union agreements, he was entitled to substantial compensation for dismissal. The amount agreed on, after adjudication, was £5,000. In March 1964, it was just what Michael and Jill needed. They had sold their Abbey Road house for £12,000 and paid out £12,000 for a handsome, roomy Victorian house a few minutes' walk from Hampstead Heath, in Worsley Road, a continuation of Pilgrim's Lane. (Worsley Road no longer exists, since Jill persuaded the authorities that Pilgrim's Lane should be the name of the whole street.) Potentially, the house was the perfect home, but it had been in multiple occupation and was in a state of ruinous decay. The cost of making it habitable was £5,000.

6

Michael was returning to a Parliament that had only a matter of months to live. Indeed, an election in the early summer was a possibility; but in April Douglas-Home announced that there would be no dissolution until the autumn. This was no surprise, as Labour was eight or ten points ahead in the opinion polls.

Michael's first *Tribune* article, on 20 March, was headed 'THE BOMB AND THE ELECTION'. He argued that Labour would be making a grave mistake by fighting the election on domestic issues rather than on the supreme issue of nuclear disarmament. The Prime Minister, it was becoming clear, intended to campaign on the necessity of the nuclear deterrent, perhaps because foreign policy and defence were the only subjects that he knew anything much about. (He had been Chamberlain's

PPS at the time of Munich and Foreign Secretary under Macmillan.) In one speech, he declared: 'There is no other way of defending our country except with a nuclear weapon.' Michael wrote:

> Everywhere he goes, he returns to the same theme with the same imbecile relish . . . Their [the Tories'] obsessive opposition to unilateral disarmament has made them the enemies of multilateral disarmament too . . . Members of CND, in particular, should welcome the contest. They, more than most others, have helped in determining the political climate in which the contest occurs.

In the run-up to the election, Michael was invited to write a campign biography of Harold Wilson. The invitation came from Robert Maxwell, owner of the Pergamon Press and Labour candidate for Buckingham (he won the seat when the election came). He was known to be a monster of egotism and a buccaneering capitalist, and was unpopular with the Labour rank and file in Buckingham, but his exposure as a notorious crook was almost thirty years in the future. The little book consisted mainly of sixty-three photographs and four Vicky cartoons; Michael had to write only fourteen pages of text. He began with an approving description of Wilson's background ('religious nonconformity and radical politics') and qualities ('a prodigious head for facts, dates and figures; an excellent physical constitution; a stunning quickness of intelligence').[40] He went on to hail Wilson as 'a *dedicated* person, dedicated to politics, to the Labour Party, to his own interpretation of Socialism'. The words 'his own interpretation' served Michael as a saving grace.

Contrasting Wilson's flexibility with Gaitskell's dogmatism, Michael wrote: 'No great party representing half or more than half the nation can expect to be, or afford to be, monolithic; this would spell death. But the internal debate can become obsessive and obstructive and sectarian. Harold Wilson's understanding of the disease of the Labour Party has been one powerful reason contributing towards its cure.' But he warned of the dangers that a Labour government would encounter: 'The weight of the old society bears heavily upon those who seek the transformation. The drive for progress loses its dynamism. Power tames and corrupts . . . These are some of the unknown hazards of the future. Harold Wilson at least has the final virtue that he knows of their existence.'

The book was, of course, ephemeral. It was not listed on the 'by the same author' page of Michael's later books. Indeed, the episode was best forgotten – not least because Michael had considerable difficulty in extracting the agreed payment from Maxwell.

In 1964, two men who had held special places in Michael's pantheon of father-figures died within a few days of each other: Max Beaverbrook and Jawaharlal Nehru. The coincidence was piquant; Nehru (with Mountbatten, the Viceroy who had paved the way to Indian independence) was on the Beaverbrook black-list and was never mentioned in *Express* newspapers unless in terms of obloquy. Michael did not write Nehru's obituary for *Tribune*, leaving the task to Fenner Brockway, who had known him since the 1920s. For Beaverbrook, he wrote a qualified eulogy: 'He recruited from *Tribune*. He employed journalists who, through political prejudice, might have found it difficult to get jobs elsewhere. He allowed some of those he liked, if they fought for the right, to say what they wanted in his newspapers.'[41]

One of the saddening aspects of growing older is witnessing the deaths of men whom one has loved or admired. Michael's thoughts inevitably went back to his youth; 1938 was the year in which he had first met both Nehru and Beaverbrook. Beaverbrook's death, at least, was in no sense a shock. Michael had last seen him at a party to celebrate his eighty-fifth birthday. Yet, with memories of so many good dinner-parties and so much entertaining conversation over the years, he was bound to be missed and to leave a gap in Michael's life. Writing about him later, Michael ended his essay thus: 'Beaverbrook's was a volcano of laughter which went on erupting until the end. No one who ever lodged for a while beneath that Vesuvius will ever forget.'[42]

Polling day in the election was set for 15 October. The Labour appeal was based on a theme that had Wilson's personal stamp: the alliance of socialism and science. He coined a phrase that became famous – 'the white heat of technology' – and told the voters: 'The choice we offer, starting today, is between standing still, clinging to the tired philosophy of a day that is gone, or moving forward in partnership and unity to a just society, to a dynamic, expanding, confident and above all purposive new Britain.' This appeal did not meet with quite the response that Wilson hoped for. The historians of the campaign concluded: 'There were references to the spirit of '45, the irrepressible upsurge of enthusiasm; but whatever excitement may have seized the party workers, it was not much in evidence in the country at large . . . The 1964 campaign struck many candidates and agents – and even more electors – as unexpectedly dull.'[43]

When 15 October came, broadcasts on the results were interrupted by startling news from Moscow. Khrushchev had been ousted from power; the new leader, Brezhnev, restored the rigidity if not the full brutality of Stalinism.

Labour won the election, but with a majority of only five seats in the Commons. Luck favoured the Tories; they won Reading by 10 votes and Eton and Slough – Fenner Brockway's seat – by 11. Brockway almost certainly lost because of his personal campaign for a law to ban racial discrimination. In Smethwick, Patrick Gordon Walker, who was Wilson's choice as Foreign Secretary, was defeated thanks to racist tactics by the Tory candidate.

In Ebbw Vale, Michael had no worries. Thanks to the restoration of the whip in 1963, he was formally endorsed as the Labour candidate, and certainly had full backing in the constituency. Neither the Liberals nor Plaid Cymru fought the seat this time; Rhys-Williams stood for the Tories again. Michael had a majority of 20,271, practically the same as Bevan five years before.

In forming his government, Wilson made several innovations. There was to be a Department of Economic Affairs, headed by George Brown. Brown was also designated as First Secretary of State, or in effect as deputy Prime Minister. But James Callaghan, the Chancellor of the Exchequer, was another Labour heavyweight, and the open question was: who would make the crucial decisions on economic and financial policy? The stage was set for power struggles between Brown and Callaghan.

Another new department was the Ministry of Technology, whose task was to overcome Britain's backwardness at a time when computers and information technology were the heralds of a second industrial revolution. Wilson's choice to head this Ministry was Frank Cousins, who could add weight to the government, coming from the leadership of the largest trade union, and was keenly interested in technological matters. Wilson had been pressing him to take the job, and he finally agreed in a midnight talk seven hours before the polls opened on 15 October. But his wife Nance, according to Cousins' biographer, Geoffrey Goodman, 'was against the idea from the beginning and she never wavered from that view . . . She believed most vehemently that his real role (an infinitely more important one in her view) was to remain general secretary of the largest trade union in the country.'[44]

Wilson had, since the 1950s, harboured strong feelings about world poverty; he had helped to found the charity War on Want and thought up the name. Now, he created a Ministry of Overseas Development. To emphasise its importance, the Minister was given a seat in the Cabinet. The job went to Barbara Castle, who tackled it with her habitual enthusiasm and energy. Sadly, after she moved on in a reshuffle in December 1965, the Ministry lost its strength and ultimately fell into the stultifying grasp of the Foreign Office.

Cousins, who was not interested in the niceties of parliamentary politics, would have liked to recruit Michael as his parliamentary secretary, or number two. He felt that he could make this proposal only through the Prime Minister, and he was told that Michael did not want to join the government. As Geoffrey Goodman remarks, 'precisely how the Prime Minister knew this remains a mystery'. It was certainly a missed opportunity; Goodman adds: 'A Cousins–Foot team at the Ministry of Technology could well have transformed the public image of what was seen by the world outside as a rather grey and unimaginative new department of State.'[45]

Wilson also appointed a Minister for Disarmament (a non-Cabinet post within the Foreign Office). It was a good idea – and would also have been a suitable job for Michael – but Wilson's choice was astonishing. The new Minister was Alun Gwynne Jones (ennobled as Lord Chalfont), who had been defence correspondent of *The Times*, was no enthusiast for disarmament and had never, so far as anyone knew, been a member or even a supporter of the Labour Party.

Another new Minister of State at the Foreign Office was Michael's brother Mac, who made his last appearance as Sir Hugh Foot and became Lord Caradon. In 1963, he had resigned from his job at the United Nations because he felt unable to defend the Tory government's policy on Rhodesia when it came under attack from Third World nations. While Northern Rhodesia and Nyasaland were winning independence under African control – as Zambia and Malawi – the Tories were preparing to grant independence to Southern Rhodesia on terms that would give power to the white minority of the population. On the understanding that the Labour government would follow no such course, Mac became Britain's chief representative at the UN.

Jennie Lee was given an appointment that was warmly greeted by an influential segment of Labour's supporters – the teachers, writers, artists, theatre directors and film-makers who were looking for a change from Tory philistinism. Labour was pledged to create an Open University, offering degree courses through home study and television and giving a second chance to people of all ages who had been unable to graduate through traditional higher education. As an under-secretary in the Department of Education, Jennie took charge of this project. She was also responsible for government assistance to the arts, which was to be significantly increased and directed towards new ventures. Although officially an under-secretary, she was given in popular parlance the title of Minister for the Arts.

As the left of the party scrutinised Wilson's government, it was seen that the key appointments were in the hands of safe right-wingers: Brown and Callaghan in the economic sphere, Patrick Gordon Walker at the Foreign Office, Sir Frank Soskice at the Home Office, Denis Healey at the Ministry of Defence. The predominant make-up of the Cabinet, as of the Shadow Cabinet before the election, was 'Czarist'. Yet *Tribune* was able to print the photographs of six old contributors who had seats in this Cabinet: the Prime Minister himself, Dick Crossman (Minister of Housing), Barbara Castle, Frank Cousins, Tony Greenwood (Colonial Secretary) and Fred Lee (Minister of Power).

— Chapter 9 —

OUTSIDE LEFT

I

Labour supporters in 1964 hoped that the government which had ousted
the Tories would usher in a bright new dawn. Instead, it had to struggle
through storm-clouds. Although Wilson and his colleagues had been
denouncing Tory mismanagement of the economy, they were not
prepared for what they found when they took over and opened the
books. Production and exports were stagnant, there was a massive
balance of payments deficit, the pound was under pressure, runaway
inflation was a real danger.

Michael saw the gravity of the situation. 'The economic situation left
by the Tories is extremely serious. Several difficult and unpopular
decisions will be inescapable,' he wrote soon after the election. But: 'The
more resolutely the boldest courses are pursued, the greater will be the
unity and enthusiasm of the Labour Party.' As in 1950–1, he urged that
the only remedy for a small majority was another election, as soon as
possible, to win a larger majority. 'Obviously one main purpose of the
new government must be to prepare the ground for a new appeal to the
country.'[1]

One bold course that some ministers favoured was a quick, surgical
devaluation of the pound. Callaghan, however, would not hear of it, and
Wilson felt that the shock might fatally weaken the government. The
alternative was a set of stringent defensive measures. Before the end of the
year, a review of all government spending was announced, an emergency
budget raised income tax and the petrol duty, Bank rate went up to 7 per
cent, and a surcharge (angrily resented by other trading nations) was
imposed on imports. The aim, of course, was to appease the rigidly
orthodox Treasury in Washington and foreign creditors or investors.
Michael did not condemn Callaghan's decisions, but grasped their
meaning. He wrote: 'What the Labour government has done in the past
two weeks, partially and with extreme reluctance, is to bow to

international pressure which it could no longer resist . . . It is not possible to build the society we want while the present desperate dependence on international finance continues.'[2]

Politically, the government's position soon became weaker still. Cousins, the new Minister of Technology, had been recruited so late that he did not have a seat in the Commons, and he was not the man to welcome elevation to the Lords. Gordon Walker was the victim of the shock defeat at Smethwick, but Wilson insisted on keeping him as Foreign Secretary. Obliged to find seats for these two ministers, Wilson prevailed on two Labour MPs – Frank Bowles at Nuneaton and Reginald Sorensen at Leyton – to accept peerages. However, both men were greatly respected in their constituencies and made no secret of the fact that their arms had been painfully twisted. Cousins held Nuneaton, but with a majority halved since the general election. Leyton, held by Sorensen since 1935, was captured by the Tories. The Labour majority in the Commons was down to three. Gordon Walker was replaced at the Foreign Office by Michael Stewart, a man who lacked any expertise in international affairs (his speciality was education) but was just as safely right-wing.

Stewart's first main task, which he shouldered without qualms, was to defend American intervention in Vietnam. In the presidential election campaign of 1964 – polling was a couple of weeks after the British election – Lyndon B. Johnson had denounced his Republican opponent, Barry S. Goldwater, for wanting to send American troops to Vietnam and had promised that he would never do so. Hailing Johnson's overwhelming victory, Michael wrote: 'Never since 1945 has an American President occupied a better posture from which he can launch a real initiative for peace.' What Johnson launched, however, was an initiative for war. He ordered ruthless bombing, the use of napalm and poison gas, and the poisoning of forests and crops. These crimes and follies (they were both) were challenged at a 'teach-in' at Oxford University. Stewart, teaming up with Henry Cabot Lodge, who headed the American presence in Saigon, delivered a speech 'prepared by a Foreign Office mandarin well trained in cold-war phraseology' – to cite the description by the chief opposition speaker, Tariq Ali, that year's President of the Union.[3] Televised by the BBC, the sparring-match was reckoned to be a disastrous defeat for Lodge and Stewart. The realisation that a Labour government was condoning the horrors of Vietnam aroused dismay and then anger on the left. While Stewart was on the American side out of pure anti-Communism, Wilson was primarily anxious to retain American support for the endangered pound. Asked by Frank Cousins why he did not take a firm stand against the US over Vietnam, he replied: 'Because we can't kick our creditors in the balls.'[4]

One of Michael's problems at this time was that – while he was the unofficial leader of the Labour left, was a conscientious constituency MP and was writing regularly in *Tribune* – he was in need of a secretary. Elizabeth Thomas found her time fully occupied as literary editor of *Tribune* and organiser of the successful *Tribune* poetry readings which she had initiated. Michael appointed three secretaries in succession but, for one reason or another, none of them stayed very long. Eventually, in 1966, Elizabeth suggested Una Cooze. Married to a surveyor, and with her children just starting school, she was looking for work; she was also a dedicated footsoldier of the Labour left and belonged to *Tribune*'s team of street-sellers. The problem was solved. Like Elizabeth, Una was a highly efficient secretary and was soon a good friend. She worked for Michael, chiefly on constituency business, until he left the House of Commons in 1992.

Altogether, this was an unhappy period in Michael's life. After completing the first volume of the Bevan biography in record time, he had plunged into the second volume and written four chapters – including a detailed account of the creation of the Health Service, based on interviews with doctors and civil servants – by the late summer of 1963. Then came the car crash. Restored to health in physical terms in 1964, he found for the first time in his life that serious writing was impossibly difficult. He continued his *Daily Herald* column until the paper finally expired, he started a signed weekly column in *Tribune* and he reviewed for the *Evening Standard*; but all these tasks required an effort which readers did not suspect, and work on the book came to a halt. Since the literary monument to Nye held deep emotional significance for Michael, the prospect of being unable to complete it for an indefinite time was painful.

These troubles coincided with terrible news about his beloved sister. Sally had managed to get a job as riding instructor at a school in Kent, but lost it within a matter of months. She was still drinking heavily and also had a drug habit; the drugs may have been very strong tranquillisers but may have been illegal psychedelic drugs, fairly easily obtainable in the 1960s. Her niece Sarah recalls that sometimes she could not speak coherently and had to be helped into bed.[5] Jennifer, Sally's younger sister, wrote to Michael in November 1964:

You may know that Sal is back here. Chris and I had to fetch her from the school in Kent in v. miserable circumstances. She is better now and plans to take her caravan down to the field by the Lynher. I know this is

Michael, Vanessa and Jill in Ebbw Vale, 1960.

Defeat . . . Joan Vickers wins Devonport for the Tories, 1955. (*Tribune*)

. . . and victory. Michael wins Ebbw Vale, 1960. (*Camera Press*)

Michael and some Ebbw Vale voters in Tredegar, 1960. (*Tribune*)

"HERETIC! STILL BELIEVES IN WHAT WE USED TO PREACH..!"

Above Cartoon by Vicky: Hugh Gaitskell and Anthony Crosland react to Michael's by-election campaign, 1960.

Left Sketch by Vicky, 1960s. The wording reads: 'Dear Michael, I'm sorry I lost my temper last night. Hope to see you soon. Yours, Vicky.'

Michael returns to the House of Commons, 1960. (*Julie Hamilton/Camera Press*)

Above In hospital after the car accident, 1963. (*Julie Hamilton*)

Opposite On the 1964 Aldermaston march: Michael with his step-grandson, Jason Lehel, and James Cameron. (*S&G*)

Left With Beaverbrook at Capponcina, 1964.

Keeping an eye on Harold Wilson. County Hotel, Durham, on the day of the Durham Miners' Gala, 1969. (*Michael Ward*)

not a good thing for her to be there on her own for any length of time, but it may be all right temporarily and it is what she wants to do . . . I feel the family should make some plan for her future . . . Most of the time she is quite all right though her ways do not fit in everywhere. With Jim [Jennifer's husband] an alcoholic, it has not been easy having her here and it would not work as a permanency.

Sally had hopes of running a riding school based on the stables at Pencrebar, but would not live in the house because she could not get on with Kitty. The field where she parked the caravan slopes steeply to the Lynher, which is a fast-flowing river, especially when swollen by spring rains. On 22 March 1965, Sally's dead body was found in the river. The verdict at the inquest was a non-committal 'found drowned'. Probably she slipped down the steep, muddy bank into the river; one speculation is that she was searching in the dark for her pills, or she may have been drunk. Suicide was a possibility that could not be ruled out. Sarah, who saw her several times in her last weeks, perceived that she was in a state of despair and did not want to go on living in her unhappy situation. John Foot was asked at the inquest whether Sally was 'eccentric'. He replied that she was 'rather unusual' and 'lived a nomad sort of life of her own seeking'.

Jennifer's reluctance to keep Sally at her home is understandable, for she was keeping pace at the bottle with her alcoholic husband; three heavy drinkers would have been living together. Later, Jim Highet tipped an eiderdown from his bed on to a paraffin heater; the house caught fire and he perished. Michael had to attend the funeral in the midst of the 1983 election campaign. Chris, the youngest Foot brother, was also an alcoholic or near-alcoholic. He had to give up working in the law firm through illness; it was diagnosed as Huntington's chorea, a disease of the nervous system, but may have had a psychological component. Dingle, by some accounts, was virtually an alcoholic in his later years. A certain strain in the family – invisible to those who saw only Lord Caradon, the Governor of Jamaica and Cyprus, Sir Dingle Foot, the Solicitor-General in Wilson's government, and Michael Foot, the famous MP – seems to persist indelibly from the character of their extraordinary father. Sarah has said: 'All the Foots are unstable. Uncle Michael is the nearest to being stable.'[6]

2

In the politics of 1964–5, the most sensitive issue was Labour's pledge to renationalise the steel industry. It was important to Michael because he saw it as the touchstone of the pursuance of 'the boldest courses'; because, in the late 1940s, it had been a similar touchstone for the Attlee government and a battleground between Bevan and Morrison; and, not least, because he was now the MP for a steel constituency. It was easy to perceive that George Brown, the Minister with the principal voice on economic strategy, was no keener on firm action on steel than Morrison had been. More awkwardly, George Strauss, who had piloted steel nationalisation as Minister of Supply under Attlee, now openly offered the opinion that renationalisation was unnecessary. Though Strauss had been a sturdy left-winger in the 1930s, a founding father of *Tribune* and an intimate friend of both Nye Bevan and Michael, he had ceased by this time to belong in any real sense to the left.

The difficulty in carrying out the election pledge was, of course, the government's tiny majority. If a new Steel Bill came before the Commons, Strauss would probably abstain. Two other Labour MPs, it transpired, were so opposed to renationalisation that they would also abstain or might even vote with the Tories. One was Woodrow Wyatt, who had been a somewhat wayward member of the Keep Left group in 1947 and was beginning a peregrination that would ultimately lead him out of the Labour Party. The other was Desmond Donnelly, one of the few men in public life for whom Michael entertained a positive loathing. Accepted as a Bevanite, Donnelly had leaked the private discussions of the group to Hugh Dalton and had then launched a dramatic attack on his former associates at the 1954 party conference. Michael was to write in the second volume of his Bevan biography: 'Few begrudged Donnelly his thirty pieces of silver, but it was somewhat provocative to appear at the gates of Gethsemane to collect it.'[7]

On 6 May 1965, there was a Commons debate on a White Paper which reiterated the pledge to restore public ownership. Brown – perhaps revealing his true feelings, perhaps affected by his morning sip of whisky – had the House in roars when he said that 'private ownership', in place of 'public', was inevitable. Wyatt proposed the compromise of a 51 per cent government stake in the major steel companies, and stated that he would have to vote against a bill that insisted on 100 per cent. In winding up the debate, Brown caused a stir by speaking of 'public control' rather than ownership, and made an unexpected offer: 'If the industry and its friends in the Tory Party will come to us and say they are prepared for the government to assume control, which we and the honourable member for Bosworth [Wyatt] agree is essential, we shall of course listen to what they have to say.' Wyatt intervened to ask if this meant control on less than 100 per cent. 'Listen, certainly,' Brown responded. Wyatt and Donnelly then voted with the government, giving it a majority of four.

Michael was outraged. He had counted on, or at least hoped for, a firm stand:

> This was the position until George Brown chucked it away in a few minutes of remarkable political imbecility . . . It was the hours of backstairs conversation between Donnelly, Wyatt and Brown which prepared the way for the fatal, fatuous minutes . . . A dog which appeared to be wagged by Wyatt and Donnelly would be the most contemptible of curs.[8]

'All the signs', the *Observer* predicted in July, indicated that there would be no Steel Bill. Michael retorted: 'They must get used to the fact that the bill goes ahead . . . Time for the Steel Bill will become available in October or November. All the signs point to a Second Reading debate taking place in one of these months.'[9] But the *Observer* was right; the Queen's speech for the 1965–6 session omitted any mention of a Steel Bill. Michael speculated ironically on the prospects for the year 2000: 'It is my expectation and hope that we shall have a prosperous and successful Labour government for the rest of my lifetime and even beyond. I daresay many years hence I shall look down from my vantage-point in some celestial place . . . I shall be interested to see whether we have got steel nationalisation by then.'[10]

For Michael, steel was not only a matter of general principle or national policy. It was also a practical and vital issue for 13,000 of his constituents who worked in the Richard Thomas and Baldwin steelworks. As a unit in a publicly owned industry, RTB could expect fair treatment. As an outsider in an industry ruled by a private enterprise cartel, the Iron and Steel Federation – described by Michael as 'the toughest, bitterest, most vengeful vested interest'[11] – it would be vulnerable to the kind of pressure that had driven Sir William Firth to the wall. Some months later, Michael named the companies which 'conducted a constant vendetta to try and squeeze RTB out of existence and squeeze Ebbw Vale out of existence.'[12] A prediction that RTB was to be closed down was prominently reported in the *Sunday Times* and cited by Woodrow Wyatt in the debate of 6 May. Michael declared angrily that it was 'a mischievous and shameful and callous lie'. He told the Commons: 'We get this scare every six months, and it is put out by some of the most sinister elements in the Iron and Steel Federation . . . Every time it is said, it sends a shiver of fear through a township which has had enough of fear and unemployment in its time.'

RTB came under fire, too, from such Tory MPs as Donald Box and Sir Gerald Nabarro, both notorious for their prejudiced attacks on national-ised industries. In February 1965, Box asked why RTB, unlike other steel

plants, was making a loss. Fred Lee, the Minister of Power and a sturdy
left-winger, replied that it had made substantial profits for ten years but
was now affected by competing developments. Michael rose to point out
that it was 'the only company which had the enterprise to go ahead and
build the biggest new steelworks in the country when private enterprise
was too cowardly to embark on the task'. But in January 1967 Nabarro
was able to say that RTB had lost £12 million in two years and added
sneeringly: 'It is the only British steel company to lose money, no doubt
aided and abetted by the honourable member for Ebbw Vale.'

Stoutly though Michael denied the gloomy forecasts, he knew that
there was reason for anxiety and for a 'shiver of fear'. The managers of
RTB, the trade unionists who formed the Works Council and many of
the workers knew it too. John Powell, an executive who came to Ebbw
Vale in 1957 and became general manager in 1965, recalls that during a
halcyon period after the war 'You couldn't make enough steel.'[13] Britain
then produced twenty-six million tons a year and targets for future
expansion were set at anything up to forty million. The Steel Company
of Wales, a private enterprise giant, built three big new plants at
Llanwern, Margam and Velindre. Sir Henry Spencer, Firth's heir at
Ebbw Vale, took over the management of Llanwern (initially, it was
called the Spencer Works). On his departure, Michael asked him whether
this new production centre might not create a threat to RTB, but Spencer
assured the anxious MP that world demand was unlimited. However,
when a Tory MP suggested in January 1967 that the position was one of
surplus capacity, Michael replied in a thoughtful vein: 'There's a great
deal in that, and if the advice of RTB had been accepted, the expansion
would have been carried out in a different way.'

While world demand was indeed growing, productive capacity was
growing faster. New, modern plants were springing up in France, in
Germany, in Japan – which zoomed by 1970 to an output of ninety-two
million tons – even in South Korea and Taiwan. In an intensive struggle
for markets, even Pittsburgh began to find life difficult. At the same time,
the development of plastics and fibre-glass reduced the demand for steel –
no longer the obligatory material for every bucket, dustbin or tobacco-
tin.

The steelworkers of Ebbw Vale could only watch helplessly as
capacity expanded along the South Wales coast, on the Lincolnshire
flat-lands and on Teesside. Finally, for political reasons and under pressure
from a vehement Scottish lobby, Ravenscraig came into existence. The
market was now contracting, with overseas customers showing a
decisive preference for Japanese steel, and the British industry was

entering the downturn that inexorably reduced its output to the present thirteen million tons. 'When they gave the green light to Ravenscraig', John Powell recalls, 'I knew we were doomed.'

3

From the day when he formed his government, Harold Wilson was holding together a team riven by policy disagreements, which were intensified by power struggles and personality clashes. The principal combatants were Brown, Callaghan and Cousins. Brown espoused the cause of higher production and economic expansion – and, to that extent, earned the approval of the left – while Callaghan adopted the orthodox Treasury view that the great danger was inflation and 'over-heating' of the economy, and hence that public spending must be sternly restrained. In Brown's department, a staff of Keynesian economists worked on the preparation of a National Plan, inspired to some extent by the famous Soviet Five Year Plans and, more directly, by the Monnet Plan, which had revived the French economy after the war. The Plan was published in September 1965, but it turned out to be at best indicative, setting targets without creating an authority to achieve them, and lacking either in the Stalinist spirit of command or French *dirigisme*. *Tribune* called it 'a non-plan with its priorities badly wrong' and complained that 'the private sector is to remain dominant and generally independent of government control'.[14]

The one form of control that Brown did institute was control of wages and prices. There, he was in agreement with Callaghan but fiercely opposed by Cousins, whose trade union background made him hostile to interference with free collective bargaining. In April 1965 (while the National Plan was still in gestation) a Prices and Incomes Board was set up with the duty of keeping prices stable and containing wage increases below a ceiling of 3.5 per cent. The board had no powers of enforcement, but Cousins rightly foresaw that these would be added in time. His temper was not improved by the appointment of a former Tory minister, Aubrey Jones, to preside over the board. To exacerbate the antagonism, Brown and Cousins belonged to the same union, though the former had been a very minor official whereas the latter had been general secretary. Brown was hurt and angry when, although the TUC responded to his speech to delegates and gave his policy a healthy majority, the TGWU voted against it. When they met, in the graphic words of Cousins' biographer, 'the two men squared up to each other like a pair of prime peacocks, spitting and clawing'.[15] In September, Callaghan (with Brown's tacit support) told the Cabinet that the prices and incomes policy would have to be reinforced by statutory powers. Cousins, we are told, 'exploded with indignation'.[16]

After a year's experience, Cousins was coming to admit that his wife had been right when she advised against his joining the government. He was not, as his best friends admitted, a good administrator. He could not get used to the House of Commons – an assembly, very unlike the TGWU conference, in which half the members were his enemies and were ready to bait and taunt him. Some of his appearances at the despatch box were disastrous. In the Cabinet, he championed the British-made TSR2 fighter aircraft against the American F111, opposed the Concorde project, protested against the Polaris nuclear submarine – and lost all these battles. His one solidly gratifying success was to save the infant British computer industry and pave the way for its growth. But, as friends like Michael knew, he was bound sooner or later to resign. Only his sense of loyalty kept him in the government until it won another election.

At the Ministry of Defence, Denis Healey was trying to carry through a review of expenditure – which would have contributed to Callaghan's economy drive and would also have pleased the left – but was hampered by Wilson's insistence that Britain should remain 'strong east of Suez'. The commitments were heavy: a conflict with nationalist rebels in Aden, a costly base at Singapore, and a confrontation with Indonesia in the jungles of Borneo. Britain was shouldering these burdens to placate President Johnson, who was demanding a contingent of British troops for the Vietnam war. Peter Shore, close to Wilson at the time, has testified: 'Enormous efforts were made by the Foreign Office, the Treasury, the Americans to get Britain wholly to identify with the war and express this with a military presence.'[17] Wilson realised that sending troops to Vietnam would be politically impossible for a Labour government. Michael spoke for the left, and indeed for some not always ranged with the left, when he said: 'It is a shameful war . . . which can never be brought to a successful conclusion.'[18] The pressure continued, however, and in 1967 Wilson confided to Barbara Castle after a visit to Washington: 'Johnson told me that if only I would put troops into Vietnam my worries over sterling would be over. Yes, I retorted, and I would be finished too.'[19]

Life would have been easier for Wilson if he had been able to silence his most formidable critic and deprive the left of leadership by bringing Michael into the government. He had missed the opportunity to take up

Frank Cousins' suggestion and offer Michael a job in October 1964, but by the spring of 1965 he decided to repair the omission. Michael was sounded out informally, first by Ernest Fernyhough, Wilson's PPS, and then by the Prime Minister himself in the members' lobby. It did not take Michael long to make up his mind that acceptance was impossible, at least in the situation prevailing at the time. He wrote to Wilson on 6 May 1965:

> I feel that, in fairness to you, I must send you a note about our brief conversation in the lobby last night. Of course, I understand that the conversation was entirely private and entirely tentative and hypothetical.
>
> I am deeply opposed to present American policies in Vietnam . . . Inevitably therefore I am strongly critical of the attitude the Government takes to these policies, particularly as I have heard it expressed by the Foreign Secretary. I try to state my criticisms in a manner which is fair to what the Government is trying to do. But it seems to me it would be impossible to join a Government when I was so much opposed to some principal features of its foreign policy.
>
> Of course, I also wish to see the Government survive and prosper, as I believe it will, if developments abroad permit. I am quite content to do all I can on the back benches to assist that purpose. Sometime this year or next, I suppose, an election will be fought. Circumstances at home and abroad may be different thereafter.

Vietnam was not the only issue that made Michael and his friends unhappy. Ian Smith, who headed a solidly white government in Southern Rhodesia (still officially a British colony) was demanding independence and refusing to extend democratic rights to the Africans. Wilson was prepared to agree to independence in return for promises to democratise Rhodesia by degrees, a scheme which was roundly denounced by *Tribune*; but Smith was impatient, and on 11 November 1965 he made a unilateral declaration of independence. *Tribune* came out with a banner headline: 'SEND TROOPS TO ZAMBIA' – something that Wilson had no intention of doing. Instead, the illegal regime was to be brought to its knees by economic sanctions. It was soon clear that these were ineffective and blatantly evaded. For everyone on the Labour left – including Barbara Castle, who was fuming at Cabinet meetings and several times contemplated resignation – the softly-softly attitude to Smith seemed to symbolise indifference to the rights and interests of people with black skins. That accusation gathered force when the Home Office issued a White Paper tightening the restrictions on immigration from the Commonwealth. Fenner Brockway, the veteran foe of racism, announced in *Tribune*: 'My head is bowed in shame.' Editorially, *Tribune* took an uncompromising line: 'The Labour Party at the incitement of its leaders has accepted the most pathetic and craven departure from principle . . . The White Paper must be contested in the House and outside until the best traditions of the party are restored.'[20]

Altogether, the Labour leadership was trying the patience of its most dedicated supporters. Michael faced the question in *Tribune* of 7 January 1966: 'What should Socialists who detest the government's policy on Vietnam, immigration and much else do about it?' One socialist and CND activist, Richard Gott, produced his own answer when a by-election occurred in Hull North, a Labour seat, by standing as the candidate of a group called Radical Alliance, primarily on the Vietnam issue. Risking the wrath of some *Tribune* readers, Michael denounced this 'wrecking candidature'. If Gott secured a substantial vote, he argued, 'the responsibility for the electoral catastrophe would be visited on the Left'; and the outcome would be a feud 'as bitter and deep and lasting as any in its [the Labour Party's] history'.

A week later, Michael went to the heart of the problem. The Labour Party, he wrote, is 'a coalition of differing interests, ideas and aspirations'. It was socialist by definition (Clause Four had been reaffirmed) 'but by tradition and practice much more social reformist and resolutely empirical'. Such was the party which Michael had learned to understand for thirty years and which he would one day lead. Looking at the immediate situation, he warned: 'If the Labour Party turns away from power at this critical moment, or tears itself to pieces for the convenience of the Tory enemy . . . we will be condemned for generations to ridicule and ineffectiveness.' Therefore, the left 'must show its desire for the party's success'. This could not be done, he added, 'by denouncing as lost souls or spirits all those on the Left who take Cabinet posts, National Executive seats or other offices'.

Labour had done badly in by-elections and local elections in 1965, but the North Hull by-election dramatically changed the outlook. Barbara Castle, now Minister of Transport, delighted the local pressure groups by promising a bridge over the Humber. The Labour majority was quintupled. (Richard Gott's vote was derisory, for Vietnam did not arouse the same passions in Hull as in Hampstead.) Wilson decided on a spring general election, with polling on 31 March 1966.

Michael, meanwhile, had to endure another sorrow. On the night of 1 March, his cherished friend Vicky committed suicide by taking an overdose of powerful sleeping-pills. The reasons were complex and deeply embedded in Vicky's melancholy temperament, but the immediate cause was a military coup in Nigeria, which was sure to be exploited to demonstrate African unfitness for stable democratic government and which faced the cartoonist of the *Evening Standard* with an insoluble problem. I was myself one of the last people to see Vicky alive, and I said to him: 'Look, nobody is demanding a cartoon about Nigeria.' Vicky answered sadly: 'I demand it of myself.' None of his friends saw him again before his death. Michael, hearing the news as *Tribune* was going to press, wrote:

> It is impossible to do him proper honour . . . Most of us are still numbed. No doubt something deeper and fuller will be attempted in the future . . . Vicky was unique. There was no one else remotely like him; never before and never again that particular combination of humour, goodness, genius, magical charm and compassion . . . He is truly irreplaceable.[21]

In his book *Debts of Honour*, published in 1980, Michael fulfilled his promise to commemorate Vicky by 'something deeper and fuller'.

On 8 March, just before the dissolution, he moved a bill to abolish the censorship of the theatre, renewing the attempt of 1949. The Lord Chamberlain, who performed this anachronistic function, had just earned added odium by refusing to license two remarkable Royal Court productions, Edward Bond's *Saved* and John Osborne's *A Patriot for Me*, for transfer to the West End.[22] Michael, an admirer and friend of Osborne, who was then regarded as a luminary of the left, told the House: 'Anyone who examines the history of the past few years will see the great liberalising effect which John Osborne has had on national life.' The bill fell into limbo because of the election, and Wilson was far from keen on it. He was apprehensive about the projected stage version of *Private Eye*'s satirical feature, 'Mrs Wilson's Diary', and warned (accurately, as time has shown) that even the Queen might be a theme for entertainment if the safeguard of censorship were removed. But the Home Secretary, Roy Jenkins, provided government time for the bill, and it eventually became law in 1968.

The election campaign of 1966 was sedate and dull. The Tories had dethroned Douglas-Home to replace him with Edward Heath, a leader who was equally unsuccessful in attracting popularity or arousing excitement. A decisive segment of the electorate decided, without ardent enthusiasm, that Labour ought to be given a chance to show what it could do with an adequate majority. The swing was enough to give the government 363 seats and a majority of 97 over all other parties. The Prime Minister's friend Ernest Kay penned an ecstatic forecast:

How long will Harold Wilson be Prime Minister of Great Britain? He believes he will be there for at least two more full-term Parliaments – for at least sixteen years of consecutive rule. That would take him up to the end of 1980 and, even by then, he will only be sixty-three . . . Some of Wilson's present Ministers believe he will be at the head of affairs until he is seventy.[23]

Such pipe-dreams are never wise. Lyndon Johnson and Charles de Gaulle, both enjoying almost imperial prestige in this year of 1966, were forced into humiliated abdication in 1968 and 1969 respectively. Wilson was to prove, politically, no more immortal than they were.

Michael again had a straight fight with a Tory – John Lovill, an insurance broker from Brighton. The only question was whether the voters would turn out, but they did; Ebbw Vale had a 79 per cent poll, four points above the national figure. Michael's majority rose to 20,584.

Naturally, *Tribune* was jubilant over the Labour victory, but it warned: 'Don't think we just have to sit back and wait for Socialism to be handed to us on a plate. No indeed. As always, Labour's rank and file will have to fight for it. There will have to be toil and argument and doubtless often bitter controversy.'[24] Even Michael did not know how quickly these words were to be justified.

4

Callaghan's first duty after the election was to present a budget. He was persuaded by Nicholas Kaldor, an economist of Hungarian origin who was much admired by Wilson, to introduce a Selective Employment Tax. Employers had to pay £1 5s a week for each worker on the payroll, but manufacturing employers got the tax refunded plus a bonus, so the burden fell on the service sector. The idea was to bring about what Wilson called a 'shake-out' – to get people out of shops, hotels and offices and into factories. Two historians of the period describe SET as 'a blunt instrument';[25] one of them points out that 'it made no allowance for good or bad firms, their relative efficiencies or their location'. In fact, though Britain in 1966 still enjoyed full employment and there were some examples of shortage of labour, these shortages were generally in the service sector, not in productive industry. Thus the workers who lost their jobs seldom found other jobs. For the first time since 1940, unemployment returned to the British scene. It became the angriest and bitterest reproach levelled by the Labour left against Wilson and Callaghan.

On 16 May, the National Union of Seamen declared a strike and ships were motionless in all British ports, and indeed all over the world. The Prime Minister and the Chancellor saw this strike as an intolerable challenge to the prices and incomes policy, but they were on weak ground for several reasons. The seamen were actually striking for shorter hours; although this could be mathematically translated into a wage increase, their demand for a forty-hour week (instead of fifty-six) was bound to evoke sympathy in the Labour movement. Secondly, the shipowners were perfectly ready to grant the demand, and the government's veto was responsible for the continuance of the strike. Thirdly, substantial salary increases had been given to judges, senior civil servants and doctors, who were all comfortably off compared to the seamen. Crossman noted in his diary: 'I was depressed by our getting ourselves into this ridiculous fight with the seamen for the sake of a prices and incomes policy which had fallen to pieces before the strike began.[26] A few months later, he was admitting: 'The price side of the prices and incomes policy is as much of a fraud as the workers suspect.'[27]

While some ministers had private doubts about the 'ridiculous fight', Wilson's posture was backed by the faithful majority of Labour MPs and, of course, by the Tories. It was in an atmosphere of mounting hysteria that Michael said in the Commons: 'Many of us believe that the seamen have an extremely powerful case which has not been fully taken into account.'[28] Barbara, after a dinner with Michael on 21 June, recorded: 'Mike was more roused against the government than I have ever heard him. He said Harold was losing his friends. Didn't he realise that he was now strong enough to stand up to the Right?'

Michael's indignation was understandable. The day before, Wilson had declared in the Commons that the strikers were being manipulated by 'a tightly knit group of politically motivated men'. He followed this up on 28 June by naming eight members of the Executive of the NUS who had Communist associations; the allegation came from the security services and was probably based on phone-tapping. Several unions at the time, including the TGWU, had elected Communists or near-Communists to their executives, so Wilson was in effect challenging the right of the members to elect whom they liked – an attitude that infuriated Frank Cousins and his chosen successor, Jack Jones. Fortunately, the NUS decided on 29 June to accept a formula recommended by a court of inquiry, phasing the reduction in working hours over a year.

However, the strike had led to a heavy deficit in the trade figures, a loss of confidence in financial markets and a fall of £38 million in Britain's gold and dollar reserves. Only three months after its electoral victory, the

Labour government was again in bad trouble – 'blown off course', as Wilson put it. In Michael's analysis, everything was connected: the refusal to dissociate Britain from the Vietnam war, the 'strong east of Suez' military commitment, the defence at all costs of the over-valued pound, the unjust and unworkable prices and incomes policy. In *Tribune* of 24 June, he delivered a comprehensive indictment under the front-page headline 'WHAT'S WRONG WITH OUR GOVERNMENT?':

> The short answer is: plenty . . . No glimmer of a changed strategy, an enlarged vision, since the election . . . The Cabinet never sat down to consider how an intelligent and intelligible incomes policy could have been operated . . . Pathetic acceptance of the Tory legacy in defence and foreign policy . . . We and our Labour government share the guilt for the continuance of the infamy [of Vietnam].

The government now decided to introduce a new and tougher Prices and Incomes Bill, with provision for the statutory powers that were anathema to Frank Cousins. To nobody's surprise, he resigned; indeed, he took his letter of resignation in person to 10 Downing Street on a Sunday morning, 3 July. His meeting with Wilson was 'a blistering crossfire of accusation and defence'.[29] He returned to his base as general secretary of his union but also stayed in the Commons in order to conduct, with the support of the *Tribune* left, a relentless struggle against the bill. The new Minister of Technology was Anthony Wedgwood Benn, known to his collegues at that time as 'Wedgy' (and thus distinguished from Tony Greenwood and Tony Crosland). His Parliamentary Secretary was Peter Shore; both were regarded as bright and brainy young men, much favoured by the Prime Minister and positioned midway between the right and left of the party.

The seamen's strike and the Cousins resignation were the prelude to (and contributory causes of) a disastrous run on the pound. Callaghan, briefly, thought that devaluation was inevitable, but Wilson ruled that the pound must be defended and the Chancellor changed his mind. Brown, however, continued to urge that devaluation was the best way out of trouble. This posed, once again, the critical question of whether the Treasury or the DEA was the economic arbiter. Outvoted in the Cabinet, Brown tried to persuade Barbara Castle and Dick Crossman to support him in a bid to dethrone Wilson and replace him as Prime Minister, but they declined and he resigned. Wilson induced him to stay in the government by giving him the job he had wanted since 1964, the Foreign Office; Stewart took over the DEA. Callaghan, a stronger political force than Stewart, took the opportunity to insist on the supremacy of the

Treasury, offered his own resignation as a calculated bluff, and withdrew it when he got his way. The DEA was on its way to the extinction that overtook it in 1968. But, while sterling hovered on the verge of collapse, the government was riven and paralysed for several critical days.

On the most critical day, 20 July, the Cabinet was rushed into endorsing the measures proposed by the Treasury. The remedies adopted were a repetition of those of October 1964: a rise in Bank rate, higher indirect taxes and cuts in investment, notably in housing and in the plans of nationalised industries. There were also cuts in the arms budget and (to the regret of Barbara Castle, but of no other ministers) in overseas aid.

Next, the government ordered a wage freeze – a total standstill for six months, followed by six months of 'severe restraint' – and pushed the Prices and Incomes Bill through Parliament. Michael described it as 'probably unworkable and likely to inflict lasting and grievous injury on the process of collective bargaining and the trade union movement'. He announced: 'I never like voting with the Tories if it can possibly be avoided . . . [but] I shall not vote for the government.'[30]

Michael – like Frank Cousins, Jack Jones, Eric Heffer and others who rejected the Prices and Incomes Bill – always made it clear that (as he said in the House during the debate) 'some form of incomes policy is required'. For socialists, the anarchic free play of the market was no more desirable in relation to wage levels than in any other sphere. What the left did consider essential, however, was a 'planned growth of wages' – that is, a rationally considered projection of what the economy would stand –a recognition of social justice as between the privileged and those in need, and the right of the trade unions to bargain freely instead of obeying commands from above. Speaking to the TUC in September 1966, Cousins said: 'You cannot have a social democracy and at the same time control by legislation the activity of a free trade union movement which is an essential part of that social democracy.'

There was no doubt that the pressure for the wage freeze and the spending cuts came from the City, the banks and the United States. *Tribune* warned: 'Bad and interested advice from the United States about the foreign burdens Britain should carry helped to kill the last Labour government and we must not allow it to kill this one.'[31] Michael declared at that year's party conference: 'All over the country there are millions of people passionately praying that this government shall succeed, and so do I. But if they refuse to take the course of challenging the power of our opponents in these central citadels, we will fail and they will be washed away in a flood of ignominy and shame.'

The only good news was in a sphere that was of close concern to Michael: the rights of the back-bench MP. In the reshuffle that followed the economic crisis, Dick Crossman became Leader of the House and John Silkin replaced Bowden as Chief Whip. They introduced a regime of tolerance, allowing MPs to abstain from supporting the government on any serious issue, and not only on the traditional 'conscience' grounds of pacifism and temperance. Wilson's attitude was changeable; he was friendly with Crossman and Silkin and inclined to give their methods a fair trial, but sometimes his temper snapped and he felt that his authority was jeopardised. Rigid disapproval of the liberal regime came from Emanuel Shinwell, chairman of the PLP, now eighty-two years old and one of the few survivors of the Attlee Cabinet, and from George Wigg, a crony of Wilson's and once a Regular Army sergeant-major.

Matters came to a head when twenty-eight Labour MPs, including Michael, abstained in a crucial division on the Prices and Incomes Bill. Shinwell demanded the withdrawal of the whip from the ringleaders of the revolt, if not all the twenty-eight. Silkin refused to take this action, and Crossman, with memories of the destructive furore over the attempted expulsion of Bevan in 1955, warned: 'The whole thing will play into the hands of the Tories and we shall be in tremendous difficulties with the constituency parties at this moment.'[32]

As a compromise, Crossman and Silkin drew up a new code of discipline which protected individual rights but forbade minorities to form organised groups. This was objectionable to the left, for such a ban had been imposed as a check on the Bevanites in 1952. Crossman described the scene at the next party meeting:

> Michael Foot got up and made a passionate speech in which he reminded us that Harold and I had led the attack on this motion when it was first moved in 1952. He was not going to give up his principles, he said. He was going to continue fighting just as before . . . I made a short speech which was not improved by a lot of suggestions on bits of paper which were being pushed to me by Harold throughout my speech. On one of the bits of paper he had written that I should say that the Bevanites accepted the decision of 1952. I was a bit doubtful but I said it.[33]

The code was accepted by a large majority and the dispute simmered down until March 1967, when sixty-two Labour MPs refused to vote for the Defence Estimates. Shinwell 'said that discipline had broken down and asked what we were going to do about it'. In the Cabinet, 'Callaghan weighed in as chief complainant. He asked for a reimposition of discipline since the new liberal system simply wasn't working . . . Only Barbara Castle staunchly came out on our side.'[34] Wilson then drafted a speech to a PLP meeting which he avoided discussing with the Leader of the House or the Chief Whip. The key sentence, which caused a sensation and passed into political folklore, was: 'Every dog is allowed one bite, but a different view is taken of a dog that goes on biting all the time. He may not get his licence renewed when it falls due.'

Crossman felt that this 'meant the end of the liberal regime' and wrote to Wilson offering his resignation. He consoled himself with the reflection: 'If I get out I should be able to see the children, live here [at his farmhouse in Oxfordshire], get to work on my books and above all I would be anticipating and resigning before the series of economic disasters which I'm afraid are now coming upon us.'[35]

While Crossman was despondent, Michael was defiant. He wrote in that week's *Tribune* (10 March) that Wilson 'seemed to want a blind, dumb, unthinking acceptance by Labour backbenchers of each and every Cabinet or Prime Ministerial decision . . . The Labour Party has never been prepared to accord this abject allegiance to any leader or collection of leaders.' In this combative mood, he was able to put fresh heart into his old friend Dick. They met; Crossman's account, naturally, describes his own side of the conversation rather than Michael's: 'I briefed him on what George and Manny [Wigg and Shinwell] were up to and told him how I was determined not to give an inch.'[36]

Michael had ended his article shrewdly: 'Wilson himself, I suspect, will recognise what a blunder last week was.' Always a nimble tactician, Wilson did recognise it and arranged to give an interview to *Tribune*, in which he said: 'Criticism is all to the good. I think the party thrives on criticism and argument.' He drew a distinction between criticism and 'dissension', which he described as 'utterly destructive', but these terms could be interpreted according to taste. All that remained was for the Prime Minister to make his peace with the Leader of the House and the Chief Whip. He drew up a statement favouring the liberal regime and read it aloud at a meeting attended by Crossman, Silkin, Shinwell and Wigg. It was now Shinwell's turn to hand in his resignation. He was succeeded as chairman of the PLP by the more amicable Douglas Houghton. Crossman recorded exultantly: 'Manny and George withdrew, clearly licked, and John and I stayed behind to have drinks with Harold.'

5

One question that came to the fore in 1967 was that of British entry into the European Community. Five years had passed since Macmillan's application had been vetoed by de Gaulle, and Labour now had a Foreign Secretary who was an ardent 'European' and vehemently advocated a new bid. Wilson was less enthusiastic, but appreciated the prospect of a diversion from his troubles and support for the pound from stronger economies, notably Germany. On 9 May, Britain formally applied to join. Wilson and Brown embarked on a tour of European capitals, prudently leaving Paris to the end of the trip.

'Europe' was not – then or in later years – a straightforward issue between right and left. Heath and most of the Tories were for joining the Community, but Enoch Powell and some others were strongly against it. In the Cabinet, the chief advocate of joining was George Brown and the most determined opponent was Douglas Jay; both were, in general terms, right-wingers. Barbara Castle was against, while Wedgwood Benn was for.

Michael did not approach the problem with his usual resolute conviction. On 8 May, speaking in the Commons during the three-day debate opened up by the government, he conceded: 'Anyone who said that there was not a balance of argument . . . would be a fool.' He was swayed to some extent by his memories of the 1940s, when he had argued for close association with Western Europe as a counterpoise to the USA and in particular for a partnership of Britain and France. However, he listed a range of objections: the provisions of the Treaty of Rome might damage the interests of Commonwealth nations, interfere with trade with the Soviet bloc and prevent the kind of regional planning that benefited Scotland and Wales. Above all: 'Part of the price, nobody can deny it, will be a diminution in the power of this House of Commons to control our own economic affairs.' His conclusion was that the application would probably not succeed anyway, so the wisest course was to tell the European nations: 'It is more advisable for us to stay out, but we wish to have the closest relations with de Gaulle and with France, our oldest ally and most indispensable friend.' At the end of the debate, sixty-two MPs voted against the motion to approve the application. Michael was among them, with such Labour left-wingers as Mikardo, Driberg, Emrys Hughes and Stan Orme (and also three Tories). But his guess was right; once again, though less brusquely than in 1963, de Gaulle made it clear that British entry into the Community was unacceptable. George Brown, who had invested considerable personal capital in the attempt, was hurt and downcast.

In this period, the two Labour politicians who tried most ardently to uphold the ideals inherited from Nye Bevan were Barbara Castle inside the government and Michael Foot outside it. They did not always see eye to eye; Barbara took a critical stand on Vietnam, on Rhodesia and on the sale of armaments to South Africa, but supported the restrictive incomes policy. Michael's view of her, however, was: 'Barbara Castle was a first-class Cabinet Minister and, over and above that – a much rarer bird – a first-class *Socialist* Cabinet Minister.'[37] Sometimes, discreetly, they worked together. On one occasion, she got wind of an arms deal with South Africa which had been concealed from the Cabinet and got Michael to table a parliamentary question. 'The lobbies were humming with excitement,' she recorded with satisfaction. At other times, she felt that onslaughts from outside the government were harmful. At the time of the July 1966 crisis, she wrote in her diary: 'I am appalled by the purely destructive mood into which the Left has got itself – not least Michael. The government is on the edge of complete disintegration of a kind from which Labour would not recover for twenty years, and I cannot see it would benefit anyone to push it over the edge.'[38]

A year later, when railway guards were on strike, she expressed herself irritably again: 'Of course *Tribune* is backing the guards on the principle that true Socialism consists of supporting any industrial claim, regardless of its effects on other workers. But to me this is nonsense . . . Left-wingism that consists of burying one's head in the sands and avoiding all awkward choices just makes me sick.'[39] Here were the roots of the antagonism that flared up with Barbara's tenure of the Department of Employment in 1968–70.

What Barbara, from her angle within the government, did not quite appreciate was that Michael too had his dilemmas, and was trying to restrain a 'purely destructive mood'. *Tribune* celebrated its thirtieth anniversary with the issue of 28 April 1967, and Michael marked the occasion with some retrospective thoughts:

> Bevinism, Deakinism, Gaitskellism all had a streak of the Stalinist temper. *Tribune* fought the disease whenever signs of infection appeared . . . But some stalwarts have stepped forward to insist that everyone but themselves must be denounced as traitors . . . One original sin of the Left is sectarianism. The pendulum swings back and forth. Sometimes the primary concern has been to curb arrogance in the leadership . . . At other moments it has been necessary to strengthen the cohesive forces within the movement.

At this time, the treasurership of the Labour Party fell vacant and James Callaghan announced that he would be a candidate for the post. Michael decided to contest the election. Like Bevan in 1954 and 1955, he did not expect to win. He would have the support of the TGWU and most of the constituencies, but that would not be anywhere near enough. The point, however, was to secure a platform for a dissenting policy. In announcing his candidature in *Tribune* of 24 June, Michael summarised his policy: cuts in the defence budget, a mobilisation of Britain's economic resources, a target of a 4 per cent growth rate. He was seeking, first and foremost, to restore the sagging faith of Labour's rank and file, and he wrote: 'A principal cause of the widespread disillusion is that a Labour government has done what it said it would not do, and that cuts even deeper than the sharp economic facts themselves. It tampers with the sources of democracy and poisons them with cynicism.'

He repeated, in a Commons speech on 10 July, that he was not opposed in principle to an incomes policy – 'Indeed, we believe that such a policy is essential to socialism.' His charge against the government was: 'They have associated incomes policy with ferocious deflation, with their whole economic policy of stringency and the deliberate creation of unemployment.' Here was the crux of the matter; by the autumn of 1967, unemployment had risen to 750,000. Working-class voters were becoming alienated, and Labour met with severe by-election defeats. Michael wrote:

It is the Tories who become the beneficiaries of political apathy and cynicism . . . There is not a Minister in the government who, prior to 1964, had not characterised the creation of such unemployment as typical of the callousness, wastefulness and blindness of Tory economics . . . Labour must break the grip of Tory economic policy . . . A Labour government which cannot do that will face disaster, and deservedly. We have not much time left.[40]

Callaghan was safely elected to the treasurership with four million votes to Michael's two million, but soon he made an untypical blunder. Sir Leslie O'Brien, the Governor of the Bank of England, said in a speech in Rio de Janeiro: 'It is impossible to manage a large industrial economy with the very small margin of unused manpower resources that characterised the British economy in the 1940s and 1950s.' Few people would have noticed the speech, had not Callaghan quoted it in the Commons and added: 'That is true . . . We must have a somewhat larger margin of unused capacity.' For the suspicious, 'unused capacity' was a euphemism for unemployment. Crossman, noting that Callaghan was 'tired and overwrought', commented: 'If you read it in Hansard you realise how terrible it was for a Labour Chancellor to say such a thing, particularly if he profoundly believed it.'[41] Michael and another left-winger, John Mendelson, immediately protested and then put down a censure motion. Two weeks later Callaghan, on Crossman's advice, made an apology to a party meeting, whereupon Michael withdrew the censure motion. But Crossman was convinced that the offending words 'were the true sentiments he shared with the Governor of the Bank of England about the pool of unemployment'.

The rise in unemployment was not the only bad news. October 1967 brought the worst trade deficit on record, and thus the onset of yet another crisis. This time, there was no alternative to devaluation, and on 18 November the pound was devalued from $2.80 (the rate fixed by Cripps in 1949) to $2.40. Callaghan, in his memoirs, described his sense of defeat: 'I felt that the three years of struggle had been of no avail.'[42] He made the best of the disappointment with a resounding speech in the Commons – 'We want a nation that is proud and self-reliant and compassionate' – which earned him a headline in the *Daily Telegraph*: 'BID BY CALLAGHAN FOR PREMIERSHIP'. However, he decided that it was impossible for him to stay as Chancellor. He moved to the safe haven of the Home Office, and Roy Jenkins went to the Treasury.

The purpose of devaluation was to win support for the pound from the International Monetary Fund, but it was not given without conditions. Jenkins signed a Letter of Intent pledging Britain to stringent deflation. Michael's reaction was: 'I was amazed and shocked. I couldn't believe that, after all the undertakings we had from the government front bench on the absence of strings and conditions, the government would have entered into such an elaborate labyrinthine commitment.'[43] To add to his distress, the letter itself was written in 'excruciating Esperanto'. Jenkins had to order the levying of charges on Health Service prescriptions, which Bevan had managed to evade in 1949, and postpone the raising of the school-leaving age from fifteen to sixteen – a decision which caused the Earl of Longford (Frank Pakenham, an Oxford contemporary of Michael's) to resign from the Cabinet in protest. Jennie Lee, too, was on the verge of resignation, but stayed.

On 18 January 1968, Michael was one of twenty-six MPs who abstained on a motion approving Jenkins' economy cuts. Surprisingly, John Silkin took a disciplinary attitude and threatened the withdrawal of the whip. Licences, it seemed, were again in jeopardy for rebellious dogs. After some tense negotiations, the twenty-six were merely barred from party meetings until the end of February.

The second rebellion of 1968 – only a matter of weeks after the first – stemmed from the emotionally charged issue of immigration control. Several African colonies had won independence in the closing years of the Tory government, thanks largely to the wisdom of a liberal-minded Colonial Secretary, Iain Macleod. One of these was Kenya, a country whose population included two minorities: the white settlers who had enjoyed a life of privilege, and the Indians who had carved out niches in office employment, shopkeeping and commercial activity. Neither of these communities looked forward happily to living under African domination. Macleod, therefore, inserted a provision in the Act conceding independence whereby any resident of the country could apply for British citizenship (as distinct from Kenya citizenship, which, since the Commonwealth Immigration Act of 1962, carried no right of entry into Britain). In 1967, the strongly nationalistic government of Kenya embarked on a policy of 'Africanisation', threatening to deprive the Indians of their jobs in the state bureaucracy or even of their businesses and shops. Availing themselves of their passports, they began to board the planes for Heathrow.

Much alarmed, and fearing an explosion of British racism, Home Office officials drafted new legislation to keep the Kenya Asians out. Roy Jenkins accepted the principle of such action, despite the obvious breach of faith with the people concerned; but, luckily for his liberal reputation, he left the Home Office after devaluation and was able to hand the distasteful task to Callaghan. Callaghan had no qualms and speedily approved a tough new bill. The atmosphere was one of panic – not least in Kenya, since reports of an imminent closing of the door stimulated a rush.

Even *The Times* described Callaghan's bill as 'probably the most shameful measure that Labour members have ever been asked by their whips to support'. In the first place, admittance to Britain would depend on the granting of vouchers at the discretion of the Home Office, and Callaghan declined to say how many there would be. Secondly, entry was guaranteed only to people of so-called 'patrial' status – that is, people with a British parent or grandparent. This protected the whites (Kenya had been open to settlement only since about 1890) while excluding the Indians, and thus set a precedent in naked racial discrimination. The final touch was that, to check the rush at the airports, the bill was guillotined and hurried through Parliament in seven days. On the day when the vote was taken, 28 February, Michael protested:

This bill is doing something which I never expected to see a British Parliament do . . . We are specifying deliberately that certain people who have United Kingdom passports shall be deprived of their rights . . . If the government seek to force through this measure tonight, not merely will it be a shameful one in its general principle, but it will be shoddy, indiscriminate and careless.

But the bill was duly forced through, against the opposition of thirty-five Labour MPs. The novelty was that the rebels were actually voting against the government, not abstaining as on previous occasions. In view of the intense passions that had been aroused (and perhaps because the Chief Whip, who was Jewish, had his own feelings about racism), there was no talk of disciplinary action.

This storm had scarcely died down when the Foreign Secretary resigned. Since George Brown's star had begun to decline – that is, since the Treasury's victory over the DEA – his relations with Wilson had become increasingly hostile. 'One of the cruel absurdities of British politics', Michael has written in this connection, 'is that two men who hate each other's guts may be forced to stump the country handcuffed together as the leaders of the same party.'[44]

Even when one examines three contemporary accounts of the night of 14 March 1968 – in the diaries of Dick Crossman, Barbara Castle and Tony Wedgwood Benn – it is hard to be certain of what happened. What can be said is, firstly, that the resignation did not arise from any serious policy difference; and secondly, that it occurred at a moment of maximum strain. Because of yet another financial crisis, it was necessary (in response to a phone call from Washington) to close the London gold market. This involved holding a Privy Council at Buckingham Palace between midnight and one in the morning so that the Queen could declare a bank holiday. It appears (according to what one believes) either that Wilson tried to summon Brown to this meeting but could not discover where he was, or that he only pretended to try to reach him. Brown may have been drunk, or Wilson may have assumed that he was – Benn, who was with him, recorded with scrupulous honesty: 'I don't know whether or not he was drunk, because you can't always tell.' Drunk or not, he worked himself into a furious temper. When the two men finally met, 'George stood up and shrieked and bellowed and shouted abuse as he went round the table, then left the room.'[45] His next appearance – the House was having an all-night session – was on the Labour back benches.

Suddenly, the government needed a new Foreign Secretary. Denis Healey, Secretary for Defence since 1964 and a former head of the Labour Party's International Department, was eager for the job. Dick Crossman and Barbara Castle were also adequately qualified. Instead, Wilson brought Michael Stewart back to the Foreign Office, where his earlier tenure had been so undistinguished and so unpopular with the Labour rank and file. Barbara fumed: 'Hasn't the man the slightest recognition of the fact that such an appointment will be like a red rag to a bull to our Party activists?'[46]

The immigration issue came to the boil again when Enoch Powell made a sensational speech in Birmingham on 20 April (incidentally, Adolf Hitler's birthday). He had been possessed for several years by the paranoid notion that white people were being victimised and terrorised by blacks – that the former, not the latter, were suffering from 'discrimination and deprivation'.[47] He had declared in 1960: 'Hundreds of thousands of our fellow-citizens here in Britain are living in perpetual dread.' Now he warned that 'immigrant communities can organise to consolidate their members, to agitate and campaign against their fellow-citizens, and to overawe and dominate the rest'.

The aspect of the speech that roused Britain's racists to ecstasy and appalled good liberals was its wild irrationality. There was the vision of racial warfare, with the famous phrase about 'the River Tiber foaming with much blood'; there were fantastic statistical extrapolations of black numbers; there were stories about persecuted old ladies which were never supported by evidence and which were simply urban folklore at a gutter level. Seldom, if ever, had a prominent politician been guilty of such glaring irresponsibility. Nor was his behaviour in any sense courageous. Michael challenged him to repeat his 'famous or infamous' speech in the Commons, observing: 'I find it remarkable that he has not chosen to try and persuade his fellow Members to accept the views he has stated outside.'[48] Powell, who was present, remained seated and silent.

However, Michael distanced himself from MPs who showed their disgust by shunning Powell. According to one political journalist: 'Foot was appalled by such behaviour, whatever Mr Powell had said. This was no way to treat a human being. Foot therefore approached Powell in a crowded Commons library, slapped him on the back and asked how he was getting on.'[49] Writing later, Michael accepted a biographer's statement that Powell was 'no racist', rejected the picture of 'the opportunist without scruple', and pointed to his 'unshakeable, almost pedantic, sense of rectitude in personal dealings'.[50] Posing the question of why he had made the speech – 'why did he fail to comprehend what fears and hatreds and antagonisms his words would help to spread?' – Michael confessed: 'I do not know the answers.'[51] In 1959, when nine Africans were beaten to death by white prison warders in Kenya, the two notable speeches denouncing the atrocity were made by Barbara Castle – and by Enoch Powell, who attacked the 'fearful doctrine' that one man's life was worth less than another's by reason of race or colour. In fact, Michael was not alone in regarding Powell as a man of baffling contradictions.

The sensation of the speech was followed by another sensation: hundreds of London dockers and Smithfield meat-porters – indisputably working class and presumably Labour voters – marched to the House of Commons to show their support of Powell. Some, as Benn witnessed, 'shouted obscene things at Labour MPs and called Ian Mikardo a bloody Chinese Jew'.[52] Michael was the target of similar abuse when walking through Smithfield on his way to the *Tribune* office. Almost as alarming as the enthusiasm for Powell was the disarray, and in some cases panic, on the left. Dick Crossman thought that Powell had 'stirred up the nearest thing to a mass movement since the 1930s' and that it was 'the real Labour core, the illiterate industrial proletariat who have turned up in strength and revolted against the literate'.[53] Barbara Castle noted a revealing conversation with Richard Briginshaw, the leader of the printers' union, who was publicly identified as a strong left-winger: 'He thought Enoch Powell had a lot of right on his side.'[54] (Under the Briginshaw regime, no blacks ever got jobs as printers.) Even the *Tribune* comment was uncharacteristically defensive and anxious:

> We do not doubt that Enoch Powell's racialist views are widely shared. We do not doubt that the demonstrations in his favour are spontaneous. We understand the difficulties and anxieties which immigration, even where there is no white racial prejudice, produces. But none of this justifies the demonstrations . . . They may end in violent racial clashes; they are sowing the seeds of generations of hatred; they must be stopped.[55]

The Powell furore coincided with the introduction of the first Race Relations Bill, which prohibited discrimination in housing and employment. The government accepted the theory that rigorous immigration control, checking the growth of the black population, would appease prejudiced whites and create an atmosphere in which racial harmony became attainable. There was little sign, however, of the validity of this theory.

By mid-1968, morale in the Labour Party, and indeed within the government, was at rock-bottom. The Tory lead in the opinion polls went as high as twenty-six points. By-election results were appalling. When George Wigg went to the House of Lords, his constituency – Dudley, in the Birmingham region – changed from a 10,000 Labour majority in March 1966 to an 11,000 Tory majority in March 1968. Altogether, in the course of this Parliament, Labour lost twelve seats to the Tories, one to the Liberals, one to the Scottish National Party and one to Plaid Cymru. *Tribune* admitted: 'All the signs point to electoral disaster for Labour in 1970 or 1971.'

The most striking phenomenon of the period – though, of course, we become fully aware of it only by reading memoirs and diaries published later – was disenchantment with the Prime Minister. Denis Healey drew this unflattering portrait:

> Since he had neither political principle nor much government experience to guide him, he did not give Cabinet the degree of leadership which even a less ambitious prime minister should provide. He had no sense of direction, and rarely looked more than a few months ahead. His short-term opportunism, allied with a capacity for self-delusion which made Walter Mitty appear unimaginative, often plunged the government into chaos. [56]

'Worse still,' Healey added, 'when things went wrong he imagined everyone was conspiring against him.' Wilson did, indeed, show distinct signs of paranoia. He worried endlessly about leaks to the press; at one time or another, he deprived even senior ministers of access to important papers; he suspected almost all his colleagues of disloyalty; he created an inner Cabinet, but changed its membership so often that it was merely a mechanism for conferring or withdrawing favour. It must be said in fairness that even paranoids can have real enemies, and Wilson was the target of undermining operations in which the security services played a nefarious role. In 1968, moreover, Cecil King, the megalomaniac proprietor of the *Daily Mirror*, tried to organise a coup against the government and sought to enlist such improbable figures as Lord Mountbatten and Sir Solly Zuckerman. But Wilson's suspicions came to dominate his mind so extensively that Anthony Crosland remarked casually to his wife: 'Harold is mad, of course';[57] while Benn, after a conversation with the Prime Minister, recorded in his diary: 'I went out shaken by this, having concluded that the man had gone mad, ought to be removed, that the great case for the parliamentary system was that it did remove people. I just felt contempt for him . . . I just feel that Harold is finished.'[58]

Such was the scene when Penguin Books commissioned Paul Foot to write a book entitled *The Politics of Harold Wilson*. As Michael remarked when he reviewed it in *Tribune*, 'that prim non-committal title turns out to be an essay in parliamentary genocide'.[59] Paul (whose first marriage had just broken up) moved into Michael's house to work intensively on the book, and ended up by giving the Penguin editors more than they had bargained for. He produced a devastating analysis of Wilson's devious political career; but he also argued the far-left case for the futility of parliamentary strategy as a route to socialism. He was writing at the time of the student revolt in France which brought the Gaullist regime into acute (if transient) peril, inspired lesser but still dramatic disturbances in Britain and America, and shaped the thoughts and emotions of what came to be called the '1968 generation'.

Michael was impressed by the book – 'a serious attempt to discuss, in political terms, why the high expectations and hopes of 1964 have been so cruelly dashed' – but he was also angered by it. He wrote his *Tribune* review in the hard-hitting style customary in the Foot family. 'How else, except by some form of representative assembly, is the State to be controlled?' he demanded. Then he took issue with Paul's criticism of plans for economic growth (another 1968 theme). 'To condemn economic growth and technological advance is about as fat-headed a perversion of Marxism as one is likely to come across outside a Stalinite seminar.' Such wrong-headed attitudes, Michael wrote, were 'a blemish on a book which should sell like hot cakes'. He wound up:

> The politics of Harold Wilson are an extraordinary mixture of opportunism, improvisation, short-sightedness and resilience . . . The politics of Paul Foot are an extraordinary mixture of first-class reporting, primitive Marxism, family wit and fantasy . . . Both may recover. The politics of Michael Foot are rejected in all quarters. Which is the reason for the general mess.

The left was fighting the left as usual, but more venomously than at most other times. On 24 January 1969, hundreds of people filled the Central Hall for a public debate between *Tribune*, represented by Michael and Eric Heffer, and the far-left journal *Black Dwarf*, represented by Tariq Ali and Bob Rowthorn. It was a dialogue of the deaf, prompting a *Tribune* reader to describe it as 'a bunch of squabbling sectarians debating obscure points of theological doctrine while Enoch Powell gleefully sharpens his axe'. Michael, too, warned that sectarianism 'could become our most fateful weakness'. He was replying to an article by the socialist historian John Saville, who accused the Labour Party of 'capitulation before the massive forces of the property owner' and remarked scathingly that the parliamentary strategy 'has survived and is surviving all practical demonstrations of its impossibility'.[60] Michael's rejoinder was to point to the impossibility of achieving socialism by battles on the streets – the victors in such battles had been Mussolini and Hitler. He urged socialists to model themselves on the Chartists: 'Their great idea was by mobilising power outside Parliament to get real power inside.' The unions were moving leftward, but this asset could 'be thrown away entirely by a reckless infantile new Leftism which scorned the policies that the new trade union leadership has fought for'. The enemy, certainly, was the City, the Treasury and the Bank of England, but victory 'depends in the end on whether Socialists have the courage and imagination to use parliamentary power to subdue these financial forces, the most powerful and irresponsible elements in modern capitalism'.[61]

6

Barbara Castle was now Secretary for Employment, a job which Wilson had pressed her to take because she was, he said, 'good at getting on with the trade unions'.[62] However, no Secretary of State who tried to enforce a statutory incomes policy could win the goodwill of the unions. The compulsory powers under the Prices and Incomes Act had expired after a year; a replacement on similar lines was bound to meet with opposition. Dick Crossman took a gloomy view: 'We're now committed to a new prices and incomes policy in which no one, except possibly Barbara, still believes.'[63] When the TUC met in September, a motion by Frank Cousins calling for opposition to the incomes policy was carried by seven and a half million votes to one million. Geoffrey Goodman was there for the *Daily Mirror*:

> In the front row of the visitors' gallery sat Barbara Castle. She did not attempt to conceal her feelings and called a news conference . . . to insist that the government's policy would go on in spite of everything. But she also called the Prime Minister to warn him that the incomes policy was now perilously close to collapse.[64]

Rhodesia was another disaster area. Wilson had rashly prophesied that sanctions would bring Ian Smith to his knees 'in weeks rather than months', but the illegal regime was still in power three years later. An alternative solution was to make a deal with Smith, and Wilson met him twice, aboard the warship *Tiger* in December 1966 and aboard the *Fearless* in August 1968. He had to move cautiously because an agreement which conceded independence without African majority rule would have led to resignations by Lord Caradon (Mac Foot), Britain's representative at the UN, by Barbara Castle, and perhaps by other ministers, as well as another revolt by Labour MPs. Wilson did, nevertheless, try to reach such an agreement, hoping to make it palatable by promises of future progress towards majority rule, but on both occasions Smith backed out of the deal after he got home. This left Wilson with the worst of both worlds – a sacrifice of principle without the advantage of success.

Undeterred by these failures, the government embarked on two more risky enterprises. The fertile brain of Dick Crossman conceived a scheme for a reformed House of Lords, whose members would be appointed by the political parties in numbers reflecting their strength in the Commons, with a smaller number of independent peers to prevent an automatic government majority. The existing hereditary peers should be allowed only to attend the House and speak, not to vote. Michael quickly perceived the objectionable features of the plan. The selection of the new-model peers would open the way to patronage on a huge scale (especially as they were to be salaried); and a more or less powerless House of Lords would achieve respectability and therefore the confidence to become a rival to the Commons.

Encouraged by promises of co-operation from the Tory leader in the Lords, Lord Carrington, Crossman introduced a bill. The problem was that a constitutional bill must be debated clause by clause in the House, not in committee, and a guillotine cannot be imposed. In the opening debate, on 3 February 1969, Michael gave clear warning of his intention to fight the bill:

> Think of it! A second chamber selected by the whips – a seraglio of eunuchs . . . In the midst of a great national crisis, with the country aflame, with everyone having forgotten who these cross-benchers are, what would we hear as the final verdict on such great issues of national policy? We would hear a falsetto chorus from these political castrati . . .
>
> Many of us will think it is our constitutional duty to argue every clause, and in that respect, if in no other, this is a bill which offers wide opportunities.

The bill faced another determined opponent – Enoch Powell. While Michael regarded the nominated chamber as an outrage on democracy. Powell proceeded from the opposite corner. He thought that, if one attempted to impose a reforming logic on the House of Lords, one might be tempted to perform the same destructive operation on a yet more sacrosanct institution: the monarchy. Diametrically opposed in political philosophy, Michael Foot and Enoch Powell were both great House of Commons men. They shared a mastery of parliamentary procedure and a keen relish in the exploitation of its opportunities. As the clauses of the Parliament Bill were subjected to ruthless and expansive scrutiny, one was often to be heard producing arguments to support an amendment moved by the other.

Callaghan, who as Home Secretary was responsible for the bill, was going through a frustrating experience:

> Enoch Powell and Michael Foot made brilliant mockery of the Bill's proposals, and by their tactics held up any serious progress for days at a time . . . Any reluctant admiration I might have felt at the virtuosity of the Bill's opponents was soon smothered beneath increasing bafflement and frustration as we failed to make progress, and lumbered on against a stream of witty, logical and devastating oratory from its two principal, merciless opponents.[65]

From January to mid-April 1969, Michael made twenty-six speeches. The question of whether peers in the Crossman-style house should be obliged to retire at the age of seventy or seventy-two evoked laudatory allusions to Churchill, Attlee, Shinwell, Lord Palmerston, Gladstone, Adenauer and de Gaulle. At various times, Michael recalled the Parliament Bill of 1911, the India Bill of 1935 and the reduction of the Lords' powers in 1948. This was only recent history. The status of Scottish peers evoked a disquisition on the Act of Union (1707). Enoch Powell intervened helpfully with an account of how Queen Anne had created new peerages to win approval for the Treaty of Utrecht (1711), and Michael, familiar with the period from his writing of *The Pen and the Sword*, took up the baton with quotations from Swift's letters to Stella.

He was frank about his loathing of the House of Lords, and made it clear several times that his own preference was for abolition. The reform 'would perpetuate a situation under which the constitution of the country is weighted permanently on the side of reaction, the elderly, the Establishment, and all other similar forces in our society'.[66] But he was equally frank about his strategy: 'We all know that the bill . . . was ridiculous to start with, but if we can pile on a few more absurd amendments, if we can push on to this ship a few more cargoes which are calculated to sink it, we shall have done a good night's work.'[67]

The Tories in the Commons, favourable to the reform plan because it enhanced the status of the Lords but averse to helping Labour ministers, maintained a prudent silence. It was for them that Michael produced his most inspired invective: 'Look at them, these unlikely novices for a new Trappist order, these bashful tiptoeing ghosts, these pale effigies of what were once sentient, palpable human specimens, these unlarynxed wraiths, these ectoplasmic apparitions, these sphinx-like sentinels at our debates – why are they here?'[68]

By February 1969, Crossman confided to his diary that the bill was 'in really serious difficulty'. He could not restrain his admiration for 'Michael Foot, on the one side, in his most brilliant, demagogic, amusing form, and Enoch Powell on the other, in his most brilliant historical form'.[69] He realised that MPs were saying: 'This bloody government, we don't want this bloody House of Lords Bill, we don't really blame people for filibustering against it.'[70] Michael sympathised with the predicament of his old friend Dick – 'What we have to do is to rescue him from his own errors.'[71] By April, Crossman, having moved on to the Department of Health and Social Security, was bored with the project himself and advised the Cabinet to admit failure. He bore Michael no ill-will and stood him a dinner at the Athenaeum. At the end of this convivial evening, 'I went away liking him more than ever before, he liking me, and both of us knowing we are in for tremendous and appalling difficulties.'[72]

The other risky enterprise on which the government had embarked was Barbara Castle's brainchild. Her project was legislation to check what she called 'unconstitutional' strikes. The government would be empowered to hold up such a strike for a cooling-off period of twenty-eight days, to order a return to work if the walkout had started, and to order a strike ballot if there was a threat to national interests. In November 1968, she produced a White Paper entitled *In Place of Strife*. This title, suggested by Ted Castle, was intended to echo Nye Bevan's book *In Place of Fear* (published in 1952). 'In fact,' Barbara wrote later, 'I was convinced that Nye would have been on my side'[73] – a dubious claim, since he had opposed a ban on unofficial strikes even in wartime. She embodied her plans in an Industrial Relations Bill, which had some provisions sure of a welcome from the unions: employers would be forbidden to prevent workers from joining a union, and workers would be given redress against unfair dismissal. It was, however, the anti-strike proposals that aroused opposition from Jack Jones, who had succeeded Cousins as general secretary of the TGWU, and other leaders. Geoffrey Goodman records: 'In my presence she was told categorically by Jack Jones on New Year's Day, 1969, that her proposals would never be accepted by the unions.'[74] Michael headed a deputation of Labour MPs advising Barbara to retreat while there was still time.

In the privacy of her diary, she confessed: 'I am swept with doubt from time to time as to whether I have entirely misjudged reactions.'[75] She was encouraged, however, by the Prime Minister: 'Harold was delighted with my ideas . . . He was already showing signs of being far more hawkish than I was.'[76] She was also supported by the Chancellor, Roy Jenkins, by Peter Shore, now heading the Department of Economic Affairs, and by the Minister of Technology: 'I had welcome support from Tony Benn . . . who knew what havoc even a small stink could cause in the complex network of modern industry.'[77] On the other hand, Dick Crossman was critical: 'I can't ask my Coventry people [his constituency] to approve another anti-labour measure, another beating of the trade unions with no beating of the employers.'[78] Tony Crosland was dismissive: 'Around the country nobody has read "In Place of Strife" and they just think that Wilson has got a massive trade union bug in him and that Barbara has gone bonkers.'[79] The weightiest opposition came from Callaghan, who warned the Cabinet that the bill would create tension between the government and the unions, would not get through the Commons and would not stop unofficial strikes even if it did become law. But, as he put it: 'Barbara galloped ahead with all the reckless gallantry of the Light Brigade at Balaclava.'[80]

On one occasion, Brian Walden (then a Labour MP) voiced the opinion that an anti-strike law was inevitable. Callaghan rejoined: 'OK, if it's so inevitable, let the Tories pass it.'[81] On 26 March, the issue came before the National Executive Committee. Joe Gormley, for the National Union of Mineworkers, moved a resolution expressing opposition to Barbara's plan. Callaghan (according to Tom Driberg's account) watched the hands go up, then raised his own.[82] It was carried by 16 votes to 5. An open clash between a Labour government and the NEC was almost unprecedented, and a vote against government policy by a member of the Cabinet was certainly a startling novelty. Taxed with disloyalty at the next Cabinet meeting, Callaghan argued that no bill had yet been introduced in Parliament, so the government had no explicit position on the matter. Wilson replied that *In Place of Strife* was a policy document, not material for discussion. He then excluded Callaghan from the inner Cabinet. Such a demotion of the Home Secretary and former Chancellor was unprecedented too.

Michael wrote in *Tribune*:

Harold Wilson and the Labour Cabinet are heading for the rocks – loudly cheered along the course of navigational disaster by a huge assorted company of well-wishers and ill-wishers: Hugh Cudlipp of the *Daily Mirror*, Paul Johnson of the *New Statesman* . . . and others who should know better . . . It is the maddest scene in the modern history of Britain . . . Such a wanton, menacing decision could

threaten to break the government and tear the movement to shreds . . .
[The government] must show that it looks to the rock whence it was
hewn and the pit whence it was dug.[83]

Paul Johnson, for one, was unaware both that these words came from the
Book of Isaiah and that they were a motto of the Foot family. In a *New
Statesman* front page, he asked petulantly: 'Leaving aside the shaky syntax,
what on earth is this supposed to mean?'[84] He was enlightened next week in
a letter from the Vicar of Scunthorpe. Michael's comment was that one
couldn't expect a Catholic to know the Bible.

Suddenly, Harold Wilson replaced John Silkin as Chief Whip by
Robert Mellish, the MP for Bermondsey. He was a right-winger and a
disciplinarian, but he was also a trade unionist and flatly opposed to the bill.
Douglas Houghton, chairman of the PLP, was against the bill too; its
prospects looked poor enough for *Tribune* of 2 May to come out with the
headline: 'THE BILL CAN BE KILLED'. Barbara noted a tense exchange: 'I told
Mike flatly that he had grown soft on a diet of soft options because he never
had to choose . . . Mike pleaded with me desperately that at least we
should postpone the introduction of my bill until after the special congress
of the TUC.'[85] After listening to critical speeches in a PLP meeting from
Michael and others, she told the MPs that they could reject the bill but 'they
could not take away from me my right to destroy myself'.

The TUC special congress duly condemned the bill by an enormous
majority. Wilson, however, promised Barbara that he would make it an
issue of confidence and resign if he was defeated. Mellish and Houghton
both warned categorically that it would be impossible to get the penal
clauses of the bill through the Commons. In the Cabinet, Jenkins, Shore
and Benn had all withdrawn their support; Benn explained that it had been
a good idea, but ahead of its time. In Barbara's account, there was an
unhappy meeting with the TUC leaders and then: 'Harold and I returned to
the Cabinet which we despised.'[86] The decisive Cabinet meeting on
17 June showed that almost all its members were ready for a climb-down.
Crossman quotes Wilson as telling them: 'You're soft, you're cowardly,
you're lily-livered.' Benn's account of the meeting reads: 'Harold and
Barbara then became extremely bitter. Harold threatened to resign several
times . . . people were completely unmoved by it. His bluff was called and
he just looked weak and petty . . . Barbara was frantic in the usual Barbara
sort of way.'[87]

It was agreed to hold over the bill to the autumn, delete the penal clauses
and work out a face-saving formula. Helpful TUC leaders produced a
'solemn and binding declaration' promising to discourage strikes. When

Wilson announced this to the PLP on 18 June (the anniversary of the battle of Waterloo) it was received, in Crossman's words, 'with somewhat cynical disdain'. As on the occasion of his own surrender two months earlier, he ended up with a pleasant evening: 'I had dinner with Michael Foot and we discussed it in detail. I really love talking to him, he is one of the people I can talk to freely.'[88]

Denis Healey's verdict was: 'The Government had wasted six months on a hopeless fight, which had caused permanent damage to our relations with the trade unions . . . *In Place of Strife* did for Wilson what the hopeless attempt to delete Clause Four from the Party Constitution had done for Hugh Gaitskell.'[89]

7

The death of Bertrand Russell in January 1970 was marked by Michael with a full-page obituary in *Tribune*. Almost forty years had passed since Michael, as an Oxford undergraduate, had first read Russell's books and first set eyes on him. After recalling that experience, Michael went on to an unrestrained encomium:

> He was always ready to pose the truly awkward dilemmas, and time and again he swam against the stream . . . Few figures in history can match his persistent intellectual courage . . . He became one of the chief glories of our nation and our people, and I defy anyone who loves the English language and the English heritage to think of him without a glow of patriotism.[90]

With the turn of the year, the battered supporters of the Labour government began to experience feelings of relief and even of hopefulness. The rigorous financial measures taken after the 1967 devaluation, while inflicting painful blows on social welfare, had also involved drastic cuts in overseas military expenditure. The costly attempt to keep Britain 'strong east of Suez' was abandoned; in Aden, the last colonial war was wound up. Roy Jenkins proved to be a successful Chancellor, achieved debt repayments which went some way to freeing Britain from the dictation of the IMF, and even built up a balance of payments surplus, reaching £440 million by the end of 1969. While the government still preached wage restraint, there was no way to enforce it; hence, wages rose by 8 per cent in 1969 and 13 per cent in 1970, comfortably ahead of the inflation rate. Unemployment, at 700,000, was still too high but was not rising. The backroom strategists in Transport House devised an election slogan: 'Now Britain's strong, let's make it great to live in'.

In fact, Wilson and his colleagues were mulling over dates for a general election. The Tory lead in the opinion polls was being trimmed. By-election results were still bad – a seat was lost in December 1969 – but no longer catastrophic. In March 1970, Wilson invited the Cabinet to consider June or October. Healey favoured June, advancing the cynical argument that 'the expectations of better times to come would be greater than the reality.'[91] Michael, in conversation with Dick Crossman, 'felt that jumping into June would be a disaster'.[92]

At this juncture, the attention of politicians was distracted by startling news from South-east Asia. The Vietnam war had been in a state of stalemate since 1968, and peace talks were in progress – though the progress was barely perceptible – in Paris. But on 30 April President Nixon announced that American troops were moving into Cambodia, a small country which had hitherto been neutral, to attack the 'sanctuaries' of hidden North Vietnamese units. The invasion was accompanied by heavy bombing. In the next few days, about 100,000 people gathered in Washington to protest and there were demonstrations in many American universities, including Kent State in Ohio, where four students were shot dead by the National Guard.

In the House of Commons, Michael asked the Foreign Secretary whether Britain intended to protest. Stewart, predictably, replied: 'I don't believe it is right for us to express judgements of that kind.' Michael therefore moved the adjournment of the House and secured a debate for 5 May. Barbara Castle cheered him on from her position in the Cabinet, but Benn was more dubious. He told her that 'we couldn't support the US. Equally he was strongly against condemning them. This was a great American tragedy and we should show acute sympathy for America's agony.'[93]

In his speech, Michael said:

The action of the United States has played into the claws of hawks all over the world – in Peking, in Moscow, in Hanoi, and no doubt on the benches opposite among the various breeds of buzzards, harriers and kites we see on that side of the House . . . We have the right to recall the part played by Chatham, Edmund Burke and Charles James Fox, who opposed a war waged by a great nation which did suffer defeat but survived because it was prepared to admit that opposition to war had justice on its side . . . The military machine of the United States can create a wilderness and desolation, but it can never win the victory, and the best friends of the Americans are those who join the growing host of brave Americans who themselves are telling the truth about this war.

Fifty-nine Labour MPs voted for Michael's motion.

Local elections in May produced good results for Labour and opinion polls showed a Labour lead. Wilson made up his mind to jump. The House was dissolved, and 18 June (once again, the anniversary of Waterloo) was fixed as the date of the general election.

When the election battle opened, the sharpest burst of gunfire was an attack on Enoch Powell by Wedgwood Benn in a speech on 3 June. He said: 'The flag being hoisted over Wolverhampton is beginning to look like those that fluttered over Belsen and Dachau . . . When hate is released, it quickly gets out of control.' Heath, although he had openly dissociated himself from Powell's racism and dropped him from the Shadow Cabinet after his 1968 Birmingham speech, criticised Benn for his 'use of emotional language on a particularly sensitive matter'. Wilson had to stand by his Minister of Technology, declaring that everyone in the Labour Party was 'agreed on detestation of Powellism'; but when Benn inquired about the party leadership's real opinion of his speech, he was told: 'Harold is furious about it.'[94]

The South Wales miners' gala in Cardiff on 13 June (attended by twenty-six Welsh veterans of the International Brigade and a delegation from the National Liberation Front of Vietnam) was a triumphal occasion. Michael, the main speaker, declared: 'The Tory Party are about to suffer the most crushing defeat in their history . . . The foundation for this great Labour victory was laid wisely when fresh agreement was reached between the leaders of the Labour Party and the leaders of the trade union movement last year.' Barbara Castle, speaking at Swansea, predicted 'the disintegration of the Conservative Party'. The diaries were in accord with the public speeches. Crossman: 'I think we are bound to win.'[95] Benn: 'My assessment is that we should win by a large majority, certainly with a working majority.'[96]

The result came as a keen disappointment. The Tories were the winners, with 330 seats against 287 for Labour and 6 for the Liberals. Both the right and the left of the Labour Party suffered losses; George Brown and Woodrow Wyatt were out, and so was Jennie Lee. Michael's majority went down to the inglorious figure, by Ebbw Vale standards, of 17,446. His brother Dingle, who had held Ipswich comfortably in 1966, lost it by 13 votes. For him – and for Mac, whose appointment as British representative at the UN was terminated by the defeat of the Labour government – it was the end of a career.

Despite all the failures and all the betrayals of principle which the left had attacked since 1964, the record of the Wilson government was not without its credit side. Barbara Castle put her Equal Pay Act on the statute book, bringing to reality a goal for which women had fought for decades. The Race Relations Act put the more blatant forms of discrimination outside the law. The Jenkins regime at the Home Office had facilitated important reforms: legal tolerance for homosexuals, easier divorce, legalised abortion, abolition of capital punishment. Comprehensive schools had become the normal form of secondary education, and the Open University was a dream come true for the culturally deprived.

Yet the big promise of 1964 – the promise of modernisation and progress and hence of rising prosperity – had not been fulfilled. In 1965, the National Plan had forecast an increase of 25 per cent in economic growth, 27 per cent in public expenditure and 21 per cent in personal consumption; the results by 1970 were 14 per cent, 11 per cent and 13 per cent. Unemployment, negligible in 1964, had become a serious threat. Confidence in Labour as the party which could solve problems had been eroded by one economic crisis after another. In the election, only 72 per cent voted, the lowest figure since 1945. Almost a million people who had voted Labour in 1966 either stayed at home or voted Tory in 1970; this was the simple reason for the defeat.

Chapter 10

INSIDE LEFT

I

For a defeated Prime Minister, the abrupt ejection from Downing Street is always something of a trauma. Churchill in the aftermath of 1945 was capable of little more than taking long holidays on the French Riviera and making speeches in America. Of Wilson in 1970, Geoffrey Goodman writes:

> Harold Wilson, who expected to win [the election], was shattered to such an extent that even his closest friends and admirers were doubtful about his capacity to recover sufficiently from that blow. His personal and political confidence seemed to be destroyed. Had there been an obvious, and an agreed, alternative to Wilson in the Parliamentary Party at that time it is doubtful whether he would have survived.[1]

All his senior colleagues, since they too had expected to win, were, if not shattered, more or less depressed. Roy Jenkins was being blamed for presenting a cautious budget in 1970 instead of giving the voters cause for gratitude. Barbara Castle, though she never admitted that *In Place of Strife* had been a blunder, was blamed for alienating trade unionists. Dick Crossman had prudently made arrangements to take over the editorship of the *New Statesman*; unhappily, he was a failure in this role and was dismissed two years later. George Brown, the major casualty of the polls, went to the House of Lords.

In opposition, the Labour Shadow Cabinet consists of the leader, the deputy leader and twelve members elected by a vote of MPs. Michael decided to stand. He came sixth, with 124 votes, and was therefore elected. He was the only member of the new Shadow Cabinet who had not held office in the last government and had indeed been a relentless critic. Wilson, however, bore him no ill-will. Their personal relationship was reasonably good; both had been Bevanites in 1951 and both had taken the position in 1960, against Gaitskell, that conference decisions should be respected. As Prime Minister, Wilson had realised that, sweeping and vehement though Michael's denunciations had sometimes been, he had always dissuaded his friends on the left from any action that might result in bringing down the government to the advantage of the Tories. Now, when it was a question of rebuilding party unity, Wilson needed him. In 1972, a profile-writer quoted a (nameless) Labour MP thus: 'Michael is now the only hope of saving the Labour Party. Unlike Harold he has not been discredited. Unlike Roy he is not a wrecker. And he sees his responsibilities at last.'[2]

The question of why Michael put himself forward as a Shadow Cabinet member calls for more reflection. Despite the agonies that he went through while he watched the suicidal course of the Labour government, life in this period had rewards for him. He could maintain his cherished political independence and speak his mind freely; he could not be accused of ambitious calculation; he moved in the world of literature and journalism as well as in the hothouse atmosphere of Westminster. All this was apparent in an interview given to the *Daily Express* in 1966:

> I think politicians can lead a very interesting life without having office. Being a back-bench member is a perfectly reputable trade and nobody has to apologise for it . . .
>
> Nye was an entirely different person, touched with genius. I'm no genius and I know it. He had powers of political leadership and imagination which I don't have and never dreamed of having . . .
>
> I could lead a perfectly agreeable life, just writing books and reading them. It's one of the frustrations that you can't live three lives at the same time . . . Doing two or three jobs is a way of keeping sane. Otherwise you're out of touch with what is happening outside this place.

Whatever his modesty, he could not be unaware that his reputation was continually growing. A leading article in *The Times* during the 1970 election campaign urged the people of Ebbw Vale to vote for him (they 'do not require advice from *The Times*', the writer conceded) and compared him to Charles James Fox, a note that Michael must have found gratifying. The praise was unconstrained:

> If one asks who is the Backbencher who makes the greatest contribution to the life of Parliament, there can at present be only one conceivable answer: Mr Michael Foot. He is a wonderful man to have in politics . . . He is certainly the best writer and one of the two or three best speakers in the place. He is a man as nearly without enemies

as it would be decent to be and has a sweetness of temper which is the preservative of the health of any Assembly. He is a good, talkative, likeable and honest man.

Reporters in the press gallery of the Commons, suffering under the weight of the flat and tedious verbosity to which they had to listen, were delighted by Michael, described by Norman Shrapnel of the *Guardian* as 'an orator to the back of his tonsils, a nostalgic echo of the great inspirational voices from the past'. Shrapnel wrote of him: 'You get the impression of a man making a last stand for his species.'[3]

Yet there was a subtle trap in this chorus of praise. Oratory – or, to use a less complimentary term, rhetoric – can be received as merely an occasion for entertainment. Several times, speakers who followed Michael in the House expressed their enjoyment but dismissed his arguments. He appeared to plant barbs in the shoulders of his opponents without striking them to the heart. To vary the sporting metaphor, an *Observer* columnist remarked: 'He is a fast bowler who does not hate batsmen, so he will never take many Test wickets.'[4]

Indeed, *The Times* comment on his 'sweetness of temper' implied a double-edged compliment. Even years later, when Michael became leader of the Labour Party, Alan Watkins of the *Observer* (who knew him well) wrote: 'He has a kind of sweetness, even innocence.' Watkins went on to quote a passage from Hazlitt with which Michael was familiar: 'Happy are they who live in the dream of their own existence, and see all things in the light of their own minds; who walk by faith and hope; to whom the guiding star of their youth still shines from afar, and into whom the spirit of the world has not yet entered . . . The world has no hand on them.'

We should be alert, at this turning-point in Michael's life-story, to a certain mistaken – and injurious, though often well-intended – view of his character and his role. According to this view, he was unsuited and indeed averse to the brutal hostilities of politics; he would have been happier, and more truly himself, had he devoted himself entirely to the study of Swift and Hazlitt; the world should have had no hand on him, nor he on the world.

Admittedly, this portrait is more than a caricature. There was, in reality, the Michael Foot who relished his relaxations, who scorned or pitied politicians for whom no world existed outside politics, who freely confessed that he 'could lead a perfectly agreeable life, just writing books and reading them'. There was the Michael Foot who found hatred difficult and could not derive it from political opposition: who could muster an empathy with Lord Beaverbrook and Randolph Churchill and Enoch Powell. Yet, if we find the whole man in this Michael Foot, we blind ourselves to the serious politician, the man of ardent and deep-rooted ideals, the convinced and purposeful socialist.

What must be understood, especially, is that Michael was aware of the trap – the trap inherent in the amiability of Tory MPs, the laudatory portrait in *The Times* and the friendliness of Fleet Street journalists whose real loyalty was to their proprietors. When he was praised for his innocence, he was capable of grasping that the word is derived from the contrary of *nocent*, harmful – that is, it means 'harmless'. In his almost forty years' experience and observation of politics, he had taken note of various instances of men who had rendered themselves harmless by just this universal acceptance and popularity. One of these was his friend Emrys Hughes, who died in 1969. Dick Crossman commented: 'I watched him running down, in a sense running to seed, as he became a kind of professional funny man . . . As often happens, one tends to parody oneself and play one's own caricature.'[5] Michael made the same point, more gently, in an obituary article in *Tribune*: 'He had the blessing of certainty. Only rarely, I believe, did politics appear to him as a business of painful choices and balancing propositions . . . His timing and his wit could command attention, and the terrible temptation was to become a parliamentary jester, to attract more attention for his eccentricity than his ideas.'[6]

It was a temptation that Michael had to evade. He was now fifty-seven years old. If he made no move to get on to the front bench, he would be seen to have rejected that option. He would remain, for as long as he stayed in the Commons, a great back-bencher, honoured for his individuality, loved for his oratorical power and his wit – but essentially, and more so as the years passed, an entertainer with little claim to be taken seriously or to have an influence on events.

The possibility of ultimately becoming a Cabinet minister, implicit in having a place in the Shadow Cabinet, must have played some part in his decision. A man who has been regarded as merely a destructive critic is likely to welcome the opportunity to show himself capable of constructive achievement. As Nye Bevan's friend and biographer, Michael knew how happy Bevan had been to become Minister of Health in 1945.

In the circumstances of 1970, there was a particular reason why Michael should wish to have a share in the party leadership. As he saw it, one of the worst disasters of the recent period was the open antagonism between the political leadership and the trade unions, and one of the most urgent necessities was to heal the breach. Never again, he believed, should the National Executive (with its union majority) find itself obliged to oppose the policies of a Labour government, as on the issue of *In Place of Strife*. Early in 1971, Jack Jones proposed the creation of a Labour Liaison Committee with six members each from the Shadow Cabinet, the National Executive and the TUC. When it was set up, the two leading figures in its deliberations and decisions were Jones and Michael Foot. The task of the moment was to fight the new Industrial Relations Bill introduced by the Tories, which perpetuated the worst features of Barbara Castle's bill and added others yet more objectionable; the long-term task was to chart the trade union legislation that might be adopted by the next Labour government. In these endeavours, Michael's role was central. It was true to say, in fact, that his main reason for seeking a position in the Shadow Cabinet was 'the estimate which he made of his own potential value as a stabilising factor inside the Labour Party'.[7]

Still, his appearance in this new role evoked some surprise and amusement even among those who understood his motives. When he made his first speech from the front bench, one journalist, Terence Lancaster of the *People*, commented: 'It was as if Mrs Mary Whitehouse had turned up in the cast of "Oh, Calcutta!".' Michael himself appreciated the irony and referred, in his opening words, to 'the novel situation in which I find myself'.[8]

When the responsibilities were allocated, he emerged as Opposition spokesman on fuel and power. It was not the job that he would have selected had he been given an unlimited choice, but he was content with it and well equipped for it. He was responsible for coal and steel, the two industries that were the life-blood of Ebbw Vale, and of which he had amassed considerable knowledge since 1960. Both were in need of defence. Although oil had not yet been discovered under the North Sea, there was strong pressure to turn to imported oil as the fuel of the future (its share in supplying Britain's energy needs had risen from 10 per cent to 44 per cent in the last twenty years) with the corollary of a cut-back in coal production. Michael asserted: 'In the past three or four years we've probably closed a hundred pits which should not have been closed.'[9] As for steel, one of the Heath government's first actions was to cripple the projected expansion of the industry by reducing investment grants.

One sacrifice that Michael had to make in his new role as a departmental spokesman was that he could no longer address the House on concerns of his own choice. He was able, however, to speak on an issue of individual human rights because it arose from a case which he had taken up as a back-bencher before the change of government. Rudi Dutschke, a young leader of a far-left group in West Germany, had suffered severe brain damage after being shot by a political enemy. Michael had sponsored his admission to Britain with the promise that he would not involve himself in British politics. Permission had been granted by Callaghan as Home Secretary and renewed by his Tory successor, Reginald Maudling. Both assured Michael that they saw no barrier to Dutschke's presence on security grounds. Now, however, Maudling accused Dutschke (without producing any evidence) of breaching the conditions and ordered his deportation. It was the old libertarian Michael Foot who delivered an indictment of Maulding on 19 January 1971:

> [The government are] guilty of the gravest possible deception and bad faith . . . They have committed an outrageous defamation of character against Mr Dutschke . . . If this kind of definition of British freedom had been applied in the nineteenth century, not only Karl Marx would have been excluded . . . but Mazzini, Garibaldi, Kossuth and Alexander Herzen would have been excluded . . . It is my belief that, thanks to the folly and worse with which the right honourable gentleman has dealt with this case, the name of Rudi Dutschke will be added to those famous names.

The philippic was in vain. On the motion for the adjournment, Maudling put up an unconvincing case but could rely on solid support from the Tory ranks. Dutschke left Britain for Denmark, where he died some years later.

2

Describing Michael's debut as a front-bencher, Terence Lancaster reported that he spoke 'corrosively, amusingly and passionately without a note'. Some of those who knew him doubted whether he could adapt his style as a back-bencher, dealing mainly in ideas and principles, to the necessity of mastering facts and details. But his excellent memory, combined with his gift for picking out essentials, came to his aid, and his oratorical talent did the rest. Barbara Castle, who had been a front-bencher for years, was impressed:

> I watched his technique with admiration tinged with envy. He would walk into the chamber whenever he had time to spare, picking up on his way in a copy of the document that was being debated. He would read it quickly as he sat on the bench, listen to a few speeches, and then join in with some penetrating analytical point. The technique worked.[10]

The stage was set for a battle between the Heath government and the miners. The NUM had put in a claim for a 10 per cent wage increase, barely enough to keep pace with rising prices, and held a strike ballot when it was rejected. There was a 55 per cent vote for strike action, but no strike ensued because the union rules required a two-thirds majority. Soon, the rules were amended to make a 55 per cent majority sufficient. Michael said: 'The country has just escaped by the narrowest margin what would undoubtedly have been a catastrophe.' Praising 'the superhuman restraint and patience on the part of the miners', he pointed out that measures introduced by the government – higher Health Service charges, higher payments for school meals, higher rents due to cuts in subsidies and the withholding of sickness benefit for the first three days – were in effect deductions from the earnings of miners and other workers. 'I sometimes wonder', Michael went on, 'whether honourable members opposite really have any understanding of what hot industrial fires they are playing with . . . What they speak for is a narrow, blinkered suburban England with no conception whatever of industrial Britain.' In another speech, on 3 December, he warned: 'We are in for fierce and angry times in this country.'

His first task was to deal with the government's Coal Industry Bill. It was not an occasion for outright opposition, because such bills – drafted by civil servants and more or less uncontroversial – were introduced every four or five years to equip the National Coal Board with borrowing powers and to authorise social benefits. A bill introduced by the Labour government had fallen when the election came, and Michael argued that the new government ought to have taken it over. Instead, they produced a bill – 'hastily concocted', Michael said – which repeated some of the same provisions but included new ones. Michael, therefore, had the tricky and laborious job of accepting some clauses, opposing others and monitoring the bill as it went through the committee procedure. He fought most energetically against provisions for 'hiving off' – an early form of privatisation – which required the Coal Board to divest itself of assets (of course, profitable assets such as pubs and hotels) which it had built up. 'One would have thought,' he remarked, 'that members opposite would congratulate the board on having the spirit and adventure to go in for these activities.'

In the debates, he had vocal assistance from twenty-seven-year-old Neil Kinnock, who had been elected in 1970 as MP for Bedwellty, a mining constituency bordering on Ebbw Vale. Angered by the Tory insistence on pushing the bill through without concessions, and without regard for the feelings of the people whom it would affect, Kinnock declared: 'Democracy will have to tread water until the next general election, when I hope the party opposite will be drowned.' Michael noted that his young follower shared his gift for the vivid phrase.

When the next session began in October 1971, Wilson shifted Michael to the position of Shadow Leader of the House. It was only a year since he had emerged from the back benches; clearly, his star was rising. He would be able to uphold the rights of the Opposition against any inroads by the Tories, and also to safeguard the regime of tolerance among Labour MPs that Crossman had introduced. But his main duty was to oppose the government's bill providing for British entry into the European Community.

It was Britain's third try. Heath had conducted the negotiations in the first attempt, in 1962, and believed that he had made fair headway until de Gaulle's veto. Unlike some Tories, he was devoted neither to the fading glories of empire nor to partnership with the United States; he was a dedicated 'European' and determined to succeed in his aim. De Gaulle had passed from the scene; the new President of France, Georges Pompidou, was a banker by profession, a pragmatist by temperament and a man who thought along the same lines as Heath. He soon announced that there would be no French veto if Britain applied again. In December 1969, the Community invited four prospective joiners – Britain, Ireland, Denmark and Norway – to open negotiations. All, including Britain under the Wilson government, accepted the invitation.

Wilson was in an awkward position. He could scarcely decline to negotiate, having attempted to join the Community in 1967 (though Brown had been the real enthusiast). On the other hand, he was anticipating an election campaign and did not want to appear more eager than his Tory opponents. He managed, indeed, to appear less eager, and in one speech he accused Heath of 'rolling over like a spaniel' at any approach from the foreigners. His formal position – and it was Heath's formal position too – was that everything would depend on the terms that could be obtained. Generally, the Labour Party tried to play down the issue. Of all Labour candidates, fewer than a quarter even mentioned it in their election addresses, and most of these adopted the formula 'if the terms are right'. A mere half-dozen came out in favour of entry on principle, and about fifty came out against. One of these was Michael, who told the voters of Ebbw Vale:

I oppose Britain's entry into the rich nations' club, sometimes called the Common Market . . . In the interests of British democracy, of the health of our economy; in the interests of Wales and our fight against a return of unemployment; in the interests of a wider peace in Europe and links with countries in the Commonwealth, I believe Britain should keep out of this narrowly conceived, Little-European Common Market.

This enabled him to say, when the parliamentary debate opened: 'When I stand here and say I am opposed to entry into the Common Market, I am saying exactly what I said at the election.'

While the 'terms' formula owed something to political strategy, there were many difficulties standing in the way of agreement. Among the problems were Britain's financial contribution, the danger to imports from the Commonwealth (notably Caribbean sugar and New Zealand lamb), the prospect of dearer food arising from the Common Agricultural Policy, and the alien system of value-added tax. Michael said in the debate:

This House and the British people will have less power to protest against VAT than John Hampden had to protest against ship-money . . . The end of the era of cheap food is no small incident in British history, even if the leader of the Liberal Party is not prepared to shed a single tear at the abandoned tomb of Richard Cobden. The instinct of the British people in these matters, particularly when it is sustained in the teeth of persistent opposition and propaganda from the main organisations and newspapers in the country, is not to be despised.[11]

Negotiations between the Heath government and the Community went smoothly and led to a Treaty of Accession, signed in May 1971. The terms involved an acceptance of the Community's established policies but eased the process by providing for a gradual transition. As Barbara Castle saw, Wilson's difficulties were far from over: 'Harold was in a trap . . . Harold knew he would have accepted the terms if they had been offered him . . . Harold, however, was well aware that a majority of Labour MPs and almost certainly the Shadow Cabinet were opposed to membership. So was a majority of the unions.'[12]

The party conference in October voted heavily for opposition and the PLP endorsed this line. Wilson's reason for entrusting the task of parliamentary opposition to Michael – rather than to Denis Healey, the Shadow Foreign Secretary, who had no strong feelings on the issue – was sensible enough. If the treaty was to be fought, it had better be fought by someone who could do it with conviction and relish, and whose record was consistent.

In reality, few people were making a judgement based on the terms. The leading figures in the Labour Party were either for or against the Common Market as a matter of principle, and in many cases very passionately. For Peter Shore, for Douglas Jay and by this time for Michael too, the prospect that the will of the British government and the British Parliament could in future be overridden by the Community was abhorrent. It would, Michael said, 'take away powers this House has had ever since it was founded, indeed almost since the Witenagemot'. But, for others, it was just this drastic change that opened the way to a splendid opportunity – a structure of European unity and co-operation that would make traditional sovereignty an anachronism.

This group included several who had held office in the Wilson government: Anthony Crosland, Harold Lever, Cledwyn Hughes, Shirley Williams. She, in particular, had earned golden opinions because of her concern for world poverty and her loathing for South African apartheid; but if she was passionate and uncompromising about apartheid, she was the same about Europe. Above all, there was Roy Jenkins, former Home Secretary, former Chancellor, and now deputy leader of the party. Jenkins was not by nature an intolerant or dogmatic man, but on this issue he had no time for anyone who disagreed with him. One observer noted that Michael 'can enter with far more charity into the spirit of Roy Jenkins' beliefs about Europe than Jenkins can enter into his'.[13] Michael decided, at the opening of the 1971–2 session, to stand against Jenkins for the deputy leadership. The same observer recorded: 'He required much persuasion – and a stern emphasis on his duty – before he put himself forward.' But it seemed to him wrong that a man who took a dissenting view on this major issue should hold second place in the party. He knew, no doubt, that he had no chance in the contest. Still, since the reason for the contest was the European issue, he did better than he might have at other times, scoring 96 votes against Jenkins' 140.

Michael Foot and Roy Jenkins had enough in common to be good friends. They were both well qualified in the literary and historical domain; Jenkins was the biographer of Sir Charles Dilke, an intriguing Victorian personality, and of Asquith. Michael had admired his record at the Home Office and his libertarian outlook. Yet they had little rapport and little instinctive sympathy. Jenkins' origins were in a South Wales mining valley, but they were origins that meant little to him and to which he was disinclined to return. He had moved away from the world into which Michael had enthusiastically entered.

The first important, though not necessarily decisive, vote on the great issue came on 28 October 1971. While a few Tories voted against the government (there were divisions in both parties) no fewer than sixty-nine Labour MPs, led by Jenkins, voted with the government, and another twenty abstained. Michael was shocked. He had spoken and voted as a rebel against the Labour leadership often enough; but it had always been against a policy, such as German rearmament or nuclear weapons, supported by the Tories too. 'I can't ever recall', he said, 'that I went into the lobbies to help a Tory government.'[14]

Nevertheless, he recognised the seriousness – and indeed the idealism, though the ideals ran counter to his own – of the attitude maintained by the Jenkins group. He said in the next debate: 'I understand the passions, the strength of feeling of honourable members in all parts of the House and in different parties . . . Of course these convictions are strong . . . They have been honestly – and I don't say this in a patronising sense – honestly and sincerely expressed.'[15]

The Tories, naturally, made capital out of the switch performed by Wilson and most of the prominent Labour leaders since 1967. Michael dealt with this easily and cheerfully. Recalling that neither Churchill nor Lloyd George had been noted for 'inflexible allegiance to the ideas he had first thought of', he commented:

> Whatever accusations can be made against me – and I daresay there are many – I do respect the House of Commons and I respect the fact that politicians have to change their minds . . . We must be a little charitable and understanding in these matters . . . I am in the happy position that I agree with my party, or perhaps I can say that my party agrees with me.[16]

The Labour strategy was to attack Heath for his reliance on his parliamentary majority to commit Britain to this historic change. In an unguarded moment during the 1970 election campaign, Heath had said that entry into the Community would require the 'full-hearted consent of the British parliament and people'. Actually, the Tories had won an election in which Europe was never a central issue, in which few candidates took an unambiguous stand and in which Tory policy was limited to negotiation. Now that the terms of entry were known, opinion polls showed a majority (though narrow and fluctuating) against going in. Clearly, no claim of full-hearted consent was credible. Michael pointed out: 'Some of us believe, especially in a world where so many nations tremble on the verge of violence, that government by consent is the most sacred cause of all.'

Labour's demand was that another general election should be held so that the people could endorse or reject the government's decision to take Britain into the Community. Obviously, however, the Tories were not inclined to put at risk the power which they had held for less than two years. Another idea was advanced: a referendum.

The originator of this idea was Tony Benn (he was divesting himself of the appellation of Anthony Wedgwood Benn). It was, in the first place, a political device; he told the Shadow Cabinet: 'This is one way in which the Labour Party can avoid dividing itself into bits.' Callaghan saw the point and remarked: 'Tony may be launching a little rubber life-raft which we will all be glad of in a year's time.'

Benn had been against joining the Community in 1967, but was now in favour of it. He was impressed by a talk with Giorgio Amendola, the Italian Communist leader, who argued that 'it was necessary to have some machinery at the Continental level to deal with international companies'. Benn recorded: 'I strongly agreed with him, whereas Peter Shore's argument is that it would be disastrous and set back socialism and so forth.'[17]

Both Michael and Peter Shore felt that a demand for a referendum would be a diversion from pressure for an election. On 28 April 1971, when Benn proposed that the referendum should be Labour policy, he failed to get a seconder in the Shadow Cabinet. With characteristic persistence, he commented: 'That was very surprising but it encouraged me to go forward to an appeal to the country and to the Party.'

Attitudes on the left were coloured by suspicion of the referendum (or, in earlier terminology, the plebiscite) as a stratagem to stampede the voters and undermine democratic debate.[18] Nevertheless, a referendum on a specific question was a regular procedure in, for example, Australia and California – states which were perfectly democratic. Churchill had suggested a referendum twice: in 1910 on the issue of female suffrage (of course, the voters in the referendum would have been men) and in 1945 on the continuance of the coalition government. But the most influential factor in bringing about a change of attitude was that, in 1972, the other applicants for Community membership held referenda. The result was a Yes majority in Ireland and Denmark and a No majority in Norway, which therefore stayed out. This left Britain as the only nation settling the issue without popular consultation. There was even a referendum in France on the desirability of enlarging the Community. It did seem absurd that the French should be voting on whether to let Britain in while the British could not vote on whether to go in.

In March 1972, Benn's proposal that the referendum should be party policy was carried, by narrow majorities, first in the NEC and then in the

Shadow Cabinet. It was 'a tremendous victory', he wrote triumphantly in his diary. Michael then urged the PLP to endorse the idea, and it did so by a majority of 129 to 96.

By this time, Michael was in the thick of the fight against the European Communities Bill, the parliamentary instrument for British member-ship. The outcome was unpredictable. Some Tories – the leading figures were Enoch Powell and Neil Marten – were so bitterly opposed to the sacrifice of British sovereignty that they voted with the Labour Party. Thus the nominal Tory majority did not suffice to get the bill through the House and Heath had to rely on the support of the Liberals. On some occasions, the government would have been defeated but for abstentions by Jenkins and his friends.

As the House began to plod through the clauses of the bill, Michael warned: 'We propose to use our parliamentary rights to the limit to ensure that these matters are properly discussed.' He held out the prospect of 'a whole variety of amendments . . . amendments to mitigate the disaster'. Once again, as in the fight against the Parliament Bill, he made ingenious use of his knowledge of procedure, contested every inch of the ground and baffled the less erudite on the green benches with a multiplicity of points of order. Once again, Powell helpfully intervened as a convergent ally. In the course of nine days in early March, the name of Michael Foot can be found forty-three times in the index to Hansard. It took the government five months to get the bill through, and there was a real possibility that it would, like the Parliament Bill, be throttled because progress could not be completed by the end of the session. To avert this disaster, the Tory whips had to fall back on enforcing the guillotine, which Michael of course denounced as 'a scandalous way for a bill of this importance to be pushed through'.

A clause envisaging future progress towards economic and monetary union was challenged because there had been no advance warning of its 'far-reaching character'. A clause authorising co-operation in defence was fought because it covered nuclear weapons which, Michael said, 'can be wielded only by dictatorial action'. There was resistance to the adoption of European rules on the steel industry, the coal industry and the film industry, and Michael was able to deploy his knowledge of all these industries – 'I agree that some of the finest films ever produced have come from Italy, Germany and France.' There were objections to the require-ment that Community documents had to be written in a Community language – the objection being that Welsh was not listed among the languages.

Altogether, there were ninety-six divisions, and on fifty-six occasions the government's majority was under twenty. The critical day (or rather night) was 3 May, when the majority in successive votes went down to four and six. Michael demanded a statement by Heath, but he did not rise. Michael taunted him mercilessly:

It's very rarely that the Prime Minister has dared to show his face during these debates . . . We know that the Prime Minister becomes especially testy and incoherent . . . but would it not be in order to ask this singularly ill-tempered Prime Minister, who dare not state his case properly, to pluck up his courage, stand on his own two feet, and say what the intentions of the government are as the bill, even under a guillotine, has no majority?

Thanks to the guillotine, the bill reached its Third Reading on 13 July. Michael kept up the attack on Heath to the last: 'The Prime Minister once said that he would ask the people for their consent. He has never done that. It is that prolonged and malicious deceit which will lie for ever on his conscience. It is that deceit which will destroy him and any of those who hope to sustain it.' The bill was carried by a majority of 17 votes, and on 1 January 1973 Britain formally became a member of the European Community. But the popular mood, as a historian comments, was 'coloured by fateful resignation rather than passionate enthusiasm'.[19]

One legacy of the episode was the opening of a gulf, and potentially a split, in the Labour Party. Tony Benn noted presciently that the Jenkins group 'really represents a new political party under the surface in Britain'. In April 1972, Jenkins resigned from the deputy leadership and two of his allies from the Shadow Cabinet.

Among the party rank and file, there was considerable anger against the MPs who had blunted the attack on Heath and, at least on one unforgotten occasion, voted with the Tories. There were demands that these MPs should submit themselves to the hazards of a new selection conference. Such demands, though advanced with arguments of democratic principle, won no sympathy from Michael. The principle that he chose to uphold was the right of the MP to defend an unpopular position and stand by his convictions. Besides, Michael hated anything in the nature of a witch-hunt. He went out of his way to speak in the constituencies of some threatened MPs and extend his protection to them.

After Jenkins' resignation, Michael again stood for the deputy leadership. Since he had earned widespread applause for his waging of the battle in the House, he might well have been elected had he been endorsed by the leader. Wilson, however, chose to support Edward Short, a colourless but conscientious toiler in the political vineyard. As no one particularly disliked Short, he won the contest. Michael was safely re-elected to the Shadow Cabinet, and at the party conference he stood for the NEC in the constituency section and topped the poll. Thus he took his seat in the party's governing body for the first time since he had left it in 1950.

The government was offering plenty of opportunities for the kind of fierce and combative opposition at which Michael excelled. The Toryism of the 1970s, breaking away from the conciliatory policies that had been followed between 1951 and 1964, veered sharply towards the rigidities of monetarism. Accepted welfare systems were imperilled; the Secretary for Education, Margaret Thatcher, earned the nickname of 'milk snatcher' by abolishing free milk in secondary schools. Industries that failed to show a profit were condemned as 'lame ducks' and allowed to close down. Unemployment rose in 1972 to what was then regarded as the appalling total of one million. Yet Heath was reluctant to go too far in this direction. Despite the 'lame ducks' rhetoric, the government rescued Rolls-Royce when it was in trouble and ended up with an expanded public sector. Even a sit-in by Communist shop stewards at the bankrupt Upper Clyde Shipbuilders led to the reconstruction of the yard with a subsidy of £35 million. The Prime Minister was beginning to reveal the lineaments of the future 'wet' and enemy of Thatcherism. Jack Jones found that 'he revealed a human face of Toryism . . . Amazingly, he gained more personal respect from union leaders than they seemed to have for Harold Wilson or even Jim Callaghan.'[20] Jones concluded: 'No Prime Minister, either before or since, could compare with Ted Heath in the efforts he made to establish a spirit of camaraderie with trade union leaders.'[21]

These contradictions were most glaring in the sphere of industrial relations. The Industrial Relations Act of 1971, bitterly opposed by the unions, set up a special court which could order a return to work, impose fines or rule that defiant unions or individual workers were in contempt of court. The unions – especially the TGWU and the Engineers, led respectively by Jack Jones and Hugh Scanlon – refused to attend the court's hearings.

In this already tense situation, the government found itself faced with the challenge of which Michael had warned in 1970: a national coal strike. Partly as a result of the disappointment of that year, the National Union of Mineworkers was under militant leadership. The President, Joe Gormley, was a Labour moderate in political outlook, but the vice-president, the Scottish miners' leader Mick McGahey, was a Communist, while the general secretary, Lawrence Daly, was a former Communist associated with the Labour left. When the National Coal Board rejected a demand for a wage increase of 8 per cent, a ballot produced an effective majority for a strike, and the pits closed down, in exceptionally severe winter weather, on 9 January 1972.

The government declared a state of emergency, a move that seemed to indicate determination to use all possible means to defeat the strike. The crucial factor was the supply of coal to power stations. Power cuts for three-hour periods hurt the average citizen more than they intimidated the miners; dinners were spoilt, families sat huddled under blankets, television was silenced, traffic was paralysed when the lights went out. Meanwhile, the power stations were blockaded by what was then the novel strategy of mass picketing. A young Yorkshire miner, Arthur Scargill, acquired instant heroic (or demonic) status by leading a column which closed the gates of a coke depot in Birmingham. The Chief Constable wisely decided not to send in the police. When the strike had lasted for over a month, the government set up a committee of inquiry under a judge. It awarded the miners a substantial increase and they won further concessions by staying on strike for two more weeks.

Victory was complete, and so was the humiliation of the Heath government. The strike had the sympathy of the great bulk of the organised working class (the mass picket was mainly drawn from engineers and other Birmingham workers, with a small vanguard of miners) and indeed of many middle-class people who were shocked to learn that miners were earning less than hotel porters or taxi-drivers. The machinery of the Industrial Relations Act was shown to be irrelevant; it did nothing to avert the strike, to stop the picketing (strictly illegal though it was) or to promote a settlement. The court of inquiry was transparently a device to get the government off the hook on terms that might have been conceded in the first place, with the saving of a vast amount of inconvenience and economic loss.

Another humiliation followed within six months. Dockers belonging to the TGWU were picketing the Midland Cold Store in east London with the aim of ensuring that work in the new container depots was covered by the union agreements established in the ports. The owners secured an order to ban the picketing, it was defied, and five men were arrested and taken to Pentonville prison. The next day, dockers all round the coast stopped work, workers in various other industries came out too, and the printers halted the national newspapers. On the verge of the greatest industrial conflict since 1926, a functionary called the Official Solicitor, of whom few people had ever heard, intervened and got the men released on a technicality. Once again, the Industrial Relations Act was proved to be useless and provocative, while Heath was seen to have stumbled into a battle he could not win.

Jack Jones and Hugh Scanlon, as the leaders of the largest and most powerful trade unions, were the prime targets of newspapers like the *Daily Mail* and the *Daily Express*. They were the 'terrible twins' – a pair of marauding chieftains, selfish and grasping, wielding the power of a sectional interest, indifferent to the higher national interest and especially to the containment of inflation. They were blamed – though the TUC and the union movement in general were also blamed – for the rejection of overtures from the government which envisaged a formal pact of wage restraint. They were not, in fact, opposed on principle to some kind of deal, but they maintained that it should cover a wide range of other considerations: welfare benefits, pensions, rents, control of prices, the impact of EC membership, and – most important – incomes other than working-class wages. Trade unionists argued that 'incomes policy' should not be a mere euphemism for wage control, and that the earnings of factory workers or bus-drivers should not be held down while those of company directors, barristers or surgeons rose freely. In the course of discussions, Jones got the impression that some such wide-ranging agreement was feasible, until Heath unexpectedly stated that these other matters were outside the scope of negotiation. Presumably, he could not carry his Cabinet colleagues with him. Agreement on these lines would have to await the arrival of the next Labour government.

The government had now lost all sense of direction. The Chancellor, Anthony Barber, adopted a policy of reflation designed to start a 'Barber boom', but it was febrile and insecure from the start. Inflation and unemployment were both higher than at any time since the war. In the House, Michael said derisively that 'everything in the garden would be looking lovely were it not for the earthquake'. He could not foresee the scale of the earthquake that Britain – and the whole capitalist world – experienced in October 1973, but his choice of words indicates his intuitive sense of the widening faults and fissures.

3

The second volume of Michael's biography of Aneurin Bevan was ready for publication at last. Although it ran to 659 pages, he felt that some valuable detail had been omitted and cursed as he struggled to condense his material – the unavoidable ordeal of a biographer. Since the publication of volume one, the firm of MacGibbon and Kee had been bought by the Granada combine, and Reg Davis-Poynter had started his own imprint. Loyal to his friend as usual, Michael entrusted volume two to the firm of Davis-Poynter. The sales – about 10,000 – were good for an expensive hardback, but smaller than those of volume one: perhaps because Bevan had been dead for thirteen years, perhaps because the autumn of 1973, when the book was published, was the time of the economic earthquake.

Now that the biography was complete, in two substantial volumes, it was hailed by general (if not quite universal) consent as a triumphant achievement. Reviewers could hardly fail to appreciate the narrative sweep, the quality of the writing and above all the sympathetic – almost empathetic – understanding of Nye Bevan's actions and reactions. Thanks to countless hours of close observation and intimate talks since 1937, and thanks to his own knowledge of the environment of the South Wales valleys, Michael was qualified beyond challenge to portray and interpret the man Aneurin Bevan.

Argument focused, and can still focus today, on whether or not the book was flawed by Michael's determination to come to Nye's defence in each and every context. Given that the biography was the work of a lifelong friend and ardent admirer, this question was bound to arise. The attacks on Nye in his lifetime had been so malicious, and often so obtuse and stupid, that the impulse to defend was natural. A tactful silence regarding Nye's faults was also natural (especially as Jennie was very much alive) but in later perspective it appears more dubious. The real Nye Bevan was over-hasty in making his decisions, brutally sharp with his tongue, inconsiderate towards his political associates and allies, reluctant to listen to other opinions or engage in discussion of his strategy and averse to self-criticism. All this was known to anyone who had been a Bevanite, and certainly to Michael, but there is little hint of it in the biography. For example, the speech in which Bevan described the Tory Party as 'lower than vermin' was explained (as indeed it can be explained) by reference to his memories of the depression years. But, in several pages on the episode, Michael never admitted that it was a rash outburst, nor that it was a gift to the Labour Party's enemies.

Of course, many readers turned eagerly to the debate on the H-bomb at the 1957 party conference, because it was the sole example of divergence between Bevan and his follower on a major issue. Michael did not try to gloss over the disagreement, nor did he conceal his view that Bevan's speech was gratuitously wounding and politically suicidal: 'He could be possessed by Lloyd George's terrible urge to claw down an enemy and on this occasion the enemy was his friends.'[22] The chapter was written with great care and scrupulous honesty, and not without emotional travail. One cannot read it without being aware of the pain that Michael endured during the episode, of his ineradicable affection for Nye and of the strain imposed on that affection.

The closing pages, which described Nye's illness and death, are surely among the most moving to be found in any biography. Nothing could be added to the sentence: 'He was like a great tree hacked down, wantonly, in full leaf.' As one closes the book, one is left in lingering meditation on the words on the last page:

> When he died, no formal or forced note was heard. The nation expressed its sense of loss unfeignedly, spontaneously, without restraint . . . It was, maybe, a sense of national guilt; a belief that he had been cheated of his destiny, that some part of his greatness had been shamefully thrown away; an awareness that he had had much to say to our perplexed, polluted world, and that we had listened only fitfully.[23]

There are in existence many inscribed copies of the book – inscribed by Michael for his friends and for old friends of Nye Bevan, or simply for people who bought the book and requested the author's signature. One copy is inscribed: 'To Abu, on the first of many visits to India.' The recipient was Abu Abraham,[24] a cartoonist whose work was rated highly by Michael, if not placed in quite the same class as that of Low and Vicky. Abu had spent several years in London, had made his debut on *Tribune* and had then been recruited by the *Observer*. After returning to his native country, he worked for the largest national newspaper, the *Indian Express*. It was in Delhi, in September 1973, that Michael and Abu met again.

Michael's sympathy for India dated back to his Oxford days, his membership of the India League and his friendship with Krishna Menon. When India became independent, Menon was the first High Commissioner in London. The Nehru policy of non-alignment was warmly praised by Bevan, by *Tribune* and by Michael. Bevan was twice invited to India, in 1953 and 1957, and greatly enjoyed his visits (for some reason, Jennie did not go with him on either occasion). As the inheritor of Bevan's mantle, Michael was pressed to visit India too, but he was averse on principle to the 'freebie' trips of which most MPs happily availed themselves. Eventually, the Deputy High Commissioner, Krishna Rasgotra, persuaded him to go as a member of what was called a delegation. The travellers were a party of four: Michael, Jill, Jennie Lee and a Labour MP named Michael English. They were in India for three weeks, arriving in New Delhi but then going as far north as Kashmir and as far south as Madras. Michael and Jill were instantly fascinated by India – by the magnificent artistic heritage, by the colour and liveliness of the streets and bazaars, by the warm and yet informal hospitality and by the level of intellectual conversation. Jill, moreover, was an admirer of the best of Indian films and, recalling her interest in town planning, was impressed with what she saw in the company of Indian architects.

However, the world's largest democracy had been going through anxious times. Indira Gandhi, Prime Minister since 1965, was faced in 1970 with a rebellion by some of her senior ministers and lost control of her party machine. The Indian National Congress split into the Congress (R), for 'ruling', and the Congress (O), for 'organisation'. After a time, the former was restyled as the Congress (I), for Indira. Indira herself campaigned on the slogan *Garibi Hatao* – 'Quit poverty', an echo of the 'Quit India' demand aimed in her youth at the British rulers. The slogan had about as much practical effect as Harold Wilson's 'white heat of technology' rhetoric, but it had an inspirational appeal for India's long-suffering millions.

In 1971, Indians were outraged by a reign of terror in what was then East Pakistan. The Indian Army was sent in, and a victorious campaign ended in securing the independence of the region with the new name of Bangladesh. Michael's memories of this event were poignant. James Cameron, his best friend since Vicky's death, was travelling in a jeep when it was struck by a heavy lorry. The accident was uncannily similar to the crash in Herefordshire in 1963; broken legs and internal injuries forced Cameron to spend months in hospital. Unlike Michael, he did not have a naturally sturdy constitution. The Bangladesh war was his last assignment as a reporter, and he wrote as a commentator and columnist until he died in 1985. But the outcome of the war was a triumph for Indira Gandhi and served her politically as the Falklands war was to serve Margaret Thatcher. She followed up the military success with a landslide election victory. When Michael met her in her impressive residence at 1 Safdarjang Road, she was on top of the Indian world.

He had never met her before, but he was predisposed to like her, to admire her and to be on her side in any controversy. She was continuing the political tradition of her father, who had always been one of Michael's heroes. He had defined India on the morrow of independence as a 'secular, democratic and socialist state'; she endorsed and often repeated these ideals. 'Secular' implied impartiality and equal citizenship as between Hindus, Moslems, Sikhs and others, and Indira set her face against intolerance by the Hindu majority. In the international sphere, she was suspicious of Nixon's America, very hostile to South Africa and a champion of the interests of the Third World. At the Commonwealth conference in 1972, she had taken the lead in attacking Heath for his persistence in selling arms to South Africa. Thus there was hardly anything on which Indira Gandhi and her guests did not see eye to eye. Michael felt that she had the qualities and the vision required in the leader of a great nation. As the outcome of long private conversations, a real and warm friendship was forged.

Jill Foot has said that she never particularly wanted Michael to be leader of the Labour Party or Prime Minister, but she would have been very happy to see him as Foreign Secretary. The new nations of the former colonial world were assuming a growing importance in world affairs, and some of their Presidents or Prime Ministers were men who, as penurious exiles in the 1950s, had been made welcome in the *Tribune* office and given sympathetic publicity by the editor. If Michael had little of the direct knowledge of the Third World that had been accumulated by his brothers Mac and Dingle, his approach to its problems was based on a consistent internationalism. At times of crisis – Suez, notably – he had understood the costs of wantonly alienating Asian and African nations. At the personal level, to treat all human beings as equals and attach value to their ideas and opinions was for Michael an effortless impulse as much as a principle. The equipment may not have been complete, but it is impossible to think of any Foreign Secretary who has possessed so much of it.

Whether he was equally well qualified in relation to the developed world is more open to argument. He had not been to the United States for a long time and his contacts with American politicians or journalists were limited. He went to continental Europe mainly on holiday and followed the routine of any tourist; he was a poor linguist, and could barely follow a speech or read an article in French. Somehow, any European (or any American) would quickly identify him as a quintessentially English person. Certainly, he had no insular prejudices; he responded easily to European culture (Italian opera in particular) and his literary heroes included Montaigne and Heine; there were Europeans – Pierre Mendès-France and Willy Brandt, to mention only two – whom he admired without reservation. Yet it might not have been easy for him, as Foreign Secretary, to give full weight to the point of view of the representative of a European nation when it came into conflict with his own.

This was a sensitive problem for Michael at a time when he was leading the opposition to entry into the European Community. In newspaper shorthand, anyone who was against it could be labelled as a Little Englander. Moreover, there were some – including some on the left – on whom the cap fitted. The rhetoric at Labour conferences verged on the insular, even the xenophobic. 'Taking orders from Brussels' could be a code for 'taking orders from foreigners'. It was tempting to appeal to a deeply ingrained feeling that the British had always managed their affairs well enough without outside interference.

To complicate matters, most European socialists – and Michael was thoroughly in favour of co-operation with European socialists – were eager for Britain to enter the Community and could not understand why there should be any objections, other than from conservative patriots obsessed with national sovereignty. Michael often protested against the classification of 'pro-Europeans' and 'anti-Europeans', and maintained that he was as pro-European as anyone. He based his argument not on sovereignty but on democracy. He was defending the freedom of the British people and the rights of his beloved House of Commons. Yet it was fatally easy to be misunderstood or misrepresented. There was a note of exasperation in Michael's complaint: 'It is dangerous to set the cause of internationalism against the claims of freedom and democracy . . . It is so dangerous to set the cause of Europe against the cause of Parliament.'[25]

An important consideration was that Michael did not want Britain to be governed in exactly the same way as other European nations, even other democracies. The distinguishing features of the British system were the supremacy of Parliament, the firm distinction between government and Opposition and hence the clear-cut choice offered to the people at elections. Most European countries had a multiplicity of parties and a proportional electoral system. The voters could not give any single party a majority; every government had to be a coalition, produced by wheeler-dealing, bargaining and if necessary the sacrifice of policies embodied in election pledges. For Michael, Ramsay MacDonald's formation of a coalition government in 1931 was a betrayal, and the willingness of some Labour leaders to continue the coalition with Churchill in 1945 was a surrender to temptation. But a Britain locked into the Community structure might tend to adopt, or reflect, the political customs of its fellow-members; and coalition would surely be the mode of government in a federal Europe or super-state, into which the Community might develop. It was hard enough to uphold the claims of principle, and of socialist ideology, without going into a political structure that, by its nature, would suppress them.

It was a relief to turn from these complexities to a scene that offered a plain opposition between good and evil. In Spain, the Franco regime was still in power (though Franco himself was feeble and senile) and there was no relaxation in the persecution of socialists, or anyone else who could be charged with 'treason', an offence that carried a death penalty. Repression was directed with particular ferocity against trade unions, known as *comisiones obreros* (workers' commissions) which were gaining strength in industrial centres. In 1973, ten leaders of these officially illegal unions were put on trial. Most were Communists, but one was a worker–priest. The case evoked a response of solidarity in Britain, partly because four of the ten worked for British companies, including Rolls-Royce and Massey-Ferguson.

A Spanish Democrats' Defence Committee was founded on the initiative of three men who had all fought as volunteers in Spain in the Civil War and were now leading figures in the trade union world. Bob Edwards (not to be confused with the Bob Edwards who had edited *Tribune*) was general secretary of the Chemical Workers' Union and also a Labour MP; Jack Jones was general secretary of the TGWU; Will Paynter had recently retired from the secretaryship of the South Wales region of the Mineworkers. Paynter and Peter Archer, a Labour MP and lawyer who was active in Amnesty International, went to Madrid to attend the trial, accompanied by Jenny Little of the Labour Party's International Department. Their presence may well have saved the lives of the defendants, who were ultimately freed after Franco's death.

Michael too went to Madrid, travelling with Paynter and Jenny Little, who spoke fluent French and some Spanish. It was a fact-finding mission; they talked to the wives and families of men facing trial, to defence lawyers, to men who had been in the hands of the fascist police and could show the scars of torture, and also to militants of the underground Socialist Party; Michael had met its young leader, Felipe Gonzalez, who was in exile in France. The authorities of course knew of their presence, but they stayed at a small, cheap hotel to avoid constant surveillance and walked to appointments in outlying working-class districts. 'If anybody's following us, they're getting a good bit of exercise,' Michael remarked to Jenny. So far as they could see, there was no one on their heels. Still, the man in the rumpled English tweed jacket, swinging his stick as he strode along, could hardly have struck the casual eye as a typical Madrileno.

4

By 1973, the Labour Party was swinging strongly towards the left. The balance of forces in the party leadership had shifted, with Michael now on the inside to reinforce Barbara Castle and Tony Benn, and Roy Jenkins in eclipse. With another general election within sight, there was a rising determination that the next Labour government should not repeat the blunders and betrayals of 1964–70 and should effect real changes in British society.

The battleground, once again, was public ownership (or nationalisation). The policy statement drafted by the NEC for submission to the party conference called for public ownership of shipbuilding and the pharmaceutical industry (in bad odour after the thalidomide scandal) and for the creation of a National Enterprise Board which could progressively enlarge the public sector. The grass-roots support for such a policy was a matter of belief rather than evidence. A survey among members of the Kemptown (Brighton) Labour Party showed that only 14 per cent of them understood socialism to mean 'public ownership of production', while the majority interpreted it as 'a better standard of living for the working class'.[26] The activists, however, were several steps ahead of the ordinary members (let alone Labour voters) and it was Kemptown that tabled a resolution for the coming conference demanding the nationalisation of twenty-five of Britain's biggest private companies.

Wilson was becoming irritated with the process of policy-making by bodies – notably the Home Policy Sub-committee of the NEC – which he felt to be out of touch with political realities. 'Sub-committees and sub-sub-committees had produced grandiose proposals for nationalising anything and pretty nearly everything,' he grumbled.[27] He was particularly angry about the 'outlandish proposal,' as he called it, to take over twenty-five big companies simply because they were big. At a poorly attended meeting of the National Executive on 30 May, it was carried by 7 votes to 6. The majority included only two front-rank leaders or ex-ministers, Tony Benn and Judith Hart, while Callaghan, Healey, Shirley Williams and Michael Foot were in the minority. Next day, Wilson (who had not been at the meeting) announced flatly that he would veto it. Nevertheless, Benn brought it before the Shadow Cabinet a month later. According to his account, 'Michael said the twenty-five company proposal was crazy and he believed I had committed an error in submitting it.'[28] Benn went on to quote Michael as asking: 'Are you *really* going for the twenty-five companies? Do you think we could win the election? Do you *want* to win the election? What are you up to?' The proposal was now the subject of open controversy. *Tribune*'s argument was: 'Nothing could suit the Tories better than to confine the national debate about public ownership to the precise item of the twenty-five companies . . . The inclusion of the phrase was likely to combine the maximum of alarm with the minimum of real commitment.'[29]

In the end, the Kemptown resolution was lost in the compositing process and was never specifically put to the conference. But the press had enjoyed a field-day over the disagreement – or, in the inevitable headline language, 'split' – between the two men most prominently identified with the Labour left. The situation had its bizarre aspect, since Michael had been identified as a wild extremist for about twenty-five years, whereas Benn had been an amiable young man, dedicated to helpful compromise, until quite recently. However, the episode of the twenty-five companies changed all that for ever. The storm signal was a leader in the *Sunday Telegraph* headed 'BOLSHEVIK BENN'. Michael, speaking at the *Tribune* meeting on the fringe of the conference, declared that it would be a scandal if intolerance by Labour MPs caused Benn to lose his place in the Shadow Cabinet. As Benn put it: 'He put his protective cloak around me.'[30]

There certainly was a change in Tony Benn's political outlook, and correspondingly in his attitude to Michael. In 1972, he aligned himself with Michael in the defence of the British Parliament against subordination to the bureaucrats of Brussels. In 1973, he was ready to pass this verdict on Michael: 'He is an elitist parliamentarian . . . he's a parlour pink to this extent.'[31] A few months later, he made the accusation sharper: 'He is what the ultra-Left accurately call fake Left, is parliamentary-oriented, although he cultivates good relations with some individual trade union leaders.'[32] That might have been taken as a saving grace, but Benn added: 'Jack Jones has completely abandoned his serious left-wing position.'

Back in 1971, Benn had reflected in his diary on a dinner-table prediction by Jill Foot that either he or Peter Shore would be the next party leader.[33] Such a remark, however lightly made, was liable to bring out a hitherto unobserved streak in his character. Tony Crosland, who had known him since Oxford days in the late 1940s when one man was a lecturer and the other a student, said: 'No one doubts his sincerity in seeing himself as a Messiah.'[34] Michael, baffled by the change, wrote later: 'It was more, I believe, a psycho-analytical than a political problem.'[35] He added that the change did not come about overnight during the IMF crisis in 1976 – 'signs of it appeared much earlier.' As one examines the record, 1973 seems to be the year when Tony Benn started to compete with Michael Foot as the hero of the rank and file and the accredited champion of the left. A shrewd observer in that year might have placed a bet that, after the departure of the senior figures in the last Labour government, Benn (born 1925) might well ascend to the leadership, but Foot (born 1913) could have no such expectation. Of course, shrewd observers are not always right.

In any case, the enthusiasts of the left were in high spirits as they dispersed after the conference. The document entitled *Labour's Programme 1973*, adopted by acclamation, met their desires more fully than any manifesto since 1945. The only trouble was that it did not excite the electorate. On 8 November, four by-elections yielded undeniably bad results. A Liberal gain from the Tories at Berwick pushed Labour into third place. The Govan division of Glasgow, a safe Labour seat since 1935, was snatched by a Scottish Nationalist. Michael reacted defiantly, but anxiously: 'Nothing could be sillier or more discreditable than the advice offered by our opponents in the press and elsewhere – namely, that we should abandon our radical Socialist proposals because the electorate has not immediately voted for them. That would merely deepen the cynicism about politics and politicians generally which is our worst enemy.'[36]

At this point, both government and Opposition were in a bad way. The best that the Tories could hope for was to coast along, hoping that the 'Barber boom' would produce some results, and prepare for a general election in late 1974 or even 1975. Events outside their control denied them the chance. On 6 October – Yom Kippur, the Jewish Day of Atonement – Egyptian forces launched a surprise attack across the Suez canal, which had been the front line between them and the Israelis since the last war in 1967. After three weeks of desperate battles, mediation by the UN secured a ceasefire. Meanwhile, oil supplies from the Middle East were interrupted and prices rose three or four times over. To make matters worse, the Arab nations were infuriated because the Dutch, who had the world's biggest tanker port at Rotterdam, continued to supply oil to Israel, and declared an embargo on all exports from their oilfields. In Britain, in other West European countries and even in the United States, petrol stations were the scene of long queues, sometimes of fist-fights and of lamentations by car-owners who felt themselves to be the victims of a deprivation worse than famine. A considerable number of households relied on oil-fired central heating, and winter was coming on.

The grim prospect was that it might be a winter not only without oil but also without coal. The miners were demanding another substantial wage increase, but the government had now turned to a policy of statutory wage control with fixed upper limits, so the National Coal Board was debarred from making an acceptable offer. The union decided on an overtime ban, which came into effect on 12 November. As in 1972, the government declared a state of emergency. As in 1972, this did nothing to resolve the crisis.

In the hope of avoiding the power cuts which had caused so much dislocation and resentment in the previous strike, the government ordered a three-day week in industry, starting after the Christmas and New Year break. Manufacturing output did not fall – a reflection on the normal standards of British efficiency. Working-class earnings, however, were sharply reduced; thousands of families were trying to sell their cars or cancelling next summer's holiday. In an atmosphere of general uncertainty, curious shortages appeared, mostly caused by panic-buying; suddenly, the shops had no toilet-paper. There was talk of milk rationing because of a shortage of glass bottles. Petrol coupons were printed, but rationing never came into force.

The overtime ban did not bring victory for the miners, so the NUM held a ballot on strike action. It produced an 81 per cent vote in favour. For Heath, there was only one way out of his difficulties. He could not surrender to the miners without endangering his position as Tory leader, and he could not be confident of defeating them when the strike began. On 7 February 1974 he announced a general election, with polling on 28 February. In the campaign, he asserted that some of the NUM leaders were 'dedicated to destroy our society' and that 'the central issue is whether we are to have a government with the will and strength to see through the battle against inflation'. But he had neither the whole-hearted conviction nor the oratorical power to rally the middle classes against the strikers in Churchillian fashion, and he was still trying to find a formula that would enable the moderate NUM leaders, such as Gormley, to call off the strike. The Pay Board, which had been created in 1973 to vet wage demands, was instructed to inquire into the relative position of the miners in the earnings table. In a speech in Cardiff on 13 February, Heath declared that 'the road to peace is open' and asked: 'Why not call off the strike while you talk?' Gormley was tempted, but McGahey was insistent that the strike must be maintained until victory, while Daly reckoned that Labour was going to win the election and it was advisable to keep the strike going until a Labour government took office.

The outcome of the election was hard to predict, for the political situation had seldom been so fluid. The Liberals were on the upgrade and had won five by-elections since 1970. The nationalist parties of Scotland and Wales were also making headway, since demands for self-government or even independence had forced the government to set up a Royal Commission on possible constitutional change. Enoch Powell had refused – 'quixotically', Michael commented – to stand again for his safe seat in Wolverhampton as a Tory, and caused a sensation by urging all true patriots to vote for the Labour Party, the only party opposed to the Common Market. How many of his admirers would follow his advice, it was impossible to say.

There were fissures in the Labour Party too. Reg Prentice, the most right-wing member of the Shadow Cabinet, had made a speech after the 1973 conference attacking the new left-wing programme and calling for a mobilisation of those who were 'sincerely dedicated to the social-democratic traditions of the Labour Party'. He was unpopular with his own constituency party and there were moves to force him to resign his seat. Dick Taverne, MP for Lincoln, another right-winger and fervent European, had been refused readoption by his constituency party in 1973; he took the gamble of fighting a by-election as Democratic Labour candidate and won a resounding victory. He was, in fact, starting the Social Democratic Party eight years too early. In the general election, he inspired a friend to contest Bristol South-east as a Social Democrat, making a deliberate challenge to Tony Benn. Michael and Jim Callaghan both volunteered to go to Bristol and speak for Benn, while Neil Kinnock sent a team of miners from his constituency. As the main target of the hostile press, Benn had reason to be anxious. After a difficult day of canvassing, he 'came back absolutely persuaded that I would lose Bristol and that there would be a Tory landslide'.[37]

In the last week of the campaign, the Pay Board found that the position of the miners had been wrongly stated because of a miscalculation. Another discovery was that they were entitled to be paid for a daily forty minutes at the pithead bath, and never had been. It became clear that they would get an advantageous settlement after the election. But in the final days the election result looked like being extremely close, and it turned out to be not merely close but indecisive.

It was certainly no triumph for the Labour Party. With 11,654,000 votes, Labour polled 300,000 fewer than the Tories. Despite the larger population and the enfranchisement of the eighteen-year-olds, the total Labour vote was far short of the peak recorded in 1951. Still more serious was the drop in the share of the poll, which, at just over 37 per cent, was the lowest since 1931. A worried commentator warned: 'Accelerating decline, which has its own momentum, is a real possibility.'[38]

With a scattering of gains here and there, Labour emerged with 301 seats. The Tories, despite their marginally bigger vote, had 296. The winners were the Liberals – with fourteen seats, their best since before the war – and the nationalist parties. The Scottish National Party broke into the Commons with seven seats, while Plaid Cymru won two.

Michael's majority was down to 15,000, mainly because Ebbw Vale had a steadily shrinking electorate. Tony Benn, after all, increased his majority and the vote for the Social Democrat was derisory.

In a House of 635 members, neither of the main parties had an absolute majority. Heath was not constitutionally obliged to resign unless and until he was defeated in the Commons. His chances of retaining power depended on winning the support of the Liberals, and he spent the weekend negotiating with Jeremy Thorpe, the Liberal leader. Thorpe was inclined to make a deal, but most of his followers saw that they had no future as junior partners of the Tories. While they hesitated, the uncertainties of that weekend prolonged the uncertainties of the last three months. Heath was invisible in Downing Street, the Queen waited in Buckingham Palace and Wilson waited in Transport House.

It was in Transport House on the Monday afternoon, 4 March, that he had a significant conversation with Jack Jones (Transport House was also the TGWU office). Jones inquired, on the assumption that there would soon be a new Labour government, who would be Secretary for Employment. He was naturally concerned, because the man who had this responsibility in the Shadow Cabinet was Reg Prentice. His later account shows that he made his attitude very clear: 'I told Harold that the trade unions would not stand for Reg Prentice being made Secretary for Employment . . . We needed a man at the Employment post who was sympathetic to our views. We agreed that Michael Foot would be the ideal choice.'[39]

Michael, at the time of this conversation, was in another room working with Shirley Williams. They had been given the task of drafting a Labour Party statement demanding that Heath should reveal his intentions to the country. Before they had finished, news came that the Liberals had turned Heath down and he was on his way to the Palace to resign. Wilson went to the Palace at half-past eight in the evening. Four days had elapsed between the close of polling and the installation of the new Prime Minister – nothing in, for instance, Italy, but a highly unusual period in Britain.

Callaghan became Foreign Secretary, and Healey was Chancellor. Jenkins was Home Secretary, a traditionally senior ranking but not a position of power in modern politics. Barbara Castle, Secretary for Social Services, recorded: 'I feel supremely confident that I can do this job and I should have hated to be left out.'[40] Tony Benn was Secretary for

Industry, with Eric Heffer as his number two. Shirley Williams, who was very popular on the Labour benches and had come top in the last Shadow Cabinet election, was given the new post of Secretary for Prices and Consumer Protection. Michael duly became Secretary for Employment, and Prentice became Secretary for Education. On 5 March, the new ministers went to the Palace to kiss hands ('Wedgie and Mike looked as though they had been camping,' Barbara noted disapprovingly) and then to Downing Street for their first Cabinet meeting.

Although Michael's appointment as a Cabinet minister had been predictable since he had entered the Shadow Cabinet, it was a source of pleasure, not unmixed with bewilderment, for his friends. Alan Taylor sent a characteristic note: 'So Max was right after all. You have climbed to the top of the greasy pole or very near it.' Alan Brien wrote:

> I'd just like to say how cheered and thrilled I was at the appearance of you in a Labour Government . . . I have never felt so optimistic about the chances of Socialism in this country since I started to read the New Statesman at the age of 12. When was the last time there was a Labour tribune of the people in office who could be described, even by opponents, as 'transparently honest'? . . . For the many young people coming up, you are our great hope for democratic Socialism.

Chapter 11

DISSENTING MINISTERS

I

At the Department of Employment, then housed in St James's Square, the ministerial team consisted of Michael Foot as Secretary of State, Albert Booth as Minister of State and Harold Walker and John Fraser as under-secretaries. Booth and Walker were working-class northerners with a solid trade union background; Fraser, a solicitor, contributed the legal expertise that would be needed for new legislation. All three belonged to the left of the party, so Michael could count on general support for his policies. He held weekly meetings with them, without the presence of officials, at which they discussed the problems of the department and sometimes broader issues too.

Wilson had given his approval to an innovation imported from France: the appointment of political advisers to ministers, who would work in government departments and be paid from public funds but would not be civil servants. Tony Benn relied heavily on two advisers who shared his views, Frances Morrell and Francis Cripps; Barbara Castle's adviser was Jack Straw, who later succeeded her as MP for Blackburn. Michael did not feel the need for a political adviser, and did not appoint one.

Nor did he feel the need for a parliamentary private secretary, but he got one all the same. The status of a PPS is ill-defined; he or she continues to be a back-bencher and is not a member of the government, but is expected to refrain from opposing government policy. Ted Short, Leader of the House in the new government, invited Neil Kinnock to be his PPS. It is hard to imagine how the staid, cautious, generally right-wing Short would have got along with Kinnock, who was described in 1984 as 'emotional, impulsive, voluble, funny, informal'[1] and in 1974 was even more so. Hastily inventing a reason to decline, Kinnock said that he had agreed to be PPS to Michael, and Michael had to give him the job. Unsuited as he was to the role of discreet observer and confidant, Neil was once told by Michael that he was the worst PPS in history. Their friendship was uninjured, but it was a relief when, in June 1975, Neil found a good occasion for resignation by voting against increased allowances for the Royal Family. Michael then decided on reflection that it was quite useful to have a PPS and appointed Caerwyn Roderick, another left-winger from South Wales. Una Cocze continued as his secretary for constituency business.

Outside the ranks of politicians and civil servants, there was only one person from whom Michael sought help and advice. Bill Wedderburn, Professor of Commercial Law at the London School of Economics, was an authority on law as it affected trade unions and workers' rights. In 1973, he had been invited by the TUC to draft an industrial relations bill to replace the hated act of 1971. Now, with Labour in office and with the framing of such a bill as a priority, Michael asked Wedderburn to take a desk in the Department. Wedderburn felt that it would be hard to combine this with his work at LSE, so he did not officially take the job, but he was much involved in planning the legislation. As a 'Marxist intellectual' – Tory demonology always depicts LSE as a preserve of the far left – he conveniently fitted the role of Michael Foot's éminence grise.

The Permanent Secretary of Michael's department was Sir Conrad Heron, described by Barbara Castle as 'kindly, shrewd and above all knowledgeable'.[2] Next to him in the official hierarchy was the Deputy Secretary, Donald Derx. He was a youngish man, a meritocrat with a childhood on a council estate, intensely hard-working and energetic, and in Michael's opinion endowed with a brilliant brain. There were others whom Michael found entirely trustworthy and very congenial. In the Labour left, it was a deeply rooted belief (enunciated by Stafford Cripps in the 1930s) that a Labour government had to expect discouragement, foot-dragging or actual sabotage from the Civil Service. This was not Michael's experience. In his first speech from the Treasury Bench, he offered this accolade: 'One of the most valuable assets we have . . . is the experience, intelligence and I would say imagination of the Department of Employment.'[3]

The officials returned the compliment; in their opinion, Michael was a better and more effective minister than most of those they had known. He was clear about what he wanted to do, his sincerity was unquestionable, he listened attentively to suggestions but was never swayed from his basic purposes, and he did not waste time on battles with other departments. The fact that he had never held junior office, apparently a handicap, may well have worked to his advantage, for it freed him to adopt the methods that suited him best. He delegated work confidently; Walker, for instance, was put in charge of the field of industrial health and safety. Probably, Michael's working practices derived from his years as an editor; any editor has to say to a member of the staff: 'I'm leaving you to deal with the Middle East' (or whatever).

The first job was to bring the miners' strike to an end. At the first meeting of the new Cabinet on 5 March, Michael was given a free hand and Denis Healey urged that a settlement should be reached within twenty-four hours. The next morning, Michael's first appointment was with Gormley, Daly and McGahey. The problem was the cost of the settlement; the NUM's full demand would call for £138 million, while the recommendation of the Pay Board meant £98 million. Michael offered a wage increase costed at £103 million (contrary to later Tory accusations, he was not handing the miners a blank cheque). A worker at the coalface would be earning £45 a week, a good wage at 1974 money values, and the miners would be ahead of the industrial average for the first time. Moreover, the settlement was to cover a range of demands relating to holidays, sickness benefit and other matters. As MP for a mining constituency, Michael was well informed on these questions and could dispense with the explanations and the pondering that a new minister might have needed. A ballot of NUM members produced a big majority for acceptance, and the pits were working again the next week.

Although a substantial wage increase for the miners was both justified and inevitable, it was bound to give a push to inflation, Britain's most alarming problem. To make matters worse, the Heath government in 1973 had instituted a system of 'threshold payments'. If and when the retail price index crossed a threshold representing 7 per cent inflation, employed workers would automatically get a monthly wage increase to compensate them for each further 1 per cent rise in the index. The scheme might have worked in a period of moderate inflation, when the threshold would have been crossed rarely or even not at all. As it was, the world oil crisis opened the floodgates to unprecedented, dizzying inflation. The payments to millions of workers, including many who had never demanded a wage increase, added to production costs and made this inflation into a vicious circle. When Michael moved into St James's Square, inflation was running at an annual rate of 14 per cent and still rising.

The statutory incomes policy, since it could be abolished only by Parliament, was still in operation, and wage demands beyond the imposed limit were ruled out of court. However, the government was empowered to make exceptions in 'special cases'. The miners, of course, were the first special case, since the strike could not otherwise have been settled. In his first few months, Michael authorised 'special case' concessions for nurses (on the insistence of Barbara Castle, who was faced with staff shortages in hospitals), teachers and postmen. Also, any increase designed to equalise pay between men and women was permissible. All these increases were justified, but they necessarily contributed to inflation and aroused resentment among other workers who did not get the same exceptional treatment. The only solution was to abolish the whole Tory structure as quickly as possible.

In principle, this meant a return to free collective bargaining. But, in the face of runaway inflation, this could not be the last word. Labour's answer to the problem was the 'social contract', a strategy which envisaged that the unions would refrain from demands likely to stimulate inflation, in return for governmental actions beneficial to the working class. Unfortunately, this concept suffered from a certain lack of precision. There never was a contract in the sense of a document negotiated, written and signed, nor was anyone able to define the terms of agreement. Even the phrase 'social contract' had slipped imperceptibly into political parlance since 1972. Wilson had originally spoken of a 'social compact', and the notion of a contract arose from the suggestion of mutual obligations, or perhaps from subliminal memories of Rousseau's title. But the TUC, in a circular to affiliated unions, listed the understood pledges: better pensions, child benefit, price control and subsidies to hold down the rents of council houses and flats.

The difficulty was that these measures did not appeal equally to all concerned. Pensions were dear to the heart of Jack Jones (who, like Michael, was sixty) but were of less immediate concern to younger union members. Child benefit – an improvement on family allowances, which dated from 1944 – was equally dear to Barbara, the minister responsible; but it would be paid to mothers and offset by a reduction in the tax allowances enjoyed by fathers, so it clashed with persisting patriarchal attitudes. Prices might be restrained but, in prevailing conditions, could not possibly be reduced. And, while council rents were important in a period when half the population still lived in public housing, home ownership was spreading. In September 1974, Margaret Thatcher scored a political point with a Tory promise of cheaper mortgages. Disappointingly, but not surprisingly, many union members – and some union leaders – preferred the traditional course of pressure for higher wages to the unquantifiable blessings of the social contract.

At best, the benefits of the social contract would need time to manifest themselves, and time was just what no one could be sure of. Lacking a majority, the government might be driven from office in a few weeks or months if the Tories were able to regroup themselves and force a showdown. The most immediate service that Michael could render was to raise the morale of the Labour benches by his inspirational eloquence. In March 1974, he had yet to prove himself an effective minister (though the settlement with the miners was a feather in his cap), but he was certainly the champion orator and parliamentarian in Wilson's team. He never failed to produce a scattering of graphic and vivid phrases; no one quite knew whether they came spontaneously to his tongue or whether he had polished them while tramping round Hampstead Heath. In his first speech as a minister on 18 March, he asserted: 'Nothing can be more absurd than the spectacle of a few fat men exhorting all the thin ones to tighten their belts.' He went on to declare: 'Relativities must be concerned with such matters as the East End and the West End, with the rich and the poor, with Disraeli's two nations.' And he wound up: 'I speak as a socialist. All my adult life I've been a socialist and it's much too late for me to start changing now.'

The effect was dramatic. Labour MPs rose to their feet in a storm of delighted applause. The Tories saw that this was not the opportunity for which they had hoped, and hastily withdrew their critical amendment without a vote. The *Daily Express* commented: 'With a superb act of exorcism, Michael Foot removed the devilment and the ugly feeling from the Commons crisis debate.'[4] Dick Crossman, gravely ill but still contributing a column to *The Times*, wrote that Michael had given the House 'a splendid mixture of the satire and ribald fun which it so much enjoyed, and the spontaneous political honesty which it so much needs'.[5] The *Sunday Times* – then edited by the left-leaning Harold Evans – called it 'the most impressive ministerial debut in living memory'. Its profile of Michael was rhapsodic: 'Parliamentary sketch-writers reached for the word "magical" . . . The one-time Devonport reject emerged as the superstar of the new Labour Cabinet . . . The extent of Foot's personal triumph is hard to overestimate.'[6]

But Michael's rhetoric had a purpose which not all the commentators discerned. While hurling defiance at the Tories, he was also seeking to impose a genuinely socialist purpose on his Cabinet colleagues. After a talk with Jill, I noted: 'He and others (Peter, Barbara) are determined to make the Cabinet a reality and challenge decisions there. But Callaghan, Healey and Jenkins have a fully worked out strategy and hold the majority. Michael is very suspicious of them and also of Wilson, and expects clashes . . . Already it's clear, he thinks, that the government is heading the wrong way.'[7]

There was, in fact, an identifiable group of ministers who were prepared to dissent from the strategy of the majority: Michael, Barbara Castle, Peter Shore, Tony Benn and Judith Hart, the Minister for

Overseas Development. They decided to meet once a week for an informal dinner. At first, the dinners were on Tuesdays at Locket's restaurant in Marsham Street, handy for the House of Commons. As Barbara narrates: 'To allay Harold's suspicions of a "cabal", wives (or husbands) were invited as well . . . The description "Husbands and Wives" dinner enabled us to book these meetings openly through our Private Offices without alerting the Civil Service network to the fact that regular political discussions were taking place.'[8]

Later, the husbands and wives deserted Locket's and gathered at their homes, taking it in turn to offer hospitality. The dinners were now on Sundays, which avoided the annoyance of being summoned by the division bell. Sometimes, the discussions continued late into the night.

The group was genuinely not a cabal. Problems which were due to come to the Cabinet were discussed, but agreement on a line to be taken was seldom sought in a systematic way. No rebellions were planned, primarily because all shared an aversion to endangering the government and allowing the Tories to regain power, and also because the Prime Minister – though regarded as devious, sly and exasperating – commanded a residual affection that went back to Bevanite times. Some of the most acrimonious spats were between the husbands and wives themselves. Barbara, and to some extent Michael and Peter, felt that Tony was seeking to maintain immaculate principles without recognising the immense difficulties that the government faced. In June, she attacked him thus: 'You with your open government, with your facile speeches, getting all the publicity, pre-empting resources . . . trying to be holier than thou and more left-wing than me.'[9]

Also in June, Barbara noted that Michael was 'furious' with Tony – or Wedgie, as she still called him – for demanding a special party conference on the European issue:

Mike is obsessed with the need to win the next election and is bitterly opposed to anything that might disrupt the party before then – and is therefore bitter about Wedgie. What interests me is how imperious Mike becomes in these discussions, getting positively irritable. But I don't object; I welcome the fact that Mike has developed such authoritativeness.[10]

Tony Benn's experience as Minister for Industry was unhappy. In July, he produced the draft of a White Paper condemned by Wilson as 'a sloppy and half-baked document, polemical, indeed menacing in tone'.[11] The Prime Minister insisted that it should be rewritten – in effect, watered down – before publication, and recorded that 'the final draft owed a great deal to Michael Foot, writing within the parameters we laid down'. Benn was advancing two 'polemical' projects. One was to draw up planning agreements between his Ministry and various industrial enterprises, committing them to approved targets of production and employment. He envisaged these agreements as compulsory, but the Cabinet decided that they should be voluntary, and in the event only one (with the Coal Board) was ever signed. His other project was that the National Enterprise Board, set up in 1974, should have powers of initiative. Wilson ruled that it should be limited to rescuing firms that were about to collapse. Sadly, the three that were rescued – with dramatic personal commitment by the Minister – all did collapse. On both these issues, Benn was allowed to go down to defeat without effective support from Michael and the other Sunday diners.

They did unite, however, on two critical issues during 1974, and it was significant that – as in the days of Attlee and Bevin – these were foreign policy issues. The socialist government of Chile was overthrown by a military coup and the President, Salvador Allende, was murdered. Britain imposed an arms embargo on Chile, but the Foreign Secretary, Jim Callaghan, insisted that the Chileans should get four British-built frigates for which they had already paid. Michael and Judith Hart supported an NEC resolution opposing this decision. In the Cabinet, Callaghan complained that some NEC members were behaving as though they were not in the government. 'Jim really is a cool one,' Barbara commented, remembering his behaviour over *In Place of Strife* in 1969.[12] But the Chilean junta got only one frigate, which had quietly sailed in the course of the argument.

Another clash soon followed. The Royal Navy base at Simonstown, South Africa, was being phased out, but a final visit by RN ships had been arranged and was permitted to go ahead. In the NEC, Tony Benn, Judith Hart and Joan Lestor (a junior Foreign Office minister) voted for a protest resolution. Michael happened to leave the meeting before the item came up; Barbara abstained. Wilson wrote to the offending three, telling them that their action was 'clearly inconsistent with the principle of collective responsibility' and demanding that they apologise or resign. When the matter came before the Cabinet, Michael said that 'Tony behaved quite reasonably' and he might have voted for the resolution too.[13] Wilson was adamant, so Benn sent the required apology – as Barbara put it, 'capitulating and leaving the other two high and dry'. Her account continues: 'Joan Lestor was furious with him. "He's a very odd chap," said Mike in his typically tolerant way.'[14]

2

Michael's main responsibility as Secretary of State for Employment was to frame, and then pilot through the Commons, three pieces of legislation which had been promised in Labour's election manifesto. The great obstacle was that the government had no majority. At every turn, he could be doomed to failure by effective Tory opposition, or by hostility from the Liberals and other minor parties, or by lack of support from Labour back-benchers, or by any ineptitude or blunder on his own part.

First in order of priority was the Health and Safety Bill, not because it was the most urgent but because a preliminary draft was ready at hand. It was based on a report made some years earlier by Lord Robens, and the Heath government had, in 1973, prepared a not unsatisfactory bill as a move to conciliate the unions. The second of Michael's projects was the Trade Union and Labour Relations Bill, which (when the bill became an act) acquired the acronym of TULRA. Michael had wanted to call it the Workers' Rights Bill, but the TUC considered this too provocative and he accepted a more formal title. Third in the pipeline was the Employment Protection Bill, but this was deferred until after the next election, which – given the need for a majority – would have to be held in the autumn of 1974 or at latest in 1975.

Michael presented the Health and Safety Bill for its Second Reading on 3 April. In his speech, he recalled that efforts to promote industrial safety went back to the first Factories Act, passed in 1819 thanks to the work of Robert Owen, and had been pursued through a history of 'fights, battles and struggles'. The toll of accidents at work had been increasing because of new technologies which were not properly supervised and new forms of pollution. Even while the bill was being debated, the dangers were dramatised by an explosion in a chemical works at Flixborough, Lincolnshire, on 1 June which claimed twenty-nine lives. Michael was quickly on the spot and drew the lesson that new technologies must be licensed – 'safety precautions are quite insufficient and much more must be done about it', he told the House. His new act, going considerably further than the Robens report or the 1973 bill, established a national Health and Safety Commission to unify an unconnected variety of inspectorates; gave this Commission powers of enforcement and initiative; authorised trade unions to set up safety committees which employers had to recognise; and extended protection to five million workers who had hitherto had none. But a House of Lords amendment excluded agriculture, in modern times a distinctly dangerous occupation, from the scope of the act.

TULRA followed quickly, with a Second Reading on 7 May. The need
for haste arose from the fact that the Industrial Relations Act of 1971 was
still in operation. Thus wage demands were being vetted by the Pay
Board; unions were being harried by the Industrial Court, chaired by Sir
John Donaldson, whom Michael described in the Commons as a
'trigger-happy judge'; and the disastrous threshold system was fuelling
inflation. Sweeping away this act was vital to any partnership between
the Labour government and the unions. Some union leaders – notably
Hugh Scanlon of the engineers, whose union was smarting under a
£75,000 fine imposed by Donaldson – pressed for a simple repeal bill
which could be pushed through the Commons in a week. But Michael,
advised by his civil servants and Bill Wedderburn, realised that this
would leave Britain with no labour law whatever and deprive the unions
of the rights (known as 'immunities') established by legislation dating
from 1875 and 1906. In any case, a repeal bill would meet with a veto by
the Lords, which could not be overridden for another year. There was no
alternative to the preparation of a comprehensive bill, re-establishing
rights such as redress for unfair dismissal. Yet it was imperative to get it
on to the statute book before the summer recess.

Michael's speech on that 7 May was rich in satire and ribald fun. Had
there been time for a White Paper on union rights, he said, it might have
been called 'In Place of Barbara' – a joke that his old friend and Cabinet
colleague probably did not enjoy. He cited an article in which Sir
Geoffrey Howe, the Tory spokesman on labour law and author of the
1971 act, had expressed a hope that 'The Red Flag', the 'Marxist hymn',
would be 'drowned by "Auld Lang Syne"'. Howe might have been wiser
not to challenge Michael in this field. After pointing out that Jim Connell,
who wrote the words of 'The Red Flag', was never a Marxist, he
explained that the man who wrote 'Auld Lang Syne', Robert Burns, was
a true revolutionary.

Essentially, TULRA guaranteed the rights cherished by the unions: the
right to recruit and organise, the right of recognition, the right to
collective bargaining and the right to strike. But Michael lost two battles
– one within the Labour Cabinet, the other at the hands of Labour's
opponents. Picketing during a strike had been legally permissible since
1906, but the picketing of those early days – a line of men standing at a
gate – was ineffective when blacklegs arrived in cars or chartered buses.
The police would have been enforcing the common law (though
unwisely) if they had stopped the mass picketing in Birmingham in 1972.
Wedderburn now produced a formula to legalise any picketing that did
not constitute 'unreasonable obstruction'. The Home Secretary, Roy

Jenkins, prompted by police chiefs, objected to it, and Michael had to drop it from his bill. The price for this decision was paid at the Grunwick factory gate in 1977 and, most notably, in the miners' strike of 1984. The other defeat was on the issue of sympathy strikes, which had been twice outlawed by Tory legislation, in 1927 and in 1971. An amendment to outlaw them again was carried in July because the Liberals voted with the Tories.

A contest that remained in the balance was on the issue of an individual's right to stay out of a trade union – in effect, the issue of the closed shop. Confronted with opposing rights – the right to join and the right not to join – Michael declared: 'To put those two rights together and seek to make them equivalent . . . is to destroy the very principle of trade unionism.'[15] A Tory amendment on this matter was defeated by one vote, but was then found not to have been really defeated because Harold Lever, who was a member of the Cabinet with the token post of Chancellor of the Duchy of Lancaster, had been 'nodded through'[16] when he was not actually in the Houses of Parliament. The amendment was then carried in the Lords. The question of the closed shop was to cause Michael plenty of trouble over the ensuing year.

TULRA passed its Third Reading just before the House rose at the end of July. The Pay Board and the Industrial Court ceased to exist. But, in order to meet the deadline, Michael was forced to accept amendments which he heartily disliked; some were accepted in the Commons to save debating time, others were inserted by the Lords. He gave notice that they would be reversed by a majority Labour government and, in a speech on 27 July, denounced the Lords for 'poking their noses into industrial relations'. He added: 'We should consider going farther and making sure that the built-in reactionary majority there is never again allowed to repeat the monkey-tricks performed by their lordships in the past two weeks.'

The way was now clear for the election. Michael wrote the key passage in Labour's manifesto, placing the social contract in the forefront of the campaign and dignifying it by capital letters:

The Social Contract is no mere paper agreement approved by politicians and trade unions. It is not concerned solely or even primarily with wages. It covers the whole range of national policies. It is the agreed basis upon which the Labour Party and the trade unions define their common purpose . . . Naturally the trade unions see their clearest loyalty to their own members. But the Social Contract is the free acknowledgement that they have other loyalties – to the members of other trade unions too, to pensioners, to the lower-paid, to invalids, to the community as a whole . . . This is the Social Contract which can re-establish faith in the working of Britain's democracy in the years ahead.

Wilson fixed polling day for 10 October. Michael took a prominent part in the campaign, speaking at meetings all over the country. His status was emphasised by his appearance at three of the Labour press conferences (Tony Benn was allowed to appear at one).

The Tories had not regained their morale (nor their confidence in their leader) since their loss of power, and were plagued by disagreements on how to pitch their appeal. They were careful not to propose a revival of their Industrial Relations Act, and offered no clear alternative to Labour's plan of voluntary wage restraint implemented by the unions. Enoch Powell was still sniping at them and stealing the headlines; much to Heath's annoyance, he was standing as a Unionist for the Ulster seat of South Down and was sure to be in the next Parliament.

The campaign was fought almost entirely on the state of the economy. Inevitably, the Tory newspapers were filled with dire predictions of imminent disaster. In a speech on 30 September, Michael accused them of 'a wicked and evil campaign of gloom and panic'. Nevertheless, there were signs that wages were getting out of control. Workers at the Ford motor plant went on strike and won a wage offer of 37 per cent, only seven months after their last rise. Under the TUC's guidelines, wage increases should have been limited to the inflation rate and spaced at twelve-month intervals. A few days later, the BBC offered its employees 28 per cent. Michael criticised the managements concerned, but admitted that the situation was very grave. According to his figures, wage increases during 1974 had been at a rate of 26 per cent (of which 12 per cent could be ascribed to the threshold system) while prices had risen by 18 per cent.

Despite all the problems, Labour politicians looked forward to victory, a victory on the pattern of the 'follow-up' election of 1966. The Tories were giving palpable indications that they did not expect to win and hoped, at best, for a hung parliament. On 5 October Heath made a revealing statement: 'I have no doubt that the real hope of the British people in this situation is that a national coalition government, involving all the parties, should be formed, and the party differences could be put aside until the crisis is mastered.' In view of the memories of 1931, no Labour leader was likely to respond to such an overture. Wilson said at his press conference: 'It is a desperate attempt by desperate men to get back into power by any means . . . Coalition would mean Con politics, Con leadership by a Con party for a Con trick.' In fact, the coalition idea was equally distasteful to socialists like Michael Foot and to convinced Tories like the steadily advancing Margaret Thatcher.

But the election result was disappointing. The Labour Party emerged with 319 MPs, a majority of only three over other parties if they combined. This was adequate authority for continuing in office, but it was certainly not 1966. The Tories had lost twenty-two seats, but the Liberals had thirteen, the Scottish Nationalists eleven (a noteworthy advance) and Plaid Cymru three. The Labour manifesto had, for the first time, promised the creation of elected assemblies in Scotland and Wales – a measure of devolution, to use the word that was coming into vogue.

Healey and Callaghan were the senior members of the Cabinet, but Michael's presence was essential because he ensured the support of the unions and the always restive left of the party. Before the turn of the year, the government was faced with the possibility of his resignation.

To Michael's mind, the credibility of the social contract, and working-class acceptance of limited wage increases, depended on an equivalent limitation in the incomes of the better paid. The salaries of judges, senior civil servants, chairmen of nationalised industries and chiefs of the armed forces were regulated by a body rather tactlessly entitled the Top Salaries Review Board, chaired by a former Tory minister, Lord Boyle. The board was now recommending increases well in excess of the TUC guidelines that applied to lesser mortals, and in excess of the inflation rate. To make matters worse, Wilson declined to grant a request from Michael for a discussion of these increases in the Cabinet.

Barbara Castle recorded on 18 December:

> At the NEC Mike passed me a rough scribble of a letter to Harold which, he hissed, he hadn't sent yet . . . In the letter Mike said that, if the announcement went ahead, the Social Contract would be in ruins and he would have no alternative but to resign. My eyebrows shot up and he looked unhappy and hesitant: obviously he is deeply uncertain about what to do. I scribbled an alternative sentence for him, 'If this goes ahead I believe it will make my job impossible.'

With this amendment, the letter read:

> I had hoped that it was agreed that, at the very least, we would have at the Cabinet on Thursday a free and uninhibited discussion about the timing of all these top salaries decisions. Of course, it is the decisions themselves which I consider to be so dangerous, but I would have

thought that my repeated representations should have been sufficient to ensure that the whole question of timing could be re-opened . . . I underline what I wrote before, that I do not think either the Labour Movement or the country at large would understand why the government had taken this action, imperilling the Social Contract, at such a moment.

I still hope that we can have on Thursday the kind of discussion I asked for. Otherwise I would feel that you had made my job as Secretary of State for Employment impossible.

Wilson yielded to the extent of allowing a full Cabinet discussion, which lasted two and a half hours. Michael was strongly supported by Barbara, Tony Benn and Shirley Williams. Harold Lever, on the other hand, thought that the increases were barely adequate and remarked: 'I pay my cooks more than some of these senior civil servants.'[17] Wilson then disclosed that he had already told the civil service unions that they would get the salaries recommended by Boyle. Michael did not resign, but he made his disapproval publicly clear: 'I don't think the recommendations of the Boyle report accord with the TUC guidelines in any sense,' he told the House of Commons.[18] In a later Cabinet discussion, he said that 'what we did about top salaries . . . was a fatal mistake'.[19]

3

In the political world, the first big event of 1975 was the advent of a new Tory leader. Heath was paying the penalty of two electoral defeats; the outcome of the first more or less democratic choice in Tory history, and of some intricate manoeuvres, was a triumph for Margaret Thatcher.

In January, Michael gave an interview to the *Gwent Gazette* and said frankly: 'The next six months are going to be very tough indeed.' This was true of the general outlook for Britain and for the Labour government, but he was referring specifically to Ebbw Vale. He had known for years that the steelworks was doomed; now, the moment of truth was near. All plans for the expansion of the steel industry had been abandoned, and its future was one of contraction and, for the less favoured units, closure. Lord Beswick, Minister of State in the Department of Industry, had been given the task of deciding the fate of three Welsh steel-making centres: Shotton in North Wales, East Moors in the city of Cardiff, and Ebbw Vale. He gave Shotton and East Moors a provisional lease of life for four years; neither survived much longer. For

Ebbw Vale, he decreed a rundown of the main steelworks and strip mill leading to a closure within months. Pleas from the local management, the unions and the MP for Ebbw Vale won a reprieve for the smaller part of the complex – the tinplate finishing plant – which saved about 3,000 jobs. However, the closure of the steelworks threw 4,600 men out of work, as well as ending a cherished tradition and dealing a cruel blow to local pride.

The decision was communicated to the unions and the Works Council on 4 February. They were angry, and scornful of the prospects of new light industries, one of which was a factory for making marshmallows. Malcolm Bourton, secretary of the Works Council, declared: 'We don't want to work in marshmallow factories or make eyes for toy dolls.' Michael bore the brunt of the anger; he was an obvious target, both as the MP and as a minister whose job was to maintain employment. Tom Coles, secretary of the local branch of the Iron and Steel Trades Confederation, said: 'This is a betrayal by Michael Foot.' Tom Thompson, chairman of the TGWU branch, told the press that Michael should have resigned from the government and the workers ought now to seek help from Tony Benn.[20]

The bad news spread rapidly through the valley, but the official announcement was made from the borough council offices at half-past two on the afternoon of Friday, 6 February. Councillor Ray Morgan, who was there, says that this was the worst possible time; hundreds of working men had just come out of the pubs.[21] According to Morgan, the bitterness was heightened by bad feeling between the production workers (belonging to the steel union or the TGWU) and the skilled workers, such as electricians, who could count on jobs in the surviving tinplate plant.

Michael was under no obligation to be outside the council office that afternoon, but he was there together with John Morris, Secretary of State for Wales. Morris was ready to announce a package of £12 million of aid, partly to ensure the future of the tinplate plant and partly to support a new industrial estate at Rassau, an area of open mountainside above Ebbw Vale. They were confronted by a noisy crowd of about 2,000 men and by improvised placards which read: 'Foot the Slayer' and 'Betrayal'. Michael borrowed a megaphone from the police and began to speak, but he could not get a hearing for about eight minutes.[22] The television crews picked up storms of booing and shouts of 'Judas!' Continually interrupted, Michael managed to say: 'I'll tell you the truth as I've always told you the truth . . . We must face this together and show some guts and determination . . . If we face the difficulties together with courage we'll overcome them.' Morris tried to speak next but was shouted down, with Michael bellowing: 'Let him speak!'

Projects earmarked for Rassau were estimated to offer 1,950 jobs, but this figure was never reached. Some promises were broken; some firms opened up and soon closed down. As fast as jobs were created in Ebbw Vale, other jobs were lost, mainly through pit closures. Unemployment in the borough of Blaenau Gwent has remained consistently high.

In the spring of 1975, Michael was much involved in working out an agreement on wage levels. Formally, it was an agreement between the government and the TUC, but the negotiations were conducted by the Chancellor of the Exchequer and Treasury officials. As the Minister most trusted by the unions, Michael played a vital role. He was thus brought into close and regular contact with Denis Healey – a contact which was something of a shotgun wedding, since they had been, respectively, protagonists of the left and the right of the Labour Party since the 1950s. Now, they were allies in their determination to maintain the Labour government and make a success of the concordat with the unions. Healey appreciated Michael's integrity and his dedication to tasks that were not naturally congenial, while Michael respected Healey's formidable intellect. Mutual respect developed into mutual trust and even into a limited degree of mutual liking.

On the union side of the table, Michael's closest friend was still Jack Jones, and he also got on well with Len Murray, who had become general secretary of the TUC in 1973. However, several members of the Cabinet were sceptical about the idea of the social contract and the viability of a voluntary incomes policy. Michael, they thought, was putting too much faith in the authority of the TUC over the various unions, or in the authority of the unions over shop stewards, or simply in the ordinary man's capacity for moderation, altruism and community spirit. Sooner or later, the voluntary system would collapse and some form of enforced wage control would be necessary. The unions, aware of these attitudes, were wary of committing themselves to a system that might not last. In the Commons on 18 December 1974, Michael stressed: 'I am bitterly opposed to any return to a statutory policy' and added deliberately: 'That is government policy.' Tory MPs interrupted him to ask whether he would resign if government policy changed. He reiterated: 'I make clear again my absolute abhorrence of any idea of returning to a statutory incomes policy . . . I don't believe there is any misapprehension in any quarter.'

After some hard bargaining, an agreement emerged, in July 1975, to remain in force for twelve months. It provided for a flat-rate increase of six pounds a week for all workers. The ceiling was set at £8,500 a year, and anyone earning more would get no increase at all. The main architect of this scheme, and the man who ensured its acceptance (by a fairly narrow majority) in the General Council of the TUC, was Jack Jones. Most of the assembly-line workers, lorry-drivers, bus-drivers and dockers who made up the membership of his union were getting less than average wages, so the six-pound increase was often the biggest rise they had ever had in their lives. (However, the leaders of the National Union of Public Employees, whose members were yet more emphatically underpaid, chose to oppose the scheme.) The idea of 'six pounds all round' was naturally less attractive to unions of skilled workers, since it eroded the differentials which they saw as a proper recognition of their training and their importance. Hugh Scanlon agreed to deliver the AEU's backing only after much persuasion by Jack Jones and by Michael, and warned that he would sooner or later seek a restoration of the differentials.

Meanwhile, Michael was fully engaged on the parliamentary front. He introduced a Trade Union and Labour Relations (Amendment) Bill, known for short as TULRA Two, to reverse the unwelcome changes that had been made to TULRA by the Lords, and followed it up with the third panel of his triptych, the Employment Protection Bill. Under its provisions, employers were obliged not only to recognise and bargain with unions, but also to provide any information they needed and to permit meetings in working time. It was, as Jack Jones has commented approvingly, 'a shop stewards' charter'. The bill also set up tribunals for appeals against unfair dismissal; required the payment of a full week's wages when work was interrupted through no fault of the workers ('wet time' in the building industry was the main example); and gave women workers guarantees of maternity leave and reinstatement. The principal legacy of this bill, however, was the Conciliation and Arbitration Service, soon known as ACAS. (The first 'A', standing for Advisory, was added as the Service took shape, perhaps to produce a handy spoken acronym.)

The Ministry of Labour had been offering conciliation in industrial disputes, and allocating civil servants to specialise in this work, for decades, but its good offices were not always acceptable to all concerned. Trade unions (and on some occasions employers) objected that arbitrators working for a government department were committed in advance to upholding government policy and fitting their verdict to the political necessities of the time. Michael decided, therefore, that ACAS should be an independent body with its own staff, its own methods and eventually its own traditions. Its finding might or might not be acceptable – in practice, the success rate was high – but in any case they were its own. The only decision made by the Secretary for Employment was the appointment of a chairman. Michael chose a trade unionist: Jim Mortimer, hitherto an official of DATA, the draughtsmen's union. Mortimer was a known left-winger, a veteran of CND and other campaigns, but he carried out his duties scrupulously and was never accused of undue partisanship.

The government was still battling for survival. Wilson's PPS, William Hamling, died suddenly in March 1975 and Labour lost the by-election at Woolwich West. Its majority was now precisely one. In one sense, the situation was worse than in 1974, since it was out of the question to hold yet another election. In this perilous situation, there was little time and little scope for hostilities between left and right. Michael, playing his pivotal role, was seen as almost – if not quite – a figure of the Labour centre. Shirley Williams sent him friendly notes or pleas for help across the Cabinet table. One that survives, dated 20 February 1975, reads:

> Michael honeybunch,
>
> Are you making a statement answering a PQ [parliamentary question] on wages today? If so, can I borrow your briefing? I've got an *hour-long* TV about prices, inflation etc. on Thames tonight.

He replied:

> Would you like (a) a brief we have on the miners, (b) a brief on comparisons of miners, railways, etc., (c) a more elaborate paper on the earnings. If so, will send it over this afternoon.

She accepted gratefully.

Tony Crosland's wife Susan recorded: 'By the early 1970s I can remember his saying: "Sweet man, Michael" . . . Sometimes he found it nearly impossible to recall the vitriol with which he and Michael Foot had assailed one another when the Left of the party was trying to destroy Gaitskell.'[23] Tony Benn's attitude to Michael was one of grudging respect. After a dinner attended by Michael, Peter Shore, Tony and their wives, he noted: 'The three of us have got to hang together now. Michael carries with him the tremendous authority of his office, his links with Len Murray and Jack Jones.'[24] A few months later, with the controversy on the European Community in mind, he was suspicious: 'Mrs Thatcher is doing the dirty work on Europe for big business in Britain, Harold is doing the dirty work for Mrs Thatcher and Michael is doing the dirty work for Harold. So there is a complete conspiracy actually not to work hard to get us out.'[25] Then, when he had been subjected to a ferocious Tory attack in the Commons, he wrote gratefully: 'Harold sat beside me and Michael, bless his heart, always supports me.'[26]

Michael, in fact, was careful not to get into conflicts with Tony which could only benefit the right-wingers of the government. He was not blind, however, to Tony's calculated nurturing of his popularity with the left, nor to his ambitions. In the 1974 voting for the NEC, always a sensitive matter, Tony came top, pushing Michael into second place, and Barbara slipped a notch and was placed below Ian Mikardo. As cheers for Tony resounded, Wilson said to her: 'He's becoming quite a young hero.' She commented in her diary: 'His ambition was in both our minds.'[27] It was certainly, and quite consciously, in Benn's own mind. In a diary reflection on the last night of 1975, which would have made interesting reading for Wilson, Barbara and Michael too, he wrote: 'It is not possible to do anything to change British society unless one is Prime Minister. Up to now I have always rather brushed aside ambition, but now I realise . . . I must be Leader of the Labour Party and Prime Minister: therefore I must do something about it.'[28]

In April 1975, Healey presented a budget which was as ruthlessly deflationary as any ever produced by Cripps, Gaitskell or Roy Jenkins. There were cuts in housing subsidies which raised council rents, cuts in food subsidies which raised the price of milk and other basic foods, and sharply increased taxes on drink and tobacco. A policy (in classic Tory mould) of requiring the nationalised industries to balance their books presaged increases in rail fares and fuel bills. Nor did the Chancellor claim that he was ordering exceptional measures to overcome temporary difficulties; he told the Cabinet that public spending would have to be kept down for at least two years.

As Healey was aware, 'almost all the spending cuts ran against the Labour Party's principles, and many also ran against our campaign promises'.[29] Barbara protested: 'His option would mean the permanent abandonment of our own policy and would destroy the party.'[30] Moreover, cuts in spending and public investment, as well as in house-building, were sure to increase unemployment, which had risen to 800,000 and threatened to reach the dreaded figure – reached only once since the war, under Heath in 1972 – of one million. Michael had said in July 1974: 'I'm not prepared to sit in this place and preside over mass unemployment'.[31] It was a declaration that, by 1975, became embarrassing to recall.

Though Michael could not halt the rise in the jobless figures, he introduced two schemes which limited the damage. Under the Temporary Employment Subsidy, an employer in an area of high unemployment who was about to make fifty or more workers redundant was given government aid, at a rate of ten pounds a week for each individual, towards keeping them in their jobs. As well as giving a reprieve to the men and women concerned, the scheme saved a number of small industries from going bankrupt. Another achievement was setting up the Manpower Services Commission, which was responsible – as an autonomous body, like ACAS – for training and job creation. Thousands of young people learned a craft at government expense; thousands more were employed on projects initiated by the MSC. In later years, these youth training schemes earned a bad name by offering dead-end jobs in the name of training and paying sub-standard wages, but in Michael's time they had the purpose of equipping the unskilled – and therefore jobless – with socially valuable skills.

4

Throughout 1975, Michael was involved in a long-running dispute which, from start to finish, he regarded as unnecessary. The closed shop, or union membership covering all workers in a given industry or workplace, was a system defended by the unions on the grounds that everyone who benefited from improved pay and conditions, achieved through union activity, should contribute to the union's strength, at least by paying dues. The Tory act of 1971 had in effect banned the closed shop, and a clause in TULRA reversed this move, by providing redress against unfair dismissal and thus enabling unions to protect the jobs of their members. Michael was at once accused of making the closed shop compulsory everywhere. In reality, he was proposing to restore the position that, at least by convention, had prevailed before 1971 – that a closed shop was legal when set up by agreement between unions and employers. He made his attitude clear in moving the Second Reading of TULRA Two: 'We have not imposed the closed shop. We are neutral about the closed shop. The government are not encouraging people to form a closed shop, but they are not forbidding them to form a closed shop.'[32] He expected a battle, since the closed shop was anathema not only to employers who wanted to weaken the unions, but also to ideologists who were aroused by what they saw as a libertarian cause. What he did not expect was that the battle would rage in a field that had been his lifelong habitat – the press.

The National Union of Journalists then had about 28,000 members and was well established in almost all British newspapers, national or local. A smaller, though older, body, the Institute of Journalists, had 3,000 members. Editors and senior executives generally belonged to the IOJ, but some were NUJ members, as Michael had been when editor of the *Evening Standard*. 'Anxieties exist,' Michael conceded in a Commons statement after a meeting with a deputation of Fleet Street editors. It was feared that an NUJ chapel,[33] having established a closed shop, might oblige everyone to join and extinguish the IOJ; that editors would then be forced to follow a political line dictated by the NUJ; and that external contributors would either have to join the NUJ and be subject to its discipline or be excluded from the paper's columns. Some of these contributors, such as book reviewers who were primarily academics, existed in an undefined borderland (an example cited in the controversy was an ornithologist who wrote a column on birds). In particular, there was some resentment in NUJ circles against recently retired cricketers and footballers who covered matches, depriving staff reporters of the job.

From his experience, Michael considered that freedom of the press was threatened much more by the arbitrary power of proprietors than by any NUJ ambitions. When faced by a Tory amendment to TULRA Two giving editors the right 'to commission and publish any article', he commented: 'I don't think Mr Murdoch gives that power to his editors.'[34] He regarded the Australian tycoon, now the owner of *The Times* and the *Sunday Times*, as an enemy, and attacked him in the Commons: 'Rupert Murdoch, who has contributed so much to the debasement of moral standards in Fleet Street, has now turned his considerable powers of befuddlement to the economic situation.'[35] Nor was he much more sympathetic to editors who had, by and large, conformed to the prejudices of proprietors: 'I say to the London editors that if they had fought for the freedom of others with one-tenth of the ardour with which they have fought for their own, we should have a world that is much more free than it is at present.'[36]

Thus Michael was not in a benevolent mood when, on 19 November 1974, he met the deputation which included Harold Evans, editor of the *Sunday Times*, and David Astor, editor of the *Observer*. He was shocked by what he saw as their misunderstanding of his intentions and their lack of trust, since Evans was on most issues a Labour rather than a Tory sympathiser, while Astor, who was conscious of the old friendship between the Foot and the Astor families and had moreover been at Oxford with Michael, was definably a liberal (in the American rather than the British sense). He told them firmly that the insecurity which hung over them was not the fault of the NUJ. In this he was proved right; within a few years, the *Observer* was acquired by a multinational company, Atlantic Richfield, and the *Sunday Times* by Rupert Murdoch.

As Michael insisted: 'Proprietors have exercised, since the days of Caxton or thereabouts, all the powers of suppression, distortion, malign influence and peremptory removal of editors to which members of my union, the NUJ, are alleged on such pitiful evidence to aspire.'[37]

Yet Michael was uneasily aware that a certain faction in the NUJ did aspire to such powers. His strategy was to fend off this faction by supporting the reasonable majority in the union. In a speech to the Media Society on 4 December 1974, he suggested that a ban on the closed shop 'might incite them to use their industrial power much more than if we tried to get a solution on a sensible basis'. Jocularly, but not entirely in jest, he alluded to 'sinister or militant elements' and added: 'I'm not referring merely to my nephew.' (Paul was editing the *Socialist Worker*.)

In the first debate on TULRA Two, he conceded: 'The unrestrained exercise of trade union power in the newspaper industry could strangle that industry.'[38] He was certainly aware that the flow of information to Britain's citizens was a value in itself, and its interruption was a menace of a different order from a strike in a car or furniture factory. In the same speech, he recalled: 'Some of the gloomiest days of my life were spent in newspaper offices when there was a strike' and concluded: 'The printed word occupies a place of pre-eminence in our society and in any democratic society. Television and radio are pitiful and pallid substitutes.'

Therefore, he invited Ken Morgan, general secretary of the NUJ, and Alastair Hetherington, editor of the *Guardian*, to draw up an agreed code that would protect both press freedom and legitimate trade union rights. By this time, however, the atmosphere had become more sulphurous. The Liberal leader, Jeremy Thorpe, denounced TULRA as 'an unprecedented assault on the freedom of the press'. The editors who had met Michael published accounts of the discussion which gave no credit to his efforts to defuse the situation, and he reacted angrily: 'The editors have produced an extraordinary combination of bad reporting, bad law, bad temper and bilious polemic.'[39] The most tendentious reporting, in his opinion, came from Nora Beloff, political correspondent of the *Observer*, who – as she recounted in a book which she later wrote[40] – had resigned from the NUJ in February 1974 in protest against a chapel meeting which delayed production of the paper. (For editors, this was one of the most irritating trade union techniques, though one must remember that it was employed far more often by printers than by the NUJ.)

The chairman of the *Observer* board, and also chairman of the Newspaper Proprietors Association, was Lord Goodman. Arnold Goodman, who had moved into public life from a base as Harold Wilson's solicitor, was a ubiquitous Pooh Bah; he had been chairman of the Arts Council and worked closely with Jennie Lee, and had been sent by Wilson on an (unsuccessful) mission to resolve the problem of Rhodesia. He now took a strongly anti-Foot stand, declaring in a speech on 20 November 1974: 'The preservation of freedom is so vital, so crucial to the preservation of our society, that we shall not tolerate any interference with it.' Michael, of course, was emphasising the vital status of the printed word in very similar words, and made the riposte: 'I absolutely deny that we have done anything to interfere with freedom of the press, either overtly or surreptitiously.'[41] What annoyed him was that Goodman, though they knew each other well, never asked him to explain his proposals and never understood his point of view. He commented: 'Lord Goodman is a very good friend of mine, but can cause Brobdingnagian confusion.'

In the debates on TULRA One, when the controversy first arose, Michael had cited his own experience: 'I've worked on newspapers for twenty years in closed-shop situations.'[42] He had in his files his contract with the *Daily Herald*, dated 28 June 1944, which stated: 'It is a condition of the engagement that you are and remain a fully paid up member of the National Union of Journalists.' Now, he reiterated: 'I have seen no examples in my experience of the kind of tyrannical acts which have been suggested and attributed to the union.'[43] Journalists, indeed, could well resent the picture that had been drawn. Michael Leapman of *The Times* wrote:

> The campaign by newspaper editors against the impending industrial relations legislation seems to underrate the intelligence and probity of members of the National Union of Journalists. A closed shop for journalists can be seen as a threat to press freedom only if you doubt our ability to run our union democractically . . . For journalists to play a part in controlling what goes into newspapers is surely no less compatible with press freedom than to leave the decision to autocratic editors and proprietors.[44]

In February 1975, as the bill was passing its Third Reading, Morgan and Hetherington produced their code. Editors were exempted from the closed shop and could continue to belong to the IOJ, or to no union. A key clause was: 'Restraints must not be placed on the rights of editors to publish contributions from a wide range of authors.' Michael told the House happily that the code provided 'protection for editors and for the press which we have never had before in our history'. Lord Houghton (Douglas Houghton, a former Labour minister) proposed to add an amendment endorsing the code when the bill reached the Lords. But, to Michael's great disappointment, the NUJ conference, meeting in Cardiff at Easter, rejected the code. In the Lords, Goodman moved amendments which made the closed shop a legal impossibility.

Without the code, Michael's bill was as vulnerable as ever. The attack was resumed with a letter in the *Times Literary Supplement* which described it as 'one of the most serious potential threats to liberty of expression that has arisen in this country in modern times'. The letter concluded: 'We urge the government to think again and to accept Lord Goodman's amendments.'[45] It was signed by, among others, Sir Anthony Blunt, Jacquetta Hawkes, Arthur Koestler, John Osborne, J. B. Priestley, V. S. Pritchett and Rebecca West. This was a severe blow to Michael, not only because the names carried weight, but still more because they included friends whom he respected.

He decided to reply, although Wilson had ruled that ministers should not write to the press. (Barbara, the year before, had resorted to writing a letter to *The Times* and having it signed by a back-bench MP.) Michael, creating a precedent, signed his own letter and *The Times* had to print it at full length; it ran across five columns.[46] He charged that 'the distinguished names were recruited to the letter by organisers who did not trouble to recite the facts'. What was not understood, he explained, was that Goodman's amendment, by banning the closed shop in newspaper offices, was reviving the most objectionable feature of the 1971 Industrial Relations Act: 'These amendments would apply a special 1971-type solution exclusively to one industry . . . Any union worth its salt would resist such discrimination, and the absurdity of the Pentonville Five might be re-enacted with journalists as the victims.'

As for the vote at the NUJ conference, Michael claimed that 'the militancy in Cardiff was largely provoked by the anti-union tirades of recent months'. This led him to write: 'The more these conflicting perils are pondered, the more people in Parliament and elsewhere may still be driven back to seek a solution along the lines which Mr Morgan, Lord Houghton and the government were following . . . Those who searched so long and earnestly for such a solution were as much concerned about freedom of expression as your correspondents.'

He was clinging to hope, mainly because Ken Morgan was submitting the NUJ's conference decision to a ballot of the membership and was confident that the code would eventually be supported. Morgan was right, but the result of the ballot was not announced until October. Meanwhile, TULRA Two was stuck in the Lords over the summer recess and Michael could not even be sure of support in the Commons. Roy

Jenkins delivered a pointed homily on press freedom,[47] and some Labour MPs who were close to the Home Secretary – Bryan Magee, Brian Walden and David Marquand – were openly critical of the bill. Six years later, they had all left the Labour Party to join the Social Democratic Party.

By the summer of 1975, Michael was not yet free of the exhausting imbroglio over the press and the closed shop. But it was only one of his worries in that troubled summer.

5

The time had come for a final decision on British membership of the European Community. In opposition, Wilson had managed to hold the Labour Party together on a skilfully devised policy: that the terms agreed by Heath were unsatisfactory, that a Labour government would reopen negotiations and try to get new terms, and that the outcome would be submitted to the people in a referendum. By the time that Labour took office, the betting among the well-informed was on continued membership. The weight of British export and import trade had, in a few years, shifted in a European direction; a reversal of this process could intensify the economic difficulties, which were already bad enough. Summarising the position in September 1974, Barbara Castle wrote: 'Expert Wilson watchers had already detected that he was determined to keep Britain in the European Community if at all possible.'[48] Callaghan, who as Foreign Secretary conducted the negotiations, took a positive line in a speech in Luxembourg on 4 June 1974: 'Let us together put these matters right and, when we do, the Community will be once again strengthened.'

Politically, the problem was that staying in would be favoured by a majority of the Cabinet, but probably not by a majority of Labour MPs, nor of the NEC, nor of a party conference. Even renegotiation was not universally popular. To get the support of the NEC for carrying on the negotiations, Wilson had to threaten to resign and go through what he called 'a weekend of button-holing, cajoling and fierce argument'.[49]

The negotiations were successful in that the nine Community governments agreed on altered terms for Britain, ratified at a meeting in Dublin on 11 March 1975. However, the changes secured by Callaghan – a new budget mechanism allowing a possible refund for Britain, and a better deal for New Zealand products – were not impressive and changed few, if any, minds. When Wilson announced that the government would advise a Yes vote in the coming referendum, he had the support of sixteen members of the Cabinet. Seven disagreed: Michael Foot, Barbara Castle, Tony Benn, Peter Shore, John Silkin, Eric Varley and William Ross. The first-named four had already gathered round the dinner- table ('Jill served up a superb meal and the red wine flowed')[50] to plan a campaign of opposition. They decided to come forward publicly as a group of members of the Cabinet and to call themselves the 'dissenting ministers'.

Wilson had agreed to permit this open dissent – which did, admittedly, break all the normal conventions of collective responsibility –with great reluctance. After a talk with Michael, he conceded that ministers might register their dissent and the public should be allowed to know that the majority view was not unanimous. However, when he heard that the dissenters were going to issue a joint statement and hold a press conference, he made a furious phone call to Barbara. 'He was almost beside himself,' she recorded. 'The venom poured out of him.'[51] She hurried to Westminster and joined Michael and Callaghan in Wilson's room. Wilson delivered a tirade lasting an hour, showing himself to be as angry with the pro-Community ministers, especially Roy Jenkins, as with the dissenters. In a Cabinet meeting (without officials) next day, he warned of the consequences of a split: 'It could be 1931 all over again . . . What I'm afraid of from this polarisation is a pro-Market coalition, a Tory-dominated coalition with perhaps a titular Labour leader.'[52]

The developments of the next month were all unwelcome to the Cabinet majority. On 26 March, the NEC resolved that 'the best interests of the British people would be served by a No vote in the coming referendum'. On 7 April, the government had to rely on Tory votes in the Commons to win approval of the Dublin agreement, for 145 Labour members voted against and only 137 in favour (with 33 abstaining). On 26 April, a special party conference voted against the government line by almost a two-to-one majority.

On 28 April, Michael was admitted to the Royal Free Hospital, near his Hampstead home, for an operation. The operation was exploratory; Michael's doctor, Gerry Slattery, suspected a possibility of cancer. On 8 May he received this letter:

All of us here assembled send you our warmest greetings and best wishes. We miss you very much – and hope you are not missing too much. Much as we feel the lack of your wisdom, guidance and comradeship, we urge you not to return to the battleground until

you are really fit. We know what these consultants can do to chaps
when they get the chance.

    Love from us all,
      Barbara
      Peter
      John [Silkin]
      Tony
On Behalf of All the Dissenting Ministers

The operation showed that Michael did not have cancer, and he was
soon able to convalesce at home. He had to prepare his referendum
speeches, draft his long letter to *The Times* about the closed shop and
consider a vitriolic article by the columnist Lynda Lee-Potter which had
appeared in the *Daily Mail* on 30 April. She had discovered that Michael
had been admitted only a few weeks after Slattery's recommendation and
that he was in a single room. He was, she charged, 'effectively getting
private treatment as an NHS patient'. Single rooms, she wrote, 'are
reserved for the dying, the chronically ill, and obscure cases who need
special nursing' – but Michael, according to the press office at his
Department, was in hospital for a minor operation. Readers were told
sardonically that Michael 'wasn't on the waiting list for three years' nor
was he 'operated on by a houseman who barely speaks English'.

The only excuse for this attack was that Michael had chosen to tell the
public, and even his friends, that he was in for a minor operation and to
make no mention of suspected cancer. Otherwise, all Lynda Lee-Potter's
facts were wrong. As Jill pointed out in a letter which the *Mail* had to
print, the Royal Free, then a new hospital, had been designed to provide
over a hundred single rooms.[53] Slattery, and the hospital staff, had
followed the regular procedure for a case of suspected cancer, and the
operation might have been performed even sooner if Michael had not
wanted to speak at the party conference. Una Cooze, Michael's secretary,
also wrote to the *Mail*, denying that there was any 'privileged treatment'
and explaining:

The nature of the operation was such that no other person showing the
same symptoms would have been placed on a waiting list . . . [He
was] admitted to his nearest local hospital . . . [He] specifically asked
that he should be placed in a public ward . . . [He had] a single room
partly because of the nature of the operation but primarily, due to past
experience, because the hospital staff feared unwarranted intrusion
from press photographers and reporters.[54]

Michael demanded an apology and, when the editor refused, issued a libel writ. Eventually, in January 1978, he secured a retraction and damages of £500.

Because of the operation, Michael took only a limited part in the referendum campaign. He spoke at several meetings, including an eve-of-poll rally on the Waun-y-Pound mountain above Ebbw Vale, where the young Nye Bevan had often walked and where, by this time, his memorial stood. Michael also wrote an article for *The Times*, in which he stressed the value of Britain's Parliament:

> No comparable institution, certainly, has shaped so continuously the life and society of any Western European state. It is the authority of our distinctive Parliament which is one of the stakes in the choice now before the people . . . The British parliamentary system has been made farcical and unworkable by . . . the semi-secret law-making process of the Council of Ministers. This last unique and ineffable invention – a dumb legislature – must surely have been the touch of some Laputan satirist . . . Historians looking back, and starting soon I believe, will be amazed that the British people were urged at such a time to tamper irreparably with their most precious institution; to see it circumscribed and contorted and elbowed off the centre of the stage.[55]

The charge that Michael was most concerned to rebut was that opponents of EC membership were advocating the isolation of Britain. On the contrary: 'We are saying we can expand our influence in the world. We are not proposing to cut ourselves off from the world in a chauvinistic manner.'[56] When the charge was made by Heath in a television debate, Michael interrupted: 'We were fighting for internationalism long before you—' The rest of the sentence was lost in a shouting-match.

Yet it was undeniable that some of the rhetoric for a No vote was tinged with xenophobia. Some prominent speakers were right-wing Tories with a reputation for racism, such as Enoch Powell and Ronald Bell. At the last press conference before polling day, Michael and Jack Jones had to share the platform unhappily with Powell and Bell. Even on the left, there were signs of a nostalgic attachment to anything British. Tony Benn's reaction to the prospect of a European passport was: 'That really hit me in the guts . . . Like metrication and decimalisation, this really strikes at our national identity.'[57]

Since Wilson had vetoed the idea that the Labour Party should campaign for the policy adopted at its conference, party activity was suspended. The chroniclers of the campaign noted: 'Many constituency

Labour parties declared themselves neutral, often locking up canvass records and loudspeaking gear to deny them to both sides.'[58] The Conservative Party, likewise, had no line binding on all its supporters. Indeed, only the Liberal Party, despite its fissiparous reputation, was united on the issue.

The rival campaigns were conducted by *ad hoc* organisations. Britain in Europe was set up in January 1975 with headquarters in Park Lane and a staff of 140. The secretary was Sir Con O'Neill, a recently retired diplomat who had played a key role in the negotiations for British entry (despite French bafflement over his first name). Great care was taken to avoid giving it a Tory coloration; the president was Roy Jenkins, with William Whitelaw merely as one of several vice-presidents. The publicity director, research director and press officer were all Labour people. There was also an autonomous Labour Campaign for Britain in Europe under the presidency of Shirley Williams, who announced that she would retire from politics if the voters turned in a No majority. This Labour campaign was backed by eighty-eight MPs and twenty-five trade union leaders.

The No organisation was the National Referendum Campaign, a successor to the Get Britain Out (originally Keep Britain Out) Campaign. It was something of a mirror-image to Britain in Europe, in that care was taken not to identify it with Labour. The chairman was the Tory Neil Marten, with Douglas Jay as vice-chairman. The committee included Michael, Barbara, Peter Shore, two Tories, Powell (now classed as an Ulster Unionist), two Scottish Nationalists and Dafydd Elis Thomas of Plaid Cymru. Tony Benn, when Jay's wife explained to him how the campaign was to be constituted, commented sadly: 'I must say it is going to be an awful ragbag.'[59] He was also given a place on the committee, but never went to its meetings.

Polling day was set for 5 June. During May, every voter received, at public expense, a folder with three statements: one from the government, one from BIE and one from the NRC. In other words, there were two statements in favour of continued membership and one against it. This disparity was reflected, or rather exceeded, by what the voters found in their newspapers. All the national papers urged a Yes vote, even the *Daily Express* with its heritage of Beaverbrookian isolationism and the *Daily Mirror* with its general support for Labour policy. There was, moreover, an overwhelming disparity in financial resources. Official returns after polling showed that BIE had spent £1,481,000 and the NRC a mere £133,000. The Liberal MP David Steel recorded his bewildered impressions of BIE: 'The basic materials which Liberals scratched hard to find or finance simply appeared: cars, aeroplanes, helicopters, film units, stage equipment, photocopiers, typewriters.'[60]

Little, if any, of the money for BIE came from sacrifices made by idealists. Donations of over £25,000 were made by Imperial Chemical Industries, Shell, Vickers, Marks and Spencer, and Guest, Keen and Nettlefold. Directors were quick to appreciate the point blurted out during the campaign by Sir Christopher Soames: 'Going into Europe is based essentially on the capitalist system.' A survey by the CBI showed that 415 major companies, out of 419 questioned, were for Community membership. Eight hundred companies, large or small, responded to the CBI's advice to appoint a 'Mr Europe' to influence their workers and to 'relate the issue to the fortunes of their companies and to the job security and prosperity of their employees'.

Looking back, Peter Shore ascribes the victory of the Yes campaign to two factors: the disparity in money and the unavoidable fact that the appeal by the No side was to upset an established situation.[61] This was shrewdly emphasised in the Yes statement written by Jenkins: 'Not to have gone into Europe would have been a misfortune. But to come out would be on an altogether greater scale of self-inflicted injury.' Whitelaw said: 'There were those who did not want us to join. I believe that many of them today have changed and now consider that once we are in, it would be catastrophic to withdraw.' The final comment of the historians of the referendum was: 'Those who denounced referenda as instruments of conservatism may have been right. The public is usually slow to authorise change . . . Before entry, to vote for going in would have been to vote radically. But after entry, it was at least as radical and unsettling to vote for leaving.'[62]

The result, in any case, was decisive. The Yes vote totalled seventeen and a half million against a No vote of eight and a half million – three million short of the Labour vote in October 1974. While the majority was lower in Scotland than in England, only the Western Isles and the Shetlands actually voted No. The percentages voting Yes ranged from 57 in Mid-Glamorgan up to 76 in Surrey.

Looking on the bright side as usual, Tony Benn regarded the No vote as 'some achievement considering we had absolutely no real organisation, no newspapers, nothing'.[63] He could certainly draw satisfaction from his own role in the episode. He had been seen on television fifty-two times, well ahead of anyone else. As the campaign closed, *The Times* commented: 'Mr Benn has been the leader of the debate . . . He was the author of the referendum and for much of the time he has managed to make his arguments the central arguments in the debate.'[64]

6

With the referendum out of the way, Wilson made some changes in the government. He wanted to dismiss Reg Prentice, whose opinions placed him outside the Wilsonian consensus and whose tactless outbursts, leading to some angry exchanges with Michael in Cabinet meetings, made him a liability. Jenkins, however, told the Prime Minister that he would resign if Prentice was dropped. Wilson agreed to keep Prentice in the government, though not necessarily in the same job.

Left-wingers did not fare so well. Judith Hart was removed from her post as Minister for Overseas Development. She was offered the Ministry of Transport, now part of Crosland's Department of the Environment. She was very distressed, partly because she cared deeply about aid to the Third World and partly because she felt insulted by the reduction in her status. Rejecting Wilson's offer, she returned to the back benches. Wilson gave the Overseas Development job to Prentice.

The most significant decision was to remove Benn from the Department of Industry. His popularity with the party rank and file and his enhanced status through the referendum campaign were just what worried Wilson and motivated him to give the 'young hero' a rebuff. Besides, however popular Benn might be in the constituencies, he was intensely unpopular with an important section of MPs and ministers. The Prime Minister's adviser and confidante, Marcia Williams, recorded: 'Tony Benn has become a cult hate figure in the way that Shirley Williams became a cult love figure . . . Never before have I seen antagonism to a leading political figure so openly expressed within his own party.'[65] The antagonism was still more acute in other circles. Paul Johnson, now writing for the Tory press, noted: 'Wherever newspaper editors, or economists, or City slickers and businessmen gather to ponder the mess and exchange horror stories of the latest national reverse, Mr Benn's name crops up and he is duly denounced.'[66] Marcia Williams reached the conclusion, evidently shared by her chief:

It became more and more dangerous for the government as a whole to allow Tony Benn to continue in the same job. With sterling as it then stood, confidence was essential . . . It was impossible to have someone running industry in whom industry, the business community and overseas interests had no confidence.[67]

Wilson decided on an exchange of jobs between Benn and Eric Varley, the Secretary of State for Energy. Varley, who was friendly with Benn, told him: 'I think Harold entered into some commitments with the City or somebody, and he has to get rid of you.'[68]

The problem for Tony Benn was that, although he was losing the job that he cherished, he was not being dismissed. Energy, with responsibility for the vital development of North Sea oil, was a position of real importance. This, indeed, was why Wilson was offering it to Benn, realising that he would be a formidable critic if he enjoyed political independence. Wilson recorded: 'He took it extremely hard, and it looked virtually certain that he would choose to retire to the back benches, the last place where I wanted to see him. Late that evening Michael Foot came to intercede on his behalf, but I made it clear that my mind was made up.'[69]

On the following day, a conclave was held in Benn's room in the House, attended by four ministers – Michael, Barbara, Peter Shore and John Silkin – and also by Judith Hart, Ian Mikardo, two other left-wing MPs, Benn's adviser Frances Morrell, and his two elder sons, aged twenty-three and twenty-one. The crucial question was whether Michael and the other ministers should protect Benn, as Jenkins had protected Prentice, by threatening Wilson with their own resignations. They decided not to make this move, much to the disgust of Mikardo, who wrote later: 'I could scarcely contain my disappointment and anger; I thought the behaviour of those ministers was both incomprehensible and gutless.'[70] The meeting broke up when Benn was due to see Wilson again. Wilson's account reads: 'When I asked him straight out whether he was refusing it [Energy] he said – not with his usual charm – of course he'd have to accept it.'[71]

Michael had become impatient with Tony. At another restaurant dinner (this time at the Gay Hussar in Greek Street), he was annoyed by Tony's statement that the first job of a Labour government was to defend the unions. Barbara recorded: 'Mike could stand no more. "You are dodging it," he exploded. "The best way to defend the trade union movement is for them to have a policy that deals with the country's problems." . . . We just could not run away from the fact, Mike continued, that inflation threatened to undermine everything we were trying to do.'[72]

There certainly was cause for concern about business confidence in sterling. In July, the pound slipped below what was regarded as the essential rate of $2.20 and the headlines spoke of yet another crisis. To win support for government policy, a White Paper entitled *The Attack on Inflation* was published and Michael presented it to the House on 22 July. He made a spirited defence of 'the much derided but still intact social contract', which had just been described by the *Daily Mirror* as a sick joke. He wound up: 'We face an economic typhoon of unparalleled ferocity, a combination of inflation and unemployment, and we can't run away from it . . . It is our duty to the House to speak plainly and boldly. I believe the response from the country may be better than collectively we deserve.'

The Tories, since they approved of wage restraint, abstained in the vote. The Liberals voted with the government, a sign of sympathy that Michael did not fail to note. But he had to face the painful spectacle of fifty-four Labour MPs voting against the White Paper, including Judith Hart, Mikardo and Eric Heffer. He must have thought wryly of the many occasions in the past when he had been the leader, not the target, of a back-bench revolt.

Worse still, the voluntary incomes policy, for which he had secured Cabinet endorsement the year before, was in jeopardy. At a Cabinet meeting on 20 June, Healey warned that a further cut in real wages, if it became necessary, would require a statutory policy. According to Benn, 'Roy Jenkins argued that a statutory pay policy had worked very well from 1968–70 . . . He favoured sanctions because non-compliance would be substantial.' Michael interrupted: 'Are you suggesting putting people into prison?'; Jenkins replied: 'We'll have to face that.'[73] Healey proposed penalties on employers who conceded excessive pay increases, not on workers or their unions. The necessary powers, he said, should be kept in reserve, to be used only if the agreed limits were breached. It was undeniable, however, that they would have to be embodied in a bill to be put through Parliament and that this would constitute a statutory policy.

Michael wrote a letter of resignation, but allowed himself second thoughts before sending it to the Prime Minister. His handwritten draft read:

I am sure that you and the Cabinet regard the measures which the Chancellor announced today as essential and urgent in the national interest. However, they do involve an attempted statutory control of wages, albeit in a different form from that imposed previously. I have myself persistently opposed any return to a statutory system and it is surely desirable that a new policy should not be administered by someone so deeply and precisely committed. I must therefore, with many regrets, resign from the Government.

Perhaps I may add that I intend to do my best to support and sustain the Government in office from the back benches. It remains my belief, confirmed rather than shaken by these latest events, that the right course for the country is for the Labour Government to carry through the policies contained in the manifesto on which we won the last two elections.

Barbara Castle wrote in her diary: 'If he resigned, I certainly would and I suspect Wedgie (and perhaps even Peter) would, too.'[74] Five ministers – Varley lined up with the left-wingers, to their surprise – decided to put up a fight in the Cabinet. Michael told Barbara: 'If things go wrong I should have to discuss my personal position with Jack Jones.'

Jones was sympathetic. He saw Michael as 'a worried and often flustered man, who genuinely wanted to help the trade unions but found he was sinking into a morass of complex problems.'[75] But he told Michael that the unions would not expect him to resign on the issue, and indeed would be very unhappy if he did. 'Don't abandon the field,' he urged.

The outcome was a compromise. When the Cabinet met again on 10 July, Fred Mulley – the new Secretary for Education, and generally a right-winger, but sponsored as an MP by a trade union – suggested that a reserve powers bill might be prepared, but not introduced unless the voluntary policy broke down. With some reluctance, Healey gave his agreement. Michael made it clear that his resignation was only held in abeyance by telling the House in the White Paper debate: 'If such a reserve powers bill were to be introduced, I should certainly have got into difficulties. Indeed, I think I should hardly be the proper person to do it.'

While enduring these trials, Michael was nursing the third pillar of his legislation, the Employment Protection Bill, through a House in which the government's majority was perpetually uncertain. A note from Jill, accompanying her present for his sixty-second birthday, read: 'No good wishing you a happy birthday with a horrible day over your Bill ahead; but all my love and here's hoping the government pulls out of the bog and that you won't have to resign.'

The debates on the bill entailed a clash over a Tory amendment proposing government funding of postal ballots in trade unions. The argument was that this procedure would strengthen 'moderates' in the unions, on which Michael commented: 'I've always been very suspicious of the word "moderate".' He was able to produce an appropriate quotation from Hazlitt: 'An affected moderation in politics is, nine times out of ten, a cloak for want of principle.' In any case, Michael pointed out, 'most of the pressure over the past year or two has been from the rank and file . . . Anyone who tries to show

that a militant leadership is dragging a slow-witted, apathetic and phleg-
matic rank and file into industrial trouble is making a great mistake.'[76]

7

In this crowded year, Michael was involved in yet another drama: the
attempted suppression of Dick Crossman's diaries.

Crossman had died on 5 April 1974. Michael's tribute to him was
warm and affectionate:

> For offering sheer sustained intellectual excitement, he had few rivals,
> and none ever paraded his riches with so little pomposity or
> conceit . . . He never lost for long the iconoclasm of his socialist ideas
> and the astringent fire of those superb mental gifts. But that was not
> why we loved him. It was not even those brains. It was the mockery,
> the irony, the ebullience, the splendid moments when he caught
> himself out in some intellectual misapprehension and turned all those
> formidable guns away from us upon himself.[77]

Almost from the day when Crossman became a Cabinet minister in
1964, his colleagues were aware – for he never practised the slightest
concealment – that he was writing a diary, recording what was said in
Cabinet meetings and in countless other political conversations. He was
accumulating evidence for a new view of the realities of how Britain was
governed. This view (first advanced by John Mackintosh, a professor of
politics who became a Labour MP) was that Cabinet government, as
described by Walter Bagehot in 1867 in *The English Constitution*, had been
replaced by Prime Ministerial government. Crossman was (with some
reservations) convinced by Mackintosh's analysis and developed it,
firstly in 1963 in a long introduction to a new edition of Bagehot, and then
in three lectures which he delivered at Harvard University in 1970.

Had he lived, Crossman would have written a more substantial study
of what he had observed in the era of Prime Ministerial government, but
an equally vital part of his project was the publication of his diaries, which
supplied detailed and indispensable evidence. Michael had read parts of
these diaries and whetted the appetites of the audience at the Crossman
memorial meeting on 15 May: 'The diaries, I'm glad to say, have exactly
the degree of malice required for the purpose. They are laden with
revelations and I've no doubt that the Cabinet Office over the next few
weeks is hardly going to be able to give its mind to any other matter at
all.'

Here, Michael knew what he was talking about. Realising in 1973 that his cancer was terminal, Crossman had asked Michael to be one of his literary executors, together with his wife Anne and Graham Carleton Greene, managing director of the firm of Jonathan Cape which had contracted to publish the diaries. Michael readily agreed, although it was easy to foresee that there was trouble ahead. Crossman wrote in a letter to the three executors: 'The main immediate task of the literary executors, if I die before publication of my ministerial diaries is complete, would be to supervise this and to make sure that the pressure, which will undoubtedly be brought both from Whitehall and from Westminster to prevent publication of parts of the manuscript, is completely rejected.' In March 1974, Michael had a visit from Sir John Hunt, Secretary to the Cabinet, who suggested that he should resign as an executor because the job was incompatible with membership of the government. Michael politely declined. It was, clearly, the beginning of the pressure.

It was an established convention that memoirs or historical narratives by former ministers should be shown before publication to the Secretary to the Cabinet, who could raise objections to certain passages or (in theory at least) to the whole book. Accordingly, on 10 May a typescript of volume one, covering the period 1964–6 when Dick was Minister of Housing, was sent to Hunt. Having read it, he asked to see the executors. They went to his office on 21 June and were told that he was flatly opposed to publication and did not see that any editing or cutting would alter his attitude. A letter to Greene next day set out his reasoning:

> Ministers will not feel free frankly to discuss and to surrender their personal and Departmental preference to the achievement of a common view, nor can they be expected to abide by a common decision, if they know that the stand they have taken and the points they have surrendered will sooner rather than later become public knowledge. Since Cabinet government depends on the mutual confidence of collective responsibility, its basis can be eroded by the premature disclosure of what has passed within the confidential relationship.[78]

Central to the argument was the myth – for all informed people knew it to be a myth – of collective responsibility, which meant that all members of the government were assumed to support Cabinet decisions. Crossman's interpretation of the doctrine was: 'The bigger the fiasco in the Department, the more tempting it is to cover it up. This is collective responsibility in its modern sense.'[79] Anyone who read his diaries could see that, if they were published, the myth would be irreparably shattered.

A further letter from Hunt on 7 August defined the disclosures that would infringe what he called the 'parameters'. These were (a) accounts of Cabinet discussions and 'the revelation of differences between members of the Cabinet', (b) accounts of advice given by civil servants, (c) discussion about Civil Service appointments, (d) 'conversations about members of the government and their policies'.

By the end of 1974, Crossman's assistant, Janet Morgan, had edited the text into final shape and the diaries were ready for publication, first in extracts in the *Sunday Times* and subsequently in book form. The proposed extracts were shown to Hunt, who refused to modify his veto. On 14 January 1975, the executors and members of the *Sunday Times* staff met in Michael's room in the House of Commons. 'Foot put up the idea that the publishers and executors should simply write back now and say they intended to defy Hunt and publish.'[80] However, the situation was complicated by advice given by the ubiquitous Lord Goodman, legal adviser to Crossman and then to the executors; he had persuaded them to give Hunt fourteen days' notice of an intention to publish. Crossman's biographer comments: 'The case for freedom of action had already been compromised.'[81] Luckily, the *Sunday Times* had given no such undertaking. The executors, therefore, gave the paper a licence to publish and the editor, Harold Evans, went ahead without delay. The first of seven extracts appeared on 26 January.

Michael was bound in honour by loyalty to his old friend and by his duty as an executor to resist the anticipated pressure. Nevertheless, his feelings about the rights and wrongs of keeping and publishing a diary were considerably more ambivalent – and became still more so in later years when the Crossman diaries were followed by the Castle diaries and the Benn diaries.

His doubts can be summarised under three heads. Firstly, the compilation of a diary added a self-imposed burden on the shoulders of an already overworked minister, putting an extra tax on that minister's alertness and efficiency. In 1975 Barbara was asking, in the candour of her diary: 'How does one solve the problem of finding time to equip oneself to be a fully effective member of Cabinet? I work sixteen to seventeen hours a day non-stop and there is still not enough time.' Michael pencilled in the margin of his copy an answer to the question: 'Stop writing a diary.'

Secondly, Michael had at least some sympathy with Sir John Hunt's view on confidentiality. He had never kept a diary himself and the man he had most admired, Nye Bevan, certainly never had. Michael reflected:

Perhaps Nye was right, as he so often was on these personal-cum-
political questions . . . He believed that public men must have private
thoughts and the means of moulding them in the company of their
friends and comrades. The notion that serious politicians should be
willing to expose to public gaze . . . all their interchanges between one
another, every nuance of opinion, every tentative tactical consideration, would have been regarded by him as, yes, *obscene*.[82]

Finally, there was the difficult question of accuracy. When Michael
read and reviewed the volume of Barbara's diaries dealing with the
1974–6 period, in which he and she had been in the Cabinet, he voiced his
reservations:

Busy, overworked, self-centred, ambitious Cabinet ministers are not
the most dependable observers . . . It must be said that not only
individual incidents but pretty well the whole picture is out of focus,
thanks to the individual angle from which everything is necessarily
seen . . . So much the worse for diaries, and not only Barbara's. They
purport to tell all, and don't. They present supposedly considered
verdicts, which in fact are perpetually disarranged by the obtruding
ego. It is the rusted nail so near the compass which can wreck the
argosy.[83]

However, in 1975 the question was not whether diaries should be
written but whether they should be suppressed. Hunt enlisted the aid of
the Attorney-General, Sam Silkin (an elder brother of John Silkin, who
was in the Cabinet as Minister of Planning and Local Government). On 9
June, a few days after Goodman had given notice of the intention to
publish the diaries in book form, Silkin applied for an injunction asking
the courts to condemn publication of 'the account kept by Richard
Crossman in the form of a diary in whatever manner the same was or is
recorded or reproduced'. The writ was served both on the firm of Cape
and on the *Sunday Times* (although all the extracts had appeared) and they
therefore came into court as co-defendants.

The case was heard before Lord Widgery, the Lord Chief Justice
(sitting alone) on 22 July – the very day when Michael was in the
Commons making a major speech on inflation – and five succeeding
days. A cross-examination of the Secretary for Employment by the
Attorney-General would have been a piquant spectacle, but most of the
witnesses were allowed to present their evidence in the form of affidavits
and the only witness who actually went into the box was Sir John Hunt.

From start to finish, things went badly for Hunt and Silkin. Hunt had to admit that the Secretary to the Cabinet was only the servant of the Prime Minister, and Wilson had prudently avoided getting involved at any stage. Sir Burke Trend, Hunt's predecessor, had expressed his alarm in 1967 when he heard about Crossman's diary-keeping, but he had also cited 'a long and honourable convention' that a minister 'is entitled before he dies to put on record his own version of the events in which he has played a part'.[84] Usefully for the defence, Crossman was undoubtedly dead. Next, it had to be admitted that neither of the two acts which Silkin tried to bring into the argument, the Official Secrets Act and the Public Records Act, had any real relevance – the former because there were no state secrets in the diary of the Minister of Housing, the latter because its imposition of a thirty-year limit applied only to documents, not to accounts of what had been said.

Then, there was ample evidence that Hunt's parameters had been ignored time and again, always with impunity. The authorised biography of Neville Chamberlain, published in 1946, quoted his diary and personal letters from his period as Prime Minister. Hugh Dalton's diaries had been quoted both in his own autobiography and in Michael's life of Bevan; an academic authority, Rudolf Klein, testified in an affidavit that they had never been submitted to the Secretary to the Cabinet and were available to any student in the library of the London School of Economics. Finally, Harold Wilson had made what Hunt would have classed as improper revelations in his book *The Labour Government, 1964–1970*.

It was now the end of July, and time for the legal vacation. Widgery wrote his judgement at leisure over the next two months and delivered it on 1 October. He gave his support to the principle that 'when a Cabinet minister receives information in confidence, the improper publication of such information can be restrained by the court'. The question was whether, in a particular case, publication was improper. Whether – or rather when, for the vital consideration, Widgery judged, was how much time had passed since the Cabinet meetings which were revealed. He remarked that 'much of the action is up to ten years old and three general elections have been held meanwhile.' Therefore, he ruled that publication of the Crossman diaries would not damage the doctrine of collective responsibility, and refused the injunction.

Widgery's ruling was criticised for its lack of legal clarity, but it had a persuasive quality of common sense. In effect, what was defined as unacceptable was the publication of the secrets of a government which was still in office. Hence, Barbara Castle's diaries of the years 1974–6 were published in 1980; and Tony Benn's diaries of the years 1977–80 were published in 1990. But if Crossman's executors and the *Sunday Times* had not challenged the attempt at suppression, none of them would ever have appeared.

8

Morale in the Labour Party was low when delegates gathered for their conference in September 1975. Unemployment had passed the limits that the rank and file regarded as tolerable; inflation too was getting worse; nerves had been shaken by the crisis in July and no one was confident that it would be the last. Thus Michael's speech to the conference was of greater political importance than any speech in Parliament. If he failed to carry conviction and to offer inspiration, the government might forfeit the loyalty on which it depended. He said:

It is indeed, in my judgement, a crisis of capitalism of a most formidable character, and we have to muster all our energies, all our skill, to deal with it . . . It is of the first importance . . . that this crisis should be faced and surmounted by a Labour government acting in the closest alliance and good faith with the trade union movement of this country. If we were to fall apart I shudder to think what would be the consequences for our people, for our young people and old alike, in unemployment and in all the consequences. I shudder to think also what would be the consequence for our democratic institutions . . .

People sometimes say: we will agree to some arrangement between the government and the trade unions about wages, but only when you have got the full panoply of socialist measures actually put into operation and in working order. I understand the argument, but I say it is unworkable. There is not a single government in the world aspiring to change society that could work upon that system of transition, whether it is Communist, Maoist, Yugoslav, anything . . .

Investment means very often, almost always, forgoing present claims in order to secure future benefits . . . You can do it by the brutal capitalist methods of the nineteenth century, or you can do it by the equally brutal, or maybe even more outrageous, methods of twentieth-century Stalinism, or you can do it by the politics of persuasion, by the social contract . . . You can do it the democratic way, which lies at the heart and soul of our Labour movement . . .

We face an economic typhoon of unparalleled ferocity, the worst the world has seen since the 1930s. Joseph Conrad wrote a book called

Typhoon, and at the end he told people how to do it. He said: 'Always facing it, Captain MacWhirr. That's the way to get through.' Always facing it – that's the way we have got to solve this problem. We don't want a Labour movement that tries to dodge it; we don't want people in a Labour Cabinet to try to dodge it. We want people who are prepared to show how they're going to face it . . . I'm not asking for any dull uniformity or anything of the sort. I am asking this movement to exert itself as it has never done before, to show the qualities which we have, the socialist imagination that exists in our movement, the readiness to re-forge the alliance, stronger than ever, between the government and the trade unions, and above all to show the supreme quality in politics, the red flame of socialist courage.

The speech, and especially the peroration, was a triumph. Barbara wrote: 'He had a horrible job and triumphed by taking the challenge full on, giving all the emotional voltage he had got. Conference rose to him with a standing ovation, only Mik and co. remaining on their posteriors . . . I myself, sitting next to him, had been almost reduced to tears by his utter dedication and sincerity.'[85] A note from Geoffrey Goodman read: 'I have heard you many, many times. But none better than today. It was a superb performance: inspiring, courageous, outstanding by any standards. Even by the standards of Nye.'

True, the speech offered no clear prescriptions for overcoming the crisis. In Conrad's deeply ironical novel, Captain MacWhirr's outstanding characteristic was not imagination but lack of imagination and inability to understand what was happening. Confronted with books of navigation, he 'ended by becoming contemptuously angry with such a lot of words and with so much advice, all head-work and supposition, without a glimmer of certitude'. But Michael's audience was not concerned with Conradian subtleties. 'Always facing it' was what mattered.

Returning to Westminster, Michael found himself still enmeshed in TULRA Two and the outcries over press freedom. Driven on by Lord Goodman's urgings, the House of Lords rejected the bill for the second time and Michael had to put it through the Commons again. The Tory leader in the Upper House, Lord Carrington, was very dubious about the wisdom of this challenge, and Lord Cudlipp (Hugh Cudlipp, a man of unrivalled experience in journalism) said that Lord Goodman might be remembered as 'the man who failed to defend the press by statute but succeeded in abolishing the House of Lords'. Michael declared: 'At a time when respect for Parliament and more especially this elected chamber is of such supreme importance in overcoming our national problems, I believe that everyone in the House should join in condemning this challenge to democratic authority.'[86]

His tolerance was further tempted at just this time by another attack connected with the closed shop. Six workers at the Ferrybridge power station in Yorkshire, where there was a closed-shop agreement, refused to join the union and were dismissed. It was then found, to the loud outrage of the Tory press, that they were not entitled to unemployment benefit. Although this ruling was in the province not of Michael's Department but of the Department of Social Security (headed by Barbara), Michael took it on himself to explain: 'A person who declines to fall in with new conditions of employment which result from a collective agreement may well be considered to have brought about his dismissal.' The Shadow Secretary for Employment, Norman Tebbit – an abrasive politician once compared by Michael to a 'semi-house-trained polecat' – denounced the decision as 'an example of pure undiluted fascism'. Picking up the theme, *The Times* on 2 December headed its main leader: 'IS MR FOOT A FASCIST?' The argument was that all-round control of an individual's fate was a hallmark of the corporate state, and the corporate state (the model being Mussolini's Italy) was a synonym for fascism. Smugly, the leader concluded that the proper question was probably 'Does Mr Foot know that he is a fascist? To that at least we can give a charitable answer.' Michael retorted that the accusation 'shows the discrimination and taste of Dr Goebbels'. In the House, he remarked: 'The editor of *The Times* throws his stone from a glasshouse of Crystal Palace proportions.'[87]

The Trade Union and Labour Relations Bill – or the Closed Shop Bill, as Nora Beloff consistently called it in her book – finally passed its Third Reading in the Commons on 21 January 1976. Goodman fought on in the Lords, attempting to delete any reference to a press code or charter, but he was now backed neither by the Tory peers nor by the Fleet Street editors and lost the crucial vote. For the Lords to defeat the bill a third time would have been pointless, since it would automatically be sent to receive the Royal Assent. Despite last-ditch protests from Goodman, TULRA Two was accepted by the Lords on 22 March 1976. Altogether, it had taken almost two years to get the bill on to the statute book.

Goodman predicted darkly: 'If the erosion of human rights continues, it will result in the destruction of democracy.' Michael, his patience exhausted, used a speech to the Foreign Press Association to declare that 'no credence whatever any more can be given to anything Goodman chooses to say on the subject' and that the whole campaign against the bill had been 'a farrago of fiction, falsehood and hysteria'.[88] Looking back today, we can see whose forecasts were right. Editors are still exempted from the closed shop; they are not subjected to the dictates of the NUJ in matters of content or policy; they still commission contributions from independent reviewers, academics or anyone else. There has indeed been a sad decline in the quality, integrity, truthfulness and ethical level of the British press – but the men to be blamed, as Michael always insisted, are the proprietors.

9

On 16 March 1976, the Cabinet assembled for what its members assumed to be the regular weekly meeting. Instead of setting the agenda, the Prime Minister told them that he had gone to Buckingham Palace earlier in the morning and tendered his resignation to the Queen.

In their own words, Healey was 'flabbergasted',[89] Benn was 'stunned'[90] and Crosland told his wife that the Cabinet were 'transfixed'.[91] Eighteen months before, Benn had predicted to Bob Mellish, the Chief Whip: 'He'll be there for another twenty years' – to which Mellish had replied: 'Oh God, I hope not.'[92] In reality, although this did not emerge until years later, Wilson had decided even before the 1974 elections to hold office for only a couple of years and to retire on, or near to, his sixtieth birthday.[93] He kept his own counsel, but on 4 March 1976 he told Barbara Castle: 'I don't intend to be in this job much longer.' He added that he had told the Queen the date of his retirement, but he declined to tell Barbara.[94]

A few people had been informed, in strict secrecy, at various times in 1975. These were the Queen (Wilson was a stickler for constitutional correctness), Marcia Williams and others of his personal staff, his old friend George Thomas, who was Speaker of the House, and another old friend, Harold Lever. Lever passed it on to Callaghan, but Callaghan was incredulous: 'I did not for a moment believe he was likely or needed to resign.'[95] The calendar for 1977 featured a Commonwealth Prime Ministers' conference, the first European summit to be held in London and the Queen's Jubilee. Callaghan is alleged to have remarked: 'I say to myself, surely the little bugger won't pass up those.'[96]

Wilson was only sixty years old and was in good health, although it had been observed that he felt – and looked – older than his age, and it is possible that he felt the first signs of the mental decline and fading memory that later overtook him. Speculation about his reasons began on that 16 March and has never ceased. He may have wanted to retire before it could be said that his departure was overdue or that he was being pushed; no Prime Minister had achieved this since Baldwin in 1937. Then, as his biographer points out, he was 'obsessively concerned about the clandestine activities which he came to believe were being directed at himself'.[97] There is much convincing evidence that elements in the security services were 'making a deliberate and carefully planned attempt to blacken Wilson's name by implying that he had illegitimate Soviet connections'.[98] But perhaps the deciding factor was that his wife Mary made no secret of her dislike of the political life and often told friends that, when she had married him, she had thought she was becoming the wife of an Oxford don. In his valedictory account, Wilson proudly listed the forty foreign visitors he had received in a year, including the Prime Minister of the Maldive Islands, the Sultan of Oman, the Foreign Minister of Somalia, the Premier of British Columbia and the Mayor of West Berlin.[99] These were not the people for whom Mary would have chosen to pour tea.

The next event was the election of Wilson's successor as leader of the Labour Party, a process which required three ballots and lasted until 5 April. For the first time in British history the monarch had to wait for a party election before appointing a Prime Minister. Michael did not immediately enter the contest, and Judith Hart wrote to him:

> I am quite clear in my own mind – and I think many others will agree – that in this situation you must be elected Leader. This means that you *must* agree to go forward: I can imagine all your personal hesitations . . . The new leader must unify the Party. And you can do it. No alternative on the scene – Jim, Denis, Roy – could do other, whatever their good intentions might (or might not) be, than increase the present tensions . . . I think you could win. No other person whom the Left would back could win. Tony? – but not now, and not yet, if only because of the campaign against him. He has time ahead of him.

Michael agreed to stand, regarding himself as the candidate of the left. There were six candidates: in alphabetical order, Tony Benn, Jim Callaghan, Tony Crosland, Michael Foot, Denis Healey and Roy Jenkins. Despite Judith's persuasions, Michael had no expectations of victory. His aim – as it had been Bevan's aim when he stood for the leadership after Attlee's retirement – was to test and if possible maximise the strength of the left. The solid fact was that the majority of Labour MPs could be classed as right-wingers and the winner was certain to be a right-wing political figure – either Callaghan, Jenkins or Healey. True,

Michael had rendered vital service to the party in the past two years, he had shown surprising administrative ability and he was a star of the House of Commons. On the other hand, he had not been tested in a front-ranking department such as the Treasury or the Foreign Office; any MP whose memory went back more than five years recalled him as a rebellious back-bencher; and, even if they had the warmest admiration and affection for him, for the most part they could not quite envisage him as Prime Minister.

In the first ballot, Michael received 90 votes, Callaghan 84, Jenkins 56, Benn 37, Healey 30 and Crosland 17. For Michael to come top of the poll was gratifying, but it did not mark him as a likely winner, since the right-wing votes were scattered. The betting was on Callaghan, as it had been from the start. Under the rules, Crosland was eliminated. Benn, who was considered to have polled well, withdrew and asked his supporters to vote for Michael in the next round. Healey did not withdraw, but Jenkins did. Keenly disappointed by getting only 56 votes, he realised that he would never overtake Callaghan. In the second ballot, Callaghan pulled ahead with 141 votes against 133 for Michael and 38 for Healey. With Healey eliminated, the final ballot was a formality. Callaghan won with 176 votes; Michael had 137.

The new Prime Minister's political assets were considerable. While he was identified with the right of the party, he had never antagonised the left to the same degree as Jenkins. He had maintained good relations with the leaders of the big trade unions, who remembered his help in the days of *In Place of Strife*. He had held the three traditional 'great offices of state' as Chancellor, Home Secretary and Foreign Secretary, a record matched by no other Prime Minister in this century. However, since he was sixty-four years old (four years older than Wilson, one year older than Michael) he had assumed that his career had touched its apogee and had given up the thought of occupying Number 10. Nor had he forgotten his early years, which had been a period of poverty, or at least closer to poverty than anything experienced by the other five candidates for the leadership, who had all been to Oxford. When Cledwyn Hughes, as chairman of the PLP, told him the result of the final ballot, he exclaimed with some emotion: 'Prime Minister of Great Britain! And I never went to a university.' Hughes pointed out that this was also true of Lloyd George and Churchill.[100]

Michael had gained in political weight by his good vote, and Callaghan consulted him about Cabinet appointments. His inclination was to give the Foreign Office to Jenkins, but Michael warned him that the left would take this badly. Callaghan, therefore, appointed Tony Crosland.

Another big job was available to Jenkins; it was Britain's turn to nominate the next President of the European Commission and Wilson, before his resignation, had offered Jenkins the nomination. Knowing that he was unlikely to rise any higher in a Labour government, Jenkins was content to make the move to Brussels.

Michael also had to consider his own future. Ted Short was ready to give up the position of Leader of the House, a vital responsibility in view of the government's practically non-existent majority. Tony Benn had told Michael: 'I've done twelve years of industrial work . . . and I think I'd like a break . . . What I would really like to do would be Leader of the House.'[101] It was not an ambition that Callaghan was likely to facilitate. His account reads: 'I consulted Michael Foot, as runner-up in the leadership election, about his personal preferences for office . . . I was happy to meet his request to be Leader of the House.'[102] Michael would have liked to stay at the Department of Employment, at least for a time, to put through the employment subsidy and other measures that he had in hand, and if possible to get the unemployment figures down. But since the job of Leader of the House was open, he was prepared to take it.

A new Secretary for Employment was needed, and Michael told Callaghan that the right man was Albert Booth, who had been number two since 1974 and was thoroughly familiar with the work, and was also *persona grata* with Jack Jones and other union leaders. Embarrassingly, Tony Benn had now set his sights on this Department and informed Michael: 'On merit, seniority and capacity to pull the trade union movement together, I would do a better job at Employment.'[103] Michael had to make it clear that Booth had been offered Employment and had accepted; Benn was obliged to stay at Energy.

These flurries were relatively harmonious by comparison with Callaghan's decision to drop Barbara Castle from the government. He had never liked her and knew that she acutely disliked him, particularly since he had checkmated her over *In Place of Strife*. In a formal letter and also verbally, Michael argued in Barbara's defence, but in vain. In their final interview, the Prime Minister told her: 'You should know that Mike has fought for you very hard. I had to tell him that this was one thing I could not give him.'[104] Barbara, however, thought that Michael could have fought harder and refused to behave like a good loser. She wrote in her diary: 'I am deeply hurt by Jim's cavalier discarding of me like so much old junk.'[105] Wounded on her own account, she was also indignant because Callaghan did not bring Judith Hart back into the Cabinet, and added: 'It shows how superficial is our party's devotion to the cause of promoting women.'

Michael left the Department of Employment with genuine regret and with farewell letters from its civil servants that went well beyond the conventional requirements. Donald Derx wrote:

I count myself lucky to have served someone who has positive aims, definite ideas on how to secure them and a generous spirit. You posed a quite exceptional challenge to my carefully nurtured powers of obstruction . . . You know my view that Ministers should not get too close to their civil servants – and vice versa. It is a good maxim and often not at all difficult to follow for either party. But I confess to feeling a special wrench on the present occasion.

A little later, after Michael had taken up his new job, he received this letter from Kathy Hegarty, who had been his private secretary:

Life in this office has been unbelievably bleak since your departure . . . I know that things will never be the same again. I am unlikely to find another Cabinet Minister who is so considerate, so warm and so appreciative; or one, for that matter, with such a lovely sense of humour . . . We miss you dreadfully and there is no doubt that this Department has lost out.

Chapter 12

PROTECT AND SURVIVE

I

In official language, Michael was now Lord President of the Council and Leader of the House of Commons. The Council over which he nominally presided was the Privy Council, whose origins went back to Norman times and whose members, in the reign of Edward I, took an oath 'to give good advice, to protect the King's interests, to do justice honestly, to take no gifts'. In the eighteenth century the Privy Council was superseded as an effective centre of authority by the Cabinet, and in modern times Privy Councillor is an honorific title, conferred on (among others) Michael's father, Isaac Foot. But the Privy Council still has to meet, in the presence of the Queen, to take certain decisions, such as the proclamation of a State of Emergency.

The Lord President is often (though not always) Leader of the House. He is often (though not always) a major political figure, freed from departmental duties to act as the Prime Minister's senior colleague. Appointment as Lord President was a sign that Michael had the status of number two in the government, or deputy Prime Minister (a position that, constitutionally, does not exist). He was also number two in the Labour Party, and this was recognised in October 1976 when, in place of Edward Short, he was elected without a contest as deputy leader.

Jim Callaghan and Michael Foot soon established a close relationship of trust and co-operation. On the face of it, this was surprising. They had never been personal friends and had certainly not been political allies, and in the last two years Michael had been critical of Callaghan's record as Foreign Secretary. But he found that Callaghan was a better Prime Minister, and easier to work with, than Wilson; he welcomed frank discussion and was open to persuasion. Political observers noted: 'Callaghan regarded Foot as his closest political confidant. While he would discuss important issues with Healey, it was Foot to whom he unburdened the deeper issues preying on his mind.'[1]

Barbara Castle, always hostile to Callaghan, complained: 'He [Michael] had been only narrowly defeated by Jim Callaghan for the leadership, but he carried his loyalty to him almost to the point of idolatry.'[2] Michael's attitude to Callaghan was actually far short of idolatry, but the loyalty was real. Callaghan was grateful and perhaps surprised, remembering that the number two in a government generally intrigued against the number one (Morrison against Attlee, Brown against Wilson). At the 1976 party conference, he paid public tribute when he told the delegates 'how deeply I appreciate the support of Michael, who, in the interests of the unity of our movement and our party, has put aside his personal feelings in order to help our party and our government'. Aware of how disastrous a rupture would be, he took care not to place Michael in a difficult position. By his own account, he ensured that the Chevaline project (modernisation of the Polaris missiles) was kept secret and never discussed in the Cabinet, partly to evade public protest, but mainly so that Michael should not be embarrassed.[3] As time passed, appreciation was transmuted into affection. In 1985, in a letter acknowledging Michael's congratulations on his peerage, Lord Callaghan wrote: 'I was caught on the hop in one of my interviews last week with the question: "Of all the people you have served with, who would you like to serve with again?" . . . My reply was instinctive. Believe it or not, I said "Michael Foot".'

Michael was now installed in a set of offices in the neo-classical buildings on the west side of Whitehall, with a direct and discreet access to 10 Downing Street. The rooms were ample and splendid. On arrival, Michael was confronted by a portrait of King James II, the legacy of the Catholic and traditionalist Norman St John-Stevas, who had occupied the rooms under the Heath government. The tyrannical Catholic monarch, evicted from his throne in 1688, was again summarily evicted and replaced by a portrait of Swift.

The Minister of State in the Privy Council office was John Smith, MP for North Lanarkshire. A Scottish lawyer, he had risen rapidly since entering the Commons in 1970 and came to Whitehall from being Minister of State in Tony Benn's Energy Department. His main responsibility was for the Constitutional Unit, which was working on plans for devolution for Scotland and Wales. His exceptional head for complex details, his legal training and his Scottish background made him ideal for the job. The senior civil servant in the Unit was the capable, if conventional, Sir Michael Quinlan. The two people closest to Michael in everyday work were his PPS, Caerwyn Roderick, and Elizabeth Thomas, his former secretary, recruited as 'special adviser'. She had moved from *Tribune* to become assistant literary editor of the *New Statesman*, but found that job unsatisfying and was glad of Michael's invitation.

In the spring and summer of 1976, Michael was working closely with Denis Healey on plans for a second year of wage restraint. The agreement reached, to run from July 1976 to July 1977, was for increases of £2.50 a week for the lower-paid, £4 for skilled workers and a ceiling of 5 per cent. The negotiations with the unions were, as Healey recorded, 'extremely difficult'. In a letter to him after the agreement was signed, Michael wrote: 'Only those who actually saw it can have the remotest idea of what it involved and what combined persistence and intelligence were required to secure it. Quite possibly it has changed the whole prospect for the country and the government; at least it has given us the chance to survive. And the achievement was overwhelmingly yours.' The last sentence was modest and generous. Jones had committed himself in a personal note to Michael: 'Whatever you decide to do regarding the present position will have my full support.' The union leaders might not have yielded to the Chancellor's demands – 'Denis Healey seemed to us intransigent,' Jones wrote later[4] – if they had not trusted Michael to preserve the voluntary system.

The typhoon was still raging. In March, the government presented a White Paper envisaging spending cuts of £1,600 million. It was labelled 'White Paper of shame' in a statement by the Tribune Group, left-wing abstentions led to a government defeat in the Commons and the government stayed in power only by securing a vote of confidence. In July, Healey was able to protect the pound only by getting a large stand-by credit from the Bank of International Settlements and promising to make the cuts. The Cabinet agreed to cuts of a billion pounds after a series of what Healey called 'appallingly difficult' meetings.[5]

The surrender bought time – but wretchedly little time. On 28 September the pound was down to $1.63 and Healey warned Callaghan that it was 'in free fall'. Nobody was in command in London, since the Prime Minister was at Blackpool for the party conference while the Chancellor was leaving for a Commonwealth conference in Hongkong. He confessed in his memoirs: 'For the first and last time in my life, for about twelve hours I was close to demoralisation.'[6] He got as far as Heathrow, then cancelled his journey. Callaghan takes up the story in *his* memoirs: 'I should have encouraged the Chancellor to go to Hongkong, for as soon as the City learned that he had decided not to go, hysterical panic set in for forty-eight hours. The markets behaved with all the restraint of a screaming crowd of schoolgirls at a rock concert.'[7]

At Blackpool, Callaghan told the delegates: 'We have been living on borrowed time . . . We used to think you could spend your way out of a recession and increase employment by cutting taxes and boosting government spending. I tell you in all candour that option no longer exists.' When Healey went on television to announce that he rested his hopes on assistance from the International Monetary Fund, Scanlon expressed his 'complete disagreement'. Judith Hart, speaking for the NEC, was cheered when she said: 'If Jim and Denis are worried about foreign confidence and the run on the pound, let them tell the IMF that we don't agree with the pre-Keynesian economics that dominate the IMF.' Healey dashed to Blackpool and began his speech with the dramatic words: 'I come from the battlefront.' With his usual tact, he went on: 'There are some people who would like to stop the world and get off,' and he told the delegates that they would have to accept 'the very painful cuts in public expenditure on which the government has already decided'. He left the rostrum amid angry shouts and returned to London to prepare for what would undoubtedly be tough negotiations with the IMF. Michael, accompanied by Jill, caught the overnight plane to Delhi.

2

The Foots were due to spend a busy week in India, visiting Kashmir, Hyderabad, Bangalore and Bombay as well as the capital. On their first day, they lunched with Indira Gandhi, watched the celebration of the Dasera festival and met Mrs Gandhi again at a dinner given by the British High Commissioner. Michael's affection for both India and Indira was undiminished since his first visit three years earlier, and he had happily accepted the invitation to another trip. However, this meeting was likely to prove more advantageous to the Indian Prime Minister than to the British Lord President of the Council. Mrs Gandhi was in dire need of friends from abroad and was anxiously concerned about her international reputation.

The High Court in Allahabad, home town of the Nehru family and Indira's parliamentary constituency, had been hearing a petition to unseat her on the grounds that she had improperly used government facilities in the 1971 election campaign. Although such offences were far from rare in Indian politics, the court ruling in June 1975 disqualified her from public office, including her parliamentary seat and her position as Prime Minister. The ruling was a godsend to J. P. Narayan, a revered veteran of the Congress movement who was already denouncing the govern-

ment for various misdeeds and promoting civil disobedience protests on
the lines of those aimed at the British Raj in 1942, in which he had played a
major part. Now, with the Prime Minister clinging to office illegally, he
called on police and army personnel to disobey orders to repress these
protests. Mrs Gandhi's response was to declare a state of emergency,
claiming that 'the security of India is threatened by internal disturbances'.

During the night of 25 June 1975, thousands of people were roused
from their beds and carried off to detention centres, including Narayan
(who was gravely ill with diabetes), the most prominent of the
government's political opponents, and 2,000 students, plus 190 of the
faculty, from Nehru University. The arrests were authorised by MISA, a
piece of legislation passed in 1973; the initials stood for Maintenance of
Internal Security Act but were often interpreted as 'Maintenance of Indira
and Sanjay Act'. The Prime Minister's vicious and disreputable younger
son, Sanjay, was a key figure in the power structure and was largely
responsible for what came to be called the 'excesses' of the Emergency.
P. N. Haksar, who had just retired as Mrs Gandhi's private secretary and
who had warned her that the Emergency would be a disaster, said sadly
when he looked back: 'It was all the fault of that wretched boy.'[8]

The case that aroused the greatest anxiety was that of George
Fernandes, leader of the Socialist Party of India. Being away from home
when the Emergency was declared, he went into hiding and started to
organise underground resistance, producing illegal leaflets and setting up
a short-wave transmitter. He was tracked down and arrested on 10 June
1976. Charged with treason, he faced a possible death sentence. When the
trial began, he was brought into the dock in chains. Thanks to his
international standing – he had attended conferences of the Socialist
International – expressions of concern came from Willy Brandt, Bruno
Kreisky of Austria and Olof Palme of Sweden. Ron Hayward, secretary
of the Labour Party, wrote to the Foreign Secretary, Tony Crosland,
who replied: 'I fully share your concern about this arrest. However, we
must clearly approach the Indians with great caution. You know how
sensitive they can be . . . Mrs Gandhi is very sensitive about the
International; I think that the less the International gets involved, the
greater the chances of success.'

Another aspect of the Emergency was censorship of the press,
gradually replaced by various forms of self-censorship or pressure. The
BBC was subjected to so many restrictions that honest reporting became
impossible and it had to close its Delhi office. The news from India, so far
as it leaked out, was a mixture of the horrific and the bizarre. Sanjay
Gandhi ordered a campaign of mass sterilisation; family planning had not

advanced sufficiently on a voluntary basis, so it was done by compulsion. According to an Indian writer: 'Villages would be surrounded, all the males rounded up and, irrespective of age, vasectomised. Or trucks halted, men turfed out and dealt with . . . Promotions, confirmations in jobs, even salaries became dependent on producing a quota of vasectomy certificates . . . Whole villages were depopulated at the sound of a jeep horn.'[9]

Naturally, friends of India in Britain and elsewhere were shocked. Natwar Singh, who was Deputy High Commissioner in London, recalls: 'It was impossible to sell the Emergency.'[10] However, a valiant effort was made by Swraj Paul, an Indian industrialist who earned Michael's gratitude by locating a factory in Ebbw Vale (when completed, it was opened by Indira Gandhi). In November 1975 he organised a dinner, attended by 300 guests drawn largely from the business world, at which the speakers were Reginald Maudling, a former Tory Chancellor of the Exchequer, and Michael Foot. As a follow-up, the Indo–British Association was created 'as a centre and forum for the promotion of Indo–British understanding', with Paul as chairman, the Tory MP Eldon Griffiths as vice-chairman, and Michael on a Council of Advisers.

The next step was to endow a Krishna Menon Lecture, to be delivered in New Delhi in memory of the fighter against imperialism who had gone on to be a key member of Nehru's government. The first lecture, in January 1976, was given by Jennie Lee. During her visit, she made it clear that she supported the Emergency, on the grounds that any democracy was entitled to take firm measures against subversion. Michael was invited to give the second lecture. Crosland was anxious about what Michael might say while in India, and instructed his private secretary to write a letter to Michael's private secretary:

He [the Foreign Secretary] believes that the Government must be careful not to appear to be taking up an attitude on India's internal affairs, for example through statements which might be interpreted as expressing public approval of the present Emergency and the existing political situation. Recent developments in India, including the arrest and forthcoming trial of Mr George Fernandes, have made this issue if anything even more sensitive politically. Mr Crosland therefore hopes that the Lord President will be guided in his talks and public statements in India by the view I have set out above.

On arrival in New Delhi, Michael received two cautions from the High Commissioner, Sir Michael Walker. He must not be surprised to find that Mrs Gandhi was surrounded by massive security precautions; and he must expect her to receive any remarks on the record of the Emergency, notably the Fernandes case, with angry resentment. However, when Michael and Jill went to the Red Fort for the Dasera festivities, they observed that Indira was fearlessly close to the crowd and had no more protection than any other democratic leader – less, indeed, than some. And, in conversation with her, Michael found that Walker's forebodings were just as unnecessary. He wrote later:

After the portrayal of her as a ruthless natural autocrat, it was stunning to meet her . . . I was warned by our all-wise Foreign Office officials how inadvisable it would be to raise a whole range of civil liberties issues with her. Even to mention them might cause a diplomatic-cum-autocratic explosion . . . We discussed at length every forbidden topic on the list. I had been told she would not tolerate intrusion in India's domestic affairs; she enlarged upon them all . . . She had a gentleness and coolness which were much more characteristic than the fury which was sometimes alleged to take possession of her whole being.[11]

Walker reported on the meeting in a despatch to Crosland:

Mr Foot asked whether, now that the political and economic situation had eased, it was proving possible to make some relaxations in the Emergency restrictions. Mrs Gandhi replied that various relaxations were now taking place and she was personally encouraging this policy and urging wider releases of those held under detention. Mr Foot . . . referred to the case of Mr Fernandes and said that he had no doubt that the Prime Minister would be aware of the international concern which had been expressed about his detention. Mrs Gandhi took this quite calmly and without demur but did not comment on the position beyond saying that Mr Fernandes would shortly come to trial . . .

Mention was made about the family planning programme and Mrs Gandhi emphasised the vital importance of ensuring a really effective policy . . . Public opinion generally was prepared to accept a compulsory policy . . .

Mr Foot was impressed by Mrs Gandhi's calm, self-confident and assured attitude . . . He was quite sure that she took no offence at all at his enquiries about Members of Parliament in prison and the position of Mr Fernandes.

On 5 November, Michael delivered his lecture and also gave a press conference. As was his wont, he spoke without a prepared text and his surviving notes contain no references to the situation in India (one note reads: 'Vietnam – age of empire over'). Memories of the press conference by Indian journalists vary, but in the gossipy world of New Delhi there was no doubt that he approved of the Emergency. For some, the mere fact that he had accepted an invitation to go to India at such a time was enough, especially when the organiser was Swraj Paul, a strong supporter of Mrs Gandhi through thick and thin, and his official host was a member of her government (the Indian Minister of Labour). At a personal level, Michael's best friend in India, Abu, was another convinced supporter of the Emergency and was then a government-appointed member of the Upper House of Parliament.

Although Michael was an experienced journalist, he could scarcely probe very deeply in eight days filled largely by official lunches and dinners, visits to four industrial establishments and a museum, and air journeys. But in a report circulated to members of the Cabinet on his return, he was emphatic:

> My main overwhelming impression is that there is strong and widespread support for the measures and general attitude which the Government of India has taken under the Emergency . . . The evidence is unmistakable and drawn from many quarters . . . The British Government will be able to influence the situation beneficially for India and ourselves only if we have an imaginative understanding of what has been achieved during the Emergency and why these achievements invoke so much popular support.

In ensuing weeks, Michael's confidence in his impressions was somewhat dented by letters from India and from Indians living in Britain. A speech which he made at a lunch with Indian journalists in London was reported thus: 'Mr Foot rejected the Western propaganda that India was moving towards dictatorship.'[12] This evoked a complaint from Mehar Chand Yadev, secretary of the Socialist Party of India: 'Your statement to Indian journalists in Britain dated 23 Nov. 76 as appeared here in India shows that you have been befooled during your visit to this country.' Michael replied: 'I assure you that I am not attempting to pass judgement on the situation in India. I did try to talk to as many people as I could and of as many varied opinions as possible. Unfortunately, I could not see everybody I wanted to during my visit because I was only in India for a short time.'

Yadev was not the only one to be shocked and dismayed. Making their own visit to India in January 1977, E. P. Thompson and his wife Dorothy observed: 'Through the length and breadth of Emergency India the media pumped out the devastating news that Michael Foot had endorsed Mrs Gandhi's regime.' Thompson attended a secret meeting of opponents of that regime:

> I must taxi here: walk there: get another taxi: meet someone by a cinema: and then . . . slide into the upstairs room of a villa where about twenty young men and women, mainly graduate students, were packed on the floor. If the meeting had been 'blown', every one of them could have disappeared indefinitely into India's overcrowded and insanitary prisons . . . Eventually the conversation came round to the point which it always did – in Delhi, Aligarh, Kerala, Bombay, Baroda – 'Why has the British Labour movement abandoned us like this? Don't people know? Why did Michael Foot support the Emergency?' Twenty pairs of pained, angry, estranged and brave eyes waited for my answer. I did not have one to give.[13]

But, for anyone who knew Michael, the answer was clear enough. Indira Gandhi was his friend, and he was always loyal to his friends. Moreover, she was the inheritor of the Nehru ideal of a democratic and socialist India. It followed that all her opponents were reactionaries (in fact, a good number of them were). It also followed that her explanation – that the Narayan campaign was a plot to overthrow a democratic government – must be taken on trust. Haksar's comment is: 'He accepted Indira's version in memory of Nehru and out of the goodness of his heart. His sympathy was right but his understanding was wrong.'[14]

Friends in England were shocked and puzzled. Michael had to listen to scathing reproaches from James Cameron, who knew India far better than he did, and from Cameron's Indian wife Moni. Geoffrey Goodman remembers a bitter argument on the subject between Frank Cousins and Michael. Caerwyn Roderick, Michael's PPS, saw that he was hurt by criticisms, casting doubt at least on his judgement and sometimes on his integrity, from old friends on the left. But, Roderick recalls, Michael remained absolutely convinced that he was right.[15]

About one aspect of the matter he was indeed proved right. In contradiction to the 'expert' view of Sir Michael Walker, who informed Crosland that the democratic phase of Indian history was over and the authoritarian regime was a permanance, he predicted that Mrs Gandhi would soon lift the Emergency and hold a free election. In February 1977, she did so. She lost the election, but she made a successful comeback in 1980.

George Fernandes, though he was still in prison at the time of the 1977 election, won a constituency in Bihar with an enormous majority. In October 1977 he came to England to attend the Labour Party conference and met Michael. He refrained from uttering any reproaches, feeling that 'it would not have been right behaviour towards a comrade'. He perceived, however, that Michael was embarrassed.[16]

3

Back in London after the busy week in India, Michael was given no respite. He had been struck by a severe headache while speaking at the Cambridge Union. The trouble was shingles, a virus infection which attacks the sensory nerves, generally those which supply the forehead and face. The pain is among the worst in the range of physical suffering. Michael had another spell in the Royal Free Hospital, and his recovery was not complete; as an irreversible after-effect, he lost the sight of his left eye.

Healey was locked in negotiations with emissaries from the IMF, who were staying under false names at Brown's Hotel. At one remove, he was actually dealing with the Republican administration in Washington and with people like Arthur Burns, governor of the Federal Reserve Bank, who cheerfully described himself (in a later interview) as 'a neanderthal conservative and naturally suspicious of a Labour government'.[17] As seen from Washington, 'the Labour government appeared, to the Americans, to be in grave danger of falling under the control of the left wing – in particular Tony Benn . . . Therefore . . . the US determined to use the IMF to force changes in British Government policy and behaviour.'[18]

Healey agreed to make expenditure cuts of one billion pounds on top of the billion enforced in July. The IMF demanded two billion and Healey finally conceded one billion in the next financial year and another billion in the ensuing year if the British economy did not turn the corner. With Callaghan's support, he presented this to the Cabinet. The balance of forces had been altered since the last crisis; Jenkins was on his way to Brussels and Stan Orme, a solid left-winger, had joined the Cabinet as Secretary for Social Services.

On 22 November, six ministers – Michael Foot, Tony Benn, Peter Shore, John Silkin, Stan Orme and Albert Booth – met and decided to oppose the cuts. They were a minority, but endorsement of the cuts was placed in doubt by the emergence of another group of opponents headed by Crosland. A later account summarised his contribution to the Cabinet meeting on 2 December: 'There was no economic case for the cuts, he said . . . Far from reducing PSBR [Public Sector Borrowing Requirement] the spending cuts would mean higher unemployment, which would in turn mean higher social security payments and lower tax revenues, thus actually increasing PSBR.'[19]

The Crosland group included Harold Lever, Shirley Williams, David Ennals and William Rodgers. Thus the left-wingers and the social democrats – future founders of the SDP – were in temporary alliance. Callaghan faced the prospect that the government would not survive. As he perceived it, Michael's attitude was: 'It would be better to stay together than to stay in government' and Crosland's was: 'In the last resort he would regard the break-up of the government as the lesser evil.'[20] But the Prime Minister was being too pessimistic. When the crunch came, both left-wingers and social democrats drew back from the brink.

The crucial Cabinet meeting was on 6 December. Michael put the case for the left:

Two billion-pound cuts and all the consequences that will flow from that are inconceivable . . . The legislation would not be passed and we would be in a position where, if the government was defeated, Labour candidates would be fighting an election in favour of cuts in social benefits . . . If we followed this course we would forfeit our agreement and our association with the unions and would be ground to death. We must connect what we do to our own beliefs . . . We want to sustain the government or, if forced into opposition, sustain ourselves in unity rather than be split into snarling groups.[21]

However, while the Foot group was solid, the Crosland group was disintegrating. Harold Lever and Shirley Williams, it seems, were indicating that they were not prepared to place the Prime Minister and the Chancellor in a minority. Crosland now told the Cabinet that he maintained his view that the cuts were wrong – economically, socially and politically – but that 'the unity of the party depends on sustaining the Prime Minister'.

The decision was to accept the IMF terms, subject to detailed discussion of where the cuts would be made. The objectors (without Silkin, apparently) gathered in Michael's room. Stan Orme was the only one who was in a mood to resign. Michael said briefly that he would not resign. One after another, Shore, Booth and Benn agreed with him. Benn made the obvious point: 'I wouldn't resign because I didn't want to bring down the government.'[22]

How long the government could survive was, in any case, an open question. On 4 November, the Tories had won two seats in by-elections: Walsall North and Workington, which Labour had held even in the disaster of 1931. Thus the government had lost its majority in the Commons and was back to where it had been before October 1974. Opinion polls reported a Tory lead of anything up to 16 per cent. Cledwyn Hughes judged, even before the by-elections: 'An election now would be disastrous for the Labour Party. We would be lucky to come back with 150 members.'[23]

November also saw a parliamentary failure which, though it did not threaten the government, was personally wounding for Michael. He had identified himself with the campaign for Public Lending Right – the right of authors to benefit financially when their books were taken out of public libraries. The scheme had first been put forward by the novelist John Brophy as 'the author's penny'; he proposed that library borrowers should be charged a (pre-decimal) penny. It was backed by the Society of Authors and discussed with Jennie Lee when she was a minister in the 1960s. While she expressed sympathy, she thought that a charge on borrowers would infringe the sacrosanct principle of the free public library, and the only alternative, payment from a government grant, was impossible in prevailing economic conditions. The writers did not accept defeat, and in 1972 the Writers' Action Group was founded by Brigid Brophy (John Brophy's daughter) and Maureen Duffy. In his capacity as a writer, Michael was an early member. Brigid Brophy was able to point out that library loans had risen to 'a stupend-ous total compared with the figures from any other western country',[24] and that the average book served forty borrowers, to the obvious detriment of bookshop sales. In 1974, MPs were lobbied by 140 writers and WAG presented its case in a House of Commons committee-room booked by Michael.

In 1976, as a key figure in the Callaghan government, Michael set himself to get PLR established, and persuaded the Prime Minister to give his backing to a government bill. It was first steered through the House of Lords by Lord Willis – as Ted Willis, a left-wing militant in the 1930s and then a successful film and television writer. In the Commons, it met with bitter hostility from a few members – two Tories, improbably named Roger Moate and Iain Sproat, and a Labour member, Michael English. They staged a filibuster and, as the government neglected to issue a three-line whip, there were only ninety-nine MPs in the House when a hundred were needed to vote for closing the debate. On the Third Reading on 16 November, the bill again (in Brigid Brophy's words) 'met a giggling filibuster of eight, each of whom was prepared to talk boringly for up to forty-five minutes, a stratagem that gave the rest of the filibuster the chance of a kip and enforce silence on the friends of PLR as the only way of giving the bill a chance to pass'.[25] The closure was prevented for a second time and, as the session was coming to an end, the bill expired. There was nothing that Michael could do except to wait for another opportunity. Meanwhile, he was facing a formidable task in the new session.

4

On 16 December 1976, John Smith moved the Second Reading of the Scotland and Wales Bill. It provided for the creation of elected assemblies in these two countries and – in the case of Scotland but not of Wales – for a quasi-governmental authority which would take over most of the functions of the Secretary of State for Scotland.

Devolution – the name given to this project – divided political opinion as deeply as the issue of the European Community, and for some it aroused equally passionate feelings. The Tories, by long tradition, cherished the concepts of 'Great Britain' and the 'United Kingdom'. They had flirted with devolution, especially when their leader was a Scottish aristocrat, Douglas-Home. They were generally the minority party in Scotland and invariably in Wales (in the election of October 1974, they won sixteen of the seventy-one Scottish seats and eight of the thirty-six Welsh seats) and they risked virtual eclipse if they did not conciliate the rising tide of nationalism. But when Margaret Thatcher became leader, she imposed her will on anxious Scottish Tories and made it clear that she would oppose the Labour government's plans.

In the Labour Party, there were two contrasting traditions. Keir Hardie, a Scot who sat in the Commons for the Welsh constituency of Merthyr Tydfil, was a strong advocate of what was then called Home Rule. The 'Red Clydesiders' who formed a vociferous left-wing group in the 1920s denounced the trampling of Scottish rights under a centralised power which was officially British but really English. The big capitalist concerns which, between the wars, condemned Scotland and Wales to worse depths of industrial dereliction and unemployment than England were controlled from head offices in London. In the political sphere, it was obvious that when the Tories won a fairly narrow electoral victory (as in 1951 or 1970) they owed it to their predominance in England. When the Scottish National Party made its breakthrough in October 1974, winning 30 per cent of the votes in Scotland and eleven seats, Labour had reason to be worried. Although most of the SNP victories were at the expense of the Tories, they ran Labour close in industrial constituencies such as Paisley and Stirling. Devolution was, at least in part, a strategy for keeping Scottish and Welsh votes in the Labour column.

The opposing tradition stemmed from a dedication to the unity of the working class – English, Scottish, Welsh and in any case British – and a belief that any concession to nationalism must undermine this solidarity. In the Second Reading debate, Leo Abse, Labour MP for Pontypool, attacked devolution as an 'attempt to placate nationalism' and argued: 'Decentralisation is one thing, but yielding to vulgar and aggressive nationalism is another.' It was a bad moment for Michael when Abse exclaimed: 'How Nye would have mocked this bill!' Indeed, Bevan had been implacably opposed to all moves towards decentralisation, even the setting up of the Welsh Office under a Secretary of State. Cledwyn Hughes recalled a conversation with him in 1945: 'I suggested that it was time we had a policy for Wales. He exploded at once and said impatiently that it was all "chauvinism", and advised me to concentrate on more important problems.'[26]

Much of the problem arose from the differences between the industrial region of south-east Wales, small in area but containing a majority of the population, and the rural areas of north and west Wales. The growth of industry had drawn many thousands of people into the mining valleys from adjacent English counties and from Ireland. This melting-pot generated an internationalist outlook with the accent on social and economic needs. Neil Kinnock, who emerged, much to Michael's regret, as one of the foremost opponents of devolution, declared in one of the debates: 'I am here to represent working-class people irrespective of their nationality.'[27] As an added complication, the Welsh language was widely spoken in the north and west but by few people in the south-east, and the issue of devolution was inextricably involved with that of the survival, or revival, of the language.

Among MPs who had been born and bred in Wales, there was a gently amused suspicion that the admiring affection for the Welsh expressed by Michael – and, no less, by Jill – was romantic, if not sentimental. In Abse's view, Michael failed to grasp that the Welsh were a hard-headed people, likely to judge devolution by its possible benefits or costs.[28] Kinnock, too, thought that Michael's enthusiasm for the rights of the Welsh exceeded anything felt by the Welsh themselves. He recalls that he and Michael had some fierce arguments, indeed 'hellish rows'.[29] However, he and Abse both stress that the arguments never caused any personal bad feeling.

Beyond doubt, Michael was passionately convinced of the virtues of devolution and saw it as a matter of principle. In this he differed from Callaghan, who went along with it partly as a political calculation and partly as an element in his concordat with Michael. For Michael, devolution was both a recognition of Scottish and Welsh nationhood and an advance in democracy. He understood the resentment felt, beyond the borders, at the centralised structure of so many institutions – the BBC, the nationalised industries, the political parties, the trade unions. Often, people who left the Labour Party to join Plaid Cymru – or voted for the Plaid, which now and again won council seats in surprising places, including Ebbw Vale – were good socialists alienated by denial of Welsh rights. Devolution, therefore, could be an instrument of reconciliation. It was Ron Evans, Michael's friend and constituency agent, who seconded the resolution supporting devolution which was carried at the 1976 party conference. Neil Kinnock, however, opposed it, remarking: 'Some, like Michael Foot, are born devolutionists; some, like the rest of the government, achieve it; others, eighty-five per cent of our people, have it thrust upon them.'

Undeniably, the subject bristled with problems. Some Labour MPs from the north of England, notably Eric Heffer, asked why centralisation should be relaxed only for Scotland and Wales and wanted a general move toward regional autonomy. The nationalist movements aimed in principle at full independence and had to convince their followers to water down this objective. Although the SNP and Plaid Cymru agreed to support devolution as a desirable half a loaf, they were critical of its inadequacies, especially the provision that the new assemblies would not have taxation powers (the Treasury had vetoed the idea). There was also the 'West Lothian question', posed by Tam Dalyell, MP for West Lothian: when Scotland had control of (for instance) education, why should Scottish MPs at Westminster have a voice in the educational system in England? No valid answer was ever produced. Given the disparity in size of the three nations comprising Britain, it was impracticable to set up a true federal system, as in the USA or the Federal Republic of Germany. Smith, in his opening speech, went out of his way to stress 'the government's unshakeable conviction of the maintenance of the Union' and declare that breaking it up would be 'spectacular folly'.

Yet another problem was the demand for a referendum, urged both by those who argued that devolution was a major constitutional change and by Kinnock and others who were sure that the vote would be a rejection and would kill the project. Initially, Michael resisted this demand. He was devoted, as always, to the authority of Parliament, and his experience of the 1975 referendum had been discouraging. He argued that Labour had won two elections with devolution in its manifesto, whereas Heath had taken Britain into the EC without making his intention clear in the 1970 election. A poll in the whole United Kingdom would lead to complaints in Scotland and Wales that the English vote was, once again, decisive. A poll in Scotland and Wales was a better idea, but had the defect that it could be held only on the existing electoral register, so that English people living in Scotland and Wales would be voting while Scottish and Welsh people living in England would not. But, by the time the debate opened, John Smith recognised that the demand for a referendum was so heavily supported that there was no chance of getting the bill through the Commons without conceding it. With Michael's reluctant agreement, he announced the insertion of a new clause authorising a popular vote in Scotland and Wales to follow the legislation.

Smith also realised, and Michael too had to realise, that it would be virtually impossible to get the bill passed without enforcing a guillotine. In 1976, Michael had shouldered the uncongenial task of imposing five guillotines – on bills to nationalise the aerospace and shipbuilding industries, to abolish tied housing, to abolish pay beds in NHS hospitals, to require local authorities to introduce comprehensive schools, and to extend the working regulations that covered the ports to container depots (this was a particular concern of Jack Jones). True, all these measures had been promised in the last election manifesto and the government had an obligation to get them passed as speedily as possible. True too, Michael was able to show that Tory governments over the past quarter-century had imposed more guillotines and allowed fewer debating hours than Labour governments. Nevertheless, past denunciations by Michael of the use of the guillotine were easy to unearth and quote.

The guillotine motion came to a vote on 23 February 1977. Twenty-two Labour members voted against it, another fifteen abstained, and it was defeated by 29 votes. Thatcher promptly tabled a no-confidence motion. The government was in mortal danger.

It could be saved only by recruiting new allies. The Liberals had thirteen MPs, the SNP eleven and Plaid Cymru three. There were also twelve members from Northern Ireland: ten Unionists, Gerry Fitt, who was the sole representative of the Social Democratic and Labour Party, and a (Catholic) independent, Frank Maguire.

On the face of it, the Unionists, who had a tradition of being virtually the local wing of the Tory Party, were the least likely prospect. However, an inducement was available. Since 1920, Northern Ireland had been under-represented at Westminster in relation to population because it had its own Parliament. In 1974, this Stormont Parliament had been suspended and the province brought under direct rule. Michael thought that an increase in representation was a reasonable demand, and hoped that it would help the SDLP to elect more MPs. He and Callaghan had a meeting with James Molyneaux, the Unionist leader, and Enoch Powell, and promised to submit the proposal to an all-party conference. The outcome was that the province was given seventeen seats instead of twelve. The deal was scarcely a resounding success. Only Molyneaux, Powell and one other Unionist voted with the government in the no-confidence debate on 23 March; the others could not bring themselves to rescue a Labour government. Fitt was offended and predicted that the change would never do his party, or the Catholic minority, much good. (The SDLP reached a peak of four seats in the 1992 election.) Still, at this critical juncture, every little helped.

Another possibility was to secure the support of the nationalist parties, who had an obvious interest in sustaining a government that was working for devolution. But the SNP cherished its freedom of action and would make no commitments, while the Plaid's three votes in the Commons were too few to make much difference. There was one other card to play – a pact with the Liberals. The idea was viewed with aversion by many in the Labour Party; Callaghan found it a hard pill to swallow. Some influential Liberals were fiercely against it. It came to fruition chiefly through the growth of understanding between Michael and the new Liberal leader, David Steel. They liked each other personally, and they both came from parts of Britain – Michael's West Country, Steel's Scotland – where the Liberal tradition was primarily one of opposition to Toryism. Still, there was some hard bargaining. The supreme Liberal objective was proportional representation, which was anathema to Michael and to Callaghan. The most that the Labour side would concede was a conditional prospect of PR some time in the future for some purposes – perhaps the European Parliament, perhaps the Scottish and Welsh assemblies. Steel was more successful in his demand for a guaranteed voice in government policy. A Liberal–Labour consultative committee, chaired by Michael, was created to discuss all government bills, major policy statements and the next Queen's speech. Moreover, each Labour minister would hold regular meetings with a Liberal spokesman – a plan which yielded more trouble than value, particularly because Healey and his Liberal counterpart, John Pardoe, agreed on almost nothing and their meetings were shouting-matches. With all these difficulties, agreement was reached only on 22 March, the day before the crucial debate. The Liberals stipulated that it was an experiment, limited to the current session (that is, until November 1977).

The Labour left greeted the pact with dismay or outright hostility. When the Cabinet met on the morning of 23 March, a few hours before the debate, Tony Benn, Peter Shore and Stan Orme recorded their protests. Shore declared that 'it went far beyond anything he had expected, would do untold damage, consultation with the Liberals would be unspeakable or impossible'.[30] In the House, Eric Heffer said that he 'would look at the agreement with the greatest suspicion' and it must be very short-term. Michael reassured the back-benchers that there was 'no question of a coalition' and the sole purpose was 'to make this session of Parliament workable'. For the time being, the government was out of danger. Although the SNP chose to vote with the Tories, Liberal support ensured that the no-confidence motion was defeated by twenty-four votes.

Michael did not pretend to be delighted with his achievement. In his political creed, he was a socialist and nothing but a socialist; he was uneasy about even the hint of a coalition; he could remember that in the 1930s he had been inflexibly averse to a People's Front alliance with Liberals. But, in the classic phrase of Mendès-France, 'to govern is to choose'. In situations that are not ideal, actions that are not ideal become inevitable – such is politics. Michael had committed himself to the maintenance of the Labour government as an absolute value, by whatever methods might be necessary. He never doubted that he had chosen rightly. Dependence on the Lib–Lab pact was no pleasure, but it was a duty.

Outside Westminster, the position was worse than ever. A by-election campaign, for the Birmingham constituency vacated by Roy Jenkins, was in progress at the time of the no-confidence debate. Paul Foot stood as the candidate of the Socialist Workers' Party; when Michael came to speak for the Labour candidate, Paul was urged to appear at the meeting and heckle him, but he scented a press stunt and refused. Uncle and nephew were still on friendly terms, but they seldom met and discussed only literary matters. Paul's vote was derisory and the Tories won the seat. A month later, another by-election produced a disaster as bad as Workington; Ashfield, a Derbyshire mining seat with a Labour majority of 22,000, fell to the Tories.

A particular disappointment for Michael was the retreat from a project which he cherished – industrial democracy. A plan embodied in a Royal Commission report (the Bullock Report) envisaged a structure of democratic decision-making in industry. Trade unions would be strongly involved; Jack Jones was a keen advocate of the idea. Michael saw it as a vital complement to political democracy. But the Liberals would not support it, so it had to be abandoned.

Even with the help of the Liberals (and they could not always be relied on in the division lobby) the government's majority was precarious. The Chief Whip, Bob Mellish, had been replaced by Michael Cocks. A macabre part of his duties was keeping watch on the health of Labour MPs. Notes passed by Cocks to Michael Foot in Cabinet meetings tell their own story: 'Tom Litterick is in intensive care unit following heart attack' . . . 'The situation has eased this morning. The specialist saw Alec Jones at 8 a.m. and he is coming up to vote.'

Without the guillotine, hopes for the Scotland and Wales Bill were fading. The Tories, naturally, used every possible procedural device to hold up progress. Labour opponents of devolution urged the government to admit its mistake and drop the project. A meeting with these rebels yielded no results, for their mood was described as 'determined if not truculent'.[31] Summer brought the end of the session within sight, and on 15 June Michael had to announce the abandonment of the bill. However, devolution itself was not to be abandoned. A new strategy was adopted: separate bills – a Scotland Bill and a Wales Bill – would be presented for Second Reading at the beginning of the next session, in November. What could not be denied was that a year had been lost, and the battle was still in doubt.

Michael was aware that the continual compromises which he had to accept, or sometimes even devise and sponsor, were hard to reconcile with his record as the unbending man of principle. Judith Hart's recollection was: 'It was a sad period in his life. He often looked unhappy and he hated being attacked by his old friends, like Mik. He just wasn't Michael.'[32] He found relief, whenever he could, in reaffirming the historic traditions that he loved. In August, he spoke at Penzance to celebrate the centenary of the Chartist leader, William Lovett, who had died in 1877. The speech can be read as a riposte to Roy Jenkins, who had visited Glasgow to make a speech interpreted by *The Times* as a 'thinly camouflaged attack on Mr Foot and Mr Benn'.[33] In Penzance, Michael said: 'Few words in the English language are more debased than "radical". Once, it could strike terror into the ranks of wealth and privilege. Now it has been purloined even by the palest and pinkest critics of the current orthodoxy.' But he had another point to make. Lovett, a 'moral force' Chartist, had waged the fight for freedom 'without resort to violence, by the politics of persuasion'. Michael commented: 'More than ever he seems to be right in the age of hand-made explosives, nuclear horrors, and such final obscenities as the neutron bomb.'

In the Privy Council office, he was always in the thick of negotiations to ensure the survival of the government. It was an incessantly laborious task and less emotionally rewarding than a triumphant conference speech, but it called for its own kind of skill and yielded its own kind of satisfaction. Elizabeth Thomas, working in the office, saw a side of Michael that Judith Hart evidently missed. On Friday afternoons, before catching the train to South Wales (and doubtless cheered by that prospect) he would remark with a smile: 'Well, we've got through another week, that's pretty good going.'[34]

The relationship with the Liberals was always under strain because of their demand for PR and also because of their enthusiasm for the European Community. The Labour left was still hostile to the Community, and Michael declared when he spoke at the 1977 party conference: 'We demand a drastic reform of the Common Agricultural Policy and the maintenance, some would say the restoration, of the authority of national Parliaments'. The former was unlikely and the latter impossible within the Community structure. One threat to 'the authority of national Parliaments' was the rival authority of the European Parliament. Britain sent a delegation to Strasbourg nominated by the parties on the basis of their strength at Westminster; the Liberals were pressing for direct elections. In Steel's words, 'the direct elections issue was a slow fuse which would smoulder through to the autumn threatening to blow up the agreement'.[35] Despite fervent protests from Tony Benn and Peter Shore, Callaghan gave in to the Liberals on direct elections while refusing to give in on PR.

The good news by the autumn of 1977 was a marked improvement in the economic situation. The IMF loan was being repaid, the balance of payments deficit had been turned into a healthy surplus, North Sea oil was beginning to contribute to the cheerful prospects, and inflation was down to 7 per cent. Unemployment, however, was still rising. There was no sign of any increase in jobs or – with tight restraints on both wages and social services – in living standards.

Despite, or perhaps because of, the stabilisation of the economy, the unions now decided that they had had enough of any agreed incomes policy, voluntary or otherwise. Jones, who was entering his last year before retirement, was defeated at the TGWU conference when he pleaded for a renewal of the agreement between the government and the TUC. Inevitably, the TUC itself voted by a large majority for a return to 'unfettered collective bargaining'. After only two years, the social contract belonged to history. Some union leaders had never supported it; others considered that it had served its purpose. It was for the government, henceforth, to lay down unilaterally a maximum of wage increases and use whatever influence it could exert to ensure that the limit was observed. Callaghan, in his speech to the party conference, warned that the limit was 10 per cent and that the alternative was a fresh surge of inflation.

Another feature of the conference was noted by political journalists and, presumably, by Michael. Not only was Tony Benn voted top of the poll in the constituency section of the NEC; not only was he loudly applauded when he spoke from the platform; but he also spoke at an extraordinary number of fringe meetings, these meetings were often organised by his political friends, and he was introduced as 'the next leader of the Labour Party'.[36] Indeed, Michael himself shared this expectation and, when advising the Minister for Energy not to antagonise the Prime Minister, had told him: 'You'll be leader of the Labour Party in time, I'm sure of it.'[37]

The relationship between Michael and Tony retained all its ambivalence. They were allies in the left bloc in the Cabinet – always the same names: Foot, Benn, Shore, Booth, Orme – but alliance did not imply real comradeship or trust. When the younger man was in danger, Michael came to his defence. At the time of the Lib–Lab pact, Callaghan threatened to sack Benn for signing a letter calling for a special NEC meeting; Michael interceded, and Benn kept his job by withdrawing his signature. In July, Callaghan accused Benn of leading a faction and Michael intervened to say: 'Tony reflects a very important element in the Party's thinking which has to be taken into account.'[38] But at the husbands' and wives' dinners Benn sensed an unfriendly atmosphere; the others resented his air of being 'more left than thou' and felt that he was less than whole-heartedly committed to keeping the government alive. After the quarrel over the Lib–Lab pact, Tony and Caroline Benn decided to stop going to the dinners – a decision which they reversed later in the year. At one dinner (the Harts were the hosts) an argument over uncontrollable wage increases had Michael shouting: 'Face the real problems!' According to Benn's account, he was 'red with anger' and 'Jill rebuked Michael for being so excitable.'[39]

Benn's diary is spattered with such expressions as: 'Michael seems an extinct volcano' (27 February 1977), 'Michael is effectively finished' (31 March), 'Michael is just a dogsbody dashing between Jim and me and trying to keep the left in order' (2 November) and 'Michael is just lost' (15 January 1978). It also records a scene, on 22 November 1977, when Michael's exasperation boiled over. Callaghan had got wind of a letter signed by Michael Meacher, a junior minister who was politically close to Benn, containing plans for a meeting of Bennite members of the government. In a confrontation in Michael's room at the House, with Shore and John Silkin present, Michael declared: 'I think it's bloody crooked that you should hold it [the meeting]' and Benn retorted: 'I won't be called bloody crooked. I am entitled to consult whom I like.' Michael went on: 'You just want the Tories in, and then we will be in the Common Market for life . . . You with your halo of martyrdom. I've been anti-Market longer than you.' Benn went to his own room and duly held his meeting with Michael Meacher, Brian Sedgemore (his PPS) and Margaret Jackson.[40]

Later in the evening, Michael went to look for Tony but failed to find him. Next morning he sent this letter:

Dear Tony,

I'm sorry you did not come back to my room last night; after Peter had come back I went up to look for you, but you had gone. If I had found you I would have said what I write now. I am extremely sorry I said what I did. I was infuriated by the meeting you had agreed to in your room. But that was no excuse whatever for describing what you had done as I did . . . We have never quarrelled before in that way, and I hope we will not – through my fault – start now . . .

I do believe that, if you left the Government or were forced out of it at this time, it would be a catastrophe for the movement . . . If we let Thatcher and Company in in the coming months, we shall become enmeshed in the Market and its institutions in a way which can be first warded off and then avoided altogether if we can get a Labour victory at the next election – with you and Peter and several others holding to key situations in the movement . . .

When Jim raised with me the question of the meeting in your room, my main response to him was to stress how disastrous it would be for the whole Government if you were pushed out. I think that on personal and political grounds, and I wish I had expressed the matter better last night. However, the main point of my writing this letter is because I did not find you last night. I had to let the sun go down on my misplaced wrath, which is contrary to the Biblical injunction which we both learned in youth.

Tony replied five days later:

Dear Michael,

Just a line to thank you for your letter which I much appreciated. I had hoped to say so personally but there was no chance of doing so last week.

His diary comment on the letter was: 'I can't quite bring myself to read it a second time,' and on the night of the quarrel he had written: 'My links with him are severed completely.'

5

'Is it worth it?' That, in Geoffrey Goodman's recollection, is the question that Jill Foot put to her husband at this point in the life of the Labour government. Michael was working tremendously hard for a man in his sixties who had been in hospital twice within two years. Sir Michael Quinlan tells of an occasion when the Lord President, after hours at the despatch box in the Commons, had to go back to his room at three in the morning because an MP who was lukewarm about devolution had requested a talk. Quinlan was impressed by Michael's patience and courtesy, which very few other senior politicians could have mustered, but observed that he was 'utterly done in'.[41]

Jill was by no means the only person who queried whether the struggle was 'worth it'. Lacking a majority, the government was making no progress towards anything that could be called socialism. When Michael reminded Neil Kinnock that he had, like other Labour candidates, advocated devolution in his 1974 election address, Neil retorted that they had also promised 'a fundamental and irreversible shift in the balance of power and wealth in favour of working people'. It might be for the best, some on the left argued, to close the chapter before further disillusion took root. If there had to be rising unemployment figures and cuts in welfare benefits, it might be wise to let a Tory government come in and take the blame.

Michael firmly rejected such counsels. He had shouldered the task of protecting the government from the assaults of the enemy and ensuring its survival – by whatever dubious devices or unnatural alliances the situation might render necessary – and he would not abandon that task. Various forms of motivation converged to shape his resolution: the undaunted persistence cherished in the Foot family tradition, the principle of 'always facing it', loyalty to colleagues round the Cabinet table and to the faithful rank and file of the Labour movement, and pride in the claim that the man who worked hardest in the cause of survival was a man of the left.

There were wider anxieties. Britain was locked into the NATO alliance, predicated as dogmatically as ever on the assumption of Soviet aggressive intentions. President Carter, elected in 1976 in the American revulsion from Watergate, was a well-meaning man and Callaghan had forged links of personal friendship with him, but he was unlikely to withstand pressure from the 'military–industrial complex'. This pressure was being exerted to install new nuclear missiles, the Cruise and the Pershing, in Britain and Germany; they would arouse fears and suspicions in Moscow and redouble the dangers of any future crisis or confrontation. Among friends, Michael was saying: 'I see all these secret reports, but nothing convinces me that the Russians have any design for world conquest. They don't know what to do about Iran. They've made a mess of things in Africa. What they're really worried about is holding on to their part of Europe. It could all go smash next year.'[42]

Certainly, there was little doubt that an election in the early months of 1978 would bring the Tories back to power. In March, another seat was lost in a by-election. But if the government kept its nerve and waited, the tide might turn before a general election was unavoidable. Perhaps this was a Micawberish hope, but it was not unreasonable to suggest that something might turn up – specifically, the economic outlook. Michael argued, therefore, that the longer the election was deferred, the better the chances.

For all these reasons, he was thoroughly committed to what may be called Operation Survival. At the same time, he realised that his championship of the operation was bound to leave him open to attacks, sometimes expressed in malicious and wounding terms. A paragraph in the *New Statesman* (written by Christopher Hitchens, then an adherent of the SWP) is an example:

Is there anything *at all* that Michael Foot will not do? I've never thought he was very nice, but there's something pitiable about his eagerness to fag for Callaghan, and to come to the microphone and take the Master's flak. Pay policy, government secrecy, expenditure cuts – you name it and Foot will find a windy justification for it.[43]

The attacks that Michael found most painful came from Labour MPs who had been his friends and allies in the Tribune Group. Sometimes these attacks were launched in the columns of *Tribune* (Dick Clements, still the editor, supported Michael but maintained the tradition of open controversy), sometimes in PLP meetings or on the floor of the House. On 15 January, the Prime Minister was moved to write to the Lord President:

You were treated disgracefully in the House this afternoon and I am very sorry indeed that you were exposed to it. It showed the difference between comrades like Ernie Fernyhough and the puffed up vanity and egotism of some others. You can bet your boots I shall be at the Party meeting tonight! I hope they haven't upset you too much – they have certainly upset me.

Meanwhile, Michael and the efficient John Smith were plodding on with devolution. This cherished project, so dear to Michael's heart, was yet another reason to avoid an early election, since it could scarcely be abandoned a second time without a disastrous loss of face and charges of betrayal from the Nationalists. The Scotland Bill and the Wales Bill, separated this time but overlapping in the parliamentary timetable, began to make steady progress once Michael secured a majority for a guillotine. When the Shadow Leader of the House, Francis Pym, protested, Michael pointed out that he had demanded more guillotines in his time and told him: 'If I am Saint-Just, he is Robespierre. Indeed, I think he might have had the decency to bring along Madame Defarge.'[44]

But on 15 February 1978 the Scotland Bill met with a serious setback. George Cunningham, a Labour MP who came from Dunfermline but represented Islington South and was opposed to devolution, moved an amendment providing that victory in the promised referendum would require a Yes vote, not only by a majority of those voting but by 40 per cent of the whole electorate. Given that an uncertain number of people on the register would have died or emigrated, or would for various reasons abstain, it was calculated that this would mean a two-thirds or even three-quarters majority of the actual voters. The amendment was carried and incorporated in the bill. It was clearly a wrecking move, and the Scottish Nationalists were furious.

With this unwelcome addition, the bill passed its Third Reading. The Wales Bill followed in May 1978, with Kinnock predicting an over-whelming No vote in the referendum. However, this was not a time for Michael to celebrate, let alone to relax. This Lib–Lab pact, on which Operation Survival depended, was at the end of its life.

The winter brought the collapse of Liberal hopes for proportional representation in the referenda. On a free vote of the House, it was opposed by all the Tories and by 115 Labour MPs, including four Cabinet ministers. By this time, Steel was getting complaints from his rank and file that the pact was useless to them; the party was doing badly in by-elections, presumably because it had to share in the government's unpopularity. In January 1978, a special party assembly authorised Steel to end the pact at his discretion. On 9 May, he informed Callaghan and Foot that he would not prolong the pact beyond the end of July. Michael, he found, reacted with 'total consternation'.[45] But in fact Michael was almost the only member of the Cabinet who was sorry. Callaghan hated governing by grace of the Liberals, Healey fumed when he had to modify his economic policies to reach a compromise with Pardoe, and the left-wingers had objected to the pact from the outset.

On 14 June the Liberals abstained in a vote of confidence, thus signalling their independence. The government narrowly survived, but clearly it was back in the same perilous situation as before the pact was made in 1977. The general view in the Labour Party was that it would be wise to dissolve Parliament in time for an autumn election, rather than to face a new session and the possibility of defeat in the House.

The question of election timing was closely related to that of the wages norm for the year 1978–9. By and large, the 10 per cent norm in 1977–8 had been observed by the unions, although the TUC had never consented to it. Callaghan decided that the new norm should be 5 per cent, which was below the inflation rate and therefore meant a cut in real wages. He announced it in a radio interview and the Cabinet had to endorse it, though Healey later recognised it as a blunder – 'we in the Cabinet should have realised that our five per cent norm would be provocative as well as unattainable.'[46] Barbara Castle was present at a meeting in Congress House when union leaders heard the news: 'The trade unionists sitting opposite to me listened in a state of bewildered shock.'[47] Len Murray, who could only guess that the figure was 'something spewed out of the computer', was sure that 'no power on God's earth could make the workers settle for it'. He had no doubts about the timing of the election: 'We said: "Go in the autumn, it'll be a bloody sight worse in the spring."'[48] Tony Benn took the same view and recalled later:

> I wrote to Callaghan in August or September 1978 saying we should go into the election earlier because, I said – and it was prophetic really – we might lose control of the situation in the winter, which is what we did. Callaghan, I think, had been advised that he wouldn't win in October '78 and therefore he decided to hang on . . . That was just what you might call a tactical error of judgement . . . but at that stage, we were heading for a totally impossible situation on the pay policy.[49]

Stan Orme – the former engineer, more in touch with working-class feelings than anyone else in the Cabinet – Geoffrey Goodman, the veteran industrial correspondent, and Caerwyn Roderick, Michael's PPS, all remember telling Michael that the unions would never accept the 5 per cent norm.[50] He replied that they were being too pessimistic. He was strongly opposed to an autumn election; he said to Roderick: 'We'd be running away.' Callaghan wrote in his memoirs: 'Michael Foot came to see me and urged that we should put the idea of an autumn election out of our minds and concentrate on preparing for the next session.'[51] Elizabeth Thomas recalls that Michael was determined to persuade the Prime Minister and that he returned one day from a talk in Downing Street to tell her jubilantly: 'I've done it.'[52] His advice certainly had an influence on Callaghan, though the decision on the election date is always the Prime Minister's own, and Callaghan made up his mind only after some solitary brooding on his Sussex farm.

At the TUC in the first week of September, he made a tantalising speech and treated the delegates to an unmusical rendering of 'There was I, waiting at the church'. He then booked a broadcast for the evening of 7 September. Cabinet ministers and journalists generally expected him to announce the dissolution; instead, he stated that the government would carry on. David Steel, who was informed of this in a phone call from Michael a few hours before the broadcast, wrote: 'My reaction was one of complete astonishment . . . Everyone was led to the wrong conclusion in his own party and indeed most of his Cabinet.'[53]

Signs of impending trouble soon appeared. Workers at the Ford motor factories went on strike for a wage increase, the management agreed to 17 per cent, and the government tried to nullify the deal by imposing financial sanctions on the company, a move for which there was no legal authority. The Tories tabled a critical motion and left-wing Labour MPs indicated that they could not support the government. Callaghan, with Michael, went to a meeting of the Tribune Group. By his account: 'Michael Foot argued strenuously that if the Tribune members abstained or voted against the government, they would fall into a trap set by the Tory Party, but even he was unable to shake the Group's resolve.'[54] Only five MPs abstained, but this enabled the Tories to carry their motion.

The decision to postpone the election to 1979 can be seen with hindsight as a mistake, but it was based on hopes that were not wholly unrealistic. There were solid indications of an economic recovery and a fall in unemployment. Michael and Denis Healey were still trying to repair the relationship with the unions; an agreement involving some modification of the 5 per cent norm in favour of the lower-paid was almost accepted by the TUC (it was in fact defeated by one vote in the General Council when Moss Evans of the TGWU went off for a holiday). But all these hopes were dashed by the wave of strikes that rolled across Britain between December 1978 and February 1979 and earned the name of the 'winter of discontent'. Since most of these strikes were in public services and transport, they caused a dislocation unmatched since the fuel crisis of 1947. And, as in 1947, the general misery was compounded by exceptionally severe winter weather.

On the roads, lorry drivers belonging to the TGWU went on strike and petrol deliveries were throttled by an overtime ban. On the railways, one-day strikes left commuters stranded on freezing platforms. In

January, all sorts of workers were on strike or working to rule: local authority office staff, refuse collectors, hospital porters, ambulance drivers, school caretakers, street-cleaners. The final bizarre and outrageous touch, a godsend to the Tory press, was added when gravediggers were not available to bury the dead. (This occurred only for a few days in one city, Liverpool, but that did not lessen the reaction of shocked revulsion.) At various times, technicians silenced BBC Television, civil servants paralysed 10 Downing Street, and thousands of people were obliged to drink unpurified water or even queue at standpipes. Almost every day brought new inconveniences, new resentments and of course new alarmist headlines.

In the first week of January, while millions shivered through blizzards and the Benns were snowed in at their country house, Callaghan flew to the Caribbean island of Guadeloupe for a conference with the Presidents of France and the USA. Pictures of the shirt-sleeved Prime Minister under the palm trees did not add to his popularity. On his return to Heathrow, he faced a barking chorus of reporters and denied that the situation amounted to chaos. The words 'Crisis – what crisis?', which Callaghan never actually uttered, made an effective *Daily Mail* headline and passed into folklore.

Callaghan had already – on 11 January, when the strike wave was at its fiercest – given the Cabinet formal notice to prepare for an election in the near future. Michael cannot have believed that Labour could win a majority in the immediate aftermath of the strikes. But perhaps, when they came to an end and calmer thoughts prevailed, the government would be given credit for doing its honest best. Perhaps the prospects would brighten in May or June.

He had one particular reason, not of major political importance yet a cause to which he was devoted, for keeping the Parliament alive. A new bill to bring Public Lending Right to birth had been introduced in November 1978. Despite determined opposition by Sproat and Moate – and by Nicholas Ridley, who demanded that Michael, as an author, should declare an interest – it was making progress. Brigid Brophy wrote: 'Michael Foot, as Leader of the House, took command of the parliamentary events. He amassed an arsenal of procedural methods, most of which he never needed to use except as bargaining counters for containing, but not stifling and thus provoking, the filibuster.'[55] The bill passed its Third Reading on 30 January and went through the Lords – in Brophy's words, 'as a result of the strategy designed and executed by Michael Foot' – on 6 March. It was only just in time.

The first of March was polling day in the referenda in Scotland and

Wales. The results were catastrophic. In Wales, devolution was crushed under an avalanche, with 243,000 votes in favour and 956,000 against. Even in Welsh-speaking Gwynedd, heartland of the Home Rule movement since Lloyd George's time, there was a two-to-one negative majority. The result in Scotland was, if anything, more of a headache. It was a narrow, uninspiring majority of 1,240,000 Yes votes to 1,153,000 No. But, thanks to heavy abstentions, this was far short of the 40 per cent of the whole electorate required under the Cunningham amendment.

Devolution was dead . . . or was it? The wording of the Scotland Act required the government to lay an order for repeal before the Commons in the event of a failure in the referendum. But Michael, as a guardian of the supreme authority of Parliament, had insisted that the referendum was consultative, not mandatory. The SNP demanded that the government should go ahead with plans for setting up the Scottish Assembly. Ingenious devices were proposed, such as laying the repeal order and advising the Commons to reject it. Michael was certainly inclined to consider any possible solution, but Callaghan was not. He was tired of devolution, which he had never much liked anyway, tired of deals with the minor parties, and wearied by all the burdens he had carried for three years.

Shortly after the convoluted events of March 1979, Michael wrote an account of what happened. It is a unique document from the hand of a man who never kept a diary and has never written his memoirs, but all the more valuable for that. Callaghan, the only person who read it, wrote: 'Your own recollection accords with mine and I have to agree with your general analysis of my attitude.' The story begins with a talk between the two men on 4 March:

I proposed to him, on the telephone that morning, that we should consider laying the orders we had to lay under the Scotland Act (and of course the Wales Act too) and urging, however, that the House should vote against the repeal of the whole Act, but insisting at the same time . . . that we would not introduce the necessary commencement order for the operation of the Act until the next Parliament . . . It was evident from the start, even from that Sunday morning conversation with him, that he was going to be hostile, that he would consider the idea, but his enthusiasm was obviously muted . . . It was primarily his idea that we should propose talks to the opposition parties, and I think he believed that this would sow some dissension in their ranks . . . I went along with it and so did the rest of the Cabinet, since it did not entirely forbid a resort to the other solution.

Callaghan was due to make a statement on 22 March, and Michael went to see him the night before to suggest putting down a motion. It would 'call on all parties in the House to respond to his invitation to talks . . . to be completed by the end of April and to enable the repeal orders to be debated within the week commencing 7 May'. Michael's account continues:

> He . . . indicated that he did not think it would be right to proceed in this way. He did not give any very powerful reason but said it was clearer to proceed in the manner of merely proposing the talks themselves. I did not try to argue the matter that evening but suggested we might discuss the matter further the next morning before the Cabinet, and he agreed. However, nothing happened and it was only on my pressure that I got to see him for a minute or two before the Cabinet started . . . He said he didn't think we should discuss the matter any further. It seemed to me then, as it did on a number of days afterwards, that his patience had suddenly snapped. He wanted to invite the election and the decision that would lead to it. It was, in my opinion, a considerable error.

By this time, the SNP had sensed that Callaghan would do nothing effective to rescue the Scotland Act and had put down a motion of no confidence in the government. Seizing the opportunity, the Tories put down a similar motion, which would be moved first since they were the main opposition party. The debate was set for 28 March.

Once again, it was Michael's task to deal with the smaller parties and try to win their support or at least to neutralise them. The Scottish Nationalists did not necessarily have to vote for the Tory motion, and some of them realised that they had fallen into – or rather dug – a trap. Unfortunately, they were subject to the authority of their National Council, which had committed the MPs to the no-confidence motion. Winifred Ewing (then an MP) declared in an emotional meeting with Michael: 'I swear on the grave of Emrys Hughes that we have no choice but to bring the government down.'[56] Two of the MPs wanted to vote with the government, defying the party decision, but discipline was strict and – in the words of the SNP whip, Andrew Welsh – 'they were whipped into line'.[57] As it turned out, this made the vital difference.

Michael had more success with the three Plaid Cymru MPs. They were poised to vote in solidarity with the Scots, but they were pressing a bill to provide compensation for men whose health had been damaged by work in the North Wales quarries. On a promise that the government would give the bill priority if it stayed in office, they agreed to oppose the Tory motion.

The Liberals, being firmly on record in favour of devolution, might have been won round to save the government, but they were averse to repeating anything like the Lib–Lab pact. Steel felt that there should have been an election in the autumn of 1978 and it was now overdue, so the Liberals decided to hasten it.

There remained the MPs from Northern Ireland. The Unionists had been given their extra seats, but their other demand, for the restoration of elected local councils, had been shelved, so they felt no gratitude to the government. Roy Mason, the Secretary of State, who leaned politically toward the Unionists, appealed to Molyneaux and Powell, but they turned him down (although two of their followers eventually voted with the government). The two non-Unionist MPs were Gerry Fitt of the SDLP and the Independent Frank Maguire. Urgent steps were taken to get Maguire, who owned a pub in County Tyrone and was an infrequent attender at Westminster, on to a London plane. But it emerged that Fitt – although he normally aligned himself with the Labour Party and was a good friend of Michael's – could not be counted on. He had been strongly critical of the government ever since it had conceded the extra seats, and he detested Mason.

On 26 March, in a meeting of a small group of ministers, Michael found that Callaghan was unsympathetic to his strategy:

> He almost urged that we should have no further talks with any of the smaller parties whatsoever. But I strongly contested this view. He seemed to be under the misapprehension that there was something discreditable about our discussions with the Welsh Nationalists . . . Denis Healey and the Chief Whip and the others present were strongly in favour of trying to do everything we legitimately could to win the vote . . .
>
> During most of these three weeks from 1 March until the night of 26 March, I had the feeling, and I think that several of my colleagues had the feeling, that Jim had made up his mind to have an election anyhow. Or at least, that his opposition to it was receding . . . For one reason or another, many of them perfectly understandable and creditable, his patience *had* snapped.

The crisis had come at the worst possible moment. A Labour MP in Liverpool had died and the by-election was due on 29 March. By going to speak there on 27 March, Michael missed what might have been a last chance to persuade Gerry Fitt. Another Labour MP was killed in a car crash in March, and yet another was gravely ill in Yorkshire and could not come to London to vote. These misfortunes may have intensified Callaghan's pessimistic mood.

However, he met the attack with a defiant speech. He dismissed the SNP with the observation that it was the first time he had seen turkeys voting for an early Christmas, and described the Liberals as 'spinning like a top'. Pointing out that the motion was supported by the Liberals, who were in favour of devolution, by the Tories, who were against it, and by the SNP, who aimed at independence for Scotland, he exclaimed: 'What a massive display of unsullied principle!'

Tension was at its height when Fitt rose and began: 'This will be the unhappiest speech I have ever made.' He hoped that Labour would win the general election, whenever it came, but he could not vote for a government who 'have not stood up to the Unionist and Loyalist extremists'.

Michael, winding up the debate, said that he had been 'deeply moved' by this speech from 'a man of great courage and great honour'. Then he launched into an attack on Thatcher – 'She leads her troops into battle snugly concealed behind the Scottish Nationalist shield, with the boy David holding her hand.' He claimed: 'No representative of any smaller party can say that I have misled him on any occasion in any conversation I have had with him.' But his peroration, delivered in the face of a storm of shouts and interruptions, was in fact the keynote speech of the coming election campaign:

> What will be the choice? Not so dissimilar from the choice in 1945, or even 1940 when the Labour Party had to come to the rescue of the country. It is sometimes in the most difficult and painful moments of our history that the country has turned to the Labour Party for salvation, and it has never turned in vain.

The division followed. Fitt and Maguire abstained, but the result was still uncertain until the tellers returned from the lobbies. A roar went up from the Tories when they saw that their motion had been carried by 311 votes to 310. Callaghan held a brief Cabinet meeting which decided on 3 May as the date for the election.

6

Moderation, common sense, practicality: these were the qualities on which Jim Callaghan relied to win the election, and he was determined that the manifesto should show the same characteristics. The procedure laid down in the party's constitution was that the manifesto should be drawn up through consultations between the Cabinet or Shadow Cabinet and the NEC. No guidance was offered as to whose will should prevail in the event of a disagreement. Thus the ground was prepared for a clash which, intermingled with other issues, plunged the party into internecine warfare over the next few years.

In December 1978, the party's research department – whose secretary was a left-winger, Geoff Bish, and which reflected the outlook of the Home Policy Committee of the NEC, chaired by Tony Benn – presented a draft manifesto based on resolutions passed at recent conferences. It called for a wealth tax, control (through compulsory planning agreements) of Britain's hundred largest companies, nationalisation of banking and insurance, and abolition of the House of Lords. Callaghan was appalled. He objected particularly to the abolition of the Lords, for he thought that the voters would see it as a doctrinaire irrelevance. He set up a working group of leading ministers, including Michael, Healey and Benn, to revise the draft. The group was deadlocked on every contentious issue and had made practically no progress when the defeat of the government injected a new element of urgency. Callaghan then instructed his personal staff to produce a new draft. It was shorter and snappier, and of course it eliminated everything that the Prime Minister did not like.

This draft formed the basis of discussion at an emergency meeting on the night of 2 April, attended by eight politicians and eight backroom figures. Acrid in any case, the meeting was made harder to endure by a strike in the Downing Street kitchen. A private secretary rustled up sandwiches and drinks, but Tony Benn was given no tea. The strike ended on the stroke of midnight; the meeting went on until half-past three. Whether by exhaustion or otherwise, Callaghan won all the disputed points. When Benn pressed for the abolition of the Lords, he said firmly: 'I won't have it . . . I am the leader of the party and I have to decide what is right.'[58]

Callaghan's authority derived, not only from the political skill he had perfected over the years, but also from the obvious fact that he was Labour's main electoral asset. While Labour was always behind in the opinion polls (except in one rogue poll at a late stage) he was consistently ahead of Thatcher in the personality stakes. The *Sunday Telegraph* praised him as 'the most accomplished purveyor of comfortable conservatism our politics have seen in many a long year'.

Whatever the compromises that Michael had made in these unhappy

Above At the party conference, 1973. Left to right: James Callaghan, Michael, Ted Graham, Ian Mikardo, Tony Benn. *(Camera Press)*

Right After a Cabinet meeting, 1975. *(S&G)*

Left With Indira
Gandhi, 1976.

Below With Callaghan
on the conference
platform, 1977. (*PA*)

Michael and Jill walk on Hampstead Heath with their dogs.
(*Harry Dempster*)

Above Tribune meeting, 1980. Left to right: Eric Heffer, Tony Benn, Michael, Jo Richardson, Neil Kinnock. (*Laurie Sparham*)

Left Michael arrives at St Patrick's Cathedral, Dublin, to lecture on Swift, 1980. (*Irish Times*)

A speech by the Labour leader, 1981. (*Camera Press*)

At the Bevan memorial on the Waun-y-Pound. (*Terry Kirk*)

Left Michael and Denis Healey on their way to Moscow, 1981. (*PA*)

Below At the Wembley conference, 1981. Left to right: Frank Allaun, Tony Benn, Judith Hart, Michael, Ron Hayward (party secretary), David Hughes (national agent). (*Camera Press*)

Michael's farewell speech as leader, 1983. (*Mike Abrahams/Network*)

With Neil Kinnock in Tredegar, 1988. (*R. L. Jenkins*)

Michael leaves the House of Commons for the last time, 1992.
Photo by Roland Boyes, MP. (*Independent*)

years, he could not be identified with comfortable conservatism and he still believed that the socialist inspiration gave the Labour Party its only hope. In his election address, he told the voters of Ebbw Vale:

The storm has blown as hard as it did in the 1930s, but this time the weak have been shielded . . . Individual men and women have been able to turn in their hour of need to a community which shows some compassion. That is what I call Socialism, or rather the beginnings of Socialism. If we had the imagination and the courage and the necessary majority in Parliament, we could carry the great idea much further . . . We have set out, despite all the hazards, on the right journey. Give us a chance, with a full majority, and we can travel faster and more safely to our desired goal . . .

It was here in these valleys that men and women first bravely mapped out the road to democratic Socialism . . . To be the Member of Parliament for Ebbw Vale is the proudest title I ever had or hope to have. I ask to be allowed to continue that work.

Tory propaganda concentrated on unemployment, which had fallen slightly in recent months but still stood at the unenviable figure of 1,280,000. Hoardings were plastered with a poster showing a line of workless men, with the slogan: 'Labour isn't working'. The men were actually members of the Hendon Young Conservatives, suitably clothed, but the poster is still cited by advertising men as one of the most effective in the history of their trade. Polls even showed the Tories nine points ahead as the best party to deal with unemployment.

However, it was the strike wave of the winter that caused a decisive segment of the voters to desert Labour, and the analysts of the election campaign wrote a verdict that cannot be denied:

The Conservatives in two short months moved into a decisive lead . . . The events of 1979 offer a good example of a government losing an election rather than of an opposition winning it . . . The Conservatives were well placed to catch the plum that fell into their laps. But it was the Labour movement that shook it off the tree.[59]

Labour candidates appealed in vain for the loyalty of people who had seen rubbish rotting in the streets or shivered in unheated homes. Indeed, the winter of discontent generated an ineradicable memory cited, as recently as 1992, to explain why victory still eluded the Labour Party.

So Labour was defeated, but there was no disaster of 1931 proportions. The Tories emerged with 339 seats against Labour's 269. The Liberals were down to eleven seats, the SNP – the turkeys slaughtered for

Christmas – to two, and Plaid Cymru also to two. The Tory share of the total poll, at 44 per cent, was by no means a resounding vote of confidence.

Michael's majority, just over 16,000, was down by 2,000 from the last election. The Tories made significant advances in the hitherto impregnable territory of Wales; they now held eleven Welsh seats, their highest score since 1874. One of the Labour casualties, in Brecon and Radnor, was Caerwyn Roderick.

The defeat was a saddening blow for Michael, and all the more so since his misjudgement had been partly responsible for the decision not to call an election in October 1978, when Labour might have won. He was sure that Margaret Thatcher's dogmatic policies would be disastrous for the country, that unemployment would soon rise far beyond the figure that the Tories had exploited in the election campaign, and that the new government would destroy the trade union legislation for which he had worked so hard as Secretary for Employment. Yet he did not despair; he believed that, for these very reasons, there was a fair chance that the Tory ascendancy might be of short duration. The task for Labour was to keep the party united, to avoid divisive recriminations and to prepare for effective opposition.

— *Chapter 13* —

DUTY CALLS

I

'Now I can write that book,' Michael had said when he lost his seat in Parliament in 1955. In 1979, his thoughts again turned to the writing of a book. This time, he was still an MP, he was deputy leader of the Labour Party and he would inescapably be in the thick of whatever struggles might develop within a party in opposition. The time when he might make literature, rather than politics, his chief occupation was still on an indistinct horizon. Yet writing – some writing, at least – was feasible; certainly the inclination and the energy were there.

His friend and American publisher, Michael Bessie, urged him to write an autobiography. The idea was discussed, but Michael Foot would not commit himself. A possibility that he considered quite seriously, at this time and again later, was a memoir of his early years: the Foot family, Oxford in the 1930s, the Socialist League and the foundation of *Tribune*. However, he decided against the project. The book that he produced in 1979 was *Debts of Honour*, published – in Britain, by Davis-Poynter – in 1980. The author sent an advance copy to Bessie with an apologetic note: 'I know this isn't the book you wanted.'

It is a collection of fourteen essays, each devoted to some notable figure regarded by Michael with admiration (total or qualified) and affection (whether boundless or more limited). These fourteen men and women would, in the original plan, have been thirteen men, but when Jill saw the list she exclaimed: 'A book without a woman!', and Michael hastened to add an essay on Sarah, Duchess of Marlborough, already a leading character in *The Pen and the Sword*. Hazlitt, of course, had his place. 'No man', Michael wrote of him, 'ever discharged with such good faith the debts of honour he owed to the favourite authors of his youth – Burke, Rousseau, Cervantes, Montaigne and a legion more.'[1] Following this example, Michael discharged his own debts of honour to some favourite authors of his youth and found a title for his book.

The subjects can be divided into classics and contemporaries. The classics, in historical order, were Defoe, Swift, the Duchess, Thomas Paine, Hazlitt and Disraeli. The essays are marked by a gaiety and a glancing wit that reveal Michael's pleasure in taking a holiday from such stern preoccupations as devolution or the IMF agreement. Defoe was described as a 'jaunty, inquisitive, bubbling, self-confident, moralising bourgeois adventurer'. Paine's writing style was praised thus: 'Suddenly the whole surrounding landscape is lit up by another streak of lightning. These are the real riches of Paine's prose, the abundance of his aphorisms, sharp, hard and glittering, like diamonds.' Disraeli was affectionately ranked as 'the inveterate opportunist, the supreme parliamentary practitioner who loved "the high game" for its own sake, and who would rather outwit Gladstone than gain an empire'. Indeed, the long essay on Disraeli was written largely to pour scorn on Lord Blake's solemnly reproving biography.

The eight contemporaries in the book were in fact near-contemporaries, since all were dead by 1979. Michael was not yet prepared to write frankly about Enoch Powell, Barbara Castle and Tony Benn, as he did in his next collection, *Loyalists and Loners*, published in 1986. In *Debts of Honour* he was revisiting his youth; he had encountered seven of the eight before 1940 – the eighth was Vicky – and they belonged to the world in which he had given his loyalty to democratic socialism without discarding his liberalism (at least with a small 'l'). The first essay, inevitably and properly, was an outpouring of affection and gratitude for his father, Isaac Foot. It began: 'My father must have been just about the happiest man who ever lived' and it closed with an evocation of Isaac's preaching in his local Methodist chapel: 'Outside, the world seemed sharply brighter than when we went in, and we would return to our Sunday dinner, the best of the week, bubbling with an unaccountable optimism, touched no doubt by the beauty of the words, the Bible's, Wordsworth's or his own, all uttered in a voice as rich and memorable as Devonshire cream.'[2]

Next – after an intermission for Hazlitt and Disraeli – came Michael's father-figure, Beaverbrook. Michael did not abate a jot or tittle of his championship and insisted on his version of Beaverbrook as a radical – 'not', he remarked parenthetically, 'as the word may be risibly applied nowadays, say to Mr Jo Grimond or Mr Roy Jenkins'. He took the opportunity to write for the first time about his own recruitment to Express Newspapers, about the fabulous evenings at Cherkley and about his dazzled adoration for Lili Ernst. The essay can be bracketed with another whose subject was Randolph Churchill: 'There were those days in 1938 and 1939, at Beaverbrook's house, when he metaphorically coshed any Munichite minister whom his host had been ill-advised enough to invite to the party.' And there was a figure from the 1930s whom few young people in 1979 could have heard of: Bonar Thompson, the star attraction of Speakers' Corner in its classic period, whose pungent commentaries drew Michael to Hyde Park almost every Sunday when he was a newcomer to London.

Three essays were devoted to men who had exerted an intellectual influence on the young Michael Foot and on others of his generation. Bertrand Russell had captured Michael's admiration in the early 1930s and retained it for forty years. H. N. Brailsford had incarnated the perfect amalgam of radical politics: 'he had a nonconformist conscience and a Marxist imagination and a romantic Shelleyan faith in the perfectibility of man and, more especially, woman'. Ignazio Silone, the irreconcilable enemy of Mussolini's Fascism, had shown how faith in socialism, even in the fellow-travelling 1930s, could be free from contamination by the base metal of Stalinism. It was to the – intrinsically Italian – richness and complexity of Silone's thinking that Michael paid homage: 'He was obsessed by the perpetual interaction of morals and politics, thought and action, ends and means, the flesh and the spirit.' Through the wording of these essays, we see how Michael had yearned to give his mind to more worthy concerns than deals with the Liberals or the Ulster Unionists. While he had not shirked the obligations of practical politics, he had remained aware of the price that they extorted.

It remained for Michael to fulfil his pledge to render 'proper honour' to Vicky. The short essay in memory of Vicky – containing, unusually in this book, hardly anything in the way of humour or irony, nor yet of personal anecdote – was the most painfully heartfelt that Michael had to bring himself to write. It had a tinge of guilt: 'I thought I really knew him. Then one cold afternoon, Charles Wintour, editor of the *Evening Standard*, rang up and told me he was dead. I had barely understood at all . . . I had no comprehension of how near his mind was to the end of its tether.'[3] Michael's last word on Vicky was: 'One cause of his unsettled mind was undoubtedly that he felt more sharply than most of the rest of the human race. He had no armour to protect himself against the twentieth-century horrors.' That was true enough, but it was a melancholy eulogy from the pen of a friend who was a survivor.

Half of the pieces in *Debts of Honour* were newly written; the others were expanded from articles, book reviews, anniversary tributes or obituaries which Michael had written for various papers – *Tribune*, the *Observer*, the *Evening Standard*, the *Sunday Telegraph* or *The Times*. It was

The Times that had, in 1978, requested a full-page article to commemorate the birth of Hazlitt, which Michael had gladly written despite his ministerial preoccupations at the time. Playfully or provocatively, he made this comment on Hazlitt's *The Spirit of the Age*:

> He pinioned, mocked, revalued or extolled some two dozen of his most famous contemporaries . . . He was no respecter of conventional judgements from left, right or centre . . . and those who usually came off worst of all were the whiffling moderates in the middle, 'ever strong upon the stronger side', like *The Times* newspaper (yes, even in those days).[4]

To its credit, *The Times* printed the sentence and the parenthesis without any cavil.

2

When the Labour Party loses power, the sequel is a rigorous, and in some quarters venomous, examination of the defects of the fallen government. There are accusations of missed opportunities, broken promises, decisions and policies that outraged the tenets of socialism, and in particular indifference to – or indeed defiance of – the opinions of the party rank and file and the resolutions of party conferences. Thus it was in 1951 and in 1970, and in 1979 it happened again.

The reproaches came most sharply from the supporters and admirers of Tony Benn, who was known to have been unhappy with the dominant trends under Wilson and Callaghan. Benn himself was reluctant to sound the first note in a chorus of disapproval, and wrote in the first issue of *Tribune* after the defeat: 'There must be no personal recriminations about the past five years. The minority Labour government which has just left office achieved a great deal that was good.'[5] But, in that same issue of *Tribune*, Chris Mullin – a member of the paper's staff who was in the process of joining Benn's circle of advisers – took a more critical line: 'Most of our leaders once in power treat the Labour Party as though it were one of a number of rather irritating pressure groups . . . We are going to need some new leaders . . . Reselection of those M.P.s who do not or will not reflect the aspirations of the party should now be pursued with vigour.'

There was, certainly, a case for arguing that the government had 'achieved a great deal that was good'. Until the final disastrous winter, industrial peace had been maintained, inflation rolled back and social justice safeguarded, while Britain's limited resources had been directed to constructive purposes. After a decade of Thatcherism, the chief economic adviser of the CBI, Professor Douglas McWilliams, judged: 'It was investment in the 1970s which carried industry on through part of the 1980s.'[6] Michael, reviewing the record in a speech in 1982, was able to claim:

> Major advances were made in the security of people's livelihood, of pensioners, of people in work and perhaps, in retrospect, most strikingly in the position of women. The first stage of equal pay, child benefit, sex discrimination legislation and employment protection laid the foundation for transforming the position of women in our society. This is an unwritten piece of history which I propose to write myself – to ensure its authenticity – when I get the chance.[7]

But this speech (which was delivered to a small academic audience, was not released to the press and was obtained by the *New Statesman*) was also coloured by what Michael called 'a penitent mood':

> It is true that we wavered in allegiance to our own doctrines . . . Mistakes and misjudgements, certainly: I would not attempt to question that charge . . . It must also be admitted that by 1977, while there was still a large measure of support for the policy [the voluntary incomes policy] there was also substantial opposition especially within the Labour movement.

At the time, in the summer of 1979, he was mainly concerned to attack the dismantling of Labour's achievements by the Tory government and to call for unity in opposition. Speaking at the Durham miners' gala in July, he said:

> Day after day, as they unveil their policies, or rather as the mask is stripped away from their furious prejudices, it is evident that the years ahead are bound to be bitter indeed . . . We need to summon the strength, unity and intelligence of the whole Labour movement to resist wherever we can, and to search out the only safe road for ourselves and for others too – the road of democratic Socialism. It would be tragic and unforgivable if at such a moment we turned aside from this supreme task to tear ourselves in pieces, if we supposed that what is needed is a constitutional wrangle within the Labour Party. That was the great folly which Hugh Gaitskell committed after the electoral defeat of 1959. I trust we can escape a repetition of such a dangerous diversion today.

However, when he gave this advice again in a *Tribune* article, Ian Mikardo retorted that Gaitskell too had sought to deflect criticism by warning the party not to tear itself apart. 'Today,' Mikardo wrote, 'Michael Foot is adopting exactly the same attitude toward his former allies and is even clothing it in Gaitskell's own cliché.'[8] He followed this up with his diagnosis: 'Our problem isn't that we don't have good policies – it is that our good policies, as the old Michael Foot regularly told us, don't get implemented.'[9]

For the dissatisfied left, this was the crux of the matter, and it was the burden of two speeches delivered from the platform at the party conference in October (to say nothing of speeches from delegates at the rostrum). It happened that the chairman that year was a committed left-winger, Frank Allaun, and he said in his opening address: 'The feeling was growing up at the grass roots about the parliamentary leaders: "Whatever we say they take no notice at all." . . . That's the real issue behind all the reforms now before this conference.' He then gave an approving outline of the proposed reforms which supplied the contentious issues at the conference. His words were soon echoed, with greater bluntness and emphasis, by Ron Hayward: 'We didn't work and spend to send an M.P. to the House of Commons to forget whence he came and whom he represents . . . Why was there a winter of discontent? Because the Cabinet, supported by M.P.s, ignored Congress and Conference decisions . . . In my forty-six years of membership of this party I've never yet seen it try Socialism in any sense.'

In retirement, Hayward recalled with jovial satisfaction that none of the ex-ministers would talk to him after he made his speech. Callaghan was highly disgruntled when he had to listen to the speeches by Allaun, who was chairman only through the rule of Buggins' turn, and Hayward, who was an appointed official – and to the applause that greeted them. The task of defending the late government was shouldered energetically by Michael:

> Some people say we should have cleared out. I wasn't in favour of clearing out because I wanted to get all that legislation through. That's why we stayed there. That's why we fought, and that's why we worked night and day as we did, and that's why we don't come and apologise for what we did . . . It's easy to say all you've got to do is obey conference decisions. Sometimes conference decisions ask for contradictory things.

The three reforms being debated in 1979 were mandatory reselection of MPs, election of the party leader by a broader forum than the PLP, and control of the party manifesto by the NEC. Callaghan was hostile to all three and was confident that his authority and prestige would suffice to defeat them, despite a warning from Mikardo that he was 'swimming against the tide of history'. Michael's attitude to all three was cautious without being entirely negative. He had his misgivings about what was demanded, but he was willing to listen to argument – especially from his 'former allies', to whom he was still linked by bonds of friendship – and his overriding wish was to reach solutions without damaging confrontations. What was certain was that there was not much time to be lost. The Labour Party had a rule that a constitutional issue, once decided, could not be debated again for another three years; thus reselection had been defeated in 1974 and was discussed again only in 1977. But in 1979 a conference vote resulted in the scrapping of this rule.

In principle, it had always been possible for a CLP (constituency Labour Party) to get rid of an MP if he forfeited its confidence. However, the procedure was slow and complicated, so the CLP generally chose to pass critical resolutions, preserve a grumbling tolerance and hope that the MP would retire or be offered a peerage. In the 1970s, thanks to the growing influence of the left – indeed, the 'hard left' – and the consequent estrangement between some MPs and their rank and file, dismissals became more frequent. In 1972 Mikardo secured the NEC's backing for the doctrine that it should intervene only when correct procedures had been infringed, regardless of the political stance of the MP concerned. Consequently, Reg Prentice was removed in 1975, Frank Tomney of Hammersmith North in 1976, and Sir Arthur Irvine of the Edge Hill division of Liverpool in 1977. Tomney has been accurately described as 'a poor M.P., on the extreme right of the party, with some notably illiberal views on homosexuality, race and capital punishment';[10] Irvine, a QC and Recorder, neglected his constituency in the interests of his legal career; Prentice proceeded to join the Tories (and later became a Tory minister), a development which was taken by many to justify his dismissal and exonerate his left-wing opponents from charges of undue intolerance.

These cases lent credence to the view that there might be a few dozen MPs undeserving of 'a meal ticket for life', and that their merits should be regularly scrutinised. By 1977, there was strong backing for a conference resolution proposing that every constituency should reselect – or refuse to reselect – its MP in the course of each Parliament. Mikardo again swayed the NEC and was able to tell the conference that it would present a workable scheme in a year's time. The prospect filled many MPs with anxiety, if not terror. John Grant, who later joined the SDP, told an interviewer: 'It was not that I was going to lose, but that I was going to be forced to spend a lot of time making sure that I was not going to lose . . . You might say that they altered the conditions of my employment.'[11] Another MP, Joe Ashton, made a more agonised plea in his speech at the 1979 conference when the issue came to a head: 'MPs are people. We've got wives, we've got kids, we've got mortgages, the same as you have. If you cut us, we bleed . . . If a man has given fifteen or twenty years to a constituency and you have fallen out with him, this sort of instant hire and fire, quickie divorce, call it what you like, won't do his party a lot of good.'

Michael sympathised with these feelings. He understood the resentment caused by the 'meal ticket for life' and had been glad to see the departure of Prentice, Tomney and Irvine; but he reacted strongly against attacks on MPs in general. At the *Tribune* meeting on the fringe of the 1980 conference, he declared: 'I won't be a party to strictures pronounced on the overwhelming mass of the parliamentary party. I don't believe they are engaged in some malicious campaign to frustrate conference or the will of the party. I know them.'

He realised, too, that the demand for reselection was being pressed in an organised way by the Campaign for Labour Party Democracy. Founded in 1973, the CLPD was in theory concerned to improve the functioning of the party and in fact had the support of people of varying political opinions, but it had inevitably become a vehicle for those who aimed at shifting the balance of power to the left – even the extreme left. In 1979, the resolution urging mandatory reselection was moved and seconded by Pat Wall and Derek Hatton, both members of the Militant Tendency (of which more will be said in later pages). It was triumphantly carried. The consequences, however, were far less dramatic than anyone had hoped or feared. In the course of the 1979–83 Parliament, only eight Labour MPs were deselected, and seven of them were over fifty-five years of age, which may well have been a factor.

The CLPD was also pressing for a change in the preparation of the election manifesto. The issue generated a great deal of heat, largely because of Callaghan's veto in 1979 on the abolition of the House of Lords. The existing rule was that the contents of the manifesto were decided at a joint meeting of the NEC and the Shadow Cabinet; the CLPD demand was that it should be drawn up by the NEC alone, as the party's governing body. It also wanted a 'rolling manifesto' – that is, a manifesto produced every year whether an election was imminent or not. In 1980, Tony Benn and Eric Heffer organised a press conference to present a manifesto approved by the NEC without consulting the

Shadow Cabinet. Callaghan and Michael, invoking their authority as leader and deputy leader, forced the last-minute cancellation of the press conference. At the ensuing party conference, the CLPD proposal was defeated by a narrow majority. It was the only setback for the extreme left in this period.

The most important and most fiercely contested struggle was over the question of the election of the party leader and deputy leader. Since the foundation of the Labour Party, the leader of the party's MPs had been automatically recognised as leader of the party, especially after 1922 when there was a real prospect of a Labour Prime Minister. Challengers to the system argued that a leader appointed in this way might not merit the trust of the rank and file, whose work was vital to the election of a Labour government; Gaitskell was an obvious case in point. They also pointed out that the leaders of other socialist parties were generally chosen at party conferences (in Canada, for example, at an American-style convention).

Michael was deeply unhappy about the opening of this Pandora's box, because it released and stimulated all the latent antagonisms between the party rank and file and the MPs. Throughout his career, he had been a dutiful and influential attender at party conferences, but also a dedicated parliamentarian. He was ready to defend the MPs, but he knew that some of them adopted a disdainful attitude to the kind of people who criticised them from the conference rostrum. There was, for instance, the Defence and Disarmament Group of the PLP, known as the 'bomber group' because its leading members – Roy Mason, Fred Mulley and William Rodgers – favoured the weaponry whose rejection was regularly demanded at conferences. It has been said of this group that 'few of its members ever attended party conference, which was often regarded as an alien hybrid body dominated by the highly politicised and therefore unrepresentative Left drawn from the constituency parties'.[12]

To begin with, the CLPD proposed simply that the leader should be elected by the conference. This meant that the choice would in effect rest with the big unions who cast the decisive votes; it also meant the complete exclusion of the MPs (who had no votes at the conference unless they happened to be delegates). Such an exclusion was unwelcome even to MPs whose main political base was the conference, including Benn. The CLPD therefore shifted its ground to develop the idea of an electoral college, in which the MPs, the constituencies and the unions would share the votes in proportions yet to be decided. But, as Jon Lansman, one of the inner circle of CLPD activists, made clear: 'We changed our position from election of leader by conference to that of the electoral college because the former was unwinnable. Our decision on the electoral college was entirely tactical.'[13]

Michael pleaded for 'no change' until 1980, when he found that this view was supported by few people except himself, Callaghan and (ironically) some of the union leaders. Then he reluctantly accepted the idea of the electoral college, which was adopted – by a majority of only 98,000 in six million votes – at the 1980 conference. In a *Tribune* article, he wrote regretfully: 'A new system would involve a serious erosion of parliamentary authority.' However, his conclusion was: 'To say that it is impossible to contrive a fair system strikes me as absurd.'[14]

Through 1979 and most of 1980, Michael's position was delicate and indeed difficult. The party was swinging hard to the left, both on policy issues on which he agreed with Benn and the Bennites (more public ownership, unilateral nuclear disarmament, hostility to the European Community) and on constitutional issues on which he did not. Unfortunately, the latter assumed much greater prominence and aroused much angrier passions than the former. Callaghan was maintaining a stubborn resistance on both sets of issues, but neither his energy nor his tactical skill were what they had been a few years earlier.

It might have been logical for Michael to desire – even, though this would have contradicted his sense of loyalty, to seek to bring about – Callaghan's retirement. Callaghan was in fact inclined to retire after the general election; he was tired after his three years in Downing Street and, in his own words, 'I was sick of it.'[15] A few words of friendly advice from Michael would, perhaps, have led him to make the decision. Far from speaking those words, Michael begged him to stay on. His chief reason for doing so was that Labour appeared, at that time, to have a good chance of regaining power at the next election. The economy was plunging into recession; both unemployment and inflation were soaring; Thatcher herself was personally unpopular and it was an open secret that half her Cabinet had acute disagreements with her. Despite his troubles in the winter of discontent, Callaghan was better equipped to win the return match than any possible successor. 'He had far more appeal to the voters than I could ever expect to have,' Michael candidly admitted. In any case, if Callaghan did retire, Michael was neither eager to make a bid for the leadership nor likely, in his own estimation, to secure it. The electoral college was a project that might never become a reality, and so long as the choice rested with the MPs the clear favourite was Denis Healey.

3

While the Labour Party wrangled over mandatory reselection or the electoral college – concepts that were esoteric or incomprehensible to most of the public – the world was not standing still. The cold war was still being waged, and the forces pressing for a new escalation of the nuclear arms race were not to be checked either by the well-meaning but fumbling President Carter in Washington or by the ailing and almost senile President Brezhnev in Moscow. Since the mid-1970s, the Russians had been developing a missile, the SS-20, aimed at targets in Western Europe. Over the same period, their American counterparts had been working on similar medium-range missiles, the Cruise and the Pershing, and on the Trident nuclear submarine as a successor to Polaris. At Christmas 1979, Soviet troops entered Afghanistan. Two weeks later, Cruise and Pershing were publicly unveiled and plans were announced to site them on bases in Britain, Germany and Italy. The Afghan blunder served as a perfect justification, both for the installation of the missiles and for a fresh wave of anti-Communist alarmism. The Americans ordered a boycott of the Olympic Games, due to be held in Moscow in 1980 – a move followed by Thatcher and endorsed by Peter Shore, now Labour's foreign policy spokesman, but deplored by Michael. The frenetic mood soon began to propel Ronald Reagan towards his victory in the presidential election of November 1980.

However, these menacing steps were met by protests of unexpected breadth and vigour. CND, moribund since the 1960s, gained a new lease of life and was able to attract 80,000 people – they included Michael Foot, Tony Benn and Neil Kinnock – to a march through London on 22 June 1980. The protests, and the arguments, reflected the growing rifts between right and left. Michael and other veterans of the Aldermaston marches were against Cruise; David Owen, who had been promoted to the Foreign Office by Callaghan in 1977, and Bill Rodgers, appointed as defence spokesman in 1979, were for it. When CND planned another march for 26 October, the NEC debated whether Labour, as a party, should support it. A motion by Shirley Williams that the party should stay aloof was defeated by 15 votes to 9, with Callaghan and Michael voting on opposite sides. Michael was one of the speakers at the rally.

Commentators in the press began to discuss the disintegration of the Labour Party as a real possibility, and holding it together became Michael's chief concern. The scenario generally sketched was this: the Bennite left, through its ruthless machinations, would seize the levers of power and force the adoption of an extremist programme; the 'moderates' would be witnessing the extinction or at least the transformation of the party as they had known it; and they would be obliged to create a new political structure, appealing for support both to alienated Labour voters and to others who were searching for a vehicle for their aspirations. In all this, a pivotal figure was Roy Jenkins. His four years in Brussels had given him space for reflection, the prestige of a 'wise man' and something of the allure of a distinguished exile. His term as President of the European Commission was to expire in January 1981, but he embraced his new future on 22 November 1979, when he delivered the Dimbleby lecture (commemorating the late Richard Dimbleby, best known for his reverential tributes to the monarchy) on BBC television. The lecture took its title from Browning – 'Home Thoughts from Abroad' – and closed with a much favoured quotation from Yeats: 'Things fall apart; the centre cannot hold.' Curiously, it was precisely the centre whose holding capacity Jenkins promised.

The text appealed seductively to everyone who felt weariness, or irritation, with the pettiness and selfishness of current political warfare. Some of the most effective phrases were:

> We could escape from the constricting rigidity – almost tyranny – of the present party system . . . Too many queasy rides on the ideological big dipper . . . A shrill and unconvincing attempt to portray almost everyone on the other side as either a fool or a knave . . . The great disadvantage of our present electoral system is that it freezes the pattern of politics and holds together the incompatible.

The key sentence was: 'If it [the electorate] saw a new grouping with cohesive and relevant policies, it might be more attracted by this new reality than by old labels which had become increasingly irrelevant.'

There was some irony in this use of the word 'new', since Jenkins' original intention, when he began to think along these lines, had been to attach himself to Britain's oldest political formation, the Liberal Party. But David Steel, the intelligent and flexible leader of the Liberals, convinced him in private conversations that he would achieve more by heading a breakaway from the Labour Party, which would work in collaboration – but not identification – with the Liberal Party. Here was the genesis of the Social Democratic Party.

The Labour personalities most likely to respond to Jenkins' appeal were Owen, Rodgers and Shirley Williams. On 1 August 1980, they published in the *Guardian* (their natural forum) an Open Letter expressing their anxiety over current trends in the party. It was a signal that their departure was not out of the question, although Rodgers was probably the only one of the three who clearly envisaged it.

These pressures were balanced by pressures from the left. There was now a cohesive group of Labour MPs – among them Dennis Skinner, Martin Flannery and Reg Race – who were quite prepared to see a right-wing breakaway as the necessary cost of swinging the party in what they saw as the desired direction. Michael felt that some of them did very little thinking, and on one occasion, when interrupted in the House by Skinner, reacted with: 'If only my honourable friend would conduct the novel experiment of listening with his ears instead of his voice, a whole new world would open to him.'[16] This segment of the left worked through a range of well-organised pressure groups: first the CLPD, then the Labour Co-ordinating Committee – founded in 1978, and concerned with policy objectives as well as constitutional changes – and finally the Rank and File Mobilising Committee, created in June 1980. The key men in this network were Vladimir Derer, who had settled in Britain as a refugee from Czechoslovakia in 1939, Victor Schonfield, who was a critic of jazz music, and the twenty-four-year-old Jon Lansman. They were unreservedly dedicated, they had no political ambitions of their own and they were in a position to work day and night for the cause without pay. Their limitation was that they had no status in any part of the Labour movement.

The groups were generally given credit for more strength than they possessed. The CLPD and the LCC had about 800 members each, and doubtless there was a large overlap. Support and financial aid were voted by four national trade unions (including NUPE and Clive Jenkins' ASTMS) and by 112 union branches, but by only 107 constituency parties out of the 635.[17] However, the strength was maximised by the technique of the 'model resolution'. In the past, conference resolutions favouring a given objective were phrased in different ways, so that the NEC member who guided the compositing session could sometimes manage to dilute their force and eliminate a vital component. Scores of identically worded resolutions gave a much greater impression of an irresistible demand.

The year 1980 was one of complex in-fighting and vain attempts to reach harmonious compromises. The NEC set up a commission of inquiry into the constitutional proposals, but it could not agree to any recommendations. A one-day special conference was called, meeting in the Wembley Centre on 31 May, to endorse a manifesto entitled *Peace, Jobs, Freedom*. Reflecting the growing strength of the left in the NEC, it advocated increased public expenditure, an extension of public ownership, control over movements of capital, industrial democracy and 'fundamental reforms' of the European Community. But it was never quite clear whether this manifesto took precedence over decisions that might be made at the regular annual conference.

By this time, it was recognised as likely that the project of the electoral college would be accepted at the October conference, and argument centred on its make-up. The paradox was that the Bennites, whose main base was in the constituency parties, wanted the unions to have the lion's share of the votes; but the union leaders – notably David Basnett of the General and Municipal Workers and the staunchly right-wing Terry Duffy, who had succeeded Scanlon as president of the AUEW – were not keen to carry this burden and wished to hand as much as possible of it to the MPs. The formula that seemed reasonable to Michael, and also to Basnett, was: 50 per cent to the PLP, 25 to the unions and 25 to the constituencies. The alternative put forward by Eric Heffer and supported by Tony Benn was one-third each.

The summer brought an uneasy lull. Callaghan told Michael that the approaching conference would be his last and he had made up his mind to retire after it. Michael, according to Callaghan's recollection, said that he would not be a candidate for the leadership. He and Jill went to Cyprus for a holiday and stayed at Paphos, where the goddess Aphrodite rose from the sea-foam. Her birthplace was almost the scene of Michael's death, for he got into difficulties in his daily swim and had to be rescued by workmen who were repairing a jetty.

At Blackpool, on the eve of the conference, he had dinner with Dick Clements, Geoffrey Goodman and Ian Aitken. They knew that Callaghan was going, and urged Michael to stand for the leadership. Clements recalls that Michael was intending to support Peter Shore, but agreed to give more thought to the matter when the journalists said emphatically that Shore could not defeat Healey.[18]

The conference proceeded to vote for the maximum programme of the left. It voted, by a two-to-one majority, that a Labour government should take Britain out of the European Community (even the manifesto adopted at Wembley in May had only suggested that Labour might be 'forced to consider' this step). It voted, by an overwhelming show of hands, for unilateral nuclear disarmament, the rejection of Cruise and Polaris, and the closing of American bomber bases in Britain. It voted for a resolution moved by another Liverpool Militant, Tony Mulhearn, prescribing the rejection of any kind of incomes policy. In this debate, Benn's speech on behalf of the NEC caused a sensation. He proposed that the next Labour government should, within a few weeks of taking office, put through an Industry Bill authorising state control of the whole of British industry, take Britain out of the EC and create a thousand new peers to ensure the abolition of the House of Lords. These pledges had never been discussed by the NEC, let alone by the Shadow Cabinet, but they were rapturously applauded.

The debate on the electoral college led to a chaotic sequence of events. Two proposals for its composition were then put to the vote: Heffer's 'one-third each' and a proposal to give the unions 50 per cent. Both were defeated. Benn and his chief allies on the NEC – Heffer, Skinner, Allaun and Joan Maynard – agreed to a compromise formula, coming closer to Michael's preference, of 40 per cent to the PLP. His coterie of advisers, with Lansman and Frances Morrell playing the dominant roles, objected. 'We thought the NEC Left had completely lost its nerve and given up far too much to the PLP,' one of them said.[19] After hours of nocturnal discussions, first in the bar of the Imperial Hotel and then in Benn's bedroom, Lansman and Morrell got the NEC back on course for a formula giving the unions 40 per cent. It looked as though this was about to be put through the conference, but Basnett secured an interval for further consideration, followed by another special conference in three months' time.

The Blackpool conference dispersed, in some disarray, on 3 October. On every issue, except the control of the manifesto, the decisions were those that Callaghan had hoped to avert (although it could be said that he had declined to fight rather than that he had been defeated). On 15 October, he announced his resignation.

Thanks to Basnett's delaying move, the electoral college was not yet in existence and could not be summoned to choose a new leader. It was still permissible for the PLP to hold a leadership election in the traditional way, although it would be the last time. But, in a speech on 16 October, Benn declared: 'Whoever they elect will be an interim leader whose term of office will automatically expire when the election under agreed procedure for choosing the leader of the whole party takes place.' He was suggesting, apparently, that there might be two leaders – of the party in Parliament and of 'the whole party'. However, the Shadow Cabinet met and, in the name of the PLP, authorised an election under the old rules.

Healey lost no time in announcing his candidacy and it was soon clear that he would be the only candidate from the right. Callaghan, though for the sake of correctness he made no public endorsement, decided to vote for Healey and expected him to win.[20] Certainly, anyone could see who was the front-runner. The well-informed political correspondent of *The Times* wrote: 'Mr Foot is understood to believe that Mr Healey could win by twenty or thirty votes.'[21]

Two anti-Healey candidates quickly appeared: Peter Shore and John Silkin. One afternoon in the summer, in a car going to Glyndebourne, Silkin had advised Jill Foot that she should stop Michael from seeking the leadership because he would be endangering his health. (In fact Silkin, ten years younger than Michael, died in 1987.) Overestimating his popularity as usual, Silkin informed the press that, if Michael did not stand, he (Silkin) would beat Healey on the first ballot, and if Michael did stand it would only delay the outcome: 'I will beat him. Already I've warned Michael Foot, sadly, that I have him beaten.'[22]

In reality, Shore was a distinctly stronger candidate than Silkin. Even so, the best judges did not fancy the chances of either man. Mikardo recorded that, when he heard that they were standing, 'my immediate reaction was to wonder how anyone could possibly imagine that either Peter Shore or John Silkin had any chance whatever of defeating Healey'.[23] The only potential candidate who did have a chance, in the estimation of Mikardo and many others, was Michael Foot. But would Michael stand?

4

Michael's leadership of the Labour Party, which lasted for two and a half years, was beset by problems that he could not resolve and difficulties that he could not overcome, was persistently mocked and derided, and culminated in electoral disaster. Therefore (though this is a classic example of the *post hoc ergo propter hoc* fallacy) it has been said that he was entirely unfitted for the role of leader and should never have accepted it. His qualities were those of the roaming guerrilla fighter, not the commander; he was at his best as a parliamentary and platform orator and as a writer. So runs the judgement – a judgement more often pronounced by detached observers, and by Michael's literary friends and Hampstead neighbours, than by those closer to the political struggles of the time.

What this judgement ignores is that Michael did have at least some of the qualities that a leader needs, particularly at a difficult period. He had a vibrant faith in the principles for which the party stood and the ability to express it in language that could be inspiring and persuasive. His integrity was recognised even by those who most sharply disagreed with him, and he was never accused of being devious in the Wilson manner. Thanks to long experience, he was skilled in negotiation and committee-handling and listened carefully to everyone whose opinions had to be considered. Even the charge most regularly made – that he was hesitant and indecisive – can be contested; sometimes he hesitated on purpose, and wisely refrained from decisions that would have intensified the existing antagonisms. If he appeared weak, there are times when being strong does the greatest harm.

The judgement ignores, furthermore, the fact that Michael – considerably more than most men – was aware of his limitations and handicaps and of how he was seen by a large part of the general public. If he had modestly indicated that he wished to continue as deputy leader, or even if he had withdrawn to work on a life of Hazlitt or an autobiography, his decision would have been treated with respect and he would have saved himself a vast amount of unpleasantness. He certainly did not believe, like Churchill in 1940, that the finger of destiny pointed uniquely to him. There might well have been a better leader; the trouble was that this imaginary better leader was not to be found and was clearly not Shore or Silkin. When Michael made the decision to stand, it was because of the necessities of the hour.

For what the judgement most glaringly ignores is the actual situation in October 1980, and the alternative that had to be contemplated. Denis Healey was not then the reflective, conciliatory statesman that he became, partly thanks to Michael's influence, in later years. He was abrasive, sometimes offensive and abusive in his style of utterance, intolerant of those who differed from him and averse to negotiated compromise. He was of course the standard-bearer of the right and was emphatically opposed to all the policies on major issues which had just been adopted by the conference. Had he won the leadership through a vote in the PLP, the sequel would have undoubtedly been a war between the MPs and the rank and file, as represented in conference, that would have dwarfed the hostilities of Gaitskell's 'fight and fight again' period in 1960–1. Given his disagreement with what was on record as party policy, his task in the House of Commons would have been impossible and the dichotomy would have been mercilessly exploited by the Tories. He would have lacked the confidence of the men and women who do the donkey-work at election times. The activists of the CLPD and the LCC were preparing to challenge his credentials as leader, and the NEC might have called a special conference to set up the electoral college and elect Benn. Thus there was a real danger of an irrevocable split in the party. In the event, it was the choice of Michael as leader – accepted, however grudgingly, both by Healey's followers and by Benn's – that averted the catastrophe. The truth about

Michael Foot's place in history is that he was the man who saved the Labour Party.

On 16 October, Mikardo phoned Michael and told him forcefully that he had a duty to stand because Shore could not win. Michael promised to think it over. Mik then spoke to Clive Jenkins, who said: 'Don't worry, I'm busy already.' Jill recalled: 'Every half-hour the doorbell rang and more telegrams arrived urging him to stand. We read them together and he finally wondered aloud whether he might be letting them all down by not participating. I agreed.'[24] Jenkins had prompted some of the messages, but many came spontaneously from people in the constituencies. Meanwhile, Stan Orme arranged a meeting attended by Shore, Silkin and Albert Booth and proposed that they should all plead with Michael to stand. Silkin angrily rejected this idea, declaring that he was sure to win.

Michael's testimony is that he was genuinely undecided and was listening to all his friends, but there is considerable evidence that he was inclined not to stand. When Peter Shore informed Michael that he was a candidate, Michael encouraged him and wished him good luck; it is inconceivable that he would have done so had he already decided to stand himself. Shore thinks that Michael was reluctant to stand but was coming under very strong pressure, 'partly organised and partly spontaneous'.[25] Both Tom McCaffrey, press spokesman for the leader, and Ron Hayward had the impression that he was unlikely to stand. Neil Kinnock took soundings among MPs and reckoned that Healey would win by 9 votes in the final ballot, so he advised Michael against standing.[26]

Michael was due to fly to Dublin on Saturday, 18 October, and to deliver a lecture on the Sunday as part of the commemoration of the anniversary of the death of Jonathan Swift. Anyone who knew Michael realised that no political crisis would induce him to cancel this commitment. The pressure continued to mount, and the veteran Philip Noel-Baker – who had made a fervent speech at Blackpool in support of the nuclear disarmament resolutions – sent a letter: 'I hope this reaches you in time. It brings you my strong conviction that you must become leader yourself. You have by far the best chance of preventing a split in the party.'[27] On the Saturday morning, Alan Watkins, political correspondent of the *Observer*, sent a telegram requesting Michael to phone him (Michael was ex-directory) and talk about the leadership. Watkins had a more than journalistic interest; a month before Callaghan's resignation, he had placed a bet of £100 at fourteen to one that Michael would be the next Labour Party leader. Michael was not obliged to ring back, but he did. He said that he was under heavy pressure, especially from union leaders, and his reply to a direct question was: 'I won't confirm anything, but you understand what I'm saying.' Watkins felt justified in writing, in a front-page story for *Observer* readers next day, that Michael had decided to stand. Michael's thoughts were now devoted to Swift and he had no intention of making a statement in Dublin. Monday's *Irish Times* reported:

> The British news media were in Dublin in great force . . . but Mr Foot was keeping his thoughts to himself . . . He said he had received many messages, telegrams and letters urging him to stand. He felt he had to consider what people said to him. Asked his opinion of other candidates, he said that Peter Shore would make a great leader of the party.

Michael found to his surprise that he was not to speak in a lecture-hall but from the pulpit of St Patrick's Cathedral, where Swift had been Dean, addressing 2,000 people. He gave them good value:

> Swift was credited with being the founder of the idea of an independent Ireland in a lecture by Michael Foot . . . He said that *Gulliver's Travels* was a greater anti-imperialist tract than anything designed by Karl Marx or his followers . . . In a curious way, said Mr Foot, Swift was the prophet of the nuclear age. He was concerned with the question of how to destroy injustice without the world destroying itself.[28]

On this Sunday morning, the left-wing MP Stuart Holland was pushing a note through the letter-box at Pilgrim's Lane with a list of twenty MPs who would vote for Michael but not for Shore. But Michael had made up his mind; before flying home, he phoned Stan Orme and told him that he would be standing. Unaware of this, Clive Jenkins had organised a dinner-time gathering to bring the pressure to a crescendo. Jill agreed to be the hostess and made a casserole, Mary Mikardo arrived with a large and rich cake, and Jenkins brought a case of claret. As well as the Mikardos and Jo Richardson, MP for Barking and an NEC member, the guests included a strong delegation of union leaders: Moss Evans of the TGWU, Alan Fisher of NUPE, Bill Keys of the printing union SOGAT and Arthur Scargill of the Yorkshire miners. Michael gave the impression that he was still listening to advice and allowed the union leaders to think that they had persuaded him. But Mik had few doubts: 'At the beginning of the evening we were pretty sure that Michael would run, and at the end of it we were quite sure.'[29]

On the same evening, Tony Benn's friends and advisers were gathering at his home in Holland Park Avenue. A few of them wanted him to stand, but the majority view was that he should ignore the PLP contest and promise to be a candidate in the 'real election'. Benn accepted this advice.

Unfortunately, Michael omitted to tell Peter Shore of his decision and Shore failed to contact him on Sunday evening. In the morning (so McCaffrey recalls) Shore went to Michael's room in the Commons to confirm that he had Michael's support and emerged much shaken by the information that Michael himself was standing. He said later that he had no feelings of resentment over Michael's lapse of tact – 'I didn't consider that I was let down or betrayed.' He had thought all along that Michael was the only man capable of beating Healey, and he would not have entered the lists if he had expected Michael to do so. He felt that he could not withdraw, having acquired promises of support, but he saw at once that 'my campaign had come to a juddering stop'.[30] In contrast, Silkin's self-confidence was not dented and he said to Clive Jenkins: 'Michael will be so hurt – can't you see I'm going to win?'

Michael announced his candidature at a press conference on Monday afternoon, 20 October. He told the reporters that he had yielded to pressure and, moreover, he had to stand because 'My wife might divorce me if I don't.' This rather laboured joke generated a belief that Jill had exerted the decisive influence. In reality, she had encouraged Michael when she saw that he was accepting the logic of the case made by Mikardo and Jenkins, but had told him that he must make up his own mind.

Now that the battle was on, Neil Kinnock swung into incessant activity as organiser of Michael's campaign, and as the days passed he became convinced that the chances were good. Mikardo, making a book on the race according to his usual practice, gave Michael and Healey at evens. In a letter written on 28 October, thanking Jack Jones for his good wishes, Michael wrote: 'I think it is going to be quite close, particularly if Denis does not win on the first ballot.' He improved his chances by an article and a speech which showed him at his best. He responded to a request from the *Guardian* for a thousand words on Labour's case against the Thatcher government, while Healey turned down the same request with a curt letter (printed by the *Guardian*) saying that his views were well known. Then, on 29 October, he wound up for the Opposition in a debate on unemployment and made effective use of a CBI report which rated the economic situation as more serious than in 1974. 'When the latest report from the CBI reads like the front page of *Tribune*, perhaps we're moving very fast,' he commented. What was needed, he declared, was a campaign against the Tory 'industrial atrocities' similar to Gladstone's Midlothian campaign against the Bulgarian atrocities. As a historical footnote, he remarked that Gladstone was sixty-eight at the time and went on to head three more governments, a piece of information which made his own age – sixty-seven – seem less of a handicap.

In 1980, as at any earlier date, the majority of Labour MPs could be classed as right-wingers, so Healey was understandably complacent about his prospects. However, there were several complicating factors. Some middle-of-the-road MPs, who would have preferred Healey in normal circumstances, considered Michael better equipped to hold the party together. Healey himself conceded: 'Without doubt the desire for a quiet life cost me the votes of some MPs who . . . feared that as leader I would have split the party.'[31] There were also MPs who hoped that Michael would protect them from the perils of reselection. Some, again, had decided to join the Social Democratic breakaway if and when it became a reality. They may have calculated – Healey certainly believes so – that a Foot victory would enable them to claim that the party was falling into the hands of the extreme left, with Michael as a Kerensky to Benn's Lenin, and give them a plausible excuse for deserting it. Healey also forfeited support, like George Brown in 1963, by his displeasing manners and short temper. Shirley Williams has said that she could name several MPs who aligned themselves with him politically but voted against him on personal grounds.[32] But Callaghan, despite his affection for Michael, voted for Healey. Asked later why he considered Michael unsuitable as a leader, he replied: 'Oh, Michael is so honest and straightforward.'[33]

The target figure was 135, and success for Healey depended on achieving it or at least getting near it on the first ballot. He polled only 112 against 83 for Michael. Silkin and Shore, with 38 and 32 respectively, were eliminated. A second ballot was held and the result was announced on 10 November. The scene has been described by the journalists who were soon to start work on a quick biography of Michael:

> Foot went into the meeting looking drawn and anxious, almost, one of his supporters said, as if he had suffered some awful shock. Several of them assumed that he had lost, though a few who knew him better guessed that this would be his reaction to success . . . The party chairman, Fred Willey, read out the result: Foot had won by 139 votes to 129 . . . One of Foot's leading campaigners, the Welsh M.P. Neil Kinnock . . . let out a blood-curdling Indian war whoop.[34]

Michael made a short speech, quoting a dictum of Nye Bevan's: 'Never underestimate the passion for unity in the party, and never forget that it is the decent instinct of people who want to do something.' Healey then congratulated the winner and said that he was willing to serve as deputy leader. He was elected to this position without any other nominations. His account confirms that Michael was looking 'nervous and unhappy', and he adds: 'I glanced at Tony Benn. His face was ashen. So I knew I had done at least one thing right.'[35]

By coincidence, the old session was ending and the new one beginning in an acrimonious atmosphere. On the day when Michael was elected, large redundancies in the (still nationalised) steel industry were announced in a written answer to a parliamentary question, instead of in a statement open to debate. The incident, Michael hastened to say, was 'one of the most extraordinary in the history of the House'. On 13 November, an unexpected 30 per cent increase in council rents was announced by the Secretary for the Environment, Michael Heseltine – also in a written answer. Roy Hattersley, the Shadow Secretary for this Department, rose to protest. The session was literally in its last minutes and, in accordance with hallowed tradition, the functionary entitled Black Rod was about to summon MPs to the House of Lords to hear the Queen's speech. A number of Labour members formed what was virtually a picket line and barred his way. Amid uproar, the Speaker suspended the session and Heseltine vanished. When the session was resumed, Michael demanded that the statement about council rents should be withdrawn, and declared: 'The rights of the House of Commons have been grossly interfered with by the behaviour of the Secretary for the Environment . . . I don't know where he is. It's deeply offensive to the House that he should not be here.' The Speaker ordered another suspension and spoke to Heseltine, who returned to say that he would withdraw the statement and hold consultations, but only in deference to the authority of the Speaker. Michael had the last word: 'The Secretary of State and the government were guilty of a grave offence against the House. It is extremely gratifying that they have now withdrawn the document, but they could have done it with much better grace.' Black Rod was then allowed to enter and the Queen read her speech, half an hour late.

David Owen and Bill Rodgers, by now on their way to an exit from the Labour Party, deplored this unruly action and accused Michael of conniving at it. This he denied, but a *Sunday Times* account judged: 'No one doubts that it was Labour's new leader who inspired, if he did not encourage, this performance.' However, the *Sunday Times* article concluded that the episode had done Michael – and the Labour Party – a power of good: 'After the lame-duck Callaghan period, there is a new atmosphere in the PLP . . . With Foot and Healey sitting shoulder-to-shoulder on the front bench, the party could at last believe that Thatcherism was the enemy transcending all its internal dis-agreements . . . Labour M.P.s have won what they see as a moral victory.'[36]

It was a stimulating start to Michael's leadership. In his first few days, he received pleasing letters from old friends. John Cripps wrote: 'How pleased Nye and Stafford would have been! All best wishes for the future.' And David Astor: 'I admire your fortitude in taking on this great responsibility . . . I was today with Arthur Koestler who was speaking of you affectionately.' Tony Benn, too, joined in the chorus of goodwill. In a friendly meeting, he volunteered: 'You and I come from old-fashioned radical liberal families, and libertarianism is what it's all about.'[37] Indeed, in the 1920s Isaac Foot and William Wedgwood Benn had been stalwarts of the radical wing of the Liberal Party.

At this point, Benn did not see his future course clearly. He thought that, if Michael were to be leader, he would make a good deputy leader, and was shaken when Healey moved easily into that position. He had also expected that the 'real election' by the electoral college would take place in the near future, but Michael made it clear that he would serve throughout the parliamentary session – that is, until November 1981. There were sound tactical reasons for getting on amicably with Michael if possible, and indeed his attitude was never one of sustained hostility. Years later, he said:

> He was very, very kind, he's a charming man, hospitable, and I had good relations with him . . . When you are very close to people in politics, if you disagree then it tends to get rather heated and it did get very heated indeed between Michael and myself. It doesn't mean, looking back on it, that I don't have a great affection for him and recognise that he played a very important role . . . You have to look at somebody's life according to the best lap they ran with the baton, and Michael's best laps, I think, were before he became party leader . . . I want to say that because I don't want you to think that I bear any ill-will towards him, because I don't, and I don't suppose really he bears all that ill-will towards me.[38]

Michael, doubtless, knew that it was no time for euphoria. If he looked 'drawn and anxious' or 'nervous and unhappy' on his first day as leader, it was because he saw the dangers ahead. The period on which he was entering could only be the most arduous and challenging of his life, even though he did not yet foresee how frustrating and unlucky it would be.

Had he been superstitious, he might have been daunted by a mishap on 12 November, when he tripped on a flight of steps in the Commons, broke a bone in his ankle, and had to have his right leg put in plaster. James Cameron commented: 'In one week Michael Foot publishes a book [*Debts of Honour*], becomes leader of the Labour Party and falls downstairs and breaks an ankle. A rich and varied life.'[39]

5

While Michael's arrival in the leadership was greeted with pleasure by most of the Labour Party, it was also the starting gun for the creation of the Social Democratic Party. In the press (naturally, those sections of the press which had never wished Labour well) the impatience could not be contained. The *Economist* lost no time in issuing its commands:

> Mr Foot's victory leaves those on the right of the Labour Party with a clearer choice than ever before . . . They can shut up, stay where they are and by their presence help Labour to another shambolic period of office when the electorate tires of the Conservatives. Or they can take their beliefs off into an exile from which could spring a new dawn on the social democratic left, a dawn which might give Britain a popular-based alternative party. The question is no longer whether they should leave the Labour Party but when. The answer is now.[40]

Back in March, a businessman named Oliver Stutchbury had circulated a report written by a partner in an advertising agency. Stutchbury's covering letter (leaked to *Tribune* in September) read:

> Following his Dimbleby lecture, some of Roy Jenkins' friends are exploring the feasibility of launching a new party of the Centre. The final decision about whether to launch or not will probably not be taken until after this year's Labour Party conference . . . I enclose a copy of a strictly confidential report which . . . treats the launch of the proposed new political party as if it were a new consumer product.[41]

The letter invited donations towards a fund of £12,000 for 'market research'. The approach may not have been to the liking of everyone who received the report, especially as it evaluated the marketability of Shirley Williams, Bill Rodgers and Dick Taverne as possible leaders. Obviously, there were two other potential leaders, Jenkins and Owen. In fact, at this stage there were more chiefs than Indians. Williams was seen as well qualified to take at least a prominent role, both because of her widespread popularity and because she was not fully identified with the right of the Labour Party, but she was not convinced that a break was either necessary or desirable. Speaking at a fringe meeting at Blackpool, in language that recalls Gaitskell's in 1960, she said: 'We are going to fight to save the party and by God we think we can. We are going to start fighting for a Labour Party worthy of the name.' Chris Mullin, who reported this meeting for *Tribune*, told his readers: 'The moderates gave the impression that they were actually going to stay in the party and argue their corner.'[42]

The social democrats were still undecided whether to form a group compatible with continued membership of the Labour Party or a new party. Another problem was to select a leader. Roy Jenkins had now returned from Brussels and the newspapers had coined the phrase 'Gang of Four' – Jenkins, Shirley Williams, Owen, Rodgers. (The original Gang of Four, the acolytes of Mao Zedong in his last years, were just going on trial in China.) Another confidential memorandum – believed to be the handiwork of David Owen – discussed the alternatives:

> Some of our closest allies see Roy still as their political leader, others count him as a friend . . . Others see him as a liability . . . The whole key to success for any initiative is that it is new, different, young and fresh looking. For every 60-year-old establishment figure there must be a late 30s early 40s radical thinker and far more than just a token woman. [Jenkins was sixty, Williams fifty and Owen forty-two.] There are strong arguments for a clean break in February . . . Premises can be found, telephones can be installed, computer space leased or borrowed and voluntary helpers enlisted.

One possibly decisive factor was that the press would award praise for bold and speedy action and pour scorn on hesitation. A writer who studied the history of the SDP found that: 'The Gang of Four, assisted by fewer than a dozen Labour M.P.s, launched the party earlier than originally planned in order to satisfy public expectations raised by the media.'[43]

In December, the elections in the PLP for twelve members of the Shadow Cabinet gave Michael trouble with both left and right. Tony Benn came thirteenth in the voting and did not win a place; this was a setback for Michael's hopes of including him in a broadly based team and enabled Benn's hard-line advisers to persuade him that he could not get a good relationship with Michael even if he tried. The chairman of the CLPD proclaimed: 'The illusion of reconciliation is over. Michael Foot cannot bridge the gap between this Shadow Cabinet and the rank and file of the party.'[44] Indeed, by *Tribune*'s reckoning, eight of the twelve elected were right-wingers and opposed to the policies adopted at the party conference.

One of the eight was Bill Rodgers, regarded with the utmost suspicion by the left. Michael, trying to assemble a balanced front bench, appointed Healey as Shadow Foreign Secretary, Shore as Shadow Chancellor, Silkin as Shadow Leader of the House and Kinnock as education spokesman. He did not renew Rodgers' appointment as defence spokesman (the post he had held under Callaghan). Rodgers was offered a choice of other departments – health, social security or Northern Ireland – but rejected them all. Although it was normal for the portfolios to be reallocated, especially by a new leader, he told the press: 'I have been removed against my will.'

Around the new year, the Gang of Four decided to set up the Council for Social Democracy. This was not explicitly the prelude to a new party, although the momentum was carrying them towards it. It would be joined by ten or a dozen Labour MPs in addition to Owen and Rodgers (Jenkins had left the Commons in 1976 and Williams had lost her seat in the 1979 election); one of them was Tom Bradley, who was also a trade union member of the NEC. The obvious time for the launch was in the immediate aftermath of Labour's special conference, which was due to meet at Wembley on Saturday, 24 January, and which was certain to be depicted in the press as a further stage in the agony of the Labour Party. As it turned out, the conference could not have been worse managed if it had been designed to play into the hands of the Gang of Four.

The conference had the task of choosing between six 'options' for the composition of the electoral college. Basnett proposed the 50–25–25 formula (50 per cent to the PLP) which was known to have Michael's support. Heffer, for the NEC, proposed 'one-third each', favoured by the TGWU. Duffy, for the engineers, proposed 75 per cent for the PLP. This was an extreme proposition, not desired by the MPs themselves; Duffy claimed that he could not cast his union's votes for any plan that gave the PLP less than 51 per cent, but few people took him seriously. The Shop and Distributive Workers' Union (USDAW) proposed 40–30–30 (40 per cent to the unions), which looked like an outsider rather than a winner. By lunch-time, none of the proposals had secured a majority. Something had to be done; the decision had already been put off for three months and could scarcely be put off again. Clive Jenkins scurried about in the lunch-hour and managed to get a critical block of votes transferred from the NEC option to the USDAW scheme. Even so, the Basnett scheme would have won a solid majority if Duffy had not clung to his pedantic purism and kept his voting card in his pocket. The

USDAW plan was declared the winner. Michael, in a short closing speech, said: 'I agreed with the case put by David Basnett. I don't disguise from you and I have not disguised from anybody that I wish conference had reached that conclusion.' He made it clear that he wanted to reopen the matter at the regular conference in October 1981, but even those who agreed with him on the merits of the case felt that it was not worth another battle. It was only in 1993, after two more leadership elections, that Labour finally adopted the 'one-third each' formula.

Next day, the Gang of Four launched their Council with what they called the Limehouse Declaration – perhaps an echo of Lloyd George's challenging Limehouse speech of 1909. Informally dressed, in the 'young and fresh looking' style of a pub-going rather than church-going Sunday morning, they met the press in front of Owen's house in the newly gentrified East End. The message of the Declaration was:

> The calamitous outcome of the Labour Party Wembley Conference demands a new start in British politics . . . Our intention is to rally all those who are committed to the values, principles and policies of social democracy . . .
>
> We recognise that for those people who have given much of their lives to the Labour Party, the choice that lies ahead will be deeply painful. But we believe that the need for a realignment of British politics must now be faced.

Michael refused to accept that anyone was leaving the Labour Party until he or she actually did so. He disclosed in an interview that he had written to Williams, Rodgers and Owen with the plea: 'For heaven's sake stay in the party.'[45] Shirley Williams, at least, was still in a state of indecision and considerable distress. She explained later that unilateral nuclear disarmament, though she was against it, would never have been a reason for her to leave the party. (It was a much more significant motive for Owen and Rodgers.) Nor, probably, would she have left because of the constitutional changes, despite her strong dislike of mandatory reselection and of the mood of intolerance which she saw as engulfing the party. The crunch for her was the conference decision that Britain should leave the European Community. Now, as in 1975, she felt that 'Britain in Europe' was a supreme issue of principle.[46]

Michael had two long discussions with her, one in August 1980 and the other just before the Wembley conference. He said, as she remembers: 'You can't leave – we need you and you have a great future.' In another conversation, Healey told her that she might 'expect high office' if she stayed in the party. There were echoes of this episode in 1985 when Williams, angered by an accusation by Kinnock that the four had been motivated by ambition, made a speech claiming that they had been 'offered positions' to stop them from leaving. Michael wrote to her to deny that such offers had been made. A sharp exchange of letters ended in his telling her: 'I don't for a moment think you left the Labour Party for reasons of ambition. However, I certainly would not give the same clean bill of health on that aspect of the matter to David Owen.'

In fact, while Michael felt that her departure would be a sad loss for the Labour Party, he could not have sincerely said the same of the others. Nevertheless, he tried to keep them within the fold. Ten years later, Rodgers told the story of 'how Labour leader Michael Foot suddenly arrived at his home in an eleventh-hour bid to prevent the breakaway in January 1981'. He recalled: 'It was a cool meeting. Michael . . . didn't bring any proposals and it was a wasted journey.' In this interview, Rodgers also disclosed that his house in Kentish Town had been the scene of 'all the clandestine meetings of the gang'.[47]

On 9 February, Shirley Williams resigned from the NEC. Her letter to Hayward, released to the press, cited the conference decisions on the electoral college, reselection and Europe. 'I have found', she wrote, 'that compromise on the NEC is another name for endless retreat. The party that is now emerging is not the democratic Socialist party that I joined.' In a letter to Michael, she wrote: 'You have tried to dissuade me from this course, and I would like to say that you have spoken to me directly, fairly and in a spirit of friendship.'

The time for peacemaking was past, and on 27 February Michael made a pre-emptive attack on those who were about to launch 'a new party, sailing under false colours, having deserted our flag and chosen to sail under one that was not even unfurled at the last election'. Rodgers retorted: 'Those who are still in the party sail in a different ship under a different captain to a different destination. They are the ones who fly false colours.'

On 2 March, the Gang of Four announced: 'We plan to establish before Easter a new political party. This intention is clearly incompatible with our continuing membership of the Labour Party. We have therefore all now ceased to be members.' The statement was accompanied by another from twelve MPs who resigned the Labour whip and decided to sit in the Commons as Social Democrats. One consequence was a strengthening of the left in the Labour Party. The departure of Rodgers meant that Benn, as runner-up, automatically entered the Shadow Cabinet. By the same process, the seats on the NEC vacated by Shirley Williams and by Tom Bradley were filled by the runners-up.

Michael was relieved to find that only twelve Labour MPs, or rather only ten in addition to Owen and Rodgers, had enlisted under the SDP flag. Gradually, however, it became clear that this was not the end of the story. Some MPs who were ready to join the SDP were advised by its founders to wait; the deliberate calculation was (with a keen eye on the media) that there were advantages in making it appear that Labour MPs were gravitating towards the new party one after another, as they appreciated its attractions and despaired of any hope of putting the Labour Party back on the correct course. As the dispassionate analyst Patricia Sykes observes: 'To maximise publicity, Social Democratic leaders instructed the converts to join at times that were calculated to steal the show from one or both of the major parties.'[48]

The question most discussed in 1981 and 1982 was whether the much heralded split in the Labour Party was really happening. A British political party – and especially the Labour Party – reckons its strength or weakness at three levels: its numbers in Parliament, its rank and file membership, and its following among the voters. At the top level, a very important dog did not bark. The established leaders of the right in the party – Denis Healey, Roy Hattersley, Eric Varley, Roy Mason – were never in the slightest degree tempted to move to the SDP. As individuals, they were deeply rooted in Labour traditions (for instance, Hattersley's mother was a distinguished mayor of Sheffield) and had close links with the party organisation and with the unions. Moreover, in the existing situation they saw good prospects of working with Michael Foot, they had a majority in the Shadow Cabinet, and although the left majority in the NEC was a problem for them, they could reckon that it might not last for ever. Naturally, the stability that they represented influenced a great many MPs to be loyal to the old regiment.

However, there was a steady drift of MPs. Some, no doubt, went through an honest change of mind; some faced deselection or were actually deselected by their constituencies, so that they had nothing to lose. By the time of the 1983 general election there were twenty-seven SDP members – twenty-four who had been elected as Labour MPs and one Tory, plus Shirley Williams and Roy Jenkins who won by-elections.

Michael exerted himself throughout 1981 to keep wavering MPs in the party and to defend them from the threat of deselection. He went to Hayes and Harlington to plead with local activists to reprieve their MP, Neville Sandelson; Sandelson was consequently saved from deselection, but joined the SDP all the same. He sent a letter of endorsement to Eric Ogden, MP for the West Derby division of Liverpool, who was fighting for his political life against a strong Militant element in his constituency.

Ogden was deselected, appealed in vain to the NEC and went over to the SDP. The same fate overtook Ben Ford, MP for Bradford North. Ford, after being displaced by the Militant Pat Wall, wrote to Michael: 'Many thanks for sending me your letter last Thursday – it was most generous. Unfortunately, it left the Militants unmoved – with the results you know.'

Emphatically, there was nothing that could seriously be called a split in the party at the grass-roots. Here and there, a few councillors or a few members of management committees changed their allegiance, but the great bulk of the party remained intact. The only event that made the front pages was the defection of sixteen councillors in Islington, who were in fact a local Irish mafia of such an embarrassing nature that the SDP kept them at arm's length. In March, the Labour Party was able to report that a total of five members had resigned from four constituencies in the north-east which had SDP MPs (including Rodgers). Indeed, the Labour Party reacted to its troubles by a recruiting drive and emerged with 74,000 more members than in 1978.

What could be seen when some of the dust settled was that the SDP appealed to a different section of the community from the Labour Party. A survey for a television network revealed 'a staggering social bias in the SDP's membership', with 57 per cent classed as professional or managerial and a mere 7 per cent as working-class.[49] This helped to explain why only a minority (perhaps a quarter) of SDP recruits came from the Labour Party. Some were Tories, alienated by the harshness of Thatcherism, but most of them had no previous political allegiance. They liked the look of the SDP because it was *not* the Labour Party or the Conservative Party and was free from what they saw as doctrinaire extremism. But it was difficult to see what, in positive terms, was the new party's political philosophy.

In their open letter of August 1980, the three incipient Social Democrats had attacked 'divisive and often cruel Tory policies' and promised 'an acceptable socialist alternative'. Owen announced: 'We are going to have a socialist party, a genuine SDP seen to be on the left, with strong links with the trade unions.'[50] There was initially some prospect of enlisting the support of a few unions, particularly the very right-wing Electrical and Plumbing Union, but this came to nothing and the SDP reverted to condemning the Labour Party for being subservient to the union bosses. As for socialism, when Jenkins was asked about it he replied airily: 'I haven't used that word for years.'[51] Rodgers told a press conference that the SDP would be 'very plainly a left-of-centre party', but this press conference featured an open disagreement between Jenkins and Owen on the one hand and Williams on the other over the acceptability of private education. Michael, in a speech at Ebbw Vale on 11 April, commented: 'If a company selling soap or soft drinks asked people to send cash on the kind of pretences adopted by the SDP, they'd be had up for fraud . . . It reminds me of the famous or infamous prospectus of the South Sea Bubble.'

Yet it was probably the ambiguity of the SDP's posture that opened the door to success at the polls. For, while the SDP won over only a fraction of Labour's rank and file and fewer than a tenth of Labour's MPs, it attracted considerably more Labour voters than anyone had expected. In a television interview on 26 March, Michael felt that it was safe to challenge the defectors to resign their seats and fight by-elections:

> Their party starts with an act of dishonour. They will never be able to wipe away the stain. They were only there as Labour members, because a lot of people up and down the country worked to get them there . . . I don't believe they will win a single seat in the next general election when they do eventually pluck up their courage to put these matters to the electorate.

In 1981, the first test came when the Labour MP for Warrington resigned to become a judge. Warrington was a solidly proletarian industrial town in Lancashire, with low wages and a high unemployment rate. In 1979 the Labour majority had exceeded 10,000 and a candidate who came forward as a Social Democrat had won 144 votes. Shirley Williams, after much havering, declined to fight the by-election for the SDP, and the apparently hopeless task was shouldered by Roy Jenkins. The sensational result on 16 July was that Douglas Hoyle, the Labour candidate, had a majority of only 1,759 over Jenkins.

This was high noon for the SDP. Jenkins and Steel easily agreed on an alliance and opinion polls rated its support as high as 44 per cent, which could have produced a parliamentary majority. In October, a Liberal standing as Alliance candidate (with a capital A) won Croydon North-west, a Tory marginal. In November, Shirley Williams stood at Crosby, a commuter suburb of Liverpool with a Tory majority of 19,000, and triumphed with a 5,000 majority. Owen offered, in an open letter to Michael, to resign at Devonport if Michael would resign at Ebbw Vale, so that they could 'put the case of our respective parties, Labour and Social Democrat, directly to the Devonport electorate'. (The proposal did not allow for a return match at Ebbw Vale.) Michael described Owen's letter as 'infantile and absurd', and told him:

You know perfectly well that I am the elected Labour member for
Ebbw Vale and have every right and duty to continue to serve the
people there to the best of my ability. You have changed your political
colours. You were elected as the Labour candidate for Devonport . . .
Those of you who were elected as Labour members at the last election
should, in honour, have resigned when you decided to leave the
Party . . . I think you sit here on false pretences.

Michael, who had kept up his friendships and contacts in Plymouth, was
certain that Owen would be defeated when the general election came. In
this, he was mistaken.

If the challenge from the SDP had been the only problem for the
Labour Party and its new leader, 1981 would certainly have been a
difficult year. But it was a year plagued by other tribulations.

6

A Labour leader needs, and Michael's predecessors had generally
enjoyed, majority support in the two arenas of decision-making: the
National Executive Committee and the Cabinet or Shadow Cabinet.
Michael's misfortune was that he could not be sure of either. In the NEC,
no analysis can be made with complete precision; some at least of its
members were liable to vote one way or the other according to their
opinions or after hearing the argument. However, a broadly accurate
description would run thus:

'Hard left' (belonging to or heavily influenced by the bloc led by Tony
Benn): five from the trade union section, five from the constituency
section, two from the women's section, one from affiliated organisations
(mainly the Co-operatives), one from the Young Socialists, plus the
treasurer, Norman Atkinson. Total, fifteen.

'Soft left' (supporting Michael on most occasions): two trade unionists,
two from the constituencies (Neil Kinnock and Joan Lestor), three from
the women's section (Judith Hart, Renée Short and Betty Boothroyd,
who had replaced Shirley Williams). Total, including Michael himself,
eight.

Right-wing: five from the trade union section plus the deputy leader.
Total, six.

Thus Michael was obliged to rely on support from the right, which
was contrary to his desire and his lifelong allegiance, and even so was
often voted down. In the Shadow Cabinet, he had three natural allies –

Shore, Silkin and Orme – but had to deal with such strong right-wingers as Roy Hattersley, Roy Mason and Gerald Kaufman. He was aware that they would have much preferred to have Healey as leader and were critical of him for being too conciliatory towards the extreme left. In their eyes, the Foot leadership was an unfortunate interregnum; they looked forward to a restoration with authority in firm hands, be they those of Healey or perhaps Hattersley. But in the short term, since Healey was committed to co-operation with Michael, there was not much they could do.

The most intractable problem was the NEC, which was after all an *executive* body, not a deliberative body like the party conference, and did not perform this function. As Michael wrote later:

> The Party's National Executive Committee ceased to be national or an executive or a committee. It was transformed into a mock-Parliament of the Labour movement in which every shade of difference was examined and broadcast, every division recorded and enflamed, every disciplinary dispute magnified, in which members were endlessly concerned in their own re-election . . . Open government was interpreted to mean perpetual disagreements openly arrived at . . . Sometimes I paused to wonder what Lenin or Trotsky (whose name might crop up in other connections) or Rosa Luxemburg would say about revolutionaries who could make such a caricature of the executive process. [52]

The power of what can fairly be called the Bennite bloc in the NEC was enhanced by its control of two key positions: Benn was (and had been since 1974) chairman of the Home Policy Committee and Heffer was chairman of the Organisation Committee. These bodies were, strictly speaking, sub-committees and their function was to make recommendations to the NEC, but in practice it was difficult to reverse a recommendation without a second time-wasting argument, and a majority on the sub-committee was likely to imply a majority on the NEC itself. The bloc did indeed vote as a bloc and pursued the line decided on in advance at a caucus meeting. Benn denied that there actually was a caucus, and it is arguable whether its preliminary meetings deserved that word, since it was a standard political procedure for people of the same way of thinking – for instance, the Bevanites on the NEC in the 1950s – to hold discussions of this kind. Admitting this, Michael observed: 'Under Tony Benn's guidance and drive, the system became more regular and efficient and demonstrably effective than ever before. More than ever, the caucus meetings and the decisions taken there about the way the later votes should be cast undermined the chance of real open debate in the Executive.'[53]

On one occasion, speaking to Benn in his office, he urged him to call off the caucus meetings or at least to 'stop the rigid prearranged votes'. The outcome was disastrous: 'He shook his head as if to deny that any such effective caucus existed, and when I persisted with the charge, he persisted with the denial. So I called him a liar, and he got up and left.'[54] Benn's account is rather more dramatic:

> He asked: 'You try to fix votes in advance, don't you?'
> I said: 'No, I try to reach a sort of general agreement about things.'
> 'You're a bloody liar,' he said.
> So I just walked out . . . I am not being called a liar by anybody. I was pretty steamed up.[55]

It was, perhaps, a question of definition. Benn argues: 'The husbands' and wives' dinners were a caucus . . . Michael probably has more medals as a caucus member than anybody else in the party . . . He's a very experienced politician and he knows perfectly well how politics works.'[56]

He had to look towards the next election for the posts of leader and deputy leader, which would be held on the day (a Sunday) before the annual conference began. The question for the left was whether to accept the Foot–Healey partnership without challenge. Benn noted in December 1980: 'Michael Foot will certainly be re-elected unopposed. My intention at the moment is to stand against Denis Healey for the deputy leadership in order to pinpoint the real issues for the Party, but I don't expect to succeed.'[57]

On the day after the Wembley special conference, he was host to a conclave of his supporters, including Derer, Schonfield, Mullin, Frances Morrell and three MPs. Although there were a few doubters, the decision was that Benn should stand. The meeting also decided that Benn should join the Tribune Group; the strange thing was that he had never joined it before.

After this, almost two months passed without any announcement, but rumours and speculation mounted. Eventually, Michael phoned Benn and asked to see him. When they met on 24 March, he said: 'I asked you to come and see me about the deputy leadership, to find out if you are going to stand, because I think it would lacerate the party if you did.' Benn replied: 'A number of people have pressed me to stand. I haven't finally made up my mind' (which, as his diary shows, was untrue). Michael told him: 'I am quite happy for you to say that I have asked you not to stand and you have responded to my appeal.' Benn (in the Wilsonian phrase) left his options open, but said that if he did stand, 'I promise I'll let you know in advance.'[58]

A couple of days later, Joan Lestor drove Tony Benn in her car to Slough, in her constituency, where he was speaking. He told her that he would be standing for the deputy leadership; she urged him to wait and talk to other left MPs, but he said that he saw no need for this and had taken his decision.[59] On 29 March there was another Sunday gathering of his inner circle. He summarised its conclusions: 'There was absolutely no doubt that I should stand as a candidate: it was unanimous. It was agreed that I should issue a statement . . . and it was agreed that the issue should not be raised at the Tribune Group on the grounds that it had nothing to do with them.'[60]

The Tribune Group was meeting the next evening, and its members were becoming suspicious. Orme took Benn aside to say: 'What's this I hear about you standing for the deputy leadership? It would be a disaster.' Allaun, though a member of the caucus on the NEC, told Benn that he could not give his support. Heffer, too, was critical. It was obvious that the secret could not be kept much longer and that Michael would be alerted by someone, probably Orme. On 1 April, Benn told Michael, as they came out of a Shadow Cabinet meeting, that he had decided to stand. Michael asked him to postpone the announcement for a week, but Benn said that 'a lot of people know about it'. This was certainly true; there was a three-line whip and the House of Commons was crowded. MPs belonging to the Tribune Group drew up a letter, addressed to Mik as its chairman, requesting a discussion on Benn's plans. They collected twenty-six signatures, decided to make the letter public and deputed one of their number, Robin Cook, to take it to the Press Association office in the building. It was now four in the morning, but the PA office was open all night. Cook hurried along the corridors, only to find that Benn had forestalled him and the announcement had gone out on the PA tapes half an hour before. Too late for the newspapers, it reached the public on radio and television.

Michael was soon reported as saying: 'I hope Tony Benn will reconsider his statement.' Members of the Tribune Group were furious and one of them was quoted as saying: 'He only joined a few weeks ago and he's already succeeded in splitting us.' Alex Kitson, who was that year's chairman of the Labour Party and also assistant general secretary of the TGWU, issued a call to Benn to 'think again and stand down' and it was endorsed by the union's executive. Heffer wrote in *Tribune* that the announcement by Benn 'without . . . having a proper joint discussion with colleagues who have worked in agreement with him for a period of time has caused worry and confusion'. Cuttingly, he added that one could favour certain policies 'and yet not agree that the standard-bearer suggested or claiming the position is the best one for the job'.[61] On the other hand, Benn was nominated by sixteen MPs, including Mikardo, who wrote that Michael was 'quite wrong' to suggest that there should be no contest for the deputy leadership. He pointed out that 'Denis Healey's policies are anathema to much of the party and have been rejected by conference.'[62]

This, of course, was the crux of the argument. Benn was insistent that he was campaigning on real and important issues and that his victory would unify, not divide, the party. It was undeniable that, on such crucial issues as Europe and nuclear disarmament, Healey was in disagreement not only with Benn but with Michael. It was harmful as well as illogical, Benn argued, to have a deputy leader holding these views. To this, Tribunites such as Kinnock replied that Healey was deputy leader, not leader, and showed no signs of embarrassing, still less fighting, Michael over the disagreements. However high-principled the contest might be (and the media, at least, would ensure that it was strongly personalised) it was bound to stress and exacerbate the tensions within the party.

The underlying issue was that of co-operation and tolerance. Since the days when the weapons of censure and expulsion had been wielded against Cripps and Bevan, intolerance had always been identified with the right. Now, there were disturbing signs of an intolerance of the left. As well as right-wingers, some Tribunite MPs such as Laurence Pavitt and Reg Freeson were threatened with deselection, and there were alarming rumours of a 'hit list'. One of Benn's advisers, Valerie Wise, said – referring not to Owen and Rodgers but to Healey and Hattersley:

> I think the sooner they go the better because the trouble with those people is that they are very much identified with the last Labour government and with previous Labour governments who betrayed the working people of this country . . . I have a gut feeling that we're not going to get rid of all the people who should leave.[63]

Benn, at the outset, believed that he had little or no chance of winning (he put this on record in his diary on 2 April) and advanced this calculation to show that the contest would not be so damaging as Michael and others feared. But, as his campaign swung into action in the constituencies and the unions, efficiently organised by the LCC and the CLPD, he became more optimistic and others more anxious. An incident on 20 May drove Michael to exasperation. Yet again, a number of

Labour MPs voted against the Defence White Paper when the Shadow Cabinet line was to abstain. Michael expressed his disapproval to the junior Labour spokesmen who had been among the abstainers but did not demand their resignations, as earlier leaders would have. However, he could not overlook the fact that Benn had gone into the lobby contrary to the decision of the Shadow Cabinet, of which he was a member. Benn recorded for his diary: 'There was a note in my pocket from Michael Foot, but I voted before I read it';[64] Michael must have realised that his appeal had been ignored. Healey commented that Benn 'loses no opportunity to kick Michael Foot in the stomach'.[65] When Michael raised the matter in the Shadow Cabinet on 3 June, Benn justified himself with a calm but defiant statement. Michael replied with a statement of his own, written and given to the press the same evening:

> In view of what he has said and done over recent weeks, and in the light of his latest statement to the Shadow Cabinet tonight, I have told Tony Benn that, in my judgement, his only honest course now is to stand against me in the coming election for the leadership of the Party. It is clear that what he is challenging is the good faith of the Shadow Cabinet in carrying out its duties under the Labour Party constitution. That is, above all and directly, an attack on my good faith . . .
>
> Let me clarify the point about the so-called collective responsibility of the Shadow Cabinet. I have never held the view that this collective responsibility needs to be, or can be, as absolute and assured as it should be in the Cabinet itself. The principle can be applied with some liberality and commonsense give-and-take . . . However, there are some matters – indeed the main matters with which the Shadow Cabinet is charged to deal – which must be conducted with a sense of common trust between those who are members of it . . . As I understand it, Tony Benn insists that he must have the right to adopt the same kind of tactics whenever he chooses . . . There can't be one rule for Tony and another for everybody else . . . That in my opinion is a recipe for perpetual discord between the Parliamentary Party and the Party Conference itself and therefore of perpetual comfort to our Tory and Social Democrat opponents.

Benn was unimpressed:

> He [Michael] went over the top on this. It was quite permissible for someone to stand in an election . . . That was quite hysterical, I thought, and it turned the whole thing into a sort of personality thing which is not what it was about . . . This theory that elections are

divisive is a very, very dangerous and undemocratic theory . . . If I'd
adopted a more cautious policy, adopted by Neil Kinnock, I might
have ended up at the top of the heap, but that wasn't what I wanted to
do.[66]

It was becoming evident that the fight for the deputy leadership was, at
one remove, a fight for the leadership. If Benn defeated Healey, he would
be excellently placed to win the leadership when Michael retired – in two
years' time Michael would be seventy – or even earlier if further
dissensions forced Michael into resignation. With this perspective, it
would have been foolish for him to respond to Michael's challenge and
stand for the leadership in the current year, and of course he did not.

A salient point made in Michael's statement was that the party ought to
be concentrating on such issues as mass unemployment and economic
depression. 'The responsibility for distracting us from these issues must
rest with Tony Benn.' Labour was mounting a campaign against
unemployment, launched in January with a successful rally in Liverpool
and the start of a March for Jobs, in which Michael joined for a short
distance despite his broken ankle. At two other rallies, in Cardiff and
Birmingham, Healey was the speaker and was shouted down by
supporters of Benn. Michael was furious:

The message was washed down the gutter by a piece of planned
hooliganism, a disgrace to the traditions of free speech for which the
Labour movement has always stood. Tony Benn's condemnation has
so far been much too feeble and temporising . . . He must bear the
primary responsibility for the deep wounds inflicted on our movement
throughout these painful months.[67]

In a long article in the *Guardian*, he dealt with the two arguments most
often advanced in the Benn campaign: the necessity of contested elections
and the supremacy of conference decisions.

Tony . . . seems to think that there is something monstrously
undemocratic in having a contest with only one candidate . . . If that's
how he feels, why did he not stand against me? The truth is, and he
knows it, that I never questioned his right to stand. I questioned its
wisdom . . . Tony never seems to have stopped to think that if you
have too many elections in too many circumstances you can undermine
the validity of the most essential elections. The voting currency, like
other currencies, can be debased . . . That is why I call the idea of
perpetual, non-stop elections the politics of the kindergarten . . .

There have been periods in the Party's history – long, agonising periods – when the conference and the Parliamentary Party or considerable sections of it have been at loggerheads . . . Time and again, as the Party has seen the peril involved in that widening abyss, they have drawn back, taken timely steps to avoid the calamity, and that is what we must do again now . . . Of course Party conference decisions must be respected but they cannot be regarded as absolute: that is, binding in every particular and upon every Labour M.P. in all circumstances . . . Defined in such terms the doctrine does not exist and any who sought to apply it with inflexible rigour in those terms would break the Party to smithereens . . . M.P.s have other loyalties too, and no less important ones – to their fellow members of Parliament, to their conscience, to their own political judgement, to their country. How simple political life would be if these various loyalties never clashed . . . Let us work together to ensure that the Party conference and the Parliamentary Party embark on a new period of partnership and understanding.[68]

For some, the choice in the contest was straightforward enough. One MP, Dennis Canavan, expressed it thus: 'Surely there is a better chance of the policies being implemented if we have a deputy leader like Tony Benn who believes in them instead of Denis Healey who opposes them.'[69] But others felt that Benn had acted unforgivably in forcing the contest, which had given the party such a long, hot and unpleasant summer, and were ready to charge him with personal ambition. 'A leadership cult is unhealthy, undemocratic and profoundly un-Socialist,' Robin Cook wrote.[70] Neil Kinnock took the same attitude: 'Socialists above all people should recognise the terrible dangers of turning justifiable admiration for an individual into a catechism of belief.'[71]

As the date of the conference drew nearer, people tried to work out the prospects and place their bets. The new system meant that the result would be expressed in unfamiliar percentage terms; an MP would have 0.1 per cent of the total, a constituency party 0.04 per cent, a moderate-sized trade union perhaps 3 per cent. There were three candidates. Shore had declined to stand, but Silkin cheerfully entered the lists and could count on the votes of the TGWU, which sponsored him as an MP and had 8 per cent of the total. However, as it was obvious (except to Silkin himself, of course) that he would be eliminated in the first ballot, it was the second ballot that mattered.

Benn, without any doubt, had an overwhelming majority of the constituencies. Healey had an emphatic, if not so overwhelming, majority of the MPs. Still, the votes of left-wing MPs were important to Benn, and cries of outrage arose when Kinnock announced in a *Tribune* article that he intended to vote for Silkin in the first ballot and abstain in the second. In the event, twelve MPs abstained, including Joan Lestor and Stan Orme as well as Kinnock. Judith Hart, Cook and Booth voted for Benn, perhaps because of constituency pressure.

The trade union votes, clearly, would be decisive. Whether they would represent the wishes of their members was another matter. Some unions never consulted their members on anything except wage claims and strike action (if that). The best solution to the problem was a postal ballot of the membership, but executive committees, with rare exceptions, decided that it would be difficult to organise and prohibitively expensive. Two unions which did hold a ballot, NUPE and the Fire Brigades Union, found a majority for Healey and accordingly voted for him; since these were strongly left-wing unions and the leaders would have preferred to vote for Benn, this was a damaging setback for his cause. The TGWU instructed its regional organisers to ascertain the wishes of the members by any methods that seemed feasible, such as votes at branch meetings or reports from branch officers. This rather dubious 'consultation process' produced a majority for Healey, but the Executive decided at the last moment to vote for Benn. Dick Clements in *Tribune* reported: 'Votes were swung around during the election with amazing rapidity and little apparent care for the reputation of the Labour movement.'

On the first ballot, Healey led and Silkin was duly eliminated. On the second ballot, Healey won by the hair's-breadth majority of 50.426 per cent against 49.574 per cent. His supporters pointed out that he would have had a handsome majority if the TGWU had voted in accordance with its 'consultation'. Bennites retorted that Healey owed his victory to the treachery of Kinnock and to MPs who stayed in the party just long enough to cast their votes and then joined the SDP. These arguments still rage in the pubs and clubs. The bitterness of the contest was not ended by the vote, but perpetuated. Benn felt that he had won a moral victory, and announced a few months later: 'Speaking as deputy leader of the party, because of course Denis Healey's entire majority has now defected to the SDP, I want to say to Labour Party people not to be discouraged but to go on campaigning.'[72] Even his friends felt that this claim was excessive. After a year of reflection, he paid an unexpected tribute to his wife (in a diary entry not published until 1992): 'Caroline felt that it was unwise of me to stand for the deputy leadership. When I look back, her advice has always been right. I think in future I will actually take her advice.'[73]

Other votes at the 1981 conference produced further bad news for Tony Benn. Thanks to a swing in the union block votes, there were five changes in the composition of the NEC and Eric Varley defeated Norman Atkinson for the treasurership; the 'hard left' majority in the NEC was no more. However, this was a mixed blessing for Michael. The victories had gone to the right, not to his friends or supporters, and he was in danger of being what the Bennites alleged – a prisoner of the right. His speech to the conference was a plea for reconciliation. Evoking Labour's alternative to Thatcherism, he said:

> We have an alternative strategy, we have an alternative policy. It was presented by Denis Healey, it was replied to by Tony Benn. I fully acknowledge to Tony from this platform the strong part he has played in the preparation of that alternative strategy and the contribution he has made to the party. I want to see a new Labour Cabinet in which Denis Healey and Tony Benn and a few others . . . play leading and honourable parts.

Taking up a reference made by Benn to the 'dog licence' threats of the past, he continued:

> I give Tony and everybody else this absolute undertaking here and now that no such dog licences for MPs will be issued by me . . . I protested against that statement then, I have protested against the idea behind it ever since, and I will go on protesting against it to my dying day . . . It's not only a question of intimidation suggested by Prime Ministers or leaders of the party. Intimidation can come from other places too. What we want to see is a proper tolerance established and sustained throughout the party as a whole.

7

While striving to hold the Labour Party together and doing his best to harry the Tory government on the issue of unemployment, Michael was also deeply concerned over the worsening international outlook. Ronald Reagan was the first US President to set his face against any kind of negotiation with the Soviet Union and any kind of disarmament even as an ultimate goal. The Russians were alarmed by this return to the most frigid era of the cold war, and Brezhnev adopted a pacific tone in his speech to the Communist Party congress in February 1981, proposing a moratorium on the development of nuclear missiles. The NEC of the

Labour Party welcomed 'this conciliatory statement'. In May, a long letter from Brezhnev, on behalf of his Central Committee, reached the leader of the Labour Party. The Soviet leaders were alive to the importance of a relationship with social democrats (as they called all Western socialists). Brezhnev wrote:

> We saw with satisfaction the resolution of your party's NEC on the foreign policy initiatives put forward at the 26th congress of the CPSU . . . Socialist and social democratic parties have influence among the masses, in trade unions and other democratic organisations of working people, they are broadly represented in the parliaments of West European countries and participate in governments. Therefore, the way the international situation will develop depends to a great extent on the activity of social democrats . . . We are ready to co-operate with you in a form acceptable to both sides.

Michael replied:

> On behalf of the British Labour Party I would like to thank you for your message and initiative concerning the important and serious questions facing the people of the world . . . As democratic Socialists, we recognise a special responsibility to ensure the peace and future of the world. Those who live in different social systems can either live together in dialogue and co-operation whilst recognising political and ideological differences or we can die together in a nuclear holocaust. We believe there is an urgent need for real discussion and real negotiations between the peoples and governments of Europe, east and west.

Contacts between the Labour Party and the Russians over the summer resulted in an invitation to talks in Moscow. As the Labour Party was in opposition, these talks would be officially on a party-to-party basis. On the British side, there was a delegation led by Michael and Denis Healey and including nine other Labour MPs. They were to face six high-ups of the Communist Party of the Soviet Union, the most senior being Boris Ponomarev, who had been secretary of his party's International Department ever since the 1940s, when Healey had held the same position in the Labour Party.

The British party flew to Moscow on 15 September and stayed for two days. There was no time for sight-seeing or social occasions; they would be returning just a week before the start of the party conference and the voting for the deputy leadership, which can scarcely have been far from their thoughts – particularly Healey's. The first day was occupied by the party-to-party session, which lasted for six hours and was conducted in the tedious formal style of Soviet tradition. Healey wrote with some irritation: 'We wasted two hours listening to a counter-productive propaganda tirade against the United States from the International Secretary, my old antagonist Ponomarev.'[74] Michael and his companions concentrated on finding out the exact terms of the proposed nuclear moratorium. But they did not avoid awkward topics, and the *Daily Express* correspondent reported: 'Mr Foot delivered a sharp rebuke over the Soviet invasion of Afghanistan. He said it was the reason for the Russians' present isolation.'[75]

The next day, the visitors went to the Kremlin for an eighty-minute meeting with Brezhnev. The Soviet ruler made a significant declaration: he was ready to reduce the number of SS-20 missiles if the Americans would suspend the deployment of Cruise and Pershing. Michael told a press conference: 'I believe that this is a big and definite advance and that it can be the basis for discussion with the USA once the negotiations begin. I believe that this Russian statement clarifies a position which has been obscure for a long time.' Western correspondents were impressed:

> It was clear from the Moscow newspapers that Foot had been taken very seriously . . . Foot and his colleagues were delighted that Brezhnev had chosen the British Labour Party to be the conduit for what they see as an important statement about Russia's newly discovered enthusiasm for arms talks. When the nitpicking is over, the visit may yet come to be seen as a diplomatic coup of sorts.[76]

Whatever the potential value of the Brezhnev offer, Michael was in a position to claim that he had taken an initiative while the Thatcher government was inertly imitating the negativism of the Americans. To counter this claim, the Minister of State at the Foreign Office, Douglas Hurd, went on the radio to allege that the Soviet Union had made a precisely similar offer in 1979. According to Hurd, the Russians had a superiority in medium-range missiles (in fact, the balance could be interpreted in various ways according to the method of calculation), and 'they are very anxious to keep that superiority without having to talk to us, so they use people like Michael Foot . . . to have the wool pulled over their eyes'.[77] Hurd's statement paved the way for a series of articles in the Tory press, more or less based on Foreign Office briefings, which depicted Michael as an innocent abroad who had been beguiled into assisting a Russian propaganda exercise. Allusions to 'Gulliver's travels' crept into this orchestrated offensive, perhaps because someone in the business imagined (or sought to suggest) a connection between 'Gulliver' and 'gullible'. It was certainly rash to join battle with Michael on anything arising from the writings of Swift, and he made a devastating rejoinder in his speech to the party conference:

> When I returned, one of those Tory newspapers referred to me, and they referred to *Gulliver's Travels*. They made a bit of a mistake there, because I know more about *Gulliver's Travels* than the Foreign Office . . . If you read *Gulliver's Travels* properly, you'll see it has some most extraordinary things. He came back from his travels in a flaming state of anger, such as I am in now, about what he had seen of the infamies being done in the world. In one sense he saw those infamies expressed in imperialism, one nation trying to subdue another nation, but even beyond that he saw it in terms of war and the infamies of war itself . . .
>
> We should see that we are not deterred by anything from the greatest crusade that our Labour movement has ever set its hand to. The world is crying out for peace as it has never cried before. I tell you – I hope I'm not boasting – I am a peacemonger, an inveterate incurable peacemonger. I ask the support of this whole movement to translate that into action.

Sadly, his troubles were far from over. Armistice Sunday fell on 8 November, and it was his duty to lay a wreath at the Cenotaph along with the Queen, the Prime Minister and other dignitaries. Michael wore a coat he had recently bought, dark green in colour and shorter than the traditional overcoat. As well as being new, it was quite a stylish garment, and the Queen Mother remarked after the ceremony: 'What a nice coat, Mr Foot' – a comment which could have served Michael well in the subsequent uproar, but which he revealed only to a few friends.[78] The coat was certainly not, as it has passed into legend, a donkey-jacket, but no doubt he would have been wiser to dress in a completely conventional manner, even if it meant hiring from Moss Bros. A malicious Labour MP, Walter Johnson, went on the radio in the afternoon to complain that Michael looked like 'an out-of-work navvy' and demand that he should be reprimanded by the party. Soon, a storm of synthetic indignation arose from such papers as the *Sun* and the *Daily Mail*.

Two days later, there was trouble with Tony Benn again. North Sea oil was the subject of a debate in the House on 10 November. The government was planning to privatise some of the assets of the publicly owned British National Oil Corporation, and in the current state of the oil boom this promised an easy profit for share-buyers. Labour policy was to renationalise these assets without compensation. However, the

Shadow Cabinet wanted to avoid being accused of aiming at confiscation, so a modified formula was evolved: 'renationalisation on terms that will ensure that no private speculative gains are made at the nation's expense'. Merlyn Rees had the job of speaking for the Opposition, but a few days earlier Tony Benn told Michael that he would like to speak too, because of his experience as Secretary for Energy, and Michael agreed. In his speech at the end of the debate, Benn advanced a version of Labour policy which was at variance with what Rees had said. As he observed: 'When I sat down Michael Foot was absolutely fuming and Peter Shore was boiling like a kettle.'[79] In an article in the *Guardian*, Benn made out a fairly strong case that he was in line with party policy. The argument – of course, there was a ferocious argument – revolved round the precise wording of conference resolutions, and whether the decisions of the special conference of June 1980 (in *Peace, Jobs, Freedom*) or those of the annual conference had greater authority. But the issue, as stated by Benn, was 'whether or not . . . the Shadow Cabinet has the right, if it chooses to do so, to change conference policy'.[80] Once again, it was a question of the relative rights or powers of the conference and the parliamentary leadership.

On the day after the debate, Michael made a prepared statement to the Shadow Cabinet:

> The dissensions and distractions in the party have injured our electoral prospects . . . After Brighton, I hoped we could make a real new start . . . I said I hoped to see Tony Benn elected to the Shadow Cabinet. And I invited Tony Benn to speak at the end of last night's energy debate, knowing his considerable knowledge of the subject and hoping also that he would pave the way to the kind of reconciliation within the Shadow Cabinet which I have striven for. I must say I have had no response whatsoever to all these overtures . . . Finally, there was the performance last night. Tony Benn's intervention has brilliantly succeeded in turning all the attack on the government into a fresh internal quarrel . . . What happened last night is a clear illustration of how necessary some form of collective Shadow Cabinet responsibility is.

He ended with the question: 'Is Tony Benn going to help us to win the next election or not? If he is going to conduct himself in relation to his colleagues as he did last night, then his presence would make the Shadow Cabinet over the next critical twelve months utterly unworkable.'

At a PLP meeting, he called on Benn to say clearly whether he would accept collective responsibility. Evidently feeling that a pistol was being pointed at his head, Benn proposed that new rules for the functioning of the Shadow Cabinet should be worked out. In a confused sequence of events, the two men failed to get together for a talk; Benn had an engagement in Bristol and Michael was not willing to wait until after the weekend. In a public statement, Michael made it clear that his patience was exhausted:

> He still will not give the clear answer I ask for. So we must all assume that his answer is No . . . He made it evident [in a phone conversation] that what he wanted to discuss were some fresh conditions to be attached to Shadow Cabinet responsibility, and I had to tell him this would not be possible . . . His answer is still No, and of course that makes it impossible for me to vote for him as a member of a Shadow Cabinet.

The Shadow Cabinet for the new parliamentary year was elected a week later. As a consequence of Michael's opposition, Benn did not win a place. Michael's feelings at this time emerged in conversation with friends:

> Michael feels he was double-crossed by Benn in the oil compensation debate. He's convinced he can't trust Benn an inch. 'Say what you like about Denis, he carries out his promises.' He thinks Benn is losing support . . . Michael then says he's got a lot of letters from Left people in the party, CNDers in particular, urging him to get tough with Benn . . . He has to assert his leadership and keep the party together and then we'll see that it won't be a right-wing party.[81]

The next blow was the Crosby by-election result. The benefit from the government's unpopularity had gone entirely to the Alliance and not a whit to Labour. A frank editorial in *Tribune* declared: 'Labour is two years from disaster' and asked: 'Will the growing challenge from the SDP push Labour back into a 1931-type position?'[82]

In this situation, another by-election could be catastrophic for the Labour Party, especially if it occurred in a Labour-held seat. Bob Mellish, a former Cabinet minister and Chief Whip, was contemplating retirement as MP for Bermondsey. He had accepted a position as vice-chairman of the London Docklands Development Corporation, which had recently been set up to turn the area of the old London docks into a free-enterprise paradise exempt from planning controls. The Labour left in this working-class part of London was heavily critical of the LDDC's policy and of a Labour politician's association with it. Mellish was entitled to a salary of £16,000 a year. As soon as he started to draw it, he would be holding an 'office of profit under the Crown' and would be ineligible to sit in the Commons. He agreed to forgo the salary for the time being and, in September 1981, responded to a plea from Michael and promised not to bring about a by-election. However, there was a potential threat which Mellish could implement at any time.

To make matters worse, the Labour Party in Southwark (the borough of which Bermondsey formed a part) was controlled by a right-wing clique, dominated by the council leader, John O'Grady, labouring under accusations, at best, of indifference to the interests of ordinary people and at worst of corruption. In the Bermondsey constituency, a rank-and-file revolt had given left-wingers a majority in the management committee. They moved to select a new prospective candidate in readiness for Mellish's retirement. Arthur Latham, a Tribunite who had lost his Paddington seat in 1979, was regarded as suitable by Michael. But, in a selection conference on 8 November, he was narrowly defeated by Peter Tatchell.

Although Tatchell was very popular with his comrades and lived in Bermondsey, several factors made him vulnerable to attack. He was Australian and had come to Britain to avoid being conscripted for the Australian contingent in the Vietnam war, thus incurring charges of 'draft-dodger'. He had been a party member for only three years (in fact, because he had been living in a constituency where the old guard avoided issuing membership cards to new applicants). It was generally known that he was a homosexual. The dockers who were well represented in the population were pictured, rather hazily, as intensely old-fashioned and prejudiced, though they were probably more tolerant than outsiders imagined. Furthermore, his political views placed him far to the left – but Jim Mortimer, the future Labour Party secretary, who had lived in Bermondsey for years and knew the political scene well, thought that Mellish had misled Michael by describing Tatchell as more extreme than he really was.[83] However, Ian Aitken reported a number of Labour MPs as believing that 'his extraordinary combination of far left opinions and militant association with gay liberation, together with the fact that he has been a member of the party for only a few years, should disqualify him'.[84]

Under the rules, any selected candidate had to be endorsed by the NEC. It was impossible to disqualify Tatchell because he had refused to fight in the Vietnam war, which Michael and most of the party had opposed, or because he was gay. Besides, the doctrine established since the early 1970s was that selections should be overruled only if there had been procedural irregularities, of which there was no sign. Thanks to this convention, eight candidates who belonged to Militant – generally regarded as a disloyal conspiracy – were endorsed;[85] and Tatchell did not belong to Militant. Nevertheless, hopes were entertained of vetoing him on account of his 'far left opinions'.

The pretext chosen was an article which he had written in May 1981 in a small journal called *London Labour Briefing*:

> Labour has long lost the radical and defiant spirit of its early pioneers. We now seem stuck in the rut of an obsessive legalism and parliamentarianism . . . Reliance on the present token and ineffectual parliamentary opposition will advance us nowhere . . . We must look to new, more militant forms of extra-parliamentary opposition which involve mass popular participation and challenge the government's right to rule.

Michael could not be expected to read with pleasure that his opposition was 'token and ineffectual', but he had many times approved of, and indeed taken part in, extra-parliamentary actions. What he did not approve of, given his dedication to parliamentary democracy, was the suggestion that the House of Commons was inherently useless and that the political battle must be waged in another arena. Tatchell's article had proposed a 'siege of Parliament' and a mass occupation of the Westminster district. Thus everything turned on a fairly semantic distinction between 'extra-parliamentary' and 'anti-parliamentary'. Later, Michael wrote to Tatchell: 'You wrote an article appearing to favour not merely extra-parliamentary activity, which has been a traditional part of Labour campaigning, but anti-parliamentary action which is something quite different.'[86] Tatchell always denied that it was fair to put this interpretation on his words.

The real anxiety was that a by-election with Tatchell as Labour candidate could see a transfer of Labour votes to the Alliance on a scale worse than Warrington – especially as fourteen Southwark councillors had just joined the SDP. On 3 December, the SDP MP James Wellbeloved – referred to by Michael as 'the inappropriately named Wellbeloved' – rose at question time in the House to ask the Prime Minister whether she agreed that Tatchell's article 'should be condemned by all those who hold precious parliamentary democracy and should not be condoned by craven silence'. For procedural reasons, the question was addressed to Thatcher, who made the expected reply, but it was clearly a challenge to Michael. He rose to say: 'Since the matter has been raised,

can I say that . . . the individual concerned is not an endorsed member of
the Labour Party and so far as I am concerned, never will be.'

Labour MPs were appalled. In the first place, 'endorsed member' was a
slip of the tongue and Michael had to issue a statement that he had meant
'endorsed candidate'. Far more important, endorsement was not a
prerogative of the leader and had to be decided by a vote in the NEC, which
might go either way. Clearly, Michael had fallen into a trap. Eric Heffer
confessed in *Tribune* that he was 'almost in tears'. Benn commented that
Michael had 'made a ghastly error', and Frank Allaun told him outright:
'You have made the most serious mistake of your life.'[87] It was another
example of the impulsiveness to which Michael was occasionally prone.

Tatchell then sought an interview with Michael and met him in his office
on 7 December. He tried to explain his views on extra-parliamentary
action, but he saw that Michael's mind was made up. His impression was:
'Foot seemed ill at ease and anxious during my brief meeting . . . [He]
acted like a paternalistic grandfather admonishing an errant child.'[88]
Michael voiced his fears that the by-election, whenever it came about,
would result in a Labour defeat, and urged Tatchell to stand down for the
good of the party. Tatchell, feeling that he had the confidence of the
constituency party, could not accept this. Their parting, as Tatchell wrote,
was 'coldly polite'.

The danger now was that the NEC would endorse Tatchell and thus
inflict a humiliating rebuff on the leader, and doubtless this would have
happened if the left had not been reduced in strength at the last party
conference. Even so, when the vote was taken on 16 December it was a
narrow squeak; endorsement was refused by fifteen votes to fourteen. The
position was still unsatisfactory, since the onset of a by-election might find
Labour without a candidate and the constituency party was not likely to
adopt anyone but Tatchell. The best that could be hoped for was that
Mellish would keep his promise and stay in the House until the next general
election. But an opposition party is supposed to look forward eagerly to
by-elections, and Labour's obvious anxiety to avoid one was an unhappy
posture.

The irony was that, with unemployment topping the three million mark
and no end to the recession in sight, the government was still deeply
unpopular. However, only the Alliance was making headway and the
general forecast for the next election was a hung Parliament. Michael was
obliged to say: 'I have to admit it, their strength is a surprise. But we let
them succeed.' His summing up for 1981 was: 'This has been a deeply
frustrating and wasted year, and it's largely our own fault.'[89]

— *Chapter 14* —

WATERLOO

I

After the *annus horribilis* of 1981, 1982 began with hopes of an improvement. Over the weekend of 5–6 January, the chieftains of the political and trade union wings of the Labour movement gathered for a planning session at the comfortable – by some accounts, even luxurious – conference centre near Bishop's Stortford maintained by Clive Jenkins' union. Officially, the business was to examine the parlous financial condition of the party and secure pledges of help from the unions in the next general election campaign, and solid progress was made in this field, but the crucial achievement was an agreement which enabled David Basnett – increasingly emerging as the Jack Jones of the 1980s – to tell the press: 'Peace has broken out in the Labour Party.' Tony Benn, who had been urged by his more fanatical supporters to stand for the deputy leadership again, realised that such a venture would be disastrous for all concerned, and it was agreed that Labour would go forward with all-round backing for the team of Michael Foot and Denis Healey. The left was compensated by a promise that the election manifesto would be based on conference decisions. Everyone began to talk hopefully of unity, comradeship and a beneficent 'spirit of Bishop's Stortford'.

There were signs, too, that the SDP bandwagon was grinding to a halt. The next by-election, on 25 March, was in the Hillhead division of Glasgow, a marginal, mainly middle-class constituency. Roy Jenkins fought the seat and won it with a majority of just over 2,000, but this was not a triumph on the Crosby scale. In seven other by-elections in the course of 1982, the Alliance failed to capture any Tory or Labour seats, only once topped 10,000 votes, and lost two deposits.

A week after Hillhead, when electoral calculations formed the staple of discussion at Westminster, startling news came from a group of small islands 8,000 miles away in the South Atlantic. On 2 April, a Friday, Argentine troops invaded and occupied the Falkland Islands.

After their discovery in the eighteenth century, these islands were claimed both by Britain and by Spain. Whether strategically or economically, they were never worth having. Dr Johnson gave his view in a passage later quoted with relish by Denis Healey: 'An island thrown aside from human use, stormy in winter, barren in summer, an island which not even the southern savages have dignified with habitation, where a garrison must be kept in a state which contemplates with envy the exiles of Siberia.'[1]

The Argentine Republic, which won its independence from Spain thanks in considerable measure to British assistance, maintained the claim to the islands, always using the Spanish name, Las Malvinas. But in 1833 the Union Jack was raised, the few Argentine settlers departed, and the islands were ranked (in British eyes and without Argentine consent) as a Crown colony. The land was taken over by the Falkland Islands Company, which granted leases to a few thousand (mostly Scottish) people who engaged in sheep-farming. The dispute over political sovereignty was dormant until after the Second World War, when a succession of Argentine dictators noisily revived their claim, partly no doubt as a distraction from internal problems. The latest among them was General Galtieri, head of a junta which seized power in 1976 and was responsible for the gruesome 'disappearances' – in fact, murders – of about 6,000 democrats.

One of the few British politicians who kept a watchful eye on the Falklands was Jim Callaghan, perhaps because of his naval background (the nearby waters had witnessed a British victory in the First World War). When he was Prime Minister, he called a meeting to discuss the threat. Tony Benn noted the attitude of the Foreign Secretary: 'David Owen has suggested a sell-out because of our great defensive weakness.'[2] Benn's general conclusion was:

If the Argentinians wished to attack the Falkland Islands they could easily crush them . . . The Argentine Government is determined to get hold of the islands . . . and the arms trade, the total spinelessness of the Foreign Office and the general decay of Britain will have combined to put us in a position where we will be unable to do anything to defend the 1950 people who live there.

There were no British troops on the Falklands other than a handful of Marines as a ceremonial guard for the Governor. There was, however, a deterrent to invasion in the form of HMS *Endurance*, an armed survey ship. A proposal to withdraw the *Endurance* as a saving in the defence budget was put up to Callaghan and, as he later told the Commons, 'I turned it down flat,' ruling that it was 'an error that could have serious consequences'.[3] Indeed, scenting a possible crisis, he ordered two frigates and a nuclear submarine to support the *Endurance* until the danger receded. Under Callaghan's influence, a Labour manifesto drawn up in 1980 included a commitment that 'Under no circumstances will the inhabitants of the Falklands Islands be handed over to any Argentine regime which violates human and civil rights.'

Thatcher, ironically in view of what followed, was much less resolute. In June 1981, after Galtieri had come to power, she ordered the withdrawal of the *Endurance* and ignored a protest from the elected Falkland Islands Council: 'The people of the Falkland Islands deplore in the strongest terms the decision to withdraw HMS *Endurance*.' Galtieri, naturally, took this as a green light.

There was another strand to British policy. Both Labour and Tory governments had given cautious consideration to a compromise formula – the word in vogue was 'lease-back' – whereby Argentina would enjoy sovereignty in principle, while the islanders were guaranteed such rights as the British legal system, English-language education and their elected Council. David Owen's number two at the Foreign Office, Ted Rowlands, had visited Buenos Aires to conduct discreet and hopeful, though inconclusive, negotiations along these lines. Thatcher's Foreign Secretary, Lord Carrington, had similar arrangements in mind and his number two, Richard Luce, had been talking in New York to the Argentine deputy Foreign Minister as recently as 27 February 1982. These discussions, likewise, were inconclusive, but after the invasion Thatcher described them as 'cordial and positive'.[4] Her anger when the invasion occurred was heightened by her feeling that Britain had been strung along by the Argentinians, much as the USA was strung along by the Japanese before Pearl Harbor.

The invasion, anyway, was a fact. By the time the House met on 3 April – the first Saturday sitting since Suez in 1956 – the Argentinians had established full control, with no loss of life on either side. Carrington and Luce, admitting that they had been outwitted, at once resigned. Thatcher, with her key ministers and Service chiefs, had been working through the night to assemble an armada for a counter-invasion. She told the House: 'A large task force will sail as soon as all preparations are complete.'

Michael, without help from Healey (who happened to be in Greece), had to make an instant decision on Labour's attitude. He did not hesitate, nor was he in two minds. What he saw was a clear case of unprovoked aggression, and he was vividly reminded of aggressions by Hitler and

Mussolini in the 1930s which were among the most emotionally powerful memories of his youth. Moreover, he had recently joined with other socialist leaders in a declaration by the Socialist International of firm opposition to political change by force. The Western hemisphere was as vulnerable to such ventures as any other part of the world. In one of his speeches during the Falklands crisis, Michael pointed to Venezuela's claim on part of Guyana's territory.[5] Our century has seen armed intervention by the US in Mexico, Cuba, Nicaragua, El Salvador and Panama. Only a year after Galtieri's troops took over the Falklands, Reagan's Marines took over Grenada.

Such was the argument on principle; but there were other considerations, advanced by some of Michael's friends in the Labour Party, which supported a view that an uncompromising demand for the restoration of the *status quo ante* might not be the only possible – or the wisest – policy. In the Callaghan government, Michael had not objected to the 'lease-back' suggestions, nor to Rowlands' mission. The best course now, in the new and disadvantageous circumstances, might be to revert to such proposals and at least try to negotiate with Argentina on this basis. No one was actually afraid that the islanders would be made to wear yellow stars or be sent to gas chambers; in fact, much larger numbers of people of British descent (notably, Welsh communities in Patagonia) were living in Argentina without suffering any discrimination. Besides, the numbers of the Falkland population were almost ludicrously small. If France had accepted the repatriation of well over a million people who gave up their homes rather than live under the rule of an independent (and undemocratic) Algeria, it should be feasible for those Falklanders who could not tolerate Argentine rule to be resettled in Britain, or to resume sheep-farming in New Zealand. The enforced transfer of the population of the Diego Garcia islands to Mauritius so that their homeland could become an American air base was a much more shameful episode (they, however, were not white or English-speaking).

Those who argued along these lines also warned that the counter-invasion, even if justified, might not be a success. Under the headline 'THATCHER'S MAD GAMBLE', *Tribune* asked: 'Will we really see an all-out attack on the Falkland Islands in an attempt to recapture them? . . . It is complete and utter madness.'[6] The editor of *Tribune* was no military expert, but the word 'gamble' was appropriate enough and the luck might have gone the other way. The Normandy invasion in 1944 had been launched with no certainty of victory, although with the advantages of a home base eighty miles away – not 8,000 – superiority in numbers of fighting men and complete air supremacy. Argentina possessed some sophisticated weaponry (much of it bought in Britain) which included the deadly Exocet missile. Nor could anyone be sure in advance that the Argentine troops would turn out to be a mass of half-trained and frightened conscripts.

Finally, while Michael's decision to support the counter-invasion was indeed morally motivated, there were moral – or at least ideological – dangers which were soon apparent. The enterprise, even if it proved successful (or rather, particularly if it proved successful) was likely to unleash a frenzy of bellicose, chauvinistic, more or less racist emotions, capable of poisoning national life for a long time to come. On a more mundane level, the political effects were predictable. At the time of Suez, when the same emotions were aroused, a Tory MP suggested: 'If our troops return home victorious . . . the government might hold a general election in which honourable members opposite . . . will be swept into the dustbin of opposition for half a century.'[7] He may well have been right – except that the Suez campaign was a failure. The Falklands campaign was a success.

The Saturday debate in the Commons – scarcely a debate, since there was no disagreement on the necessity of an effective riposte – has gone into history as memorably as the Norway debate in 1940. A left-wing critic has given a scathing account: 'To listen to that parliamentary debate on the radio was to enter into a kind of collective inanity . . . Some leapt for joy, others scurried, many panted to catch up, plenty caught the whiff of intimidation.'[8] Michael rebutted this version: 'I know there are some people who say that the House reacted in a spirit of impetuosity. I believe . . . it was the expression by the House of its feeling of moral outrage.'[9]

The Prime Minister struck the note that everyone expected, rising to the expectations of her supporters:

> I am sure that the whole House will join me in condemning totally this unprovoked aggression . . . It has not a shred of justification and not a scrap of legality . . . The people of the Falkland Islands, like the people of the United Kingdom, are an island race. Their way of life is British; their allegiance is to the Crown. They are few in number but they have the right to live in peace, to choose their way of life, and to determine their own allegiance.

Michael, though he eschewed the 'British way of life' sentiment, was equally categorical:

> The people of the Falkland Islands have the absolute right to look to us

at this moment of their desperate plight . . . They are faced with an act of naked, unqualified aggression, carried out in the most shameful and disreputable circumstances. Any guarantee from this invading force is utterly worthless – as worthless as any of the guarantees that are given by this same Argentine junta to its own people . . . There is the longer-term interest to ensure that foul and brutal aggression does not succeed in the world. If it does, there will be a danger not merely to the Falkland Islands, but to people all over this dangerous planet.

Some on the Labour benches felt that he was pitching it too strong, and Healey wrote later that, had he been in London, 'I would have tried to moderate some of Michael's rhetoric.'[10] Labour MPs were happier with the rest of the speech, devoted to attacking the government for its lack of foresight, and other Labour speakers concentrated on this theme. Silkin charged: 'All the indications are that heretofore they have blundered and bungled,' while Rowlands, evoking the phrase that Michael had made unforgettable, declared: 'The guilty men should not go scot free if we do not retrieve the islands as quickly as possible.' Michael was relentless:

It seems that the British government have been fooled by the way the Argentine junta has gone about its business. The government must answer for that as well as for everything else . . . The right honourable lady, the Secretary for Defence and the whole government will have to give a very full account of what happened, how their diplomacy was conducted, and why we did not have the information to which we were entitled. Above all . . . what happened to our power to act? The right honourable lady seems to dismiss that question. It cannot be dismissed.

He warned that in due course there must be a full debate, perhaps a motion of censure, and an inquiry. His accusation was that the Falklanders had been betrayed, and he wound up: 'The government must now prove by deeds – they will never be able to do it by words – that they are not responsible for the betrayal and cannot be faced with that charge.' This 'deeds not words' passage, seen as an advance endorsement of any military action ordered by Thatcher, was often cited in later controversy by Michael's critics on the left. However, the only action that he specifically supported was the sending of the task force. His requirement was that Britain should somehow get the Argentinians out of the islands, whether by actual force, threat, pressure, mediation, diplomacy or whatever method proved effectual. This was reasonable enough, but it was soon evident that armed force was regarded in some quarters as the only possible course, and even as possessing some moral or therapeutic value. In the debate, Enoch Powell bitingly challenged Thatcher to prove that she deserved her title as the 'Iron Lady' and laid down that the only correct reaction was 'direct and unqualified and immediate willingness – not merely willingness, but willingness expressed by action – to use force'. A *Times* leader on the Monday enunciated the doctrine that 'the national will to defend itself has to be cherished and be replenished if it is to mean something real'. This seemed to imply that Servicemen were asked to sacrifice their lives not merely to liberate the Falklands but to 'replenish' the national will.

While the task force steamed majestically towards its destination, efforts to resolve the crisis peacefully were being made by Alexander Haig, the US Secretary of State, and by Javier Perez de Cuellar, the Secretary-General of the UN. Michael told the Commons on 14 April that he supported the despatch of the task force and that, if the Labour Party opposed it, 'one of the consequences would be to injure the world-wide support we have received'. But he also said: 'We shall continue to act and respond in what we conceive to be the best interests of our country. Included high among those interests in this dispute is that the matter should be settled peacefully.' Doubts were beginning to spread in the Labour Party. Judith Hart, in this 14 April debate, condemned the 'intolerable aggression' but proposed that the task force should be halted to allow 'a pause for peace'. Tony Benn went further and demanded that it should be withdrawn. Michael had to take up the argument on the floor of the House, remarking that some Labour MPs 'put too great a store on General Galtieri's good nature'.

From mid-April, however, he put the emphasis on the hopes of mediation and on Thatcher's inflexibility. On 26 April he was asking the Prime Minister: 'How are we to ensure that there will be no dangerous escalation of this crisis?' and telling her: 'The Opposition remain firmly, unshakeably and persistently committed to fresh initiatives in the search for a peaceful settlement.' Next day, he rebuked her for turning down an appeal from Perez de Cuellar not to escalate. If she did not respond positively to this UN appeal, 'she will inflict a grievous blow on our country's cause'. Unexpected support came from Admiral Woodward, the commander of the task force, who was quoted as saying: 'Unless people say "Let's stop" it will be a long and bloody campaign, and to my mind it is absolutely fundamental to try to avoid it . . . There has to be a political will to go on negotiating.' Michael seized on these remarks: 'I say that the admiral on this occasion was talking more sense than the amateur warmongers . . . I say that we have to try and try again to secure that peaceful settlement.'[11]

The task force was now in position off the Falklands, and on 30 April the Argentine cruiser *Belgrano*, although it was outside the 'exclusion zone' ordered by the British, was torpedoed with the loss of over 300 lives. Perhaps because of this incident (or perhaps not – the evidence is inconclusive) a peace plan sponsored by Perez de Cuellar and by the government of Peru came to nothing. Four days later, an Exocet sank HMS *Sheffield*. Nevertheless, Michael issued a statement insisting: 'The diplomatic solution to the crisis to which we are all pledged must be sought more urgently and strenuously than ever.'

Thanks to his dual-track policy, Michael was getting solid support in the Labour Party. On 28 April, a motion by Tony Benn urging a ceasefire and withdrawal of the task force was defeated in the NEC by fifteen votes to eight. But at this critical moment, much to Michael's chagrin, *Tribune* became a Bennite organ. Dick Clements was giving up the editorship which he had held for twenty-two years, to replace Liz Thomas as Michael's political adviser. Despite his scepticism on the military prospects, he had given Michael his backing. His successor, chosen by a selection process in which the staff participated, was Chris Mullin. He held his first editorial meeting in his flat and invited Benn, plus the entourage of Morrell, Derer, Lansman and the rest.[12] The outcome of this meeting was a front page featuring a reprint of the famous 1956 headline 'STOP THIS SUEZ MADNESS', a new echoing headline 'STOP THIS FALKLANDS MADNESS', and a demand for the recall of the task force.[13] In vain, Clements tried to point out to Mullin that the UN, which had condemned Britain as an aggressor in 1956, was now condemning Argentina.

The next week, Michael was confronted by an open letter by Anthony Arblaster headed 'WILL THE REAL MICHAEL FOOT STAND UP?' Arblaster conceded that Thatcher had neglected to look after the Falklands properly, but asked: 'Do you really think that the right way to atone for this neglect is to . . . bomb and shoot our way back on to the islands? . . . It is a war of petty prestige and the crudest chauvinism. It amazes me that you should have allowed yourself to be carried along by this tide of revived imperialist fervour.'[14] Invited by the editor to reply, Michael wrote:

He [Arblaster] succeeds in writing about my views on the Falklands crisis without once mentioning the role of the UN, the UN Charter or the UN Secretary-General. Quite an omission, since these form the core of the Labour Party's case . . . I don't suppose that any but a few sectarian stragglers will follow your advice, but my fear is for *Tribune*.

Never for long has *Tribune* been afflicted by the disease of infantile Leftism. I hope the paper survives the present bout.[15]

Michael was still hoping against hope for a peaceful outcome, and on 17 May, in a letter to Thatcher requesting another debate, he wrote: 'It would be intolerable if moves were made from the diplomatic field to full-scale military operations without the House having a chance to judge for itself the nature of the diplomatic settlement available.' By this time, however, everyone knew that a landing and a decisive battle were imminent. There was a debate on 20 May, ending in a vote in which the Labour Party line was to abstain. Thirty-three Labour MPs defied this decision and voted against the government, a fairly limited number by the standards of the many revolts since Bevanite days. This time, Michael was not inclined to be tolerant; the three front-bench spokesmen who had been among the rebels were required to give up their posts.

The day after this debate, it was announced that men of the Parachute Regiment were ashore and advancing towards the little capital of the Falklands, Port Stanley. The news in late May and early June was dominated by fighting on the desolate moors and by successes for which some of the invading force – such as fifty men of the Welsh Guards at Goose Green – paid with their lives. In London, there were two diversions. On 6 June, another CND march drew about 200,000 people. It was a protest against nuclear weapons and particularly against Cruise, but there were many placards and slogans directed against the Falklands war. On the following day, Reagan arrived for a state visit. Thatcher was determined to exploit this occasion as advantageously as possible. Her plan was that Reagan should address a joint session of the Lords and Commons in Westminster Hall. This hallowed edifice had not been used since the ceremonial farewell to Winston Churchill in 1954; Michael made it clear that there would be complaints, and perhaps a boycott, if it were put to such a controversial purpose. Thatcher had to give in and Reagan made his speech – an anti-Communist tirade – in the Royal Gallery, a little-known part of the House of Lords.

The final surrender at Port Stanley came on 14 June. Two hundred and fifty British lives had been lost, enough to justify patriotic mourning but not enough to provoke, like the loss of 70,000 American lives in Vietnam, a disillusioned revulsion. Michael said in the House: 'The sense of relief is very great and we are all grateful for the fact that the bloodshed is now coming to an end.'

Thatcher celebrated the victory in an exultant speech at a Tory rally on the racecourse at Cheltenham on 3 July:

When we started out, there were the waverers and the fainthearts . . .
The people who thought we could no longer do the great things which
we once did . . . that Britain was no longer the nation that had built an
empire and ruled a quarter of the world. Well, they were wrong. The
lesson of the Falklands is that Britain has not changed and that this
nation still has those sterling qualities which shine through our history.

In this speech, she coined the expression the 'Falklands factor'. As the
months ticked away before the next general election, it was a phrase that
acquired a potent meaning.

2

For Michael, 1982 was not quite so difficult as 1981. The NEC no longer
denied him a majority, and there was no second contest for the deputy
leadership. Yet he was still forced to devote an inordinate amount of time
and effort to the internal problems of the party. Of these, the most
intricate, the most exasperating and unfortunately the most headline-
catching was the problem of the Militant Tendency.

Under Clause Two of the party constitution, an organisation which
had its own 'programme, principles and policy' and had 'branches in the
constituencies' could not affiliate to the Labour Party, nor could any of its
members belong to the Labour Party. This rule was directed against the
Communist Party, and some of its members were therefore instructed to
join the Labour Party without admitting that they belonged to another
party.

This strategy, known as 'entryism', was gradually abandoned by the
CP, only to be imitated by smaller parties or groups which looked for
inspiration not to Stalin but to Trotsky (although Michael Foot, who
cherished a lifelong respect for Trotsky, remarked that he 'would surely
have disowned with one sweep of his pen the breed of modern
Trotskyists').[16] These groups had a bewildering series of splits and a
variety of names over the years, but the one that refined entryism to an
almost professional technique was the Revolutionary Socialist League.
Unlike the CP, it was truly minuscule in size and had no prospect, in the
most favourable conceivable circumstances, of ever rivalling the Labour
Party in popular support or votes; entryism was its only chance and
virtually its only activity. It created (or, it might be truer to say,
transformed itself into) the Militant Tendency. *Militant* was the name of a
weekly paper, started in 1964; members of the organisation maintained

that the paper was an independent organ, like *Tribune*, and that the meetings or conferences they attended were gatherings of supporters or readers of the paper. The word 'tendency' was a translation of the French *tendance*, applied to people of a certain way of thinking within a large party, and was chosen in preference to 'league', 'society' or 'group' to disavow any impression of firm structure. Members of the Tendency succeeded, just like members of the CP in earlier years, in securing significant positions in the Labour Party, becoming candidates and MPs, and gaining control of the youth organisation (the Labour Party Young Socialists) which in the 1970s was given a seat on the NEC.

The secretaries of the Labour Party – Ron Hayward and Jim Mortimer, who succeeded him in 1982 – never had any doubt that Militant had its own 'programme, principles and policy' and for that matter its own discipline. Hayward enjoyed telling the story of how, in a talk with Ted Grant, a key figure in Militant, he charged that some of the 'supporters' had sexist attitudes to women, to which Grant replied: 'Oh, that's not true, we'd have expelled them.'[17] This power of discipline was one hallmark that distinguished Militant from other minority groups in the Labour Party, such as the Socialist League in the 1930s or the Tribune Group later. The real difference, however, was that the latter recognised a loyalty to the Labour Party, whereas the loyalty of Militant members was to Militant (sometimes referred to in secret documents, indeed, as 'the party'). One such document laid down: 'All members holding public office, paid or unpaid, shall come under the complete control of the party and its organs . . . All members are required to enter the mass organisations of the working class under the direction of party organs for the purpose of fulfilling the aims of the party.'[18] Another revealing document dealt with Militant groups within local Labour parties: 'These groups will meet and decide tactics before Labour Party meetings. They should be centrally linked by a committee which should give the responsibility to someone to organise this work, setting model resolutions, keeping a record of members and contacts . . . initiating local area meetings and conferences to discuss work and programmes.'[19]

It was in the 1970s that the Labour Party began to get seriously worried about these developments. The NEC commissioned Reg Underhill, the national agent, to make an investigation and present a report. He completed his report, citing documents of the type quoted above, in November 1975. The NEC, by a vote of 16 to 12, decided that it should not be published and no further action should be taken – partly, so Hayward recalls,[20] because some of Underhill's evidence came from informants who wished to be anonymous and therefore appeared unreliable, partly because it would offer the hostile press a field-day, partly because it would evoke a demand for action and there was no agreement as to what action would be justified. Underhill, although he was no ferocious right-winger, was naturally annoyed. In 1979, when he retired and became Lord Underhill, he gave his report to the press.

The decision not to publish had been taken by a sub-committee consisting of Michael Foot, Eric Heffer, Ron Hayward and two right-wingers who were outvoted. Michael held as a matter of principle that the only way to defeat people with harmful ideas was to work through free debate for the triumph of better ideas. He keenly remembered the Bevanite days, when the right-wing leadership had sought to penalise or expel any dissenters. Repressive action against Militant might not stop there, and in view of Militant's secrecy it was hard to establish who belonged to the 'tendency' and who did not. All Michael's instincts cried out against anything that might grow into a witch-hunt. The strongest demands for expulsions came from the incipient Social Democrats, who formed a clearly defined 'tendency' of their own, held confidential meetings and were moving towards leaving the party. In a speech in February 1980, Shirley Williams said: 'It is not unreasonable for a party to protect its principles and methods from being destroyed and to do so by accepting into membership only those people who embrace both.' Clements, in *Tribune*, retorted sharply: 'Is she suggesting that those found discussing a Centre Party should be expelled?'[21]

However, in the course of 1981 Michael reluctantly admitted that something had to be done. Militant was going from strength to strength; it was credited with over 4,000 members, was well entrenched in a number of constituencies, and was even believed to have a bigger full-time staff than the Labour Party. A special stronghold was Liverpool, presciently designated by Grant in 1955 as a base from which the organisation could expand 'first in Lancashire, then to London, then nationally'.[22] The fact that three of the city's five Labour MPs went to the SDP provided an obvious opportunity; Heffer was the only one who could be respected as a socialist, and he never condemned Militant. Thus Militant was able to control the city-wide Labour Party and the city council and to get some of its leading figures, such as Derek Hatton, selected as parliamentary candidates. That a group with its distinct 'programme and policy' could bring about the deselection of Labour MPs and nominate future MPs was a situation that Michael, as leader, could not view with equanimity.

The problem now was how to strike a blow against Militant without hitting all those, including many sincere and idealistic young people, who had enlisted under its banner. Michael, with the support of Hayward and of friends such as Neil Kinnock and Joan Lestor, was insistent that the Militant leaders should be penalised for their conspiratorial techniques and not for their opinions. In particular, *Militant* – the paper – should not be the target. In 1954, when a Trotskyite paper called *Socialist Outlook* was proscribed by the NEC, Michael had written a scathing article in *Tribune* denouncing this violation of Voltairean principles; his words were much quoted by defenders of *Militant*, or Militant, in the 1980s. Thus it was necessary to prove that Militant actually was an organisation, not a body of people who read and supported a weekly paper.

However, one issue of political opinion, or doctrine, was involved. It was generally agreed that a person who was opposed to elective institutions could not be called a democratic socialist and had no proper place even within the 'broad church' of the Labour Party. Michael, therefore, prepared the way for action against Militant by writing two long articles in the *Observer*, reprinted as a pamphlet, under the title *My Kind of Socialism*. It was among his more eloquent, as well as erudite, essays, replete with quotations from Oliver Goldsmith, Hazlitt, the Chartist Julian Harney, Engels, Herzen, Tawney, Silone and Bevan. Others who received favourable mention were Marx, John Strachey, William Morris, Orwell, Koestler and Jill Foot, whose early opposition to high-rise blocks was cited as an example of socialist humanism. Michael showed that the Levellers, the Chartists and the suffragettes, regarded by some as exemplifying alternatives to Parliament, in fact supported his argument because their aim was to make Parliament fully democratic. His conclusion was:

> Whatever its other manifold deficiencies, Parliament can still symbol-ise the attempt to settle disputes by better methods than brute force. Any democratic Socialist who overlooked that connection would hardly deserve the name . . . For those who accept that only by profound Socialist change can the deeper disease of our society be cured, the dominant need is to turn the nation's mind to parliamen-tary action . . . [Trotsky] would never have been guilty of the infantile, querulous condemnations of Parliament and parliamentary action which some of his self-styled followers adopt . . .
>
> Of course, I am well aware that these cautionary admonitions and invocations . . . will be cited as evidence of how my own Socialist convictions have become soft or mellow or something worse; how I have become shackled or suborned by events or pressure or, heaven help us, the corruption of power. Heaven help me, and my con-

stituents and the Labour movement! It is the absence of power – the signs that the prospect might move from us – which enrages me.

In December 1981, on Michael's initiative, the NEC set up a new inquiry into Militant, to be undertaken by Hayward and Underhill's successor as national agent, David Hughes. This report, updating and enlarging on Underhill's evidence, was presented in June 1982. It recommended an ingenious plan: groups which wished 'to be recognised and allowed to operate within the party' must apply to be placed on a register. The test would be their compatibility with Clause Two of the constitution. Militant, as Hayward and Hughes frankly predicted, would be rejected. Consequently, the individuals controlling this impermissible organisation would be in line for expulsion.

The scheme – and, as no one doubted, the crackdown on Militant – had to be endorsed by the 1982 conference. Michael put his weight fully behind it. Ian Aitken (anticipating Admiral Woodward with his choice of adjectives) had written: 'It will be a long and bloody campaign, but he has now given notice that he does not intend to flinch from it.'[23] Another well-informed journalist, John Cole, wrote on the eve of the conference:

> Foot believes that if Downing Street is not to remain a mirage, both for himself and Labour, he must tackle *Militant* head on . . . Foot, it is said, will argue that the whole central core of *Militant* must be cut out – not just the editorial board but also the Labour parliamentary candidates who profess loyalty to *Militant*, as well as the paper's full-time, paid representatives.[24]

Mortimer, moving acceptance of the register, stressed that no indiscriminate witch-hunt was intended: 'We must distinguish between the inner organising group of the Militant Tendency and a wider circle of sympathisers . . . I don't regard this Militant Tendency sectarianism as part of the genuine Left of the Labour movement . . . All who observe the rules have a legitimate place in the broad stream which constitutes our party.'

Michael replied to the debate, an exceptional decision (normally, the leader makes only one speech in conference week). He struck the same note:

> What was I to do as leader of the party? If I recommended that we set aside that report, that would have been a gross betrayal of my duties . . . That would have been a recipe for the destruction of good faith in this party . . . You must do it in a manner that does not infringe

the proper rights of free association, free debate and free argument in the party.

The voting for the NEC produced an emphatic setback for the Bennites. On any issue which found the right and the 'soft left' in agreement, they now had a clear majority, and the crackdown on Militant was such an issue. Benn was removed from the chairmanship of the Home Policy Committee and Heffer from that of the Organisation Committee. The register scheme was endorsed by a conference vote of five million to one and a half million. Thus it seemed to be a foregone conclusion that the 'inner core' Militants would soon be out of the party. In Mortimer's timetable, the first step was to reject Militant's application for inclusion in the register.

But it was not, after all, plain sailing. The Militant leaders – strictly speaking, the editorial board of the paper – declined to apply. According to them, there was no organisation, no membership, no 'programme, principles and policy' – nothing but a weekly paper. Lawyers were found to submit a case in the law courts that expulsions without specific charges and impartial scrutiny were contrary to natural justice. Michael reproached the strategists of Militant for seeking a rescue in the 'capitalist courts', so often denounced by revolutionaries; but they had no scruples about this, and Lord Denning upheld the 'natural justice' plea. The register had to be abandoned, leaving the NEC with only two options: to admit defeat or to declare Militant a proscribed organisation. This was an embarrassing course, since the 'proscribed list' was identified with the intolerance of the 1950s (when Mortimer had been expelled for holding office in the Society for Anglo-Chinese Understanding) and had been abolished in 1973. However, it was now the only solution.

Time was passing, the newspapers were gloating over the difficulties, and there was a danger that the saga would stretch out until the approach of the general election or even beyond. It was only in December 1982 that the NEC was able to decide on the proscription; and it was only in February 1983 (since individuals threatened with expulsion had a right to plead their case) that Ted Grant and four other members of the so-called editorial board were actually expelled. Even this was not final. Like Stafford Cripps in 1939, the five had a right of appeal to the next party conference. In October 1983 they exercised this right and made time-consuming speeches. The expulsions were upheld, but only five of the thousands of Militant 'supporters' were excluded from party membership. The Militant grip on Liverpool, in particular, was not broken until 1986.

The most serious effect of the delay was to make it impossible to get rid of Labour candidates adopted through Militant's machinations. As John Cole had correctly reported, this was an important part of Michael's programme. There were eight of these candidates, almost all Liverpudlians but adopted in Bradford, Coventry and other places. In order to dislodge them, it would be necessary first to declare Militant a proscribed organisation, secondly to prove that the eight belonged to it, and thirdly to cancel their endorsement and hold a fresh selection. There was no time to do all this before the election came round, and Labour therefore entered the 1983 election with candidates who, in view of their generally known allegiance, should not have been playing the humblest part in the campaign.

By the autumn of 1982, the 'Falklands factor' was overshadowing the political scene. Television showed the return home of the warriors, ship by ship and regiment by regiment, all cleverly spaced and stage-managed. With their swaggering demeanour and their loudly voiced scorn for the 'Argies', they clearly could have nothing to say to Michael Foot, nor he to them. The opinion polls, which were studied by Labour MPs with all the obsessive nervousness of a vain woman scrutinising the lines on her face, showed the Tories coasting comfortably towards electoral victory. And, wide though the gap between the parties was, the gap between their leaders was emphatically wider. In the 1979 election, Thatcher had been less popular than her party; now, she was ahead of it and was clearly an asset. Michael's standing provided a cruel contrast. His 'doing a good job' rating sank as low as 13 per cent, the worst since polling was invented. A mood of dissatisfaction with his leadership began to spread dangerously in the Labour Party.

One irremediable reason for this mood was his age. He would be seventy in July 1983 and he certainly looked no younger. With a man of this age, questions about his health inevitably arose. The lingering after-effects of the car crash, the spells in hospital, the weakened eyesight – all were listed and pondered. When directly challenged by an interviewer, he had his answers: 'I've been for an hour's walk on Hampstead Heath this morning. People a good deal older than myself are still active in politics in the world.'[25] But the walk on the Heath with the dog, for which Michael was famous, looked like an old man's recreation; younger men had a session at the gym or took up aerobics. As for the septuagenarians 'still active in politics', the examples that came to mind were Churchill in his declining last phase, Adenauer, de Gaulle, Mao Zedong, Reagan and Brezhnev – decidedly not the heroes of the Labour Party. While Labour men and women sighed, Labour's enemies put the boot in. Bernard Levin professed to feel sorry for Michael, 'half blind and at least a quarter crippled'.[26] George Malcolm Thomson, a colleague of Michael's in Beaverbrook days, pointed out in a letter that this was an accurate description of Nelson – but Nelson never had to stand for election or submit to a polls rating.

'Do you seriously want this old man to run Britain?' the *Sun* asked its readers, in a front page featuring a photo of Michael on the Heath, when the election came. The fact was that Michael was old; the perception was that he was out of touch, that he lived in a bygone age. Everything contributed to this impression: the casual clothes which were not like present-day casual clothes, the book-lined study, the stick invariably depicted in cartoons (half a century ago, young and healthy men had often carried sticks, but they did so no longer). Michael was a superb platform orator and capable of mastery of the House of Commons, but these were the qualities of half-remembered politicians, such as Lloyd George, and he was much less effective on television. His style was wrong, and he was too old to learn a new one even if he had cared to.

In the 1950s, when Michael was the star attraction of *Free Speech*, one could take part in a television programme just as in an argument or conversation in social life. By the 1980s, it was already more like appearing for an examination or a job interview. A not unfair judgement was: 'Mr Foot acquitted himself more honourably than many of his critics allowed, but a prolixity and discursiveness which ill suits modern television were compounded by a casualness about preparation which contrasted with Mrs Thatcher's thorough briefings.'[27] Barbara Castle's verdict was sharper:

> It is absolutely essential for a leader in politics to master the television arts. They should work at it, they should take pride in it, they shouldn't be ashamed of it. The more left-wing they are, the more important it is that they should learn the art of presentation. The pose, the sophistica-tion, the clever diversion, the outwitting of your opponents – and there was Michael on telly sitting hunched up with his collar all out of place. Why didn't someone tell him? I wanted to. Why wouldn't anybody take him in hand? He believed that genuineness was all, but actually the visual media can distort so much that genuineness just looks like boorishness.[28]

Just before the summer recess, Anthony Bevins of *The Times* wrote: 'The despair of Labour M.P.s has now plumbed such depths that there is speculation at Westminster that James Callaghan might stage a come-back, returning to the leadership. This nonsense serves as an indication of the near-total lack of faith in Michael Foot's lame leadership.'[29] It seems, in fact, that some MPs sounded out Callaghan to see if he was at all interested in the idea, which he was not. After the new session began in November, the same journalist, making use of leaks from an unhappy PLP meeting, reported:

> Front-benchers and back-benchers rounded on Michael Foot for his 'abject failure' to pull the party together . . . Sources on all wings bar the hard Left, and at all levels including the Shadow Cabinet and the whips' office, agreed that the party was seething with rage against Mr Foot . . . At one secret meeting of more than a dozen representative M.P.s, there was repeated criticism of Mr Foot's leadership.[30]

The reference to the whips' office was significant, for Dick Clements recalls a conversation with Michael Cocks in which the Chief Whip expressed the view that the leader should resign. As for the Shadow Cabinet, it had a consistent majority of right-wingers who had never wanted Michael as leader in the first place. They were able to show their power when they vetoed his plan to appoint Neil Kinnock as front-bench spokesman on employment in place of Eric Varley. Chris Mullin's *Tribune* rallied to Michael's defence against the right, but by no means in complimentary terms: 'Michael Foot owed his election as leader of the Labour Party to the Left. But no sooner was he elected than he set about trying to appease the Right . . . Now they want Michael Foot to resign. He has outstayed his welcome and they are openly plotting his downfall . . . There is only one way out. Michael Foot must come back where he belongs.'[31]

Exactly who was plotting, or at least hoping for, Michael's downfall it is still impossible to say with any certainty. A book dealing with Kinnock's political career names Jack Straw, Jeff Rooker, Joe Ashton and Robert Kilroy-Silk.[32] Other names suggested by political observers are John Cunningham, Gerald Kaufman and Dale Campbell-Savours. Michael has left it on record that, in this November, Rooker 'openly urged me to my face to resign'.[33] The only MP who was willing to be quoted in the press as favouring a resignation was Walter Johnson, the protagonist of the 'donkey-jacket' affair.[34] There is no doubt, however, that the reports in *The Times* were substantially accurate and that a significant number of MPs would have welcomed Michael's departure with relief. It must be noted, too, that the names which have been mentioned are those of left-wing as well as right-wing MPs (Straw, Rooker and Ashton were members of the Tribune Group). But *The Times* was accurate, once again, in referring to 'all wings bar the hard

Left'. Tony Benn and his friends had no wish to see Michael go, with the obvious risk that the new leader would be a right-winger, presumably Denis Healey.

Despite this troubled atmosphere, there were Foot loyalists with considerable status in the party and especially in the left: Stan Orme, Judith Hart, Joan Lestor, Neil Kinnock. In a speech on 6 September, aimed at bringing any possible plot into the open before it could gather strength, Kinnock said: 'There is no justification for anyone who diverts attention from the pursuit and presentation of our policies by a formal or informal campaign to replace Michael Foot.' This was enough to show that Michael had defenders, but not enough to stop the speculation. Michael himself had to speak out firmly in a speech on 30 November: 'I have a duty to this party placed on me when I was elected. I propose to discharge it to the best of my ability to the close of poll on election day, and thereafter as the duly elected democratic Socialist Prime Minister.'

One relevant question with no obvious answer is: why did the MPs who wanted a change of leadership (and, *a fortiori*, the Shadow Cabinet members) take no action? The most that has been suggested is that someone began to circulate a round-robin and collect signatures, and even this may not be true. Michael, after all, was no monster of vanity, nor was he the sort of leader who would punish the disloyal by blocking their hopes of advancement. In principle, there was nothing to stop these MPs from forming a deputation and speaking frankly to him. Indeed, the press reports, the poll ratings and the conversation with Rooker were already enough to make him ask himself whether resignation might be the right course. As he recorded later: 'I considered the possibility with the utmost care.'[35] An hour with an impressive and representative deputation might have convinced him.

One deterrent was that everyone, or almost everyone, liked Michael and contemplated the task with distaste. Then, even if there were blunders in his record – such as the 'deeds not words' speech and the handling of the Tatchell affair – he had performed with fair success the essential duty of holding the party together. The left gave him credit for upholding the policies adopted by conference and acceptable to the rank and file; the right, for keeping at bay the advance of Tony Benn and taking firm action against Militant. No alternative leader was likely to have a better all-round record. Also, MPs knew that the problem was not Michael Foot, the real man, but the way he was seen by the public at large. As one (anonymous) MP put it: 'We all know that Michael Foot is a man of decency and integrity. But outside they don't, they just see a vacillating, white-haired old man.'[36] What 'they' saw was shaped by the press and television, and aversion to the power of the 'media' was deep-rooted in the Labour Party. Many, on the right as well as the left, felt that a surrender to this power would be grossly unfair to Michael and wrong in principle. Many would have agreed with his argument:

> The newspapers which had claimed my scalp so often . . . would legitimately present themselves as the victors. They certainly would have played their part in choosing the leader of the Labour Party and, having re-acquired the taste for such public executions, they would not be likely to lose it thereafter . . . It would not have been by itself a healthy event for the Labour Party or even, putting the point not too pompously, I trust, for British politics . . . The more I examined this course of action, for all its immediate attractions so appealing to the Tory Press, the more distracting, futile, even cowardly I thought it to be.[37]

There was a further question: what would happen if Michael resigned? In the short term, his place would be filled by the deputy leader. But, if there were no early general election, there would have to be another contest in Labour's electoral college. It would be as venomous, divisive and time-wasting as the deputy leadership contest of 1981, and there was no guarantee that Healey, the man assumed to have the greatest mass appeal, would be the winner. And if he did become leader, was he to repudiate all those conference decisions and tear up the existing manifesto, or to enter the election campaign tied to policies in which he plainly did not believe? Dauntingly, the prospect of renewed civil war in the party loomed again. Healey could make these calculations as well as anyone else; he preferred a good working relationship with Michael, cemented in the days of the social contract and recently on the trip to Moscow, to the possible leadership of a warring and fragmented party. His realistic opinion was that Michael 'simply did not look like a potential Prime Minister . . . we had no chance whatever so long as he was leader'.[38] But he gave no encouragement to any plotters who might appear and firmly rebuffed speculation: 'I think Michael will lead the party at the next election. I intend to remain his loyal supporter.'[39]

Yet this was an unhappy time for Michael. He realised that his party was retaining him as leader because, on balance, it was more advisable to do so than to get rid of him. Since the Falklands war, he had also realised that the election would bring defeat, perhaps disaster. For Jill, the cruel cartoons depicting the man she loved as a feeble dodderer, the vicious articles by journalists she despised, the television interviews in which Michael was harried – all these were painful, and she knew that, for all his fortitude, they were painful for Michael too. They would both be relieved when it was all over and he could honourably retire from the leadership.

In accordance with the law that if anything can go wrong, it will, there was more bad news from Bermondsey. On 2 August 1982, Mellish relinquished the Labour whip and announced that he was an independent MP. It was a clear prelude to leaving the House and forcing a by-election. There was no prospective candidate; a selection conference would have to be held, but the party in Bermondsey was sure to select Peter Tatchell again. He was invited for a talk with Michael, and found that it made a contrast with his earlier encounter: 'I was immediately struck by the immense warmth and friendliness of his welcome . . . Foot stopped short of confirming that he would support my future endorsement, saying he could not guarantee it . . . [but] I left the meeting feeling that he would no longer oppose my candidature.'[40]

Michael was making the best of a bad job and hoping against hope that Mellish would stay in the House until the general election, but on 1 November Mellish resigned his seat. A by-election in Peckham (also a part of the borough of Southwark) on 28 October had yielded a very low poll and a poor result for the new Labour MP, Harriet Harman. Tatchell drew the obvious conclusion: 'The general opinion among us was that he [Mellish] wanted to inflict the maximum damage possible on the party he claimed to love so much . . . If he delayed his resignation much longer, there might not be a by-election.'[41] Michael took the same view, and was furious with Mellish for breaking his word. He accosted Mellish in the members' lobby and told him that his action was a flagrant breach of his promise. Mellish made no reply. The by-election could be deferred until the new register came into force in February 1983, but not longer. It was bound to be at least as bad as Peckham.

The year ended with another event that Michael could have done without – a battle for control of *Tribune*. In the worst capitalist tradition, it was a take-over bid with ownership of shares as the weapon. To comply with the law, Tribune Publications Limited was a company, but the shares had never paid a dividend and it had never mattered who owned them. Back in 1937 when *Tribune* was founded, there had been twenty-six shareholders. All were now dead except Michael Foot, Jennie Lee and Donald Bruce, who held sixty shares each, and three other people who owned a few. Bruce (Lord Bruce, a Labour life peer) had once written a short polemical book jointly with Michael[42] and had been one of the Bevanite group, but was now a forgotten figure. Together with John Silkin, he conceived a plan to get rid of the directors appointed by the staff (an innovation of the 1970s) and install a board of directors that would check the ultra-leftism of Mullin's editorship. Silkin owned no shares and had never had much to do with *Tribune*, but Jennie Lee was persuaded to appoint him as her proxy for the next shareholders' meeting. Mullin fought back by appealing to readers to contribute to a fund, administered by Jo Richardson, which would enable the paper to keep going on the existing basis. With financial advisers and lawyers taking a hand, the imbroglio became wearisomely complicated.

Although Michael strongly disapproved of Mullin's conduct of *Tribune*, he was disgusted by this manoeuvre and refused to do anything to help Bruce and Silkin. He tried to stay out of the battle, but agreed to a request from the staff to act as arbitrator. A compromise was reached, with Bruce and Silkin as directors, two other directors representing the staff, and a chairman nominated by Michael. Michael's choice was Norman Buchan, a Tribunite MP who saw it as his role to safeguard editorial independence. Bruce and Silkin were left without effective power over policy, and in time the whole affair simmered down.

On Christmas Day, Michael and Jill visited the peace camp which had been set up by women protesters at the gates of the Cruise missile base at Greenham Common, greeted the women and donated a food parcel. It was a generous and principled gesture, but not deemed to be a prudent one; the press knew nothing of it until later.

3

With Tatchell duly selected and endorsed, polling day in Bermondsey was set for 24 February. John O'Grady, the old right-wing stalwart of Southwark Council, had stormed angrily out of the selection conference and now came forward as a candidate, styling himself the Real Labour Candidate. At the outset of the campaign, he was tipped to beat Tatchell, with the Liberal, Simon Hughes, and the Tory (confusingly, another Hughes) as outsiders. Tatchell, by this time, was on the receiving end of vitriolic press attacks and even of personal assaults, perhaps perpetrated by O'Grady's supporters, perhaps by the National Front, which had a certain following in the district. He recorded: 'Even doing my shopping or going to work became an ordeal of running the gauntlet of abuse and threats . . . Bottles and bricks were hurled at me from flat balconies and passing cars, and I was once chased and menaced by two youths with an iron bar.'[43]

Tatchell alleges that he had very little help from Labour headquarters, in contrast to the efforts made a few months earlier in Peckham. Jim Mortimer denies this, but in any case relations between Bermondsey and Walworth Road were soured when the national agent, David Hughes, insisted on the pulping of thousands of leaflets which had been printed by a press connected with Militant; the cost had to be deducted from the election expenses. Almost certainly, the by-election was written off as a lost cause, with regret in some quarters and without regret in others. 'There is no doubt at Westminster', reported *The Times* on 15 February, 'that several Labour figures would like to see Mr Tatchell defeated, if only as a signal to the party's hard Left.'

The campaign was as dirty as any in political history. O'Grady openly exploited Tatchell's homosexuality and went round the streets in a traditional horse and cart chanting, to the tune of 'My old man's a dustman':

> Tatchell is a poppet, as pretty as can be,
> But he must be slow if he don't know he won't be your MP.
> Tatchell is an Aussie, he lives in a council flat,
> He wears his trousers back to front 'cos he don't know this from that.

Michael spoke in Bermondsey on 21 February and denounced the smear campaign:

> I urge you to vote Labour not only in the interests of our party but in the name of decent politics . . . I ask you to repudiate all the slurs, slanders and smears . . . I was not in favour of an immediate by-election . . . I thought it should be delayed because it might be an election in which the Tories and some of their hangers-on would try to push aside the real issues and fight on smears and scares . . . I tried to persuade the parties concerned, Peter Tatchell and Bob Mellish, that it would be in the best interests of Bermondsey and of the Labour Party as a whole that we should not have a by-election. Peter Tatchell kept his word. Bob Mellish broke his.

The various smears – on Tatchell's extremist political views and on his evasion of military service – made his prospects hopeless, but the sexual smears may have been a relatively minor factor. His own estimate is that, of the 12,000 votes that Labour lost by comparison with the last general election, only about 2,000 were lost because of sexual prejudice. Many people who would not vote for him were nevertheless repelled by O'Grady's behaviour, and opted for the Liberal, who fought straightforwardly on his policy. The result, in any case, was a disaster for Labour:

Simon Hughes, Liberal	17,017
Peter Tatchell, Labour	7,698
J. O'Grady, 'Real Labour'	2,243
R. Hughes, Conservative	1,631

The immediate consequence was that Michael's leadership was again imperilled. Even in advance of polling day, the *Sunday Times* claimed: 'Labour leaders are preparing for an immediate challenge to Michael Foot's leadership if Peter Tatchell loses the Bermondsey by-election.'[44] On the day when the result was known, Anthony Bevins in *The Times* stated that a majority of the Shadow Cabinet thought that Michael should go – which brought a quick denial from Healey. But at least one Shadow Cabinet member (anonymous, to be sure) was quoted as saying: 'Michael is mortally wounded. Labour can't win under his leadership.'[45] Confronted in a television interview on the Sunday after the by-election, Michael said: 'It's my firm intention to carry out what I was elected to do. Labour leaders are not elected by the polls or newspaper campaigns.' The interviewer went on to ask whether Michael would resign if Labour lost Darlington, the next pending by-election. He replied firmly that he would not. But Dick Clements, looking back today on this anxious period, says: 'If we'd failed at Darlington, it would have been the end of Michael.'[46] In fact, the main reason why no 'immediate challenge' was made after Bermondsey was that those who were contemplating it decided to wait for Darlington – in other words, to give Michael one more chance.

Darlington had none of Bermondsey's exceptional characteristics. It was a marginal seat, held by Labour in 1979 with a majority of just over 1,000. It could be won by any of the three parties; the Liberals had come a poor third in 1979, but the Alliance had made its mark on the political map since then and had gained encouragement from the Bermondsey success. Labour strategists felt that prolonging the uncertainties, including the speculation about Michael's fate, could do nothing but harm. Polling day was fixed for 24 March.

Michael went to speak in Darlington on 11 March. At a well-attended meeting, he highlighted the issue that had primary importance in his mind: 'We want a government which will play a leading part in stopping the nuclear arms race.' But he had to repeat at a press conference: 'I am not in any circumstances contemplating a departure from the Labour Party leadership.' Jill, accompanying him, was equally emphatic: 'I can say with absolute certainty that Michael will not be hounded out by any campaign mounted against him by the media.' She added that she had just had a heart-to-heart talk with Edna Healey, Denis' wife: 'We agreed completely that it is a team job and our respective husbands are easily the best team.'[47]

Fortunately, Labour had an excellent candidate, a polytechnic lecturer named Oswald O'Brien whose democratic socialist beliefs and loyalty to the leadership were impeccable. Fortunately, too, the SDP put forward a decidedly weak candidate. The Labour campaign was as resolute and determined as it had·been dispirited in Bermondsey. Not only was the seat held, but the slender majority was doubled.

It was a reprieve, but only a reprieve. Analysed with the aid of a computer, the figures showed that the Tories were well placed to win a general election. Thatcher's advisers were urging her to take the plunge; Labour hastened to make urgent preparations. A 'campaign document' was produced with the title *New Hope for Britain*. Michael wrote a foreword with a forthright attack on the Thatcherite ideology:

> She worships the profit motive, the money test. Nothing else, no other value in life, is allowed to count. She extols Victorian values without even a passing comprehension of the human suffering and indignity which the mass of our people had to endure . . . [The Labour Party] came into being to vanquish the hard, pinched values of Victorian Britain.

The document incorporated all the proposals contained in resolutions passed at party conferences. This, as Michael saw it, was the best way to show proper respect for decisions duly debated and adopted and avoid the accusations of picking and choosing that had been made in 1979 against Callaghan. However, when the election came this scrupulously democratic procedure proved to be a handicap. In a subsequent criticism, Healey pointed out: 'The party was unable to produce a short, popular and lively manifesto and we fell back on the campaign document, which was verbose, over-detailed and badly argued.'

The probable approach of the general election seemed to close off the threat to Michael's position, but it was revived for an unexpected reason. The Australian Labour Party had lost confidence in its leader, William Hayden, and, on the point of going into an election campaign, had replaced him by Bob Hawke, a robust character somewhat in the mould of Denis Healey. Now, news came that Labour in Australia had won the election despite – or even perhaps because of – this unorthodox move. All the speculation started up again.

On 9 May, a Monday, Margaret Thatcher went to Buckingham Palace and obtained a dissolution of Parliament with polling on 9 June. Four

days later, she opened her campaign with a speech to Scottish Tories at
Perth. The rhetoric was well prepared: 'What a prize we have to fight for!
– no less than the chance to banish from our land the dark divisive clouds
of Marxist socialism . . . If we keep our standards and our vision bright,
what we have begun will end not only in victory for our party, but in
fulfilment of our nation's destiny.'

Michael too was planning to open his campaign in Scotland, with an
important meeting in Glasgow, but on 16 May he was in his office to see
Gerald Kaufman, who had requested an appointment. Like most Labour
politicians, Kaufman saw no chance of winning the election. He had
passed a sleepless night, thinking of friends who might not be returning
to Westminster (his own seat, in Manchester, was reasonably safe).
Perhaps some of them might survive, thanks to an Australian-style rescue
operation? He told Michael frankly that a resignation from the leadership
would be in the best interests of the party. In Michael's words: 'He put his
point courteously and I replied, I trust, with equal courtesy, and that was
that.'[48] Kaufman recalls that Michael listened carefully and replied that
his resignation would not, in his opinion, do any good.[49] The conversation was brief; Kaufman took his leave after assuring Michael that it
would remain confidential. He went to catch a train to Manchester and
Michael went to catch a train to Glasgow. It was not the happiest of
overtures to an election campaign.

4

One way of describing the 1983 election is to say that, while the Tory
experience was of a single campaign, the Labour experience was that two
campaigns were going on at the same time. For the Tories, every
technique of achieving victory was synchronised and summoned at the
most effective moment, as the conductor of an orchestra might call upon
the strings, the brass, the drums and the cymbals according to their place
in the score. The instruments, to pursue this metaphor, were the big
meetings addressed by the leader (of which, deliberately, there were
few), the prepared statements at press conferences, the broadcasts on
radio and television, the interviews through these media, and the news
items supplied to journalists on sympathetic newspapers. All these were
supplemented by the day-to-day work in the constituencies of canvassing, arranging for postal votes, providing cars for the sick and the aged,
and so forth; but the Tories, while they were indeed more efficient than
Labour in these respects, never made Labour's error of supposing that

constituency work would win the election. No Tory canvasser was likely to ring a doorbell at a time when his leader was on the air.

Whether the media are a decisive and unbeatable weapon in a modern election is open to debate, but a comparison of the Labour victory in 1945 and the Tory victory in 1983 is instructive. In 1945 two of the 'big four' newspapers supported Labour (the *Daily Herald* and *Daily Mirror* versus the *Daily Express* and *Daily Mail*) and there was a rough balance of readership on either side. By 1983, three-quarters of total readership belonged to papers supporting the Tories. In 1945 there was no television and it was possible to listen reflectively to appeals on the radio, cast in the traditional mould of speeches at public meetings. In 1983 the broadcasting time was still numerically equal, but the technique of making a television programme, in which the Tories were much more adept and sophisticated as well as better financed, was modelled on advertising. The Tory programmes were critically, if with reluctant admiration, analysed by the most perceptive observers of the campaign:

> The programmes adopted a rapid-fire approach in which dramatic visuals and frequent changes of shot (the average duration of which was under ten seconds over the first four programmes) drove the message home in a way which allowed no time for reflection . . . At its worst it led to comparisons between unemployment in Britain, Germany and Japan being fired at the viewer, lovingly double-checked in Central Office, yet utterly misleading. But before the brain could fully register this, the shot had raced on. [50]

The effects of manipulation and shock tactics, elbowing argument and debate aside, were reinforced by the incessant battering from the opinion polls (again, a contrast with 1945) which had become news events in themselves and were often the most prominent items on television and in the papers. After the election, the report from the London Labour Party noted sadly: 'Many agents told us that they went home from a hard, and what they thought was successful, day's campaigning only to learn of the latest opinion polls and become dispirited.'

This comment illustrates the salient fact that two campaigns were in progress: the one to which the agents, party members and volunteers devoted their time (and, unfortunately, their attention) and another which was passing over their heads. In the former, everything went well. The meetings were enthusiastic, concealing the fact that only about 2 per cent of the voters ever went to meetings, and then mostly to support their own side. The welcome given to Michael and other leaders in the streets was gratifying. The canvassing returns were good, though the regional organiser for Wales grasped that they were too good to be true, and wrote: 'The need for personal contact is still important, but our efforts in this field should now be to convince electors to vote for us, and not merely to identify our supporters, because we are finding that when they are identified they are not our supporters.'

But the experience of campaigning was heartening enough to be impossible to reconcile with newspaper reports and opinion polls which showed Labour heading for defeat. Michael, as much as anyone, shared in the puzzlement:

> Carmarthen was warm, expectant, exultant . . . Liverpool, too, overflowed with enthusiasm and high spirits . . . There *was* a new spirit of exhilaration among our own members, even of unity in the face of the enemy . . . There was a gulf indeed, wider than anything I had ever experienced before, between the fighting spirit in our rank and file and the mood of the general electorate. Another election altogether was being conducted on the television screens.[51]

Healey, in his post-election report, recognised that the election had been lost in the preceding two years: 'The party acquired a highly unfavourable public image, based on disunity, extremism, crankiness and general unfitness to govern.' But he went on to pinpoint the essential flaw in the conduct of the campaign:

> We did not properly appreciate the importance of the media, especially radio and television, through which the overwhelming majority of electors actually follow the election. We concentrated on traditional election methods, especially public meetings, at times to the detriment of getting the Party's spokesmen and message on to radio and television.

Because of this outdated approach, Michael shouldered a programme that, within twenty-three days, took him to eighty constituencies in all parts of the country. On 17 May, the day after his Glasgow meeting, he did four walkabouts in Lancashire towns and spoke at two outdoor meetings and one indoor meeting. In a shopping precinct at Skelmersdale, he was almost pushed through a plate-glass window by a crowd of young well-wishers. 'We'd have called the police if they'd been hostile, but they were on our side,' Clements recalls. In the mêlée, he was separated from Jill; she campaigned separately on subsequent days. On 19 May, he spoke at meetings in Banbury, Oxford and Slough, finding time to visit a hospital, a hostel for the mentally handicapped, a centre for the unemployed and the Banbury market. Another peak day was 1 June, filled with a press conference at Walworth Road, three walkabouts and five meetings. He stood up to the strain with unfailing resilience, and indeed he was in his element. But there was never enough time to rest, nor to reflect on strategy and consult with Healey or other colleagues, nor – and this was a fatal disadvantage – to see recordings of the day's television and follow the 'other campaign'.

In the propaganda battle, Labour never equalled Tory skill. The Tory posters and press advertisements, dishonest though they may have been, were cleverly devised, and rebuttals always came too late. It was only in February that Labour had, reluctantly overcoming rooted prejudices, commissioned a polling organisation, MORI, and an advertising agency, Johnny Wright. The agency produced the vacuous slogan: 'Think positive, act positive, vote Labour', which appeared at the end of every television broadcast. It is a measure of Michael's lack of control that he permitted an appeal coined by someone who could not tell an adjective from an adverb.

The campaign committee at Walworth Road, with twenty members and a fluctuating attendance, was much too big and pseudo-democratic to work as an effective directing staff. Mortimer, with his background in a minor trade union and ACAS, had neither the experience nor the flair for election politics. On 27 May, he astonished the press by suddenly announcing: 'At the campaign committee this morning we were all insistent that Michael Foot is the leader of the Labour Party and speaks for the party . . . The unanimous view of the campaign committee is that Michael Foot is the leader.' According to Michael: 'It wasn't a vote of confidence or anything of the sort. It was just an affable word of encouragement.'[52] But it naturally made the headlines and prompted the question of why the committee had felt it necessary to examine Michael's position.

Another gift to the Tories was Michael's appearance on the same platform as known Militants, including Derek Hatton in Liverpool and Pat Wall in Bradford, whose candidatures he had tried – but failed – to block. The reasonable excuse was that the meetings were in important towns with several constituencies and other candidates were on the platform too. But if Michael's tour had not taken him to so many places, the necessity would not have arisen.

Jill, meanwhile, was visiting constituencies in London and the south of England, including Reading. On 1 June, the *Reading Evening Post* quoted her as saying that Michael would resign as leader if Labour lost, and furthermore: 'Even if the party wins, I shouldn't think he would stay on for long because it would be time to make way for a younger man.' In itself, the statement was sensible enough. Had Michael become Prime Minister, he probably would have chosen to lay down the burden after a couple of years. The effect, however, was to create another press sensation and focus attention on Michael's age. Jill's recollection is that she had been chatting with Labour supporters and did not realise that a reporter was in the group. Hasty repair work proved unconvincing. Michael said: 'The story is based on a considerable misapprehension of what my wife said,' and Jill: 'One makes a remark which is twisted and distorted and taken out of context.'[53]

But these mishaps and organisational deficiencies, even taken together, do not account for the loss of the election. Aside from the disasters of the preceding two years, which really meant that the election was lost in advance, the defeat must be explained by Labour's failure to win the argument on the two issues which were chosen as its main themes: unemployment and disarmament. The impression that a Labour government would have no cure for unemployment, and might indeed make it worse, was given strength early in the campaign when the *Daily Mail* headlined a story that the Japanese car firm, Nissan, had decided to cancel its plans to build a large plant in Britain if Labour won and that 35,000 jobs would be forfeited. Nissan head office in Tokyo issued a denial, and it is still uncertain whether the story came from a junior executive or whether it was a pure fabrication. In any case, the damage had been done.

Unemployment had spread like a plague in Thatcher's first two years in power, touching a total of almost three million, but now it was falling. The fall was largely achieved by statistical manoeuvres, such as omitting men over sixty who were allegedly not 'available for work', but the figures caught the headlines; during the election campaign, they showed a fall of 121,000 in the last month. As for inflation, it was at its lowest rate since 1968.

Still, the economic issues were relatively fertile ground for Labour by comparison with nuclear disarmament. According to the polls, support for unilateral renunciation of nuclear weapons had slipped since 1981 from 32 per cent to 16 per cent. The Tories hammered at Labour's alleged intention of 'leaving Britain defenceless', and particularly at contradictions in Labour policy. Unilateral nuclear disarmament and disarmament by negotiation were both advocated in conference resolutions, which, as Michael had pointed out several times, were not always consistent with one another. The difficulties of the subject had been revealed to *Tribune* readers when Michael gave an interview to Chris Mullin in 1982:

There are many complications which can't be stated in simple terms . . . I don't believe it's fair for those who are unilateralists, as I am, to say we're not going to take any notice of the rest of the obligations and undertakings in party policy . . . I know there is some illogicality, people can say, in emphasising unilateral action and multilateral action, but it is much better to try to co-ordinate the two.[54]

A further problem was that Denis Healey, Labour's deputy leader and Shadow Foreign Secretary, was not a unilateralist and, despite his desire to keep in step with Michael and avoid causing embarrassment, could not pretend to be. Michael, for his part, could not disavow the hallowed beliefs of an old Aldermaston marcher. In an interview in October, he introduced the concept of gradual progress: 'What we want to do is get rid of those weapons as soon as we can, but I don't believe it can all be done in one fell swoop.' When the election came, he repeated this approach (in a television interview on 25 May): 'What we're going to try to do is to get rid of the nuclear arms race by a stage-by-stage process.'

The unavoidable question was: what about Polaris? The nuclear submarine, roving the Atlantic but based in Holy Loch, twenty miles from Glasgow, presented a clear danger of retaliation if it were ever to fire its missiles. Michael's Glaswegian friends, Norman and Janey Buchan, had campaigned against it with a song: 'It's suicide / To base it on the Clyde – / We don't want Polaris.' But, in the talks with Brezhnev, Michael and Healey had named Polaris as the weapon which Britain should relinquish in exchange for a Soviet relinquishment of the SS-20. It was Labour policy to give up Polaris as a matter of principle, and it was also Labour policy to bargain with it; the inconsistency was palpable. On 20 May, Healey came out with what most of the public accepted as a common-sense answer: 'We don't get rid of them [the submarines] unless the Russians cut their forces aimed at us . . . No trade unionist is going to succeed in a negotiation if he tells the employer he's going to give up the object of the negotiation anyway, whatever happens in the negotiations.'

When Michael was asked about it at his press conference on 23 May, Mortimer did not improve matters by trying to rule out the question because it was not on the agenda. The questioner insisted, and Michael explained: 'What we propose is that Polaris should be put into the negotiations'. Three days later, asked on television whether there were any circumstances in which he would keep Polaris, he replied: 'No, I don't believe there are.' The question persisted until, in a BBC interview on 6 June, Robin Day asked whether it was the case that Michael would never order or threaten its use. He replied: 'I can't conceive of any such circumstances in which it would be anything other than criminal insanity . . . To say that you're going to use a weapon which is going to involve mass suicide for this country and mass genocide as well, to say that you're going to use such a weapon is in itself incredible.'

The apparent rift between the leader and the deputy leader, inevitably magnified in the newspapers, would have been damaging in any case; but, just when the difficulties were at their worst, Jim Callaghan chose to exacerbate them. Speaking in his constituency on 25 May, he applauded the rejection of unilateralism by British governments, his own and (presumably) Thatcher's: 'Our refusal to give up arms unilaterally has brought better and more realistic proposals from the Soviet Union.' The Polaris submarines, he said, should be retained because 'they have a further life-span of ten to twelve years, and perhaps longer, as effective deterrents.'

The effect, as a politician so experienced as Callaghan must have been able to see, was disastrous. Since Michael and Healey were making efforts to mend the breach, the *Guardian* headline was apt: 'CALLAGHAN WRECKS POLARIS REPAIRS'. In Ian Aitken's words: 'The former Labour Prime Minister took the unprecedented step of repudiating the defence policy of his own party in the middle of a general election campaign.' The *Sunday Times* reported: 'Foot's supporters regard the Callaghan speech as a major act of betrayal.' Privately, the Welsh regional organiser told Walworth Road: 'The raising of the unilateralist issue by J. Callaghan certainly had an effect on the morale of activists in Wales and we lost a week of campaigning, due to this unnecessary speech.'

A year later, after Michael had criticised the speech with deliberate mildness in his post-election book, Callaghan wrote a letter of self-justification:

What you call a 'compromise' on Defence was to put it vulgarly a 'fudge'. . . The trouble with the non-nuclear strategy was that the British people saw it was a fudge and they didn't care for it. I was on the doorstep *every* day and listened to the direct questions that were put by Labour voters. Our policy was not credible *in their eyes* . . . My postbag will show that *our* people wanted me to speak about the issue; and with my background and my commitments in the past, I simply could not stomach our policy. I took no pleasure in it . . .

All I can say is that nothing would have made me swallow that policy – not even (I hope) the thumbscrews, but I am truly sorry to have added to your concerns. I hope and trust that we remain friends.

Labour had another ex-Prime Minister – Harold Wilson. Two days after Callaghan's speech, Wilson gave an interview to the *Daily Mail*. It appeared under the headline: 'WHERE MY PARTY HAS GONE WRONG'. Michael was criticised for tolerating Militant (in fact, he had taken action from which both Wilson and Callaghan had refrained), for 'pulling out an issue a day', and for subjecting the Labour Party to the power of the unions. The subject of Militant (the interview appeared on the day when Michael spoke with Pat Wall) and the subject of union power were two of the major themes trumpeted by the Tories in the campaign. Michael's subsequent comment was bitter but just: 'Mrs Thatcher herself could have approved every word. The whole piece might have been another brilliant advertisement designed by Saatchi and Saatchi.' He made a distinction between Callaghan's speech – 'an expression of view on the subject about which he felt most deeply' – and Wilson's interview – 'a gratuitous display of vanity'.[55] Wilson's letter of excuse was decidedly lamer and less credible than Callaghan's:

Let me say right away that I did *not* write the article which appeared in the *Mail* during the election. [It appeared as an interview and the *Mail* never presented it as an article.] I never put pen to paper. What happened was that on 26 May, I think, I had a long-standing engagement involving a speech in the City . . . The *Mail* lobby man was there and thumbed a lift back to the House with my driver. He was sitting in front of me and I could not see that he was writing . . . What he put together was based on his own construction . . . I very much regret that you were at the receiving end of all this skulduggery.

On 2 June Michael was in Bristol speaking for Tony Benn, who noted in his diary: 'He was friendly.' Benn's seat, Bristol South-east, had been wiped out by redistribution. He honourably turned down the offer of a safe seat in Scotland, was beaten by Michael Cocks in selection for Bristol South, and ended up as candidate for Bristol East, which was un-winnable. Michael went on to Plymouth and made a vehement attack on David Owen, who had been elected as a Labour MP for Michael's old seat, Devonport, and was fighting to hold it for the SDP. Michael noted: 'No one I met that Thursday believed he would win Devonport, and nor did I'[56] – but Owen did win it.

On the last Sunday of the campaign, Michael was in Hyde Park to greet another March for Jobs; the marchers, or some of them, had tramped from Glasgow to London. That afternoon, Thatcher was speaking at Wembley to a Young Conservative rally. Also in the spotlight was the comedian Kenny Everett, who began his act by yelling 'Let's bomb Russia!' and followed it up with 'Let's kick Michael Foot's stick away!' The *Daily Mirror* reported: 'They cheered their heads off.' Indefatigably,

Michael went to Birmingham, Manchester and Kent before reaching Ebbw Vale on the eve of poll. Touring Manchester on the open top of a bus, he was hit by a tomato, but the thrower was not representative of what *The Times* called 'cheering and affectionate crowds'.

Up to the end, a strange optimism pervaded the Labour camp. The national agent, David Hughes, reckoned on a surge of support and assured the campaign committee on the eve of poll: 'Labour canvassers report that they began to detect this surge on Monday of this week and they report that it has increased considerably day by day as polling day approaches.' The truth was exactly the opposite. The canvassers were themselves deceived, as the East Midlands organiser concluded later: 'Many former Labour supporters were reluctantly withdrawing their support and did not want to tell us . . . We have been guilty of talking among ourselves and not talking and listening enough to those whom we wish to represent.'

In his final speech in Ebbw Vale, Michael spoke anxiously and movingly about the human as well as the economic consequences of unemployment. He referred to Toxteth (in Liverpool) and Brixton, where there had been serious riots since the Tories came to power and hope receded for many young people. He said:

> If they say to young people here: 'You are not going to have any life in our country, no jobs for you' . . . our young people will not endure that insult to their manhood and their womanhood . . . To say it to growing legions of them, which is what is happening up and down the country today: I say that way lies disaster as well as shame. If our people are instructed that political action cannot produce economic results, then again, as Nye taught us, the consequences for our democratic political institutions will be immeasurable.

His peroration was:

> I am not seeking to diminish the nature of the previous battles fought here in Ebbw Vale, Abertillery and Tredegar: battles fought by our party and our movement when our resources were much more slender than those we have now; fought by people who were fighting almost on empty stomachs; fought by people who had to risk their own homes and their own lives and their own families in order to stand for democratic socialism . . . Let us go about these great tasks in the spirit they gave us. They gave us the greatest democratic movement in the world. We believe that here in these valleys, here in Wales, we have shown how that gift should be treasured.

The results, as they came in during the night of 9 June and the next day, were a terrible shock for Labour's self-deluding optimists and almost as much of a shock for those – Michael among them – who had foreseen defeat but not anticipated its scale. His own majority was bigger than ever, thanks to the redistribution which had given him 20,000 additional voters in Brynmawr and Abertillery, but this was little consolation. Nationally, the Tories had 43.5 per cent of the votes, Labour 28.3 and the Alliance 26.[57] The Labour share of the poll, eclipsing the low point of 1931, was the worst since the Labour Party became a serious contestant in 1918. Clearly, Labour voters had turned to the Alliance in unexpected numbers and it was only by a narrow margin that Labour held second place. A detailed analysis only made things gloomier. Labour did not have majority support among either men or women, among either the old or the young, among either skilled or unskilled workers, or even among the unemployed.

In the new House of Commons, the Tories had a majority that gave them a revenge for 1945, with 396 members against Labour's 209. Tony Benn was missing from the depleted Labour benches; so were Joan Lestor, Albert Booth, David Ennals and Oswald O'Brien, whose tenure as MP for Darlington was about the briefest in political history.

The peculiarities of the British electoral system ensured that the Alliance, despite its percentage of the popular vote, had only twenty-three MPs. The Liberals were up from eleven seats to seventeen, but the SDP was down to six. Only five of the defectors from Labour won re-election under their new colours; they did not include Shirley Williams or Bill Rodgers. The emergence of the Liberals as the senior partner set up strains which, eventually, the Alliance could not contain. The Scottish Nationalists and Plaid Cymru kept two seats each. But only close students of politics were interested in the precise make-up of the opposition. The salient feature of the next period of British politics was the Tory supremacy.

5

A car with a police escort roared up the M4 through the night, touching a hundred miles an hour. Michael and Jill were on their way to Walworth Road to thank the staff for their election work. When they arrived at 5.25 in the morning, they found the building almost deserted. Jim Mortimer was still there, but few others had cared to stay and contemplate the wreckage of their hopes.

The press quoted Michael as saying: 'It was a deeply reactionary and offensive campaign fought by our opponents. That makes all the more scandalous and unforgivable the treachery of those who helped to enable the Tories to win – defectors from our own ranks.' Another comment was: 'It was the verdict of the electorate not only on our campaign but also on the whole period prior to it.' But on Sunday, 12 June, when he went north to speak at the Northumberland miners' gala, he struck a more cheerful note: 'I'm rejuvenated already . . . We've had a setback, but it's only a setback . . . I believe that the Labour movement over the coming weeks and months will greatly renew its strength.'

What the Labour movement had to do in those weeks and months was to choose a new leader. On the morning after the election, Moss Evans of the TGWU and Clive Jenkins of ASTMS breakfasted and agreed that, in the predictable event of Michael's resignation, they would pledge their votes to Neil Kinnock. In the evening, Jenkins was at the Foots' house for supper. Michael asked: 'What will happen if I resign?' Jill quickly supplied the answer: 'They'll nominate Neil.' Jenkins explained that two big unions could already be counted as Neil's supporters. Michael expressed his satisfaction and phoned Neil to tell him.[58]

The executive of ASTMS met on Saturday. Jenkins told them that Michael was declining renomination, and they decided unanimously to nominate Kinnock. Jenkins sent out a press release to this effect and informed television viewers himself on the Sunday morning programme, *Weekend World*. Having (so he believed) stage-managed Michael's decision to stand in 1980, he was happy to stage-manage Michael's departure. He explained later that his executive happened to be due for a meeting and it happened to be the right time of year to consider nominations; no one believed that this was pure chance. Tom McCaffrey, as head of Michael's office, was annoyed. As he saw it, Michael was due to offer his resignation formally to the NEC on the following Wednesday and Jenkins had robbed the occasion of its dignity. However, Michael had no feeling that Jenkins had behaved badly, and was glad to see the Kinnock campaign getting off to a flying start. Michael and Clive, with their wives, went to the cinema on Tuesday evening and were photographed chatting amicably. They saw a political satire, *The Ploughman's Lunch*.

In theory, Denis Healey was a possible candidate for the leadership, or even perhaps the obvious candidate. Nevertheless, he would be seventy by the time another election came round and he realised, or was told, that there was a strong feeling in favour of skipping a generation. Neil Kinnock, forty-one years old, would be the youngest leader in Labour's history. Roy Hattersley, who emerged as the candidate of the right, was fifty. Peter Shore (fifty-nine) and Eric Heffer (sixty-one) were nominated, but attracted little support. John Silkin, for once, did not enter the lists. Tony Benn, as he was no longer an MP, was not eligible.

At the time and later, it was said that Michael exerted himself to ensure that Kinnock was his successor. It was true that he had a high regard for Kinnock's talents, and Kinnock was the accredited standard-bearer of the Tribunite left. Few people were more warmly welcomed at Pilgrim's Lane than Neil and Glenys. However, the 'father–son relationship', which made a neat story for profile-writers in the press, was somewhat exaggerated. It was in Neil's character, and also in his interests politically, to be 'his own man', and this was understood by Michael. In any case, there was no need to worry about his chances in the leadership election. From the day of the nominations, a Kinnock victory was taken as a foregone conclusion. When the votes were cast at the party conference in October, Kinnock had 71 per cent, Hattersley 19 per cent, Heffer 6 per cent and Shore 3 per cent. It had been agreed that the winner would support the runner-up for the deputy leadership, so Hattersley moved into that position.

Neil made a short speech, devoted partly to a determination to lead Labour to a future victory and partly to a tribute to Michael:

> We thank Michael Foot for his special strengths of decency and courage in the face of the unmitigated adversity of the last three years. I want to thank him for a past, present and future in which he is and will be a glowing inspiration to all of us who believe that the purpose of socialism is the gaining of liberty for humankind.

Officially, Michael was still the leader until the end of the conference and it was his duty to make the main speech from the platform, known constitutionally as the parliamentary report. He spoke, as usual, without a written text, he digressed to tell funny stories and he was aware that he was going on too long. As he told the delegates, he had been warned by Jill not to 'do a Beethoven'. He explained: 'She thinks – maybe she is misguided about this – that Beethoven had a bit of difficulty in finishing some of his symphonies.' The core of the speech, however, carried a message that evoked an assenting response from everyone in the hall and even from the press table:

> I understand the scale of the defeat which we suffered at the general election . . . I am deeply ashamed that we should have allowed the fortunes of our country and the fortunes of the people who look to us

for protection most . . . to sink to such a low ebb . . . I'm not one of those who believe you can blame the election defeat solely on the media or the newspapers . . . [but] the debasement of journalism is worse in Fleet Street today than at any time I can recall . . . Fleet Street is a place where Gresham's Law applies with particular ferocity. The bad drives out the good, the evil drives out the shoddy, the tenth-rate drives out the second- or third-rate . . . Every decent journalist in the country knows the truth of what I'm saying.

Then he stressed once again the theme that, despite all the confusions, he had tried to pursue during the election campaign:

The nuclear powers are not the only countries in the world. It's not only the Russians or the Americans or the British or the French or the Chinese who are the only people with a right to speak; all the others can be blown to pieces too . . . We will use all the efforts, all the power, all the imagination, all the new cohesion that I believe we can have in our party . . . to try to stop this hideous nuclear arms race.

He ended, as he had so often, with a quotation from Aneurin Bevan, taken from a speech made on 10 November 1937: 'Nye said on the day before Armistice Day 1937: "We don't come here to bury the dead – we come here to bring life to the living." That's what we are doing at this conference – life to the living – both in our own country and elsewhere, a new hope for our stricken country and our frightened world.'

The three-minute standing ovation at the conference is sometimes a synthetic routine. On this day in 1983, no one doubted that it was far more than that.

— *Chapter 15* —

RECESSIONAL

I

In the months following the general election, Michael wrote a book about the campaign. The news that he was writing it was received with some surprise; no other party leader, winner or loser, had reverted so quickly and in such detail to the story, although some had presented their reflections or grievances in their memoirs. Not everyone grasped, even when *Another Heart and Other Pulses* was published, what its purpose was. Michael told the readers, rather negatively: 'This book does not purport to be a diary or a batch of memoirs or a polemic or a personal apologia or, least of all, I trust, a mere record of the 1983 general election. It does contain a fair dose of all these ingredients.'[1]

His real aim was to express the significance of the election as a confrontation between two political and social ideologies and, beyond that, two concepts of morality. This would have been clearer if all readers had known the context of the title in a sonnet by Keats, which Michael (or the publisher, Collins) unfortunately neglected to print as an epigraph:

> Other spirits there are, standing apart
> Upon the forehead of the age to come.
> These, these will give the world another heart
> And other pulses. Hear ye not the hum
> Of mighty workings –
> Listen awhile ye nations and be dumb.

The structure of the book was a day-by-day chronicle of the campaign, which did give it the appearance of 'a mere record'. A good deal of space was devoted to the injustices of which the Labour Party, or Michael personally, had cause to complain: the biased press headlines, the scare about the Nissan factory, the allegation that Michael was being pushed into the background and Denis Healey was taking over the campaign. British convention despises a bad loser, and no very positive effect was created by raking over such episodes. The justification was that the imbalance in the press and the exploitation of opinion polls amounted to a qualitative change in the way elections were fought, and a real danger to democracy. The book did impel serious readers to think about these issues, and some who were not Labour supporters found themselves obliged to agree with Michael.

However, the vital message was stated in the concluding chapter, 'The Hope Next Time'. Here, Michael insisted that 'politics are concerned with competing philosophies, moral choices, historical developments, designs for the future'. He recognised the truth of a charge made by Barbara Castle: 'that we had allowed Mrs Thatcher and her Conservative Party to seize the moral initiative'. He went on:

> The safest rule with Mrs Thatcher herself is to assume that she believes what she says . . . She does believe that it is these individualist virtues which make the world go round . . . Yes, there was and there is such a thing as Thatcherism . . . the moral shield for the re-establishment of that older society, the full-scale counter-revolution on which we are embarked not only here in Britain but in many other parts of the Western world.[2]

What was needed, he maintained,

> is the exposure of the moral insufficiency and shoddiness of Thatcherism, and how it can be replaced only by the morally superior Socialist society. This is not to claim that politics is solely concerned with morals; it is concerned too with clashing interests, the guiding of historical forces. But if Socialists desert the arena of morals the Conservatives may seek to occupy the forsaken territory. And furthermore, the Socialist case, the case for collective action to deal with deep-seated wrongs and evils, *and as the only effective means of dealing with them*, has always been much more of a moral case than many Socialists, and not only the Marxists, have been willing to admit.

Then came a melancholy but eloquent prediction:

> The profound immorality of the Thatcherite society will be exposed year by year as the economic crisis of the 1980s deepens. The interval between slumps will grow briefer, as they have done already in the past decade. The clash between rich and poor will become sharper and less easily masked. The condemnation of greater stretches of our country to industrial dereliction and social degradation will grow more widespread and intolerable. Our precious Earth will grow more polluted.

Britain will cease to be a great industrial nation . . . Some of these will have been economic choices, choices made in our thraldom to a deadening economic theory. But they are moral choices too; moral certainly in the sense that the only alternative, the only remedy, must be sought in collective action.

2

If there was one year in which the conflict between the values of Thatcherism and those of 'collective action to deal with deep-seated wrongs and evils' was played out with particular intensity, it was 1984. That year was also unique in being observed, not as an anniversary or centenary, but as the title of a prophetic – or, as its author intended – a minatory book. While the paperback trade and television profited from *1984* in a way that might have drawn sardonic comments from George Orwell, Michael unveiled a plaque on the Hampstead house in which the writer had briefly lived, and Paul Foot delivered an incisive lecture on his life and work.

The great drama of 1984 was the miners' strike, which made Arthur Scargill a hero to his admirers and a bogeyman to the Tory press to a degree not exceeded even by Tony Benn. It began in March when the National Coal Board ordered the closure of some Yorkshire pits, of which at least one, Cortonwood, had been recently given an assurance that it was safe. There was never much doubt that Mrs Thatcher was throwing down the gauntlet to destroy Britain's most militant trade union and intimidate all those who resisted her economic policies. She spoke darkly of 'the enemy within', and *The Times* declared: 'There is a war on. It is an undeclared civil war instigated by Mr Scargill, his squads of pickets and his political associates.' Michael wrote a letter of protest:

Representing a mining constituency, I believe these insults add greatly to the injuries they feel. If it takes a long time to restore a decent, democratic tone of controversy in this country, *The Times* and Mrs Thatcher will bear much of the responsibility.

There is no war in this country as described by *The Times*, unless it be the old class war which H. G. Wells used to define as a pastime of the ruling class, and it is both foolish and dangerous to resort to such terms. There is a most serious industrial dispute which started and has continued partly because Mrs Thatcher's ministers, with the insensate support of *The Times*, abandoned all the normal processes of industrial conciliation . . . If the closure of Cortonwood was justified and can be thus repeated in the same manner, all the miners' fears are upheld and fortified.[3]

Michael was indeed keenly concerned, if only because the Marine pit at Cwm, in Ebbw Vale, was a crucial source of employment in the valley after the closure of the steelworks. The miners of South Wales played a loyal and honourable part in the strike, and it was the only coalfield in which there were no blacklegs, and no pits could be worked, until the final hopeless months of the struggle. At the Marine pit, not a man deserted the strike until the very end.

At the same time, the NUM leaders in Wales realised from the start that the chances of victory were poor. March was the wrong month to begin a strike, coal stocks were unlikely to be exhausted, foreign coal was freely imported, it was clear from the first days that pits in Nottinghamshire and other districts would go on working, and the government was determined to break the strike, using the police as a paramilitary force. In private, the Welshmen were strongly critical of Scargill for launching the strike without a national ballot, for scorning the efforts made by Labour MPs, particularly by Stan Orme, to get a negotiated settlement, and for his 'verge of victory' rhetoric which was increasingly at odds with the facts.

After the strike had gone on for almost a year and had plunged the mining communities into acute deprivation, it had to be admitted that the government was getting through the winter without any of the emergency measures that had been necessary in 1972 and 1974. The NUM was now ready for negotiation, but the Coal Board, clearly under orders from a government that pretended to be merely holding the ring, demanded an acceptance of the closures before any peace talks. ACAS, the conciliation service which had been created by Michael precisely to forestall such a deadlock, had never been allowed to step in. Michael spoke angrily in the Commons: 'ACAS would have told them that such a demand was intolerable . . . How many months did we have to listen to the tale of combined fraud and deceit from Ministers that they were not intervening? . . . The Prime Minister's claque was sent in to destroy any chances of a decent honourable agreement.'[4]

In this desperate situation, it was the Welsh miners who insisted on an orderly decision that the strike was over, rather than a ragged drift back to work. In the valleys, the miners marched to the pitheads in disciplined columns headed by their cherished brass bands, showing their unity even in defeat. Yet it was a bitter moment, and the bitterness would not soon be healed. A 'Welsh day' debate gave Michael the opportunity to say:

> Month after month, year after year, there will be more closures. Shops are closing in the streets of Welsh towns. We have to fight against the same type of problems as those against which we fought during the twenties and thirties. Of course the valley towns will not give in. The Tories will not beat us today any more than they were able to do before. We shall fight them at every turn.[5]

There were indeed more closures. A year after the end of the strike, the Coal Board ordered the closure of the Marine pit, although the manager as well as the workers argued that it was in good shape for staying in production. Out of more than a hundred pits that had been thriving in South Wales at its industrial peak, and twenty-two that were still open at the time of the 1984 strike, only one survived into the 1990s.

Michael was again a back-bencher, as he had been before 1970, free to speak as the spirit moved him, ready to intervene on a wide range of topics, and always able to fill the House. He supported the bill to protect and advance women's rights moved by Jo Richardson:

> Just as in race discrimination it is necessary to have the assistance of the law to sustain decent behaviour, so that is also necessary with sexual equality . . . In some areas there is no provision whatever for any type of nursery education . . . Women are being denied the right to choose. They apparently have the right to choose whether they want to work . . . but by being denied nursery education for their children, the mass of women are in reality denied such choices.[6]

He managed to bring several subjects into a debate on the environment, starting with the endangered future of Hampstead Heath in view of what he called 'the fatal, miserable and squalid decision to abolish the Greater London Council'. He warned: 'The organisations that have protected Hampstead Heath in the past, which have said that every inch of it is in effect holy territory and not to be invaded, destroyed or vandalised, will fight once more to protect it.' Then he moved on to the cuts in the budget for school books implemented by the Thatcher government: 'The trouble is that a strong streak of barbarism runs through the government, which is illustrated by their elevation of money to the highest place in their estimate of what should be done . . . At times of stress and strain, when people's lives are being uprooted, the government should increase support.' Before he sat down, he had castigated the government for its refusal to return the Elgin marbles to

Greece: 'Their attitude is all part of their streak of barbarism, but I expect a solution from the next civilised government we have.'[7]

He spoke in support of a bill moved by Janet Fookes, the Tory MP for the Drake division of Plymouth, to authorise the televising of debates. It was argued that this would change the way the House conducted itself, but Michael pointed out that the same objection had been made to newspaper reporting: 'The character of that eighteenth-century House was changed by the reporting of proceedings, and a very good thing too . . . Parliament and the country have the power, strength and ability to take the changes and to weave them into past traditions and prepare them for the future.'[8]

He was still closely following Indian affairs and corresponding with Indira Gandhi. The Sikhs in the Punjab were demanding a separate Sikh state, to be called Khalistan. This demand, pursued by methods of violence and terrorism, ran counter to the concept of a secular India and Mrs Gandhi was determined not to yield. When armed Sikh militants barricaded themselves in the Golden Temple at Amritsar, she ordered the army to storm it. In Britain, a Khalistan government in exile was formed, headed by Karamjit Singh Chahal. There were bitter complaints in India because he was allowed to carry on his agitation and raise funds to sustain the terrorists.

There was violence in Kashmir too. In its overwhelmingly Moslem population, large numbers had never accepted its accession to India. Mrs Gandhi learned with indignation that a Labour MP, Richard Caborn, had assured a delegation that a Labour government would support self-determination for Kashmir. She wrote to Michael: 'All this talk of self-determination in Kashmir is quite meaningless,' and asked whether she ought to complain to Neil Kinnock. Michael replied:

I can understand how infuriating these reports may be when they reach India, but I doubt whether it is necessary or desirable for you to intervene . . . If any proposal were to arise about the alteration of the Labour Party attitude towards Kashmir, I can assure you there are some of us here who would take part in the discussion and remember how the question was settled before.

In October 1984, Indira Gandhi was shot dead by her Sikh bodyguard. In a frenzy of revenge, thousands of Sikhs were massacred in Delhi. Her son Rajiv, former airline pilot and reluctant politician, became Prime Minister and won a landslide election victory. In January 1985, Michael was in India again as guest speaker at a Rotary conference. He had a talk with Rajiv, who complained about the tolerance that the

Khalistan organisation received in Britain. Michael conveyed these complaints to the Foreign Office and also to the Attorney-General, but it was never possible to reconcile sympathy for India with the protection of freedom of expression.

'Violence, non-violence and the moral order' was one of the themes for discussion at a conference in memory of Indira Gandhi, held in Delhi in January 1987. Michael took part together with a remarkable assemblage of personalities, including Germaine Greer, Archbishop Huddleston, Jack Lang, Iris Murdoch, E. P. Thompson and Simone Weil. On the back of his programme, Michael noted a quotation from Voltaire: 'Those who can make us believe absurdities can also make us commit atrocities.'

Through 1985 and 1986, the Labour Party was regaining its morale under Neil Kinnock's leadership and preparing for the next election. Michael was busy with a new literary project and, now that he had no leadership responsibilities, was free to retire from the House of Commons if he chose; but there were no hints, let alone pressure, from his constituency party and he decided to stay in the Commons, at least for one more term. What he certainly did not intend to do was to go to the House of Lords. Although it had become pardonable for people with impeccable socialist beliefs to accept peerages – including Jennie Lee, Barbara Castle and Fenner Brockway – Michael preferred not to contradict his denunciations of patronage and privilege. One day in 1986, lunching with Sheila Noble of the *Tribune* staff, who had been brought up as a Catholic, he wrote and signed this document: 'I hereby swear (affirm), in response to an absolute pledge from Sheila Noble (née Catholic) that she will not be entering the kingdom of heaven, that I give the same assurance respecting the House of Lords.'

The election came in May 1987. Michael spoke in a number of constituencies, mostly in Wales, and gave more time to canvassing in his own constituency than he had been able to manage when in the party leadership. His majority rose to 27,861. But, in view of the unprecedented swing that would have been needed for Labour to win the election, the Tories were confident of retaining power, and shed only twenty of the seats they had won in 1983. Michael would never sit on the government benches again.

3

After the publication of *Another Heart and Other Pulses*, Michael's next book was a compilation, *Loyalists and Loners*. Like *Debts of Honour*, it consisted of essays devoted to men and women whom he wished to commemorate. Of these twenty-eight essays, some ran to only a few pages and were simply reprints of articles or book reviews, some were expanded from their original form, and some were written specially for the book. The subjects were mostly political contemporaries – including Jennie Lee, Barbara Castle and Tony Benn – but the collection also reached into the past to discuss Lady Astor and George Orwell, and further to pay tribute to Herzen, Heine and Stendhal. It appeared in 1986. It is still well worth reading for a scattering of pungent phrases and thought-provoking judgements, but for Michael it was an easy task while he prepared to tackle a major work, *The Politics of Paradise*. These three books were published by Collins; Michael's dealings with the firm were satisfactory enough, but he ended the connection when it was acquired by Rupert Murdoch.

Published in 1988, *The Politics of Paradise* – Michael's 'vindication' of Byron – is, next to his biography of Bevan, his most substantial work. It has 397 pages and was written in two years, an extraordinary feat for a man in his seventies who was also a dutiful constituency MP and was steadily producing book reviews for the *Observer*, *Tribune* and the *Hampstead and Highgate Express*. It is hard to say whether the pace of writing is more remarkable than the range of Michael's reading (especially in view of his limited eyesight). He read all of Byron's poetry, letters and journals, which fill several volumes; he was able to refer to deleted or altered lines in the poems, to be found in manuscript, and to Byron's only short story, which was never published and was discovered in the archives of the publisher, Murray, in 1985. This scrupulous reading yielded a title, for it was Byron, in a letter explaining the purport of his verse play, *Cain*, who dashed off a phrase about 'the politics of Paradise'. Moreover, Michael read an impressive number of the books written about Byron from the 1830s to the present and praised their insights, debated their interpretations or denounced their slanders in lengthy footnotes.

There was a certain affinity between Michael and Byron himself. Both had Scottish mothers who were women of strong character; and, although most people would place Byron as an aristocrat, he inherited his title unexpectedly from an uncle at the age of eleven after spending his childhood years, as one authority quoted in a footnote put it, 'in middle-class and pious circles' – like the young Michael Foot, in fact. It seems that in his early years he read *Don Quixote*, *Roderick Random* and a good deal of history and 'acquired an intimate knowledge of the Bible'.

It was, in large part, the idea of 'vindication' that spurred Michael to write the book. In his lifetime, Byron had scandalised respectable society both by his personal life and by his writings – 'it will be impossible for any lady to allow *Don Juan* to be seen on her table', one critic declared in tones that remind us of the prosecuting counsel in the *Lady Chatterley* trial. The predominant view was one of shocked condemnation even in the early twentieth century, when a considered view (voiced, incidentally, by a descendant of Coleridge) was: 'It was not only the loftier and wholesome poetry of Wordsworth and of Tennyson which averted enthusiasm from Byron, not only moral earnestness and religious revival, but the optimism and the materialism of commercial prosperity'[9] – a sentence which can well be seen as a challenge to Michael Foot. In 1924 the governing clerics of Westminster Abbey were still rejecting a plea for a Byron plaque, which was eventually granted in May 1968 (a highly appropriate date). Michael's book was published in 1988, the bicentenary of Byron's birth. He was wryly amused when a card from Geoffrey Goodman, posted in Moscow, carried a Byron commemorative stamp; the British Post Office had declined to produce one. 'Either they had never heard of Byron or they had heard stories about his misdemeanours,' Michael remarked, pouring scorn on the postal philistines in a Commons debate on the arts. He wound up: 'For generations the truth about Byron was suppressed, but he has won through in the end.'[10]

Part of the truth about Byron – an aspect to which Michael, unlike most biographers, gave careful and ample attention – was that he was seriously concerned about the political problems of his time. He was a young man when the ideals of the French Revolution were being tarnished by the despotism of Napoleon; everyone who had been inspired by those ideals faced the dilemma of either renouncing them, like Wordsworth, or remaining loyal to them despite the disappointment. Few readers grasp – but Michael pointed out – that this faith without illusions gives full meaning to the familiar lines: 'Yet, Freedom, yet . . .' It was a dilemma of a kind that had recurred in Michael's own youth. An intriguing essay by Isaac Deutscher draws a comparison between men who maintained their revolutionary ideals in Napoleon's time and socialists who refused to abandon the ideals of the Russian Revolution because of Stalin.[11]

The most startling of these correspondences was a poem entitled 'Darkness', written by Byron in 1816. It is not very well known; after discovering it, Michael began to read it aloud to friends in considerable excitement. The opening lines will demonstrate the point:

> I had a dream, which was not all a dream,
> The bright sun was extinguish'd, and the stars
> Did wander darkling in the eternal space . . .

> And men forgot their passions in the dread
> Of this their desolation; and all hearts
> Were chill'd into a selfish prayer for light:
> And they did live by watchfires – and the thrones,
> The palaces of crowned kings – the huts,
> The habitations of all things which dwell,
> Were burnt for beacons; cities were consumed . . .

A century and a half after the poem was written, thinking people were concerned about the devastating effects of nuclear weapons ('cities were consumed') and then in the 1980s about the threat of the 'nuclear winter' – the obscuring of the sun's light, always a source and symbol of human happiness. Michael had made speech after speech about these dangers, which weighed inexorably on his mind. It was uncanny to find that a poem written in 1816 'describes what might happen more graphically than the modern nuclear scientists have been able to do'.[12] And Michael's commentary pressed home another point: Byron did not confine himself to prophecy, but denounced 'the makers of wars and those who offer the altars and trumpets of religion to excuse what they achieve, the ultimate desolation'.[13]

Once Michael began to extend his reading of Byron, he felt the fascination that only two other writers had exerted upon him – Swift and Hazlitt. They were all subjects for his 'vindication', and he gave them all a place in his book. He used Hazlitt as a sort of prism, viewing Byron's creative achievement through the thinking of the most perceptive contemporary critic. He had, in fact, thought of writing a book about Hazlitt; but Byron had priority, so the potential Hazlitt biography took the form of a long opening chapter in *The Politics of Paradise*, with the somewhat odd result that readers did not come across Byron until page 72. A particularly awkward aspect of the matter was that Hazlitt never appreciated Byron properly and was indeed hostile to him, on one occasion calling him a coxcomb and on another occasion writing: 'I do not mean to vindicate the immorality or misanthropy in that poem [*Don Juan*] – perhaps his lameness was to blame for this defect.' The best that Michael could do was to regret that Byron and Hazlitt never met and got on to terms of mutual understanding, and to comment sadly: 'By some miserable intervention of fate they were always finding themselves at cross purposes.'[14]

Swift presented an easier problem, for Byron, towards the end of his life, came to admire Swift almost as much as his literary idol, Pope. When he sailed on his last journey to Greece, he took with him Swift's collected works in nineteen volumes (no question of excess baggage arose). Swift's incisive wit, his savagery when roused to indignation, his denunciation of the futility and absurdity of war, his contempt for the pomposity of power, his frank enjoyment of sexual pleasure – all these found an echo with Byron.

As everyone knows, Byron's sexual impulses were powerful and unashamed (there are still people who know hardly anything else about him). However, Byron never confused sex with love or gave them the same value. It was W. H. Auden who pointed out (as Michael noted) that Don Juan, in the course of a very long narrative poem, has full relationships with only four women; Byron's hero has nothing in common with the calculating scalp-collector of Molière's play and Mozart's opera. What Byron proved, in life and with the pen, was that he was a man who understood women – and they understood him. Indeed, Michael offered a thesis of his own: 'The women understood Byron better than the men: Goethe's daughter-in-law better than Goethe himself; Lady Melbourne better than her husband; Jane Welsh Carlyle better than Carlyle; Mary Shelley (marginally) better than Shelley; Fanny Brawne better than John Keats.'[15] Another point made by Michael was that the women who were important in Byron's life, starting with his remarkable mother, influenced his ideas. In 1792, a year when the guillotined aristocrats were martyrs in most British eyes, Byron's mother was writing that she was on the opposite side to her family and she was 'quite a Democrat' – an assertion as bold as being 'quite a Communist' in McCarthyite America.

Teresa Guiccioli, the woman whom Byron loved most deeply, was dear to him because of her ardent dedication to the cause of Italian liberation as well as for other reasons. Two verses of *Don Juan* commemorate the daily ride that the lovers took through the Ravenna pine forest, passing the neglected tomb of Dante, a poet of whom Teresa knew long stretches by heart. Byron, the exile from England, was bound to feel in tune with Dante, the exile from Florence. Above all, he responded to Dante as the poet not only of Florence or Rome or Milan, but of Italy – an Italy, in the nineteenth as in the thirteenth century, fragmented, parcelled out among petty tyrants, and a prey to predators from north of the Alps. It was then – because of Teresa, because of Dante, and because he had found a new homeland – that, as Michael wrote, 'his political association became something much more real, an immediate throbbing commitment to the Italian cause'. He was influenced, he learned and he changed. As Michael wrote a few pages later: 'Byron's political view was always being propelled forward by his own reading of the events he saw around him, by the spectacle of the human cruelties he saw inflicted, or by the resistance to such encroaching horrors.'[16] Thus, in 1821, he and Teresa identified themselves passionately with what became an abortive national uprising and saw their friends executed or imprisoned. He wrote to an English friend: 'There will be blood shed like water, and tears like mist; but the peoples will conquer in the end. I shall not live to see it but I foresee it.'

Yet Byron the fighter for freedom was also Byron the hater of war, wrestling with the same dilemmas that confronted Michael Foot in a political lifetime that stretched from the Oxford Union debate of 1933 to the Gulf war of 1991. In 1809, he witnessed the ferocity of the Peninsular war and wrote: 'The barbarities on both sides are shocking.' It could be said of Byron, as Michael said of Swift: 'He was concerned with the question of how to destroy injustice without the world destroying itself.' And the problem was rendered more agonising because the barbarities of war were permitted by a God assumed to be both omnipotent and benevolent. Byron had rejected conventional Christianity, but he could not divest himself of belief in some kind of God. At times, he found himself denouncing God as he would have denounced an infinitely powerful king or emperor.

He uttered his defiance in his epic, *Cain*, over which argument still rages. Only such an iconoclast as Byron could have made a defence of the original murderer, held up to reprobation by centuries of theology and literature. Michael understood the purpose of *Cain*, but was nevertheless amazed:

> As he felt his full powers as a poet, he wanted to settle his scores with his old Calvinistic God . . . Byron examined the facts honestly, as he often did, and found them shameful and shocking and insulting to his reason and his humanity. Above all, the persistence of cruelty and torture, the way men and women were ready to flay one another, and the animals too, might not this evil tradition owe something to the burning sacrifices which we had been taught to bow down before and adore? . . . The idea of choosing Cain, the first murderer, to confound the Christians can still stun the imagination.[17]

Byron was not the first great English poet to present the devil as a more fascinating, and indeed more heroic, figure than the deity. But even Milton's Satan did not make out a braver or a more persuasive case than Byron's Lucifer. To Cain's baffled query: 'But why *war*?', Lucifer replies:

> You have forgotten the denunciation
> Which drove your race from Eden: war with all things
> And death to all things and disease to most things
> And pangs and bitterness. These were the fruits
> Of the forbidden tree.

It was not, in other words, the sin of Adam, nor the weakness of Eve, nor the machinations of the serpent (who was not, as Byron, the student of the Bible, noted, instructed by any devil) that brought murder or war or death into the world – it was the vengeful and pitiless decree of God. If this decree was divine, the reproach levelled by Byron was human – and, in the profoundest sense, humane.

So Michael, in his closing pages, linked Byron's message of imaginative humanity to the perils of our own time and to our chances of salvation:

> It was all these virtues and passions, raised to their highest pitch, which made him the poet who exposed most faithfully what was truly meant by modern war . . . What other poet has shown so resolute, so revolutionary, a political will? . . . He told in *Darkness* how warring creeds could destroy the universe: the claim is not too high . . . He wrote with all his wits about him, and with a contempt for contemporary restraints which transfigures his whole life. He knew what he was doing, and would not allow anyone or anything to stop him. Such courage and such imagination can save us.[18]

4

Certain adjectives recurred with increasing frequency in Michael's speeches and writings after 1983: decent, civilised, intelligent. They evoked values derived from the beliefs and teachings of Isaac Foot, from the old radical Liberalism of the West Country, and from his education at Leighton Park and Oxford. Socialism, the political philosophy which he had embraced early in his adult life and successfully synthesised with these older values, never lost its primary importance for him. But, now that he was in his seventies, he had to recognise that he would not see the swift socialist transformation of society envisaged by the ardent spirits of the Socialist League and that he would live out the rest of his life under some kind of capitalism. What mattered now was that capitalism did not have to be ineluctably marked by the crudities of Thatcherism; that choices might be made which were civilised, intelligent, conceivably even decent. Hence, he exerted himself to defend the best traditions of the BBC, to safeguard Britain's museums from vulgar commercialism, to uphold surviving standards of integrity in the press and publishing.

There was another factor: the balance between the attractions of politics and literature, oscillating in Michael's mind ever since Oxford, was tilting in the latter direction now that leisure permitted a relaxation of the pressures of responsibility. It was a pleasure to allow himself time for careful and reflective reading, to join in discussions with people of the same inclinations, to lecture to sympathetic and appreciative audiences; and he was now free to indulge in these pleasures without any sense of guilt. He was able to see more of friends whose names – and whose line of talk – would have meant nothing to most of the occupants of the Labour Party front bench, such as John Hillaby, the chronicler of literary London and Hampstead in particular, or Ian Norrie, the owner of the independent High Hill Bookshop.

There were also two annual gatherings which Michael seldom missed. One was the Wordsworth conference at Dove Cottage in the Lake District, the poet's home. Michael did not attend merely as a listener, but always prepared a contribution to Wordsworthian studies. He was there only a few weeks after the bruising ordeal of the 1983 election, and it gave him the recuperation that other defeated leaders might have sought on the holiday beach or the golf course. The other was the Chelten-ham festival of literature. It was dear to Michael's heart largely because the man who had initiated it, Alan Hancox, was a bookseller, the owner of a private library laboriously and lovingly assembled, and an auto-didact with little formal education – in fact, a man in the mould of Isaac Foot. When Hancox died in 1992, Michael put unmistakable devotion into his obituary:

> He understood the central part which literature should play in the life of the nation and he made his festival the best expression of it . . . Ted Hughes, Seamus Heaney and a few of the others could command much larger audiences than the fading politicians . . . So many of those who graced his festival platforms had often found themselves ostracised or patronised elsewhere. Alan made them at home, for he too detested the suffocating orthodoxies of his time . . .
>
> He knew how rich was the English tradition which had nothing to do with money. He knew how little some of the greatest writers – again the poets among the foremost – had been paid for their priceless first editions. He hated the idea that money should rule society and he must

have been happy to see his festival outlasting the ignoble period of Thatcherism.[19]

During these years, Michael spoke at a memorial meeting for Jack London, a writer in grave need of rehabilitation. He went to Ireland to take part in a scholarly commemoration of Swift, but also to offer his tribute to the orator of Speaker's Corner, Bonar Thompson. He lectured on Byron often and in various places – once in Venice, which gave him special enjoyment. He spoke – once in Brixton and once at Wellesley College in the US – in honour of C. L. R. James, the black historian who had rescued the Caribbean past from oblivion and incidentally extolled the triumphs of West Indian cricket. Lectures like these (and there were others) were marked by careful research and often reinterpretation. When Michael received honorary degrees – at the Universities of Wales, Nottingham, Exeter, and the new University of Plymouth – these were not merely acts of courtesy, but signs of academic respect.

Of course, he spoke as readily about political history as about literature. He spoke in Manchester at a commemoration of Peterloo, and in Nottingham to render belated justice to the frame-breakers whom Byron had defended in the House of Lords. He was in Paris for the bicentenary of the storming of the Bastille, taking part in a television programme organised by Melvyn Bragg. And he lectured three times on Thomas Paine – at a Paris symposium, in New York and at the University of Indiana (this visit was arranged by Jill's daughter Julie, married to the Professor of Music). In the New York lecture, Michael told the audience:

> Paine, in his lifetime, commanded a notoriety and popularity such as only pop-stars may have today . . . He was already acclaimed for his pre-eminence by contemporaries whose fame soon became much more securely established than his own – by George Washington, by Thomas Jefferson . . . It was from such heights that his name and glory were dragged down into the dirt, and the more one looks back upon the episode, the more one is driven . . . to accept the notion of a kind of sinister Establishment conspiracy . . .
>
> Nothing could shake his own conviction that within his own lifetime or shortly afterwards – and thanks largely to his own Atlas-like exertions – the world would be turned upside down. He knew he possessed the implement which could work the miracle – the power of free speech, free writing and free thought . . . No other figure in history can ever have believed in the power of freedom – and not merely its virtue – with Paine's single-minded intensity . . . And the

words are still there, still burning on the page. They retain their force today, in Asia, in Africa, in the old continent and the new ones.

At this time, Michael was making his own defence of free speech, free writing and free thought. In 1988, he was chairman of the panel of judges for the Booker Prize. His choice for the prize was Salman Rushdie's *The Satanic Verses*; he was excited by its boldly imaginative quality, he was entertained by its wit and its verbal jokes, but above all he applauded its derisive assaults on religious bigotry. In all this, there was a flavour of Swift to which Michael warmly responded. The other judges all preferred Peter Carey's *Oscar and Lucinda*. One of them, Sebastian Faulks, wrote in an account of the final meeting: 'Michael Foot argued that the daring handling of contemporary scenes made Salman Rushdie's novel outstanding, but the other judges, while expressing great admiration for Rushdie's work, were adamant.'[20] Michael said tersely: 'I surrender.' Some of the judges felt that he might have converted them if he had pursued the argument, and were surprised by this ultra-democratic behaviour, rare in literary circles. The meeting, the shortest in the Booker's history, ended after only twenty-five minutes, with Carey as the winner. Those who deplore the decline of the English novel may be reminded that the unsuccessful entries in 1988 included Bruce Chatwin's *Utz*, Anthony Sher's *Middlepost* and Doris Lessing's *The Fifth Child*, which was not even short-listed.

In his speech at the presentation dinner, Michael emphatically voiced his praise for *The Satanic Verses*, and he reiterated his view on BBC radio next day. Then the storm broke. It had not occurred to any of the Booker judges that a few short passages in the novel might be construed as an insult to the Prophet Mohammed and the Moslem religion. Michael was inundated with letters, identical in phraseology although handwritten, reproaching him for his support of the outrageous book. One letter, from the secretary of Balham Mosque, told him: 'Now that you are at the fag end of your life, you would do well to reflect on matters of the hereafter. To this end I, on behalf of the South London Moslem community, am sending you various books on Islam.' A councillor in Newham reminded him pointedly: 'Over the years the majority of Muslims have supported the Labour Party and to maintain this vital support Muslims' feelings have to be respected.'

Rushdie wrote to Michael:

I just wanted to let you know that the generosity of your words at the Guildhall last night and on the radio this morning has meant a lot to me, not least because it contrasts so sharply with the patronising, mean-spirited rancour of some British critics of my book . . . I am planning to leave England for the United States in a few months, abandoning English literature to the likes of Anita Brookner and Piers Paul Read; and when I go, your kindness will go with me.

Michael replied:

I am shocked, if possible, about the way in which some people have received your book. However, I have no doubt that it will, by its own merits, surmount all these difficulties. I think it was even better when I read it the second time . . .

It occurred to me, after the Booker dinner, that the comparison I should have drawn was the attempted suppression of Jonathan Swift's *A Tale of a Tub*. Swift thought that was his best book, and it certainly was a satire on all religions. It was said to be the reason why Swift was never given a Bishopric, and I think I should have told the Booker audience that I cannot rate very highly your chances of an episcopal preferment.

The furore spread and intensified. Moslem organisations demanded that the book should be banned; many bookshops were intimidated into declining to stock it, or else avoided displaying it and sold it only on request; in some towns, notably in Bradford, angry marches were organised and copies were publicly burned. Some MPs with significant numbers of Moslem constituents aligned themselves with the outcry. A Tory MP from Hyndburn, Ken Hargreaves, tabled a motion: 'That this House regrets the distress caused to Muslims in the United Kingdom by the publication of *Satanic Verses* by Salman Rushdie . . . and reminds authors that freedom of speech goes hand in hand with responsibility to ensure the accuracy of what is written'. Evidently, Hargreaves did not grasp that the book was a novel. Max Madden, a former member of the staff of *Tribune* and now Labour MP for Bradford West, proposed that the publishers should insert a statement written by Moslem critics, and argued that 'Freedom of speech is pretty meaningless in a society where substantial ethnic minorities and religious minorities feel their views are not adequately understood or represented.'[21] Michael noted, in fairness, that the Militant MP for Bradford North, Pat Wall, took a courageous stand in defence of tolerance.

Soon, an incredulous world learned of the decree, or *fatwa*, issued by the Ayatollah Khomeini, which proclaimed that the killing of Salman Rushdie would be a meritorious act. In theological terms, the justification was that he was a renegade, having been brought up in a Moslem family (in fact, a family that was by no means bigoted or even devout). He was immediately given police protection and disappeared into hiding. Michael maintained his sympathy for the writer and, by courtesy of the police, they met on several occasions.

5

The later 1980s and early 1990s brought political changes, especially in the Communist world, of a far-reaching character which hardly anyone had anticipated (although a persecuted dissident, Andrei Amalrik, had once written a book entitled *Can the Soviet Union Survive until 1984?*). After the deaths of Brezhnev and of two short-lived successors, Mikhail Gorbachev moved into the Kremlin in March 1985. Changes followed swiftly: economic reform and decentralisation, freely contested elections, an unprecedented measure of freedom for the press and literature. Michael became an enthusiastic admirer of Gorbachev and was greatly impressed by the book, *Perestroika*, in which the Soviet leader expounded his novel political ideas. The best news of all was that Gorbachev and Reagan came to terms on the first genuine disarmament (as distinct from arms limitation) agreement since the onset of the cold war. It happened that Michael was going to New York to lecture on Paine at the precise time when Gorbachev went to sign this agreement in Washington. In his lecture, Michael said:

As I came across, flying to New York to take part in this occasion . . . I thought it was a stunning time to come to such a meeting as this in New York, all arranged under the auspices of Thomas Paine, of course. Indeed, it might be said that he had fixed most of the arrangements and that neither of the two chief leading people who are engaged in ceremonies elsewhere throughout this week would have been able to carry through their operations at all if it had not been for Thomas Paine . . . I was also partly prompted in these thoughts because, muddled up in my mind with Thomas Paine, whom I was also reading as I came across through the night, I was reading . . . the latest book by Mikhail Gorbachev, and I recommend everybody to read it. He is not as good a writer as Thomas Paine, I may say, but it is a very good book none the less . . . There is one sentence there that struck me, and again I am sure it would not have been written if it had not been for the existence of Thomas Paine, for Mikhail Gorbachev writes in his book, describing the atmosphere of what is happening in the Soviet Union:

'Today it is as if we were going through a school of democracy again,' and I hope he is . . . I do believe that it is something different from what went before in the Soviet Union. It is not the kind of democracy which was the tired, debased use of the word which previous operators in the Soviet Union have employed . . . Maybe Thomas Paine was watching over Mikhail Gorbachev when he wrote those parts of the book . . .

Here now, I believe that in this week the world has seen by far and away the most hopeful development since the invention of nuclear weapons, and I believe that it can lead the world along the path to the total abolition of these weapons . . . If Paine were writing today . . . I cannot believe that he would not be giving his full support to the pursuit of the abolition of nuclear weapons in their entirety.

By 1989, it was possible to claim that the nuclear arms race was over, and so was its cause and justification, the cold war. Since it was built in 1961, the ugliest symbol of the cold war had been the Berlin wall. When it was breached and then demolished, the monolithic structure of the Communist regimes in Eastern Europe crumbled and collapsed within months. The German Democratic Republic ceased to exist and was absorbed into what had been West Germany. Soon, an intransigent strike leader was President of Poland and a banned playwright was President of Czechoslovakia.

But, if 1989 was the happiest year since the overthrow of Nazi power, the imbibing of champagne was followed by painful hangovers. East Germany became a scene of mass unemployment, social disintegration and virulent racism. In Poland, in Hungary and most wretchedly in Romania, the task of constructing a viable non-Communist society presented formidable obstacles. Even peaceful and well-ordered Czechoslovakia fell apart and frontier posts went up between separate Czech and Slovak states. The genie that escaped from the bottle, once the stopper put in place by Stalin was removed, was a passionate and uncompromising nationalism. In the Soviet Union itself, Armenians fought Azerbaijanis, Georgians fought Ossetians, the Baltic republics broke away, and the whole vast territory began to groan and crack like a frozen lake in a spring thaw.

The Gorbachev regime, which had begun so hopefully and earned the plaudits of democratic socialists like Michael Foot, did not last. The command economy was replaced by a fluctuating, chaotic system that was neither socialism nor capitalism, neither democracy nor dictatorship. Ordinary Russians, instead of seeing improved standards after the stagnation of the Brezhnev era, faced shortages and soaring prices. In 1991, Gorbachev survived an attempted coup only to find that power had slipped from his hands into those of Boris Yeltsin.

Nor did the ending of the cold war and nuclear arms race lead to an era of universal peace. On 2 August 1990, Iraqi troops invaded and occupied Kuwait. President George Bush, Reagan's successor, ordered massive American ground and air forces to the region. Margaret Thatcher, contributing a British task force, reached into her wardrobe for the armour that had served her in the Falklands war. She never had a chance to wear it. For reasons that had nothing to do with Kuwait, the solid centre of the Conservative Party decided that she had outlived her usefulness. By a sequence of highly questionable stratagems, she was forced to resign. When Michael Heseltine, having narrowly failed to pick up the fallen crown, paid a tribute to her in the Commons, Michael Foot commented that it was 'the first assassination scene in which the envious Casca tried to pass himself off as Mark Antony'.[22]

The clock was ticking towards the launching of hostilities in the Gulf. No suggestion of compromise, or of any solution other than the use of force, was considered in Washington. Saddam Hussein, for his part, was as wildly confident as General Galtieri. John Major, now Prime Minister, punctiliously followed the Thatcher line and endorsed every American decision. However, sharp criticism came from four political veterans who were listened to attentively in the Commons, who could not be accused of personal ambition and who had between them almost 160 years of parliamentary experience. These critics were Michael Foot, Denis Healey, Tony Benn and Edward Heath.

Heath, who went to Baghdad and talked to Saddam Hussein in the course of the waiting period, argued that Iraq could not make an abject retreat without losing face, so the obstacle to peace was American inflexibility. Healey warned that the use of force could lead to unpredictable perils, and declared that it was the third time he had seen a great nation 'sleep-walking to disaster with its eyes open and its mind closed' – the other occasions being Suez and Vietnam. Benn attacked the hypocrisy of claiming that the Western Allies were motivated by principle, when they were really concerned about oil. Michael concentrated on economic sanctions as a way of making an impression on Iraq without bloodshed.

In a debate on 15 January 1991, he said: 'I don't believe that the government or its allies have fully considered the effects and possibilities of sanctions . . . We should think not twice but four, five or more times to try to find a different way out.' He referred to the large peace demonstrations which had been held in London, Paris and elsewhere;

the marchers were not all pacifists but were 'saying that the sanctions alternative was a much more civilised and intelligent way of settling the dispute'. He went on to rebuke *The Times* for calling sanctions 'the notorious appeaser's remedy'. When Abyssinia was attacked by Mussolini in 1935, *The Times* had supported appeasement and ruled out sanctions as too dangerous. Michael said sternly: 'One would have thought that the hand of a *Times* leader-writer would wither before he dared to write such words.' He wound up:

> We could have stopped the Second World War by taking effective collective action, starting with economic sanctions and taking further action if they did not succeed . . . The time has not yet come to abandon that option and resort to methods that would have incalculable consequences for the Middle East and indeed the world as a whole.

In the opinion of George Bush and his generals, however, the time had come to start the war. Soon after this debate, the Allies struck at the Iraqi defences with devastating power.

The year 1991, which began with the Gulf war, saw the descent of Yugoslavia into disintegration and chaos. For several reasons, this was intensely painful for Michael. Since 1948, when Tito had broken away from the Communist bloc and defied Stalin, the Yugoslav experiment in grass-roots decision-making and industrial self-management had been admired and praised by Aneurin Bevan and Labour left-wingers in general. In particular, Tito (who was a Croat ruling from the old capital of Serbia) had won special credit for ensuring equal citizenship for the various ethnic groups in the Federal Republic, in contrast to the centralised domination enforced throughout the Soviet Union by Stalin. Besides, Michael and Jill had been spending their holidays in Dubrovnik for several years, and cherished a great affection for it. By 1991, Dubrovnik had suffered (fortunately, not extensively) from Serbian shellfire from the surrounding mountains. Knowing and loving Dubrovnik as an irreplaceable cultural gem, Michael agonised over its fate as he would have agonised over a threat to Oxford, Paris or Venice. He remained faithful to it; despite the travel difficulties, he and Jill twice revisited Dubrovnik and made a film – with Jill as director and Michael as narrator – to pay tribute to the endangered city. The title was *A Foot in Dubrovnik*.

In 1991, there was savage fighting along the borders of Serbia and Croatia. In towns such as Vukovar, where a mixed population had been living without any apparent discord, the Croats were either killed or driven out by the Serbs. The repulsive euphemism 'ethnic cleansing' entered the political vocabulary. In 1992, worse horrors descended on Bosnia, whose people – an inextricable mixture of Serbs, Croats and Moslems – had tried hard to avoid taking sides in the fratricidal warfare and to maintain their region as an island of peace. Michael's admiration went to Yugoslavs who had fought side by side in the Partisan war and upheld freedom as a value for all citizens. He wrote: 'They had this peculiar love for their own homes which proved stronger than any other instinct. Without that, fascist Germany would still be in control of the Balkans as the Turks were for centuries and every house in Dubrovnik would now be in the possession of some Serbian stormtrooper.'[23] In a speech in the House of Commons on 5 March 1992, he took a clear stand:

> The immediate and overpowering cause of recent wretched events was the way in which the federal army was let loose. The federal army rampaged up the coast and used its might in a way that it thought would enable it to impose itself by widespread intimidation not only there but throughout the country, including Bosnia . . . Their doctrines had taught them that military power was all that would count in the end, if they used it with sufficient force and venom . . .
>
> I was present as a reporter in 1945 at the establishment of the United Nations in San Francisco. Conflicts similar to these led people to say that we must have an international authority with the power and the capacity to send in troops speedily and the authority to settle disputes . . .
>
> I hope that the government will remedy some of its past actions . . . We held back at critical moments. I hope there will be no more such holding back, because for the solution to this problem and for the future of the world, we must hope that this United Nations force will have the necessary backing for as long as is necessary to try to establish real peace in the area.

This was Michael's last speech in the House of Commons.

He had informed the Blaenau Gwent Labour Party in good time that he would not stand at the next election. He was hoping that the new MP would be Marilyn Pitman, who had been an outstanding leader of the borough council. It would be a healthy development, he thought, for a woman to be chosen; whatever virtues might be claimed for South Wales, it had never been in the vanguard of feminism. However, for personal reasons Mrs Pitman did not wish her name to go forward. The candidate selected was Llew Smith, a man whose qualities Michael strongly respected.

It remained for Michael to sum up his parliamentary experience. Suitably, the vehicle offered to him was the *Evening Standard*:

Has the House of Commons lost its place as the central forum of the nation? Has the art of parliamentary oratory been fatally impaired? Have radio and television together put an end to these ancient, honourable pursuits of the English people? Enoch Powell, one of the last great exponents and defenders of our parliamentary system, might pass these verdicts . . .

But wait. Others before the prophetic and incorruptible Enoch detected the death-throes of the British Parliament, and it lived to flourish more gloriously thereafter . . . It is instructive to recall that one of the moments when the disease was supposed to be most deadly was in the years just before the First World War. Leading parliamentarians like Asquith and Lloyd George were shouted down – often by the scions of what still passed for the British aristocracy. Maybe the din which came from those Tory benches then was not so different from the massed chorus of estate agents, accountants, publicity merchants and other spokesmen of the secondary professions . . .

At the height of the Thatcherite dominion, it looked for a while as if the executive mastery over the Commons might become complete and irreversible. Measures such as the poll tax were pushed through with an unprecedented resort to closures and guillotines . . . Mostly these decisions are made by ministers who have little experience of life on the back benches of the House of Commons, but it is there that the real vitality of the place is preserved, there that the chances of renewal are sustained . . .

As this poll-tax parliament reaches its ignominious end, all these various voices, past, present and future, can help remind us of the most potent truth more celebrated in this century than any other. No other British institution has shown the same capacity to turn defeat into victory; no other has had so much practice in this perilous game.[24]

6

The Parliament elected in 1987 had to be dissolved, constitutionally, in June 1992 at the latest. The date chosen for the general election, 9 April, was in fact the one generally expected. Michael had to relinquish his spacious office in the Norman Shaw building overlooking the Thames and to crate or package the mass of papers which had accumulated in its recesses. He could look back on almost half a century of political and parliamentary history. Because of his absence between 1955 and 1960, the title of Father of the House eluded him, but he was nevertheless the only MP who had taken his seat in the historic year of 1945.

He was often asked: 'Won't you miss the House of Commons?' Of course, every corner of the building – the chamber itself, the lobbies, the bars, the tea-room and the dining-room, the terrace – held a palimpsest of memories for him. He turned his back on them firmly. In ensuing months, when an MP invited him to lunch, he made the proviso that they should meet at a restaurant. Revisiting the Commons as a guest – or ghost – was something he preferred to avoid. But his answer to the question was, sincerely, that he would miss Ebbw Vale much more than Westminster. The House of Commons was, after all, a stage on which the actors performed their roles and ultimately made their bows; the Welsh valleys were a living community of which he had become a loyal, though an adopted, citizen. The annual dinner-dance of the constituency Labour Party was a date that, through thirty years, he had never missed. When he spoke at this dinner for the last time, on 26 February 1993, it was a profoundly emotional occasion.

The 1992 election was the first in Michael's adult life in which he was not a candidate. He undertook a speaking tour for the final week of the campaign, offering his services by choice in marginal seats in Wales. He spoke in Monmouth, the scene of his first contest in 1935; Labour had captured it in a 1991 by-election and was fighting to hold it. In North Wales, he spoke at Cefn Mawr in Clwyd, Conwy, Llangefni in Anglesey, and Machynlleth. Next on the itinerary was Pembroke, represented by Nicholas Bennett, a Tory whom Michael particularly disliked and to whose defeat he was eager to contribute. His eve of poll meeting was at Ystradgynlais, an archetypal mining community which belongs geographically and socially to the Swansea valley but is, by an electoral quirk, included in the sprawling Brecon and Radnor constituency.

Labour's activists were confident of winning this election. A long sequence of discreditable episodes had left the Tories, apparently, disheartened and reeling; economic recovery, predicted for 1991 and then 1992, was not yet a reality. It did not seem possible that the Tories would, for a fourth time, secure a victory which they had done nothing to deserve. Nowhere was the optimism greater, and the evidence for it more persuasive, than in Wales. As I walked with Michael through the streets of Holyhead and Caernarvon, we were delighted by the ready handshakes, the Labour stickers smilingly accepted, the assurances that 'You'll be all right this time.'

Ystradgynlais, a place of proud collective spirit, has a population of only 11,000 but a civic hall, built in recent years, with good equipment for drama or music and seats for 400. Half an hour before the meeting was due to begin, people were pouring in to fill every seat. They stood to cheer Michael when he appeared on the stage, when he began his speech and when he ended. He spoke for an hour, and no one here seemed to need an apology for doing a Beethoven. He said:

> I thought of the terrible Thatcherite years; it's rather a tragic thought, you know, but also in a sense an encouraging thought that if it had been left to us in Wales and Scotland we would never have had the Thatcher years at all. We had a very good result in Wales last time . . . Despite all the difficulties, whatever the troubles, Wales voted for decent socialist policies . . . Aneurin Bevan used to say that the purpose of getting power is to be able to give it away – much too clever for any of the Tories to understand. But you know, we have to teach them, we have to teach the English, and sometimes it takes a lot of teaching . . . I'm partly English myself, but I can assure you I learned lots of things in Wales. But you see, the English get on all right if they've got some good Celts to assist them, but if you leave them to themselves – then you get Thatcher, you know . . . The greatest political leaders must combine courage and imagination. If you've only got courage, you may just turn into stubbornness, and for us that's the nicest thing you could say about Mrs Thatcher, I suppose. If you've only got imagination and you haven't got the guts and the courage to fight for it over long periods, it will lead you into merely romantic hopes . . . As the very greatest leaders from Wales have always shown, you must combine the courage and the imagination, and it is, I believe, a great historic moment in our country's history, because a new leader from Wales is going to go into Downing Street and show the country and the world how those two qualities can be combined . . .
>
> It's not all going to happen immediately, but I tell you it'll be another great proud day, the end of the wretchedness and the squalor of this past thirteen years, the most corrupt government in British history – not quite as bad as the one that plunged us into the war in the thirties, but almost as bad . . . Well, those evil days are coming to an end.

I left the hall while the cheers were still resounding. The next day – polling-day – I drove Michael from Tredegar to London. No doubt it was strange for him to spend that day without polling stations to visit, without a count to attend. It was a beautiful spring day as we went from Wales into England: from the untamed uplands above the heads of the valleys, with the wild ponies and the thin grass over the coal-tips, across the Severn to the sleek comfort of Gloucestershire and the Cotswolds. We stopped for lunch in an old pub in Stow-on-the-Wold and browsed in one of those second-hand bookshops that, when Michael is the guide, form a network from coast to coast. We talked about books and ideas – largely, I recall, about Wells and Shaw and the Fabian Society. Of course, we knew that Labour had won the election. Neil Kinnock said later that he had sensed the victory slipping away in the last four days of the campaign; but in the Welsh heartland, in places like Ystradgynlais, we had sensed nothing of the kind.

In the evening, we were at Melvyn Bragg's house for the election-night party, hosted jointly by the Braggs and the Foots. Staring incredulously at the television, we learned what had happened. Wales had done well, but not well enough; Pembroke had been won, but not Brecon and Radnor, and Monmouth had been lost again. What kept the party going was that Glenda Jackson had won Hampstead.

Michael had already moved into his new office. He had a quite large study at home, but he has always stuck to the journalist's habit of the daily journey to work. He arranged to take a room in the *Tribune* offices on the fourth floor of the TGWU building in Gray's Inn Road. So he was back at *Tribune*, though not in the Victorian building where he edited the paper. At Gray's Inn Road there are computers (not in Michael's room, however) and a modern lift, an elegant contrast to the shuddering cage with its clanking gates in which Nye Bevan, George Orwell and Michael Foot made their slow ascent. Most of the staff were not even born when *Tribune* attacked Hugh Gaitskell's Health Service charges and defended itself against Arthur Deakin's attempts at suppression. Yet Michael is at home in their company, not as an incarnation of tradition but as a comrade.

Since finishing *The Politics of Paradise*, he had been considering what to write next. He had sketched out a book on the sources and traditions of socialist political thought, somewhat along the lines of Edmund Wilson's *To the Finland Station*. However, he had not got beyond making notes when he was invited by Doubleday to write a biography of H. G. Wells. Publication is planned for 1996.

It was in 1934 that Michael first read Wells' *Tono-Bungay*, taking it with him on the trip to Paris when he celebrated his twenty-first birthday. He has said frankly that he found *Tono-Bungay* even more fascinating than Paris. He was equally attracted by the sweep and vigour of the novel, by its scathing criticism of Britain's social structure, and by the discovery that Wells' taste in reading had anticipated his own. The narrator (*Tono-Bungay* has a strong autobiographical flavour) says of his boyhood: 'I read and understood the good sound rhetoric of Tom Paine's

Rights of Man . . . Gulliver was there unexpurgated, strong meat for a boy perhaps, but not too strong.' It could be Michael Foot remembering his foragings in the book-filled house of his own boyhood.

Four years later, he met Wells in person as a fellow-guest for a Beaverbrook weekend. They kept in touch, and Michael paid this tribute many years later: 'Among his other virtues he gave constant encouragement to young writers, and I, when I worked on the *Evening Standard* in the late Thirties and early Forties, was a beneficiary of his kindness and instruction.'[25] It could be said that Wells was a beneficiary too, for the *Standard* under Michael's editorship published a series of articles by him which, because of their mordant criticisms of the Churchill government, might not have easily found another outlet. When Wells died in 1946, Michael wrote:

> It is sad, indeed, that we shall hear no more of that splendid scorn and soaring imagination. But while we honour him first of all for his genius, let us also recall his great qualities without which his match-less gifts would not have been spent so unsparingly in the service of all mankind.
>
> First we should reckon among them his courage, the most attractive quality of all. It was shining and indomitable . . . Courage, human-ity, and strongest of all, patriotism. Not, of course, the vulgar, flagwagging variety . . . but a deep, abiding love for the best spirit of England and all it had given to the world . . . England should honour him above all other nations which he yet sought without respect for colour, race or creed to join in allegiance to his Rights of Man. He belongs to them all, but first to us.[26]

In that article, Michael noted that some obituaries of Wells were written in a patronising tone and minimised his achievements. Over the years since Wells died, his reputation has not been secure against attacks – any more than the reputations of Swift, Hazlitt and Byron. In 1993, Michael reviewed a biography which he described as 'a wretched caricature'. The biography that Michael himself is writing will be, once again, a vindication. It is a task that he has always found stimulating and enjoyable.

The former editor, former MP, former minister and former party leader is still what, in his heart or a significant part of it, he has always been: a writer. The last chapter of Michael Foot's life is certainly not the least happy.

NOTES AND REFERENCES

CHAPTER 1
On Freedom Fields

1 Michael Foot: *Debts of Honour* (Davis-Poynter, 1980).
2 *Encyclopaedia Britannica*, 1910 edition.
3 Letter to members of Devonport Labour Party, 1938.
4 In *The Pleasure of Reading*, edited by Antonia Fraser (Bloomsbury, 1992).
5 Sarah Foot: *My Grandfather, Isaac Foot* (Bossiney Books, 1980), p. 73.
6 *Evening Standard*, 19 October 1965.
7 *Cherwell*, October 1933.
8 The text of an interview between H. G. Wells and Stalin, with comments by Shaw and others, was published as a *New Statesman* pamphlet in 1934.
9 *News Chronicle*, 4 April 1934.
10 *Cherwell*, October 1933.
11 Hugh Dalton: *The Fateful Years* (Muller, 1957), p. 149.
12 Michael Foot: *Aneurin Bevan*, vol. 1 (MacGibbon & Kee, 1962), p. 156.
13 *Young Oxford and War* (Selwyn & Blount, 1934).
14 Castle diary, 20 March 1975.

CHAPTER 2
The Making of a Socialist

1 Hugh Foot: *A Start in Freedom* (Hodder & Stoughton, 1964), p. 87.
2 *New Statesman*, 21 March 1936.

3 *New Statesman*, 3 October 1936.
4 In *Tribune*, 19 September 1947, in *Debts of Honour*, and in the first part of *The Politics of Paradise*.
5 Interview.
6 Sarah Foot, *op. cit.*, p. 51.
7 Letter to members of Devonport Labour Party, 1938. In fact, Michael had not yet been to America or Liverpool when he first went to South Wales.
8 *Bevan*, vol. 1, p. 164 note.
9 *Bevan*, vol. 1, p. 181.
10 *Bevan*, vol. 1, p. 260.
11 Michael Foot: *Armistice 1918–1939* (Harrap, 1940), p. 168.
12 Eric Estorick: *Stafford Cripps* (Heinemann, 1949), p. 141.
13 *New Statesman*, 7 March 1936.
14 *Hampstead and Highgate Express*, 7 December 1984.
15 Barbara Castle: *Fighting All the Way* (Macmillan, 1993), p. 78.
16 Castle, *op. cit.*, p. 81.
17 C. H. Rolph: *Kingsley Martin* (Gollancz, 1973), p. 291.
18 Gabriel Jackson: *The Spanish Republic and the Civil War* (Princeton University Press, 1965), p. 248.
19 *Time and Tide*, 6 August 1938.
20 *Armistice*, p. 184.
21 'French efforts to persuade the British to change their position, such as the visit to London of Jules Moch, assistant to Blum, on 30 July . . . proved unavailing.' (Glyn Stone in *Paths to War*, edited by Robert Boyce (Macmillan, 1989), p. 213).
22 Dalton, *op. cit.*, p. 100.
23 *Tribune*, 17 August 1937.

24 Ben Pimlott: *Labour and the Left in the 1930s* (Cambridge University Press, 1977), p. 95.
25 Pimlott, *op. cit.*, p. 34.
26 *Tribune*, 7 May 1937.
27 Interview with Ted Willis.
28 Castle, *op. cit.*, p. 84.
29 *New Statesman*, 1 August 1936.
30 *Reynolds' News*, 30 August 1936.
31 *Tribune*, 18 February 1938.
32 George Orwell: *Homage to Catalonia* (Secker & Warburg, 1938), p. 142.
33 Speech at Albert Hall, 7 February 1937.
34 Ruth Dudley Edwards: *Victor Gollancz* (Gollancz, 1987), p. 267.
35 Andrew Roberts: *'The Holy Fox'* (Weidenfeld & Nicolson, 1991), p. 156.
36 Viscount Templewood (Samuel Hoare): *Nine Troubled Years* (Collins, 1954), p. 344.
37 *Tribune*, 11 February 1938.
38 B. H. Liddell Hart: *Memoirs*, vol. 2 (Putnam, 1966), p. 82.
39 G. E. R. Gedye: *Fallen Bastions* (Gollancz, 1939), p. 300.
40 Ernest Jones: *Sigmund Freud*, vol. 3 (Hogarth Press, 1957), p. 233.
41 Orwell: *Selected Essays, Journalism and Letters*, vol. 1 (Secker & Warburg, 1968), p. 272.
42 *Bevan*, vol. 1, p. 279.
43 *Tribune*, 17 August 1937.
44 *Bevan*, vol. 1, p. 243.
45 Quoted in F. M. Leventhal: *The Last Dissenter* (Clarendon Press, 1985), p. 257.

Chapter 3
The Finest Hour

1 It was an off-the-record briefing for American and Canadian correspondents; Chamberlain's remarks were thus paraphrased in the *Montreal Star*.
2 Quoted in A. J. P. Taylor: *The Origins of the Second World War* (Hamish Hamilton, 1961), p. 176.
3 Quoted in Keith Middlemas: *Diplomacy of Illusion* (Weidenfeld & Nicolson, 1972), p. 277.
4 *New Statesman*, 8 October 1938.
5 Andrew Rothstein: *Munich* (Lawrence & Wishart, 1958), p. 174.
6 Rothstein, *op. cit.*, p. 196.
7 This compares interestingly with a phrase used by Bevan after Suez: 'They [the Tories] have support among many of the unthinking and the unreflective who still react to traditional values.' (Commons, 5 December 1956).
8 Simon Hoggart and David Leigh: *Michael Foot* (Hodder & Stoughton, 1981), p. 69.
9 *Debts of Honour*, p. 73.
10 Hoggart and Leigh, *op. cit.*, p. 76.
11 *Debts of Honour*, p. 79.
12 *Debts of Honour*, p. 73.
13 *Debts of Honour*, p. 74.
14 Anne Chisholm and Michael Davie: *Beaverbrook* (Hutchinson, 1992), pp. 348–50.
15 *Tribune*, 15 March 1946.
16 D. N. Pritt: *From Right to Left* (Lawrence & Wishart, 1965), p. 103.
17 J. Alvarez del Vayo: *Freedom's Battle* (Heinemann, 1940), p. 268.
18 Taylor, *op. cit.*, p. 231.
19 Roberts, *op. cit.*, p. 170.
20 Commons, 3 October 1939.
21 The meeting was private, but a verbatim record has been published in *About Turn*, edited by Francis King and George Matthews (Lawrence & Wishart, 1990).
22 *Bevan*, vol. 1, p. 337.
23 Foot: article on Frank Owen in Dictionary of National Biography.
24 Roberts, *op. cit.*, p. 224.
25 *Guardian*, 5 July 1990.
26 *Debts of Honour*, p. 89.
27 Quoted in Richard Lamb: *The Drift to War* (W. H. Allen, 1989), p. 296.
28 Liddell Hart, *op. cit.*, p. 193.
29 Middlemas, *op. cit.*, p. 50.
30 Middlemas, *op. cit.*, p. 82.
31 Morrison had replaced Burgin as Minister of Supply.

32 *Debts of Honour*, p. 72.
33 *Debts of Honour*, p. 96.
34 Hoggart and Leigh, *op. cit.*, p. 86.
35 *Evening Standard*, 8 June 1965.
36 Interview.
37 *Debts of Honour*, p. 79.

CHAPTER 4
Victories

1 Frank Wintle: *The Plymouth Blitz* (Bossiney Books, 1981), p. 20.
2 Wintle, *op. cit.*, p. 41.
3 *Bevan*, vol. 1, p. 347 note.
4 Evidence to Royal Commission on the Press, 1949.
5 Quoted in Chisholm and Davie, *op. cit.*, p. 434.
6 Angus Calder: *The People's War* (Cape, 1969), p. 616.
7 *Tribune*, 22 October 1943.
8 *Western Morning News*, 28 June 1945.
9 A poetic echo; it was Shelley who had first written of 'old Custom, legal Crime and bloody Faith'.
10 *Daily Herald*, 19 December 1944.
11 *Daily Herald*, 5 January 1945.
12 *Daily Herald*, 8 December 1944.
13 *Daily Herald*, 19 December 1944.
14 *Evening Standard*, 19 May 1993.
15 Emanuel Shinwell: *The Labour Story* (MacDonald, 1973), p. 172.
16 *Western Morning News*, 9 June 1945.
17 R. B. McCallum and Alison Readman: *The British General Election of 1945* (Oxford University Press, 1947), p. 142.
18 McCallum and Readman, *op. cit.*, p. 165.

CHAPTER 5
Cold War Years

1 Ben Pimlott: *Hugh Dalton* (Cape, 1985), p. 413.
2 *Tribune*, 21 September 1945.
3 *Tribune*, 12 September 1947.
4 Kenneth Harris: *Attlee* (Weidenfeld & Nicolson, 1982), p. 295.

5 Alan Bullock: *Ernest Bevin, Foreign Secretary* (Heinemann, 1983), p. 72.
6 Commons, 7 November 1945.
7 *Tribune*, 19 October 1945.
8 Commons, 26 October 1945.
9 Cabinet minutes quoted in Bullock, *op. cit.*, p. 123.
10 *Daily Herald*, 14 December 1945.
11 *Evening Standard*, 19 May 1993.
12 The film has been transferred to video and can be seen at the Fawcett Library, London.
13 *Evening Standard*, 23 March 1971.
14 Commons, 1 July 1946.
15 Quoted in Anthony Howard: *Crossman* (Cape, 1990), p. 119.
16 Howard, *op. cit.*, p. 114.
17 Commons, 1 July 1946.
18 Peter Weiler: *British Labour and the Cold War* (Stanford University Press, 1988), p. 197.
19 *Tribune*, 4 January 1946.
20 *Tribune*, 7 June 1946.
21 Commons, 4 June 1946.
22 *Daily Herald*, 23 April 1946.
23 *Daily Herald*, 25 April 1946.
24 *Tribune*, 8 March 1946.
25 Ian Mikardo: *Back-Bencher* (Weidenfeld & Nicolson, 1988), p. 101.
26 *Daily Herald*, 31 May 1946.
27 *Debts of Honour*, p. 102.
28 *Tribune*, 17 January 1947.
29 *Tribune*, 4 March 1949.
30 *Tribune*, 25 April 1947.
31 *Tribune*, 5 September 1947.
32 Mikardo, *op. cit.*, p. 110.
33 Rolph, *op. cit.*, p. 110.
34 *Tribune*, 6 June 1947.
35 Bullock, *op. cit.*, p. 407.
36 *Tribune*, 11 July 1947.
37 *Tribune*, 19 December 1947.
38 Testimony to a Senate committee, quoted in Weiler, *op. cit.*, p. 101.
39 *Daily Herald*, 3 May 1948.
40 Interview.
41 *Tribune*, 30 April 1948.
42 Bullock, *op. cit.*, p. 557.
43 *Tribune*, 25 April 1948.
44 *Tribune*, 25 April 1948.
45 Commons, 30 June 1948.
46 *Tribune*, 2 July 1948.
47 *Bevan*, vol. 2 (Davis-Poynter,

1973), p. 230.
48 *Tribune*, 26 November 1948.
49 Commons, 12 May 1949.
50 *Tribune*, 25 March 1949.
51 *Tribune*, 6 May 1949.
52 *Tribune*, 20 May 1949.
53 *Debts of Honour*, p. 103.
54 *Tribune*, 1 July 1949.
55 Commons, 25 March 1949.
56 *Tribune*, 21 May 1948.
57 *Tribune*, 14 October 1949.
58 Interview.
59 Quotations in this section are from the *Western Morning News*.

CHAPTER 6
The Bevanites

1 James Cameron: *Point of Departure* (Barker, 1967), p. 49.
2 Peggy Duff: *Left, Left, Left* (Allison & Busby, 1971), p. 73.
3 Cameron, *op. cit.*, p. 85.
4 Beaverbrook claimed no credit, and the facts came to light only when A. J. P. Taylor examined the Beaverbrook papers in 1970.
5 A. J. P. Taylor: *A Personal History* (Hamish Hamilton, 1983), p. 251.
6 Quoted in Asa Briggs: *Sound and Vision* (Oxford University Press, 1979). A detailed account of *In the News* is on pp. 599–606.
7 Taylor, *op. cit.*, p. 253.
8 BBC Written Archives.
9 Commons, 29 June 1950.
10 An extended summary of the discussions is preserved in the Museum of Labour History, Manchester.
11 *Bevan*, vol. 2, p. 301.
12 *Tribune*, 30 June 1950.
13 I. F. Stone: *The Hidden History of the Korean War* (Turnstile Press, 1952), p. 7.
14 *Tribune*, 21 July 1950.
15 *Tribune*, 1 September 1950.
16 *Tribune*, 1 December 1950.
17 *Daily Mail*, 6 December 1950.
18 See Kenneth O. Morgan: *Labour in Power* (Oxford University Press, 1986), p. 443.

19 *Bevan*, vol. 2, p. 296.
20 Duff, *op. cit.*, p. 29.
21 Philip M. Williams: *Gaitskell* (Cape, 1979), p. 250 note.
22 *Tribune*, 20 April 1951.
23 Morgan, *op. cit.*, p. 453.
24 Quoted in *Bevan*, vol. 2, p. 340.
25 *Bevan*, vol. 2, p. 334.
26 Leslie Hunter: *The Road to Brighton Pier* (Barker, 1959), p. 42. Hunter was the political correspondent of the *Daily Herald*.
27 Duff, *op. cit.*, p. 34.
28 Duff, *op. cit.*, p. 36.
29 Hunter, *op. cit.*, p. 47.
30 Hunter, *op. cit.*, p. 56.
31 *Bevan*, vol. 2, p. 350.
32 *Tribune*, 14 December 1951.
33 *Tribune*, 28 December 1951.
34 Harris, *op. cit.*, p. 504.
35 *Bevan*, vol. 2, p. 379.
36 Williams, *op. cit.*, p. 305.
37 Howard, *op. cit.*, p. 178.
38 Mikardo, *op. cit.*, p. 152.
39 *Tribune*, 26 November 1954.
40 *Tribune*, 14 May 1954.
41 *Tribune*, 13 August 1954.
42 Letter to *News Chronicle*, 11 May 1955.
43 His official title, dating from the seventeenth century, was Captain-General.
44 *Debts of Honour*, p. 106.
45 Robert Edwards: *Goodbye Fleet Street* (Cape, 1988), p. 55.
46 Williams, *op. cit.*, p. 343.
47 Harris, *op. cit.*, p. 529.
48 Hunter, *op. cit.*, p. 98.
49 *Sheffield Star*, 9 June 1955.
50 Hoggart and Leigh, *op. cit.*, p. 117.

CHAPTER 7
The Clash

1 Michael Foot: *The Pen and the Sword* (MacGibbon & Kee, 1957), p. 18.
2 *The Pen and the Sword*, p. 273.
3 *The Pen and the Sword*, p. 352.
4 *Daily Mail*, 9 January 1958.
5 *Observer magazine*, 24 February 1991.
6 Williams, *op. cit.*, p. 363.

7 *Bevan*, vol. 2, p. 496.
8 My diary, 16 January 1956.
9 *Still at Large* (*Tribune* pamphlet).
10 Interview.
11 *Bevan*, vol. 2, p. 520.
12 *Evening News*, 31 October 1956.
13 Keith Kyle: *Suez* (Weidenfeld & Nicolson, 1991), p. 440.
14 *Bevan*, vol. 2, p. 556.
15 *Bevan*, vol. 2, p. 562.
16 *Bevan*, vol. 2, p. 567.
17 Interview.
18 Interview.
19 *Bevan*, vol. 2, p. 575.
20 Interview.
21 Jennie Lee: *My Life with Nye* (Cape, 1980), p. 235.
22 *Bevan*, vol. 2, p. 580.
23 *Bevan*, vol. 2, pp. 583–4.
24 *New Statesman*, 2 November 1957.
25 Michael Foot in *Kingsley Martin: Portrait and Self-Portrait* (Barrie & Jenkins, 1969), p. 26.
26 Duff, *op. cit.*, p. 121.
27 *Bevan*, vol. 2, p. 602.
28 *Bevan*, vol. 2, p. 580.
29 In 1981, I heard her recall it with satisfaction at a social gathering at which, among others, Michael Foot, Dick Clements and Peggy Duff were present.
30 See Duff, *op cit.*; *The CND Story*, edited by John Minnion and Philip Bolsover (Allison & Busby, 1983); and *The Disarmers*, by Christopher Driver (Hodder & Stoughton, 1964).
31 *Bevan*, vol. 2, p. 601.
32 Quoted in John Cox: *Overkill* (Peacock Books, 1977), p. 214.
33 Angus Maude.
34 *Bevan*, vol. 2, p. 537.
35 This story was made public by K. S. Karol in *L'Express*, 30 May 1958.
36 *Tribune*, 2 January 1981.
37 Imre Nagy was executed on 16 June 1958, which enables us to date this letter approximately.
38 *Western Morning News*, 9 October 1959.
39 From the title of J. K. Galbraith's book *The Affluent Society*.
40 Hugh Foot, *op. cit.*, p. 161.
41 Bernard Levin in the *Spectator*.
42 *Bevan*, vol. 2, p. 651.

CHAPTER 8
Ebbw Vale

1 *Bevan*, vol. 2, p. 654.
2 Lee, *op. cit.*, p. 252.
3 *Tribune*, 22 July 1960.
4 *Western Mail*, 24 September 1960.
5 Interview.
6 Speech by Harry F. Spencer, Firth's successor at RTB, quoted in *Bevan*, vol. 1, p. 217.
7 Interview.
8 Susan Crosland: *Tony Crosland* (Cape, 1982), p. 103.
9 Hoggart and Leigh, *op. cit.*, p. 142.
10 Quoted in Duff, *op. cit.*, p. 166.
11 A full account of this episode, and particularly of the role of Schoenman, is in Caroline Moorehead: *Bertrand Russell* (Sinclair-Stevenson, 1992), chs 19 and 20.
12 Crosland, *op. cit.*, p. 104.
13 Commons, 25 January 1962.
14 *Tribune*, 6 October 1961.
15 Commons, 9 July 1963.
16 Commons, 17 November 1961.
17 Commons, 22 February 1962.
18 *Tribune*, 2 March 1962.
19 *Daily Herald*, 24 April 1962.
20 *Tribune*, 20 April 1962.
21 *Tribune*, 9 March 1962.
22 Commons, 9 July 1963.
23 Commons, 30 July 1963.
24 *Bevan*, vol. 1, p. 11.
25 *Bevan*, vol. 1, p. 192.
26 These were First World War battles involving, respectively, Canadian and Australian troops.
27 *Tribune*, 5 October 1962.
28 Denis Healey: *The Time of My Life* (Michael Joseph, 1989), p. 211.
29 Commons, 11 February 1963.
30 *Tribune*, 25 January 1963.
31 *Tribune*, 22 February 1963.
32 Commons, 27 June 1963.
33 *Daily Herald*, 2 August 1963.
34 *Tribune*, 18 October 1963.
35 Interview.

36 *Tribune*, 14 December 1962.
37 Interview.
38 *Daily Herald*, 13 March 1964.
39 *Daily Herald*, 13 March 1964.
40 Michael Foot: *Harold Wilson* (Pergamon Press, 1964), p. 9.
41 *Tribune*, 5 June 1964.
42 *Debts of Honour*, p. 108.
43 David Butler and Anthony King: *The British General Election of 1964* (Macmillan, 1965), pp. 152 and 155.
44 Geoffrey Goodman: *The Awkward Warrior* (Davis-Poynter, 1979), p. 384.
45 Goodman, *op. cit.*, p. 433.

CHAPTER 9
Outside Left

1 *Tribune*, 23 October 1964.
2 *Tribune*, 4 December 1964.
3 Tariq Ali: *Street Fighting Years* (Collins, 1987), p. 51.
4 Goodman, *op. cit.*, p. 493.
5 Interview.
6 Interview.
7 Donnelly issued a libel writ, but died before the case came to trial.
8 *Tribune*, 14 May 1965.
9 *Tribune*, 1 July 1965.
10 Commons, 16 November 1965.
11 Commons, 6 May 1965.
12 Commons, 4 November 1965.
13 Interview.
14 *Tribune*, 17 September 1965.
15 Goodman, *op. cit.*, p. 464.
16 Goodman, *op. cit.*, p. 465.
17 Ben Pimlott: *Harold Wilson* (HarperCollins, 1992), p. 388.
18 Commons, 26 April 1966.
19 Castle diary, 22 July 1967.
20 *Tribune*, 1 October 1965.
21 *Tribune*, 4 March 1966.
22 The Royal Court Theatre was technically a membership club and was therefore not subject to censorship.
23 Ernest Kay: *Pragmatic Premier* (Frewin, 1967), p. 233.
24 *Tribune*, 8 April 1966.
25 Kenneth O. Morgan: *The People's Peace* (Oxford University Press, 1990) and Clive Ponting: *Breach of Promise* (Hamish Hamilton, 1989). The second quotation is from Ponting.
26 Crossman diary, 14 June 1966.
27 Crossman diary, 1 October 1966.
28 Commons, 24 May 1966.
29 Goodman, *op. cit.*, p. 495.
30 Commons, 3 August 1966.
31 *Tribune*, 23 September 1966.
32 Crossman diary, 26 October 1966.
33 Crossman diary, 2 November 1966.
34 Crossman diary, 2 March 1967.
35 Crossman diary, 5 March 1967.
36 Crossman diary, 7 March 1967.
37 Michael Foot: *Loyalists and Loners* (Collins, 1986), p. 45.
38 Castle diary, 25 July 1966.
39 Castle diary, 25 September 1967.
40 *Tribune*, 29 September 1967.
41 Crossman diary, 7 November 1967.
42 James Callaghan: *Time and Chance* (Collins, 1987), p. 219.
43 Commons, 2 December 1967.
44 *Loyalists and Loners*, p. 84.
45 Benn diary, 14 March 1968.
46 Castle diary, 16 March 1968.
47 Commons, 16 November 1965.
48 Commons, 9 July 1968.
49 Alan Watkins in the *Observer*, 16 November 1980.
50 *Loyalists and Loners*, p. 188.
51 *Loyalists and Loners*, p. 191.
52 Benn diary, 21 April 1968.
53 Crossman diary, 27 April 1968.
54 Castle diary, 24 April 1968.
55 *Tribune*, 26 April 1968.
56 Healey, *op. cit.*, p. 331.
57 Crosland, *op. cit.*, p. 185.
58 Benn diary, 24 July 1969.
59 *Tribune*, 27 September 1968.
60 *Tribune*, 7 February 1969.
61 *Tribune*, 14 February 1969.
62 Castle, *op. cit.*, p. 398.
63 Crossman diary, 26 May 1968.
64 Goodman, *op. cit.*, p. 566.
65 Callaghan, *op. cit.*, p. 502.
66 Commons, 18 February 1969.
67 Commons, 12 February 1969.
68 Commons, 25 February 1969.
69 Crossman diary, 25 February 1969.

70 Crossman diary, 26 February 1969.
71 Commons, 12 February 1969.
72 Crossman diary, 15 April 1969.
73 Castle, *op. cit.*, p. 418.
74 Goodman, *op. cit.*, p. 574.
75 Castle diary, 15 January 1969.
76 Castle, *op. cit.*, p. 418.
77 Castle, *op. cit.*, p. 419.
78 Crossman diary, 4 January 1969.
79 Crossman diary, 27 April 1969.
80 Callaghan, *op. cit.*, p. 274.
81 Peter Kellner and Christopher Hitchens: *Callaghan: The Road to Number Ten* (Cassell, 1976), p. 96.
82 Kellner and Hitchens, *op. cit.*, p. 95. No mention of the NEC meeting can be found in Callaghan's memoirs.
83 *Tribune*, 18 April 1969.
84 *New Statesman*, 25 April 1969.
85 Castle diary, 7 May 1969.
86 Castle, *op. cit.*, p. 424.
87 Benn diary, 17 June 1969.
88 Crossman diary, 18 June 1969.
89 Healey, *op. cit.*, p. 341.
90 *Tribune*, 6 February 1970.
91 Benn diary, 8 March 1970.
92 Crossman diary, 22 April 1970.
93 Castle diary, 5 May 1970.
94 Benn diary, 4 June 1970.
95 Crossman diary, 7 June 1970.
96 Benn diary, 17 June 1970.

CHAPTER 10
Inside Left

1 Goodman, *op. cit.*, p. 582.
2 Patrick Cosgrave in the *Spectator*, 15 July 1972.
3 *Guardian*, 2 January 1968.
4 *Observer*, 14 May 1967.
5 Crossman diary, 24 October 1969.
6 *Tribune*, 24 October 1969.
7 Christopher Farman in the *Illustrated London News*, October 1972.
8 Commons, 29 October 1970.
9 Commons, 25 February 1971.
10 Castle, *op. cit.*, p. 446.
11 Commons, 25 October 1971.
12 Castle, *op. cit.*, p. 444.
13 Cosgrave in the *Spectator*, *op. cit.*
14 Hoggart and Leigh, *op. cit.*, p. 163.
15 Commons, 3 November 1971.
16 Commons, 17 February 1972.
17 Benn diary, 13 January 1971.
18 Defending Nehru's refusal to hold a plebiscite in Kashmir, *Tribune* wrote: 'A plebiscite settles an issue irrevocably on a single day . . . with the voters asked to say Yes or No to a narrow and perhaps a loaded question.' (*Tribune*, 1 March 1957).
19 Morgan, *op. cit.*, p. 317.
20 Jack Jones: *Union Man* (Collins, 1986), p. 262.
21 Jones, *op. cit.*, p. 259.
22 *Bevan*, vol. 2, p. 576.
23 *Bevan*, vol. 2, p. 658.
24 'Abu', the signature on the cartoons, was a contraction of the surname Abraham. Abu was a Kerala Christian; Biblical names are common in this community.
25 Commons, 13 July 1972.
26 *New Statesman*, 28 September 1973.
27 Harold Wilson: *Final Term* (Weidenfeld & Nicolson, 1979), p. 29.
28 Benn diary, 20 June 1973.
29 *Tribune*, 9 June 1973.
30 Benn diary, 3 October 1973.
31 Benn diary, 25 May 1973.
32 Benn diary, 26 September 1973.
33 Benn diary, 18 July 1971.
34 Crosland, *op. cit.*, p. 210.
35 *Loyalists and Loners*, p. 116.
36 *Tribune*, 16 November 1973.
37 Benn diary, 11 February 1974.
38 Mervyn Jones in *New Statesman*, 8 March 1974.
39 Jones, *op. cit.*, p. 281.
40 Castle diary, 5 March 1974.

CHAPTER 11
Dissenting Ministers

1 Ben Pimlott in *Times Literary Supplement*, 12 October 1984.
2 Castle, *op. cit.*, p. 404.
3 Commons, 18 March 1974.
4 *Daily Express*, 19 March 1974.
5 *The Times*, 20 March 1974.
6 *Sunday Times*, 24 March 1974.

7 My diary, 14 March 1974.
8 Footnote to *The Castle Diaries,
   1974–1976* (Weidenfeld &
   Nicolson, 1984), p. 45.
9 Benn diary, 11 June 1974.
10 Castle diary, 18 June 1974.
11 Wilson, *op. cit.*, p. 33.
12 Castle diary, 17 November 1974.
13 Benn diary, 31 October 1974.
14 Castle diary, 17 November 1974.
15 Commons, 7 May 1974.
16 An MP who is unwell can have his
   vote counted without walking
   through the division lobby, provided that he is on the premises.
17 Benn diary, 19 December 1974.
18 Commons, 23 January 1975.
19 Castle diary, 22 May 1975.
20 *Western Mail*, 5 February 1975.
21 Interview.
22 *Western Mail*, 8 February 1975.
23 Crosland, *op. cit.*, p. 295.
24 Benn diary, 5 January 1975.
25 Benn diary, 7 April 1975.
26 Benn diary, 6 August 1975.
27 Castle diary, 28 November 1975.
28 Benn diary, 31 December 1975.
29 Healey, *op. cit.*, p. 401.
30 Castle diary, 22 May 1975.
31 *Daily Mirror* interview, 24 July
   1974.
32 Commons, 3 December 1974.
33 The traditional name for an NUJ
   branch.
34 Commons, 15 October 1975.
35 Commons, 5 November 1974.
36 Commons, 12 February 1975.
37 Letter to *The Times*, 18 February
   1975.
38 Commons, 3 December 1974.
39 Commons, 12 February 1975.
40 Nora Beloff: *Freedom Under Foot*
   (Temple Smith, 1975), p. 49.
41 Commons, 12 February 1975.
42 Commons, 10 July 1974.
43 Commons, 3 December 1974.
44 *The Times*, 17 January 1975.
45 *Times Literary Supplement*, 25 April
   1975.
46 *The Times*, 9 May 1975.
47 Beloff, *op. cit.*, p. 95.
48 *The Castle Diaries, 1974–1976*,
   p. 190.

49 Wilson, *op. cit.*, p. 53.
50 Castle diary, 2 March 1975.
51 Castle diary, 19 March 1975.
52 Benn diary, 20 March 1975.
53 *Daily Mail*, 9 May 1975.
54 *Daily Mail*, 12 May 1975.
55 *The Times*, 23 May 1975.
56 Interview in *The Times*, 17 May
   1975.
57 Benn diary, 4 December 1975.
58 David Butler and Uwe Kitzinger:
   The 1975 Referendum (Macmillan,
   1976), p. 140. Most of the facts in
   this section are taken from this
   book.
59 Benn diary, 17 December 1974.
60 David Steel: *A House Divided*
   (Weidenfeld & Nicolson, 1980),
   p. 20.
61 Interview.
62 Butler and Kitzinger, *op. cit.*,
   p. 280.
63 Benn diary, 6 June 1975.
64 *The Times*, 5 June 1975.
65 Marcia Falkender: *Downing Street in
   Perspective* (Weidenfeld & Nicolson,
   1983), p. 207.
66 *Daily Telegraph*, 4 January 1975.
67 Falkender, *op. cit.*, p. 209.
68 Benn diary, 9 June 1975.
69 Wilson, *op. cit.*, p. 143.
70 Mikardo, *op. cit.*, p. 196.
71 Wilson, *op. cit.*, p. 144.
72 Castle diary, 18 June 1975.
73 Benn diary, 20 June 1975.
74 Castle diary, 5 July 1975.
75 Jones, *op. cit.*, p. 284.
76 Commons, 23 June 1975.
77 *Tribune*, 12 April 1974.
78 Quoted in Hugo Young: *The Crossman Affair* (Hamish Hamilton and
   Cape, 1976), p. 14. This book is the
   source for most of the facts and
   quotations in this section.
79 Crossman: *Inside View* (Cape,
   1972), p. 59. This is the text of the
   Harvard lectures.
80 Young, *op. cit.*, p. 25.
81 Howard, *op. cit.*, p. 6.
82 *Listener*, 25 September 1980.
83 *Observer*, 9 December 1984.
84 Young, *op. cit.*, p. 114. Trend was
   giving evidence to the Franks

Committee on official secrecy.
85 Castle diary, 29 September 1975.
86 Commons, 12 November 1975.
87 Commons, 9 December 1975.
88 Beloff, *op. cit.*, p. 123.
89 Healey, *op. cit.*, p. 446.
90 Benn diary, 16 March 1976.
91 Crosland, *op. cit.*, p. 310.
92 Benn diary, 3 November 1974.
93 Ben Pimlott: *Harold Wilson* (Hutchinson, 1992), p. 651.
94 Castle diary, 4 March 1976.
95 Callaghan, *op. cit.*, p. 386.
96 Kellner and Hitchens, *op. cit.*, p. 168.
97 Pimlott, *op. cit.*, p. 719.
98 Pimlott, *op. cit.*, p. 712.
99 Wilson, *op. cit.*, p. 87.
100 Hughes diary, 5 April 1976.
101 Benn diary, 29 March 1975.
102 Callaghan, *op. cit.*, p. 401.
103 Benn diary, 8 April 1975.
104 Castle diary, 8 April 1975.
105 Castle diary, 5 April 1975.

CHAPTER 12
Protect and Survive

1 Hoggart and Leigh, *op. cit.*, p. 199.
2 Castle, *op. cit.*, p. 508.
3 Interview.
4 Jones, *op. cit.*, p. 307.
5 Healey, *op. cit.*, p. 428.
6 Healey, *op. cit.*, p. 429.
7 Callaghan, *op. cit.*, p. 428.
8 Interview.
9 Raj Thapar: *All These Years* (Penguin India, 1991), p. 425.
10 Interview.
11 *Telegraph* (Calcutta), 19 November 1984.
12 *Times of India*, 25 November 1976.
13 E. P. Thompson: *Writing by Candlelight* (Merlin Press, 1980), p. 146.
14 Interview.
15 Interview.
16 Interview.
17 *Sunday Times*, 14 May 1978.
18 Kathleen Burk: 'Money and Power', in *History Today*, March 1993.
19 *Sunday Times*, 21 May 1978.
20 Callaghan, *op. cit.*, pp. 436 and 437.
21 Benn diary, 6 December 1976.
22 Benn diary, 6 December 1976.
23 Hughes diary, 25 October 1976.
24 Brigid Brophy: *A Guide to Public Lending Right* (Gower Publishing, 1983), p. 51.
25 Brophy, *op. cit.*, p. 126.
26 Cledwyn Hughes: *Referendum: The End of an Era* (lecture reprinted by University of Wales Press, 1981).
27 Commons, 9 May 1978.
28 Interview.
29 Interview.
30 Benn diary, 23 March 1977.
31 *The Times*, 10 May 1977.
32 Interview.
33 *The Times*, 2 July 1977.
34 Interview.
35 Steel, *op. cit.*, p. 58.
36 *New Statesman*, 7 October 1977.
37 Benn diary, 24 March 1977.
38 Benn diary, 29 July 1977.
39 Benn diary, 9 October 1977.
40 Benn diary, 22 November 1977. Margaret Jackson, then a Benn supporter, is now Margaret Beckett, deputy leader of the Labour Party.
41 Interview.
42 My diary, 26 December 1978.
43 *New Statesman*, 6 October 1978.
44 Commons, 15 November 1977.
45 Steel, *op. cit.*, p. 136.
46 Healey, *op. cit.*, p. 462.
47 Castle, *op. cit.*, p. 507.
48 Interview.
49 Interview.
50 Interviews.
51 Callaghan, *op. cit.*, p. 514.
52 Interview.
53 Steel, *op. cit.*, p. 150.
54 Callaghan, *op. cit.*, p. 535.
55 Brophy, *op. cit.*, p. 128.
56 Interview. Emrys Hughes had been MP for South Ayrshire.
57 Interview.
58 Benn diary, 2 April 1979.
59 David Butler and Dennis Kavanagh: *The British General Election of 1979* (Macmillan, 1980), pp. 339–40.

CHAPTER 13
Duty Calls

1 *Debts of Honour*, p. 24.
2 *Debts of Honour*, p. 21.
3 *Debts of Honour*, p. 145.
4 *Debts of Honour*, p. 22.
5 *Tribune*, 11 May 1979.
6 *Independent*, 25 October 1992.
7 *New Statesman*, 26 November 1982.
8 *Tribune*, 17 August 1979.
9 *Tribune*, 18 September 1979.
10 Eric Shaw: *Discipline and Discord in the Labour Party* (Manchester University Press, 1988), p. 189.
11 Patricia Lee Sykes: *Losing from the Inside* (Transaction Books, 1988), p. 35.
12 G. L. Williams and Alan L. Williams: *Labour's Decline and the Social Democrats' Fall* (Macmillan, 1989), p. 55.
13 David Kogan and Maurice Kogan: *The Battle for the Labour Party* (Kogan Page, 1982), p. 63.
14 *Tribune*, 31 October 1980.
15 Interview.
16 Commons, 29 November 1979.
17 Figures from Kogan and Kogan, *op. cit.*, p. 42.
18 Interview.
19 Kogan and Kogan, *op. cit.*, p. 85.
20 Interview.
21 *The Times*, 13 October 1980.
22 *The Times*, 20 October 1980.
23 Mikardo, *op. cit.*, p. 204.
24 *Western Mail*, 27 May 1983.
25 Interview.
26 Interview.
27 *Tribune*, 31 October 1980.
28 *Irish Times*, 20 October 1980.
29 Mikardo, *op. cit.*, p. 204.
30 Interview.
31 Healey, *op. cit.*, p. 479.
32 Interview.
33 Interview.
34 Hoggart and Leigh, *op. cit.*, p. 1.
35 Healey, *op. cit.*, p. 478.
36 *Sunday Times*, 16 November 1980.
37 Benn diary, 18 November 1980.
38 Interview.
39 *Tribune*, 21 November 1980.
40 *Economist*, 15 November 1980.
41 *Tribune*, 26 September 1980.
42 *Tribune*, 3 October 1980.
43 Sykes, *op. cit.*, p. 108.
44 *The Times*, 6 December 1980.
45 *The Times*, 15 November 1980.
46 Interview.
47 *Hampstead and Highgate Express*, 1 February 1991.
48 Sykes, *op. cit.*, p. 119.
49 Williams and Williams, *op. cit.*, p. 114.
50 Quoted in Sykes, *op. cit.*, p. 97.
51 *Sunday Times*, 15 February 1981.
52 Michael Foot: *Another Heart and Other Pulses* (Collins, 1984), p. 162.
53 *Loyalists and Loners*, p. 120.
54 *Loyalists and Loners*, p. 125.
55 Benn diary, 27 January 1981.
56 Interview.
57 Benn diary, 26 December 1980.
58 Benn diary, 24 March 1981.
59 Interview.
60 Benn diary, 29 March 1981.
61 *Tribune*, 17 April 1981.
62 *Tribune*, 10 April 1981.
63 Quoted in Kogan and Kogan, *op. cit.*, p. 123.
64 Benn diary, 20 May 1981.
65 *The Times*, 21 May 1981.
66 Interview.
67 Article in *Daily Mirror*, 24 September 1981.
68 *Guardian*, 10 September 1981.
69 *Tribune*, 25 September 1981.
70 *Tribune*, 12 June 1981.
71 *Tribune*, 18 September 1981.
72 Benn diary, 16 December 1981.
73 Benn diary, 13 November 1982.
74 Healey, *op. cit.*, p. 514.
75 *Daily Express*, 17 September 1981.
76 *Sunday Times*, 20 September 1981.
77 Letter to Mid-Oxfordshire Conservative Association, 21 September 1981.
78 He quoted the Queen Mother's compliment four years later when a Tory MP raked over the incident. Commons, 20 November 1985.
79 Benn diary, 10 November 1981.
80 *Guardian*, 18 November 1981.
81 My diary, 13 December 1981.
82 *Tribune*, 4 December 1981.
83 Interview.

84 *Guardian*, 2 December 1981.
85 A tense battle was waged over the endorsement of Pat Wall in Bradford North. He was finally endorsed over Michael's opposition in July 1982.
86 Letter of 9 January 1983, after Tatchell had been selected again and endorsed.
87 Benn diary, 7 December 1981.
88 Peter Tatchell: *The Battle for Bermondsey* (Heretic Books, 1983), p. 65.
89 Interview in *Daily Star*, 10 November 1981.

CHAPTER 14
Waterloo

1 Healey, *op. cit.*, p. 493.
2 Benn diary, 4 July 1977.
3 Commons, 9 February 1982.
4 Commons, 3 April 1982.
5 Commons, 14 April 1982.
6 *Tribune*, 9 April 1982.
7 Lord Hinchingbrooke, Commons, 31 October 1956.
8 Anthony Barnett: *Iron Britannia* (Allison & Busby, 1982), p. 27.
9 Commons, 20 May 1982.
10 Healey, *op. cit.*, p. 496.
11 Commons, 29 April 1982.
12 Benn diary, 2 May 1982.
13 *Tribune*, 7 May 1982.
14 *Tribune*, 14 May 1982.
15 *Tribune*, 21 May 1982.
16 *Observer*, 17 January 1982.
17 Interview.
18 John Callaghan: *The Far Left in British Politics* (Blackwell, 1987), p. 194.
19 John Callaghan, *op. cit.*, p. 193.
20 Interview.
21 *Tribune*, 8 February 1980.
22 John Callaghan, *op. cit.*, p. 191.
23 *Guardian*, 8 December 1981.
24 *Listener*, 23 September 1982.
25 *People*, 14 November 1982.
26 *The Times*, 1 December 1982.
27 David Butler and Dennis Kavanagh: *The British General Election of 1983* (Macmillan, 1984), p. 168.

28 Interview.
29 *The Times*, 29 July 1982.
30 *The Times*, 26 November 1982.
31 *Tribune*, 10 September 1982.
32 Robert Harris: *The Making of Neil Kinnock* (Faber, 1984), p. 197.
33 *Another Heart*, p. 20.
34 *The Times*, 26 February 1983.
35 *Another Heart*, p. 20.
36 *Observer*, 27 February 1983.
37 *Another Heart*, p. 21.
38 Healey, *op. cit.*, pp. 499 and 502.
39 *Observer*, 27 February 1983.
40 Tatchell, *op. cit.*, p. 100.
41 Tatchell, *op. cit.*, p. 112.
42 *Who Are the Patriots?* (Gollancz, 1945).
43 Tatchell, *op. cit.*, p. 106.
44 *Sunday Times*, 20 February 1983.
45 *Observer*, 27 February 1983.
46 Interview.
47 *Daily Star*, 12 March 1983.
48 *Another Heart*, p. 41.
49 Interview.
50 Butler and Kavanagh, *op. cit.*, p. 150.
51 *Another Heart*, pp. 38 and 91.
52 *Another Heart*, p. 82.
53 *The Times*, 2 June 1983.
54 *Tribune*, 12 February 1982.
55 *Another Heart*, pp. 85 and 87.
56 *Another Heart*, p. 117.
57 These figures are from Britain. Slightly different figures, applicable to the United Kingdom, are sometimes quoted.
58 Interview with Clive Jenkins.

CHAPTER 15
Recessional

1 *Another Heart*, p. 11.
2 *Another Heart*, p. 168.
3 *The Times*, 4 August 1984.
4 Commons, 4 February 1985.
5 Commons, 28 February 1985.
6 Commons, 9 December 1983.
7 Commons, 14 June 1984.
8 Commons, 20 November 1985.
9 E. H. Coleridge in *Encyclopaedia Britannica*, 1910 edition.
10 Commons, 20 May 1988.

11 In *Heretics and Renegades* (Hamish Hamilton, 1955).
12 *The Politics of Paradise*, p. 187.
13 *The Politics of Paradise*, p. 187.
14 *The Politics of Paradise*, p. 241.
15 *The Politics of Paradise*, p. 191 note.
16 *The Politics of Paradise*, p. 271.
17 *The Politics of Paradise*, p. 293.
18 *The Politics of Paradise*, p. 397.

19 *Guardian*, 5 February 1992.
20 *Independent*, 28 October 1988.
21 Letter in *Guardian*, 23 January 1989.
22 Commons, 22 November 1990.
23 *Tribune*, 15 May 1992.
24 *Evening Standard*, 5 March 1992.
25 *Evening Standard*, 14 January 1993.
26 *Daily Herald*, 15 August 1946.

BIBLIOGRAPHY

BOOKS BY MICHAEL FOOT

Armistice 1918–1939 (Harrap, 1940)
Guilty Men (Gollancz, 1940)
The Trial of Mussolini (Gollancz, 1943)
Brendan and Beverley (Gollancz, 1944)
The Pen and the Sword (MacGibbon & Kee, 1957)
Guilty Men 1957 (Gollancz, 1957)
Aneurin Bevan, vol. 1 (MacGibbon & Kee, 1962)
—— vol. 2 (Davis-Poynter, 1973)
Harold Wilson (Pergamon, 1964)
Debts of Honour (Davis-Poynter, 1980)
Another Heart and Other Pulses (Collins, 1984)
Loyalists and Loners (Collins, 1986)
The Politics of Paradise (Collins, 1988)

OTHER WORKS

Benn, Tony, *Against the Tide: Diaries 1973–76* (Hutchinson, 1989)
—— *Conflicts of Interest: Diaries 1977–80* (Hutchinson, 1990)
—— *The End of an Era: Diaries 1980–90* (Hutchinson, 1992)
Bullock, Alan, *Ernest Bevin, Foreign Secretary* (Heinemann, 1983)
Callaghan, James, *Time and Chance* (Collins, 1987)
Cameron, James, *Points of Departure* (Barker, 1967)
Castle, Barbara, *The Castle Diaries 1964–70* (Weidenfeld & Nicolson, 1983)
—— *The Castle Diaries 1974–76* (Weidenfeld & Nicolson, 1984)
—— *Fighting All the Way* (Macmillan, 1993)
Chisholm, Anne, and Michael Davie, *Beaverbrook* (Hutchinson, 1992)
Crossman, R. H. S., *The Diaries of a Cabinet Minister* (3 volumes, Cape, 1975, 1976, 1977)
Crosland, Susan, *Tony Crosland* (Cape, 1982)
Davies, Russell, and Liz Ottaway: *Vicky* (Secker & Warburg, 1987)
Duff, Peggy, *Left, Left, Left* (Allison & Busby, 1971)
Foot, Hugh, *A Start in Freedom* (Hodder & Stoughton, 1964)

Foot, Sarah, *My Grandfather, Isaac Foot* (Bossiney Books, 1980)

Goodman, Geoffrey, *The Awkward Warrior* (Davis-Poynter, 1979)

Harris, Kenneth, *Clement Attlee* (Weidenfeld & Nicolson, 1982)

Healey, Denis, *The Time of My Life* (Michael Joseph, 1989)

Hoggart, Simon, and David Leigh, *Michael Foot* (Hodder & Stoughton, 1981)

Howard, Anthony, *Crossman* (Cape, 1990)

Jones, Jack, *Union Man* (Collins, 1986)

Kogan, David, and Maurice Kogan, *The Battle for the Labour Party* (Kogan Page, 1982)

Lee, Jennie, *My Life with Nye* (Cape, 1980)

Mikardo, Ian, *Back-Bencher* (Weidenfeld & Nicolson, 1988)

Morgan, Kenneth O., *Labour in Power* (Oxford University Press, 1986)

—— *The People's Peace* (Oxford University Press, 1990)

Pimlott, Ben, *Labour and the Left in the 1930s* (Cambridge University Press, 1977)

—— *Hugh Dalton* (Cape, 1985)

—— *Harold Wilson* (HarperCollins, 1992)

Shaw, Eric, *Discipline and Discord in the Labour Party* (Manchester University Press, 1988)

Shore, Peter, *Leading the Left* (Weidenfeld & Nicolson, 1993)

Sykes, Patricia, *Losing from the Inside* (Transaction Books, 1988)

Taylor, A. J. P., *A Personal History* (Hamish Hamilton, 1983)

Wilson, Harold, *Final Term* (Weidenfeld & Nicolson, 1979)

Williams, Philip, *Hugh Gaitskell* (Cape, 1979)

Young, Hugo, *The Crossman Affair* (Hamish Hamilton & Cape, 1976)

INDEX

Machiavelli's Children
EDWARD PEARCE

The Prince, Machiavelli's short, luminous text on political necessity, caused shock and outrage when it was first published in 1513, and has since become a model for cunning and unprincipled statesmanship. In *Machiavelli's Children*, Edward Pearce has applied the Florentine thinker's ideas to our own times. Referring to the political practice of such figures as Hitler, Stalin, John F. Kennedy, General Sharon, Harold Wilson and Margaret Thatcher, Pearce brilliantly reveals the true motives and calculations which underlie the pious forms of twentieth-century politics. Ironic, authoritative and wholly original, it also demonstrates that *Il Principe* will always be pertinent as long as men – and women – itch for power.

'A superb read, laced with insights' – Tam Dalyell, *The Scotsman*

'Excellent . . . enlightening, witty and consistently entertaining' – *Mail on Sunday*

'Pearce integrates Machiavelli seamlessly into his own acute style to bring out the hypocrisy and humanity of leading politicians and princes . . . He is one of the most perceptive of modern political correspondents, with an insight and a turn of phrase which is sometimes so clear as to be cruel. It is the source of his strength' – Graham Allen, *The House Magazine* (The House of Commons magazine)

'He delights in paradoxes and learned references. He is often stimulating and seldom boring . . . At the end I wanted to re-read *The Prince*' – Peter Riddell, *The Times*

ISBN 0 575 05798 X

Publication due April 1995

Heroes and Villains
An Anthology of Animosity and Admiration
Introduced by
JOHN WALSH

Invited by the *Independent Magazine* to name their hero or villain, some of the best writers in the English language have responded by eulogising and vilifying a wide and unpredictable range of characters: Cleopatra and Colette, Barbara Cartland and Klondyke Kate, the Singing Postman and the Pope, Bernard Manning and Bluto . . . The choice of subject often provides fascinating insights into the writer's inspirations and influences, and frequently challenges the reader's preconceptions about public figures. Here are fifty-four examples of first-class prose from an extraordinary roll-call of literary talent: provocative, polished and highly entertaining.

ISBN 0 575 05839 0

Handel
The Man and His Music

JONATHAN KEATES

An elegant, witty account of Handel's colourful life – from his youth in Germany, through his brilliantly successful Italian sojourns, to the opulence and squalor of Georgian London – interwoven with vivid commentary on the composer's vast output. In its combination of scholarship, insight and sheer enthusiasm, this is unsurpassed among Handel biographies.

'Full of extremely penetrating, well-judged observations on both man and music' – Nicholas Kenyon, *The Times*

'Will still be valued in a hundred years' time . . . the book as a whole is an event' – Peter Phillips, *Spectator*

ISBN 0 575 05481 6

Partners in Protest
Life with Canon Collins
DIANA COLLINS

Canon John Collins, for many years a canon at St Paul's Cathedral, was one of the most dynamic and radical Christian activists of this century. A founder member of CND alongside J. B. Priestley, A. J. P. Taylor and Bertrand Russell, he was a central figure in the anti-apartheid movement, working with Nelson Mandela, Oliver Tambo and Trevor Huddleston, and a constant thorn in the side of the Church Establishment.

Sharing his life – his beliefs and commitments – was Diana, his wife and companion for forty-four years. Their campaigning work took them all over the world; they were both invited to speak at the UN and John was nominated for the Nobel Peace Prize. *Partners in Protest* is Diana Collins' vivid, touching and amusing account of a unique loving and working partnership.

Shortlisted for the Marsh Biography Award

'The best book ever written by a wife about her husband . . . She has done full justice to a truly Christian man' – Lord Longford, *Catholic Herald*

'A very good biography . . . remarkably honest, warm, impulsive, courageous and loving' – *Contemporary Review*

'The best account of a married partnership I have ever read' – *The Tablet*

'Often fascinating, often entertaining, often charming and beguiling narrative. Her description of the RAF camp where John served as a chaplain is funny enough to bring Evelyn Waugh to mind' – *Guardian*

ISBN 0 575 05753 X

Hons and Rebels
JESSICA MITFORD

'Whenever I read the words "Peer's Daughter" in a headline,' Lady Redesdale once sadly remarked, 'I know it's going to be something about one of you children.' The Mitford family is one of the century's most enigmatic, made notorious by Nancy's novels, Diana's marriage to Sir Oswald Mosley, Unity's infatuation with Hitler, Debo's marriage to a duke and Jessica's passionate commitment to communism. *Hons and Rebels*, unveiling the children's isolated and eccentric upbringing between the wars, fills in the background to *Love in a Cold Climate* and *The Pursuit of Love*. Along the way it pinpoints, with that brilliant humour characteristic of the Mitfords, the origins of the sisters' remarkable individuality.

'Reads like extravagantly mannered fiction, except that it is all fabulously true . . . at once touching and wildly funny, there is not one of her highly coloured characters that is not violently alive and uncomfortably kicking' – *Tatler*

'Extremely entertaining' – *Penelope Mortimer*

'More than an extremely amusing autobiography . . . she has evoked a whole generation. Her book is full of the music of time' – *Sunday Times*

ISBN 0 575 04533 7